Designing Instruction For Open Sharing

Shalin Hai-Jew

Designing Instruction For Open Sharing

Springer

Shalin Hai-Jew
Information Technology Services (ITS)
Kansas State University
Manhattan, KS, USA

ISBN 978-3-030-02712-4 ISBN 978-3-030-02713-1 (eBook)
https://doi.org/10.1007/978-3-030-02713-1

Library of Congress Control Number: 2018959754

This Springer imprint is published by the registered company Springer Nature Switzerland AG
The registered company address is: Gewerbestrasse 11, 6330 Cham, Switzerland

Preface

One of the more salutary aspects of the age of the current Social Web (or Web 2.0) has been in the sharing of learning resources. Amateurs to experts create learning contents, and they share their experiences with others—through narrated demo videos, slideshows, simulations, games, and codes. People can go online to acquire new knowledge and skills, shore up old ones, and explore other people's specialties, expertise, experiences, interests, and perspectives. For some of the more basic activities, one may emulate others' skills and gain self-confidence: "That looks pretty easy! Hey, I can do that!" That confidence may extend further to, "Hey, I can create learning objects and sequences for others online!" After all, people all have their own expertise that may interest others. If this is something you have considered, then this how-to book may be for you.

The vision for an online world of open-shared learning objects has been around for decades, and it goes something like this. Content experts from around the world have insights to share, and they individually and in teams co-create contents that others may use at no cost, through the affordances of the Web and Internet. The reusability enables there to be less wasted human effort in creating similar learning resources. These endeavors are complementary to the commercial space and occasionally competitive to it. The open sharing efforts are informed by humanistic ideals to entice learners to explore, to bring others in the field forward, to advance the fields themselves, to enable broader spaces for author voices and expression, and to better unite humanity across shared interests for learning. Those who may not directly access higher education and other learning endeavors may discover and develop their inner talents. This effort democratizes the world's knowledge, and it lessens some of the vagaries of birth by introducing increased and egalitarian access. Open-shared learning resources are predicated on having more level playing fields.

In terms of contributors, this is an inclusive space. Anyone who wants to contribute may, in the same way that anyone who wants to be electronically social may engage; however, the space is also highly competitive, with people individually and collectively being highly protective of their attention and time. Just because something is free does not mean that it will necessarily be taken up and used. For the potential contributors, the bare outlines of the open-shared learning resources challenge reads like this:

> For a budget of $0, an individual or a team peruses the online learning environment, identifies a possible gap in publicly available information, defines a number of learning audiences with possible interest in the topic, and conceptualizes a learning object that he or she may create in a unique and learner-centered way. He or she (or they) collects information and creates digital learning objects and learning sequences in a way that stands up to legal scrutiny around issues of copyright, information privacy, media law, and others and is risk-controlled. He or she tunes the learning to a wide potential range of learners. Along the way, he or she uses research resources that can easily top thousands of dollars, software suites and stand-alone programs that range in the thousands of dollars, and professional time that equals some thousands of dollars. The created learning resources are released to the public with all its potential scrutiny. In most cases, the work is in the environment but does not result in any public notice or acclaim. Bylines are sometimes used, but such objects are not usually cited nor credited. Digital learning objects are not usually cited to advance careers. Typical usage may be in the double digits up to the quadruple digits of users.

If that is a value proposition that sounds appealing, then this book may be the one for you.

The essential premise of this text is that there are approaches and methods that may be taken to design more effective instruction for open sharing on the Web and Internet. If the current age is about user-generated contents being shared widely on social media platforms, it is actually also the age of generous sharing of expert insights by individuals and groups, who enable free and global access to their works. For some, such a share is a one-off, and for others, such shares are part of regular work. The open share of an online learning object or learning sequence requires more forethought and effort than a social media share, such as a quick image capture or Tweet or posting or up/down vote. So for such a complex topic, where is a reasonable place to start? Full disclosure: Initially, this was to be an edited text, but when the initial calls for proposals did not reveal committed interest by potential contributors, I asked the publisher if they would be willing to go with an authored one, and they said yes! (Timing is everything, and the mass mood for a topic has to be right to attract sufficient commitment to an authored project. Also, with the shift to an authored text, what is gained is a more individual author point-of-view, but what is lost are some of the diversities of voices that could have been—had the momentum been different.)

My point-of-view informs the text's framework. I assume that real-world information is critical to this work, so I draw on decades of educational and instructional design experiences in this space. I strive to surface relevant tacit knowledge (in a generalizable way), and I assume that practical decision-making will be important. I assume that many readers will be working as designer/developers on their own open-shared projects, in part because many such objects are often single bylined and because teams are hard to bring together for such work and are less common. I also assume that there may be the occasional team, so I address both approaches. Another general assumption is that readers will be working on single projects or short learning sequences—not major instructional design projects—in part because this seems to be a more common sharing market than large-scale funded open-shared learning endeavors (like many massive open online courses or "MOOCs"). I am envisioning creative projects: apps for engaging a physical environment, serious games, assessments, AI bots engaging in immersive virtual worlds, virtual tutors, game-based learning scenarios, slideshows, interactive webpages, exploratory learning spaces, digital photo albums, electronic books, interactive kiosk experiences, and anything else people may want to build to share.

I am informed by my work life, which has included decades of work in higher education, the public sector, and the private sector. The field of instructional design is not a settled one. It is lively with a range of different accepted approaches and much on-ground decision-making by its practitioners. This book provides the best state of the art that I could create in this year of development, and the writing provides general guidelines and approaches, but the decision-making and choices are left rightly in the reader's hands.

The goal is to avoid superficial and click-bait contents and go for building something that will last and have a longer impact than fleeting views. The insights in the text can apply to the larger-funded projects, but the main focus is on the smaller efforts. The level of generality is purposeful, to be as inclusive as possible, given that there are so many types digital objects. This book also takes a "dot your i's and cross your t's" sort of approach because the professional field requires that, because accuracy serves learners well, and because precision protects the designer/developer.

This text is structured as a fairly comprehensive but general work sequence, beginning with the initial interest in possibly creating a learning object or sequence for open sharing, going through exploratory and planning stages, reviewing the extant applied laws and ethics, designing the object, developing it, testing it, launching it into the world, and considering how to support its users and ultimately learn from the experience. This textbook is practically hands-on, with various learning features at chapter level: defined learning objectives, keywords, interspersed reader tasks, practical assignments, explanatory visuals, what-if scenarios, sidebars, web resources, main point reviews, critical thinking questions, and reference resources, among others.

The tasks are indicated by a clipboard icon with a checkmark.

The "Live Examples (on the Web)" resources are indicated by a WWW icon.

The what-if scenarios are indicated by customized word clouds created from the respective chapters. These represent the contents of the chapter because the decision-making scenarios draw from the contents of the chapter.

Other visuals in this work are data visualizations. These are cited and described in the text near the figures and tables.

The Table of Contents (TOC): This textbook does not focus on any particular subject matter areas or learning domains or disciplines, and it is written at a fairly general level—so as to be usable in a variety of applied contexts. A wide range of types of objects, sequences, and contexts are considered, but the main focus is on using a disciplined approach to build to pedagogical quality and legal standards (albeit without tedious prescriptions). The process described includes everything from conceptualization to launch, with a special focus on testing to ensure quality. In a sense, this text contains nothing novel in and of itself, but the novelty may be in the open sharing approach, informed by decades of instructional design and updated technologies.

The general Table of Contents (TOC), set up as a comprehensive sequence of steps for creating an open-shared learning object, follows:

These are more guidelines than full step-by-step delineations. The chapters, of course, do not fully specify the potential work involved; that would not be possible because of the diversity of work in this space. The contents were written here at a generalist level. The characteristics of the target projects will most certainly change how the chapter sequences are viewed. Also, in all likelihood, going down a few levels in granularity will affect the different projects in very different ways. Given the dynamism in the technologies used in this space, it is not likely possible to have a base source for all the design and development work using particular tools. These steps will be beneficial in helping an individual or team get started and walk through a sequence with the necessary specificity as practiced in the field. However, this book does not describe all the respective branches.

Representing sequential work steps, the respective chapters may be thought of as a modular structure, with additional pieces that may be interspersed with the existing sequences and with pieces and parts that may be taken out. It is assumed that there are as many ways to approach instructional design and development as there are designers and developers and work contexts to support this work. (In one sense, every learning design is "boutique" and original; in a converse sense, every learning design is generic.) This systematized approach is not to be applied in lockstep, and this should not be conceptualized formulaically. The same textbook may be harnessed by different users, and even with the same defined contents and learning objectives, they will likely come out with very different learning objects and sequences. There will be equifinality of quality (as defined by the designer/developer) but not of method, content, or style. There is something very expressive and human in learning designs, as it should be. There will also be some transparency about how decisions were arrived at and insights about the instructional design work.

Target Readers. This work does not assume that the reader has any background in either instructional design or in open sharing of learning objects and/or learning sequences. Rather, the assumption is generally that the reader is a content expert in a field and is attracted to the idea of sharing some insights about his/her/their field. If the reader has some instructional design experience or some open sharing experience, this textbook may still be helpful and shed new light on some aspects of this work.

The "idealized reader" is a known approach for writers, so that they can write beyond themselves as the "first reader" but to a sense of an audience. My ideal reader for this book is someone who is open-minded, curious, well read, exploratory, engaged with the world, analytical, and generous, someone who has something to share with the broad public and is willing to work hard to enable that. The share may be a one-off, something that a reader has on a bucket list, or it may be a continuing share, with new shares over time. (Each learning object or designed sequence after the first one seems to come a little easier. Even more important, with each newly shared object or sequence, the individual and/or team can go more ambitious and risk-taking—with growing earned confidence and senses of self-efficacy.)

Also, this textbook may be used in a formal higher education setting, for both undergraduate and graduate work. It may be used in nonformal learning contexts, such as trainings, noncredit short courses, seminars, and conferences. It may be used in an informal learning context, as part of self-discovery learning or lifelong learning.

The Original Inspiration. For me, books start as intense inspirations but hazy ideas. I know that the information is there, but until I actually try to articulate them, I do not know what I know or think, in depth. "Write what you know" goes the old advice of my writing teachers. Better yet, look back at what you have been doing for the past many years, and draw out the salient themes from those times. Indeed, I have been working on the design and development of online learning contents since the late 1990s—in private industry and in the public sector. I grew up using many of the courseware tools and watched as the space evolved over time, with ever more sophisticated learning management systems (LMSes) and authoring tools and then so much more! I have built learning objects free-form and others with rigorous templating and rules.

What have I learned in these years that help inform the text?

- Defined work processes can be set up to ensure better quality outcomes.
- Conducting an environmental scan of the context (online and offline) can inform designs that benefit from contemporary methods and technologies.
- Design decisions do better when they are made consciously and purposefully (even when the designer is under heavy and tight deadlines); however, inspirations for designs can come from anywhere (so the designer does well to sample broadly).
- Design is about conventions and the familiar, and it is about avoiding arbitrariness in the creation of learning experiences and sequences.
- Understanding potential target learners and considering their likely central needs informs an effective instructional design.
- Considering how humans perceive and learn and remember informs an effective instructional design.
- Learning designs should be informed by empirical research and data. It is important to test designs in the real world.
- Alpha (α) testing and beta (β) testing ensure that the learning objects and learning sequences meet standards and are engaging and beneficial to learners.
- Developing customized testing for particular learning objects benefits the ultimate quality and polish of the unique works, based on unique focuses for different projects.
- Post-launch care of users of learning objects may be important to their use of the learning materials.
- Those who create open-shared learning objects benefit from having a plan for revising the objects and sequences as needed (based on defined standards).
- Competition for human attention online is fierce, and if one's resource is not a destination site (findable in the top few pages of a Google Search), it will languish (and will have to find a theorized user base in the future or not at all).

Probably the most important insight is that people can be motivated by much more than money to create contents for others' benefit (both now and into the future). People may be driven by the need to share their expertise. They may want a side project around which to build new knowledge, new skills, new technological savvy, and new professional connections. That said, this is hard work, and while the rewards may be many, it will still be a minority of designers and developers who will take on this hard work. (Those who pursue such projects to advance careers and earn tenure will contribute their work to achieve their goals, but they will not have the hunger to go beyond the one-off, from what I have seen. The world is not zero sum, where one person's gain is necessarily another's loss); however, it is not a fully positive sum game either, where there is a net gain for those involved. Creating a "win-win" will require principled efforts and sufficient considerations. Designing and developing open-shared contents involves real costs as well as opportunity costs, and one should not be blithe or unthinking in these endeavors.

I have learned that if one is positioned to offer some object or sequence of value, that moment, if not seized, passes, often never to return. It also helps to know the rules of the game, to know how to make decisions and how to plan processes, and to know what to look for to inform choices, particularly in environments with complex phenomenon. And it helps to occasionally break rules strategically and purposefully, with eyes wide open.

This textbook, *Designing Instruction for Open Sharing*, then, is my small effort to pause time and to share some of what I have learned in decades working in public higher education both in the USA and abroad and in private industry. If we can all pay it forward and share something of our respective expertise, we can enrich each other's lives and benefit those into the future.

Finally, it may seem "rich" to write about open-shared learning objects when this book itself is published with a for-profit publisher. For me, I chose to go this route for purposes of publisher reputation and support, the book's distribution, and the structure needed to create and evolve this from an idea. In reality, book publishing pays very little, maybe just enough to keep me in notepads and Sharpies, black teas, and an occasional book, for a few years. When that is enough, you know you are on to a good topic. Ultimately, the only real money is time, and we have to spend it with care doing things that are meaningful and relevant, for ourselves and others.

Thanks!

Thanks to Susan Lagerstrom-Fife and Caroline Flanagan at Springer Publishing, Inc., for supporting this project.

Thanks also to Anthony Dunlap, Saveetha Balasundaram, Sam Daniel, and others on the extraordinary team for their fine work in laying out this book creatively and clearly.

My home institution of Kansas State University has enabled me to share online learning contents over the years, for which I am grateful. The open sharing work itself has sharpened my skills and benefitted my mainline work projects. While the temptations are rife to leave the work place when everyone else does, actually investing in one's profession counts for something, among them, that one's ideas can be made real.

Thanks also to all the readers of this work. I hope you find this somewhat useful.

Manhattan, KS, USA Shalin Hai-Jew

Acknowledgments

This book is dedicated to those engaged in designing and developing for open sharing. There are rewards and surprises in this path.

This is for R. Max, Lily, and Asher, who mean the world to me.

Contents

About the Author

Shalin Hai-Jew has been working as an instructional designer at Kansas State University since January 2006, and she has worked on a number of projects, including those related to biosecurity, turf grass management, grain science, game design, one health, public health, PTSD, mental health, social justice, and other federally funded projects. She has also worked on hundreds of online courses in her line of work. She has worked as an instructional designer here since 2006. She has created open-shared learning objects (all bylined) for a number of years, and these have been shared through a variety of publications, slideshow-sharing platforms, websites, and other spaces; some of these are listed in learning object referatories.Dr. Hai-Jew earned BAs in English and psychology and an MA in English from the University of Washington (in Seattle), and she earned an EdD from Seattle University (where she was a Morford Scholar). She has continued her learning with university courses, both undergraduate and graduate, since her formal degree-based studies. She has received a number of scholarships and awards in higher education. She tested into the University of Washington at age 14 and started her studies there at 15 and earned two baccalaureate degrees by the time she was 18 and her first graduate degree by 20. She is a major believer in the power of education at all levels to change lives.In her professional life, she has worked in the public and private sectors. In general, she has worked as a college professor, both in the USA and abroad. She worked as a college instructor in the People's Republic of China for 4 years (1988–1990, 1992–1994), the latter 2 years with the United Nations Volunteer Programme (UNV) of the United National Development Programme (UNDP). She worked for The Boeing Company as a faculty fellow for two consecutive summers. She worked for Catholic Community Services, a nonprofit organization, for one of her first jobs out of university.She has edited a number of academic texts and authored a few, with multiple major publishers. She is interested in human learning; online teaching and learning; research design, quantitative and qualitative data analytics methods, machine learning, and data visualization; and other related fields. She is working on multiple publishing projects currently, including an edited text on online survey research and an authored text on mapping electronic hive minds on the Social Web and Internet. She has served on a number of editorial advisory boards related to publications focused on educational technologies. She has served on the steering committee for Colleague 2 Colleague (C2C), a nonprofit professional organization for a number of years, and she co-edits the *C2C Digital Magazine*. For some more information and some basic third-party metrics:

ORCID ID: 0000-0002-8863-0175

Researcher ID: J-3022-2018

Publons Profile: https://publons.com/author/1268346/shalin-hai-jew#profile

Google Scholar Citations: https://scholar.google.com/citations?user=0ungL5gAAAAJ&hl

Comments may be sent to haijes@gmail.com.

Part I
The Open Sharing Ecosystem

Chapter 1
Understanding the Open Sharing Learning Environment Online and Local Starts

Abstract Those interested in possibly contributing open-shared digital learning contents would do well to acquire a sense of the sharing ecosystem and of their distinct possible roles in that space. This chapter introduces the topic of open-shared learning online as a phenomenon with roots going back several decades. This chapter takes the learner through an environmental scan of the open-shared learning space and some methods to identify what the reader may contribute to this space—by evaluating his/her/their organizational context, skill set, interest in contributing, and other related factors.

Keywords Environmental scan · Internal organizational scan · Subject domain · Open sharing · Online learning resource ecosystem · Open sharing · Learning object · Learning sequence · Learning resource

> 'Commons' refers to a particular institutional form of structuring the rights to access, use, and control resources.
>
> –Yochai Benkler, *The Wealth of Networks: How Social production Transforms Markets and Freedom* (2006, Ch. 3, p. 60)

> Sharing is good, and with digital technology, sharing is easy.
>
> –Richard Stallman (1953–)

> Sharing is the essence of social media.
>
> –Zoe Sugg (1990–)

> The Internet has introduced an enormously accessible and egalitarian platform for creating, sharing and obtaining information on a global scale. As a result, we have new ways to allow people to exercise their human and civil rights.
>
> –Vint Cerf

S. Hai-Jew, *Designing Instruction For Open Sharing*,
https://doi.org/10.1007/978-3-030-02713-1_1

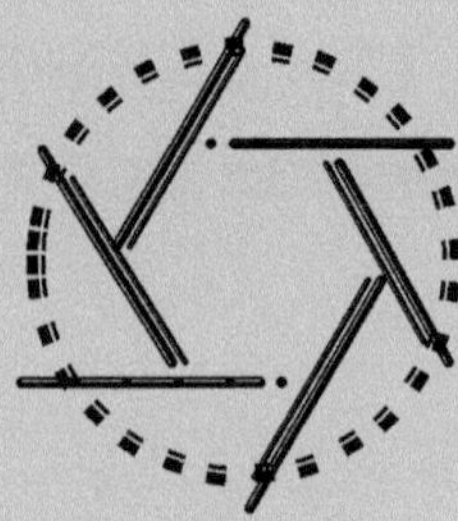

Opening Scenario

Opening Scenario: Openness to a Side GIG Creating Open-Shared Learning Resources?

You are a professional in a field. You have privy knowledge about some issues, which are not for public consumption; however, you also have access to knowledge, discrete information, resources, and skills that may benefit the general public and would garner public interest. You have benefitted from the uses of open-source materials, for research, for project design, and for projects development even. You are somewhat interested in exploring open sharing but may not have engaged in open sharing or publishing before. You may have had some experiences with designing instruction for employees of the organization. You have created contents for public presentations, to be delivered in person and virtually.

You may have something to offer the larger community by creating learning objects. Better yet, your company may have an interest in contributing to the public good and would encourage such sharing as an innovative side project—to maintain employee engagement, and the supervisors are open to having company technologies used for such projects albeit in lulls between intense project work. Maybe there is even some leftover digital contents that may be used for such learning objects. You have conducted a basic environmental scan and have identified some gaps in what is available to the broad public in the particular domain. You may be able to fill that gap with your expertise. (Good intentions do not replace actual expertise. People's expertise has to be developed over the years, and there are no cases of talent coming out of nowhere. For most who have achievements in their fields, they have been hard at work for much of their lives.) Your environmental scan has enabled you to develop a sense of what learners may expect of learning resources based on what others have shared. This baseline understanding is set accurately at least for the next short while.

Should you share? Does your local work environment enable such work? Is there excess capacity anywhere? Or a willingness to use your own time to create the digital learning object?

Some Early Questions to Consider

Is there local interest in pursuing the design and development of some sort of instruction for open sharing?

What would be some motivating ideals that would drive you?

What are some practical considerations you would have to make before endeavoring to create such an open-shared object? What professional considerations do you have to make?

What is your professional standing, and does it enable you to take on a particular topic credibly?

Are there some ways to strengthen your standing as an expert on this topic? How so?

Who is your competition, and why do you see them as your competition?

How do you conceptualize yourself as an instructional designer (or a designer of instruction)? A developer?

How do you conceptualize your relationship to learners? The general public? What sort of point-of-view would you take?

How would you communicate your sense of relationship to the general public?

Would you have support in your workplace to pursue creating open-shared learning objects? Is there a way to achieve this without zero-sumness (your workplace taking on the costs and liabilities of your endeavors)? Is there a way to set up win-wins for all those involved?

Learning Objectives
Learners will…

Open-Shared Learning Ecosystem

- Consider some definitions of open-shared learning contents and historical movements that contribute to open sharing
- Conduct an environmental scan of the generic open sharing learning ecosystem online
- Identify some of the more cutting-edge technologies in use and the related enablements by reverse-engineering available learning online (both proprietary and open)
- Identify the main funders of open sharing learning and their stated interests in this space, and name the main contributing individuals and entities to the open sharing learning space, and list their stated and apparent objectives
- List the types of online and face-to-face (F2F) social supports available for those who create open-shared learning objects

Domain-Specific and Interdisciplinary Topical Exploration

- Conduct an environmental scan of some available open-shared learning contents based on specific targeted subject areas
- Explore the proprietary learning ecosystem online around learning subjects/topics of interest
- Explore potential gaps in available open-access learning in a particular domain in an open sharing context

Local Workplace and Designer/Developer Life Conditions

- Define the local workplace or organizational context (for issues of domain expertise, interests in open-shared learning) and some cost-benefit considerations as precursors to possible designing and developing for open sharing
- Evaluate one's own readiness for engaging in creating learning content for open sharing

Learning Resource Project Doability

- Evaluate how "doable" a particular learning resource project is, practically speaking.

1.1 Introduction

The design and development of "open-shared" learning objects and sequences are common practice and have been for years. In early days, programmers would share their code and apply licensure to release their code based on conditionals. Then as online learning became more popular, people created ways to advance social sharing of learning resources—with defined common technical standards, shared metadata systems, intellectual property licensure releases, content-sharing-based learning platforms, and others. This book on designing open-shared learning conceptually builds on the movements of open-source (coding), open-access (publishing), open educational resources (ideals for humanity), and common practices in this space. The distribution of open-shared learning contents is not a new thing, so this work is somewhat an observation of the current present, but with a formalization of the standards and methods applied to the creation of such objects. For years, the thinking has been that if users are generating contents for free, then it is hard to ask them to abide by shared standards for content creation. However, that thinking is starting to change with so many assuming expertise that they do not actually have to drive traffic to their media channels, and with so many professionally created learning objects not attracting much of a learning audience and acquiring low reuse [estimated generally at about 20% according to published research (Ochoa 2018; Ochoa 2011)]. For years, the only informal evaluation of such shared objects has been through commenting and upvotes/downvotes, enabled by some of the online platforms. More formal critique on learning object repositories and referatories has been through limited peer review by (mostly volunteer) individuals who are identified to personally identifiable data (PII) and their professional profiles (and not ambiguous handles). A definition of an open-shared learning object or sequence then is an evolved one, which borrows aspects from open-source, open-access, open-educational resources, and other concepts.

An open-shared learning object or sequence, then, is broadly shared learning content specifically designed and developed for others' learning. Learners optimally have anytime-anywhere access through any device, in any number of contexts. In this book, these are digital objects, not analog ones (although they may be in whole or in part). These are conceptualized as content created in alignment with professional standards, informed by research and theory about human learning. And these are envisioned as aligning with legal requirements—for intellectual property, accessibility, and other applicable laws. These are conceptualized as being broadly accessible to a wide range of learners, who may be invited to the contents or who may merely find their way there. These are released through various generous licensure, and some may be released to the level of the editable code. Generous licensure may ensure that users into the future may use the work and even update it in customized ways, in some cases.

Open-shared learning objects are generally identifiable to an actual author or authoring team (or if absent that, a particular organization). This concept includes the idea of an "author hand," a unique signature of the designer/developer or team. Even if multiple developers are assigned the same topic, they will invariably emerge with highly variant learning objects and sequences because their prior work experiences, aesthetics, points-of-view, senses of taste, and accesses to resources, are all different. Some works are understood through just a personality frame, a force of personality. (The "designer/developer" concept is one of an instructional designer who often creates the design and develops the object. There is a thin line between designing and developing, especially given the capabilities of authoring tools and courseware, which close the thinking-doing gap. Many times, the designed learning object is designed as it is developed, developed as it is designed.)

This textbook aims to describe the process of beginning with a concept of a learning object and ending with a fully functional and actualized learning object/sequence that may be broadly publicly shared. The described sequence is fairly comprehensive, and it is possible to skip some steps for an expedited development cycle, once one has achieved a high level of professional practice. Without that experience, though, it may be risky to skip some of the steps. More on this will follow later on. Figure 1.1 shows the importance of conducting an external environmental scan and an internal one to assess for local starts.

Some Motivating Ideals For all the methods and techniques in the world, a project will not be actualized without some seeding life-infusing actualizing deep motivation or drives. Think of what humanity can do if all of its members had access to the knowledge in the world. The vision for open-shared learning contents is couched around ideas of inherent human rights to education from K12 through university. People are valuable, and they should have every right to fully actualize themselves in all their capabilities, including full access to formal education through university level and have access to lifelong learning (Dinevski 2008, p. 117).

Yet, there is a worldwide gap in supply and demand with challenges of availability, accessibility (with "legal and administrative barriers, financial obstacles, discriminatory denials of access, obstacles (fees, distance, schedule)," acceptability (including "parental and adult choice, minimum standards (quality, safety, environmental health), language of instruction," and others), and adaptability ("minorities, indigenous people, workers, people with disabilities, migrants, travelers") (Geith and Vignare 2008, p. 107). In the U.S., one of the rationales for open education is the completion gap, in that many who enter higher education never complete a degree (Geith and Vignare 2008, p. 109).

Open learning resources, which are made broadly accessible to all through the Web and Internet, may fill some gaps for those who do not have access to university

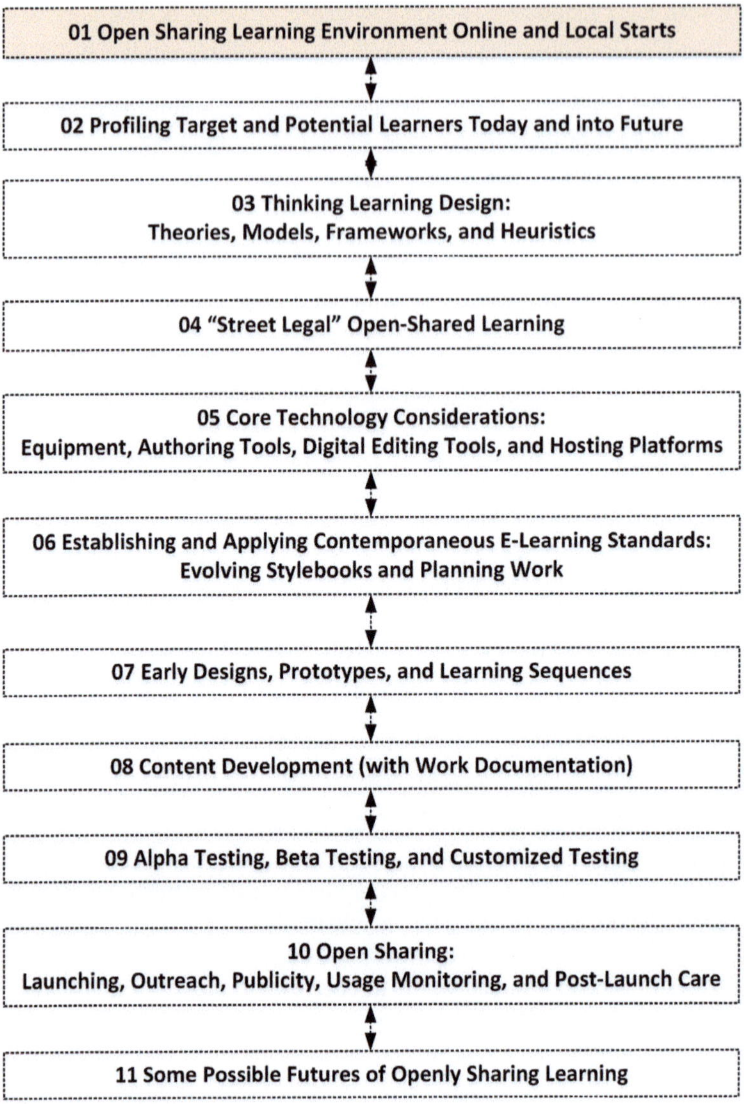

Fig. 1.1 Step 1 in the open-shared learning resource development sequence

studies, and it may expand the available learning for all. The open-access means that there are no barriers (like paywalls, like memberships) to accessing the contents, and the open-source refers to the fact that the underlying code may be viewable, sometimes editable, and non-proprietary. The ideal is one of professional care and beneficence. Such openness and *pro bono* work in higher education is motivated by "generosity, sharing, and giving," or some "core values of education" (Wiley 2010). For many people are transitioning from an industrial society to a knowledge one that requires "continuous learning, meaning processing, and knowledge creation"

(Tuomi 2012, p. 11). Open learning resources stand to promote "a worldwide knowledge society" (Richter and McPherson 2012, p. 201) and even "educational justice throughout the world" (Richter and McPherson 2012, p. 204).

The thinking goes that if one can reach a sufficiently wide audience—in the near term, the mid-term, the long term, and maybe the far future, that the work would be justified. The concept of an audience may be a powerful motivation for such work in part because it brings out the social performative aspects of people. Understanding a potential current user base not only motivates the open sharing effort, but it may inform the actual instructional design since learning has to focus on learner needs—whether the learners range anywhere on the amateur and novice to expert ranges; whether the learners are pursuing formal, nonformal, or informal learning; no matter what the background knowledge of the learners are, in relation to the subject domain; no matter the level of perceptual and learning capabilities, and other variables. Learning objects and sequences that are shared may be used in any number of learning contexts: fully online, fully face-to-face (F2F), and in blended contexts. In many cases, they may be used on a range of devices—large screen and small screen. The shared learning contents may be mashed-up or combined with other contents.

The designer/developer also will have no control over what point in the learning sequence their object is slotted in and used—whether it is used as a lead-up object to an other-created learning sequence, or as a lead-away object from someone else's learning sequence, or whether it is embedded as part of a case study, or it is analyzed as a sample learning object. Anything released into the wild may be harnessed any number of different ways, for both intended and unintended effects. Security wraps around particular learning objects only have limited utility, and there are a number of tools online that enable scraping online data, recording online videos, and otherwise capturing the object and re-rendering it or hosting it elsewhere or re-editing it. This is even in the face of limiting licensure. Depending on the design and development, and the underlying technologies, it may be very hard to know what the learners are taking away from the learning object and intervening to head off misunderstandings. The more complex the learning, the more pre-learning assumptions there may be for learners to be able to use the learning object. For example, if the open-shared learning object is a research article, an accurate read would require deeper-than-average knowledge on the following: research design and methods, statistical analysis, professional ethics, prior lead-up research, analytical implications, and other insights about the domain. Knowledge of learner understandings helps control for negative learning. Or a shared game might require some understanding of rules of gameplay and gameplay interfaces. Or an open-shared simulation should be coherently navigable and able to be oriented to/understood. Or a slide deck should have clear references for informational understandings, for users to fill in knowledge gaps and to optimally augment muddy points with definitions. Also, the way learning is designed has to "pass muster" with each learner, or else, that will risk loss of learner interest and attention. Learners have to be attracted to a learning object—which means that Web searches have to identify the resource as a relevant one in the top few pages of results, that people have to be aware of the resource and willing to recommend others to it, that the work may be shared through various platforms, that the work may be embedded in others' online learning resources, and so on. Those who come to the learning resources cannot be turned off by what they find because negative word-of-mouth (via commenting, upvotes/downvotes, social media messaging, and other details) can have a dampening effect on others' usage.

The harnessing of the capabilities of the Internet and WWW for shared learning has been in the works for many years. Digital goods can be created and re-used into perpetuity with negligible marginal costs after the initial design and development work, particularly if ways can be found to preserve such objects against the "slow fires" of technological change. The objects may be experienced by anyone globally, at scale, no matter where they are on Earth (and even in space, in low-Earth orbit).

An Evolved and Emergent Infrastructure for Open Sharing Over the years, many parts of the information technology structure have been built to enable people's distributed interconnectivity through intercommunications: text messaging, emails, voice over IP, social networking, web conferencing, digital content sharing, and others. Those who create code and digital contents can collaborate with others with ease, in real time and asynchronously. Contracts are signed all the time through encrypted digital means. Meeting face-to-face (F2F) is the exception, not the rule, in most online collaborations. These are some of the realities of this online collaboration space.

In 2001, Lawrence Lessig started the Creative Commons licensing scheme to enable people to more easily release their creative work for use by others. This was seen as an extension from the free software and open-source software movements of the 1980s. For open sharing, the pursuit of copyright permission can be "very time consuming and expensive" (Fitzgerald 2005, p. 1).

Common features of Creative Commons licenses are as follows: "licensees are granted the right to copy, distribute, display, digitally perform and make verbatim copies of the work into another format; the licenses have worldwide application that lasts for the entire duration of copyright and are irrevocable; licensees cannot use technological protection measures to restrict access to the work; copyright notices should not be removed from all copies of the work; and every copy of the work should maintain a link to the license (and) attribution of the creator or author must be given" (Fitzgerald 2005, p. 5).

The term "open educational resources" (OER) was coined during the United Nations Educational, Scientific and Cultural Organisation's (UNESCO) 2002 Forum on Open Courseware, and it was defined as "the open provision of educational resources, enabled by information and communication technologies, for consultation, use and adaptation by a community of users for non-commercial purposes" (UNESCO 2002, p. 24). Over the years, other works have been prepared to define OERs and to on-board any who wanted to participate (Butcher 2011).

Following that opening salvo, various governments came forth with declarations advocating for open access publishing and other endeavors increasing global access to knowledge. Since then, all sorts of learning contents have been shared: standalone digital "learning objects" (articles, videos, slideshows), collections (imagery, historical documents), simulations, immersive virtual worlds (with automated agents and scripted objects), massive open online courses (MOOCs), and others.

Wiley (2010) suggests that such shared contents may be licensed to the public for the "4 Rs": reuse, redistribution, revision, and remix, with each additional "R" involved with more rights to users. Lawrence Lessig's Creative Commons licensure (2001) setup involves dimensions of licensure including attribution (crediting), share-alike, commercial/noncommercial usage, derivation/non-derivation (editing rights), and others.

And now, years out from that initial splash and heightened sense of promise, indeed, there are many open-shared learning resources which are freely accessible (not behind a paywall) and many open licensed to enable others' extended usages of the resources. A closer look shows that the resources are from some learning domains, but their coverage is somewhat patchy, and the quality of the respective works vary. System-wise, this open sharing of learning objects is social: it not only involves encouraging those with expert knowledge to create digital contents but for those in formal teaching (K12 through higher education), nonformal education (trainings), and informal education (self-learning, lifelong education), to choose to adopt (and occasionally revise) the respective shared resources. There are roles for workplaces and organizations to support the work of those who create open-shared learning. Occasionally, there are roles for funders who may support such projects. A virtuous circle is one in which people take part in relevant and interdependent ways and support the creation and use of effective open-shared learning contents. By contrast, a vicious cycle may be one in which many learning contents are not created and shared, or the ones that are are of low quality or created for advertising and other non-learning reasons. Per the standards of academia, open-shared learning objects and learning sequences generally benefit from neutrality as regards political or marketing positions. Including hidden messaging, manipulations, and advocacy positions may not only interfere with the learning message but show the creator as a biased agent. Up through the present moment, this open-shared learning seems to be part of an ongoing experiment, and it is not clear what the right balance of incentives and rewards may be for those engaged in the creation and use of such learning objects and sequences. From early days, various authors have questioned how sustainable such endeavors may be (Wiley 2007).

Few people would approach the creation of open-shared learning objects or sequences without some forethought. After all, the work requires complex professional skills, including original content creation and highly technical specifications. Releasing learning objects to the broad public entails some risks, including legal and reputational. For example, what would happen to a designer/developer's reputation if a historical work was found to advance an inaccurate paradigm or model? To include rookie mistakes? To be poorly revised and/or edited?

The value proposition of such objects and sequences is elusive since many such endeavors are unfunded, leaving designers/developers with having to fund the objects themselves, collaborate with others to share the burden, crowd-source parts of the work, or barter for the necessary resources. There may be endeavors to force down costs (Wiley 2007). In lieu of payments, the designer/developer or sharer payoff is supposed to be some combination of the following:

- advancing professional development
- acquiring new skills or reinforcing and extending current skills
- having a voice related to an issue (expressivity)
- building a professional portfolio or collection of works
- creating a public professional reputation
- paying it forward (benevolence) to help others, and
- making the world a better place (an ideal).

For organizations that support such endeavors of their staff, they may benefit from higher morale and sense of larger purpose among the workforce, employees with a broader range of skills and capabilities, burnishment of their brand, and positive public relations messaging.

For all the idealism and good will, cold hard costs and effortful expert inputs are balanced against something that sometimes feels like whimsy. The readiness to create relevant open-shared learning objects and the readiness to accept them are fleeting opportunities. For example, a current project from which spinoff open-shared works may be created may be relevant and active only for a particular time period. On the Social Web, the competition for attention is brutal, with an over-abundance of user-generated contents for virtually every interest. To be competitive on a Web search, for example, a source should be on the top few pages of the search (out of millions of results.

This chapter explores the open-shared learning ecosystem and some of its dynamics. It walks the reader through conducting subject-specific domain-specific topical explorations of the open-shared space. Then, it suggests ways to explore the local work conditions of the readers to see if there may be fit with the creation of open-shared objects for the world, and for the peoples of today and the future. This first chapter follows the general framework of the text, with a focus on practicality.

1.2 Review of the Literature

The power of "open" is an important point in the sharing of learning contents. Openness is understood in a number of different dimensions:

> the freedom to use the work and enjoy the benefits of using it; the freedom to study the work and to apply knowledge acquired from it; the freedom to make and redistribute copies, in whole or in part, of the information or expression; the freedom to make changes and improvements, and to distribute derivative works (Wenk 2010, p. 435, with some small punctuation changes).

The Open Learning Object model defines an *open* learning object as "any *open* digital resource that can be reused to support learning," where contents are in "open format (e.g. Open Document) or content in closed format whose source files are also available (e.g. Adobe Flash). Moreover, our vision of reusability is not simply based on combining LOs but goes beyond this towards a pedagogical concept of reusability in which a LO can evolve to meet specific educational requirements" (Fulantelli et al. 2008, p. 6).

Broadly speaking, "open educational resources" (OERs) emerged as a concept and a practice in 2002 at a UNESCO conference. The idea was that the world lacked the higher education infrastructure to fully educate the world's youth, which would be coming of age soon. To harness their capabilities, having OERs freely available would enable more to access higher learning. Also, OERs could enable the fulfillment of the human right to education *through higher education* and not just K12. Originally, OERs were created for uses in formal learning settings (Wenk 2010, p. 435) but have evolved to be applied to nonformal and informal settings as well. One description suggests that OERs online are "quasi-courses" that are openly provided and "enabled by information and communication technologies, for consultation, use and adaptation by a community of users for noncommercial purposes" (De Vries 2013, p. 56 and 59). These may include "lecture materials" and "educational software like computer-based simulations and experiments" (Wiley 2007, p. 4), among others. Others add larger-size elements: courseware, learning management systems, learning object repositories, and educational courses (Koohang and Harman 2007).

A few years later, the concepts expanded further, to be inclusive of learning content (defined as "courses, modules, learning objects, exercises, references to collections and archives"), software, hardware, an "implementation resource" (such as "creative commons licenses, best practice design principles"), interoperability standards, and media ("images, audio recordings, videos") (Wenk 2010, p. 436). OERs are "liberally licensed for re-use" and often "free from restrictions to modify, combine and repurpose the content" (Geser 2012, p. 20).

The impetus was also based on technology—based on the sense that (intangible) digital goods were non-rivalrous and could accommodate any number of users after an object was created. While most would not argue technological determinism, certainly the enablements played a role in mass human sharing. The OER endeavors require sufficient infrastructure, so the resources may be used, including: "technology (hardware, software, connectivity, standards, etc.); organization (technical competencies, training, standardization communities), policy (openness, business model)" (UNESCO 2002a, as cited in Downes 2007, p. 33).

As one example, the year prior to the coining of "OERs," MIT OpenCourseWare was founded to make available the Massachusetts Institute of Technology's courses to a wider audience.

> Annual budgets for MIT OCW projected from 2007 through 2011 average just over USD 4,300,000 per year, with the most resources allocated to staff (USD 2,095,000 per year), technology (USD 1,046,000 per year), and contracted services (USD 562,000 per year). An average spend of USD 4,300,000 per year on an average of 540 courses produced per year makes for an average cost of just under USD 10,000 per course. (Wiley 2007, p. 8)

Those numbers are from over a decade ago, and the costs have certainly risen. The types of objects included as OERs have also broadened. Certainly the development of larger learning contents are costly, but the ability to reach learners at a mass scale may justify the inputs (Rodriguez 2013).

One conceptualization about the types of open educational resources shows the simpler level ones as those for individual learning experiences; on the more complex end are those that are configurable and personalized (OER III) and at their most complex, "exponential" and "collaboration"-based (OER IV), including "a large interrelated cluster of cultural-historical, activity-theoretic, socio-cultural, situated, ecological, distributed, and extended cognition models" (Tuomi 2012, p. 12).

The logistics of actualizing the vision of open-shared learning resources has evolved, from "*de facto* standards" for various types of digital files (Wiley 2007, p. 13) and required (metadata) annotations for re-use (p. 14; Fulantelli et al. 2008, p. 7). There have been in advancements in metadata schemes, methods to enhance learning object findability by both humans and computers, more effective ways to segue from one learning sequence to another, standards-setting for legal and accessible learning contents, licensure schemes to enable clearer releases, more sophisticated user interface designs, mobile-friendly contents, and other endeavors.

The shared contents come in various sizes or granularities. The understanding of digital object granularity (size) in the online learning context depends in part on the context of re-use and the item conventions and technologies. Small granularity objects may be "slide presentation components" but also "images in encyclopedia articles"; medium granularity objects may be "learning modules" for online courses as well as "software libraries"; large granularity objects may be "courses" and "web services" that enable mashups (Ochoa and Duval 2008, p. 323).

Adoption of Open Learning Objects While the created learning contents are often available for free, people down the line have had to invest into the objects and learning resources. The rationale for this funding and investment is the benefit to learners who receive the learning contents. User demand for the resources are often the main metric for these endeavors, and who users are and what their needs are are critical to understand:

> The question of use and user demand is itself intimately tied to questions of cost and sustainability: There is no avoiding the fact that sustainability of open educational resource initiatives will be determined ultimately by actual user demand (Harley 2008, p. 198).

Multiple researchers suggest that the adoption of OER has been somewhat slower than initial expectations might have suggested. One writes: "The theoretical benefits of Open Educational Practices (OEP) have become understood in the academic community but thus far, the use of OER has not been rapidly adopted" (Atenas et al. 2014). Barriers to OER adoption by academics have been explored: "language barriers, quality of the resources, difficulty finding content, time consuming, adaptability of the resources, relevance of the resources, licensing issues, lack of training, (and) technological challenges" (Atenas et al. 2014, p. 37).

While the Global South has "a dearth of quality materials" (Kanwar et al. 2010, p. 65), that need alone has "not translated into concrete and tangible results" (p. 68); problematically, "the flow of OER is happening in one direction only, from the global North to the global South" (p. 68), raising concerns of external OER development dominance. The authors note that there were some OER endeavors in the developing world, namely in India, China, South Africa, and Vietnam, then (Kanwar et al. 2010, p. 68). Some open learning contents have no takers, and it is important to explicitly bring on local partners to encourage buy-in even if such a "bottom-up participatory approach requires much longer time frames" (Kanwar et al. 2010, p. 69 and 71). Local users in the global South need to be empowered to use OER and go through a process of "domestication" of the OERs (involving the four phases: "appropriation, localization, incorporation, and conversion" (Kanwar et al. 2010, p. 76), which results ultimately in the integration of the individual into a global community of OER developers and sharers.

Globally, many objects are built that do not transfer well over the digital divide. Some content requires high Internet connectivity and complex graphics card capabilities to function appropriately. Or the learning may be designed using English alone (Willems and Bossu 2012), when a third of Internet users "never or rarely ever visit English language Web sites (DePalma et al. 2006, p. 4, as cited in Richter and McPherson 2012, p. 204). Some learning objects are not mobile friendly, limiting their use in developing countries where mobile phones are the devices of choice for online learning.

One of the necessary requirements is to build open learning resources in ways that are inclusive and designed for uptake and usage. If the success of commercial goods are measured by their sales, the success of open shared learning resources are measured by their adoption and reuse, and their ability to find an audience. In general, the adoption of shared educational objects tend to be mapped as a power law, with a few objects receiving a lot of attention and a long tail or rarely or never used objects. Researchers found a 10% adoption rate for open educational textbooks on one platform (Straumsheim 2016) and a 20% learning object reuse rate across the board (Ochoa 2011, 2018). Most such shared learning contents are mostly left in the realm of the Great Unread or the Great Unused; they are non-performing, delivering benefit only at the point of their creation but not offering value in their finished form. This is even though the barriers to learning object publication are so low, and openness is thought of as a way to reach wider audiences:

> Kansa and Ashley (2005), for example, point to statistics showing that only 27% of research papers are published, and only five percent of research shared. The value of research data, they argue, increases ten times on openness (Kansa and Ashley 2005, as cited in Downes 2007, p. 30).

While open educational resources may be free to access, they are not actually costless to use. Some main challenges to the reuse of educational resources involve "*flexibility*, *context* and *pedagogical expertise*" requiring mitigations such as "*configurable objects, learning scenarios* and an *integrated work environment for educators*" (Klebl, et al. 2010, p. 937), approaches combining information, metadata, interoperability technologies, and other mitigations—which may apply beyond the particular system to which these capabilities were built. Even developers who plan to re-use OERs have to acquire new skills to integrate these (De Vries 2013, p. 56). Repurposing OER "involves additional levels of complexity to designing a learning activity from scratch; namely that the OER first needs to be understood, deconstructed and then redesigned" (Conole et al. 2011, p. 14).

The power to remix learning objects is seen as value-adding to the original resource (Tuomi 2012, p. 5) and creating a sense of "emotional ownership" over the OERs (Clements and Pawlowski 2012, as cited in McKerlich et al. 2013, p. 92). A researcher has defined a four-phase collaborative development cycle of OER: Design & Develop → Redesign → Reuse → Republish (Pawlowski 2012, as cited in McKerlich, Ives, McGreal 2013, p. 92), which suggests value from versioning a work beyond the initial released version. Indeed, an improved OER resource that is redistributed is thought to have achieved the "level where a new accumulative and expansionary dynamic of resource development emerges, as users can become producers who work on the received resource" (Tuomi 2012, p. 6).

Researchers have explored how the size of the shared learning objects may affect their adoption and reuse. Early research suggested that more finely granular objects were more adoptable than more fully packaged and larger-size learning objects. Follow-on research suggests that such generalizations may not be particularly informative and that the local context is important.

> The percentage of object reuse was similar regardless of the granularity of the object. Courses were even reused more often than slide components. Merging the theory with the empirical finding leads to a new interpretation of the role of granularity in the reuse of learning objects. This new interpretation involves also the granularity of the context of reuse as the determining factor. Objects that have a granularity immediately lower than the object being built are easier to reuse than objects with a much lower or higher granularity. For example, when building a course, it is easier to reuse whole lessons than reusing complete courses or individual images. (Ochoa and Duval 2008, p. 324).

If teachers are needing contents for a course, for example, the granularity of the course will determine the type of granularity of object that they would choose.

In a later study, based on survey research, survey respondents were queried about the level of likelihood of their using different types of OER, and the most common types of OER used were (in descending order): scholarly journals, videos, images, textbooks, and audio (McKerlich et al. 2013, p. 95). In terms of the types of OER being created, their range seems to have broadened, including tutorials, quizzes, audio files, video, images, groups of lessons, textbooks, "scenarios case studies," software, other, game, animations, and maps, in descending order (McKerlich et al. 2013, p. 97). Factors that may increase the "use and creation of OER" were found to include "academic quality, course team, knowledge, hardware/software, admin support, time," cost reduction for students, the environment, and recognition" (McKerlich et al. 2013, p. 98).

The collaboration around open educational resources goes beyond the general sense of distributed community. Some groups have stepped forward as volunteers to adapt OER for "language, culture, and relevance" (Albright 2005, as cited in Richter and McPherson 2012, p. 204).

Organizational Considerations for Going Open Learning The open-shared space captures a sense of clash between the "social economy" and the "market economy" (Lane 2008), with activities in both economies affecting the other. While profit-seeking is a necessary part of business survival, corporations are not just about profit-making. "B Corp" corporations help companies promote prosocial and pro-environmental impacts (Certified B Corporation 2018). If organizations are persons, these "persons" also have a moral compass. (Some open-source contents may displace commercial products and upend markets, and vice versa.) At heart, both systems have to focus on sustainability and continuance. For open educational resources to continue, there has to be participation by the various stakeholders, and the resources have to be technologically accessible, the learning contents and designs relevant, the resources available, and designers-developers willing to create and share. One commonly cited approach to defining OER initiatives is defined as comprising five main features: "(1) open courseware and content; (2) open software tools (e.g. learning management systems); (3) open material for e-learning capacity building of faculty staff; (4) repositories of learning objects; and (5) free educational courses" (Hylén 2005, as cited in Downes 2007, p. 30).

Non-profit organizations like higher educational institutions seem to be better positioned to straddle the social economy (of sharing) and the market economy (of survival and sustainability through profit-making). In this sense, it is easier for institutions of higher education to create the space for participating in the OER community.

> There may be different reasons for an institution to launch an OER initiative. They can be categorized as *altruistic,* where there are benefits to individual learners (who are not paying fees to the institution), to other educational institutions (often in developing nations) and to the wider society; *commercial,* where the university increases its visibility through an OER initiative leading to increased student recruitment or other funding possibilities; and *transformational,* where there are positive impacts on the structure, processes and content of the institution carrying out the OER project (Sclater 2009, p. 3).

Those organizations that take on OER generally have to either have the excess capacity or a funding stream to support the work. Otherwise, the work only occurs on the margins.

Some Effects of "OER" Beyond Learning Open educational resources are conceptualized as creating a larger space for human development globally. Other effects are hypothesized as well. There is the political sense that increasing access to education has political impacts in how learners are viewed (as autodidacts or self learners) and are empowered through education (Phelan 2012). If designed using inclusive pedagogy, learning objects may enhance diversity and promote "social inclusion by cultivating an awareness of the complexity of student diversity among university teachers whose traditional forms of pedagogy often fail to maximize intercultural learning, address inequalities, handle tension, and deal with sensitive issues" (Hockings, et al. 2012, p. 250). Shared learning objects may highlight the variation in people's "practices, ethnicity, and belief alongside class, locality and gender" (Hockings, et al. 2012, p. 250).

There is also the sense that "releasing content openly imposes evolutionary pressures that accelerate change and work around barriers" (Lane and McAndrew 2010,

p. 1). These can serve as a forcing function for teaching and learning practices, with more of a focus on learners and the power of learner expectations. In a sense, the social norms around academic output have evolved, and part of academic output may be digital scholarship (Scanlon 2014, p. 12) even though such channels for publishing and dissemination may be less formal. Currently, there are not common citation conventions for shared learning objects, however.

A core concept of the OER movement is that "the world's knowledge is a public good and that technology in general and the World Wide Web in particular provide an extraordinary opportunity for everyone to share, use, and reuse that knowledge" (Smith and Casserly 2006, p. 10). That vision of open sharing is not without costs nor risks, and sustainability has been a concern, given the protectionism around research information in higher education and "the strains of anti-intellectual-ism and protectionism that run deep in parts of the world all threaten the open spread of knowledge. These threats can only be offset by the enthusiasm, imagination, and commitment to open knowledge that we see in people as we travel throughout the world (Smith and Casserly 2006). In real space, though, personal enthusiasm only carries people so far. That is not to say that there were not early identified headwinds, including copyright, "fears of low recognition for OA publications," competition for scarce resources, and competition with commercial goods, among others (OLCOS 2007, as cited in Yuan et al. 2008, p. 5), as identified by Open e-Learning Content Observatory Services (OLCOS). In the longer term (identified through 2012), anticipated inhibitors include difficult business models, a "lack of institutional policies and incentives for educators to excel in OER," insufficient investment in "training and support" to ensure that teachers can create and share such contents, costly educational metadata creation, and a gap in the "advanced tools and services for educational repository" (OLCOS 2007, as cited in Yuan et al. 2008, p. 6). Now, well beyond the long term of the initial thinkers on this issue, what is the state of open educational resources?

Where some see limited resources, others see plenty, even a glut. "Now, instead of scarcity of educational resources, in this new technology age we are faced with open content, open resources, open learning, open architecture in design of physical and virtual spaces, open source, and open knowledge, all of which have blossomed in the last 10 years" (Batson et al. 2008, p. 90). There may be a potential for industrial level production of open learning contents (Tuomi 2012). And yet, there are some learning domains that are more over-built and others that have been barely explored.

1.3 Environmental Scans of the Open Sharing Learning Environment and Local Starts

Understanding the operational environment is critical to successfully creating and deploying effective open-shared learning resources (both objects and sequences/sets). An environmental scan can show the "state of the art," or where this practice is at in terms of content and technologies. In this context, an environmental scan is an exploration of the external ecosystem—the open-shared learning environment on the Web and Internet. The scan informs what the market will bear, or what the learner market is interested in and what the public learner expectations are for the learning resources. To achieve a sense of what is possible for open-shared learning, it is important to explore both what is in the world currently through an environmental scan and what may be possible to contribute locally based on limited resources. From the observations of the space, designer/developers may apply abductive reasoning or abductive inference to arrive at some plausible understandings of the space.

A History of Open-Shared Learning Contents At present, there are no clearly defined taxonomies of open-shared learning contents in the academic literature. As noted earlier, these may be analog or digital. There are broad ways to sketch these. One major differentiator between the types of open-shared learning objects are by whether these are large-scale funded endeavors with elicited contents (usually from respected universities and recognized experts) or unfunded endeavors with self-offered user-generated contents.

The first funded set tends to have recognized big-name experts, mixed-skills development teams, full courses (with analogs or comparatives to credit-based university courses), mid-to-high level production values, and often a loyal user base (such as for "massive open online courses" or "MOOCs"). The contents tend to feature original contents and high production values and a sense of refinement. The technologies supporting such contents may be custom-built online learning platforms, adaptive hypermedia, high-end simulations, and more complex technological builds.

By contrast, the latter unfunded set tends to have mixed expertise. This group includes non-experts who create "click-bait" contents to drive traffic to their respective video or slideshow-sharing or other such social media sharing accounts, for fleeting and non-committal low-engagement interactions. There are limited development teams (often only the individual content expert), single learning objects or limited online learning sequences, low-to-mid level production values, little adherence to extant applicable laws, and no defined user base (except in the occasional cases when the subject matter expert (SME) has brand recognition). For these objects, there are rarely concerted outreaches to potential user audiences.

Funded endeavors may involve human-led courses; in most of the cases, open-shared learning contents are non-human-led but automated. In terms of formal learning, the funded endeavors tend to offer a majority of resources that meet formal learning needs (with credit offered). In terms of nonformal learning, learning from non-credit but structured experiences like seminars, both funded and unfunded sources provide learning contents for these. Finally, in terms of informal learning, the unfunded user-generated contents set seems to contain more for informal learning. Also, large-scale funded contents seem to often be delivered via custom-created hosted systems, with varying levels of downloadable contents; many of these seem to be about delivering a full online learning experience, with instructor(s) and co-learners

Table 1.1 Learning object types and sequences from raw to processed, fine granularity to coarser granularity

Raw materials (analog and digital)	Analog and digital learning objects	Integrated elements, portable digital objects	Online learning series and sequences	Higher digital immersion spaces
Imagery Audio Video Text Data Collections of items at this granularity	Image Map Figure Drawing Timeline Slide Paragraph or section Screen grab Audio snippet Data visualization Sequences Definitions Acronyms Animated GIFs	Slideshow Digital poster Article E-book Photo album Audio files Video Podcast Chapter Data table Lecture notes Assignments Assessments	Series of any of the prior Image set/collection Datasets Mixed sets of curated or uncurated objects Websites Learning portals Wikis Publications Sequences of any of the prior: full courses, massive open online courses (MOOCs), dataset collections, and others	Game Simulation Virtual world E-book Case Story Problem-solution Scenario Short course Play Long course Sequence LMSes Repositories Environments

and even in-world events. These systems capture a range of data about the learners, and some of this data have appeared in academic publications about the learners and their performances. Unfunded self-created contents seem to be less bounded to hosted systems and may be available on one or more content-sharing social media platforms, which may be harnessed for the sharing of learning objects.

In terms of accessibility accommodations, funded instructional projects seem to meet these standards more consistently than unfunded ones. For the first, the videos have closed captioning or timed text transcription, and the images have alt-text (alternative text), and the interactivity are keyboard enabled (instead of necessarily requiring a mouse). There may be downloadable or copyable transcripts. In terms of the unfunded contents, accessibility may be happenstance, such as the inclusion of captioning with some imagery, and accessibility may not always designed for or addressed.

Given the breadth of open-shared objects and sequences for learning, another way to think about open-shared learning objects is by “size” and “granularity”. One approach may be seen in Table 1.1, with the smallest granular pieces in the leftmost column and the most integrated coarser granularity items to the right. The small sizes of the elements in the left-most column may be automatically transcluded into various documents and pages as needed, based on the sense of learning relevance for the particular learner or the learning context.

Sometimes, concepts precede actions. As precedents for open-shared learning, related concepts may be the following: the “cathedral and the bazaar” (CatB), learning objects, non-rivalrous digital goods, open educational resources, learning object reusability, open-access, open-source, crowd-sourcing, and others. Early funders to this effort include both non-profit foundations and governments and institutions of higher education.

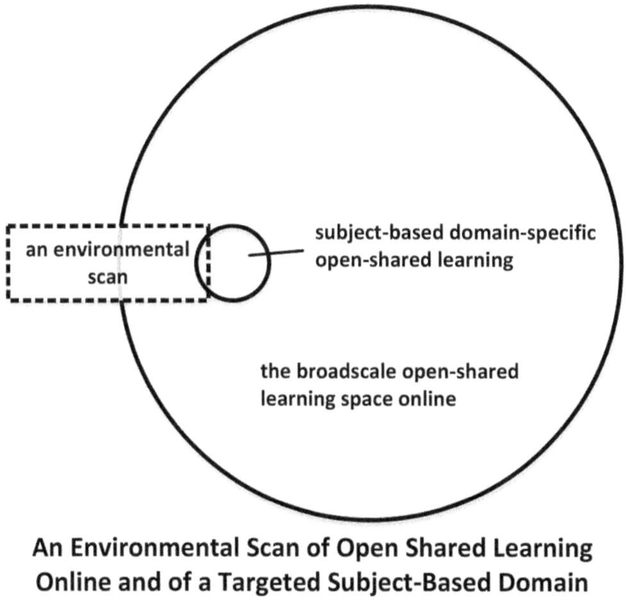

Fig. 1.2 An environmental scan of open shared learning online and of a targeted subject-based domain

State of the Open-Shared Learning Ecosystem Online For open-shared learning objects and sequences, the ecosystem is generally found online, on the Web and Internet. This scan may initially focus on subject-based domain-specific open-shared learning and then broaden to the larger ecosystem (Fig. 1.2). Collections may be found on websites, learning object referatories, learning object repositories, databases, learning management systems, content management systems, wikis, virtual immersive worlds, and other web-facing locales. The membership (stakeholders) include those with various interests: the funders, the educational institutions, the government agencies, the corporate technology-makers, the designers-developers, the learners, and others. Among these entities and individuals, there are a mix of interactions and interests, some mutual and some in conflict.

A brief scan shows that there are destination sites for particular topics and for types of learning, which may suggest a crowd-sourced rush to quality. (This same dynamic may be seen with free software, music, and other digital contents shared online.) In general, the most trustworthy sources seem to be those with solid and regular funding, often with proprietary technology platforms (Khan Academy, Coursera, MIT OpenCourseware, and others). At the fringes are smaller objects created to meet local needs that have been shared globally in case others may find value in the objects.

The reasons to conduct an environmental scan are several-fold. They help individuals understand how the space has evolved given real-world pressures and real-world incentives. They help an individual or team understand what resources are available around particular topics and around particular learning groups (particularly split out in age categories). They showcase what technologies are used. They enable people to see where the funding is coming from and what the apparent interests of the funders are. They give a sense of what the general public uses in terms of the available contents…and what they ignore. The point of an environmental scan is also to identify the standards applied to the design and development of learning objects and sequences not for emulation's sake, but for standard setting.

Once a brief environmental scan has been conducted of the larger space, it helps to think about how the individual designer/developer may relate to that space.

Conducting an External Environmental Scan What are some ways to conduct an external environmental scan around the open sharing of learning objects? An initial approach may involve a skim of the overall ecosystem to understand what is generally available, what technologies are generally used, who the main participants are, the general quality of the contents, and other dimensions.

A subject domain-based environmental scan may explore what open-shared learning objects are available for the particular topic, who seems to be creating them, the quality of the objects, the types of objects (informational, procedural, demonstrative, analytical, or others; types of learning approaches; technologies used; types of learner actions required; levels of learning and intrinsic cognitive load required for the topic and the expected germane cognitive load required for schema- and sense-making and others).

Then, more targeted explorations may be done, such as based on particular search terms, technologies, developers, platforms, and so on. It helps to begin with a direct search of relevant related terms to the search phenomena. List the various links, and explore them. Go to the Social Web, and identify the main individuals, entities, groups, and others on that space. Explore their messaging and endeavors. Explore the online communities around the use and creation of open-shared learning contents. Explore the repositories and referatories made for learning objects. Explore virtual immersive worlds to see what learning contents are available there. Further out, explore the technologies related to this space.

Task #1: Exploring the External Environment
Do a broad general search and identify some platforms with open-shared learning objects, and explore some of what is available in your area of expertise. Write a paragraph each to describe the respective learning objects.

Applied Technologies The types of technologies used for online learning objects and sequences include the following types:

- Digital recording tools (hardware like scanners, digital cameras, audio recorders, sound mixing boards. and others; software like screen recorders, *machinima* tools, and others)
- Digital editing tools (for media like imagery, audio, video; websites)
- Digital authoring tools (for creating diagrams, learning objects, simulations, and others)
- Courseware systems
- Learning management systems
- Immersive virtual worlds
- Scripting languages

There are certainly others as well.

Main Funders of Open-Shared Learning Resources According to the "OER World Map," the main OER funders are a mix of foundations (family and corporate) and government agencies, and most are located in the U.S. and Europe (OER World Map n.d.) The funders of particular topic-based learning objects differs based on the stated objectives of the organizations and how such objects may promote those.

Funding for creating open resources may come from endowments for "base funding," coalitional memberships of contributing organizations for open educational resource development and sharing, community donations, a conversion model of changing users of free resources to paying customers, contributor-pay models (in which those who develop resources pay for their distribution), sponsorship support (in which payers for a resource are recruited but the created goods are shared freely to the public), an institutional model (a higher educational institution co-sponsors the content development), a government model (with grant-funding by government agencies), voluntary support models (likened to a "tip jar"), and others from the research literature (Wiley 2007, pp. 15–17). Certainly, there are combinations of the above approaches and others as well. The general model assumed in this book is of *pro bono* work by professionals and subject matter experts with the good will to share, content to distribute, and the skills to actualize the work.

Online and F2F Supports for Creators of Open-Shared Learning Objects Designing and developing learning resources for open sharing can be challenging work, with advances occurring in fits-and-starts. As with writing, designer/developer work can be somewhat alone work. The work can take anywhere from several hours to months and even years. If people are working in teams or in partnership, the members can provide mutual support to each other. This is so whether they are co-located or distributed.

Beyond local support, people may find support online, in virtual communities. These may include social networks built up on social media platforms, software technology communities (which are often designed explicitly for mutual support

Task #2: Social Supports for Builders of Open-Shared Learning Objects
There are some groups on social networking sites to support those who build (design and develop) open-shared learning objects. Identify as many as you can with an initial search, and then identify a few that may be ones that you might want to join. Identify what features of these groups feel welcoming to you.

and tip sharing), and other social care. Depending on the level of social support needed, it is important for people to engage with others constructively for their own mental health and resilience in the face of stress, and for the advancement of the work.

1.3.1 Domain-Specific and Interdisciplinary Topical Exploration

In terms of what is available in the open-shared spaces, there may be high variances depending on the subject matter. Before proceeding to create learning contents, it may help to conduct an external environmental scan to see what open-shared learning contents are already available, what the most cutting-edge technologies are in-use, and where there may be gaps in available contents (through a gaps analysis). The environmental scan involves looking at both what is there (what exists) and what is not there (what should exist). This scanning approach ensures that the individual or team is using the most recent and most informative design and development approaches available. Further, the individual or team will better understand the social competition for limited attention. It is hard to go to Google Search and find nothing on virtually any known topic in the world, in general. Identified informational "dead zones" are purposeful blanks based on protectionist governments, commercial companies, organizations, and individuals, all savvy about what should be protected.

While the current age is all about the "sharing economy," the "sharing" is more about access to what was conceived of as private goods (cars for ride shares, housing for brief stays, and other possessions) put out for public use for earning money (and maybe using fewer natural resources); the "sharing" is not about beneficent generosity in this sense. The "sharing economy" is about the economy.

After all, if an issue has already been addressed, then anything created thereafter loses any novelty value, and its draw may be much more limited. This is not to say that others cannot challenge resources that already exist by creating a competing resource—especially if designers/developers can conceptualize improved ways to approach the content. This open-shared space is not an unlimited playing field. This is not a case of "build it and they will come"; there are constraints on attention and willingness to explore. Sometimes, reputations can be made based on complementing or augmenting others' existing learning objects; sometimes, reputations can be made by undercutting others' works. That said, building learning objects is not costless, and perhaps, efforts may be spent elsewhere more productively. The better part of valor may also be to acknowledge when one is outclassed—if someone else is already offering a solid learning object or learning sequence on the particular topic.

That said, if there are no competing works in existence as-yet, then basic information may be sufficient to corner the market for a time. If there are extant works, then any newcomer needs to differentiate by offering some combination of the following: updated data, fresh pedagogical approaches, different learning experiences, unique packaging, different authoring technologies, and so on. If the designer/developer is leery of being unduly influenced by the existing open-shared learning resources, he or she may peruse the environment, identify the competitor objects, scan them briefly, design their own in depth, and then re-review the competitor objects in depth for analytical purposes and to make sure that there is no unintended overlap. In general, one does not purposefully design something to be a counterpoint to an existing open-shared learning object. In some cases, competing viewpoints may be addressed with head-to-head combatting learning objects. In such cases, for learner interests, the consumption of both together may be informative.

During the environmental scan, it is important to skim the top-level of available learning objects and sequences *to set the baseline* for design and development. The assumption generally is that the quality learning objects and resources garner the most attention over time as the general public is selective and chooses what is most relevant to them. (However, massive amounts of human traffic can be attracted by cats on Roombas and other sorts of social media spectacles.) The top links in a web search show the most popular destinations for particular search terms, so that recognition alone may not directly testify to quality but be one possible proxy indicator. Reputational indicators may be important since people are willing to share their assessments on social media platforms and on social media features of learning object repositories and e-learning systems. Then, too, there is the ability to evaluate the learning objects and sequences for quality directly.

Some basic common threshold requirements of open-shared learning objects and sequences may include some of the following. The learning contents have to be *credible* or believable based on the source, the factuality of the contents, the up-to-datedness of the contents, the originality, the informational value, the objectivity, and professionalism of the presentation (clear writing, respectful and consistent tone). The contents should also be designed for *learning value*, with proper and logical sequencing, full technological functionality, properly designed experiences/assignments/assessments, applicable information, and so on. It should also be *usable*, with full functionality, full accessibility, clear navigation, and aesthetically pleasing touches. These three boldfaced elements are summary ones. How these features are perceived is partially subjective. All learning objects have their tradeoffs, with strengths and weaknesses. Also, there are likely decisions made based on the perceived *suitability or fit* of the learning object or sequence to the learner and to the task and the context. For shared learning objects, the contents may not be novel in the way research contents generally have to be; for example, a learning object that is packaged in a way that is understandable to a learner new to the subject matter may have high learning value.

Why are the most effective learning objects (in a particular topical domain) used as the baseline for a new learning object? Well, the usual available learning objects are several years old, and as such, they are lagging indicators for what is going on in the field. The idea is not to build to the old but to use what exists as a baseline minimum.

It is important to identify the leading creators of the learning objects and explore what their offerings are as well. This scan will inform any designs, which should meet all the required in-house standards for legality, ethics, accessibility, usability, and so on, but also out-class any of the publicly available open-shared learning contents. The idea is to ensure that whatever is created actually contributes something important…and is accepted in the space.

More importantly, during the environmental scan, a *topic-based sampler* of extant online learning objects should be collected. These may include both open-shared contents as well as proprietary ones. Those that may not be downloaded may be screenshot or recorded and described (for in-house usage), so that the contents are clearly represented. This curated set should be analyzed to answer some of the following questions:

- What learning objects and learning sequences are most effective? Why?
- What learning objects and learning sequences are the least effective? Why?
- What technologies are being used to build these objects?
- What operating systems are being built to? What web browsers? What platforms? What devices?
- What are the explicit depictions of the topic in the respective learning objects and sequences?
- What are the implicit assumptions made in the respective learning objects and sequences?
- Where are the gaps in available learning objects and learning sequences for this topic? Why do such gaps exist? What contents may fill such gaps?

This curated set may serve both situational awareness and informed design inspiration. This approach is not about being directly emulative or mimicking but about learning from what works and what does not work, what the "competition" looks like, and how to advantage-seek through proper design, development, and available features. One strength of a designer/developer is that he or she is a "prosumer," both a producer of and consumer of learning resources.

A Proprietary Learning Ecosystem Around Topics of Interest In the same way that the open-shared space is of interest, the proprietary one is important. Such proprietary sources include book publishers, filmmaking companies, learning management system (LMS) companies, and others in the space. Those working in academia should have access to many of these materials as part of their work. Many companies are amenable to having instructors review proprietary materials for possible adoption. These proprietary materials may be assessed also for informational contents, technologies used, and possible topical gaps.

1.3.2 Explore Potential Gaps in Available Open-Access Learning in a Particular Domain in an Open Sharing Context

To simplify, a "gaps analysis" is an effort to define a desirable ideal state and the distance between that state and the present. A version of a "gaps analysis" can be an ideal available open-shared learning sequence and the present, which would involve defining a desired sequence and then seeing what is available in the world…and mapping the gaps. This approach does not use direct learner needs as a basis for identification of "demand" but rather a theorized learning sequence: "for learners to get from this understanding "A" to understanding "B," they need to be exposed to these concepts and activities. And at present, they lack access to such materials."

A "gaps analysis" approach may enrich the environmental scan. This analysis involves exploration of the environment in order to look for gaps in available open-access educational and training information online. How to understand a gap is important here. There are multiple ways to approach this. If a learner wants to acquire certain topical awareness, knowledge, skills, or attitudes, where could they go to acquire this? What navigational paths can they cobble through a learning sequence, and how coherently can those learning sequences be created? Or what gaps are there in these learning sequences? (A more complex gaps analysis may look at what other open-shared learning contents may be accessed to substitute for missing contents.)

What if the learners have differing needs, such as if their interest in the topic is as an amateur (an individual who wants to know some light information but not to study the field in depth) or a novice (an individual with little expertise in the topic but who aspires to expertise at some point) or a pro (an expert in the topic who is evaluating the learning objects for usage for teaching or some other purpose)? Or what if the learner is approaching the topic from variant age backgrounds: pre-school, kindergarten, Grades 1–3, Grades 4–5, Grades 6–8, Grades 9–12 (high school), undergraduate studies (higher education), graduate studies (higher education), post-graduate studies, post-doctoral studies, professional lives, lifelong learning, and others? Or what if a potential learner is interested in acquiring new information about the topic vs. a person acquiring information for review? In other words, for a given topic, is there a gap in available learning materials for individuals with varying learning needs based on their varying backgrounds? The idea is that gaps may be fulfilled by unique objects to meet unique custom or boutique needs, in some cases; in others, multiple gaps may be fulfilled by single objects or series.

If there are extant learning objects available, but these are poor quality, inaccurate, incomplete, dated, or inaccessible, those are show-stoppers, and these objects should not be listed in the available category. The idea is that a gaps analysis should identify learning object needs that are as-yet unfulfilled based on the environmental scan. Also, if resources are available, but the cost is prohibitive (they are hosted behind a paywall) and the code is proprietary and unavailable, then for the purposes of the gaps analysis, the contents are unavailable in the open-shared learning space.

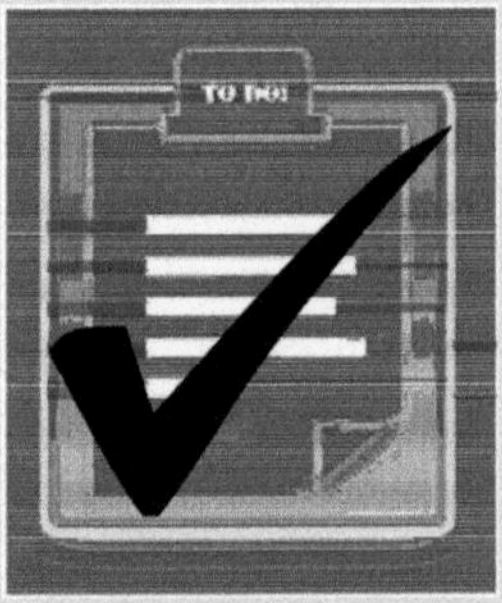

Task #3: Domain-Based Gaps Analysis
List your subject domain of interest. Review some of the learning resources in that domain, and identify half a dozen unaddressed topics in that domain. Consider why these observed gaps might exist.

1.3.3 Local Workplace and Designer/Developer Life Conditions

Another early assessment involves evaluating the local workplace and the designer/developer life facts in order to understand capabilities, interests, and goals. A critical partner in this endeavor may be an enlightened workplace which has sharing and community values as a goal (or a work place which chooses to turn a blind eye if some of its technologies are used for open-shared learning resources on off-hours). This cooperative relationship is considered here.

1.3.4 Define the Local Workplace or Organizational Context (for Issues of Domain Expertise, Interests in Open-Shared Learning) and Some Cost-Benefit Considerations as Precursors to Possible Designing and Developing for Open Sharing

People acquire knowledge and skills in different ways. Most commonly, these are acquired in workplaces and in personal-interest pursuits. If an individual wants to create open-shared learning objects under the auspices of their employer, he or she will need to acquire appropriate permissions to do so, especially if workplace technologies and resources may be used, even in off-hours. In ideal circumstances, designing and building open-shared learning objects may involve whole-of-organization supports. Of course, there may be whole-of-organization interests in the public-facing aspects of open-shared learning objects, for reputation management, brand building, public relations, and other concerns. The relationship is not necessarily one-directional, and there can be a symbiosis.

If a workplace is brought into the building of open-shared learning resources, the members of the team should remember that workplace interests come first. The open-shared learning resources are a non-priority relative to the mainline work unless the organizational leadership suggests otherwise. And the uses of the technologies and workspaces are *de minimus* usage only.

In work places, the cost-benefit calculation is not about designer/developer largesse alone. Or about one-directional altruistic efforts towards enacting social justice. The creation of open-shared learning objects is a way to use up any over-capacity, and it is a way to develop and maintain high levels of skills among the workforce. It is a way of creating and maintaining positive public relations. It may serve as a bridge to the sales of products and services. In many sense, whether to take on the creation of open-shared learning resources is about "fit" to the organization's interests and "timing" (how much the new work impinges on current work). These endeavors may benefit the workplace and the workers and ultimately the field. (If a commitment is made to create open-shared learning contents, organizations tend to rationalize and explain the decision—as individual persons will. An important point is not to trade the real for the fake, real costs for illusory gains. This would suggest that accurate measures would be important to understand the actual implications of open-shared learning resources.

The organization may also benefit from engaged employees who feel good about the work place and who are enhancing their work-based skills with various projects and who are engaging the larger social environment as professionals.

Conducting an Internal Organizational Scan To these ends, an "internal scan" of the organization may be necessary to better understand organizational interests, the leadership, the available resources, and possible open-shared projects that may align with the organization. Certainly, the authorizing environment (how the influencers around an individual affect his/her decision making and actions, often as delimiters) around each individual will differ, and the authorizations will shape what is possible and what supports are available. In institutions of higher education, such work may be allowed during project down times and in the service of professional presentations—but there is little excess capacity otherwise.

In every workplace, there are some types of information that may be protected and cannot be released because they might compromise commercial interests, safety, security, people's identities, branding, or other corporate interests. Clearly, competitive advantage, safety, security, individual privacy, branding, and such, are all more important than sharing learning objects and learning sequences as acts of social generosity. A lack of awareness of priorities can be dangerous to the designer/developer and to the organization.

What are some questions to ask in an internal scan to test its readiness for supporting open-shared learning endeavors?

- What are the main objectives for the organization's or business's existence (their *raison d'être)*? What are the organization's values? What are the messages in the organization's brand?
- Who are the leaders in this organization that may be interested in open-shared learning objects?
- What are resources that may be available for building open-shared learning objects and learning sequences?
- What are bureaucratic endeavor that may be harnessed for the building and sharing of learning objects and learning sequences?
- Are there any *natural* partnerships that may be created? Within the organization? Outside the organization?
  - How much may be reasonably asked or expected for such open sharing endeavors? Why?
  - What are objective ways to test these propositions?
- What are public-facing organizational interests that may be promoted with open-shared learning objects?
  - What are some ways to monetize open-shared learning objects, such as by leading individuals to paid products and services?

For some whose organizations will not explicitly fund such efforts, they may engage in so-called "feral" development off-the-books. "Feral" work in an information technology context refers to systems built in the wild to meet employee needs but often without the approval of central administration (Kerr et al. 2014). Such work may result in risks to the organization, not only of resource mis-use but also the purposeful or accidental release of sensitive or proprietary information. On the public facing side, off-message text/subtext communications may cause harm to the brand. However, some feral projects may be constructive and fruitful for the organization as well; they may prove rewarding to employees in the workplace.

Screening by project topic may also be done to determine whether there is fit to "the culture, resources, or available talent" of the organization (Hsu et al. 2011,

p. 514). Practically, it would make more sense to start with topics of mutual interest.

Considerations of I/O (Inputs and Outputs) Another way to approach the question of whether a particular open sharing project should be taken on involves the balance between necessary inputs and likely potential outputs (Fig. 1.3). Ideally, the best leveraged work is to have low costs (inputs, investments) but high value outputs (gains), or colloquially, the "low-hanging fruit". In terms of a quality focus, only what should result in high value outputs should be pursued, but that may include the "high costs, high value" quadrant.

In many cases, whether to proceed with an open-shared project or series of such projects is a personal calculation, for the individual and for the team members. This is because the work requires heavy personal agency and investment. Building learning objects will not be sustainable if it is a road to nowhere. End of story. Optimally, what works best seems to be a mix of internal motivation and external motivation. For example, a designer/developer has a background in a particular topic but would like to learn more (internal motivation); he or she will be participating in a regional conference on an aligned topic and has proposed a topic about which he or she can use the building of the learning object to learn more (external motivation). Perhaps there is a topic that a designer/developer wants to pursue and needs just a little extra motivation to follow through. Or he or she prefers the ephemera of public attention as an ego stroke. The alignment of incentives may provide a path forward to actualize an open-shared learning object in the world, to benefit the creator(s) in the local context, to enable actualization of the designer/developers, and to optimally benefit many others in the larger global context. (The "who benefits" consideration is important because there may be intended beneficiaries as well as unintended ones. Designers/developers do not want to give advantage unthinkingly to various entities, whether commercial or non-commercial, private or public. It helps to think a few degrees out in terms of implications.)

The simple math suggests that the costs are many—for overhead, technologies, the design work, the development work, the testing, the launch, and the post-launch support, among others. A deeper look suggests that the years spent in formal education and practice means that most learning objects are serious loss leaders. (The popularized 10,000-h rule to acquire high-end expertise may actually be a low number given the complex skill sets of professionals today in developed countries.) For those who may rely on their workplaces to absorb some of the costs of development, the designers-developers are not shouldering the actual full costs of their efforts. They are not having to respond to market pressures, and worse yet, they may learn dependencies on others' resources in order to achieve this work. Learned inefficiencies are not helpful to their own competitiveness, particularly if they habituate to such protected contexts. Their open-shared work would be vulnerable to workplace sensitivities and shifts. Separate from their support contexts, their endeavors would not be sustainable in the real world.

The ties of open-shared learning objects and sequences to people's reputations and egos, to people's self-expression and self-actualization, to people's studies and

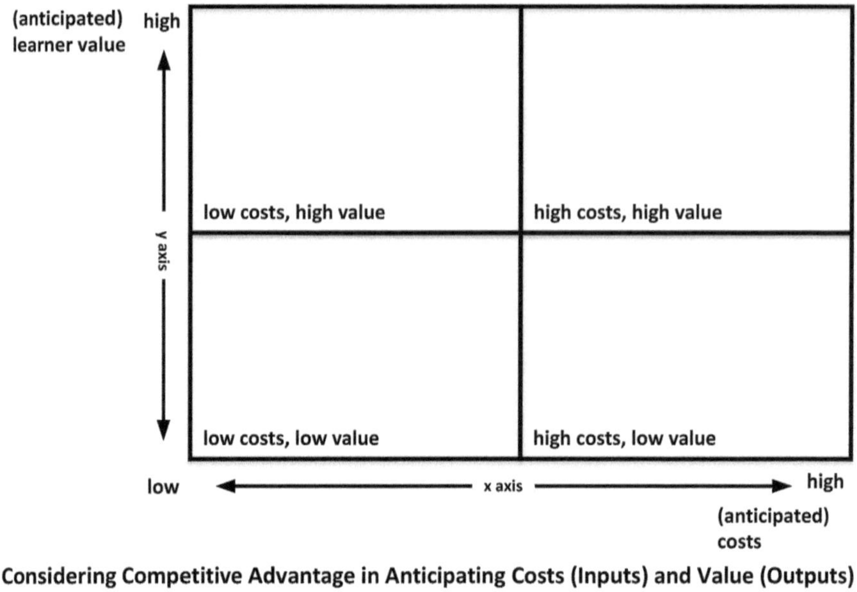

Fig. 1.3 Considering competitive advantage in anticipating costs (inputs) and value (outputs)

workplace ambitions, may muddy the waters of the actual dynamics of costs-benefits calculation. After all, how much does one value learning objects that are the extensions of the self in the world? And yet, it is important to bring in these various factors because they are part of the equations for many.

Some digital contents may entail additional costs. There may be unforeseen risks, which may entail legal costs. Balanced against this is usually a paycheck of $0, which suggests a severe asymmetry. (Ironically, in this context, if one offers work that is not free, one is already priced out of participating in this market. The reasons for this are complex and not necessarily fiar. Unless there is a financial stream—from commercial products and services, from tuition, from charitable donations—those who host such items do not have direct financial gain either. Learning objects do not have obvious monetization streams at present. Without a funding stream, no entity can be faulted for not funding the purchase of some object. The value proposition has to work for all members of the value chain.) On the individual front, if bylines are included with the release of the object, the name recognition is hard to monetize. In terms of knowledge, skills, and abilities development, or staying limber and in practice, those creativity aspects are beneficial—but those same skills can be attained in more directly monetarily rewarding ways. The sense of personal achievement at providing an actual contribution in a particular space may be sufficient reward for some.

In some contexts, designers/developers invest fairly hefty sums into equipment, technologies, research, digital contents, and labor—in order to actualize the work. This may be because they anticipate some return on investment (ROI) beyond general use of the learning resource. They may assume changes in their work lives. Or they may be enthusiasts with inner drive to share, regardless of the costs. Their energy to share may change up from they calculate costs.

People's attention is thin gruel, but their learning may lead to distributed social benefits for both them and the broader world. Another calculation may be that open-source resources may benefit those who contribute as well—because they are not only designers/developers, but they may also consume others' works, but this is a diffuse logic. It is critical to have some reasoned approach in this context because potential would-be contributors to the open-shared space can "defect" at any time in the process, based on any number of challenges, and they may actually even retract works that were once released. (Open-shared works shared under open licensure are not retractable, but if they are no longer hosted or findable, then they only exist in the versions that have been archived and stored…or in downloaded versions. They are no longer really easily accessible.)

Also, while a work may be created with skill and the best of intentions, going broadly public entails some risk—of learning resource mis-use, of informational mis-representation, of malicious messaging, of reputational risks, and even of law-suits. Any actual cost-benefit calculation has to consider risks (ranging from potential ones to wildcard ones). Building a work properly with professional standards can go a long way to mitigate most known risks, but unknown risks are in the environment as well.

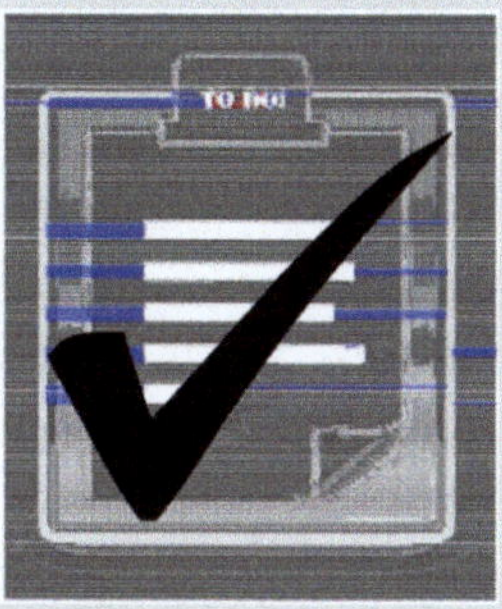

Task #4: Inputs and Outputs

Consider a learning object that you have created before, and calculate the inputs you invested to design and develop and deploy that resource. Then, calculate what you gained from that resource…and what other benefits were captured by others from the sharing of that resource. Consider intended and unintended benefits.

This is not to say that there is not a go-it-alone option, if work places are not amenable to supporting the development of open-shared learning resources. Basic equipment needs are not that expensive, relatively speaking. There are sufficient open-shared technologies that may be used for the development of content. Sometimes, all that is needed is knowledge, skills, and initiative (an inner drive or fire).

Evaluating Self-Readiness for Creating Open-Shared Contents In his famous work, *The Cathedral and the Bazaar,* Eric Raymond observes: "Every good work of software starts by scratching a developer's personal itch" (2000). Another dimension of this is Jim Collins' observation of the criticality of human passion in human endeavors—both for individuals and organizations: "You can't manufacture passion or 'motivate' people to feel passionate. You can only *discover* what ignites your passion and the passions of those around you" (Collins 2001, p. 109). In the same way, those who would create open-shared learning objects often find motivation from personal-based passions and interests. Being motivated by an internal spark or two may be a necessary antecedent to any contribution to the open sharing space.

The cost-benefit calculus has to be done at the individual level, even if the designs and developments are actualized as a team. And in all likelihood, the calculation will not be a pure one because other factors like ego and skill and reputation come into play. The decision making about whether to continue with a work is decided ultimately at the individual level. Some have a personal drive to self-express and to share, and open-shared learning objects may be one such channel. For this calculation, the individual should use the best information available, and they should include the less obvious and non-obvious costs. Creating learning objects based on authorizing documents (like grant funding agreements) is one thing, with everything spelled out. Conceptualizing a learning object *cold* and creating that from scratch is something else and requires much more initiative, creativity, self-drive, and focus.

With an official budget of $0, it becomes even more important to understand where the potential costs may come from and to avoid under-counting. A basic resource for project budgeting follows in Table 1.2. If designed poorly, one can add "legal counsel" to the costs, which results in even more expensive costs.

If the costs are not a non-starter, then it may be helpful to consider an additional potential cost or risk: going public and sometimes going it alone. In Fig. 1.4, this binary decision tree describes a process of individual decision making about whether to pursue making a particular learning object or sequence for open sharing. In this conceptualized sequence, the individual has to have an initial interest in open sharing learning contents. Then, he or she has to assess whether he or she has the requisite expertise…and has to be able to identify a relevant topic from that body of expertise that may stir interest in learners in the broad general public. He or she has to have access to relevant information and contents from which to build a learning object, and then he or she has to have the required resources, including technologies and time and skills. If a basic cost-benefit analysis makes sense, then, he or she may decide to proceed, do the work, check for quality and mitigate for risk, and then launch the object or sequence to the public. This decision tree is set up as a decision sequence for a particular project only because there is not a once-and-for-all decision about creating open-shared learning objects for all contexts and conditions. The social ecosystem may not be equally receptive to a particular work. Also, in this decision tree, any breakage in the sequence can stop the effort in its tracks. Such commitments can be fragile and transient, and people can sometimes be easily dissuaded. While this decision tree describes a process that may be seen as fairly generic and linear, there may be any number of decision sequences that add additional steps or that remove particular steps…and that occur in somewhat different order.

Beyond the decision tree, it may help to ask more granular and specific questions. A basic back-of-the-napkin analysis may be helpful in assessing interest and then professional readiness. The following ten question areas offer a basic start to considering this issue.

1. Are you familiar with the *open sharing (learning) ecosystem* and some of the basic rules of play? Is there *interest in creating learning objects/sequences/resources* that may be valuable to the larger public or to particular targeted publics? How receptive is the social and learning environment to a new learning object? Is the issue fairly timely and relevant in the present or near-present?
2. Are you comfortable *being in public* (or being a public persona) and engaging with strangers now and again? Do you have a sense of a public self for a "personality frame" around the digital learning objects? Do you have a likeable public persona? Are you open to different points-of-view and opinions about your work? Do you empathize with general learners? Are you comfortable with the inherent risk-taking of engaging with people in public space? Are you understanding of some of the diversities of individuals that are reached with a broadly public work? Are you comfortable finessing messaging so as to be inclusive of others and non-offensive in messaging? (The public presence is indirect here, but sharing contents publicly does mean having a public-facing side.)
3. Do you have *a unique and in-depth expertise of interest to learners in the world*? Do you have professional niche expertise and knowledge? Are you well positioned to be able to address the target topic based on professional training and work (and other related) experiences? Do you have unique and in-depth professional experiences of interest to them? Do you have standing and a public identity from which to address the issue? Do you have a fairly neutral stance regarding the possible target topics, so you can approach the topic fairly and comprehensively? Are you willing to share mental space regarding this topic? Is there an internal drive to share knowledge? Do you have *a unique point-of-view* related to the target domain? Are you positioned in a way that is advantageous for creating open-shared learning resources from a fresh perspective?

Table 1.2 A checklist to estimate project costs for the created learning resource(s)

	Costs
Subscription databases for research	
Travel for research	
Software authoring tools	
Analog and digital content costs	
Software technologies	
Equipment	
Designer/developer time	
Office supplies	
Others	

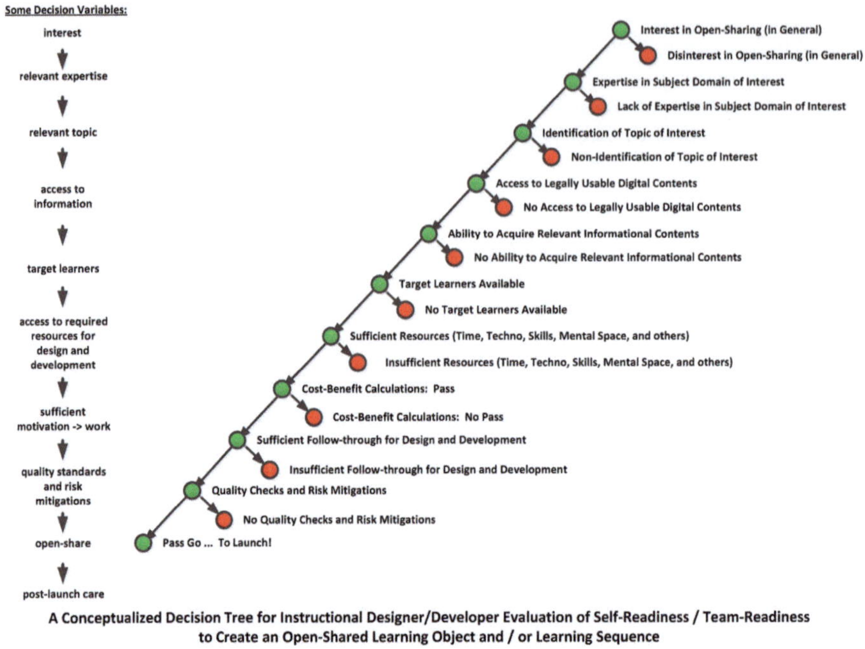

Fig. 1.4 A conceptualized decision tree for instructional designer/developer evaluation of self-readiness/team-readiness to create an open-shared learning object and/or learning sequence

4. Do you have *legal access to unique information and digital resources* that may be integrated into a coherent learning object or learning sequence? Do you have access to experts (aka "subject matter experts" or "content experts")? Are you able to differentiate between "public" information and more sensitive "protected" information? Are you *aware of the basic laws* related to publishing, media, intellectual property and copyright, accessibility, and other requirements? Do you have the skills to uphold these relevant laws (yes, it's good to be a rule follower…in many cases)?
5. Do you have the *necessary pedagogical design and technological skills* to create digital contents that function accurately? Do you understand how people learn and what barriers exist to learning? Do you have the necessary grit to work through frustrations and design/development challenges? Do you have the ability to take accurate notes? Do you have research experience? Are you familiar with the technologies required for creating learning objects and learning sequences?
6. Do you have the wherewithal and patience to *constructively review and critique your own work* using objectively observable standards and *revise* based on those evaluations? Are you comfortable with being spot-checked and critiqued by fellow peers in the field? Are you able to receive constructive critique from outside learners, especially if such critiques appear on public (social media and other) venues? (Are you able to objectively review and critique others' learning objects and sequences as well?)

7. Are you *comfortable being a "creative"* and generating something that has never existed before? (How do you feel when you are looking at a blank digital file with a flashing cursor at the beginning of a project?) Are you comfortable being different? Are you comfortable making project decisions? Are you comfortable creating a style wrap around your work? Does the work give you a sense of flow (per Mihalyi Csikszentmihalyi) and excitement ("all engine and no brakes")? Do you strive for "personal bests" or achieving the highest and greatest within one's limits? Are you motivated to create open-shared learning objects because of alignments with your own interests (instead of merely theorized interests)?
8. Are you willing to *meet the needs of others*? Are you open to conducting light research to learn what learners may need and how to meet their needs? For many who are offering something for free, they may take an initial attitude that they can create whatever they want, and that users will just have to take what is available. A more constructive approach is to understand the open-shared learning space as a competitive one. Learning objects and sequences need to be practical for learning and attractive to learners, to build a user base. Some users will use a learning object once, and others may return to it again and again as a reference. Meeting the needs of learners requires that those who build the learning have *a sense of responsibility for their well-being and a sense of respect for their personhood.* It also helps to be flexible to package contents differently to meet learner needs in various contexts: packaging for style, for culture, for devices, for access/non-access to the Internet, and other factors.
9. Do you have the *skills to manage a project* and the thousands of files required to actualize a work to standard? Are you aware of documentation standards, and are you able to meet them? Are you able to create a reasonable schedule, stay on it, and meet deadlines?
10. Are you *familiar with mass media and social media*, in order to effectively launch the results of an open-source learning project? Are you familiar with how to create a media plan and to execute on it? Are you capable of creating an engaging media presence to engage with others?

It is important to note that it is likely that everyone has some gaps in the question list identifying their readiness for engaging in open sharing, but these are generally shortcomings that may be addressed. To review personal readiness, Table 1.3 may be filled out with personal information as an early light assessments.

This first chapter is about taking stock to understand what is possible based on the professional context and on the personnel. Another approach may be to identify pros and cons of the work in terms of work-based interests for the designer/developer (Table 1.4).

Creating works for open sharing enables an individual to not only benefit from what others have put into the open-shared space but to directly contribute and to have a unique voice into the space. The secondary benefits of the effort are many. For many topics, there is little competition in the space because of the large gap between "cheap talk" vs. "costly signaling" (e.g. people may express interest in doing something, but it takes much more effort to actualize the work and make it real). In many cases, the work may be like the Russian folktale of the Little Red Hen.

Strategic Considerations for the Individual Besides the designer/developer's readiness and standing to contribute, there are some strategic considerations.

The most important is the relevance of the topic to the designer/developer because the project will require his/her mental attention for a length of time. It will require his/her expertise (or access to expertise). The topic should have learning value, for professional development, or for other types of advancement. One approach is to see whether the topic has personal traction is to see how much personal enthusiasm it evokes. One useful thought experiment is to ask, "If an unknown individual asked me to create this learning object for free on my own time with my own resources for no compensation, how would I respond?" A more raw way to think about this is if a stranger or group of strangers asked, "May I impose on you for the following: your expertise, your time, your resources, your reputation, and your hard work?" After all, once a learning object is costed out, its inputs can easily range in the thousands of dollars for the prior listed investments. The asking-a-favor thought experiment conjures the real world because the object will benefit others at a cost to the self. In a volunteer context, the inspiration may have to come from self-drive within, but that impetus also has to work against one's own inertia and other commitments. The "ask" or the "proposition" should still make sense even if the other-benefit is explicit and stated. (The counter argument is that while the work may cost individuals and team members unduly, the cost becomes much less in a different per-user count if that number can be ascertained and extended over time into the near-future. Of course, learner attention requires learner awareness of the resource and their willingness to engage it. An open-shared learning resources may have a lifespan usage of several years if it is designed well, and possibly even longer. Of course, if there is no initial inclination to create open-shared learning, those experts will not find any proposition for designing learning objects for either love or money because the work itself is simply too hard. It helps to be more than a little obsessive about the topic, and it helps to have some personal investment and interest. That personal satisfaction may make the terms of $0 budget, 20% uptake, guaranteed hard work, and some risks easier to accept. This is not to say that a particular shared work won't be the anomaly and an outlier, but based on "priors" and likelihood based on research and experience, the general context is clear and challenging to change.)

Another strategic consideration is how strategically valuable the topic is to address in order to advance professional agendas and professional development. Which ones would be more tactically easy to execute on, with sufficient certitude of information? (How the topic is depicted will affect long-term reputation. Going with less certain information may be risky because the designer/developer will then have gone on record with inaccurate information. At least, the object will seem dated. At worst, the author may be seen to have over-reached.) Whatever topical territory is mapped out will also affect how much of an audience the author will reach because of the "installed base" of potential learners for that particular topic.

Some topics may have more potential to build on, and others may be less open. Strategically, those who may design open-shared learning objects may want to consider the utilitarianism of pursuing which topics and the impacts of that decision on his/her/their careers. What a person puts out in public space helps define his/her

Table 1.3 Assessing personal readiness to engage in the creation of open-shared learning resources

	Sufficiently familiar	Insufficiently familiar or outright unfamiliar
1. Open sharing learning ecosystem		
2. Public persona and public space		
3. Unique expertise and point-of-view in domain		
4. Legal awareness and compliance		
5. Pedagogical design knowledge and ability		
6. Acceptance of review and critique		
7. Being a creative		
8. Meeting the needs of others		
9. Project management and documentation skills		
10. Publicity and mainstream media and social media		

Table 1.4 Pros and cons of designing and developing an open-shared learning object or learning sequence

Relevant variables	Pros	Cons
Research and discovery		
Learning and knowledge		
Work-based skills		
Reputation		
Career enhancement		
Effects on broader publics		
Social capital		

professional persona. This reputational tie can be a downside if it forces work contributions for which the individual is not compensated. People may unwittingly sign on to long-term commitments to projects simply because their names are publicly linked. The designer/developer's free will decision-making should be maintained throughout.

Also, if a person chooses to create open-shared learning contents, he/she may start leaning towards continuing contribution because of the prior investments (or sunk costs) into the endeavor. A more balanced approach is to realize he/she may reconsider what is working or not working in this setup and decide whether or not to continue, with provisional commitment. In this space, there are no long-term commitments per se. There are all sorts of freedoms to maneuver in terms of selected topics (based on prior expertise and research and new learning), forms of digital learning objects and sequences, distribution platforms (learning object repositories, learning management systems, courseware, social media platforms, and others), and learning communities and publics to speak into with the shared contents.

In the open sharing space, unfunded contributors may think about playing the long game. This will require the following: maintaining technologies and technology skills, maintaining pedagogical design skills and acquiring new ones, continuing and accurate situational awareness of the space, continuing inspirations, personal encouragements and senses of value for the work, and others. Burnout can end contributions for the future, and it should be avoided. (A lot of self-discipline comes from knowing how to "hack" oneself to take on difficult work. It has been said that writers have an "ego" which drives their work, and in the same way, many "creatives" seem to share this sense of self and the sense that one has something to say to a larger audience. This ego can be harnessed as work motivation through self-manipulation.)

A Physical Place and Space to Be Creative For the designer/developer, it helps to have a comfortable and dedicated work place, a space that enables thinking, inspiration, research, design, and development. Optimally, the space would be ergonomically sound and with proper lighting and creative media. This may include tablets and styluses (or their analog equivalents, notepads and pens). There would be online connectivity and access to online resources. There would be access to the necessary software and the various devices on which the learning objects may be tested. This would be a space without distractions or with the preferred level of pleasant distractions. Until people are without such resources, such requirements may be fairly invisible.

A Sharing Context For the individual, they may also have had a commissioned project that does not ultimately get accepted for any variety of reasons (the funder may have changed directions or pulled a project). In those contexts, it may make sense to get the project released, assess it for legal rights releases for the open-shared space, make adjustments, and proceed to the share. If done right, this gives the resource a "second life" or at least an initial use life.

1.3.5 Learning Resource Project Do-ability

Another important factor for "local starts" may be the viability of creating a particular or multiple linked learning resources.

- Evaluate how "doable" a particular learning resource project is, practically speaking.

A simple feasibility run-through of practical considerations for a learning resource project may include the following questions:

- Is there a built audience or user base of learners for the planned learning resource? Do the learners have interest in the topic? Do they have the necessary lead-up knowledge? Do they have access to the technologies to enable them to experience the learning object? Are there ways to reach these learners to notify them of the learning resources (once these are created)? Can the designer/developer offer sufficient novelty to capture their attention? Or if it's the first of its kind topic-wise, can the designer/developer do the topic justice?

- Is there sufficient access to raw contents (with the proper legal releases)? Is there sufficient access to investment funding (as needed)?
- Is there sufficient access to the necessary technologies for every phase of the work?
- Does the developer/designer have access to the skills to achieve the work? (Or can he/she acquire the necessary skills in the required time period/) Is the designer/developer sufficiently motivated, experienced, and focused?
- Is there sufficient time to achieve every phase of the work?
- Is there some local workplace benefit, if the work is created under the auspices of the workplace?

These questions assume that there should be a need for the learning object or sequence in a practical way and that the builder has access to the resources, skills, and wherewithal to execute. These questions also assume a pre-design through post-launch sense of feasibility with the idea that the open-shared learning resources have a positive future (and ideally no blowback).

Understanding how viable a project is may increase the probability that, if pursued, the work will be to quality and with sufficient (informational and resource and effort) backing. Considering the likelihood of successful actualization of the work is important because getting from an impulse or a concept to something tangible requires plenty of real-world investment and work (Fig. 1.5).

Fig. 1.5 A Word Cloud of Chapter 01: Understanding the Open Sharing Learning Environment Online and Local Starts

What-If: Understanding Breakpoints and Workarounds

You've decided to take on the challenge of creating an open-shared learning object. Even better, you've been able to assemble a talented team of researchers, writers, instructional designers, developers, graphic artists, editors, and several content experts. The dynamics within the team are healthy, with the members communicating effectively and working together to help each other. While the members do not all know each other directly, they are interconnected through trust networks. The team knocks ideas around to consider what to co-create. The team members have different preferences for what the target learning object should be and what platform it should be built to and whether it should be part of a sequence or a stand-alone object.

Decision point #1: stop or advance. If advance, how should the decision be made? What should be developed first, and what should be developed later?

The team agrees on some goals, and the work commences. As time passes, it becomes clear that one or more of the team members have gone silent and are not responding. For example, a graphic designer has gone silent, and he has not left copies of any of the work with any team members. It turns out that his supervisor has forbade his work on this unpaid project, and his professional life has become demanding. And an editor has only viewed some of the contents and left work partially edited. When pressed, the two suggest that they are no longer interested in continuing. This means that the team will have to break up these individuals' work and do it themselves, hire out for the work, recruit other volunteers, or do without the look-and-feel style design and the editing.

Decision point #2: stop or advance. If advance, how should the gaps left by the individuals be addressed? Is it possible to advance even without these tasks being completed a particular way?

The team recruits another graphic artist, and the team members divide the editing work among the team members. As they commence with the work, they suddenly find out that the images they had planned to use are actually under copyright. They reach out to the company running the web database with the images, and the company's lawyer suggests that all rights are reserved. The sales division proposes a price in the four figures, which means that the team is effectively priced out from using the images. The images were to be play a major role in the designed learning object or sequence. A review of open-source images shows that there is nothing that can directly substitute for the images. Other commercial competitors offer some workable images, but their billing regimes are as expensive as the initial company.

Decision point #3: stop or advance. If advance, how will the team make up for the missing images? Should they substitute in digital drawings? Should they create visuals using video? Should they reconceptualize the learning objects and/or go with new designs? Should they fund-raise to pay for the visuals? Should they negotiate with the respective companies and bargain for the image resources by offering some service? Should they use their own skills to self-create the images? Should they use a combination of approaches to address this issue of the "missing images"?

The team moves forward, and they use a combination of approaches to meet the shortfall. They execute on the design plans. They move beyond their prototypes and create functioning objects.

However, as they are just about ready to conduct alpha- and beta-testing on their work, they discovery that a new open-shared learning object has been posted online by a competitor team. The learning resource is well made and memorable.

Decision point #4: stop or advance. If advance, the team will have to create something unique and value-added in its own way. The designers have to decide whether to go forward with their original planned work and just finalize their work, or they may review the competitor work and build around it. They may choose to challenge the primacy of the other work directly. Ignoring competitor works is not a real option. Situational awareness is important to maintain throughout the project.

The team decides to advance. They analyze and review the competitor learning resources. They identify areas in which they can excel and differentiate themselves from others. They can compete by offering advantageous features—fresh and novel information, different learning experiences, different expertise, high-dimension data, and others. They decide what they can practically achieve, and they continue.

They conduct the alpha test and revise the objects. They conduct the beta test with outside learners, and they may some additional revisions. They are now ready to launch the learning resource to the broad public. Suddenly, there comes word that one of the content experts (aka "the talent") has decided to withdraw permission to use her video. She wants the information to be portrayed a particular way, but the other content experts want a more mainline approach. When the team goes back to check its records, it turns out that they had failed to acquire her signature on a media release. Since her role was a central one, the team has come to a breakpoint. They cannot legally use anything with her likeness in it—nothing of her image, her voice in audio, her likeness in video, her name, and others.

The team can try to negotiate with her and acquire her agreement and signature. The team can change how they depict the learning to align with what she wants. The team can scrub her likeness from the project.

Decision point #5: stop or advance. If advance, the team will have to decide how to handle this challenge. They can work with her to come to agreement about the learning object and rework it. They can scrub her from the work and go with what they have. They can try to change up her incentives to acquire her freewill agreement.

The team decides to continue. They negotiate with the content expert and reconfigure her role to explain her position to her satisfaction, but this also means that they expend more energy and resources to create an additional video. At the end, all are satisfied, and the team has its legally acquired media release.

The team releases its learning object to the public, with both soft launches to target audiences and hard launches to the broad public. The team is thrilled with the launch, and most of the word-of-mouth (WOM) is highly positive and encouraging. In the commenting sections, some of the learners seem to be misunderstanding part of the teaching and learning. The team can decide whether they want to interact with users, or if they want to be open to redesigning the learning object based on public interactions.

Decision point #6: stop or advance. If advance, the team can work on how they want to interact with users into the future…and if they want to revise published learning objects based on public responses. Will there be a threshold for how long the team will respond to the public? Do they want to be responding to learners even years later, and with what level of commitment? Do they want to update learning objects or sequences as new information comes in…or new comments come in? What will the standards be for when they might update?

The team decides…

The What-If Debriefing

This "what-if" makes the point that instructional design projects come up on a number of different decision junctures, and these may be breakpoints at which a project is interrupted and changed, or it ends. For a project to "make," the design and development team has to have workarounds. They have to have the resilience and creativity; they have to have resources to draw from. Also, the point is not to let project breakpoints sneak up on the team but to be able to anticipate some of these and to address them sufficiently early. All teams work in time and sometimes against time. All teams have a vested interest in preserving the work even if there are unexpected events. All teams generally need to share leadership because the work requires it, even if there is a formal leader or point-person.

Self-indulgence of any sort by the team members or contributors to the project can be expensive to the shared effort and the ultimate resulting work.

Also, teams require grit and stick-to-it-iveness. Challenges do not necessarily come in the form that one might expect. It might be something as simple as boredom or technology crashes or a painful criticism or a bout with whimsy. The point is to pick "advance" over "stop" at every breakpoint, where that makes sense. And the point is to make the right calls, based on the possible.

Real-world projects will not have so many challenges. In the real, maybe one or two challenges may arise, and they are generally worked through without too many problems. Of course, this depends on the complexity of the project and other factors. In an open-shared context, though, with no formal budget and only volunteers who are there because of their own interests and a sense of goodwill, such efforts may be much more fragile and sensitive to challenges.

Live Examples (on the Web)

The open sharing space is a fairly dynamic one, but some of the following sources are of sufficient quality that they may well be around for many years.

The U.S. National Sciences Digital Library (2000–) enables federated searches across a range of contents around science, technology, engineering and mathematics education. The searches may be filtered by grade level and other attributes.

The MERLOT (Multimedia Educational Resource for Learning and Online Teaching) referatory (1997–) points to various digital learning contents hosted online. This is a program of the California State University System.

Khan Academy (2007–) offers a range of free online courses with narrated videos and practice. Digital badging is offered as part of this.

Various courses and course parts are available through various massive open online course (MOOC) platforms. Some of the most notable include Coursera and edX. Some learning management systems host free learning resources as part of their general service.

Certainly, proprietary learning objects may be informative as well. Lynda.com is known for having quality courses. These are widely available through commercial licenses but are mostly hosted behind a paywall. Some excerpts of their videos are available on the Open Web as samples.

These provide a start, but this list is by no means comprehensive. This list may also be somewhat West-leaning.

Discussion Certainly, in the open-shared space, user-generated contents posted on social media platforms are *sometimes* open learning resources. Some of these are high-end videos by high-achieving individuals with insights about their work and professionally collated image sets and other digital contents; however, the uses of social media platforms also mean that some "learning" contents may be superficial works created by non-experts who want to attract mass attention in order to start or maintain a funding stream. Discernment between the expert and non-expert contents is critical. (There are inevitable gaps between non-experts' "mental models" of a topic and experts' "conceptual models." Learning through non-experts may result in mental disconnects and minimized and even mistaken understandings. That said, if modern online learners are more trusting of peers and non-expert knowledge, that will be a challenge for those who design learning based on expert portrayals.)

Short-Listing Topics for Design and Development What are some engaging potential topics? Initially it helps to brainstorm broadly and to maintain this list of possible ideas to use into the future. Among those identified by a gaps analyses, candidate ideas for the individual or team should be the "low hanging fruit," those ideas that are close to the members' expertise and the available resources. Learning resources that are a byproduct of other projects (such as presentations for conferences) may offer sufficient access and momentum because other project's deadlines will drive development. The costs for preparing the learning object are borne by the event. Once one has attained practice, then it's easier to take on more distant and challenging projects. A long-term interest in the domain is needed to keep the work on track.

The benefits to the learners should be at the forefront of considerations, beyond even direct personal interests. In learner centered design, the focus is on meeting the understood requirements of learners. The "best interests of the student" approach informs decision making in education, as informed by standards of the profession, professional codes of ethics, ethics of the community, personal codes of ethics, and individual professional codes (Shapiro and Stefkovich 2001).

Teaming Sometimes, working on a design and development team may make better sense than going it alone. A team may bring more resources and skills to the endeavor, and shared efforts may shorten the time needed to arrive at a completed digital object or learning sequence. It helps if team members have prior shared co-work experiences, so there is mutual trust and understandings of each other's skills, interests, personalities, and work styles. Lean teams work much better than larger ones simply because they are less unwieldy, and often, there may be more accountability. The team members need to trust each other sufficiently to share ideas freely across areas of specialization, and it helps when each respects each other's differences. The selection of team members is critical to the success of a project—as plenty of research indicates, and those that are included need both integrity and skills. This is not a space for rookies with naive assumptions. Those who deliver stay on board and receive byline credit, and those who do not should be left off. Often, "past is prologue," so it helps to understand people's "priors" in terms of such projects.

A Seeding Inspiration Finally, there is something to be said for an initial powerful inspiration as the driver to creating open-shared learning resources. Sometimes, these are sufficient to carry the work to a polished deliverable and beyond even potential "sharing creator's remorse". (Similarly to buyer's remorse, sharing creator's remorse may stem from feeling like the designer/developer overpaid—over-invested in a resource for which he or she did not get proper returns. Or they may be unexpected negative repercussions or legal liabilities. Or the work itself may have not been sufficiently rewarding. There are many other potential reasons for a sense of remorse. Doing a favor for someone else with some expectation of return is a challenge, particularly in the academic space, because people keep score differently and because people may not be sufficiently positioned to return a favor. Ideally, creators will go into a project *without* "starry eyes" and outsized expectations but with accurate knowledge of what to expect. It also helps for creators to place others' opinions and expectations in proper context, with awareness that people come at their work from different places and will have a range of opinions, not all positive.) For individuals and teams, being self-aware of what is inspiring can be the difference in unlocking the potential of the sophisticated open-shared learning resource.

side bar

Differentiating Quality Open-Shared Learning Objects and Sequences from Non-Expert User-Generated Social Shares

Some shared informational works do not go beyond a superficial headline level of expertise. There are videos on a well known video-sharing platform that shows a range of top-ten lists that seem to be gleaned after viewing a few television shows with a top-ten listing of screen grabs and light inexpert commentary. There are many videos that purport to be analytical ones with learning value but end up having been created to sell a social video channel, a product, or a technology. This phenomenon extends to whitepapers, learning objects, and other digital artifacts shared online. Self-anointed experts claim expertise in a wide range of fields, and the focus on impression management means that skills and capabilities are often inflated. Accurate self-representations are not sufficiently common. In many areas of innovation, people will "fake it until you make it," which does not result in candid representations.

The hard work of acquiring and maintaining expertise is critical for people to understand an area well and to engage that space with their full capabilities. Creating the contexts for appropriate professional roles to position individuals to constantly learn and develop in their areas of interest are no small feat, and protecting this context is important to maintaining skills. There are foundational differences between experts with accurate conceptual modeling and non-experts with inaccurate mental modeling.

If the current age of sharing and social technologies encourage the "here comes everybody" effect, with amateurs willing to step up and share as if they were experts (Shirky 2008), the risks of a cultural death of expertise (Nichols 2017) may be imminent but should be resisted.

In many of these cases of mash-ups, the cost of creation is low, and many use mashups in lieu of actual original contents. The spell check may not have been engaged, and the images may actually be copyrighted by others (although cartoonish image overlays and annotations may have enabled the creators to get away with using others contents based on "fair use"). In many cases, images are stretched, without correct aspect ratio, and object sizing is not considered. Images are not white-color balanced. Information is offered without supporting source citations. The quality standards for the development are not kept. And yet, because of screaming headlines and the promise of titillation and spectacle, many of these draw millions of views, likely for the mindless distraction or entertainment value. Lower-quality objects often share various features:

The poorer learning objects do not demonstrate expertise on the particular topic.

The creators may be self-identified experts, without actual professional training or background in the area.

This means that the data may be cherry-picked and that there may be oversimplifications in representing contents.

The harnessed media contents and information may not have clear provenance.

Production values tend to be low: videos with poor lighting, unfocused imagery, poor writing, poor functionality, and so on. Contents may be unoriginal, and the object may be a mere mash-up.

There is not clear respect for learners nor consideration for what the shared learning may mean for those who apply the learning in life. (There is not apparent thinking about second order and third order effects, beyond the learning.)

The source is unaffiliated with a professional organization and is "freelancing." In many cases, the source cannot be identified to a person, only to a user handle, and there may not be an easy way to reach the individual or group behind the work. Such distancing behavior is a red flag for poor quality. Such ambiguity of identity enables disavowal of authorship, even as they are legally liable. (Of course, some people prefer a lower profile than taking on a high profile public role.)

No matter the hosting platform, there are always risks of "vanity publishing" (Lane 2008). Going to learning object repositories and referatories may result in more substantive learning contents. Many of these are curated; many are peer reviewed and/or editor reviewed. The contents here are not regurgitated and derivative mashups, in general, and many of the works are substantive, original, academic, and more clearly defined for learning value. There are clearer efforts to protect people's identities for those depicted in the media. There tends to be some controls against negative learning (by avoiding using misleading information and offering more explanatory depth). Quality learning objects deal with actual hard problems in learning; they involve consideration of learners and their needs in the design. They demonstrate expertise and design skills and development skills. There is clear thought into not only first-order learning effects, but also second- and third-order effects when learners put the learning to use and make decisions based off of the shared information. The language is accurate and well vetted.

1.4 Conclusion

This first chapter summarizes some research on movements leading up to the open-shared learning objects and sequences moments; it makes the point that understanding the open learning object ecosystem is important, along with reviewing available open and proprietary resources around subject matter areas. Also, the point was made that an internal scan of the reader's workplace may be helpful to know whether or not official support may be available for taking part in open-shared learning resource creation. Finally, readers are advised to better understand their own motivations and standing to engage in the creation of open-shared learning resources. Once a designer/developer decides to start on an open-shared project, the potentials are broad and promising. He or she or they do not need a full plan at the beginning. Their work can evolve over time. They can improvise as they go. They can take on the challenges as they arise. Sometimes, an effective and inspired start is all it takes to come up with something workable. If a full commit to a larger project is not possible early on, then something more manageable and minimalist may be desirable.

Sharing, though, is not a natural state. For many, withholding something that might even be costless to share may be the natural state. Sharing is risk-taking and effortful and often thankless. For unfunded endeavors, these seem to only be able to be worked on the margins. The unfunded efforts that seem to work are only those that collate mass human efforts in which a large group of people put in a little each and a few put in a lot (as the power law frequencies might suggest).

However, if the current time is about a G-Zero world where every country's peoples fend for themselves, with little sharing and little caring of others' plights, what can be the direction of open sharing, which on its surface and at its heart is a "dominated strategy" (an inherent losing approach to those who follow that strategy)? Will this sharing impetus disappear?

Is it possible to change social norms in a way that would motivate people beyond their local interests to care about those of others' and to invest actual resources into their well-being? Maybe. This will require leadership and people modeling such generosities. This will require community building around topics, with people collaborating around shared contents as builders and as users.

Are there ways to incentivize this work? Are there barters that may be set up that encourage the creation of such open-shared objects—such as by those who sell authoring tool software or who host learning management systems (LMSes) trading access to services for quality developed shared objects or sequences. Such content goods may drive viewer traffic to the respective commercial tools and may raise awareness about how these tools may be harnessed. If specific talent may be attracted and brought to bear, such shared works may be canonical ones. Are there companies that may offer small grants as incentives to the building of open-shared learning objects, around particular related domain fields?

Are there ways to encourage open sharing maybe for the development of lesser and non-expert contents, such as making these in higher education, as part of undergraduate and graduate student work? Is there value to edited and peer-reviewed student-created learning resources?

People benefit themselves and others when they express their insights on a learning topic. In the open sharing space, there is room for quality learning content. The idea is to venture something ultimately for social gain.

1.5 Reviews and Assignments

1.5.1 Main Points Review

- Open-shared learning contents (analog and digital) are generally freely available, freely accessible, freely experience-able learning that is distributed globally.
- Various licensure frameworks enable various applied uses of the open-shared learning contents, including revision, adaptation, commercial usage, and other specific releases.
- Open-shared learning contents are generally created for free or on shoestring budgets, with the designer(s)/developer(s) covering the costs.
  - The works are not typically commissioned nor invited (say, by a publisher or by a learner group) but self-generated by the designer/developer.
- Open-shared learning online is made globally scalable because of the nonrivalrous nature of digital goods and the reality that after an object has been created, there is a near-zero marginal cost for each new user thereafter. The numbers of those using the particular object will not diminish others' usage of the resource.
- An "environmental scan" may shed light on the state of the open sharing ecosystem online, including the learning domains addressed and some of the technologies used.
  - Such scans may help people identify familiar forms and to define potential learner expectations for such objects. Designer/developers often build to learner expectations as a goal.

- It is possible to view a digital learning object or learning sequence and reverse engineer how the object was built, what sorts of informational contents were harnessed, and what likely technologies may have been used in the object's/ sequence's design and building.
- At present, there are some main funders (entities and individuals) of open-shared learning.
- There are some online communities that may be joined that provide social supports for those who create open-shared learning objects.
- Different subject domains have different types and numbers of open-shared learning objects and learning sequences.
- Studying closed and proprietary learning objects and learning sequences may be beneficial to the creation of open-shared learning.
- To decide what open-shared learning objects may be of value on the Social Web, it may help to identify gaps in available open-access learning.
- To assess whether or not a workplace or organizational context may be suitable for creating open-shared learning objects or sequences, a number of factors may be considered—such as the leadership, the available expertise, the available resources, excess capacity, and cost-benefit analyses for engaging in such endeavors.
- A personal assessment of one's readiness for engaging in creating learning content for open sharing include honest assessments of interests, motivations, skills, and other factors.
- An early assessment should include how practically doable particular projects may be.

1.6 Critical Thinking Questions

Benefits from Open Sharing

- In the give-and-take dynamic of the Open Web, what are some ways to benefit from the open-shared learning resources shared by others?
- To increase the value of raw shared imagery, sound files, video files, understanding the provenance is important. What are some ways to offer validated provenance of digital contents online (and to avoid fraud)?
- What are some ways of encouraging academic citation of shared learning objects and learning sequences, so as to increase crediting of those who might share (and so directing some professional benefits in their direction)?

Understanding the State of the Art

- In conducting an environmental scan, people see what exists and some of what is possible. Why is it important to learn the state-of-the-art from the world? And further, how can one reach beyond what exists to something more in terms of creativity?

Strategic Partnering

- What are some creative ways to build partnerships with others who are building and sharing learning resources online and offline?
- What are some ways to change the social norms and culture around the creation and sharing of learning objects and learning sequences? (For example, should public grants encourage "publication" of such objects—as they do the findings of research?)

Incentivizing Sharing

- What are some effective workplace propositions for the creation of open-shared contents? What are some benefits that may accrue to those in a workplace context? What are some arguments that are less likely to work?
- Given the ease of "defection" from the open-shared work, what are some ways to address and face down the following challenges: discouragement of such endeavors in the workplace, a lack of resources, time pressures, constructive criticism, technological challenges, hosting platform changes, and others. How can online social communities support some of the work, particularly during particular work or other challenges?
- What are some effective ways to identify topic gaps about which to create open-shared learning contents?
- In terms of subject domains, are there ways to identify interdisciplinary approaches? Ways to bridge domains in a valuable way?
- What are some strategies to create the "go-to" or "destination" learning objects and learning sequences? What are the most important considerations to users of open-shared learning contents?
- What are some effective, healthy, and constructive ways to balance regular work and *pro bono* work, without lapsing into over-work?

Domains and Topics

- What are ways to differentiate between critical "seed corn" resources and the extraneous ones that may be used for open-shared learning contents? What are some circumstances in which using core resources may be justified for open-shared learning contents?
- What are some ways to rethink cost-benefits of creating open-shared learning resources that may make the proposition more reasonable? For example, being able to speak into the public on important issues may justify some personal and/or organizational costs.
- How can learning objects and sequences be designed and deployed to accommodate the diversity of applications in an open-shared global learning context—including formal, nonformal, and informal learning? How can open-shared learning resources be designed and deployed to bridge gaps among the various learning types—formal, nonformal, and informal?

Diverse Learners

- What are some ways to understand the diversity of learners in a global context?
- Given the advances in automated language translation approaches, how should open-shared learning be written?

Studying Impacts

- What are some objective and evidence-based ways to understand what impact a particular shared learning object or learning sequence has on the larger environment?

Designer/Developer Expressivity

- If the author hand is important in literature, and the director hand is important in filmmaking, is there an analogical signature for the creation of open-shared learning objects for designer/developers? If so, what could the signatures be, and why?
- What are practical considerations for how doable a learning project may be or not?

1.7 Assignments

Directions The Assignments are divided into two sections, Basic and Advanced. The Basic section is for those who may not have much instructional design experience or background in the area of creating instructional contents for open sharing. As such, these are set up to familiarize them with the chapter-related knowledge, skills, and abilities. The Advanced section is for those who already have some knowledge of this general space and who may benefit from more challenging work.

In a formal learning context, these assignments would benefit from expert feedback and further applications of the learning contents. In a nonformal or informal learning context, including self-directed learning, these assignments would benefit from both reflection and practice. These assignments are built to be extensible, to have elements added to benefit the learners. They are designed to be assigned selectively and not in full. The setup of this textbook is as a work sequence, and similarly, the assignments may be set up as tasks to be completed by the learner in a sequential way…that takes them through the fairly complete and sequential *open-shared learning design → development → test → revision → launch → post-launch* process.

1.7.1 Basic

Assignment 1.1: Exploration of the Open Sharing Online Learning Environment for a Specific Subject Domain In your area of specialty (or learning domain), conduct a search for all open-shared learning contents. Maintain a list of the name of the resource, the creator, the funder (if available), the hosting platform, the URL, and write a paragraph or two describing the resource.

Assignment 1.2: Exploration of the Proprietary Online Learning Environment for a Specific Subject Domain In your area of specialty (or learning domain), conduct a search for all proprietary learning contents. Maintain a list of the name of the resource, the creator, the corporation, the cost, the hosting platform, the URL, and write a paragraph or two describing the resource.

Assignment 1.3: Workplace or Organizational Readiness to Create Contents for Open Sharing Conduct a light analysis of your local work context. How amenable is the leadership to having staff create learning contents for open sharing? Does your organization benefit from open-source online learning? If so, how so? What sorts of content expertise is available? What sorts of contents are available? What sorts of technologies are available for online learning design and development? Does the organization have a history of open sharing of learning contents? Are there projects for which open sharing learning contents may be a natural byproduct? Are there staff interested in engaging with open sharing projects?

Assignment 1.4: Identifying Informational and Learning Gaps in the Available Online Learning In the target learning domain, what are some informational and learning gaps in the available online learning? Are there weaknesses in terms of the extant learning objects? Most importantly, are these gaps that may be addressed by the learner or the group or the organization?

1.7.2 Advanced

Assignment 1.5: Evaluating Real-World Learning Objects/Courses/Sequences Identify half-a-dozen of the top-flight learning objects you have encountered in the environmental scan of the online learning environment for the particular domain. What are some of the top quality features? What are some of the signature aspects of online learning experiences that are particularly effective? Why?

Assignment 1.6: Creating Strategies for Dealing with Time-Sensitive Online Learning Contents Virtually all learning and information has a shelf life. Human attention itself is fleeting and has limits. All open-shared learning objects will fall into disuse over time. The market for an object or learning sequence may evolve and change, but in generally, most attention that a learning object will attain spikes early on and diminishes over time, sometimes with short bursts of attention but an overall decline. What are ways to "future-proof" a learning object or sequence as much as possible? What are ways to retrofit an object to make it more relevant in that moment (without incurring excessive costs)?

Assignment 1.7: Reverse Engineering Top-Flight Learning Objects/Courses/ Sequences If you were to "reverse engineer" the object/course/sequence, how would you think that the object was designed and created? What technologies do you think were used? What sorts of designs were probably used to inform the development? Why? What level of confidence do you have about your impressions? What aspects of these online learning experiences may be emulate-able (indirectly)? Which aspects may be too expensive or too sophisticated to emulate?

Assignment 1.8: Mapping Learning Sequences If you were to map learning sequences to particular work-based skills, how much is publicly available? For example, some workplace skills that may be helpful may include the ability to use particular technologies, or soft skills such as working effectively on a team, or others. What is the quality of what is available? What are some mistakes in the learning sequence? What are some possible misunderstandings? What skills are possible to attain through open-access and open-source learning online?

Assignment 1.9: Individual Readiness to Create Contents for Open Sharing With the focus on practical considerations in this chapter, how ready are you to create open-shared learning contents on the open Web? Do you have some relevant learning contents to share, legal access to the underlying data, the skill set to achieve end-to-end creation of the learning objects, target learner groups who may benefit from the shared objects, and the will to give up some of your free time and *pro bono* skills and resources to this? What sort of "signature" do you think you have in your authorship of digital learning objects? If you see yourself as a "creative," what do you find inspiring? What sort of package of incentives and disincentives affect you? What do you see as your "end game" in the creation and publishing of open-shared learning resources?

Assignment 1.10: Defining Learning Object Success/Failure Based on the environmental scan of learning objects of a particular modality (form or type), subject domain-based, or other set, create a sense of what makes for a "successful" learning resource vs. an "unsuccessful" one. What metrics would you use for success/lack of success? Explain your reasoning. Can you find examples of learning objects that may be successful in some contexts but not others? Are there universal measures for a learning object's success or non-success? Or is success relative and context-sensitive and learner-dependent? Is there a sense of space for all learning objects, or do you think only some of them should be hosted and made available to a broad audience? Write a short essay to engage these and other relevant issues.

Key Terms and Definitions

Altruism A self-less care for others

Authorizing document An official document that authorizes particular work to be done, such as for an instructional design project

B Corp Corporations that make commitments to enable prosocial and pro-environmental impacts

Crowd-Source The act of going to people who are active in online communities and spaces to acquire information, resources, work, and other goods

Electronic textbook An electronic textbook, often created with multimodal features

Environmental scan A fast exploration of a particular context, often to understand opportunities and threats

Granularity The size of an item, ranging from fine to coarse granularity

Internal scan An evaluation of an in-organization environment to understand particular features

Non-rivalrous The feature of an object (such as a digital learning one) being able to be used by large numbers of people without being diminished or materially limited

Open access Able to be accessed/experienced/read without cost or other common barriers

Open educational resources (OER) Openly available learning contents, often released to extended use through licensure

Open shared Resources made available to the broad public often via the web and internet and through generous licensure releases and often with the fewest barriers as possible (no or low paywalls, no or few proprietary technologies required, no membership requirements, and so on)

Open source A software program with its underlying code publicly available

Personal best The optimal achievement for any individual, which is often higher than the individual may assume

Reusability The ability to use an object or sequence in a different context

Sharing creator's remorse A sense of regret for expending time, talent, and treasure in creating open-shared learning resources publicly and for free

Topic-based sampler A collection of open-shared and proprietary online learning objects based on a particular subject matter

Transclusion Act of including part of an electronic document via hypertext

References

Atenas J, Havemann L, and Priego E. Opening teaching landscapes: The importance of quality assurance in the delivery of open educational resources. *Open Praxis 6:* 29 – 43, 2014.

Batson T, Paharia N, and Kumar MSV. A harvest too large? A framework for educational abundance. Ch. 6. In T. Iiyoshi and M.S. Vijay Kumar's *Opening Up Education: The Collective*

Advancement of Education through Open Technology, Open Content, and Open Knowledge. Cambridge: The MIT Press. 89 – 103, 2008.

Butcher N. A Basic Guide to Open Educational Resources (OER). Commonwealth of Learning. United Nations Educational, Scientific and Cultural Organization. 2011.

Certified B Corporation. http://www.bcorporation.net/. 2018.

Collins J. *Good to Great: Why Some Companies Make the Leap…and Others Don't.* New York: HarperCollins Publishers. 2001.

Conole G, McAndrew P, and Dimitriadis Y. The role of CSCL pedagogical patterns as mediating artefacts for repurposing Open Educational Resources. In: Pozzi F. and Persico D., Eds. *Techniques for Fostering Collaboration in Online Learning Communities: Theoretical and Practical Perspectives.* Hershey, USA: IGI Global. http://oro.open.ac.uk/23040/. 2011.

De Vries I. 2013. Evaluating open educational resources: Lessons learned. *Soc Behav Sciences* 83: 56 – 60, 2013; https://doi.org/10.1016/j.sbspro.2013.06.012.

Dinevski D. Open educational resources and lifelong learning. In the proceedings of the ITI 2008 30th International Conf on Information Technology Interfaces. June 23 – 26, 2008. Cavtat, Croatia. 117 – 122, 2008.

Downes S. Models for sustainable open educational resources. *Interdisciplinary Journal of Knowledge and Learning Objects* 3: 29 – 44, 2007.

Fitzgerald B. Open Content Licensing (OCL) for open educational resources. In the proceedings of OECD Expert Meeting on Open Educational Resources, Malmö, Sweden. Retrieved May 10, 2018, from http://eprints.qut.edu.au/archive/00003621. 1 – 24, 2005.

Fulantelli G, Gentile M, Taibi D, and Allegra M. The Open Learning Object model to promote open educational resources. *Journal of Interactive Media in Education.* 1 – 24, 2008. https://doi.org/10.5334/2008-9.

Geser G. Open educational practices and resources: OLCOS roadmap 2012. Open eLearning Content Observatory Services. 1 – 150, 2012.

Geith C, and Vignare K. Access to education with online learning and open educational resources: Can they close the gap? *Journal of Asynchronous Learning Networks* 12: 105 – 126, 2008. https://eric.ed.gov/?id=EJ837472.

Harley D. Why understanding the use and users of open education matters. Chapter 13. In T. Iiyoshi and M.S. V. Kumar's *Opening Up Education: The Collective Advancement of Education through Open Technology, Open Content, and Open Knowledge.* Cambridge, Massachusetts: The Carnegie Foundation for the Advancement of Teaching and The MIT Press. 197 – 211, 2008.

Hockings C, Brett P, and Terentjevs M. Making a difference—Inclusive learning and teaching in higher education through open educational resources. *Distance Education* 33: 237 – 252, 2012. DOI: https://doi.org/10.1080/01587919.2012.692066.

Hsu JS, Liang TP, Wu SPJ, Klein G, and Jiang JJ. Promoting the integration of users and developers to achieve a collective mind through the screening of information system projects. *International Journal of Project Management* 29: 514 – 524, 2011.

Kanwar A, Kodhandaraman B, and Umar A. Toward sustainable open education resources: A perspective from the Global South. *The Amer. Jrn. of Distance Education* 24: 65 – 80, 2010. https://doi.org/10.1080/08923641003696588.

Kerr DV, Burgess K, and Houghton L. *Feral Information Systems Development: Managerial Implications.* Hershey: IGI Global. 2014.

Klebl M, Krämer BJ, and Zobel A. From content to practice: Sharing educational practice in edu-sharing. *British Journal of Educational Technology* 41: 936 – 951, 2010.

Koohang A, and Harman K. Advancing sustainability of open educational resources. *Issues in Informing Science and Information Technology* 4: 535 – 544, 2007.

Lane A. Reflections on sustaining Open Educational Resources: an institutional case study. *eLearning Papers* 10: 1 – 13, 2008.

Lane A, and McAndrew P. Are open educational resources systematic or systemic change agents for teaching practice? *British Journal of Educational Technology* 41: 952 – 962, 2010. https://doi.org/10.1111/j.1467-8535.2010.01119.x.

McKerlich R, Ives C, and McGreal R. Measuring use and creation of open educational resources in higher education. *The International Review of Research in Open and Distance Learning* 14: 90 – 103, 2013.

Nichols T. *The Death of Expertise: The Campaign against Established Knowledge and Why it Matters*. New York: Oxford University Press. 2017.

Ochoa X. Learnometrics: Metrics for Learning Objects. Slideshow. Retrieved May 18, 2018, from https://www.slideshare.net/xaoch/learnometrics-metrics-for-learning-objects-presentation. 2008.

Ochoa X. Learnometrics: Metrics for Learning (Objects). In the proceedings of LAK 2011. Retrieved from https://www.slideshare.net/xaoch/learnometrics-keynote-lak2011. 2011.

Ochoa X, and Duval E. Measuring learning object reuse. Times of Convergence. Technologies across Learning Contexts. Third European Conference on Technology Enhanced Learning. Maastricht, The Netherlands. 322 – 325, 2008.

OER World Map. n.d. https://oerworldmap.org/.

Phelan L. REFLECTION: Politics, practices, and possibilities of open educational resources. *Distance Education* 33: 279 – 282, 2012. https://doi.org/10.1080/01587919.2012.692070.

Raymond ES. The Cathedral and the Bazaar. Thyrsus Enterprises. Archived copy on Internet Archives Wayback Machine. Retrieved May 20, 2018, from https://web.archive.org/web/20030424100429/http://www.catb.org/~esr/writings/cathedral-bazaar/cathedral-bazaar/. 2000.

Richter T, and McPherson M. Open educational resources: Education for the world? *Distance Education* 33: 201 – 219, 2012. https://doi.org/10.1080/01587919.2012.692068.

Rodriguez CO. MOOCs and the AI-Stanford like courses: Two successful and distinct course formats for Massive Open Online Courses. *European Journal of Open, Distance and E-Learning.* 1 – 13, 2013.

Scanlon E. Scholarship in the digital age: Open educational resources, publication and public engagement. *British Journal of Educational Technology* 45: 12 – 23, 2014. https://doi.org/10.1111/bjet.12010.

Sclater N. The organizational impact of open educational resources. In: Ehlers, Ulf-Daniel and Schneckenberg, Dirk, Eds. *Changing Cultures in Higher Education: Moving Ahead to Future Learning.* Berlin: Springer. http://oro.open.ac.uk/18765/. The Open University. 2009.

Shapiro JP, and Stefkovich JA. *Ethical Leadership and Decision Making in Education: Applying Theoretical Perspectives to Complex Dilemmas.* Mahwah, New Jersey: Lawrence Erlbaum Associates, Publishers. 2001.

Shirky C. *Here Comes Everybody: The Power of Organizing without Organizations*. New York: Penguin Press. 2008.

Smith MS, and Casserly CM. The promise of open educational resources. *Change: The Magazine of Higher Learning* 38: 8 – 17, 2006. https://doi.org/10.3200/CHNG.38.5.8-17.

Straumsheim C. Where open textbooks are used. *Inside Higher Ed.* Retrieved May 19, 2018, from https://www.insidehighered.com/news/2016/07/26/study-finds-use-open-educational-resources-rise-introductory-courses. 2016.

Tuomi I. Open educational resources and the transformation of education. *European Journal of Education* 48: 1 – 20, 2012.

Wenk B. Open educational resources (OER) inspire teaching and learning. IEEE EDUCON Education Engineering 2010- The future of Global Learning Engineering Education. Madrid, Spain. 435 – 441, 2010.

Wiley D. On the sustainability of open educational resource initiatives in higher education. OECD Centre for Educational Research and Innovation (CERI). Paper. 2007.

Wiley D. Openness as catalyst for an educational reformation. *EDUCAUSE Review* 45:14 – 20, 2010. https://er.educause.edu/articles/2010/8/openness-as-catalyst-for-an-educational-reformation.

Willems J, and Bossu C. Equity considerations for open educational resources in the glocalization of education. *Distance Education* 33: 1 – 16, 2012. https://doi.org/10.1080/01587919.2012.692051.

Yuan L, MacNeill S, and Kraan W. Open educational resources—opportunities and challenges for higher education. *Educational Cybernetics: Reports.* Paper 1. 2008.

Additional Reading Section

Benkler Y. *The Wealth of Networks: How Social Production Transforms Markets and Freedom.* New Haven: Yale University Press. 2006.

Merriam SB, and Caffarella RS. *Learning in Adulthood: A Comprehensive Guide.* 2nd Ed. San Francisco: Jossey-Bass Publishers. 1999.

Steers RM, Porter LW, and Bigley GA. *Motivation and Leadership at Work.* 6th Ed. Boston: McGraw Hill. 1996.

Walters K, and Brody M. *What's Language Got to Do with It?* New York: W.W. Norton & Company. 2005

Chapter 2
Profiling Target and Potential Learners Today and into the Future

Abstract Conducting an early learner profile for a particular subject domain may help identify whether there is a potential market for the conceptualized open-shared learning objects and sequences…and may inform learning designs for target and potential learners. This chapter focuses on the importance of learner-centered design or the general idea that the design of learning accommodates understood learner needs and interests. This is not to say that all learner needs are accommodated because there are learning benefits for those who are able to adjust and adapt to the learning context. This chapter describes the importance of rough learner profiling as a framework, some relevant dimensions of such profiling, and how to use such profiles to enhance the design, development, and delivery of open-shared learning contents. This work shows the importance of using empirics to profile target and potential learners, and also to use profiles to constructive ends, not any potentially harmful ones (such as stereotyping and limiting learner options or denying access to particular groups). Also, this work emphasizes the efficacy-testing of learner profiling on learning resource designs and development and the resultant learning.

Keywords Target learner · Potential learner · Learner profiling · Learner-centered design · Usability · On-the-fly behavioral profiling · Demographics · Great unused

> In times of change learners inherit the earth while the learned find themselves beautifully equipped to deal with a world that no longer exists.
>
> –Eric Hoffer (1898–1983)

> Stereotypes should never influence policy or public opinion.
>
> –Janet Reno, Attorney General of the United States of America, in a June 12, 1998, speech at the American-Arab Anti-Discrimination Committee Conference on "Shaping the Future"

S. Hai-Jew, *Designing Instruction For Open Sharing*,
https://doi.org/10.1007/978-3-030-02713-1_2

Opening Scenario

Opening Scenario: Know Your Potential Learners and Their Needs?

In a commercial context, the success of a publicly available product is measured by sales, by reputation, and by contributions to the public good (among other things); in an open-shared content context, the success of a free and open-shared object is partially measured by "audience" or the numbers of users who have adopted and are using the open-shared object, reputation, and contributions to the public good.

Usage of a shared learning object by the general public is not necessarily a given. Their adoption of a learning object is not costless. There is effort required in seeking and assessing potential learning objects. Instructors have to integrate the learning objects into their courses; learners have to adapt to the learning object. Their selection of one object may mean that they leave others unexplored or unused. The open sharing learning environment is a competitive one, with various individuals and organizations vying for and seeking public attention. In many cases, there is zero-sumness in terms of learning object usage (if a person experiences a learning object on a topic, he or she may not seek out others on the same topic). In the era of Web 2.0 or the Social Web, electronic word-of-mouth (WOM) matters: a high influence individual can drive traffic to and from various sources. It is one thing to be philosophical about reception of one's work, but in the real, attracting learners is important.

When such objects are designed and developed, there will be considerations for how to make the learning object "safe" for users to inherit and use by being accurate, legally created, and non-offensive, for example. In an attention economy, adoption of a learning object may depend on the polish of the object, its look and feel, the personality of presenters, and the wooing of the content creators, and incentives, among others. Prior to the outreach, though, one core issue involves understanding learner needs and creating objects that meet those needs.

Prior to committing to creating an open-shared object, it may be helpful to consider the targeted learners. Who would you be sharing open learning with, and why? How would you understand their particular learning needs for the particular topic? How would these potential learners practically learn about your online learning resources?

For formalized learners, it is generally possible to map their formalized curriculum through the various credit-bearing course experiences. To understand a general public, though, which includes "amateur learners" (those who want to learn about a topic lightly and do not aspire to expertise in the future) and others who may be outliers in a learning population, profiling generally may be done by harnessing a variety of less traditional tools. After all, a public mind may be informed by fictional contents (think video games, movies, television shows, books, and other media) as well as academic contents. Individuals may be informed not only by what is broadly available but by esoterica, impressions, and one-offs. In some cases, broad "hive minds" may be mapped around particular topics, but in other cases, the profiling work may have to be for sub-populations and with limited insights.

One tool, Google Correlate, enables explorations of web-scale word associations around web searches. In other words, when people go to learn about an issue, they tend to also look up other related terms. These mass-scale word associations may be insightful. Note that the words are listed in descending order by level of correlation. The terms may be clustered by related meanings for a macro sense of the search topic. To understand a mass-scale association with "open learning," in the U.S., a list was brought up that may suggest that the global center of this endeavor leans more towards England. Some technologies and technology companies are also suggested in the list. (Fig. 2.1)

Some Early Questions to Consider

If you are to offer a back-of-the-napkin profiles of the possible learners for an open-shared learning object that you would create, how would you characterize these learners? Who are the likely users of the open-shared learning objects, and why?

If you were to design to target learners, who would they be, and why? What would their most salient characteristics be as learners? How would you design learning objects to meet their needs?

Who are the majority of these potential learners? How may they be accurately characterized? What are ways to target the center mass of this group with effective learning resources?

If there is a potential for niche populations of learners, who would these niche groups be, and why? What does/do the "long tail(s)" of this potential population of learners look like? Who are some of the projected niche groups? Why? What are their unique needs? What are their needs, motivations, and objectives? Why would they have an interest in this topic?

What methods would be most effective in learning about these potential learners? What methods would be the least effective in learning about these potential learners?

How would you move from the learner profiles to their needs? What aspects of people are most indicative of their respective learning needs? Why?

Who are the potential future learner groups, and why? What if the learning resources are available indefinitely?

What are some ways to anticipate the needs of future learners and to design for those today in the here-and-now?

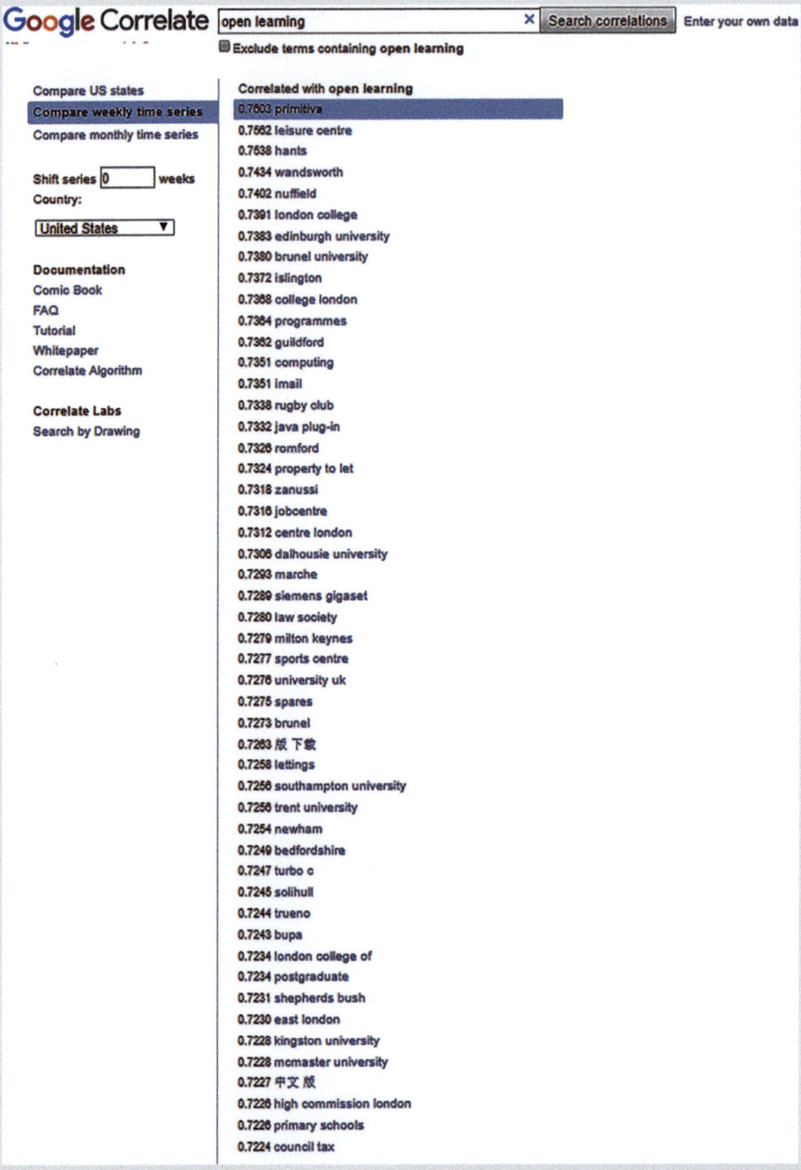

Fig. 2.1 "Open learning" search on Google correlate in the U.S. by Weekly Time Series

Learning Objectives
Learners will…

Importance of Pre-design and Pre-development Learner Profiling

- Consider the importance of roughly and accurately profiling potential groups of users of particular open-shared learning objects and sequences …pre-design and pre-development
- Consider questions including the following:
  - What do the learner profiles suggest about the demand-side for learner needs and interests related to the topic? What may be discovered about demand-side forecasting?
  - How self-aware are these target learners about their learning?
  - How knowledgeable are these target learners about the particular subject matter? What sorts of mental models do they have of the topic vs. the professional conceptual models?
  - How comfortable are these target learners with online learning technologies?
  - What types of learning will these target learners be comfortable with? How do they expect to be addressed and why?
- Consider the possible roles of potential learners in participatory design of online learning

Some Dimensions of Learner Profiling

- Consider a conceptual "universal learner" profile as a baseline
- Profile the target learners (demographic features, their current knowledge, their learning needs) who may benefit from open-shared learning objects, courses, and sequences
  - List specific and potential benefits to the target learners of well-made open-shared learning objects, courses, and sequences
  - Consider what may attract the target learners to the particular designed online learning resource
- Consider the pros and cons of profiling learners on-the-fly based on their learning behaviors with digital learning objects and their behaviors on learning management systems (including learner privacy interests)
- Conceptualize an imaginary "idealized learner" for learning resource development
- Imagine future learners and their learning needs
  - List dimensions of the future learner as most relevant to their learning needs
  - Consider the most common ways that future learners might differ from contemporary learners and explain why

Reaching Target Learners Through their Social Networks

- List some possible "project partners" in reaching possible learners using the open-shared learning objects and sequences (to benefit from social networks)

- Identify individuals who may serve as knowledgeable informants of the respective communities that may benefit from the open-shared learning
- Consider some initial ways that the potential learners and "project partners" may be reached via the Web and Internet (and through organizations and social agglomerations of people)

Connecting Learner Profiles and Learner Needs in "User Models"

- List possible unique needs of particular learners and learner groups in user models
- Conduct some early thinking about some ways to begin to meet those possible learner needs through design, strategic messaging, informational content, multimodality, style, and other endeavors
  - Consider some effective possible outreaches to target learners through various publicity and outreach efforts

2.1 Introduction

When a learner or group of learners first experiences an online learning object or learning sequence, they explore what is there and consider how closely the learning resources align with what they need (or perceive that they need). If they see a mismatch, they may simply move on. Commitments to "found" objects online are fragile. If the learning resources are especially negative (if there are clear inaccuracies, poor designs, a lack of respect for users of the object, and others), some users will post derogatory comments and down-rate the resource. In most cases, there are no second chances. After all, the designers/developers are not easily reachable (and many do not even share their actual names, choosing to go with handles). Even when some learning objects are interactive (by design), there is no human intervention to mediate understandings, except maybe from third-party co-learners who are active on that social space.

A critical part of designing for open-shared learning resources is to profile the target learners during the initial needs assessment for the project. (A "needs assessment" is an inquiry process early in a design sequence to best understand the parameters of a project as a way to advance the work.)

The profiling of target learners involves several basic assumptions. One assumption is that global learners using open-shared learning resources are heterogeneous, not homogeneous. As such, learners have different points-of-view and subjectivities; also, they come from different learning contexts and have different motivations for using learning objects in different ways. The "universe" is actually a "multiverse," in terms of people's experiences. Another assumption is that learner profiles only capture sketches of individuals and people groups, not full profiles. For individuals and people, only some aspects are visible.

Ethically, the learner profiling should be as transparent as possible. Those in power who create profiles and can make decisions affecting people's access and their learning experiences have an extra large responsibility to ensure that this effort is accurate and pro-learning and ultimately beneficent for all involved. The transparency may ensure that others have inputs on the processes, so no undue influences should go into the profiling, and critically, no harm comes from the decisions from such profiling. The learner profiles should be open to revision and reconsideration. It should not be intrusive and should not compromise learner privacy (and often not even be trackable to personally identifiable information). In the literature, there is already debate about the re-use of learner profiles (or personal data in "learner models" in innovative learning environments research) and the different interests of those who are teachers, learners, families, institution, and scientists (Eyssautier-Bayay et al. 2009, p. 265). Learner profile-informed designs should be inclusive of the target learner groups without being exclusionary of out-groups or others outside of the target learners. This inclusiveness is important even for customized boutique learning designs to very specific target learners. For open-shared learning, people are not designing to cliques but to potentially everyone (but practically to some).

Target learners, by definition, are thin-sliced segments of a broader population. There are no absolute indicators for what should be included in the profile; however, based on past practice, there are some common elements. For example, the target learners' ages are important because of the link between age and developmental state (and often capabilities). (This is not to say that there are not variances to the respective populations. Often, there are some extreme outliers in the respective populations, but populations generally fall into normal curves, which enable some predictivity. However, every profile is necessarily limited and should not be used to negatively stereotype, cast aspersions on "other" people, or exclude people from opportunities, and a profile and should never be used unethically—such as to deny people access to learning topics of interest.) Performances on standardized tests, represented by scores, are often used as indicators for academic achievement. The challenge is to find factual data about populations that enable understandings of their learning needs to strengthen learning designs. Ideally, these profiles would be fairly sparse and simple, with bare relevant sketched details to inform the design. These assumptions of the relationship between profiles and learning preferences then have to be tested with actual designs and actual learners, to test the assumptions.

This chapter addresses the importance of learner profiling in the pre-design and pre-development phases, so that this information may be integrated into the design of the respective open-shared learning resources. This considers a base model of "universal learners" initially and then discusses various other applied methods to extract theorized learner profiles for open-shared learning resources. Those learner profiles are then analyzed for perceived learner needs, for learner-centered designs. They inform adaptivity to the learners' learning needs through user modeling (Brusilovsky 2003). These profiles are used to engage in "demand side forecasting" or trying to ascertain the amount of need for the particular open-shared learning resources among learners. The higher the potential demand, the higher the potential justifications for expenditures and work.

This chapter suggests the importance of reaching actual target learners to enable connecting when the learning resources are ready for primetime but also to test the posited learner profiles along with understood learner needs (and the efforts to meet those needs with learner-centered designs). This chapter is the second in the sequence (Fig. 2.2).

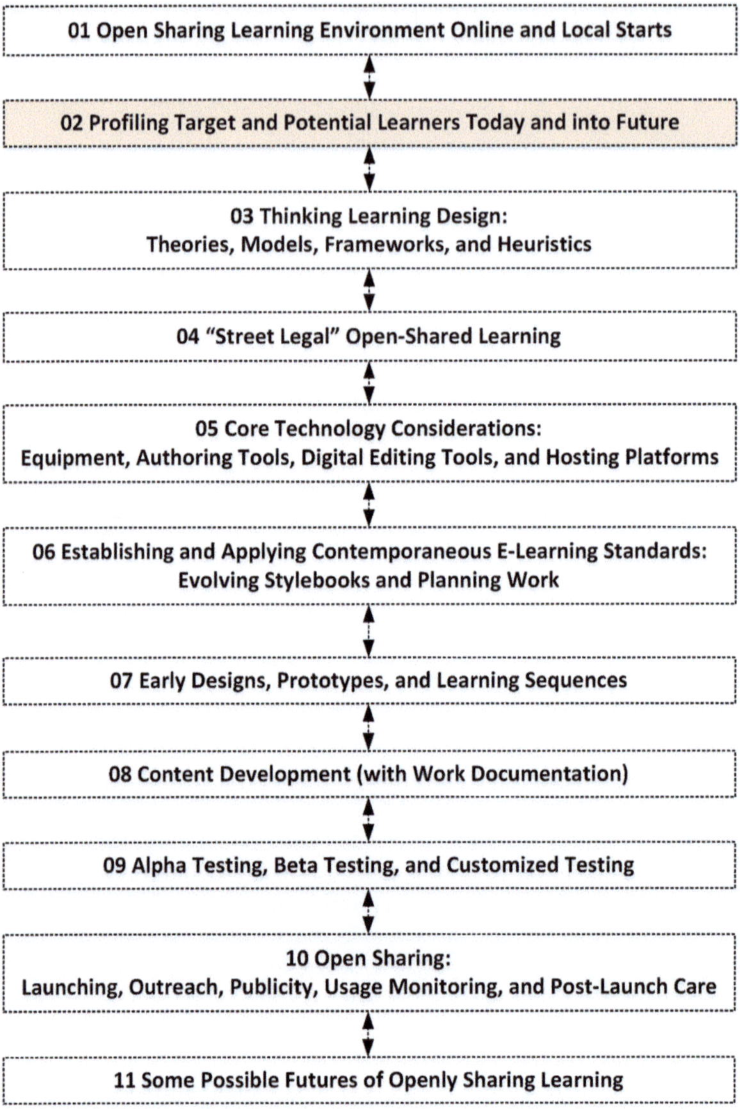

Fig. 2.2 Step 2 in the open-shared learning resource development sequence

2.2 Review of the Literature

A core assumption in learner profiling in learning is that better understanding the learners enables better learning designs, improved delivery of services (with recommender systems, online automated tutors, auto-selected learning, and human instructional interventions) with increasing learning and proficiencies, and ultimately, improved learner success and learner awareness of their success.

What is a "Learner Profile"? On one level, a "learner profile" is not one simplistic thing but a multi-dimensional and complex representation, involving various research methods, technologies, mixed data, and various concepts. Learner profiling may occur at any point in the learning process—prior to a customized learning sequence or during the learning and even after the learning (Fig. 2.3).

The idea of building learning to learners is certainly not a new one. Profiles may be static, based on parameters that do not change a lot, such as some demographic characteristics. Or, they may be dynamic, and in flux, such as behavioral parameters. Profiles are mostly done in groups, but with more recent computational capabilities, they may be more individual-focused. For the group profiles, depending on the size of the subpopulation, the members are assumed to fall on a normal curve, with learners that tend to coalesce around "averages" and "medians" and with outliers (few by definition) on the tails.

Traditional learning profiling has involved basic demographics, the academic record, course history (transcript information), and professional experiences (Skourlas et al. 2007). In higher education, learner profiles have been applied to a wide range of applications: admittance to degree programs; scholarship selection; hiring; career advancement, and others. In terms of learning design, learner profiles have been used to design (especially customize or adapt) and deliver learning, through adaptive online learning systems, e-learning platforms, virtual learning environments, learning sequences, learning objects, and others. Learner profiles have informed thinking work, like conceptual modeling and others.

In the academic field, extant questions related to learner profiling include the following:

- Which learners should be targeted, and why?
- How should learners be targeted? What are the practical channels to use to reach them? What messaging may be most influential?

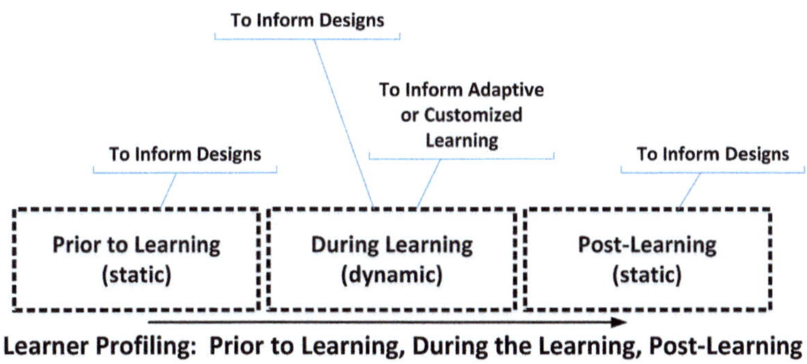

Fig. 2.3 Profiling learners before, during, or after the learning

- What aspects of target learners are most salient to understanding how they learn, and why? What aspects of target learners are not directly relevant to understanding how they learn?
- How do distinct and individual learner profiles relate to learning designs? How can individuals learners be effectively profiled? What aspects of individuals are most salient to a particular learning context and a particular learning design?
- How can learning designs be actualized to support some target "in-group" learners without dispossessing, harming, or denying other "out-group" learners?
- What are some typical use case scenarios for the respective learner groups, and why?

The challenges have always been about how to most effectively build learning to particular learners without excluding others (causing harm) and without stereotyping people groups (or individuals) and without over-generalizing. In public endeavors, whether they are commercial or not, there are high risks of causing offense, annoying or irritating users, and ultimately falling out of favor. The challenges also stem from the fact of nuanced humanity, with people tending towards sensitive responses to various signals and messaging in the world. People may trigger based on fleeting impressions and aesthetics; they may be petty and responsive to minutiae. People can respond to stimuli in unconscious ways. They may experience and view learning contents through egocentric and personalized ways. Some tailoring of learning to particular learners may mostly have to do with messaging and making changes at the margins.

User modeling, representations of common users (particularly their knowledge in particular areas and their user preferences related to the service), has long been integrated into the design of Web services because individual knowledge and preferences affect usage and accessibility mitigations. The IMS Global Learning Consortium has created technological specifications for learner accessibility needs in the IMS Accessibility Learner Profile (IMS ACCLIP), which "enables the description of user preferences (visual, aural or device)" and enables "tailoring (of) learning contents" for electronic learning (Salomoni et al. 2007, p. 85). The "learner information package" (LIP) is comprised of the following categories: identification ("bibliographic and demographic data about learner"), goal, QCL ("qualifications, certifications, and licenses granted by recognized authorities"), activity ("any learning-related activity in any state of completion"), transcript, interest ("hobbies and other recreational activities of a learner"), competency ("skills, knowledge, and abilities of a learner"), affiliation (professional organization memberships), accessibility ("learning preferences as well as language capabilities, disabilities, and eligibilities"), and others (Atif 2011, pp. 265–266). Another design approach involves an approach focused on characterizing "learning situations" instead of learners to "advocate dynamically a composite learning service, which mimics a learning pattern specification" (Atif 2011, p. 265). With sufficient information collection, it is possible to identify "advocated patterns of learning which have proven their pedagogical effectiveness" (Atif 2011, p. 259); learning may be delivered based on learners' learning styles based on how people prefer to perceive and process information, per Kolb's experiential learning cycle (Atif 2011, p. 268), with the harnessing of "existing experiences or examples" for learners who prefer "concrete experiences," opportunities to reflect for learners who prefer "reflective observation," "inductive reasoning to distil reflection into models" for those who prefer "abstract conceptualization," and the application of "intuition and deductive reasoning" for those who prefer to test implications (p. 269). Certain learning styles have been found to be dominant in certain cultures (McLoughlin and Oliver 2000).

Another work explored user characteristics like "visual, cognitive, and emotional processing parameters as well as the 'traditional' user profiling characteristics that together tend to give the most optimized, adapted and personalized result" for web-based technologies are studied and responded to (Germanakos, et al. 2008, p. 1434).

In recent years, related to online learning, learning profiling has been applied in various ways. Learner profiling has been harnessed to improve learning platforms to have more of a service orientation (Dagger et al. 2007). If the core strategies for building first-generation e-learning platforms were "monolithic," and the second-generation ones were "modular," the third-generation ones are "service-oriented" with a focus on users through the harnessing of adaptive hypermedia and Semantic Web technologies (Dagger et al. 2007, p. 31).

Another approach to learner profiling involves examining a learner's performance and work output to better understand their learning progress. For example, profiling language use (such as through "vocabulary profiling") leads to understandings about the language user's thinking and language capabilities (Yoon et al. 2012). Hierarchical clustering has been used to profile learners based on their handling of mathematical issues online (Taraghi et al. 2015). Another approach involves using learner questions to profile their level of understanding (Harrak et al. 2018). There may be gaps between what people report in their own profiles and what may be observed based on their learning behaviors online.

Researchers have mapped adult learners' knowledge taxonomies and identified errors to aid in their profiling (Abyaa et al. 2017, p. 3) and created systems to report back to them about their error frequency, the relevance of the errors, and corrections. Another research work captures learner information in order to identify at-risk learners based on various indicators, such as "academic expectations, subject interest, understanding ability, exam nervousness, (and) mathematical ability" (Pellow et al. 2005, p. 11).

In virtually all cases, learner modeling is multi-dimensional and involves multiple channels of information. Some harness informative learning models like Kolb's Learning Style Inventory applied to online behaviors and resulting in classifications of learners with particular behavior sets ("Explorers" and "Observers") and potential accommodations (Liegle and Janicki 2006, p. 885). Some more recent research involves augmenting learning profiles of learners taking MOOC courses with data traces from Social Web presences to augment available data (Chen et al. 2016).

Understanding learners' emotional states during the learning process is another aspect of learning profiling. In one research work, a static learner profile (their goals, preferences, age, skills, and computer usage) is combined with a dynamic capturing of learners' emotional responses (stress, confusion, boredom, frustration), as inferred from physiological signals, in-learning-system behaviors, and learning performance (Jraidi et al. 2013, p. 273). Another approach uses pedagogical texts to understand learners and their learning experiences and emotional states (Montero and Suhonen 2014). Some recent research has used various indicators of learner affect (such a psychological distress) to change how learning is delivered—its pacing, its contents, its sequences, and other elements—to accommodate learners and to strive for their well-being.

Some research works have explored the importance of mutual social supports to enhance learner retention. Instructors have experimented in terms of how to combine learners into dyadic, triadic, and small-group teams, based on informal profiling. Should learners be combined with other similar members, or should there be cross-functional and mixed teams? Is there some relational alchemy that may benefit learning? Certainly, current-day e-learning platforms contain a range of tools that enable learner intercommunications, interactivity, co-creation, and sharing of digital files. Persistent profiles enable learners to interrelate often well past the end of a formalized learning experience. Other technologies enable persistent web-scale collaboration. For example, annotation systems have been created that enable people to learn from each other's insights via the Social Web (Su et al. 2010). One research study showed some ambivalence of the introduced sociality, with less than high enthusiasm for sharing social profiles in online learning contexts and only 40–50% or so viewing their peers' profiles (Kear et al. 2013).

Cultural-based learner profiles have also been used in teaching and learning contexts. For example, a training for American Indian/Alaska Native (AI/AN) middle school students on sexual health were designed to be "culturally sensitive and relevant, and that they not inadvertently negatively affect youth's cultural values, competencies, or language" (Shegog et al. 2017, p. 29). Culturally inclusive online learning is achieved through "flexible, adaptable and relevant" pedagogy and curriculum for cross-cultural learning (McLoughlin 2001, p. 7).

For many of the early generation and current generation applications, learner models help select which contents to capture and deliver to learners, often combining multiple streams of information (learner data, pedagogical data, personality data, LMS experience, cognitive data, (and) device" data, in one meta-analysis of multiple studies (Heng et al. 2018, p. 1176). A core through-line in much of the resource is that such models identify learner "modalities" and enable the enhancement of learner performance (Heng et al. 2018, p. 1172). Dynamic learning sequences may be delivered based on unique learner needs.

Other research focuses on how learners conceptualize of themselves as learners and how they set goals to motivate themselves to seek challenge and to be persistent to push out the edges of the possible. Having appropriate learning goals stand to increase competence and agency. When facing difficulty, learners can take on attitudes that result either in "facilitation" or "debilitation"; if they continue to believe in the value of their effort and apply themselves with "undivided, intensified attention," maintain positive affect, and experience intrinsic rewards by striving in their learning (Dweck and Leggett 1988, p. 262), they stand to better achieve their learning goals. How people set goals has been found to be informed by their implicit theories about themselves, their minds, and their capabilities, namely a "growth mindset" vs. a "fixed mindset" (Dweck 2015). The first involves thinking of human mental capabilities as malleable and influenced by effort while the latter involves erroneously thinking that human learning capabilities are fixed by nature (genetics) and unable to be changed. Understanding the importance of effort in learning encourages people to take risks in their learning and to problem-solve their way through learning frustrations. Whether learners take a "deep" or "surface" approach to learning is also important to learner profiling. (May et al. 2012). The ability of learners to tolerate ambiguity in learning contexts may affect learning, such as the acquisition of foreign language learning, with a lack of "familiarity and logic" and the absence of typical predictability Mäntysaari 2013, p. 34). Intrinsic differences among people may be adapted to to optimize learner performance based on a range of human factors, including "cognitive style, visual working memory span…and anxiety" (Tsianos et al. 2008, p. 1).

Open learner models (OLM) focus on supporting self-regulated learners in their own metacognition (self-awareness of their own perception and thinking), self-motivation, and agency: "Open learner models (OLMs) are learning tools that take an internal model of the learner maintained by a computer-based adaptive or tutoring system and shows it to the learner" (Guerra 2016, p. 329). (Learner profiling can be obvious to learners or made non-obvious, and for much of the research, these profiles seem to exist more on background for system functioning only.) These tools enable "better personalization and adaptive mechanisms" for self-regulated learning (Guerra 2016, p. 329).

Dynamic Profiling In terms of dynamic data capture of learners, this is often done from either the electronic learning platform (whether repository, LMS, MOOC platform, immersive virtual world, virtual learning environments, computer-supported learning environments, computing environments for human learning, simulation space, intelligent learning environments, or others) or the platform hosting the learning object or learning sequence. A "runtime" profile of a learner is how a learner instantiates based on behaviors and actions in the online space, and this is often captured tactically based on targeted log or trace data.

The capture of learner behavior, actions, and learning performance can be informative of a profile even if an earlier pre-learning profile was not directly captured. This information capture bypasses some of the weaknesses in people's self-reporting as well. Often, multiple methods are harnessed for on-the-fly profiling, including "behavioral, physiological and self-reporting methods" (Çimen Summer 2003, p. v). One exploratory study around math learners used the following: "surveys aiming to measure participants' epistemological beliefs, metacognitive strategies and the levels of mathematics anxiety; behavioral data including audio-visuals and screen capture embedded with eye-tracking, and physiological data including heart, respiration and eye blink rates" and mixed research methodology cross validating analytics across the data types (Çimen Summer 2003, p. v). Another research team has created a fairly granular learner profile (comprised of their behavior, knowledge, skills, interactions, and "design") in order to deliver pedagogical activities and necessary assistance in an online learning context (Kear et al. 2013).

On various massive open online courses (MOOCs), learner engagement is measured (Kizilcec et al. 2013), and learners' help-seeking behaviors are used to create clustered group learner profiles (Corrin et al. 2017). Such learner trace data is used to enable adaptive learning in some cases. Targeted digital trace data from social media platforms have been used to inform simulated environments built for experiential learning (Ammari et al. 2012). An effective MOOC is one that works well for a broad diversity of learners (with highly variant profiles and backgrounds) (Garcia-Peñalvo et al. 2014). Learner motivation has been a dimension used to profile learners on massive open online courses (MOOCs), based on their online learning behaviors, including the following four types: completing, auditing, disengaging, and sampling (Kizilcec et al. 2013, p. 172).

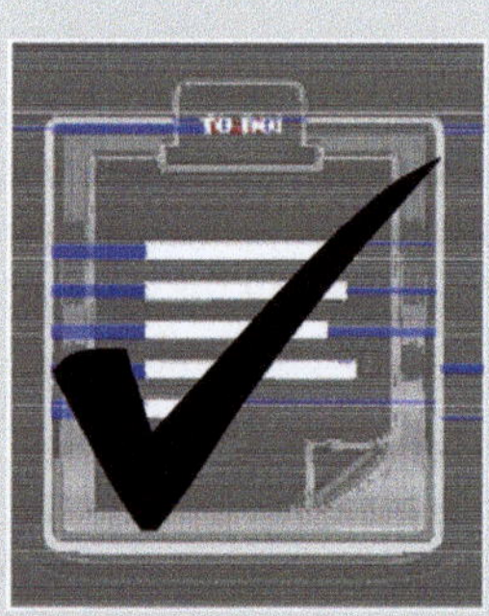

Task #1: Profiling the Typical Learners with Whom You Connect
Think about the learning groups that you usually address with your work. What do you know of them *for a fact?* What are some inferences that you can make of them? Why? How do you design to their needs?

Do you have ways to validate or invalidate your senses of these learners? How much of your insights are particular to individuals and not the larger group? How generalizable are your observations?

2.3 Profiling Target (and Potential) Learners: Current and Future

One core concept behind learner profiling actually comes from the information sciences, particularly Claude Shannon's information theory (1948), which addresses the importance of the accurate receipt of informational content to control for entropy or uncertainty. While online learning has far advanced beyond the concept of learning as passively receiving of information, the idea of understanding learner needs and their preparedness for particular learning has come to the fore. The idea is that learners have to be accurate receivers of the learning, and the information senders need to understand what the receivers prefer and are capable of handling. (A corollary concept is Lev Vygotsky's concept of a learner's "zone of proximal development" or ZPD, which suggests that learners are at particular points of readiness and receptivity to learning, and with designed teaching supports, they may be able to make some additional advancements beyond what they can achieve alone. However, this learning progress is within a certain proxemics range from where they are. Beyond this range, their sensemaking would be difficult or even impossible. This concept suggests the need to know where learners are in their learning and to build to that. Without a certain level of subject familiarity, learners would be lost, even those with a high tolerance for ambiguity.)

Those who teach for a living may profile their learners as part of any learning design because they have to use whatever they create with learners and often acquire instant feedback about what is working and what is not. For many who have well practiced, they may make such observations and design choices intrinsically, and much of this may be left unspoken and unsurfaced. The benefit in articulating assumptions about target learners is that it brings the concepts top-of-mind, and it enables individuals to assess their own thinking, test their own theories, consider whether learner needs are met (and to use empirical methods to test their own assumptions), and continue to build on their store of pedagogical and design knowledge.

In an open-shared learning resource context, though, there is no close working relationship with learners, and adjustments to the resources cannot readily be made. Given this situation, it helps to address who the target learners may be and to profile them, and to include profiling of most likely potential learners (with a broad potential client base) and future prospects.

Some assumptions of learners who will pursue open-shared learning resources may begin with some basic assumptions. The potential learner groups may be categorized into three types:

Assumption A (Savvy and/or Formally Guided Mainstream Learners) Learners who access open-shared learning resources are from the mainstream population of learners who access online learning. They may be pursuing formal (credit-based studies), nonformal (non-accredited learning), and informal (learning as a byproduct of other activities) learning objectives. They may want to augment their other learning using available public resources. They may be pursuing work-based objectives. They are informed by their prior learning experiences and need to recognize the learning value of the objects and sequences made available in the open space.

Assumption B (Self-Motivated and Unconventional Self-Regulated Super Learners) Learners who access open-shared learning resources are self-regulated learners who are driven by a need to learn, and innate and reinforced curiosity. They are self-starters, and they tend to be more resilient than mainstream learners in terms of following through with their learning. They are savvy users of online resources.

Assumption C (Dabbling and Exploratory Learners) Learners who access open-shared learning resources are just exploring. They are not particularly motivated to learn but just want to see what is out there. They are finding a way in to a topic. If something does not capture their attention early on, they will not continue with their use of the learning object or learning sequence.

Individuals and groups may be in different categories in different learning contexts and with different learning topics. For example, a learner may access a formal MOOC course to acquire knowledge about wielding a particular technology as part of a workplace learning team on the one hand but be a dabbling explorer when acquiring quilting skills by watching videos on YouTube. Regardless of the category, the uptake of learning objects requires some learner receptivity.

2.3.1 Identifying "Target" and "Potential" Learners

"Target learners" are those for whom the designer/developer is especially focused on in the contents, and "potential learners" are those who may not be direct targets but who may find their way to the resource and to use it nevertheless. In general, target learners tend to be more homogeneous sub-populations, and potential learners tend to be more heterogeneous subpopulations (Fig. 2.4). In general, the range of potential learners will include those with little background in the subject matter (amateurs, novices, neophytes) all the way to those with intensive expertise (professionals, experts). In designing and developing open-shared learning resources, considering members of both of these groups may ensure that the learning contents are more effective. In terms of designing trainings for organizations, the learning design

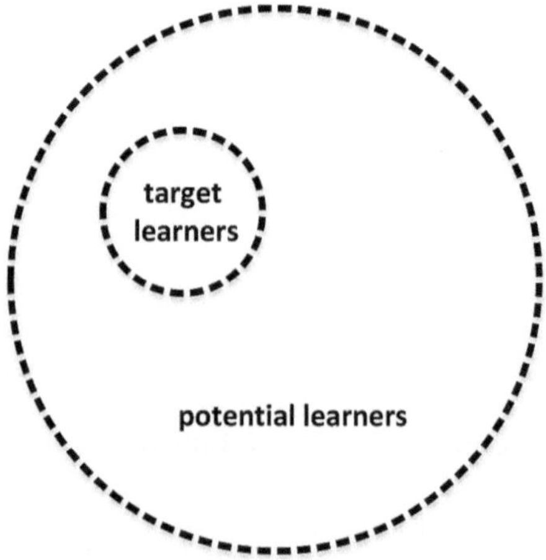

Fig. 2.4 "Target" and "potential" learners for particular open-shared learning resources

is informed by studies of the external environment, the organization's internal environment, and employee needs defined as workplace performance requirements (Rothwell and Cookson 1997).

Learner profiling, the act of sparsely describing learners based on their most salient characteristics, may occur at any point in the design, development, launch, and post-launch sequence. A learner profile may inform the learning design, the development of learning objects and sequences, how learning contents are launched and publicized, and how the learning contents are being used and whether effectively or not. Figure 2.5 shows how basic learner profiling may inform each stage of the design-development-launch sequence.

For this textbook, early learner profiling will answer two important questions: First: Is there an extant market for the potential open-shared digital learning objects and sequences? Or is there room to create just such a market from scratch based on individuals who have a peripheral interest? If yes, then this may inform the decision of whether to go forward with the work or not. The next question then answers how to possibly proceed with the work. Second: What are the learning needs of the "target" and "potential" learners? What sorts of learning designs would the target and potential learners respond to and find helpful (Fig. 2.6)? Question 1 focuses on whether there is a need for the particular product, and Question 2 considers how to design for the likely users. If an initial learner profile does not show any likely users, then throwing resources into design-development-launch will only result in a net loss of effort with no gain and no upside. There will just be more contents contributed to the Great Unread. (In Chap. 1, the prior environmental scan will inform on whether competitor learning contents already exist and how these are effective or ineffective.) The point about understanding whether there is a need in the population for the learning is built on the assumption that people have limited attention to spend, and many will not choose to engage in learning on their off-time. If the market share is already captured by an existing resource, it is likely much harder to convert those users to the new learning objects, and it is possible that there are fewer others in the general population who may be wooed to a particular learning experience or sequence.

Learner profiling may be the difference, in part, in making an open-shared learning object or sequence more competitive. Unless a learning object is in the top few pages of a Google Search (in the very top ranges of a web search), it will not generally find an audience. To be relevant, a learning object needs to be the "go-to" or destination one. The baseline for learning object adoption seems to be about one in five (Ochoa 2011). If success of open-shared learning resources is measured by adoption, then the failure rate is high (80%). While some learning repositories (collections of learning objects hosted by one provider) and learning referatories (web portals that point to learning objects hosted externally to the site) may maintain various relevance metrics (based on user evaluations, and other variables), there is no consensus-based or widely acceptance evaluation measure for learning object or learning sequence quality.

Ideally, there would be a topic area in which one is a recognized expert about which there is public interest and a potential installed base of learners who would be

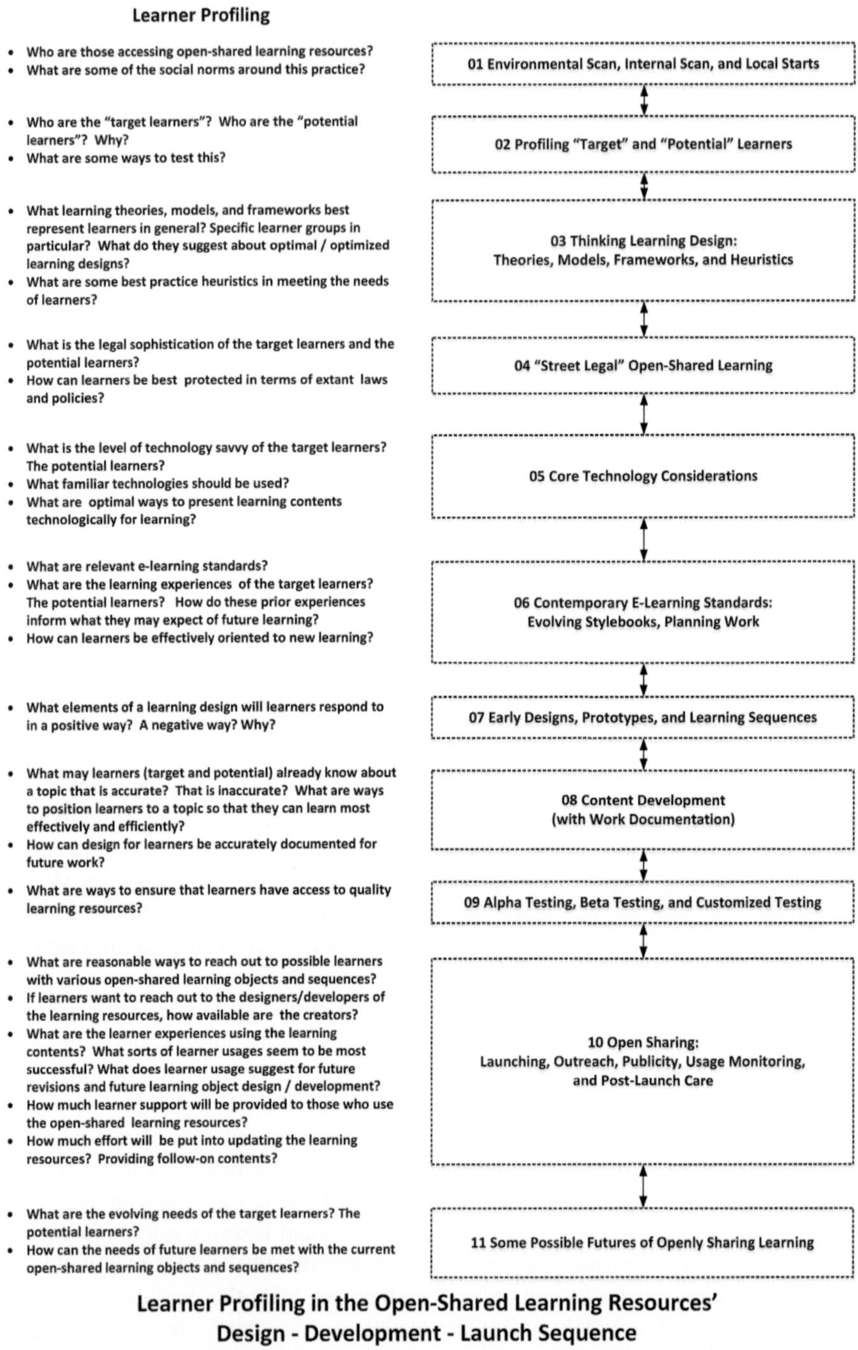

Fig. 2.5 Learner profiling in the open-shared learning resources' design-development-launch sequence

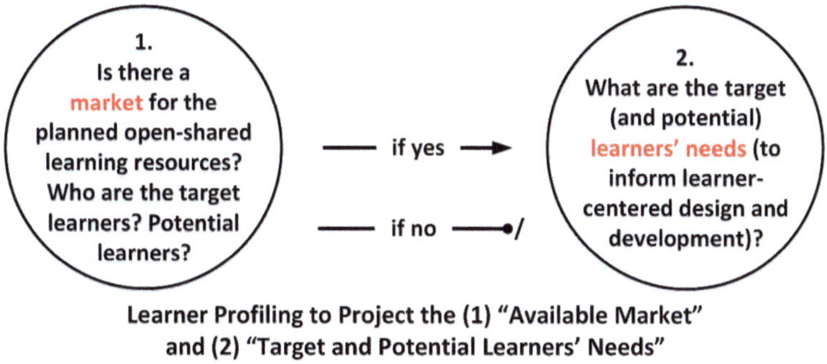

Fig. 2.6 Learner profiling to project the (1) "available market" and (2) "target and potential learner needs"

receptive to open-shared learning resources. Another way to approach this is to identify learner populations that have been thus far left unaddressed and try to understand what their learning needs are and to build to that. Being the first to address a particular topic or a particular learning community may be highly rewarding, even if a little intimidating. The novelty factor is important. The contexts of usage are likely too broad to depict, but technologically, these may be described as fully online (including with mobile-only), blended or hybrid, and face-to-face.

For this chapter, the learner profiling is considered most effective prior to the design and development phases, so the learner profile(s) may inform all the processes that follow (Fig. 2.2). However, this also means that the learner profile has to be multi-sourced and partially speculative and as-yet untested.

side bar

Profiling Online Learning Communities

On the Web and Internet, there are numerous defined online learning communities coalesced around different topics of interest. Some may be found coalesced around particular technologies like massive open online course (MOOC) courseware, social content sharing sites, social networking site communities, microblogging sites, news-sharing sites, and others, both *within* as well as *across* a number of such sites. Some of the learning communities are self-named and self-identified on the respective online spaces. Others are less obviously coalesced "communities" and may be more dispersed but share common interests.

Regardless, it is possible to access publicly available information to better understand the particular learning communities. By looking at the digital residua from such sites, it is possible to reverse-engineer a learner profile from such sites.

What are some possible signals or indicators? Some informative details may include the following (and more):

the types of interactions: the conversations (the text and the subtext, the stated values, and others), the questions posted (and answered), the shared digital files, members' treatments of each other, and others

the events (both in-world and virtual): presentations, guest speakers,

the membership: the personally identifiable information (PII), the identifier handles, the individual profiles, the represented geographical locations, and others

the languages: member languages

the funding and resources (if any): foundations, personal, other

From the interactions, the shared resources, and the problems-solutions posted to the community, it is possible to infer the topic-based sophistication of the learning community. It is possible to see the social norms practiced by a majority of the learning community members, especially in terms of how they intercommunicate (what they profess, how they embody what their values may be), and what they share. What people do may be revelatory of their internal agendas, in general, except for when they are trying to create a false persona or miscommunicate intentions (deception). How new members are treated—the learning community's inclusiveness or exclusiveness—may be understood as well, particularly if the researcher is willing to engage and join such communities.

To understand opportunities to participate, it may help to identify apparent unmet needs here. For example, what questions go poorly answered or unanswered altogether? What other types of expressed needs are not being met? Who are the members for whom the space is constructive and effective, and for whom is this not working? What sorts of new members may be recruited for the betterment of all?

Live Example: @MOOCList on Twitter

A surface impression of the @MOOCList on Twitter may suggest that it is an aggregator of MOOC information. The followers of this list may be those who want to stay up-to-date on what is available in the world of MOOCs. A light exploration using computational data extraction might complement initial impressions.

A profile of the @MOOCList account on Twitter will be conducted to try to better understand this community. The account is out of Portugal and joined in December 2012. Its profile reads: "A complete list of Massive Open Online Courses (free online courses) offered by the best universities and entities." The landing page is at https://twitter.com/MOOCList. At the moment of the data capture, there were 8841 Tweets, 50 following, 17,313 followers, 438 likes and 1 list. The following accounts include a range of individual and organizational accounts, featuring English and Spanish. The data extraction of the most recent Tweets on the @MOOCList Tweetstream using NCapture of NVivo 12 Plus resulted in 3,232 messages.

A map of the account shows most activities occurring in Portugal. This belies the large-scale name which might be more suggestive of a global following and membership (Fig. 2.7).

Fig. 2.7 Account and activity map for the @MOOCList account on Twitter

A social network graph map of its membership also seems to show little intercommunications activity (including retweets and mentions) (Fig. 2.8). It is possible that this capture caught the account during a lull.

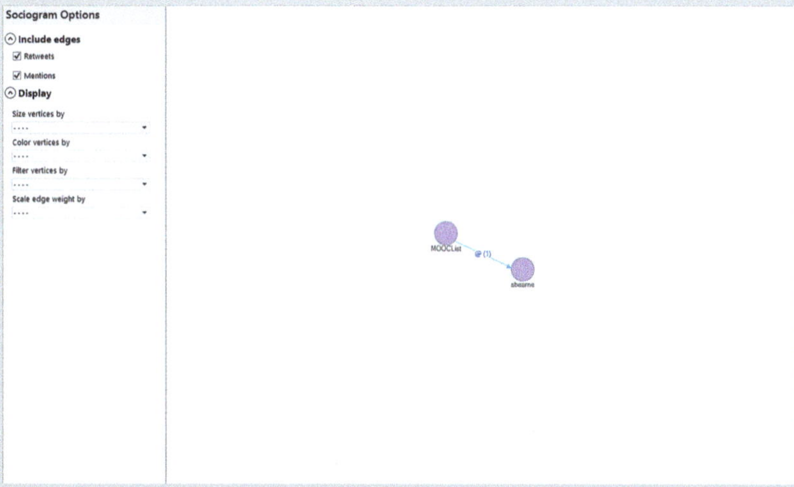

Fig. 2.8 Sociograph of the @MOOCList on Twitter

A simple word frequency count identifies some common hashtag (#) campaigns, a lot of pointing to different URLs, and other themes (Fig. 2.9)

Fig. 2.9 A word cloud of the top-1000 words messaging @MOOCList on Twitter

In terms of basic topic modeling, autocoded themes were all of a kind and based around one term "moocs" instead of a broad range of terms. A treemap diagram shows the autocoded themes in Fig. 2.10. This suggests a one-to-

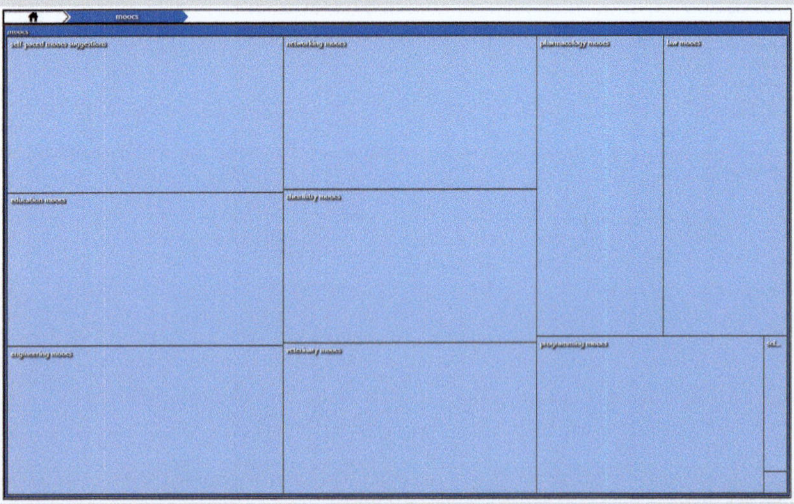

Fig. 2.10 Autocoded themes from the @MOOCList tweetstream sample on Twitter

many communications dynamic announcing available massive open online courses (MOOCs), based around subject domains like education, engineering, networking, chemistry, veterinary, pharmacology, programming, law, and others. This account disseminates information of varying levels of interest to its community.

A cell-level analysis of sentiment resulted in a pattern of "very negative" sentiments (Fig. 2.11). This finding, based on the built-in sentiment dictionary in NVivo 12 Plus (set to English), may suggest that users use the space to review their MOOC course experiences and maybe even to rant (which is not unheard of on a microblogging site).

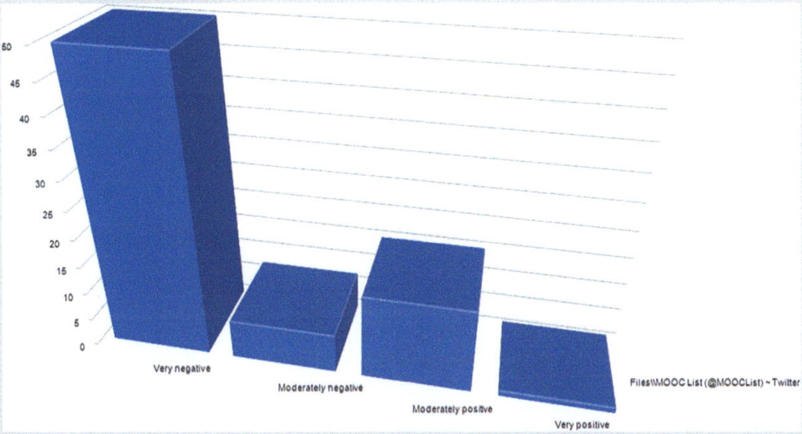

Fig. 2.11 Very negative sentiment @MOOCList on Twitter

A text query of the topic of "MOOC" reveals a sparse word tree with just a few branches, which further gives the sense of a lull in messaging currently (Fig. 2.12).

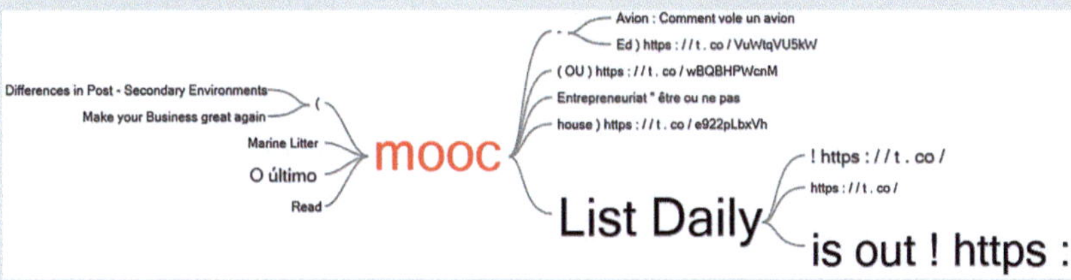

Fig. 2.12 A word tree around "mooc" in the @MOOCList account on Twitter

In the collected data, one is able to capture all social account usernames (whether they are handles or whether they are personally identifiable information to actual names). A listing of URLs highlight outlinks. A Location Coordinates column shows the location of the device sharing the Tweet. A reading of profiles may lead to email and other ways to contact the individuals. The data table may be exported for analysis using other tools (like SPSS, LIWC, and others) (Fig. 2.13).

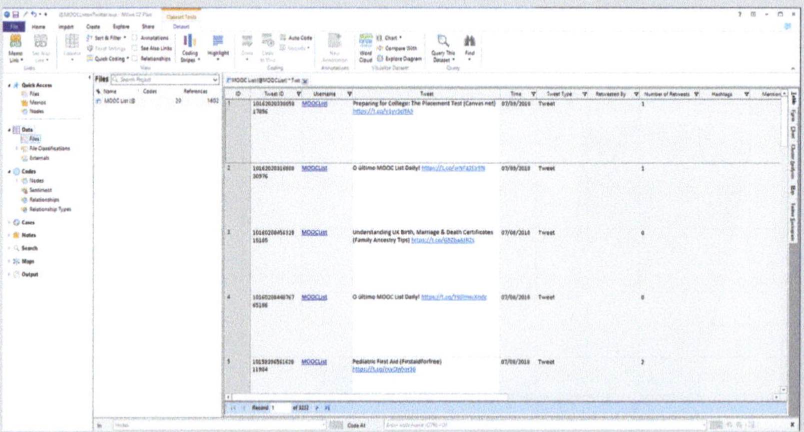

Fig. 2.13 An exportable and informative data table from the @MOOCList account on Twitter

Owners of the social media accounts have to enable access to their data through their privacy settings. If that is allowed, then the broad general public (whitelisted into the respective platforms with validated accounts) may access a selection of the most recent data from social media platforms are accessible through respective application programming interfaces (APIs). Some platforms are rate-limited, which may mean a longer period of time to access the desired information. In almost no cases are there an N of all in terms of data capture.

On Facebook, the platform enables the collection of a larger set of post-stream data, but other information such as graphing networks and identifying locations is missing. #hashtag networks may be captured and illustrated into graphs using Network Overview, Discovery and Exploration for Excel (NodeXL), an add-on to Excel, but the tool itself sets collection limits.

What follows next are some ways of profiling learners in the open-shared learning space. These approaches will draw from facts and from the human imagination. They are described in fairly practical and applied ways, so they may be harnessed by people in various contexts. Each approach begins with a different starting point or starting node, so that the conceptualizations can be wide-ranging and rich and applicable to a variety of contexts.

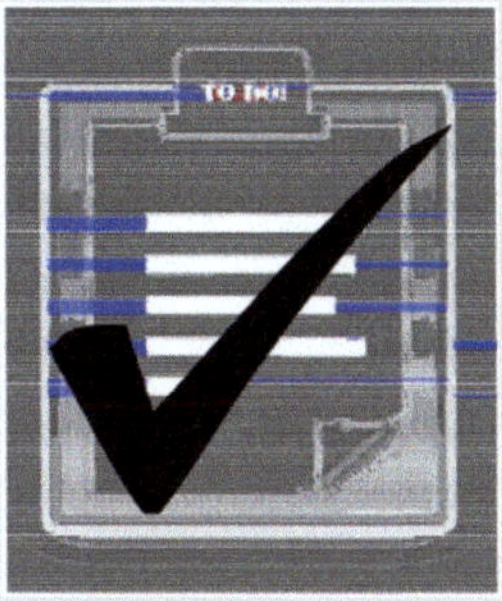

Task #2: Informal Learner Profiling
Think about some of your go-to's in terms of methods for profiling learners. How good is the information you get about them? What confident are you in the results? Why?

Some Possible Back-of-the-Napkin Sequences in Learner Profiling At present, there are no available defined or mapped way to approach learner profiling in the open-shared learning space. There may be some methods written into socio-technical systems. There may be particular approaches for unique cases or technologies. There is nothing generally applied to this open-shared learning space. To meet the need, a dozen straightforward back-of-the-napkin (implying: drafty, casual, incomplete, nonformal, and quick-study-ish) approaches are proposed here.

In this textbook, the learner profiling approaches are summarized in three main categories, based on starting points to the learner profiling. The first category is comprised of inanimate starting nodes (those based on inanimate start points): a learning topic, a target learning skill, a type of advanced learning context, and a technology platform. The second category is comprised of animate starting nodes (those based on people): macro- to micro- populations, target cultural populations, target language populations, organizations, idealized learners, and actual learners. The third category is a tactically synthesized approach combining both inanimate and animate elements. Each approach highlights different aspects of the profiled learners, and each evokes different insights.

These profiles should, of course, be evaluated to see how they may inform learning design…and the efficacy or in-efficacy of the respective designs should be tested with live learners (within the constraints of human subjects research review).

Some less formal ways to profile "target" and "potential" learners of open-shared learning contents follow in this section. A "string of pearls" approach is used, beginning with a starting node at the far left of the timeline and advancing the analysis to a group learner profile. Where an analysis starts can influence what is perceived. A dozen or so approaches are introduced here, and they are not conceptualized as stand-alone approaches but can be mixed and matched for different insights, for one project. These are based on both empirical data and the human imagination. The first set of approaches begin with nodes that are "inanimate" (not alive); the second set of approaches begin with nodes that are "animate" (alive); the third category combines the inanimate and animate approaches for synthetic ones.

2.4 Set One: Inanimate First Node in the Learner Profiling Sequence

Beginning with inanimate (non-living) nodes enables people to begin with the target learning and skills, or technologies, or platforms, in order to backwards infer who the target and potential learners may be.

A Learning Topic Approach to Learner Profiling To run a learner profile effort from a particular learning topic, it may help to understand how the learning topic is generally approached, who the traditional learners tend to be, their general learning roles (based on extant numbers if such statistics are collected—as they often are), to arrive at a group learner profile.

This approach assumes that there are natural learner constituencies for particular topics. This also suggests that for complex topics that there may be a diminishing pipeline of potential learners as dependencies for that learning mean fewer and fewer are able to fully appreciate the topic (at least with full understanding). This is not to say that learners without the full preparatory backing for a topic cannot approach a topic and gain some learning from it, but it may be that they may not achieve full dimensional understandings. Learning pipelines are thought to begin at pre-school age and extend through the lifespan of an individual. Certainly, if a topic is novel and relevant, new constituencies of learners may be created by the existence of the learning opportunities (Fig. 2.14).

Within topics and subject domains, people may be profiled into sub-groupings such as those who follow certain beliefs or concepts, and those who follow certain practices. These are important to know because of the stubbornness of initial ideas and worldviews (whether with a factual basis or not). Taking into account prior ideas may help in addressing learners with different perspectives, those lightly held and those tightly held.

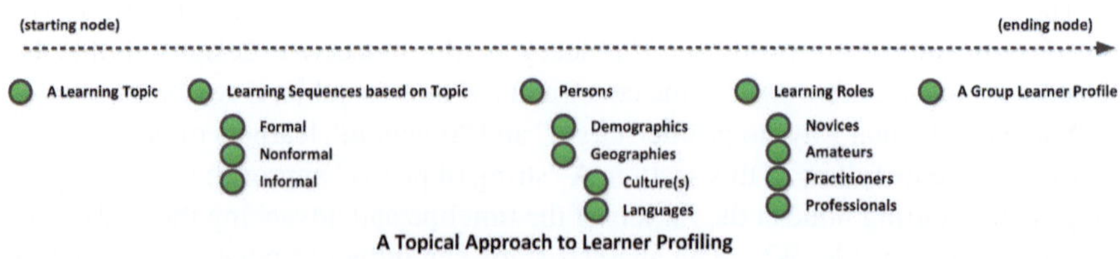

Fig. 2.14 A topical approach to learner profiling

A Target Learning Skill Approach to Learner Profiling Another starting node to profile learners may be based on a target learning skill. The target learning skill may be defined initially, to understand its formal and informal definitions, its applications, people's motives for acquiring the skill, and their learning needs, to create a group learner profile. It would be helpful to know what the most common learning sequences are and where the gaps are for those who are on different learning paths but who need a particular target skill. (At a more zoomed-out level, "learning progressions" focus on developments of learners as they build knowledge in a particular domain. These progressions may be informative of macro-scale learning and macro-scale learning needs, and these may inform people in a field of the need for particular formalized learning sequences.) Of special interest are the sequences made possible through open-shared learning objects and sequences (Fig. 2.15).

A Type of Advanced Learning Context Approach to Learner Profiling Another form, inspired by academic research, profiles learners based on the needs of a particular learning context and the technologies [The particular work that inspired this approach profiled learners to assess their suitability for serious game-based learning. To that end, the authors studied "the level of ICT skills and competencies, profile levels of familiarity with using games, and…types of games used, and the learning preference within the user group" through both qualitative and quantitative means (de Freitas and Jarvis 2009, p. 223)]. In this riff off of that concept, the profile begins with various complex forms of advanced learning, and it backwards induces the group learner profile from there. What required knowledge and skills and technologies are needed for this learning? What are the motivations of learners? Then, based on those requirements, the learners may be targeted. This approach may involve profiling for an assignment, a series, a short course, a long course, and other types of learning (Fig. 2.16).

Fig. 2.15 A target learning skill approach to learner profiling

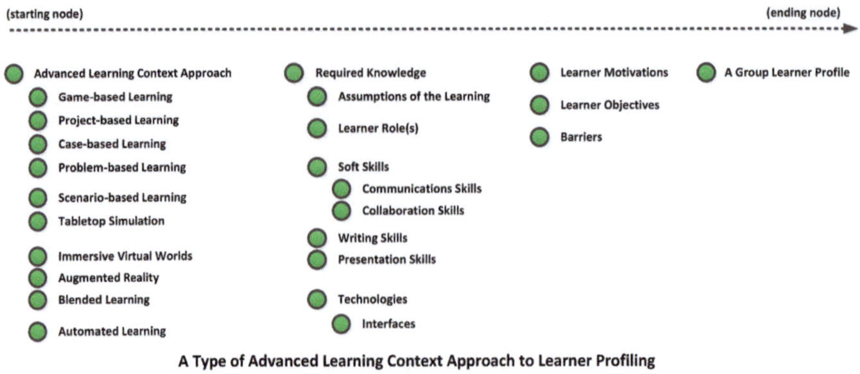

Fig. 2.16 A Type of advanced learning context approach to learner profiling

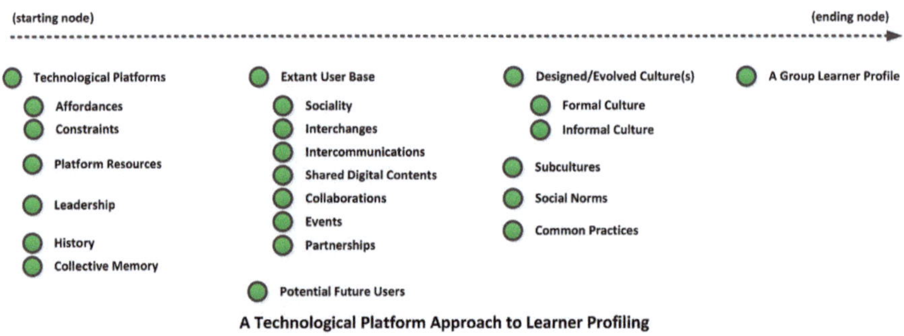

Fig. 2.17 A technological platform approach to learner profiling

A Technological Platforms Approach to Learner Profiling One can begin with a technological platform in order to identify the user base and profile learners from there. These platforms may be understood as socio-technical spaces, including MOOC platforms, learning management systems, content-sharing social media sites, and others with built-in user bases. People who congregate around shared interests on particular platforms often co-evolve a sense of community, shared social norms, shared values, and common practices (to varying degrees). This learner profiling sequence may initially capture the affordances and constraints of the technological platforms; the extant (and potential future) user base; the designed and evolved culture(s) and subculture(s); and the resultant group learner profile. The approach is to think about the profiling as a back-of-the-napkin exercise, so the focus is on observational research and abductive reasoning or logic, not about studying the user data from the platform based on log data (which would not be available to outsiders anyway) (Fig. 2.17).

2.5 Set Two: Animated First Node in the Learner Profiling Sequence

Another approach can involve starting with "animated" (living) first nodes for the learner profiling sequence. These are listed from the largest to the smallest group sizes. These all start with people groups and individuals. This set contains the one imagination-based profile.

A General (Macro- to Micro-) Population Approach (Based on Formal Borders) to Learner Profiling Another approach to learner profiling involves starting with profiling the general population at a macro level. The population is described using demographic data, culture, language, geographical features, and other details. The population's experiences with learning is mapped, and that is followed by observations of the population preferences for learning. From this information comes a group learner profile. If the population is profiled at the macro level, the profile itself will be fairly macro; if the population is profiled at a micro level, the profile itself will be more micro and focused on a sub-population. How much data is available will depend on the society and the information-capture practices. The populations here may refer to national ones, regional ones, and other ways to define populations by formal borders (Fig. 2.18).

One "micro-" level population may be the older adult. To provide a sense of this, work centered around prototyping "maker" learning included an evidence-based profile of "the elderly":

> The 'older adult' audience encompasses a wide age range and varied interests and ability levels (with numerical source citations removed). The group is characterized by age (often age 60 or 65 and older) and occupation (retired from full-time work). This period of life is associated with increased free time, self-reflection, and personal growth. Those who are social and actively engaged within this group are less likely to be depressed. At the same time, their activities are increasingly shaped by digital technology" (Farina and Nitsche 2015, p. 11).

Fig. 2.18 A general (macro- to micro-) population approach to learner profiling

While the underlying data sources are recoverable based on the in-text citations (which were removed in the block quote), the assertions are broad-scale and general. They are also suggestive of particular design features.

Once the population is profiled, designer/developers may want to know what a "mass mind" is about particular learning topics. There are many ways to capture baseline understandings, such as reviewing the mainstream press, social media, web search data (such as with Google Correlate), social image data, and others. Then, too, there are more direct methods such as conducting interviews, focus groups, survey research, and others, from a random sampling of the general population.

A target Cultural Population Approach to Learner Profiling A "cultural" population refers to a group of people who share a common culture (defined broadly as collective practice based on shared norms, values, senses of history, and other features), no matter where they physically reside (Fig. 2.19). While a majority of the world's peoples stays in their original countries of birth, there is a small minority that are displaced (due to disease, natural events, war, famine, and other issues) or who travel to pursue opportunities elsewhere. Various diasporas in human history have resulted in people groups settling in shared geographical locations and building cultural (and racial and ethnic-based) communities. For this approach, it helps to begin with a culture and a history…and to understand how those inform a worldview. Aspects of culture that may be especially important for understanding learning preferences may include a sense of history, the values, the worldviews, the society's leaders, the language(s), and other aspects. The history of teaching and learning is important. And certainly, with any macro-scale group, there can be analyses at the sub-group levels.

This analysis may be enriched through various cultural theories and models. Hofstede's five-parameter model (1967–1973), based on power distance, masculinity/femininity, individualism/collectivism, uncertainty avoidance, and time orientation—is still fairly widely used. A ranking of 50 cultural dimensions related to human-computer interaction include ten dimensions from Hofstede and others.

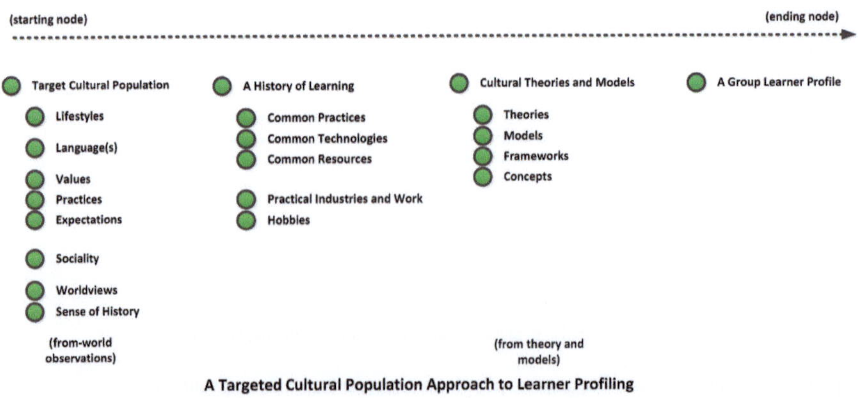

Fig. 2.19 A target cultural population approach to learner profiling

Fig. 2.20 A target language population approach to learner profiling

> The first 10 dimensions are: context, technological development, uncertainty avoidance (Hofstede), time perception, power distance (Hofstede), affective vs. neutral, face-saving, activity orientation, nonverbal communication, and individualism vs. collectivism (Hofstede). Hofstede's time orientation dimension came in at number 11 and his masculinity vs. femininity dimension at number 14. (Baumgartner 2003, as cited by (van Biljou and Kotzé 2007, p. 4)

In the target cultural population approach, there may be social justice considerations such as the identification of under-represented audiences, whose needs may be built to, for beneficent aims.

A Target Language Population Approach to Learner Profiling People with shared languages often share common understandings and some common culture and some common history. (The Sapir-Whorf hypothesis suggests an influence of language on how people perceive the world and how they think) (Fig. 2.20).

An Organizational Approach to Learner Profiling If a particular organization is the focus of the open-shared learning resources, the organization itself may be the starting node of a potential learner profiling sequence. A next step may be the regulatory environment that the organization works under in terms of external regulators and then also the internal policy environment. The training within organizations often have to align with the regulatory requirements. Next, the learning culture may be of interest, with the stated and unstated values. Then, too, the history of trainings may be informative given how experiences inform learner expectations. At the end of this process is a rough-cut organizational learner profile. If possible, more nuanced profiles may be extracted, such as by dividing the members of the organization into sub-groups of learners with varying needs and expectations (Fig. 2.21).

An "Actual Learners of Similar Learning Resources" Profiling Approach to Learner Profiling Another approach can begin with learning objects that are similar to the ones that the designer/developer is pursuing designing/developing and profiling the actual learners who use those resources. These may include both static and dynamic profiles. This is a backwards profiling approach based on frequency data about who is actually using the similar learning resources. This is not a projec-

Fig. 2.21 An organizational approach to learner profiling

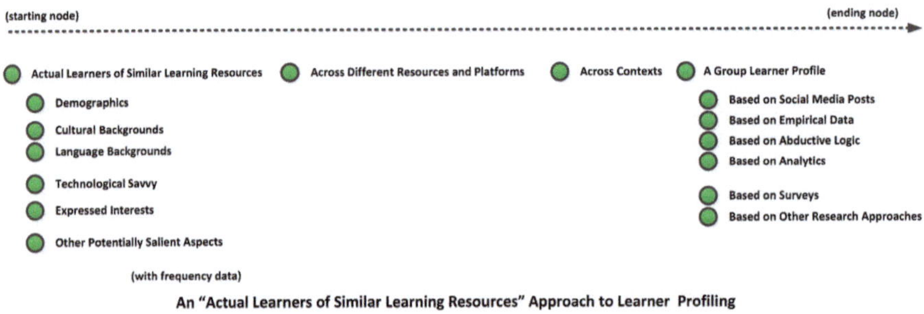

Fig. 2.22 An "actual learners of similar learning resources" approach to learner profiling

tion from assumptions but more firmly linked to empirical and real-world data of actual learners. This sequence begins with similar learning objects and sequences from various platforms and acquiring learner data from those to create a composite profile. Some of the approaches may be direct, such as with data from the platforms and with surveys (direct elicitations of information), and others may be indirect and inference-based, such as based on learner commentaries on the respective sites (Fig. 2.22). This approach may be vulnerable to the "cold-start" problem in which there is insufficient base data from which to build understandings.

Another variation of actual learner profiling is a dynamic on-the-fly profiling approach. Some e-learning platforms enable learner tracking (with varying levels of specificity) and varying levels of convenience in accessing learner data. In these cases, how learners progress through the learning may be understood and may provide insights for profiling learners going through similar learning contents. Some questions that may be asked in such cases include the following:

- Behaviorally, what do the online learners prefer in terms of learning sequences?
- Where do the online learners encounter hurdles, and how do they get by them (if they do)?
- What sorts of cognitive scaffolding do they access, and why?
- What sorts of misconceptions do the learners have based on the performance on assignments and assessments? And so on…

An Idealized Learner Approach to Learner Profiling In the same way that writers sometimes write to an idealized reader, designer/developers may sometimes design and develop to an idealized learner. This approach can be helpful in several ways. First, it is easier to design to a theorized individual than a theorized mass of people in some ways. What can be shared to a group differs from what may be shared with an individual and particular learner. It is easier, generally, to have a conversation with one other person than with a large group. Second, this approach humanizes the idealized learner because the learner may be a composite of real-world learners that the designer/developer has encountered. In some cases, the idealized learner is a fantasy version of the designer/developer himself or herself. Generally, making this personal is not a great idea because designing to the self is a very self-limiting strategy. An idealized learner is a work of the imagination, informed by empirical observations and data. This conceptualization can free up the imagination for more creative learning objects and sequences. Third, an idealized learner may be defined with idiosyncrasies and peculiarities; this character does not have to be a generic one. The human-ness of an idealized learner may kick-start the creative process for more creative learning designs. An idealized learner may be based on a real-life person whom the designer/developer knows and who somehow embodies learning.

This sequence of starting with an idealized learner conceptualization and taking it all the way to a learner profile is depicted in Fig. 2.23.

Time may figure into how this idealized learner is conceptualized. Every learner has a past, a present, and a future. Keeping this in mind may enhance the learner profile and the related design, so that the content is designed to an understanding of the learner's past experiences (and what extant "knowledge, skills, and abilities" or KSAs the learner comes with), the learner's present context, and the learner's anticipated future (to enable harnessing of learner motivations). From the learner view, motivation-wise, the past may be an inspiration, and the future may exert a motivational pull on the present (Tables 2.1 and 2.2).

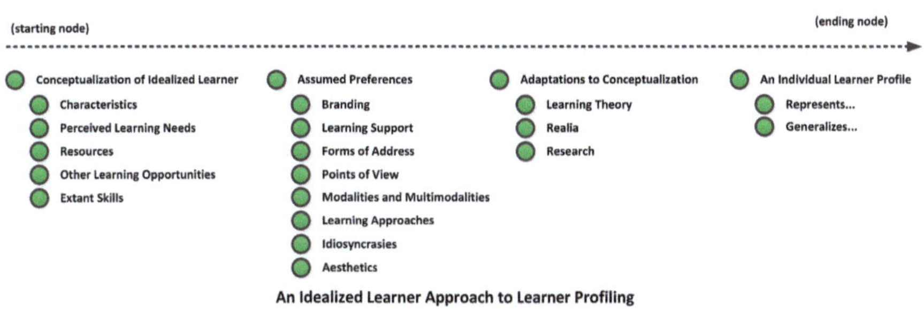

Fig. 2.23 An idealized learner approach to learner profiling

Table 2.1 Extended time factors in learner profiling: the learner's past, present, and future

Learner's past	Learner's present	Learner's future
Prior learning Attitudes and beliefs Language(s) Culture(s) Values Expectations based on prior experience Personality	Human factors Perceptions Capabilities Motivations Attitudes Beliefs Available technologies/devices (access to resources) Available learning contexts Available learning resources Social resources Other available resources	Goals (career, personal, and others) Incentives Disincentives How they may use the information How they may use the learning

Table 2.2 Some pros and cons to profiling learners on-the-fly during their online learning

	Pros	Cons
Learning	• May advance learning • May enable more adaptive learning designs • May identify formerly unknown learning sequences and performance indicators • May enable adjustments to learning on-the-fly	• May define learning sequences that are not appropriate for some based on online learning behavioral profiling
Privacy	• May involve designs that mask privacy	• May compromise individual learner privacy (by connecting profiles and IP addresses to online behaviors and learning performance) • May involve privacy compromises invisible to learners (even with mitigations and "informed consent")
Technologically	• May be automated for efficiencies	• Will require sophisticated pedagogical and developer analysis
Data	• May surface new insights	• May include noisy data that will require accurate interpretation
Learner choice-making	• May be the difference in enhancing learner performance albeit without their conscious choice-making	• May not be clear how much decision making and branching is done based on "black box" algorithms • May take away learner choice-making about learning experiences/sequences/ other factors

A naïve or rookie design approach sometimes involves a designer/developer teaching to the self. The designer asks what he or she would prefer in terms of learning and assumes that others may be similar. Essentially, the teacher is teaching to the self. An extension of this phenomenon is the act of "social reproduction," in which a teacher tries to create versions of himself or herself from the students. This tendency may muffle the unique interests of the respective learners and lessen attentiveness to actual learner needs. Human creativity starts with the self, and that is unavoidable, but stronger work transcends the self and reaches for more externally informed understandings.

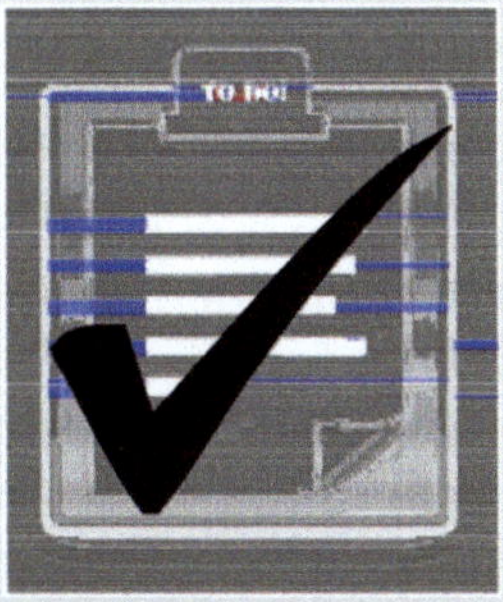

Task #3: Learner's Past, Present, or Future

Let's engage in a thought experiment. Between a learner's past, present, or future, which is the most critical for your learning designs? Why?

Why are the other aspects less important to you?

An Actual Single Learner as Embodiment Approach to Learner Profiling Another single-individual learner profiling approach can be based on an actual individual. Here, one would select an individual who represents some particular type of learner. That individual is profiled for salient characteristics. There may be a priori hypothesizing based on a theory or model or framework, and there may be ad hoc hypothesizing, and there may be post-hoc hypothesizing. Given the limitation of a single example and the subjectivity in the analysis, the generalizability of this profile may be somewhat limited, but the insights may still be refreshing (Fig. 2.24)

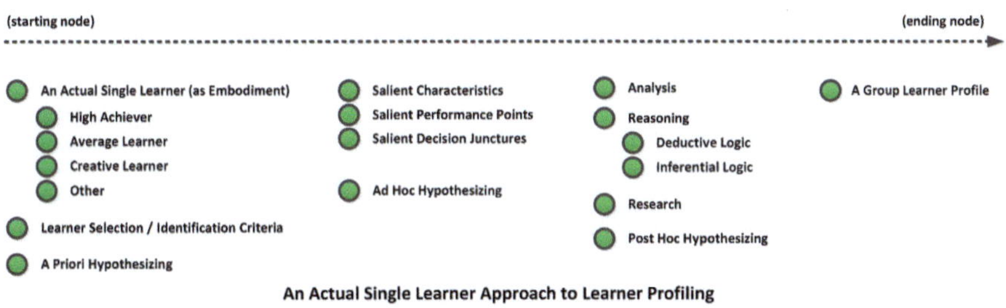

Fig. 2.24 An actual single learner approach to learner profiling

2.6 Set Three: An Integrated, Synthetic Approach

This final and third set is a kind of catch-all category. It is possible and sometimes fruitful to use both inanimate and animate approaches to profile learners, for particular contexts. This approaches is somewhat more suggestive of some early a priori hypothesizing to set up the synthetic approach.

An Integrated Synthetic Approach to Learner Profiling Learner profiling may also be approached from an integrated synthetic way. This approach combines both inanimate and animate details to profile learners for a particular specific context. The emphasis may focus more on one than the other. The idea here is that thin-sliced insights may be available by analyzing various dimensions of learners. This approach can be worked top-down from theories and frameworks, or it can be worked bottom-up from data (Example: Here is a high-performing learner group based on their behaviors, and what makes them different?) (Fig. 2.25)

The prior 12 learner profiling approaches are generalist ones that were evolved from applied practice. They are not thought to result in equifinality or coming to the same conclusions about particular learner groups but to possibly enable complementary insights. While there are references to theories and models and frameworks in some of these, the approach is not an a priori coding one but more of bottom-up coding in many ways. All but one of the approaches is based on factual empirical data, and one is built from the imagination. The core goal of learner profiling for the open-shared learning environment is to identify target learners (those for whom the learning is designed) and potential learners (the opt-in learners from the general population who may be attracted to the particular learning objects)...gauge their potential need and usage for a particular learning object or sequence...and to design to their apparent learning needs and preferences. The idea is to be inclusive of target learners and potential learners, without excluding others. The initial profile may evolve based on other information streams from learners, to update and adapt understandings.

Once the target learner group features are identified, the next step is to identify the most salient variables that will be informative of how they learn and why they learn. These insights then inform the design. All learner profiles are held lightly, with the idea that while there may be a "center mass" to the groups, there are outliers as well. And for every rule, there are likely many exceptions.

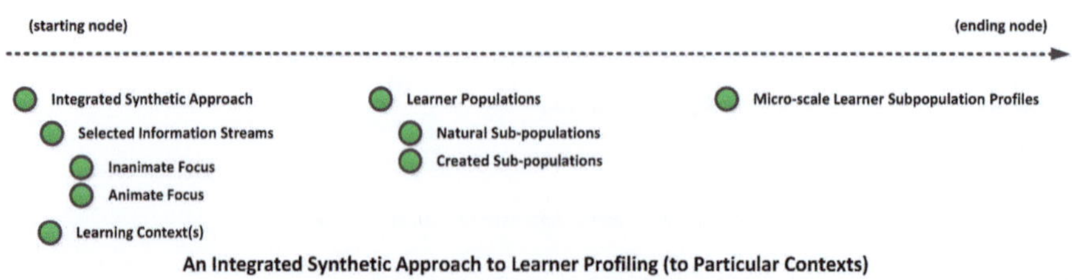

Fig. 2.25 An integrated synthetic approach to learner profiling

2.6.1 *Importance of Pre-design and Pre-development Learner Profiling*

Creating brief "target" and "potential" learner profiles early in the design and development process stands to inform all the work stages that follow. If profiling is not done until the work plans are drafted, the prototypes are made, and some contents developed, changing courses will be much more expensive and time-consuming.

Profiling potential learners for their particular learning needs in a specific domain may enable some demand-side forecasting. In other words, if a designer/developer costs out a project on the supply-side, will there be sufficient demand by potential users to "justify" the cost, as it were? Will there be sufficient usage of the learning resource?

Designer/developers would do well to exercise empathy with the target learner groups and the projected potential learner groups. Getting into the headspace of the target learners—their metacognition, their familiarity with the subject matter, their mental models of the subject (vs. professional conceptual models), their familiarity with online learning technologies, their motivations for learning, and their familiarity with different types of low-touch (mostly automated) teaching and learning methods—may enhance the learning design. It may enable using the language that direct speaks to the respective individuals. After all, it is important to understand how to respect learners' individuality and dignity and self-identity. It is important to understand the pace of learning they prefer. It helps to understand what (de)motivates them, in order to engage them at a motivational level. If learners have prior knowledge and attitudes that are counter-productive for learning, those have to be addressed early on, so the learning is not hindered.

In the spirit of participation and contribution, some learners may be interested in sharing their insights and expertise with those designing and developing online learning objects and sequences. These learners may go further and engage in participatory design of such learning resources by co-designing and co-developing the resources. The advantages of having people with interests in the topic are that these individuals may bring new insights, ideas, and resources to the work. They will help designer/developers understand what learners may bring to the learning experience.

2.6.2 *Some Dimensions of Learner Profiling*

The idea of a "universal learner" is a necessary fiction. It provides a bare outline of what a human learner is and what motivates him/her and what their basic capabilities are. For example, some basic assumptions are that a human pursues pleasure and avoids pain. A human is thought to learn as an innate interest, and learning can be inherently pleasurable (with learners in a state of "flow") even when it is difficult.

In terms of limits, people also have natural limits based on their biology. The challenge with designing to human capabilities goes beyond perception but entails a whole range of human capabilities:

1. *Perception*: human sensing systems in engaging the external and internal environments
2. *Cognition*: sense-making from sensory input and experiences
3. *Learning*: acquisition of knowledge and skills from study and experience
4. *Memory*: recall in short- and long-term contexts
5. *Decision Making*: selecting from possible actions
6. *Action-taking*: following through on a course-of-action (Hai-Jew 2016, Slide 15)

Another way to think of so-called universal learners is based on their level of knowledge and skill with the learning topic. Novices are new to the field but aiming towards expertise ultimately even though they are just starting out. Amateurs are new to the field but not aiming towards expertise ultimately; their interest is partial and may be satisfied with selective and partial learning. Experts are knowledgeable individuals to the field with formal training and plenty of formal practice.

A universal learner then is a very basic conceptualized generic human learner based on research and theorizing. The basic thinking is that when one designs learning in a "neutral" sense, it is to a generic universal learning, and then accommodations are made from that design for other more specific learner groups. This assertion is controversial because of the political implications. After all, the "generic" may just be the socially dominant group, and all other groups are treated as lesser and are expected to adapt and make their adjustments. That is not the intention here, and it would help to think through what a generic would look like while being inclusive of many diversities in that generic representation.

A counterfactual case can be made that building "neutral" (if that is possible) may offer other benefits by forcing all learners to adjust and adapt to learning contexts that are not fully directly suited to them. A "neutral" learning design might be simple, facts-only, and devoid of cultural factors (beyond the built-in culture in language). The point-of-view would be in the third-person objective view. In theory, this design would be for the middle part of a normal curve, and special accommodations would be made for the outliers in the tails. By definition, one of the tails may include "slow learners" (Wettasinghe and Hasan 2007), who may be accommodated with supportive learning designs.

Particular subject domain-based contents may have natural constituencies that they may appeal to. Using that as a premise, it is possible to identify possible learner groups of interest based on extant formal, nonformal, and informal learning sequences. It is possible to address this by profiling current known users of similar learning contents from the particular domain space.

On-the-fly profiling of learners is often done via e-learning platforms (like learning repositories, MOOC platforms, learning management systems, and others), and they may show the following: learning sequences, learner performances, and other details. Some of this data may be available on the back-end data portals, and/or others may be viewable on user dashboards. In some cases, the data is summary data about the learners as groups. In other cases, the information may be identifiable to a person. In some cases, both types of data are available.

For many stand-alone learning objects, the learner profiling feature may not be available and even if available not in a context-aware way. (Some learning systems with context-awareness capture data about the learning service, content, the learning process, the individual in the learning, and other details. Combined with learner profiles, this data may inform on new learning and learning design insights.) Learners' learning sequences may not be available. The learner device information may/may not be available. Locational data and time data may/may not be available.

A naïve instructional designer builds learning to himself or herself instead of to the target learners, and this is a challenge that most trained instructional designers are aware of. One way to get around this fallacy is to go through the formality of defining an actual "idealized learner" to whom learning is designed. An idealized learner is a fantasy figure who typifies the target learner, and having a defined figure helps a designer/developer to focus on who he/she is designing to. It helps them get in the right state-of-mind and focus to deliver the necessary learning contents. For some creatives, they will have visual representations of this idealized individual in their workspace, for a human point-of-reference.

It would be hard to gauge the longevity of particular learning objects over time. It may be a safer bet to suggest that well-funded open-shared learning endeavors buoyed by government may be used longer into the future than individual-made contents without backing. For individual-made works, while there is no guarantee that they will find an audience, one could assume that an object will find some users in the near-term future right after release. Without knowledge of competitor works being created, it is hard to know if the work will be supplanted by other learning resources in the near-term, mid-term, or long-term. There is no sense of whether a topic will be perceived as relevant by future learners. Human attention is expensive and rare, and people generally try to spend their attention mindfully.

What militates against a learning resource's future use are many factors: advances in a field and changes in paradigms, competitor contents, the "slow fires" of various technologies, the advances of "killer apps," evolutions in culture, evolutions in language, and others. Non-attention to open-shared learning contents is tantamount to "product death" and the Great Unread/Great Unused. If groups of people deride learning, usage of open-shared learning resources will drop. No matter how designer/developers try to "future proof" their work, many of the factors are beyond their knowledge and their control.

2.6.3 *Reaching Target Learners Through their Social Networks*

With a budget of $0, attracting project partners may have to be done on the basis of shared interests. For example, maybe a corporation wants to train its personnel in a particular field, and any learning objects created locally can be used by their personnel. Or a software company may want to raise its profile by having its technology used for the creation of open-shared learning contents. Or a hosting platform may want to sponsor development of particular learning sequences for their user base.

Who these partners may be may differ depending on the topic and the designer/developers.

Project partners may be closer to home, with work places and nonprofit organizations supporting the work. Open-shared learning resources may be byproducts of funded projects, presentations for conferences, and of personal hobbies and personal learning.

Part of early profiling of potential users of open-shared learning objects is to ensure its usage once it is completed. Online, there are self-organized online virtual communities of interest, like groups in virtual worlds, on social networking sites, on video and image content-sharing sites, on news sharing sites, and others. Based on these networks, it is possible to identify influential members—formal declared leaders as well as informal leaders (those who act in the role of leader and are respected by others as such based on their capabilities and personality). Identifying individuals who may serve as effective contacts would be helpful.

There are a number of ways different entities (educational institutions, businesses, organizations, clubs, and others) may partner with a designer/developer of open-shared learning objects. There may be the sharing of resources. Or teams may co-design and co-develop contents. Perhaps partners may help with the beta-testing of contents. Or there may be mutual work to host contents. Whatever the scenario, partnering with others may broaden the distribution of the open-shared learning resources. In that spirit, designer/developers may want to identify potential partners—often through personal connections and relationships—to explore potential areas of shared interest.

Of course, coordinating such relationships takes effort. It also helps to have all agreements written in documented format.

2.6.4 Connecting Learner Profiles and Learner Needs in "User Models"

If a universal learner contains generic learning needs for a theoretical mainline learner, what are the unique needs of identified target and potential learner groups who may be accessing the forthcoming learning objects or sequences? "User models" are generalized representations of what the learners know in terms of the domain and related topics and their preferences for the learning.

- If there are high school students who may access the learning, what are some unique needs they might have? Middle school students? Undergraduate students? Graduate students?
- If there are professionals in the field who will be accessing the contents, what are some unique needs they might have?
- If there are amateurs dabbling in the field, what are some needs that they might have?
- What about lifelong learners?
- What about learners with low socio-economic status (SES)?

- What about learners from particular cultures? Language groups?
- How may those accessing contents with mobile devices and slow connectivity be addressed?

How can the unique needs be addressed effectively, with various learning designs, styling, versioning, add-ons, downloadables, and others? And how can the efficacy or inefficacy of the various design features be tested with the various target learner groups?

What Learner Profiling Influences The learner profiling, which may be achieved discretely in time or throughout the project lifespan at different start points, stands to inform every aspect of the project thereafter: the learning design, the addressing of legal standards, core technology selections, the work planning, the early designs and prototypes and sequences, the content development, the beta testing, and the launch and support for learners. The profiles are not absolutely deterministic nor definitive but are used to support the design and development work. In theory (and in some practice), learner profiles may affect the following: the informational content, the presentation of the information, the sequencing of learning experiences, the depiction of people and situations in the learning, the language/visuals/audio/video used, the learning technologies, the cognitive scaffolding, the look-and-feel and other styling, the assignments, the assessments, and other aspects of the learning resources. This is not the space to over-think this because subjectivities are not fully considered in any learning context and not directly designed to per se.

Learner profiling is in many ways still in a nascent state. There are no consensus-based accepted methods of learner profiling. The research literature offers a wide range of learner profiling approaches for different projects and learning systems technologies and contexts, but these are discrete and not particularly universal. Many articles do not describe any closing the loop by testing with extant learners or sample audiences. Having some way to validate or invalidate learner modeling would be helpful, and confirming/disconfirming various learning design approaches would also be important.

Learner profiles help designers and developers address some issues, but the need to ensure universal access overall tempers what may be changed. It may be argued that there are some universal learning formats (with forms and conventions) that are recognizable across cultures, such as slideshows and videos. There may be universals of clear information organization and presentation. Universals may be the primary aim in learning design first, and then specific needs of specific target groups may be considered albeit more on the margins. For example, novice learners to a topic may have their needs met with cognitive scaffolding features that they can opt-in but which are unobtrusive to the main target learners. Or language versioning may be offered to learners whose first or second languages are not the primary base language used in the design, but this is a versioning option. Or particular cultural groups may have accommodations in terms of depictions and language and sequencing as a complementary option. Or groups with low wireless connectivity may be offered downloadable contents for consumption instead of having to stream contents (with high latency).

Learner profiles should not be misused or turned into negative people group stereotypes. For example, suggesting that some people groups cannot learn or do particular things would be highly negative. "Stereotype threat" has been empirically shown to degrade the performance of those under stereotype, even with very nuanced suggestions (Steele and Aronson 1995; Spencer et al. 1999). If the point of open-shared learning is to benefit people, then surely something this negative should be avoided. The promotion of derogatory views of people groups should be avoided. For example, one of my colleagues showed me a learning object she had created using an African American female alone to depict recipients of "welfare" in a mostly Caucasian state with majority Caucasian recipients of said welfare. Stereotyping has no place in learner profiling. The learner profiling should ensure inclusiveness of learners without the exclusion of others and without negative side effects.

Keeping the goal of creating effective open-shared learning objects by meeting the needs of anticipated learners may help mitigate some potential misdirection. The learning resources are being created in the service of the learners, and their profiling is to ensure that the objects meet their needs and do not offend or frustrate them.

Learner Group Connections Then, too, the next steps after the initial learner profiles may be to understand shared interests and affinities between learners and learner groups. These mutualities may provide areas to build learning to meet the needs of multiple groups. There may be other leverages to those connections, such as in accessing informational and human resources for building the learning.

Live Examples (on the Web)

Task: Identify a target online learning community (that may be interested in a particular open-shared learning resource. What are some leads to use to find online learning communities?

There are two general approaches to identifying online learning communities.

Declared online learning communities. In some ways, the more obvious way is to find a self-identified or declared one that is manifested on a particular social media platform or organizational website. These communities may be spinoffs of professions. They may be hobbyist groups. There may be formal numbers about the membership and defined rules for membership and defined activities, and so on.

Platforms to explore include dedicated websites, massive open online courses (MOOCs), news sharing sites, and others.

Some current online spaces to explore include the following: Coursera (MOOC), EdX (MOOC), Reddit (news-sharing), and others.

In this approach, formalized organizations for learning communities are important start points.

Informal online learning communities. Another approach may be to map informal online learning communities that coalesce temporarily around particular issues of interest or subject matters. These communities may be distributed over multiple online environments, including video sharing sites, image sharing sites, social networking sites, microblogging sites, news sharing sites, slideshow sharing, and so on.

Some current online spaces to explore include the following: YouTube (video sharing), Vimeo (video sharing), Flickr (image sharing), Instagram (image sharing), Facebook (social networking), Twitter (microblogging), Reddit (news sharing), slideshow sharing (SlideShare), and others

In this latter case, those in informal online learning communities use multiple platforms for their respective learning.

Or, another approach may be to begin with learning platforms and expand the exploration from there. The snowball research methods can expand from any part of the informal online learning community by following links (link analysis), message analysis (content analysis, image analysis, text analysis, and others), human relationship analysis (social network analysis), and others.

Discussion Whatever are the profiles arrived at, it seems wise not to prematurely lock in to understandings and to keep the learner profiles provisional and flexible. It makes sense to hold such profiles loosely and not to be doctrinaire in how these inform learning designs. After all, people are complex, and each person fits into multiple groups and categorizations. Their individual learning needs are complex even if they share membership with others along various dimensions. The "intersectionality" of various aspects of identity also means more complexities in identities, with complex interrelationships between identity attributes. People and groups are constantly changing, so profile information will have to evolve to capture those changes and to be relevant. (Some aspects of a learner profile may be more relevant for longer periods than others.)

The mental models of learners should be accurate to actual learners as much as possible, within the limits of knowability. It is important to keep the informational channels open to understand how the learning resources are being experienced, to inform revisions (if those are pursued) and the creation of follow-on learning objects and sequences. Learner profiles also have to remain flexible because different people will be coming across the learning objects, and the user populations will continue to evolve over time.

There are practical hedges against exclusion of other learners outside of profiles by making the learning as inclusive and accessible and multi-cultural as possible.

There are ways to avoid negative stereotyping by using broad informational channels, keeping learner profiling channels open (and considerate of new information), by holding profiles lightly, by using non-judgmental approaches, by avoiding derogatory conceptualizations, and others. Some aspects of a learner profile may be broad and general, and others may be zoomed-in and specific. Learner profiles may be held lightly and provisionally, so these may be updated with new information. The value of "First, do no harm" should apply in every context, so meeting the learner needs of one group should not necessarily exclude others.

Learner profiling for open-shared learning resources can take many forms, and the resultant information may be used in a variety of ways depending on the available technologies (like e-learning systems), human resource skills, and delivered learning resources. The most sophisticated applications are likely in the massive open online course (MOOC) space and other large-scale teaching-and-learning platforms, and the least sophisticated applications may be in the stand-alone learning object and stand-alone learning sequence space. The latter context is more common because it does not require massive infusions of funds, but it also enables the fewest technological interventions. The expressed designs in this context tend to be deterministic and not adaptive. The learning objects tend to be componentized, and there are no spelled-out paths between "unrelated" learning objects. It is early days for this application.

Then, too, linking learner profiles with learning needs and ways to meet those learning needs add more complexity and risks to accuracy and efficacy. And then how the learning is instantiated may introduce further challenges (Fig. 2.26).

Fig. 2.26 A Word Cloud of Chapter 2: "Profiling Target and Potential Learners Today and into the Future"

What-If: Profiled Learner Personhood → Learning Needs → Inclusiveness Design

You and your colleagues and friends have decided to document how to use a complex data analytics tool. Each of you will take different sections of the tool and conduct the research and do the functional walkthroughs, take the screenshots, and do the writing. Another part of the team will evaluate the documentation for accuracy, and then, the contents will be made available to the broad public. This project stands to benefit the team by encouraging them each and collectively to learn more about this complex tool.

Then, one of the members asks, "Well, who are we creating this leaning resource for?"

"For us!" answers one of the smart alecks of the group.

"For the software company!" chimes in another. That brings up some questions for the group. How will a commercial company that makes the resource respond to an open-shared learning resource about their software? How will the "folk" created resource compare with more formalized help documentation? What will be the competitive advantage of using one or the other?

The group mulls over these details. They agree that they can offer a resource that would complement the training videos offered by the company. They will not really undercut the training market that the company offers commercially.

Decision point #1: stop or advance. If advance, the team will have to ask the following questions. Who will most likely use this resource? What would their motivations be for using the resource? What would their expectations be? What levels of expertise would they have coming at the tool? On what basis are the team members making assertions about the potential users, and how confident can they be in the results?

"Well, let's do a light learner profile," suggests another.

They peruse the learning resources offered by the company, and they infer the various users—ranging from total newbies to expert users. The company has offered short open-access videos focused around user-based contexts (you are analyzing interview data…you are conducting a review of the literature…) ranging from "how to get started" all the way to complex applications. The team reviews the terms-of-use for the software, and they realize that the software makers enable a low-cost license for enrolled students at the low end, discounts for educational usage in the middle, but at the commercial high end, a software license costs in the low-four figures.

The software tool itself has a dozen different base languages that may be used based on UTF-8. The team decides that the potential users around the world would mean that whatever they would create would be used in a number of different languages. That said, the team will design and build in clear English, and they will hope that their work translates well to other languages with online tools (like Google Translate) and on web browsers like Google Chrome.

What about the ethics of creating contents for users of a commercial tool? The team checks, and none of its members have any secret ties to the commercial company. They decide that they can legally create their own unauthorized version of support for the tool given the extant laws. They agree to consider the basics of the Technology Acceptance Model (Davis 1989), but they also know that they will report strengths and weaknesses of the tool, and they will not take any advocacy role regarding the adoption of the software. (The TAM approach suggests that people consider the possible usefulness of a technology and its ease-of-use before making a choice. In general, the team thinks the tool is useful, but the learning curve is fairly high. The software is easy to use only after a lot of hours of study and experimentation.)

The team writes up their findings on a shared folder on Google Drive, and then one of the team members asks, "While we're at it, should we start a collective consensus stylebook?"

Decision point #2: stop or advance. If advance, the team will have to define the basic standards that they will build to, to help with the work coordination. What should the writing style be? What should the over-arching tone of the work be? What sorts of digital contents will the deliverables be, and why? What are the legal standards the team will adhere to? How much work documentation will they create? And so on. If they don't, they will have to spend time re-contacting everyone who contributes to ask them to submit materials to standards and in the right forms.

The team has decided to use Google Drive to post an evolving stylebook. At the start, the team has agreed to use the third-person point-of-view in the their writing. They have agreed to use the APA citation method for published academic sources, if they choose to cite them. The screenshots will have to be about 350 ppi (pixels per inch) for clarity. The annotations will be in a defined red, with box sizes at 2.25 line weight, and the font at Calibri-12. The team has defined the respective technologies to use, including Microsoft Visio, MS Office Suite, Adobe Photoshop, and others. They have spelled out their legal standards—which are common among them because of their shared professional history. The team decides on an open-shared e-book and have decided on a particular platform.

You and the team members each get to work, and the content start rolling in. The developers put the e-book together, and they host it on the site in a closed way, so the team can review it. During the review, the team realizes that the content that they've created is skewed toward those with graduate degrees in research and professionals, and they have left out the newbies altogether. The team wants to be accurate to the complexity of the tool, but they don't want to discourage would-be users. Each of the team members started out as new users of this software years ago, and they may not be as empathetic to new users as they could be. Another comments that the writing is non-inclusive of researchers outside the Western milieu. And a third mentions that the learner targeting has not really considered possible future learners and what their needs might be.

Decision point #3: stop or advance. If advance, the team has to decide what adjustments to make to be more inclusive. How can they simplify complexity for new users? What tasks can they suggest for new users that would give them a sense of self-efficacy but still not mislead them about the software tool? Or the team can decide that the "target" learners that they want to support are the high-end users, and they can leave the newbies to use what already exists in the world.

Also, how can they ensure a sense of inclusiveness for users of the software from various regions around the world without being exclusivist? How can they think beyond their own uses of the tool to show the full range of applications of the software? Or the team can determine that the learning resources are sufficient for their aims and advance the project to the next stage to finalize the work and launch it.

Or the team can flow the additional design and development work to a future follow-on section to the open-shared e-book.

As to the future users, the team decides that they don't want to try to anticipate where the data analytics software will go in the future, or where the state of research is headed per se. It seems safer to stay with the extant details and the facts and current practices.

And there are other options as well.

The team decides…

The What-If Debriefing

This scenario offers a somewhat simplified version of how a design and development team may collaborate in a distributed way and how learner profiling may become a natural and integrated part of their work. This scenario mentions some common challenges with learner profiling, namely, the failure to meet some of the needs of some of the target and potential learners. This scenario provides a sense of very real costs to designing for and delivering contents to a wide swath of the population. Also, this makes the point that learner profiling is valuable as a form of informed design and critique, even if the team does not accommodate some parts of the potential learner population and some aspects of their needs. Also, practically speaking, all design goals and efforts entail efforts, investments, and costs.

2.7 Future Research Directions

As mentioned earlier, the dozen sequences to arrive at learner profiles here were back-of-the-napkin methods, based on spontaneous on-ground practices and unschooled approaches. These casual tactics, while using both extant data and the human imagination, enable initial impressions of target and potential end users, but they unduly rely on prior experiences of the designer/developers in the space. These understandings also benefit from complementary environmental scans to understand the ecosystem and what competitor resources are available. What users end up with are initial impressions to inform a design but not much more. Using theory-informed, formal, and tested methods to profile learners would be an improvement to what is available here. In terms of future research: What are some improved and formalized ways to profile learners for the design of open-shared learning resources?

The uses of learner profiling to create learning resources is a type of anticipatory design to meet the perceived needs of the target and potential learners. One critical aspect here is to empirically evaluate how effective such profiling is to designs and to the delivered learning contents, with the actual learning measured as objectively as possible. After all, if the profiles are inaccurate or if they are not particularly informative, that could be problematic.

In terms of future research, learner profiling seems to exist mostly in groups instead of individuals. It may be helpful to explore learners in dyads, triads, and other forms of "motifs" and small-group combinations. Are there strategic ways to pair learners and group learners, based on their respective profiles, for more effective learning, for more mutually motivated learning? (These may be activities like "think-pair-share," "write-pair-share," and others.)

Learner profiles may be captured in both broad strokes or in zoomed-in particulars, with varying efficacy of each approach. Different methods of target and potential learner profiling may be explored—in static, on-the-fly, and other ways—and in various phases of the design-development-launch sequence. Connecting learner profiles to learner needs (in "user models") may be better established through research. Researchers may explore improved ways to harness learner profiles (particularly specific indicators) and connect these to effective learning designs.

How to protect learner privacy, their identities, their thinking, their skills, is also of importance in this space, particularly with the capturing of learner behaviors and performance in online learning systems. How the personalized information is captured, used, stored, and disseminated will be important to online learning.

Little work has been done on anticipating the needs of future learners (those who may come to the resource in the near-, mid-, and far- futures). There is not a clear sense in terms of how online learning communities may evolve over time or how their membership may change. How to conduct such future profiles and how to "future proof" learning resources will be important. It would also help to conduct longitudinal studies to see how accurately these profiles were and how effective the resultant learning designs were as well. Such information will be especially important to know given the potential headwinds of automated cobbling of learning sequences on the Semantic Web. If work spaces are saturated with only a few quality learning resources, this will mean less space for people to create contents and find responsive audiences. This means that reaching out to potential learners will be important to attract and maintain a learning audience for open-shared resources. Those who create learning contents would do well to express respect for and encouragement of learners, now and through time.

2.8 Conclusion

In many ways, people have been studying each other since the beginning of time. Profiling "target" and "potential" learners not only stand to benefit learning designs and development, but they may provide strong motivation for people to create the open-shared learning contents. People can be excited by and motivated to reach out to others. Understanding an audience can help designer/developers to calibrate what they create to a response.

It may help to conclude with some reasonable caveats. People are complex, and they are constantly evolving over time. They are products of the environment and genetics, with a majority of the influence from the first and a minority from the latter. People profiling is a moving target, and there is very little in the research that is doctrinaire about learner profiling. Each learner is his or her own person, but he or she shares some characteristics with others, and that overlap is what is targeted in learning designs. This approach though should not detract from the fact that every learner is original and has a unique combination of needs. Not all those needs can be ascertained nor directly met with any learning object or sequence. In open-shared learning, learners opt-in, and they opt-out. How committed or fragile they are will depend on a range of factors. Whether the learning is aligned or non-aligned with their learning background and preferences may affect their persistence to some degree, but learners can benefit from non-aligned presentational and teaching methods, too. The alignment with learner learning preferences is not necessarily deterministic of learning success, and the converse of disalignment leading to learning failure is also not accurate. A perfect fit to learners is not necessarily desirable nor particularly pro-learning.

The current thinking is that people tend to have cognitive biases. They habituate to certain expectations of the world, and any new information builds on existing knowledge (confirmation bias). In the same way that the broad public can spark to outrage with small triggers, individuals can do the same. People are informed by their expectations, and those expectations create a baseline for reality. In general, people do not take well to change, and they do not like surprises unless they are positive ones. Learners can "turn off" based on trivial and nuanced details, but it is better for them if they can push through annoyances and stay the course. While profiling can provide some insights and inform some designs, there are some real limits as well, and not all learners can have their needs met in ways that may align fully with their preferences. Learners themselves have to develop resilience and follow-through, even with learning objects that may not be to their liking (occasionally).

The public sense of "profiling" may have negative connotations because of how profiles have been used in policing stateside, apparently resulting in stereotyping and biased treatments of particular segments of the population. In a learning context, however, profiling learners to enable learner-centered learning designs has been commonly and effectively harnessed.

In an open sharing context, the designer/developer releases contents into the wilds of the Web and Internet, and who accesses the objects is outside their reasonable control. While the potential scale is users is high, actual users are actually much smaller than assumed. It can generally be assumed that both people and robots (scripts) will be accessing the contents and harnessing them for any number of purposes. While those with pedagogical backgrounds may want learners to have particular topic-based learning backgrounds, to experience the learning in particular sequences, to practice adaptive learning behaviors, to pace their learning a certain way, to go through the necessary assessments, they actually really have no impact on independent and self-regulated learner decisions. A common behavior online is to sample and explore as needed (and to view contents as harnessed for just-in-time consumption).

Learner profiling enables designers/developers to not just put something out into the ether and hope that it has value for someone. Certainly, the other path is to develop contents in a "learner unprofiled" way and focus more on supply-side delivery of contents and ignore the demand-side. This one-way approach may save on the effort and time for learner profiling, but it means that the design is less learner aware and less designed for learner (perceived) relevance.

There is a body of theoretical work about just how to best match learning to learners (more on this in Chap. 3).

2.9 Reviews and Assignments

2.9.1 Main Points Review

- Conducting some rudimentary learner profiling *prior to* designing and developing open-shared user-centered learning objects is important to inform the design and development work.
- Early learner profiles may evoke some learner-based demand-side forecasts to anticipate possible uses of the learning contents.
- Various dimensions of learner profiling may be pursued to better understand what the learner needs may entail in relation to the target topic.
- Learner profiles may be used to identify individuals who may engage in (or inform) participatory learning design.

- Learners may be profiled by their static descriptors (like demographics), or they may be profiled by their online learning (and other) behaviors in a dynamic way. They may be profiled by their social media activities from outside systems as well.
  - The various types of profiling may infringe on learner privacy. Where would you draw the lines in terms of information collection of learners, especially personally identifiable information (PII)? What are learner expectations for privacy?
- Part of a learning design of an open-shared learning object or sequence should involve ways to attract learners, in a highly competitive environment.
- An "idealized learner" is an imaginary individual, for whom a learning design is made. For different designer/developers, they will have different idealized learners with different imagined characteristics and different imagined needs.
- Future learners may have different learning needs than today's learners. Being able to project to future needs may help "future proof" the shared learning contents.
- When engaging with the larger open public, there may be project partners who may have some shared interests in the open-shared learning contents. They may have social networks that may benefit from knowledge of the particular open-shared learning object project.
- When engaging with the public, there may be knowledgeable informants who may provide information of respective communities that may benefit from the open-shared learning.
- Many potential "project partners" may be identified through their public-facing sides, such as through the Web and Internet.
- Once learners have been profiled, it is important to connect those profiles to particular learners needs and how to meet those needs. This involves inductive logic and inferential thinking and abductive logic, in part. It is important to spell these out in detail, however, in order to surface assumptions and test the logic.

2.9.2 Critical Thinking Questions

Understanding Target Online Learners and their Respective Needs

- What aspects of a person are most revealing about his/her learning needs, and why? (If removing age, educational history, IQ tests, personality, culture, language capabilities, and others, what are the most revealing aspects of a person?)
- For potential learners who opt-in to learning opportunities online, what are their most common motivations? What accounts for their taking initiative? What might this suggest about how they engage the open-shared online learning?
- How would you generally profile those in the mainstream population who use open-shared learning objects? Why do you think they access these particular

objects? What needs are they meeting through their online learning? What are their core motivations in pursuing such learning?

  - If they were to pursue commercial learning online, where would they go to acquire these contents and learning experiences? Why?

- Why is it important to create effective learner profiles (or sketches) prior to the design and development of online learning objects? What does "learner centered design" mean, and why?

  - What are the main features of a learning object that would change based on different learners, and why?
  - What cognitive scaffolding may be needed to help high school learners adjust to content usually thought of as higher education contents? Why?
  - What can be offered to expert learners who are reviewing more basic domain information?

- If the typical focus of profiling is to enable the targeting of a majority of learners, what are some cases when you would be targeting niche populations?

  - How might niche learners' have different needs than mainstream learners? How can these unique needs inform a learning design?
  - When might the needs of those on a long tail come before those of the vast majority of learners?

- Look at an open-shared learning object or learning sequence, and reverse-profile the target learners (their likely demographic features, their level of domain knowledge, their learning needs), and consider how they may benefit from this learning resource.

  - Profile learners who would *not* find this particular learning object or sequence appealing or useful, and explain why. (This is a reverse profile of those who would not be the target for the open-shared learning resource.)

Avoiding Stereotyping

- When profiling learners, what are some of the risks of stereotyping? What are solid ways to avoid typecasting those in the general learner population and in niche groups? How can generalizations be created without negative and inaccurate information?

Openness to Participatory Design of Learning

- How may potential learners be encouraged to take part in participatory design of learning objects?

Considering and Designing for Learner Interests

- Ideally, what benefits would a well-matched learner acquire from well-designed online learning objects and sequences? What would they learn about the domain? What experience would they go through? What downloadable resources would they have access to, and why? What direct first-order effects would a learner receive from the learning experience? Second-order effects? Third-order effects?

Strategic Partnering

- Based on the particular target learners and others who may have interests in these learners, are there some possible project partners who may have a shared interest in co-creating open-shared learning objects and sequences? In contributing contents or talent to the building of such resources? In publicizing such resources to potential learners?
- When thinking about possible "project partners" for various aspects of an open-shared learning object, can you think of some who may be interested in taking part during any of the phases (from the environmental scan through the design through the technology selection through the development, the launch, and other endeavors)? Where are points of mutual interest: the learning, the training, the technologies, and others?

Latent Insights

- Sometimes learning about particular potential learner groups may require information that is not available in a "surface" way (if you will). Which individuals could you reach out to that may be knowledgeable informants of the respective communities who may benefit from the open-shared learning resources?
  - What would you need to know from informants around the particular topic domain? Where would you go to find that information?
- What are some initial ways you could possible use the Web and Internet to find particular project partners? What social groups (networks) would you go to, and why?
- What are some unique needs of particular learners? Particular learner groups? Why? What are the scientific and data-driven explanations for these particular needs?
  - What are some ways to use design, strategic messaging, informational content, style, and other endeavors to meet these unique learner needs?
  - Is it sufficient to version the learning for different groups, or are the changes more fundamental?

Automating Adaptivity Solutions

- Some adaptive or intelligent online learning systems use algorithms to customize the learning contents and sequences that learners experience. The delivered learning may be based on initial profiles and assessments, and/or they may be built off of learners' online behaviors in the learning system. If you were writing some of these rules, what would they be, and why? Further, how would you know if your rules were correctly written? How would you ensure that the rules do not unethically restrict learners' access to experiences that may be beneficial to them?

Designing to Idealized Learners

- As a point of inspiration, some writers will write to "idealized readers." If you are designing and developing for "idealized learners," who would these be, and why? What would their main characteristics be? Is this idealized learner "you" (self-concept) or an instantiation of you? What are ways to create an idealized learner who would inform a learning design?
- Do you find it helpful or harmful to have idealized learners that you are focusing on? What should the role of the imagination be in understanding others? How grounded should the assertions be in objective and evidentiary details?

Projected Learner Profiles and Projected Learner Needs

- What are the relationships between learner profiles and learner needs?

Understanding Future Learners

- As each new generation of learners comes forward to learn a particular topic, they will come at the topic with unique experiences and insights, facility with particular technologies, and other realities. What are some ways to build learning objects in future proofed ways? Why?
- There are limits to future proofing, however, given the reliance on language, culture, technologies, social context, and other shared understandings. What are ways to ensure that shared learning resources are relevant even when they are dated?

2.10 Assignments

Directions The Assignments are divided into two sections, Basic and Advanced. The Basic section is for those who may not have much instructional design experience or background in the area of creating instructional contents for open sharing. As such, these are set up to familiarize them with the chapter-related knowledge, skills, and abilities. The Advanced section is for those who already have some knowledge of this general space and who may benefit from more challenging work.

In a formal learning context, these assignments would benefit from expert feedback and further applications of the learning contents. In a nonformal or informal learning context, including self-directed learning, these assignments would benefit from both reflection and practice. These assignments are built to be extensible, to have elements added to benefit the learners. They are designed to be assigned selectively and not in full. The setup of this textbook is as a work sequence, and similarly, the assignments may be set up as tasks to be completed by the learner in a sequential way…that takes them through the fairly complete and sequential *open-shared learning design → development → test → revision → launch → post-launch* process.

2.10.1 Basic

Assignment 2.1: Self-Awareness of Learning Preferences…and the Resulting Learner Model Identify a learning topic of interest, and conduct an analysis of what is available through open sharing on the World Wide Web (WWW) and Internet. Explore some of these learning objects and sequences, and document which ones you enjoy and which ones you do not.

Explore why you have certain positive responses and also why you have some negative ones. Then, write up a personal learner profile for yourself. Identify what demographics, cultural influences, language, and other dimensions are the most impactful for your learner profile. Consider how your preferences may or may not be informed by your learner profile. (You can pre-write a learner profile for yourself and evolve it over the span of the assignment…or create one after you've engaged with the respective learning objects and sequences. The idea is to use facts for the profile, as well as your actual responses to the shared learning. What surprised you about your learning profile? Why?)

Identify linkages between the two. Also, identify non-linkages between the two. (What parts of your learner profile do not align with how you actually responded to particular learning objects?) A simple table follows below to enable the capturing of this information.

Personal Learning Preferences (from engaging with open-shared learning objects and sequences)	Personal Learner Profile
→	

Extra: Start with your identified learner profile. Then, generalize from your unique descriptors. If you were universalized as a learner, what sort of a community would you represent?

Self Learner Profile	A Universalized Learner Profile
→	

Assignment 2.2: Potential Target Learners for Target Learning Domain By analyzing the available open-access and open-source learning objects, courses, and sequences, who do the main potential target learners seem to be? Why? In terms of demographics, how would you characterize the learners, and why? What percentage are from which age groups? Gender groups? Cultural backgrounds? Dominant languages? Nationalities? Other aspects? How confident are you about your initial senses, and why?

Assignment 2.3: Learner Uses of Shared Online Learning Contents Based on your analysis, how do you think the potential learners are using the available online learning materials—as stand-alone contents? Augmentary learning contents? Why?

Assignment 2.4: Pre-requisite Understandings Required to Use Particular Digital Learning Objects/Courses/Sequences What sort of basic background in the domain field is required for them to engage effectively with particular digital learning objects, courses, and sequences? What pre-requisite knowledge, skills, and abilities do they need? Why? In terms of learning outcomes, what will the learners acquire from particular learning objects, courses, and sequences? What competitive advantages are possibly available? Why? How so? (What sorts of lead-up knowledge, skills, and abilities may be developed before a more complex learning sequence?)

Assignment 2.5: Specific Learner Group Targeting In the domain, what are some of the specifically targeted learner groups? How can you tell that these groups are specifically targeted? What are some of the different contents and instructional strategies used for the respective different groups? Why?

Assignment 2.6: Learning Resource Versioning for Different Target Learners What are some ways to version the online learning contents to accommodate the needs of various learner groups? What parts of the learning are the easiest to change, and which parts of the learning are hardest? Why?

2.10.2 Advanced

Assignment 2.7: Culture as a Tool for Profiling Learners "Culture" is a broad-scale term that deals with various aspects of human practice passed forward from history into the present and co-evolving in the present moment. Culture itself is a multidimensional term evoking various aspects of human practice. Using culture, or selected aspects of culture, profile learners based on salient aspects, and explore how these cultural aspects may affect an instructional design. This assignment involves the hard work of operationalizing culture.

Assignment 2.8: Post-hoc Learner Profiling from Performance Another approach to learner profiling is to observe learner behaviors and performance in a particular learning context (using open-shared learning resources). The sequence generally goes like this:

- How do the respective learners perform, and what differentiates the high performers from others?
- What does the learner experience seem to be? What aspects are pro-learning, and which are not? (High-stress in learners is often considered negative for learning, for example.)
- What differentiates the high performers from others? Are there differences in demographics? In learning strategies? In decision making? In interactions with the content, the other learners, the learning system?

Write a short exploratory essay about the potentials of profiling learners from their learning behaviors and their performance. How generalizable can such findings be? What are some common hypotheses you can come up with about learners who do well in your area(s) of specialization? Why?

Assignment 2.9: Profiling Learners from Social Media and the Web and Internet Another approach in the research literature to learner profiling involves capturing information about the learners from personally identifiable information (otherwise known as PII). These indirect profiles are often culled from social media platforms and the Social Web as well as the Internet. What are some strengths and weaknesses to using this type of data? What may be informative about learners and their needs from their social media data? Their general Web data?

Extra: Should unshared information be used to profile learners? Should Deep Web data be used to understand learners?

Assignment 2.10: Multiple Strategies for Reaching Learner Groups Broadly speaking, there are several approaches to creating learning contents for learners. One is a generic approach to creating learning contents, without considering particular groups, but making the learning as accessible as possible, based on the ideas of "universal design." Here the works are usually written in an objective way, and trust comes from expert credentials and the shared contents. Another approach is to identify target groups and build to their knowledge base, culture, points-of-view, values, and so on. This is to make the learning as comfortable as possible for the targeted groups, in order to encourage their uptake of the learning. Between these two poles, which approach do you find more comfortable, and why? What are the strengths and weaknesses of each approach? Why is it likely that you'll use both strategies at various points in your designs and developments of open-shared learning objects and sequences?

Extra: Identify a small open-shared learning object/sequence project. Create some basic informational contents. Use a universal design approach to engage the contents first.

Then, use a targeted design approach to an identified likely learner group for those contents. Document the work, and identify the differences and strengths/weaknesses in the different approaches.

Key Terms and Definitions

Cultural profiling Applying an individual or group's cultural background as a filter through which to understand the target individual or group (with "culture" defined as the collective values, thinking, and practices of peoples at particular times and spaces)

Data mining The identification of intrinsic patterns in data and information

Demand-side forecasting Projecting user interest in a product or service based on empirical and other data and research methods

Demographics Statistical data about human populations and sub-populations, including counts of people by age, race, class, and other factors

Language profiling The application of native language(s) as part of understanding individuals and groups

Learner profiling The describing of learners by rough details, usually based around particular dimensions and indicators

Potential learner A profile of individuals and groups who may find a particular open-shared learning resource of-interest for their own learning

Profile extraction The uses of user-based log data to describe learners

Target learner A profile of individuals and groups who have a learning object or sequence built in anticipation of their needs and wants

Usability Fitness for use

User model A representation of target learner group's knowledge related to the domain topic and related topics and their preferences for the learning (in context)

References

Abyaa A, Idrissi MK, and Bennani S. An adult learner's knowledge model based on ontologies and rule reasoning. In SCAMS '17. Oct. 25 – 27, 2017. Tangier, Morocco. Association for Computing Machinery. 1 – 6, 2017.

Ammari A, Lau L, and Dimitrova V. Deriving group profiles from social media to facilitate the design of simulated environments for learning. In LAK'12. Apr. 29 – May 2, 2012. Vancouver, BC, Canada. 198 – 207, 2012.

Atif Y. An architectural specification for a system to adapt to learning patterns. *Educ Inf Technol* 16: 259 – 279, 2011. https://doi.org/10.1007/s10639-010-9125-9.

Brusilovsky P. Developing adaptive educational hypermedia systems from design models to authoring tools. In Murray T., Blessing S.B., Ainsworth S. (eds). *Authoring Tools for Advanced Technology Learning Environments*. Springer, Dordrecht. 2003.

Chen G, Davis D, Lin J, Hauff C, and Houben G-J. Beyond the MOOC platform: Gaining insights about learners from the Social Web. Websci '16. May 22 – 25, 2016. Hannover, Germany. 14 – 25, 2016. https://doi.org/10.1145/2908131.2908145.

Çimen OA. Mathematics learner profiling using behavioral, physiological and self-reporting methods. Thesis. Simon Fraser University. 2003.

Corrin L, de Barba PG, and Bakharia A. Using learning analytics to explore help-seeking learner profiles in MOOCs. In LAK '17. Vancouver, B.C., Canada. https://doi.org/10.1145/3027385.3027448. 1 – 5, 2017.

Dagger D, O'Connor A, Lawless S, Walsh E, and Wade, VP. Service-oriented e-learning platforms: From monolithic systems to flexible services. *IEEE Internet Computing*. 28 – 35, 2007.

Davis FD. Perceived usefulness, perceived ease of use, and user acceptance of information technology. *MIS Quarterly* 13: 319–340, 1989; https://doi.org/10.2307/249008.

De Freitas S, and Jarvis S. Towards a development approach to serious games. In T. Connolly, M. Stansfield, and L. Boyle's *Games-Based Learning Advancements for Multi-Sensory Human Computer Interfaces: Techniques and Effective Practices*. Hershey: IGI Global. https://www.igi-global.com/chapter/towards-development-approach-serious-games/18797. 2009.

Dweck C. Carol Dweck revisits the 'growth mindset.' *Education Week*. 2015.

Dweck C. and Leggett EL. A social-cognitive approach to motivation and personality. *Psychological Review* 95: 256 – 273, 1988.

Eyssautier-Bayay C, Jean-Daubias S, and Pernin J-P. A model of learners profiles management process. In the Proceedings of the 2009 Conference on Artificial Intelligence in Education: Building Learning Systems that Care: From Knowledge Representation to Affective Modelling. IOS Press. Amsterdam, The Netherlands. 265 – 272, 2009.

Farina K, and Nitsche M. Outside the brick: Exploring prototyping for the elderly. In the proceedings of the British HCI 2015. July 13 – 17, 2015. Lincoln, United Kingdom. 11 – 17, 2015.

Garcia-Peñalvo FJ, Hermo VF, Blanco AF, and Sein-Echaluce M. Applied educational innovation MOOC: Learners' experience and valorization of strengths and weaknesses. In TEEM '14. Oct. 1 – 3, 2014. Salamanca, Spain. 2014. https://doi.org/10.1145/2669711.2669892.

Germanakos P, Tsianos N, Lekkas Z, Mourlas C, and Samaras G. Capturing essential intrinsic user behavior values for the design of comprehensive web-based personalized environments. *Computers in Human Behavior* 24: 1434 – 1451, 2008.

Guerra J. Open social learner models for self-regulated learning and learning motivation. In UMAP '16. July 13 – 17, 2016. Halifax, NS, Canada. 329 – 332, 2016; https://doi.org/10.1145/2930238.2930375.

Hai-Jew S. Designing online earning to actual human capabilities. In the College and University Professional Association for Human Resources (CUPA-HR) Midwest Regional Conference 2016. https://www.slideshare.net/ShalinHaiJew/designing-online-learning-to-actual-human-capabilities. 2016.

Harrak F, Bouchet F, Luengo V, and Gillois P. PHS profiling students from their questions in a blended learning environment. In LAK'18. Mar. 7 – 9, 2018. Sydney, NSW, Australia. 102 – 110, 2018. https://doi.org/10.1145/3170358.3170389.

Heng LE, Sangodiah A, Muniandy M, and Yuen PK. Integration of learner's model into learning management system environment. *Journal of Fundamental and Applied Sciences* 10: 1771-1778, 2018. https://doi.org/10.4314/jfas.v10i6s.141.

Jraidi I, Chaouachi M, and Frasson C. A dynamic multimodal approach for assessing learners' interaction experience. ICMI '13. Dec. 9 – 13, 2013. Sydney, Australia. https://doi.org/10.1145/2522848.2522896. 271 – 278, 2013.

Kear K, Chetwynd F, and Jefferis H. Knowing me, knowing you: Personal profiles in online learning. *eLearn Magazine*. 1 – 7. 2013.

Kizilcec RF, Piech C, and Schneider E. Deconstructing disengagement: Analyzing learner subpopulations in Massive Open Online Courses. In LAK '13. Leuven, Belgium. 170 – 179, 2013.

Korchi A, Elidrissi NE, Jeghal A, Oughdir L, & Messaoudi F. A modeling learner approach in a computing environment for human leaning based on ontology. *Int. J. Comput. Eng. Technol* 6: 21-31, 2013.

Liegle JO, and Janicki TN. The effect of learning styles on the navigation needs of Web-based learners. *Computers in Human Behavior* 22: 885 – 898, 2006.

Mäntysaari M. Ambiguity tolerance as an instrument of learner profiling: A Q methodological study of how upper secondary school students' perceptions of EFL reading reconstruct a learner variable. Master's thesis. University of Jyväskylä. 1 – 136, 2013.

May E, Taylor C, Peat M, Barko AM, and Quinnell R. An application of student learner profiling: Comparison of students in different degree programs. In the proceedings of UniServe Science Assessment Symposium: 89 – 96, 2012.

McLoughlin C. Inclusivity and alignment: Principles of pedagogy, task and assessment design for effective cross-cultural online learning. *Distance Education* 22: 7 – 29, 2001. https://doi.org/10.1080/0158791010220102.

Montero CS, and Suhonen J. Emotion analysis meets learning analytics – Online learner profiling beyond numerical data. In Koli Calling '14. Nov. 20 – 23, 2014. Koli, Finland. 165 – 169, 2014.

Ochoa X. Learnometrics: Metrics for Learning (Objects). In the proceedings of LAK 2011. Retrieved from https://www.slideshare.net/xaoch/learnometrics-keynote-lak2011. 2011.

Pellow AJ, Smith EM, Beggs BJ, and Fernandez-Canque HL. Assessment of a-priori and dynamic extended learner profiling for accommodative learning. In Proceedings of the 9th CAA Conference. Loughborough, Loughborough University. 2005.

Rothwell WJ, and Cookson PS. *Beyond Instruction: Comprehensive Program Planning for Business and Education.* San Francisco: Jossey-Bass Publishers. 1997.

Salomoni P, Mirri S, Ferretti S, and Roccetti M. Profiling learners with special needs for custom e-learning experiences, a closed case? In W4A '07 Proceedings of the 2007 international cross-disciplinary conference on Web accessibility. 84 – 92, 2007. Banff, Canada. May 7 – 8, 2007. https://doi.org/10.1145/1243441.1243462.

Shegog R, Rushing SC, Gorman G, Jessen C, Torres J, Lane TL, Gaston A, Revels TK, Williamson J, Peskin MF, D'Cruz J, Tortoero S, and Markham CM. NATIVE-It's Your Game: Adapting a technology-based sexual health curriculum for American Indian and Alaska Native youth. *J Primary Prevent* 38: 27 – 48, 2017. https://doi.org/10.1007/s10935-016-0440-9.

Skourlas C, Sgouropoulou C, Belsis P, Pantziou G, Sfikas C, and Fosses N. Learner profiles In the higher educational context. In *Proceedings of E-Ra 2nd International Conference Information Technology to Science, Economy, Society and Education.* 2007.

Spencer SJ, Steele CM, and Quinn DM. Stereotype threat and women's math performance. *Journal of Experimental Social Psychology* 35: 4 – 28, 1999. https://www.sciencedirect.com/science/article/pii/S0022103198913737.

Steele CM, and Aronson J. Stereotype threat and the intellectual test performance of African Americans. *Jrn Personality and Social Psychology* 69: 797 – 811, 1995. http://mrnas.pbworks.com/f/claude%20steele%20stereotype%20threat%201995.pdf.

Su AYS, Yang SJH, Hwang W-Y, and Zhang J. A Web 2.0-based collaborative annotation system for enhancing knowledge sharing in collaborative learning environments. *Computers & Education* 55: 752 – 766, 2010.

Taraghi B, Saranti A, Ebner M, Müller V, and Groβmann A. Towards a learning-aware application guided by hierarchical classification of learner profiles. *Journal Of Universal Computer Science* 21: 93 – 109, 2015.

Tsianos N, Lekkas Z, Germanakos P, Mourlas C, and Samaras G. User-centric profiling on the basis of cognitive and emotional characteristics: An empirical study. In: Nejdl W., Kay J., Pu P., Herder E. (eds) Adaptive Hypermedia and Adaptive Web-Based Systems. AH 2008. Lecture Notes in Computer Science, Vol. 5149. Springer, Berlin, Heidelberg. 214 – 223, 2008. https://doi.org/10.1007/978-3-540-70987-9_24.

Van Biljou J, and Kotzé P. Profiling mLearning students according to cultural dimensions: Is that possible? UNISA Institutional Repository. http://uir.unisa.ac.za/handle/10500/3137. 2007.

Wettasinghe M, and Hasan M. Exploring the efficacy of IT with slow learners: Case studies in primary schools. In Conference ICL 2007. Sept. 26 – 28, 2007. Villach, Austria. 1 – 11, 2007. https://telearn.archives-ouvertes.fr/hal-00197252/document.

Yoon S-Y, Bhat S, and Zechner K. Vocabulary profile as a measure of vocabulary sophistication. In the 7th Workshop of the Innovative Use of NLP for Building Educational Applications. Montréal, Canada. June 3 – 8, 2012. 180 – 189, 2012.

Additional Reading Section

Blake R, and Sekuler R. *Perception.* 5th Ed. Boston: McGraw Hill. 1985.

Joseph PB, Bravmann SL, Windschitl MA, Mikel ER, and Green NS. *Cultures of Curriculum.* Mahwah, New Jersey: Lawrence Erlbaum Associates, Publishers. 2000.

Sousa DA. *How the Brain Learns.* 4th Ed. Thousand Oaks, California: Corwin. SAGE Publishing. 2005

Wanigasinghe [illegible] Exploring the efficacy of IT with slow learners: Case studies in [illegible]

[illegible]

Part II
Building to Standards

Chapter 3
Thinking About the Learning Design: Theories, Models, Frameworks, and Heuristics

Abstract People have been studying how humans learn and theorizing about ways to support their learning for many years. This chapter addresses the importance of using relevant concepts and empirical-based knowledge of human learning to inform the design and development of the open-shared learning objects and sequences. This chapter may be one of the more challenging ones given the number of potential concepts and data that may inform design practice, and also given that there are many different preferences that open-shared learning designers and developers may have in their selections. The core idea is that designing for learning centeredness benefits from knowledge of human learning and thought-through and informed processes in learning design.

Keywords Learning design · Analysis Design Development Implementation Evaluation (ADDIE) · Models · Framework theories · Universal design · Flow · Kolb's learning styles and experiential learning cycle · Bloom's taxonomy · TPACK framework (technological pedagogical content knowledge)

> For me, I am driven by two main philosophies: know more today about the world than I knew yesterday and lessen the suffering of others. You'd be surprised how far that gets you.
>
> —Neil deGrasse Tyson, March 1, 2012, on Reddit "IAmA…Ask Me Anything" subreddit (https://www.reddit.com/r/IAmA/comments/qccer/i_am_neil_degrasse_tyson_ask_me_anything/c3wgffy/)

S. Hai-Jew, *Designing Instruction For Open Sharing*,
https://doi.org/10.1007/978-3-030-02713-1_3

Opening Scenario

Opening Scenario: Have the Knowledge and Tools for Informed Learning Designs?

At the very beginning of an instructional design project, it is possible to begin just with some learning contents in a domain or field, some general learning objectives, and the general group of target learners. Beyond those basics, a designer/developer has to decide how to package the learning contents to make it engaging and comprehensible for learners, and how to ensure that the desired learning occurs. One of the tools that he/she may use to inform the learning design is to select relevant theories, models, and frameworks. These tools enable a more systematized way to think about the learning design, multimedia presentation strategies, instructional strategies and tactics, technology selections, learner experiences, assessment design, and other features.

Beyond theory, oftentimes, empirical research is applied to instructional designs and development.

Finally, this is not to say that all designers and developers *have to* use a conceptual basis or a research data-driven basis for their designs. Certainly, some subject matter experts or content experts may prefer to create in a more freeform and intuitive way.

To enable the share, what are some ways to think about how to best design and create the learning objects?

Some Early Questions to Consider

What empirical research informs how people perceive, learn, remember, make decisions, and apply their learning?

If you are to choose empirical research on online learning, what are some go-to studies?

If you are to choose a handful of theories and/or models and/or frameworks to inform your design of learning objects, what would you select, and why?

In terms of your learning domain of interest, what aspects of that domain inform how it may be taught most effectively?

Learning Objectives
Learners will…

General Learning Theories

- Identify the main learning theories that may influence open sharing instructional designs
  - Include any theories from other areas that may apply
- Select the most salient learning theories for the particular design and development context (and explain why they are the most relevant ones)
- Identify the implications of the selected learning theories on how learning should be designed

General Learning Models

- List the main models that may influence open sharing instructional designs
  - Include any models from other areas that may apply
- Choose the most important models for the particular design and development context (and explain why these are critical)
- Name the implications of the selected learning models on how learning should be designed

General Learning Frameworks

- Recognize the main frameworks that may influence open sharing instructional designs
  - Include any frameworks from other areas that may apply
- List the most applicable frameworks for the particular design and development context (and explain why these are important)
- Recognize the implications of the selected learning frameworks on how learning should be designed

Relevant Applied Heuristics for Learning Design and Development

- Based on prior practice, research, and concepts, list the most relevant heuristics (rules of thumb) for learning design and development
- Place these in order of relevance from most relevant to least relevant, and explore this list, and continuous add to it

Baseline Theories, Models, and Frameworks

- Synthesize the most relevant theories, models, and frameworks, and form a general sensibility about the following: who learners are, what their needs (learning and otherwise) are, how to meet their needs

How Humans Learn

- Identify some of the more salient research about how humans learn, based on the academic research literature and empirical data from related fields

- Create some baseline understandings about how humans perceive, learn, retain, think, and make decisions, and why
- Consider how this information about human factors may inform the design and development decisions

Target Learning Domain

- Describe the learning domain of your subject area of specialty
- Conduct some light research to better understand how the teaching for this learning domain is done (and why)
- Explain why the conventions of the area will affect what is designed to the area

3.1 Introduction

Let's begin with a thought experiment. In the design and development of learning resources, a person or team may begin with a *tabula rasa*, and from there, he or she or they have a range of options. They can justify various design and development paths. However blank the slate at the beginning, there are many elements that are already somewhat pre-defined.

Any number of decisions have to be made in the design and development of learning resources. Some of these decisions are informed by pre-defined laws that apply to instructional design: intellectual property (IP) law, accessibility law, media law, privacy law, and others. (More on these follow in Chapter 4.) Then, there are the requisite accessibility accommodations required for the various forms of media and multimedia. There are the technological decisions, with limited choices at each phase, in order to output the ultimate digital resources desired. Many of these decisions are made in almost a mechanical way to follow the rules.

Then there are decisions made based on the state of the art—the quality of the learning objects that are available in the world at the moment enabled by the available technologies and talents and resources. There is a kind of forcing function based on these works that normalize or regularize the shared works. These features are also expressively tangible and objectively observable.

Then, there are other more ephemeral judgments made that inspire and animate the learning. These are conveyances of enthusiasm and personality and professional insight. These are based on intuitions into the particular domain based on experiences. Underlying all learning resources are implied values and ideals, conceptualizations of learners, and worldviews. These may be articulated or silently expressed. In some cases, these concepts may be uninformed and inchoate. These conceptual influences may be partially inferred, with some level of ambiguity and some level of confidence, from the learning resources—through reverse engineering. Others have suggested that "a functional analysis of a generic instructional artifact provides a set of subcategories for the organization of instructional theory at a more detailed level" (Gibbons 2009, p. 2).

Those who have a background in designing instruction are well aware that there is over a century of theorizing and scientific research work into how people learn. From these efforts, there are theories, models, and frameworks; from practices, there are known best practice heuristics. There are thousands of research studies about teaching and learning, and hundreds about instructional design. This chapter introduces some general categories of learning theories; select learning theories, learning models, learning frameworks; select heuristics, and some applicable insights. The core thinking is that purposeful and informed design trumps scattershot any day. From the theorizing work, the research (in learning and other related fields), fact patterns emerge that can better inform the work.

The thinking about the learning design is Step 3 in the work sequence (Fig. 3.1).

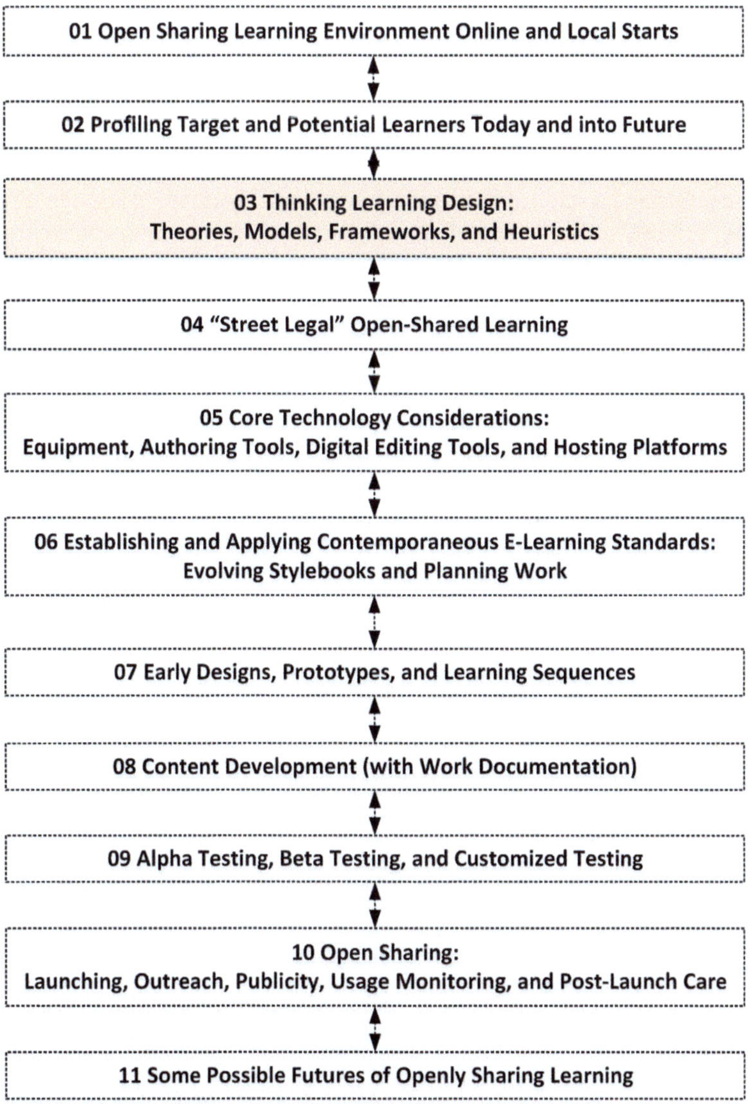

Fig. 3.1 Step 3 in the open-shared learning resource development

This work does not suggest Sequence that there is only one normative or one correct way to think about teaching and learning. Certainly, the local conditions of a learning context will be much more informative. And there are so many moving parts to a learning design that asserting one right way would be quite far-fetched. Getting the fundamentals right is important, though, and additional changes at the margins may be the difference in smaller ways. Also, the unique local conditions of the learning context (if these are define-able in the open sharing sphere) may inform additional research that may inform the work.

3.2 Review of the Literature

At heart, instructional design as a "technology" which is used to create instructional experiences to make learning "more efficient, effective, and appealing" (Merrill et al. 1966, p. 5). In this conceptualization, instruction is a "science" and its effects are observable and testable. From another viewpoint, instructional design is a "prescriptive science" with "a set of prescriptions for determining the appropriate instructional strategies to enable learners to acquire instructional goals" (Uden and Alderson 2000, p. 67).

A "learning design" is defined as "an application of a pedagogical model for a specific learning objective, target group and a specific context or knowledge domain" (Koper and Olivier 2004, p. 98). The "7Cs of Learning Design" include the following steps of the designer/developers: vision (conceptualize), activities (create, communicate, collaborate, consider), synthesis (combine), and implementation (consolidate) (Conole 2016, Slide 38).

A Long History of Instructional Design One researcher suggests that instructional systems design has a long history. She writes:

> As a formal discipline, Instructional Systems Design has been a long time in the making. The early contributions of thinkers such as Aristotle, Socrates and Plato regarding the cognitive basis of learning and memory was later expanded by the 13th century philosopher St. Thomas Aquinas who discussed the perception of teaching in terms of free will… (Crawford 2004, p. 413)

In more recent history, some foundational ideas in instructional design originated in the 1960s, including "task analysis, objective specification, and criterion-referenced testing…linked together to form processes, or models, for systematically designing instructional materials" (Reiser 2001, p. 61). In the 1980s, cognitive psychology methods came to the fore, and the wider uses of "microcomputers for instructional purposes" were major influences on the field (Reiser 2001, p. 62). Then, a focus on performance technology meant "more careful analyses of the causes of performance problems," including poorly designed trainings (Reiser 2001, p. 63). In the present, instructional design focuses on human factors, various modes of learning, unique harnessing of a range of technologies and methods, and rigorous learning and performance measurement. Instructional designs can be high impact and can directly affect learner engagement in the learning and interest in the field (Nolen and Koretsky 2018).

In this space, there is no "theory of everything" or coherent framework that incorporates the thinking, research, and practice. And there is no sense that one will arise anytime soon. Generally, the design of instruction may be informed by concepts (theories, models, and frameworks), research, practices (heuristics), technologies, and other factors.

A few simple definitions follow. "Theories" refer to interrelated ideas or principles that explain an in-world phenomenon. Some may be seen as fairly accepted given research in a particular field or area, and others may be hypothetical and even as-yet un-tested. "Models" refer to theorized representations of systems or dynamics. These represent entities and objects and the interrelationships between these objects to represent a phenomenon. They represent a portion of a system. "Frameworks" refer to underlying structures to a phenomenon, and these may be descriptive (showing how things function), prescriptive (how things should function), proscriptive (how things should not function), and so on. Theories, models, and frameworks are informed by in-world observations, research, experimentation, data, and other sources. "Heuristics" refer to practical problem-solving techniques and rules-of-thumb in a particular context.

At a high level, sequentially, there have been a few major paradigms that inform human learning. Initial thought centered around behaviorism, the idea of learners responding to stimuli and understanding those patterns. Later, behaviorism was added to with the idea of the "social" that affects human learning. Next, there was cognition, which conceptualized learning as information processing through the human senses, the brain's processing of signals, the interpretation of those signals, and sensemaking of the world and storing that into memory. Then, constructivism came to the fore with the idea that the respective human learners formulate their sense of reality themselves, and in coordination with (Payne 2009). At present, people are conceptualized as each having different mixes of intelligences and learning preferences (but not "learning styles"). The human mind is seen as "plastic" and malleable. More recent theories have looked at human learning for behavior change, in order to modify people's health behaviors, lifestyles, and other aspects, and through the support of the larger social environment.

In earlier days, instructional design theory was conceptualized as addressing four main areas:

> Instructional design theory can be thought of as being concerned with four major aspects of instruction: (1) ways of organizing instruction, which include such concerns as sequencing and formatting the subject-matter content, (2) ways of delivering instruction, which is usually a matter of media selection, (3) ways of motivating students, which may be intrinsic or extrinsic, and (4) ways of managing the student's use of the other three aspects of instruction (Reigeluth and Merrill 1979, as cited in Reigeluth 1979, p. 8)

Today, there are theories that address design at the macro-, meso-, and micro-levels, those aspiring to be complete high level theories and many partial theories that explain aspects of instruction.

In education and training designs, there are thought to be four main paradigms: instrumental (to aid planning and intercommunications), communicative (to include stakeholder inputs), pragmatic (to enable efficiencies in design), and artistic (to represent unique designer inspirations). Each of the four paradigms has strengths and weaknesses (Visscher-Voerman and Gustafson 2004, p. 87).

Instructional designs may be based on particular "centrisms": media-centrism (the technologies), message-centrism [with "primary importance on message-related constructs" and using "media constructs (main idea, explanation, line of argument dramatization, etc.) secondarily, according to the demands of the message"], strategy-centrism ("the structured plan of messaging and interaction as a main source of instructional effectiveness"), and model-centrism ("the system and model constructs that lie at the base of subject-matter knowledge")(Gibbons 2003, pp. 22–23). The design goals depend on the layer:

> A set of design goals unique to the layer, a set of design constructs unique to the layer, a set of theoretic principles for the selection and use of design constructs, a set of design and development tools, and a set of specialized design processes (Gibbons 2003, p. 23).

In this conceptualization, the design layers age out on different timetables and are handled in different ways (Gibbons 2003, p. 23). While a particular centrism may come to the fore, the other centrisms may have an influence on the design.

In other conceptualizations, the learning designs are based on the learning subject (expressed as ontologies, knowledge structures, structured informational relationships, and semantics), human learning capabilities (and the biological functions of the brain and body as learning instruments), the desirable learning outcomes and performance outcomes, and other aspects. "Teaching to the test" is considered negative and overly focused on one goal at the expense of more important ones. If informational content is somewhat related, it is thought that with proper presentational sequencing, "higher levels of learning, synthesis, retention, and affect" may be achieved (Reigeluth 1979, p. 8). Instructional design methods focus heavily on evaluation, and there is the sense that refining learning resources is never finished, and a learning resource is "never 'final', but merely in a stage of evaluation" (Crawford 2004, p. 417).

One thinker identifies the following seven models as important to the instructional design space: situated cognition theory, sociocultural learning theory, the ADDIE Model, Merrill's Principles of Instruction, individualized instruction, Bloom's Taxonomy of Learning Objectives, and the SAM Model (Successive Approximation Model) (Pappas 2017, pp. 3–4).

The work of instructional design is highly demanding because designer/developers face ill-structured problems, with any number of possible appropriate solutions but also many opportunities for dead ends. One team describes the work this way: "The practice of instructional design (ID) has been found to involve complex thinking, a systematic design approach, strategic global planning, the use of iterative processes, and the reflective selection of design strategies." (Akondy and Murthy 2015, p. 53).

3.2.1 *"Theories" to Understand Human Learning and Learners*

Theories are simplified hypotheses about how the world works (and should work, in some cases). These are interrelated principles and ideas that describe particular aspects of the world. In some cases, they explain; in others, they recommend actions and discourage others. In the educational realm, as in other sciences, theories should be "falsifiable" (able to be proven false in theory through experimentation and objective observations). They should be logically aligned and not self-contradictory. Strong theories are thought to have construct validity, so they focus on the construct coherently; to have internal validity (such as the absence of internal contradictions), and external validity (in that they represent something real in the real world).

So what are some of the predominant theories in applied design of instruction today? A brief, limited, and selective summary follows. The main precepts are bolded, and the respective informing theories and theorists are briefly summarized.

Build learning to the Desired Capabilities and the Levels of Learning Some of the most widely accepted theories applied in the design of instruction will be touched on here, as an opening to the wider fields related to human learning. Benjamin Bloom created a taxonomy of learning domains in 1956, and this hierarchical model suggests that human learning may be conceptualized as built on base capabilities and enable more complex ones. At the base of the Bloom's Taxonomy expressed as a triangle, there is first knowledge, then comprehension, application, analysis, synthesis, and evaluation; in 2001, this was updated as follows (from the base of the triangle to the top): remember, understand, apply, analyze, evaluate, and create. The concept is that human creativity is a pinnacle enabled by the prior affordances (Anderson et al. 2001). People learn various types of knowledge, with differentiations between "declarative" and "procedural" knowledge. Other learning models inform human learning to the cognitive domain, the affective domain, or the psychomotor domain (or a combination).

Help Learners Actively Engage in their World and Reflect on their Engagements and Test their Hypotheses In 1984, David Kolb's learning styles model was introduced, which suggests that when people reflect on their lived concrete experiences, they may form abstract conceptions about that experience (and novel ideas as well), which they may then test in the world. The steps are as follows: concrete experience (feeling), reflective observation (watching), abstract conceptualization (thinking), and active experimentation (doing). (Kolb 1984)

Meet Learners Where They Are in their Learning Lev Vygotsky conceptualized the Zone of Proximal Development (ZPD) from approximately 1924–1934, during the last decade of his life. His idea was that properly designed learning supports may enable a person to accelerate their learning in ways that they could not achieve alone; however, this advance is only within a certain proximate distance from the level of learning the learner has achieved so far. This concept suggests the importance of knowing where learners are at in their learning in order to tailor and target the learning tactics.

Motivate Learners with the Proper Level of Challenge Mihalyi Csikszentmihalyi (1990) proposed the concept of "flow" in his book *Flow: The Psychology of Optimal Experience*, which suggests that when people are deeply engaged in an activity, they will bring their complete selves to the task and engage at a high leve. This work suggests that creating challenging tasks (sometimes called "hard fun") that trigger learners' intrinsic motivations may be most effective. If the challenge is too hard for the learner at the particular stage in their learning, they may become frustrated and give up; the challenge is too simple, they may be bored and give up. Core preparatory study skills for college-age learners focus on self-management and goal-setting, to enable them to self-regulate their learning. A wide range of theories on human motivation enable self-regulated learners to set goals and meet them (Code et al. 2006).

Consider the Context and the Social Lave and Wenger (1991) highlighted the importance of building "communities of practice" in which people co-learn together and experience learning in a situated way (similar to a real-world context), in their book *Situated Learning: Legitimate Peripheral Participation.* They brought in the importance of the social aspects to learning.

The design of instruction usually borrows from multiple theories, each of which address different aspects or parts of the design. The unique features of an instructional design context require a synthesis of theories.

3.2.2 "Models" to Build Learning

If theories are fairly macro- in their approach, models tend to be more meso- and micro-, in that they represent systems (entities and relationships and dynamics). These are sub-units within a macro world.

"Andragogy" refers to how adults learn, and "pedagogy" technically refers to how children learn. Andragogy has been studied since the 1920s. Malcolm Knowles was one of its later proponents in the West, and he emphasized the importance of intrinsic motivation for adult learners, who tend to focus on practical needs for their learning. Understanding what motivates various individuals to want to learn is an important part of learning design.

Cultural models of learners have also been harnessed to make learning more aligned with perceived learner needs. One classic model that is the basis of much of this research is by Geert Hofstede with his Cultural Dimensions Theory (1967–1973) and its implications for intercultural communications. Over time, he added a sixth dimension to his original model. The dimensions (which exist on continuums) include the following factors: (1) individualism—communalism, (2) power distance, (3) masculinity—femininity, (4) uncertainty avoidance (high or low uncertainty avoidance), (5) long-term orientation—short-term orientation (focus on the past, present, or future, and in what amounts), and indulgence—restraint. In this space, how history is portrayed, how maps are drawn, how humans are depicted, how humans are shown interacting in different relationships, assumed macro-level learning styles, and other elements come into play. A number of research works focus on instructional design to engage "culturally diverse learners" and meet their learning needs (Sabin and Ahern 2002).

The ADDIE Model (sometimes referred to as a "framework") is both descriptive and prescriptive. Its name is an acronym, which stands for "Analyze, Design, Develop, Implement, and Evaluate". It originated in 1975 as the work of the Center for Educational Technology at Florida State University. Over the years, respective steps have been elaborated on, and spinoff models have been added (including the "Dick and Carey" Systems Approach Model for Designing Instruction in 1978 by Walter Dick and Lou Carey and James Carey; the rapid prototyping approach by Steven D. Tripp and Barbara Bichelmeyer in 1990; and others). There are multiple contributions of this model—such as the formalization of the analysis and design to inform the development, the implementation (launch), and then the importance of evaluating the efficacy of the learning resources to inform further work on all the prior steps (analysis, design, development, and implementation). The sense of continuous improvement is another critical aspect of this model.

The TPACK (Technological Pedagogical Content Knowledge) Model (sometimes referred to as a "framework") was originated by Mishra and Koehler (2006) as a way to ground educational technologies theoretically. These researchers conceptualize instructional work as the interface between content, pedagogy, and technologies (depicted as a three-circle Venn diagram). Teachers then need technological content knowledge, pedagogical content knowledge, and technological pedagogical knowledge, and at the intersection, technological pedagogical content knowledge or TPACK (Mishra and Koehler 2006). Besides putting technology into the teacher responsibility in a central way, this framework was conceptualized to apply to teaching, instructional design, research, analysis, and other work in academia. For many teachers and instructors, instructional design work is considered part of their skillset. There are formal efforts to advance the work of instructors in terms of instructional design (Utschig et al. 2005).

Clark and Mayer (2016) have combined Sweller's Cognitive Load Theory and Mayer's Cognitive Theory of Multimedia Learning (CTML) into a practical empirical-research-based book with advisement on how to effectively use multimedia to promote learning. Their principles include the Multimedia Principle (about using words and graphics rather than words alone), the Contiguity Principle (about aligning "words to corresponding graphics"), the Modality Principle (presenting words as speech "rather than on-screen text"), the Redundancy Principle (about explaining visuals in words "in audio OR text but not both"), the Coherence Principle (about limiting contents and avoiding extraneous material), the Personalization and Embodiment Principles (about using "conversational style, polite wording, human voice, and virtual coaches"), the Segmenting and Pretraining Principles (about "managing complexity by breaking a lesson into parts), and other insights (Clark and Mayer 2016, pp. 2–5). The concepts here suggest that learning should be built to human capabilities and particularly how people process signal data that they perceive and then how they process and encode that data. The dual-processing model of multimedia learning suggests that attention should not just run on one channel but both the visual and auditory cognitive processing channels in working memory for effective learning (Mayer and Moreno 1998; Moreno and Mayer 1999).

A study of how instructional designers make instructional strategy decisions found that there was a heavy reliance on "interaction with others both as a means of making instructional-strategy decisions and of learning about new theories, trends, and strategies" (Christensen and Osguthorpe 2004, p. 45), so professional social networks are important. Only half of the respondents in this study regularly used theories to make instructional strategy decisions, and they were "eclectic in their underlying philosophical assumptions" (Christensen and Osguthorpe 2004, p. 45). In terms of the most influential theory categories by frequency, they were as follows: constructivism, social constructivism (26), cognitive theories (17), instructional theories (17), motivational theories (11), behaviorism, S-R (stimulus-response) theories (10), and andragogy theories (9) (Christensen and Osguthorpe 2004, p. 57). Various philosophies, values systems, understandings of human learning, philosophical systems, political aims, and mass-scale paradigms have informed human education systems (Ozmon and Craver 2003). Such competing interests may be seen in the choices that instructors make. Constructivism has had a long history in formal education (Bruner 1960; Payne 2009).

3.2.3 "Frameworks" as Structures for Learning Design Methods and Learning Contents and Sequences

Many use "models" and "frameworks" interchangeably. A focus of a framework is on a "structure," an arrangement, or an assembly.

In this context, a framework will be applied to various types of learning resources. In the research literature, there is in the design of different types of learning experiences or modalities, such as face-to-face (F2F), blended, and fully online. There is research focused around particular designs for types of learning: problem-based learning, project-based learning, authentic learning, active learning, over-learning, complex learning, discovery learning, inquiry-based learning, simulations, immersive virtual world learning, ubiquitous learning, and others.

Then, too, there is research on how to frame serious games, pervasive games, slideshow lectures, multimedia for learning, interactive videos, "flipped classroom" lectures, adaptive learning sequences, virtual labs, remote labs, datasets for learning, interactive electronic books (e-books), and so on. Researchers have shared information on how to create "active multimodal presentations" (Hartley 2005); learning based on a "hypertext instructional design methodology" (Mengel et al. 1997); "multimedia presentations with animations" (Moreno and Mayer 1999), and other digital contents. Another shared on how to most effectively create assembly instructions based on cognitive psychology research and visual communications (Agrawala et al. 2003).

There is research on massive open online courses (MOOCs) and everything related to that approach. There is research on the design of computer-based trainings (CBT) (Bayer 1991), which still have relevance today given how different learner populations come online in different paces around the world.

There are frameworks for trainings in vocational spaces for adult learners to meet compliance guidelines.

There are particular applications to particular learning domains like nursing or engineering or mathematics, and meta-domains like STEM fields (science, technology, engineering, and math).

There is research on online learning communities and their creation and maintenance over time and across different technologies.

There is research on how to harness virtual reality and microworlds for learning. Then, there is augmented reality, with head-mounted devices and other equipment.

There is research about how to achieve unusual outcomes such as high level creativity and innovation. A class of contents deal with generative learning and ID patterns that promote exploration of open-ended solutions (Brophy and Velankar 2006). Sometimes, target values serve as guideposts for learning designs.

There are masterful works on how to create effective forms of assessment, assignments, and aspects of learning. There is research on how to provide effective examples, and others on providing effective feedback.

There are fairly unique conceptualizations, such as "powerful learning factors" used to inform instructional design strategies. These factors include "personal interaction with mentor/expert teacher"; "active experience; doing it"; reflection; motivation to learn; support of peer group; visual reinforcement of points spoken; "independence, ability to control one's own learning" and "informal, low-pressure environment," for example (Rowland and DiVasto 2013, p. 23). Another creative work demonstrates conveying aspects of works of literature in visual designs and graphics (Latiff et al. 2009). These are refreshing and less conventional approaches.

There are pedagogical patterns identified in one area applied to others. For example, inspirations from Massively Multiplayer Online Games (MMOGs) have been applied to m-learning (mobile learning) or "Massive Multiplayer Online M-Learning" (Khalid and Kameyama 2008) in one case and also to Massive Open Online Courses (MOOCs) (Voulgari and Sampson 2014). There are designs of religious instruction in various learning contexts. There are hybrid builds like "edutainment" and "gamified courses." Theories may be hybridized in instructional designs, such as one based on motivation theory and constructivism (Jin 2009). There are designs for specific learning, such as game programming based on an industry curriculum framework (Wu 2014).

Much of the research involves case-based works and other one-offs with insights that may be transferable to other contexts. The research is myriad in this sense.

Some frameworks are instantiated into technologies to inform the instructional design, such as LMSes with rich social interaction components. There are various efforts at automating instructional design (Ellis et al. 2004). Some systems seem to disintermediate the work of human instructional designers to enable subject matter experts to "plug and play" with providing contents only.

3.2.4 *"Heuristics" as Working Best Practices in Learning Design*

And fourth, "heuristics" are common practices to best achieve certain practical outcomes. In the design of instruction space, these include tips for efficient and effective work.

"Design research," with its focus on practical approaches, seems like an effective method to identify helpful instructional design heuristics. One team writes:

> Design research requires that faculty members: explore significant educational problems, rather than conduct research for its own sake (and) define a pedagogical outcome and create learning environments that address it (Reeves et al. 2005, p. 109)

The steps of one process for evolving instructional technologies may apply to general instructional design as well. It reads as follows:

- Emphasize content and pedagogy rather than technology.
- Give special attention to supporting human interactions and nurturing learning communities.
- Modify the learning environments until the pedagogical outcome is reached.
- Reflect on the process to reveal design principles that can inform other instructors and researchers, and future development projects. (Reeves et al. 2005, p. 110)

The design and development work is done first, and then lessons are drawn from that work. [Others have observed that design research can be used to develop and refine theories and may be particularly effective for "domain theories, design frameworks, and design methodologies" (Edelson 2002, p. 105) but are difficult and costly ways to "refine educational theories" (p. 118). Capturing insights about the respective theories may be a positive byproduct of actual designs. How well these conceptualizations (theories, models, and frameworks) inform work is an important function.]

Open Instructional Designs? In 2009, a research team called for a radical transparency of instructional designs so that learners may seen what went into the design of their learning. The authors argue:

> Without prudent application of Instructional Design, the process of learning simply boils down to an optimistic experimentation rather than an enlightened guidance. Predominantly, learners are not exposed to the instructional design process that the instructor followed to rationalize the resultant pedagogy. In fact, learners are led to believe that learning is a by-product of effective exposure to instructional material and instructional activities. We challenge that learners be allowed to inspect the instructional design processes adapted by the course designer and the chosen instructional design product, and use them as a guideline for a better understanding of their learning. (Kumar et al. 2009, p. 42)

Further, they describe co-designed learning between instructors and learners. They conceptualize instructional design as "an open process of formulating, applying, evaluating, and reasoning a theory of effectiveness of learning in a given context, open not only to instructors but also to learners" (Kumar et al. 2009, p. 42).

Learner Group Profiling Another way to understand how heuristics may be surfaced comes from learner group profiling. For example, there are common practices of trying to understand subpopulations of learners by their "generation" and tailoring learning to their worldviews based on what they may have experienced. There are works describing how to reach the "gamer generation" with learning that aligns with a gaming worldview. A recent work suggests that the brain's plasticity has been changed with the consumption of electronic media, and learners today may find it harder to concentrate for longer periods of time to enable them to consume works of literature (Wolf 2018, as cited in Chen 2018), for example. Some works are informed by one defining theory, like active learning, but with project limitations based on other defining characteristics of the learning context (Belcadhi and Ghannouchi 2013). Research teams have focused on particular culturally related learner groups, like indigenous learners in Malaysia, including follow-on testing with learners to see how accurate the design was (Zaman et al. 2005).

In the current space, research work on human learning done in a range of semi-related fields to education (psychology, economics, neuroscience, nutrition, and others) are contributing knowledge on how to advance human learning, and they are suggesting a number of best practices.

Altogether, these theories and methods offer ways to think about a learning situation that is more systematized and informed by what is known about human learning. They offer an ability to select concepts that may inform the design. These offer ways to translate concepts to practices and procedures. However, given the complexity of the space, there are also challenges with aligning theories, models, and frameworks, so there are not outright contradictions where possible.

From Concept → Practice ... How?

Theorizing is used in academic fields and practices to help people better understand a particular phenomenon in the world and to better navigate through it. The first challenge is to identify which theories are most salient to a particular design context and why. If there are "universals" that apply to a range of contexts, those should always be taken into account. If there are "specifics" that apply to a particular learning design context, then those should be taken into account. The challenge is to articulate clear and reasoned standards for the uptake of particular theories, models, and frameworks.

Once applicable theories, models, and frameworks have been identified, one has to decide how to operationalize the principles. How will the abstract ideas transfer to different contexts? How will the various fact patterns apply to new circumstances?

The next challenge is how to interpret a particular theory, model, or framework, and then to understand what it may mean for a particular design. How directively should the approaches be taken? Should the theories be used to inform assessment of the learning design? Should they be used to inform work processes (and if so, how)?

Then, too, the unique design requirements of a particular context may affect how applied theory is expressed.

Will an applied theory/model/framework affect how learning content is presented? What the user interface looks like? What technologies are used? What assignments are created? What assessments are created? The look-and-feel of learning resources?

3.3 Learning Design Theories, Models, Frameworks, and Heuristics

Those who would design open-shared learning have hundreds of years of documented human thought about human learning, decades of instructional design theories and models, and a "long tail" of specific frameworks and heuristics. This information may be used to broaden design thinking, align designs with what is known about human learning, and harness research to inform the work. Designer/developers will come at the work with their own strengths and weaknesses of the design hand, and all likely will benefit from a solid understanding of this space.

3.3.1 Part 1: Theories

Macro-level theories are concepts that explain in-world phenomena, and sometimes prescribe certain courses of action (while discouraging others). Some theories will "speak to" designer/developers more than others. Regardless of the individual responses, they would benefit from a full and accurate understanding of each theory, the implications of each, and how these might affect the learning design and development work. No ideas should be rejected out of hand without fair consideration. Of course, not everything read will be thrown into the design mix; rather, the designer/developer will have to select what is relevant.

For a particular design, some helpful questions about theories may include the following:

- What theories relate to the "target" and "potential" learners?
- What theories relate to the content domain?

- What theories relate to teaching and learning methods effective for the learning objectives and learning outcomes?
- What theories relate to the technologies that will likely be used?
- Of the selected theories, how well do they mesh? Are there logical conflicts, and if so, what? How would one resolve the conflicts?
- Which learning theories may be most simple to apply to good effect? To operationalize to the design and development work?

Task #1: Worldview About Learners and Learning
In some (or even many) scenarios, people may start a learning resource without pre-planning or work. Some may be novices who parachute into the space, create a work, and move on. In other cases, these are experts in learning designs who have a collection of heuristics and internalized organizational structures and standards; in many cases, such experts will follow their work with a rigorous assessment during which any issues are corrected. Neither scenario is optimal because the advances in the learning space are continuous, and spending a little time to think through what might inform a learning design and a learning resource would benefit the work and the resulting contents.

In this spirit, first, conduct a review of your worldview regarding learners (who they are) and learning (how people learn). List where your insights come from and why.

Then, update your knowledge base. Identify a dozen relevant and recent articles and/or sources, and read up on these topics. Make a record of what you have learned.

Task #2: Relevant Theories for the Design of Learning

A theory generally seeks to explain a system or dynamics by identifying entities and interrelationships. A theory may be conceptualized as appearing in the world in different ways, and a theory is researched in different ways. A theory does not try to explain the whole of a phenomenon but an aspect, given the complexity of the world.

Human learning is a complex phenomenon, and the human being himself/herself is a complex individual. Based on your knowledge of theories related to learning (from education, from psychology, from neuroscience, from economics, from instructional design, and other fields), choose your top six theories, and write down the main assertions from each of these theories. List the main thinkers for each of the theories. Analyze the design implications of each of the theories individually, and then the implications from the synthesized mix of theories.

3.3.2 Part 2: Models

Models are conceptual representations of systems in the world, and these are usually at the meso- and micro-levels (no global-scale macro models currently for learning although there are aspirants for "universal" models). Models tend to be sparse and parsimonious.

To select relevant models, designer/developers may consider the following questions:

- What models would best inform the work sequence and include all relevant steps?
- How do the selected models interact? Do they complement each other, or do they clash?
- What are the implications of the respective models? How would it be best to operationalize the models?

To thread the needle for a learner-based approach to instructional design, through the creation of a "user model," Fig. 3.2 provides some early work.

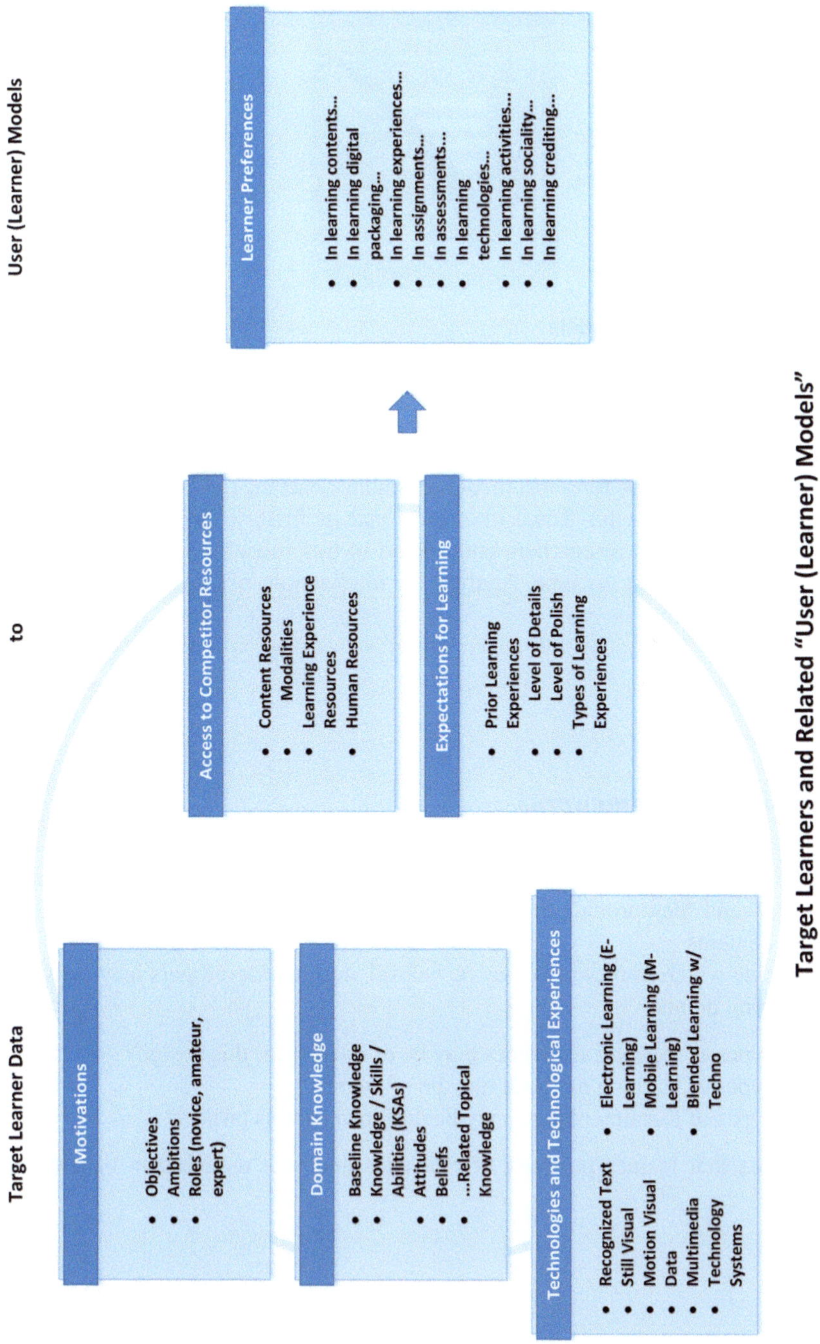

Fig. 3.2 Target learners and related "user (learner) models"

Task #3: Relevant Models

Models refer to representations of systems, the entities and dynamics within and without (outside) those systems. In the learning space, models cover unique parts of this sphere in some cases but also overlapping parts in others.

Choose one of the foremost models of human learning (and design to meet human learning needs). Trace its origins and its history. Explain what the major thinkers and researchers contributed to this model. Explain how the model has evolved over time. Analyze the implications of this model for the design of learning.

3.3.3 Part 3: Frameworks

Frameworks in this case are structures applied to the building of various learning resources—and they provide direct guidance and support for the development of learning contents.

To decide which frameworks may be helpful, designer/developers may consider the following points:

- What types of learning sequences may be of interest for this design?
- What types of learning methods may be of interest?
- What types of learning objects may be designed for this project?

The idea that learner profiling of relevance and user models can benefit the design

Task #4: Relevant Frameworks

Frameworks define underlying structures of a phenomenon. As noted earlier, they may be descriptive, prescriptive, proscriptive, or others.

Select a framework that you may use for the design of a learning resource. Identify its main purpose—to describe, prescribe, proscribe, or some other purpose. Support your analysis with facts and details.

Then, apply the framework to a learning design for a learning object that you intend to create. Analyze how this framework is useful or informative to your work.

3.3.4 Part 4: Heuristics

Heuristics are practical rules-of-thumb based on common practices. As noted above, there are a wide range of these, with multiples of these per each published work in the learning design literature. For instructional designers, there are best practices for working with clients and subject matter experts and videographers; conducting research; following laws; creating data visualizations and diagrams; designing interactivity; creating learning contents, and so on. These are best described as various processes and procedures (along with accompanying rationales).

To select the relevant heuristics to a project, developer/designers may consider some of the following:

- Have I encountered this context before, and if so, what was it, and what were applied best practices in the prior project (and why)?
- What case research would apply to the learning context, and why? From this research, what makes sense to at least try? What makes sense to avoid?
- Based on the technologies in this instructional design build, what are best practices, and why?
- What heuristics make sense for me based on my own personal preferences and knowledge, skills, and abilities (KSAs)?

Task #5: "Climate for Learning"

Identify an adult learner population and a topic of interest. If you were building a learning ecosystem combining various socio-technical and technological and social media platform capabilities, how would you create the space? What functionalities would you provide? And how would you create a "climate for learning"?

3.3.5 Part 5: Defining Local Realities

Baseline Conceptualizations…and How Humans Learn Baseline theories, models, and frameworks are fundamental ones that inform on who learners are, what their needs and motivations are, and how to meet those learning needs. To these ends, some relevant ones include the following:

- biological bases for human learning
- psychological bases for human learning
- developmental stages of human learning
- social aspects of human learning

It is important to know, too, about how humans learn, how to avoid negative learning (misunderstandings) given the difficulty in writing over old learning (and the difficulty of "forgetting"), and how to enable humans to learn for particular learning objectives. Researchers have explored learners' "naïve reasonings" and how to control for them in the learning designs (Nasr et al. 2009). It is important to understand human limits and the cognitive biases built into the human brain and how to counter those for more accurate learning and more accurate decision-making.

Target Learning Domains In particular subject domains, depending on how the field has evolved, there are accepted and conventional ways of teaching and learning. Such conventions inform learners in the space, and these conventions can be targeted to align new learning with familiar constructs and approaches. There are many culturally informed ways of understanding learning conventions. One example is how "rote memorization" is considered in different cultures for initial learning in the K12 context.

Task #6: Concept(s) to Applied Practice(s)

Idea #1: To practice how a concept may affect a design, consider the practice of the priming of human memory. Priming occurs in non-conscious ways and may be harnessed to enhance human learning or to inhibit it, and it can be used for benefit or for harm.

If your work is to prime learners to be open to learn in a particular context with particular domain contents, how would you set up the priming and then the follow-on learning?

Idea #2: Cognitive Load Theory (by John Sweller, late 1980s) suggests that learners expend cognitive effort to organize structures of knowledge ("schemas") in particular domains. It is thought that germane cognitive loads may be lessened through explanatory depth, worked problems, the provision of structured information, and other efforts.

If your work is to manage learners' cognitive loads to enable them to engage with schema creation with high levels of cognitive ability, what would some of your efforts go? What would you do to create more efficient learning opportunities for learners?

Task #7: Experience-based Heuristics and Best Practices

For this task, think about your experiences building learning resources. Brainstorm a list of your best practices in these applied contexts. Cluster these in groups of similar ideas. Create a structure of heuristics (with sub-heuristics), so that the ideas are all at the right level of generality and specificity. Then list these from most important to least important (in descending order). This can look like an outline, or it can look like a data visualization. Read your list, and consider why these are your go-to heuristics and what they provide for you. Consider exceptions to these heuristics.

If you had more time, more resources, and more of whatever it is that your work would benefit from, how would you change these practical heuristics? Why?

Discussion If one might have assumed that bringing in concepts and practices into a learning design might have simplified the space, it may have in some ways; however, depending on one's comfort level with abstractions, this may have also introduced complexity. In every design, there will be multiple influences and multiple right ways to execute on that design. Every design, no matter how effective and elegant, will involve tradeoffs. The substantive basis for a design for one person or team may make no sense to others. This chapter does not suggest that different teams will necessarily converge on a shared solution to a design challenge. The field is not a settled one with consensus around the necessary theories, models, or frameworks, or the proper heuristics, but rather a disparate field with competing assertions. Rather, the awareness of the research work in the field of human learning and instructional design is to enable the individuals and teams to be better informed when they create (principled) designs and develop the learning contents. The resulting work will not be arbitrary but built with more of a sense of purpose and direction.

Is it possible to get lost in so much theorizing? Certainly, but a healthy application of Occam's razor ("simplest solution is the right one") and practical design and development work may help balance some of the complexity.

3.4 Future Research Directions

Currently, there is already ongoing theorizing and research work on learning and evolving paradigms of how to best depict human learning. At local levels, there is shared work on design advancements, technologies, and development. Interestingly, there is no sense that the field is closing in on the far edges of the learning space, and it looks like there will be many more generations of work to come (Fig. 3.3).

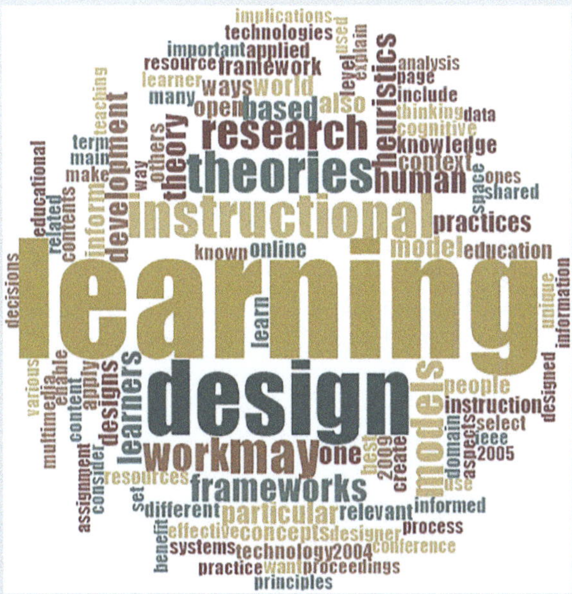

Fig. 3.3 A Word Cloud of Chapter 03: "Thinking about the Learning Design: Theories, Models, Frameworks, and Heuristics"

What-If: A "Principled" Learning Design
You want to build an open-shared learning resource to one of your favorite online communities: research authors.

You begin with a back-of-the-napkin depiction of the learners. You assume that you will attract a range of novices/amateurs on one end and professionals on the other end, and every level of experience in between. You assume that some of those who access the resource will be from the U.S. but also that you will have many from countries from around the world. You assume that not all users of your resource will have English as a primary or first language, but you also know that there are resources online that enable translation to a multitude of languages of the world (expressible using UTF-8).

You brainstorm about the domain. You need to cover the rationale for publishing. You need to cover the publication rules. You want to cover peer review and editorial oversight—two topics that may be very intimidating to new authors. You want to introduce the technology side of things. And you want to those who use your resource to disabuse themselves of the fantasy of large paychecks (or any paychecks in many cases).

You want the resource to be easy to access. You want it to be downloadable in case a user wants to have a copy for later reference because the learning is fairly complex. You decide that you could make a web page with downloadables (that are printable). Or you could do a slideshow that is itself downloadable.

You decide to be personality forward and make a video where you will directly address readers, too.

You want to create a principled design… so that the work aligns in theory, and is informed by relevant models, and fits in with appropriate frameworks. You think that this would require extra effort, but you also think it might simplify your work in other ways. But you also want to be able to get this work done soon, and part of you just wants to go straight to development.

What do you do next?

Decision point #1: Stop or advance. If advance, do you do some research on applicable theories, models, and frameworks? Heuristics?

You go online, and you start searching through a scholar-based web search. You go into subscription databases. You download a number of digital files into a folder. You start to read. All of this is very interesting (you're a wonk), but how do you begin to select what is relevant to you?

What do you do next?

Decision point #2: Stop or advance. If advance, what standards will you use to select theories, models, and frameworks? What will you choose for heuristics?

You believe that cognitive scaffolding would be necessary to ensure that the respective users of the learning resource will be accommodated.

You will align your work with the best accessibility guidelines out there.

You decide that a basic sequence-based work heuristic is necessary.

You decide to follow the dual coding through multimedia learning approach and will record a slideshow with voice. You will handle telepresence with just a still image at the beginning to personalize the slideshow. You decide against a video.

What do you do?

Decision point #3: Stop or advance. If advance, what work process will you use, and why?

You start by brainstorming the full range of contents that you want to cover. You also want to research for new insights that you may not have thought of…

Over time, you evolve a complete learning sequence, with a basic host website and a downloadable slideshow.

You want to make sure that this work aligns with the needs of the target and potential learners. You want to make sure that the cognitive scaffolding makes sense. You want to make sure that the language is appropriate and respectful and warm.

What do you do?...

The What-If Debriefing

This scenario begins with an objective and shows how that objective for the open-shared learning resource already somewhat delimits the possible theories, models, and frameworks…and heuristics…that may apply. It describes some of the hard work of bringing in secondary research and theorizing to the work.

This also shows how a designer/developer is the ultimate decision maker in terms of how the respective theories, models, and frameworks affect the design, including through the assessment process. The thinking in general is that it helps to be aware of the rules, so that when one breaks them, it is purposeful and to particular effects.

3.5 Conclusion

Having more than a passing familiarity with the theories, models, and frameworks related to human learning, in combination with practical heuristics, can achieve benefits for the designer/developer by…

- encouraging exploration and broadening informed design thinking;
- aligning the learning design with what is known about human learning (up to the present);
- expanding research methods in the space;
- encouraging the meeting of high-level standards in the work;
- providing sufficient supports for learners to acquire the learning and to extend their self-efficacy and agency;
- extending the software tool capabilities through sophisticated design and development usages, and
- optimally strengthening the work all around.

The theorizing, research, and analysis contribute aspects to the design and development; they do set normative standards per se, and they are not directive. This chapter posits a foundational level of understandings that would benefit the designs and developments but also suggests that particular research and information may be used to address the unique aspects of the work. There can be too much of a good thing with over-thinking the design and development, too.

3.6 Reviews and Assignments

3.6.1 Main Points Review

- Learning theories are arrived at in a variety of ways, with from-life observations, research, data, data models, theorizing, the imagination, and other sources. Learning theories tend to be macro-level ones, but there are some which are at meso- and micro-scale.
  - Optimally, learning theories should be falsifiable (found to be untrue using empirical research). If they are not falsifiable, they cannot be considered a testable theory.
- Models are representations of systems in the world, comprised of entities and relationships and dynamics.
- Frameworks are structures representing phenomena in the world. In this context, they are conceptualized as structures of different types of teaching and learning, content objects, and others.
- Understanding standards for acceptance of a learning theory, model, or framework would be important because not all concepts are created equal, and not all concepts are sufficiently back-stopped with sufficient research or evidence or reasoning.
- Heuristics are applied work practices for problem-solving and other applications. Some heuristics are "best practices" for a given context.
- For a principled design, it may help to include learning theories that apply generally to most learning contexts…and then specific models and frameworks and heuristics unique to the design.

3.6.2 Critical Thinking Questions

Selecting theories, models, and frameworks

- What standards should be applied to the harnessing of a particular theory or model or framework for a learning design or project? If there are competing concepts, how should those concepts be "adjudicated"? Which should predominate, and why?
- In terms of heuristics (as in common practices and rules of thumb), how should these be selected? What makes sense, and what doesn't make sense?

Cultural influences on theories, models, and frameworks

- What is the role of culture in the acceptance or non-acceptance of certain learning theories/models/frameworks and practices? Why is it risky to misunderstand culture in design and development?

Universals

- In setting a baseline of fundamental ideas that would apply to virtually all learning resources, what would these include, and why? What would you leave off, and why?

Domain-specific thinking

- In terms of the specific target domain that you work in, what are some common accepted theories of learning? Practices of learning? Common heuristics?

Learning research

- What are some risks to over-generalizing from learning research, such as applying adult learning theory to non-adults, or applying a social learning theory to a non-social context? What are some ways to prevent such mis-applications? And why is it important to go back to the "fine print" to understand theories, models, and frameworks?

Project-based concepts

- In terms of specific and unique instructional projects, what are some unique applied concepts and practices, and why? Unique heuristics, and why? (Based these on actual work experiences.)
- Designer/developers apply theories, models, and frameworks in different ways. It is very possible to have very different design outputs and learning resources from a similarly informed set of prompts, directions, and theories. What are some standard ways to understand how people respond to abstractions by creating tangibles?

Live Examples (On the Web)

In online spaces, people are constantly engaging with contents and with each other. In this spirit, there are many updates on the learning theories, models, frameworks, and heuristics mentioned in this chapter.

It is possible to search for a theory and view many uploaded images linked to that particular model. These visualizations may offer fresh insights on the thinking that may not be as easily apparent in text.

Also, there are videos that offer people's "takes" on particular conceptualizations.

There is formal reported research and available datasets.

There are also stories online of people's design heuristics as they relate to the creation of open learning.

These may be explored in depth based on your conceptualizations of interest!

3.7 Assignments

Directions The Assignments are divided into two sections, Basic and Advanced. The Basic section is for those who may not have much instructional design experience or background in the area of creating instructional contents for open sharing. As such, these are set up to familiarize them with the chapter-related knowledge, skills, and abilities. The Advanced section is for those who already have some knowledge of this general space and who may benefit from more challenging work.

In a formal learning context, these assignments would benefit from expert feedback and further applications of the learning contents. In a nonformal or informal learning context, including self-directed learning, these assignments would benefit from both reflection and practice. These assignments are built to be extensible, to have elements added to benefit the learners. They are designed to be assigned selectively and not in full. The setup of this textbook is as a work sequence, and similarly, the assignments may be set up as tasks to be completed by the learner in a sequential way…that takes them through the fairly complete and sequential *open-shared learning design → development → test → revision → launch → post-launch* process.

3.7.1 Basic

Assignment 3.1: Learning Theories for Instructional Design Learning theories offer conceptual frameworks from which learning designs and development may be built. Theories are principles or hypotheses of real-world phenomena and how things work. Some common theory types are categorized under behaviorism, cognitivism, constructivism, transformative, multiple intelligences, and others. Each theory is thought to have implications for practice in that they inform on issues such as on how people learn, what efforts to take to enable human learning, and other details. Select one learning theory, and write a short essay about why you chose that theory, the main facts and assertions of that theory, and what the implications of that theory are for designing and developing online learning (generally) or of a specific real or conceptual digital learning object.

Assignment 3.2: Learning Models for Instructional Design Learning models may also inform instructional designs these represent various systems related to learning. Models are conceptualizations of real-world phenomena. These models may be of human perception, learning, and thinking; they may be about interactions between learners and technical systems; they may be about other related phenomena. Select one learning model, and write a short essay about why you chose that model, the main facts about the model, and how that model informs the design and development of online learning (generally) or of a specific real or conceptual digital learning object.

Assignment 3.3: Learning Frameworks for Instructional Design A framework is a conceptual explanatory structure describing a particular real-world phenomena. A learning framework is a set of standards (or learning outcomes) that inform what a learner should be able to know and do after going through a learning experience. Identify a learning framework to use. In a short essay, write a factual summary of the framework, and analyze what the framework's implications may be for the design and development of online learning (generally) or for a specific real or conceptual digital learning object.

Assignment 3.4: Concepts to Affect the Learning Design. How Should the Concepts Be Selected? And Why Should the Selected Ones Be the Ones Chosen? And Why Should the Ones Left Off Be the Ones Ignored? Consider which learning theories, models, and frameworks may be harnessed for particular instructional designs *and why*. Consider how the selected learning theories, models, and frameworks may apply to particular instructional designs and decision making. Given the universe of learning theories, learning models, and learning frameworks, how will you select the ones to use on a given instructional design project? Why? What are your standards for selecting these contents? How practical do the ideas have to be? How familiar? And if you adopt particular models, how flexible are you to work outside of the concepts as well?

Assignment 3.5: Seeking Constructive Critics For most (all?) creative works related to human learning, it helps to have other sets of eyes constructively critiquing the work. Critics will have different points of view, insights, and expertise. They will notice areas to improve that the original designer/developer may not. What sorts of constructive critiques are most useful to you and why? Where can you practically acquire such supports?

3.7.2 *Advanced*

Assignment 3.6: Measuring the Efficacy of Online Learning In the research literature, there are a number of ways to measure the efficacy of online learning—specifically, how much learners learn and why. Based on the open-shared learning that you are creating, what are some ways to assess the learning that is occurring? Gaps where learning is not occurring? How would you "operationalize" the research? In an open-shared learning context, learning may not be measured to the individual but broadly and en masse. Are there ways to improve the capture of learning metrics for open-shared learning objects and sequences? How so?

Assignment 3.7: Role of Research and Analysis in Instructional Design It is rare for individuals or teams to have complete information at the beginning of an instructional design project. Research involves the seeking of additional new relevant information to inform the work. Design-based research is focused around research to inform a design. Consider the role of research in design projects, to inform the work, to inform the actual learning resource, and in terms of post-launch learning. How helpful is topic/domain-based research? Specific research into learning-type methodologies (game-based learning, problem-based learning, etc.)? What are common sources of information for the research at every stage? What are the standards for understanding the information?

Assignment 3.8: Basic Understandings of How and Why People Learn The basic conceptualizations that designer/developers have about how people learn may inform his/her work. Based on this idea, how do you think people learn? What motivates people to learn? What needs are they meeting? How can these interests be harnessed for effective learning? How can people's long-term memories be written to through deep learning?

Assignment 3.9: Multimedia and Human Learning Multimedia may be designed to align with people's perception, cognition, working memory, and other aspects. What does the empirical research say about how people learn? What sorts of designs are most effective for human learning and why? What are some of the cognitive channels understandings of how people learn?

Assignment 3.10: Concepts to Practices, and Practices to Concepts An extant question in instructional design is just how concepts affect practices, and how to reverse-engineer concepts from observed practices. After all, theories, models, and frameworks are supposed to inform the work. First, in your own work, identify how a particular concept affected a design and development of a learning resource. Second, identify one of your prior created learning resources, and extract what concepts went into that design.

Assignment 3.11: Heuristics and "Best Practices" Plenty of insights may be gained from on-ground work, and many of these heuristics (rules of thumb) and "best practices" may not necessarily be informed by concepts (theories, models, or frameworks). Some practices may arise from observations in the world and abductive reasoning. What are some of your tried-and-true heuristics and "best practices" based on hands-on experiences? When do these apply, and what are exceptions? Also, in terms of observations based on others' work, what heuristics and "best practices" have you gleaned from them?

Keyterms and Definitions

Abductive Reasoning Observing in-world phenomenon and providing the simplest likely explanation through logical inference

Analytics Computational analysis of data

Framework Underlying structure to a phenomenon (defined in this case as a learning resource)
Heuristics An applied problem-solving technique
Model A theorized representation of a meso- or micro- system or dynamic in the world, often comprised of entities and relationships and dynamics
Theory A system of interrelated ideas and/or principles explaining an in-world macro phenomenon (often expressed as principles and concepts)

References

Agrawala M, Phan D, Heiser J, Haymaker J, Klingner J, Hanrahan P, and Tversky B. Designing effective step-by-step assembly instructions. ACM SIGGRAPH '03. 828 – 837, 2003.

Akondy V, and Murthy S, 2015. From novice to expert instructional design: A training based on cognitive apprenticeship model. In 2015 IEEE Seventh International Conference on Technology for Education. 53 – 60.

Anderson LW, Krathwohl DR, Airasian PW, Cruikshank KA, Mayer RE, Pintrich PR, Raths J, and Wittrock MC. A taxonomy for learning, teaching and assessing: A revision of Bloom's Taxonomy of Educational Objectives. Allyn and Bacon. 2001.

Bayer NL. Instructional design: a framework for designing computer-based training programs. In the proceedings of the engineered communication (PICC 91). Oct. 30 – Nov. 1, 1991. IEEE Xplore. https://doi.org/10.1109/IPCC.1991.172789. 1991.

Belcadhi LC, and Ghannouchi SA. An instructional design approach for e-active courses. In TEEM '13. Nov. 14 – 15, 2013. Salamanca, Spain. 119 – 126, 2013.

Brophy S, and Velankar Y. Work in progress: Cataloging instructional design patterns that facilitate generative learning. In the proceedings of the 36th ASEE/IEEE Frontiers in Education Conference. Oct. 28 – 31, 2006. San Diego, California. T2J-3 – T2J-4, 2006.

Chen A., 2018 A neuroscientist explains what tech does to the reading brain: It's not a zero-sum game. *The Verge.* https://www.theverge.com/2018/8/27/17787916/reader-come-home-maryanne-wolf-neuroscience-brain-changes.

Christensen TK, and Osguthorpe RT. How do instructional-design practitioners make instructional-strategy decisions? *Performance Improvement Quarterly* 17: 45 – 65, 2004.

Code JR, MacAllister K, Gress CLZ, and Nesbit JC. Self-regulated learning, motivation and goal theory: Implications for instructional design and e-learning. 1 – 3, 2006.

Conole G. Designing for learning in an open world. In the Learning and Teaching Day, University of Suffolk. Slideshow. 2016.

Crawford C. Non-linear instructional design model: Eternal, synergistic design and development. *British Journal of Educational Technology* 35: 413 – 420, 2004.

Edelson DC. Design research: What we learn when we engage in design. *The Journal of the Learning Sciences* 11: 105 – 121, 2002.

Ellis TJ, Hafner W, and Mitropoulos F. Automating instructional design with eCAD. In the proceedings of the 34th ASEE/IEEE Frontiers in Education Conference. Oct. 20 – 23, 2004. Savannah, Georgia. T1H-1 – T1H-6, 2004.

Gibbons AS. A theory-based alternative for the design of instruction: functional design. In the proceedings of DESRIST '09. May 7 – 8, 2009. Malvern, Pennsylvania. 1 – 5, 2009. http://delivery.acm.org/10.1145/1560000/1555633/a10-gibbons.pdf.

Gibbons AS. What and how do designers design? A theory of design structure. *Tech Trends* 47: 22 – 27, 2003. https://link.springer.com/content/pdf/10.1007%2FBF02763201.pdf.

Hartley R. Active multimodal presentations (AMPs), instructional designs and learner autonomy. In the proceedings of the Fifth IEEE International Conference on Advanced Learning Technologies (ICALT'05): 1 – 2, 2005.

Jin H. A hybrid instructional design model for the combination of motivation theory and constructivism. In the proceedings of 2009 4th International Conference on Computer Science & Education: 1652 – 1656, 2009.

Khalid MFM, and Kameyama W. Instructional-designed strategy for Massive Multiplayer Online M-Learning. *In the proceedings of 2008 IEEE International Symposium on IT in Medicine and Education:* 781 – 785, 2008.

Kolb D. Experiential learning. *Experience as the Source of Learning and Development.* 1984.

Koper R, and Olivier B. Representing the learning design of units of learning. *Educational Technology & Society* 7: 97 – 111, 2004.

Kumar V, Lee S, Manimalar P, Somasundaram T, El-Kadi M, and Sidhan M. Open instructional design. In the proceedings of the International Workshop on Technology for Education (T4E). Aug. 4 – 6, 2009. Bangalore, India. 42 – 48, 2009.

Latiff SA, Ahmad WFW, and Sivapalan S. Design and development process model of converting literature texts into graphical metaphor. In the proceedings of iiWAS 2009 ERPAS. Dec. 14 – 16, 2009. Kuala Lumpur, Malaysia. 613 – 617, 2009.

Mengel SA, Adams WJ, and Hagler MO. Using a hypertext instructional design methodology in engineering education. In the 1997 Frontiers in Education Conference: 648 – 652, 1997.

Merrill MD, Drake L, Lacy MJ, Pratt J, and the ID_2 Research Group. *Educational Technology* 36: 5 – 7, 1966. http://mdavidmerrill.com/Papers/Reclaiming.PDF.

Mishra P, and Koehler MJ. Technological Pedagogical Content Knowledge: A framework for teacher knowledge. *Teachers College Record* 108*:* 1017 – 1054, 2006.

Mayer RE, and Moreno R. A split-attention effect in multimedia learning: Evidence for dual processing systems in working memory. *Journal of Educational Psychology* 90: 312 – 320, 1998.

Moreno R, and Mayer RE. Deriving instructional design principles from multimedia presentations with animations. IEEE: 720 – 725, 1999.

Nasr R, Hall SR, and Garik P. Understanding naïve reasonings in signals and systems: A foundation for designing effective instructional material. IEEE: 720 – 725, 2009.

Nolen SB, and Koretsky MD. Affordances of virtual and physical laboratory projects for instructional design: Impacts on student engagement. *IEEE Transactions on Education:* 1 – 8, 2018.

Pappas C. Top 7 instructional design theories & models for your next eLearning course. *ELearningIndustry.com.* 1 – 7, 2017. https://elearningindustry.com/top-instructional-design-theories-models-next-elearning-course.

Reeves TC, Herrington J, and Oliver R. Design research: A socially responsible approach to instructional technology research in higher education. *Journal of Computing in Higher Education* 16: 96 – 115, 2005.

Reigeluth CM. In search of a better way to organize instruction: The elaboration theory. *Journal of Instructional Development.* 1979.

Reiser R. A history of instructional design and technology: Part II: A history of instructional design. *Educational Technology Research and Development* 49: 57 – 67, 2001.

Rowland G, and DiVasto T. Instructional design and powerful learning. *Performance Improvement Quarterly* 26: 9 – 42, 2013.

Sabin C, and Ahern TC. Instructional design and culturally diverse learners. In the proceedings of 32nd ASEE/IEEE Frontiers in Education Conference. Nov. 6 – 9, 2002. Boston, Massachusetts. 2002. S1C-10 – S1C-14.

Uden L, and Alderson A. Teaching and learning using instructional design. *IEEE:* 67 – 70, 2000.

Utschig TT, Elger DF, and Beyerlein SW. Key issues surrounding faculty development of expertise in instructional design. In the proceedings of the 35th ASEE/IEEE Frontiers in Education Conference. Oct. 19 – 22, 2005. Indianapolis, Indiana. T3F-18 – T3F-23, 2005.

Visscher-Voerman I, and Gustafson KL. Paradigms in the theory and practice of education and training design. *Educational Technology Research & Design (ETR&D)* 52: 69 – 89, 2004.

Voulgari I, and Sampson DG. Applying lessons learnt from Massively Multiplayer Online Games (MMOGs) to Massive Open Online Courses (MOOCs). In the proceedings of the 2014 IEEE 14th International Conference on Advanced Learning Technologies. 14 – 15, 2014.

Wu P. A game programming instructional design model. In the proceedings of the4 CCSC Northeastern Conference. 57 – 67, 2014.

Zaman HB, Mukti NA, Sembok TMT, and Ahmad A. Indigenous multimedia content development for next generation smart schools: A cognitive instructional design approach. In the proceedings of the Fifth IEEE International Conference on Advanced Learning Technologies (ICALT'05). 1 – 2, 2005.

Additional Reading Section

Bruner J. *The Process of Education: A Landmark in Educational Theory.* Cambridge, Massachusetts: Harvard University Press. 1960, 1977.

Clark RC, and Mayer RE. *E-Learning and the Science of Instruction: Proven Guidelines for Consumers and Designers of Multimedia Thinking.* Hoboken, New Jersey: John Wiley & Sons. 2016.

Csikszentmihalyi M. *Flow: The Psychology of Optimal Experience.* New York: HarperPerennial. 1990.

Lave J, and Wenger E. *Situated Learning: Legitimate Peripheral Participation.* Cambridge, United Kingdom: Cambridge University Press. 1991.

Ozmon HA, and Craver SM. *Philosophical Foundations of Education.* 7th Ed. Upper Saddle River, New Jersey: Merrill Prentice Hall. 2003, 1999, 1995, 1986, 1981, 1976.

Payne CR. *Information Technology and Constructivism in Higher Education: Progressive Learning Frameworks.* Hershey, Pennsylvania: Information Science Reference, IGI Global. 2009.

Chapter 4
"Street Legal" Openly Shared Learning

Abstract Creating open-shared learning resources for global use means that the works have the potential to be high profile and widely accessed. This means that it is especially important to get the legal and ethical aspects right. Designer/developers need to be aware of all the potentially relevant laws right and to adhere to them, in both the letter of the laws and the spirit. The ethical implications should be recognized as well. Following the law serves to control for designer/developer risk, communicates respect to the other stakeholders in the publishing and learning spaces, "future proofs" the learning resources, encourages broader usage of the resource around the world, and ultimately benefits the open sharing work. Being aware of the legal requirements early on saves on the overall amount of work needed to ensure that the legal standards are sufficiently met. Legal considerations are present at every stage of the design and development and launch work. This chapter has at its center the idea that whatever is created to benefit people in open learning should not also cause harm to anyone. This chapter addresses legal concerns (including controlled information, intellectual property, (IP) software, accessibility, media law, data handling, ethical research, and others). It also highlights the challenges with global publishing and distribution, given the patchwork of laws in different nation-states and the risks therein.

Keywords Controlled information · Intellectual property · Creative commons licensure · Accessibility · Universal design · Disability laws · Accommodations · Universal design for learning · Media law · Privacy protections · Defamation · Libel · Trespass · Data handling · Ethical research · Human subjects research review

> So uncritically do we accept the idea of property in culture that we don't even question when the control of that property removes our ability, as a people, to develop our culture democratically.
>
> —Lawrence Lessig in *Free Culture: How Big Media Uses Technology and the Law to Lock Down Culture and Control Creativity* (2016, Lulu Press, Inc.)

> Two things awe me most, the starry sky above me and the moral law within me.
>
> —Immanual Kant (1724–1804)

S. Hai-Jew, *Designing Instruction For Open Sharing*,
https://doi.org/10.1007/978-3-030-02713-1_4

The safety of the people shall be the highest law.
—Marcus Tullius Cicero (106 BC–43 BC)

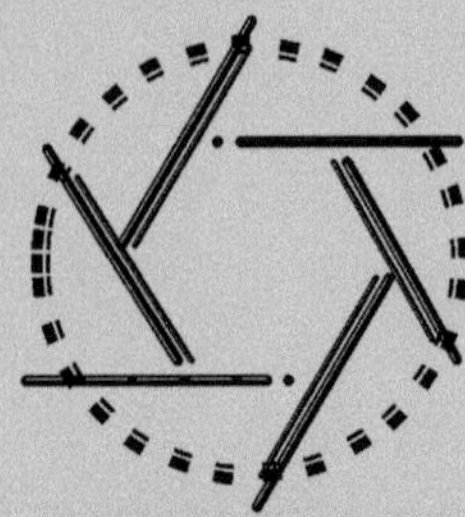

Opening Scenario

Opening Scenario: Checking the Boxes for Legal Requirements?

Those who would created open-shared learning objects, generally speaking, may be willing to do the work without pay in some instances, but most will not consciously want to incur further risks or unexpected costs once they have released the object into the wild. It may also be a safe assertion to suggest that most instructional designers and developers agree with the concept of *primum non nocere* ("first, to do no harm" in Latin). What that means in the development of open-shared learning objects is that the designer/developer will not misrepresent information, misuse others' information, make recordings of people without their knowledge or permission for the learning object, put a work into the world that is not accessible, and so on.

What is important to consider so that any sharing is done in a street legal way?

Some Early Questions to Consider

Based on your experiences designing instruction, you have developed a sense of the laws that you have to abide by. What are the most important laws that you keep top-of-mind in your professional work?

What are ways to approach a project that encode the values and ethics of the profession in your work processes?

What are ways to ensure that legal and other standards are met and that corners are not cut even in a context of unfunded learning content development?

Have you heard of alpha tests? Beta tests? What is the difference between these?

Learning Objectives

Learners will …

Legal Requirements for Distributed Open-Shared Learning Objects

- Review the relevant legal requirements related to the open sharing of learning, including the following: controlled information, intellectual property (creative works, trademarks (TM) and registered marks (R), rights releases through licensure, and others); software acquisition; accessibility require-

ments; media law applied to broadcast and publications (including privacy rights, defamation, libel, and others); legal and ethical research (including human subjects research review and oversight), and so on
- Consider some of the implications of the respective laws conceptually and in actual work practice
  - In controlled information
  - In intellectual property (and copyright)
  - In pirated software
  - In accessibility requirements
  - In media law
  - In privacy protections
  - In data protections
  - In use of data
  - In the capture and use of data of children and youth
  - In legal and ethical research
- Create a checklist of legal requirements (including "showstoppers") that must be met before a project may be released to the public and which legal issues may be most problematic in the local work context (and why)
- Consider some practical ways to efficiently address the legal requirements by building in certain oversight, training, practices, and practical work situations
- Consider some of the most common legal offenses in the open-shared digital learning objects, courses, and sequences

Legal Requirements for Going Global

- Conduct some research about legal requirements for publishing in particular regions (like the European Union) and particular countries.
- Explore differing sense of privacy protections for people, and others.

Ethical Guidelines for Distributed Open-Shared Learning Objects

- Review the ethics and values that may affect the design and development of open-shared learning (through and beyond extant laws and policies)

4.1 Introduction

Online publishing is not a legal-free zone, not even when the sharer is motivated by good intentions and generosity.

For designer/developers, they need to closely adhere to relevant laws, so whatever they share in public …

- does not release sensitive information into the public space
- has clear content provenance (sourcing, origins), with everything legally acquired (without fraud, without deception, without duress)
- shares only accurate information and with sufficient nuance
- does not plagiarize others' works

- does not use anything that belongs to others (not without a legal release)
- is not built on pirated software
- is accessible and offers multiple ways to access and engage the contents
- does not defame any individual or entity
- does not contravene others' privacy protections, and does not trespass on others' private spaces, and
- does not use data from illegal or unethical research.

Close adherence to laws will mitigate risks to the designer/developers; convey respect to other stakeholders in the publishing and learning spaces; protect the longevity of the learning resources; encourage broader usage across a range of locales, and benefit the work ultimately. A car that is "street legal" is one that meets all legal requirements for use on the roads, and an open-shared learning resource that is "street legal" is one that is ready to traverse the information highways at full speed. Making sure that the work is legally achieved is Step 4 in the work sequence (Fig. 4.1).

This chapter highlights some of the legal requirements relevant to open-shared learning objects and shows how the legal concerns affect every stage of the work. The requirements include protected or controlled data, intellectual property, accessibility, media laws affecting publications and broadcast, data handling, legal and ethical research, and others. This work points to some regional differences in different countries and jurisdictions. This work also highlights some of the ethical consideration behind some of the laws.

Disclaimer This chapter and this book is informational only and is not advisement. The author is not a lawyer. These understandings here come from years in the fields of instructional design, publishing, and mass communications instruction (as a faculty member). The framing of this will be more on applied practice than on the laws themselves. For actual legal questions, please consult your legal counsel.

4.2 Review of the Literature

If one were to describe the main areas of legal considerations that arise around the creation of open-shared learning resources, one can point to the following: (intellectual) property rights (who owns what creative content and what can they legally do with it; what software can be legally used, etc.), accessibility requirements for online learning, people's privacy protections, people's reputational protections against defamation (for people depicted in public space), the conduct of ethical research, and the conduct of ethical data handling. The creation of open-shared learning resources involves conducting research, creating learning contents, and publishing those out to the broad public. In the content creation, they will be representing truth about individuals and entities, and the target subject matter domains. At every step of this work, there are legal considerations. (More on this follows in Table 4.1.)

Controlled Information "Controlled information" refers to identified information that is considered relevant to national security and trade protections, that, if shared with foreign nationals, may result in serious harm to the country. Such information

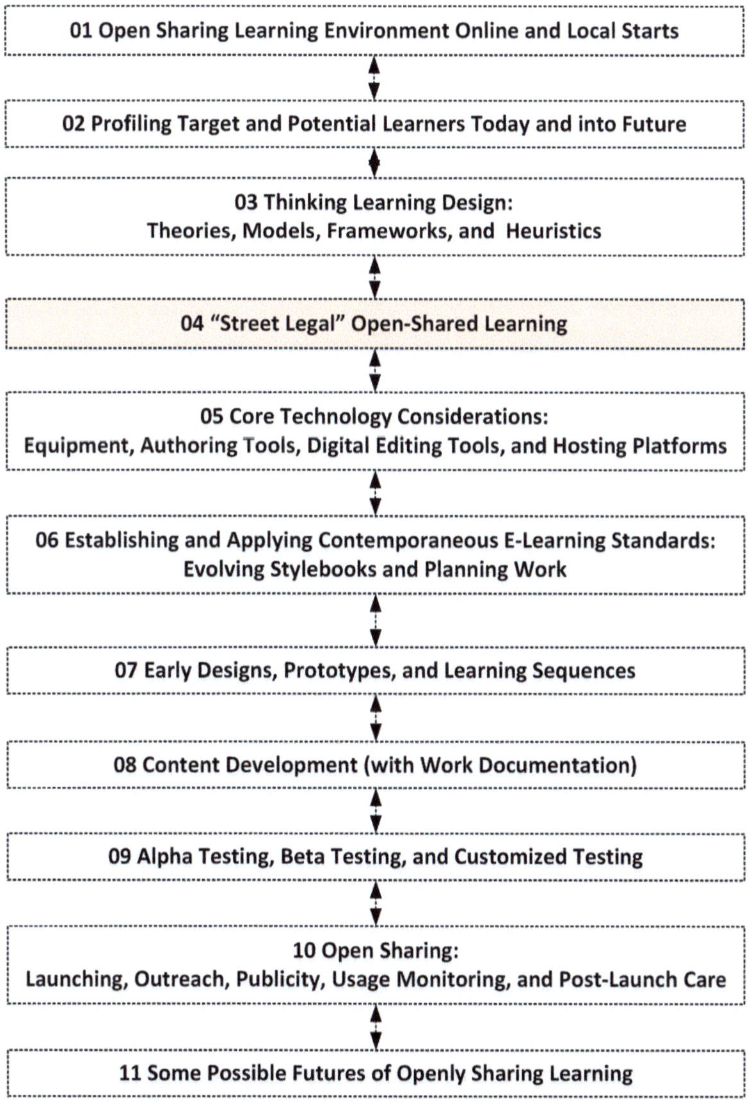

Fig. 4.1 Step 4 in the open-shared learning resource development sequence

is under "export controls" and are forbidden from being shared abroad or domestically with a foreign national.

Beyond such information, there may be a range of sensitive information that a person may have access to—such as EXIF (exchangeable image format) metadata riding on imagery—that may cause harm if released. There may be information that belongs to a workplace and not the individual. Just because an individual has access to information and data does not mean that he or she may use it for open-shared learning resources.

Table 4.1 A checklist for assessing legality

Topical area	Question	Passes	Fails
Controlled information	Is the learning resource free of any sensitive controlled information (or even side references to such information) that may cause harm to national security and/or harm to trade?		
Intellectual property	Is there clear provenance for all contents (of all modalities) in the learning resource?		
	If copyright releases were acquired for some of the contents, did the signer of the releases have legal standing (as the actual copyright holder) to release the respective works?		
	Have all research sources been cited accurately (to avoid plagiarism)?		
	Have all trademarks and registered trademark marks been properly labeled?™® (ctrl + alt + t) and (ctrl + alt + r)		
	Has self-plagiarism been avoided?		
	Is the design wholly original (or does any part of the design emulate others' designs?)?		
	If works released to the public through various forms of licensure have been used, has the designer/developer or team properly followed through on the requirements?		
Software acquisition	Are there legally acquired licenses on all the commercial proprietary software used? (Has pirated software been wholly avoided? Has questionable freeware been wholly avoided?)		
	Does the acquired software meet the requisite accessibility requirements?		
Accessibility	Are there multiple means of representation, multiple means of action and expression, and multiple means of engagement for the learning? (per universal design standards)		
	Do all audio and video files come with closed captioning and/or transcription?		
	Are the written contents conveyed in clear and simple English (or the base language)?		
	Do all images have sufficient alternative "alt" text (that are the informational equivalencies of the visual)?		
	Is information not represented by color alone (but in text and numbers and other representations)?		
	Is textual information placed in a hierarchy and tagged or styled based on the textual roles (header text, subheader text, body text, and so on)?		
	Do all interactive objects, applications, and websites have keyboard access (without requiring a mouse)? (Assistive devices use the keyboard shortcuts to input commands into computers and enable a range of different input devices using eye blinks, breaths of air, and other ways to interact.)		
	Are all downloadable files based on universal file types? And are they named in informationally informative ways?		
	In the uses of color, are the colors sufficiently high-contrast? And are the colors avoidant of common color blindness challenges (with blue and yellow, red and green)?		
	Are HTML data tables properly coded to enable accurate screen reader navigation through the cells (with clear column and row headers for each cell)?		

(continued)

Table 4.1 (continued)

Topical area	Question	Passes	Fails
	Do users of videos and simulations have the sufficient controls to start, stop, pause, speed up, slow down, the experience?		
	Do videos and games and simulations avoid any strobe effects or sequences (which may trigger epileptic seizures)?		
	If live events are part of the learning, are accessibility accommodations included [including live notetaking and/or live American Sign Language (ASL) translation]?		
Media law	Have all who contributed their likeness (image, voice) and talent to the project signed media releases? (Have they been properly acknowledged and compensated, where relevant?)		
	Have all media been legally acquired (including b-roll)? Have recordings been done in public spaces where individuals do not have a reasonable expectation of privacy?		
	Have individual and entity reputations been protected against the distribution or false defamatory information through libel (in publication) or against slander (in broadcast)?		
Legal and ethical research	Have all formal releases been acquired for the use of research data?		
	Did the researchers acquire proper permissions from the proper oversight groups for the particular research? (For example, if the research involved human subjects, did the research go through the Institutional Review Board or an equivalent body?		
	Is the data handled appropriately?		
	Is personally identifiable information (PII) protected?		
	If information is collected about protected groups, like children, is that information handled appropriately?		

Provenance of Information and Data and IP Rights Where digital contents originate may be unclear or even obfuscated online. A lot of contents are shared online through various types of licensure releases, but sometimes, people are releasing contents that they do not actually own. To find the original owner of an image, for example, designer/developers may access reverse image search tools to find the oldest postings of an image on the Web and Internet … visit those websites … and contact them to try to track down ownership. Sometimes, tracking ownership can take days to weeks. In some cases, those who run particular websites may choose not to respond. Having rights released to contents by anyone other than the copyright holder is not particularly helpful.

One helpful aspect of intellectual property (IP) regimes and copyright laws is that there are some common treaties (Berne Convention) and shared practices around the world. One author writes:

> However copyright law which takes definition from international conventions and is similar in most countries provides that you cannot reproduce or communicate copyright material (literary, dramatic, musical and artistic works, films and sound recordings) without the permission of the copyright owner subject to exceptions for fair use/dealing, private use and educational use. Private use and educational use exceptions are usually subject to the payment of a statutory levey, royalty or license fee (Fitzgerald 2005, p. 1).

Another aspect of "provenance" or "origin" that is relevant involves the context in which an image, audio, video, or other information was captured. Without that data, it is hard to accurately represent the contents being depicted. Many of the sharers of such contents on social media platforms may not themselves have that information (unless they took assiduous notes or have a perfect memory). If the digital contents are being used in a somewhat superficial way where the original provenance is not necessary, then this may be a lesser issue.

One researcher suggests making open educational resources (OERs) using one's own resources is simpler than "(1) incorporating materials taken from other sources, or (2) incorporating materials that contain photographs of private individuals who have not given you their consent" (Bissell 2009, pp. 98–99). The author notes that how to proceed varies "from country to country" … with laws varying "substantially" (pp. 98–99).

Factuality On the Web and Internet are all sorts of news stories professing to be objective news instead of opinion. Likewise, there are all sorts of fraudulent claims about what is being depicted or how factual an assertion may be. For learning objects and resources to be effective, they need to be unassailably accurate, so designer/developers need to apply high standards for validating information.

Originality In terms of competitive advantage, one of the most important aspects of a learning resource has to be its originality—in shared information, in design, in development and execution, in presentation, in look-and-feel, in socio-technical implementation, and other factors. One basic way to start working towards building this originality is to use new research data that is available nowhere else. Arriving at this data in an ethical way is important, by adhering to the professional standards for the conduct of primary research. If that is too much effort (and it often is), then the content creators may use secondary research published by others but cite their sources and package the learning in a refreshing way. If they are acting on derived inspirations from others' works, that may be worth a mention. There are many technological ways to identify influences to a work, and even nuanced influences may be technologically discoverable. Ideally, designer/developers would apply high standards to their own work, and they would be rigorous in citing others' works when those are used.

Accessibility Accessibility has long been the law of the land in the U.S. and around the world, as parts of human rights and civil rights impetuses. Section 504 of the U.S.'s Rehabilitation Act of 1973 protects the civil rights of learners with disabilities, and Section 508 of the same act requires that information and communication technology (ICT) be accessible to persons with disabilities, and a "refresh" in 2017 updated the standards and guidelines to "harmonize with international voluntary consensus standards" ("Section 508 of the Rehabilitation Act," 2018).

Web Content Accessibility Guidelines (WCAG) are international web standards by the World Wide Web Consortium (W3C), with v. 1 published in 1999 and v. 2 in 2008. In this standard, there are four principles of accessibility design: that contents be "perceivable," technologies "operable" and "understandable," and "robust" with current assistive technologies. "Perceivable" contents are those that are versioned in multiple ways. For example, non-text contents should have text alternatives that "can be changed into forms people need, such as large print, Braille, speech, symbols or simpler language," for example (Poore-Pariseau 2010, p. 150). "Operable" contents provide a clear sense of orientation and navigation for users, and they enable "all functionality" from a keyboard. "Understandable" contents are well written so the contents are "understandable," and web pages function in predictable ways. "Robust" contents "maximize compatibility with current and future user agents, including assistive technologies" (Poore-Pariseau 2010, p. 150).

The universal design approach emphasizes three main principles: "provide multiple means of representation," "multiple means of action and expression," and "multiple means of engagement (The three principles of UDL 2014) ." Various combinations of these approaches may be applied to create accessible learning. Universal design is commonly applied to ensure that higher education is as accessible as possible (Burgstahler 2015).

Online accessibility has been described as involving "the ability to use online content without vision, without hearing, without pointing or manipulation, and without speech by persons with cognitive limitations, with language disabilities, with low vision and limited or no hearing, and with alternative languages (Vanderheiden, Harkins, and Barnicle as quoted by Schwartz 2004, p. 1, as cited in Poore-Pariseau 2010, p. 148)

The highest level of web accessibility is AAA, with the standard level sufficient for Section 508 as AA, and then a substandard A level. At the code level, there are different approaches that may be used to create accessibility, with as with hierarchical markup tags, data table summaries and code span labels (for columns and rows), the uses of buttons for actions like submittal and navigation (via clicking) and links to navigate (to "divs"/divisions and "spans"/span elements), with information built into button labels, semantically labeled icons, semantically named downloadable files, and other practices. Sufficient color contrast ratios are at the AA level at 4.1:1 and the AAA level at 7.02:1 on a monitor or smalls screen. (There are automated tools that may be added on to browsers to test for contrast failures, and with hexadecimal color code suggestions to pass the contrast requirement.) In forms, labels and blanks have to be clearly labeled and defined. Form fields should be structured in a consistent way so that fields are seeable for those with peripheral vision challenges … as well as for those with core vision challenges. For touchscreen accesses, touch areas have to be of sufficient finger size targets (45–57 pixels for an adult finger size). Images require informative alt text. The speed of portrayed contents should be controllable by users. Accessibility testing for applications and websites should be run on both a laptop or desktop computer and mobile devices because they will present differently.

In the learning space, some argue that it should be sufficient to offer alternative equivalent learning experiences and propose an approach to create these through a system they call Transformation, Augmentation and Substitution Service (TASS) (Gkatzidou and Pearson 2009b). This approach goes against predominant thinking currently that the original learning resource should be as accessible as possible based on universal design approaches (design for all).

In the literature and in applied technologies, there are various tools to assess for accessibility ("a11y," an ICT-based referent to "accessibility" with the "a" and the "y" bookending the 11 letters in between for a clever abbreviation) and then to enable it. Authors share tested methods to enable accessibility, such as for vodcasts, given the technologies of the day; the accommodations are not of one dimension but include design, pedagogical, technical adaptations, and accessibility enhancements (Gkatzidou and Pearson 2009b, p. 298). There are advances in terms of creating highly targeted devices, such as to help persons with aphasia self-express (Al Mahmud et al. 2010).

Reputational Protections When going public with information depicting others, it is important to fully verify the information to be accurate, and doubly so if the information is potentially defamatory. There are strict anti-libel and anti-slander laws in place through which people may seek damages. There are also privacy protections against the broadcasting of private information of individuals who are non-public figures.

Finally, there is the question of whether it would make sense to break the rules to achieve "legal ends" ultimately. For example, would it be right to use unethical research to acquire data to create a learning resource that may benefit learners? Or would it be fair to trespass into others' privacy in order to capture imagery to use in a learning resource? The means-ends argument is sometimes used to suggest that the ends justify the means (if the ends are sufficiently critical), and the counterview is that the means and the ends have to be aligned and legal and justified. In general, the ends of an open-shared learning resource do not justify illegal or unethical means.

4.3 "Street Legal" Open-Shared Learning

There are a range of laws and requirements for the design, creation, and deployment of learning resources. What do these mean in actual practice?

Legal Requirements for Distributed Open-Shared Learning Objects A brief review follows.

Controlled Information In terms of controlled information, which are clearly indicated as so, these should never been purposefully or unintentionally shared in learning resources. People are on a constant trawl for sensitive information online, and every so often, they will make direct requests for sensitive data. Sensitive information is controlled in work places, and most maintain some surveillance over accesses. There is no logical reason to share controlled information with the broad public.

Intellectual Property Intellectual property involves a wide range of restrictions to the usage of contents created by others except for when they are in the public domain or legally released through open sharing licensure. Just finding a resource online with a generous sharing license does not mean that the object belongs to whomever released the image, that the image has relevance provenance, that the image is usable, or that the current project's restrictions enable following through on the licensure requirements. There is work to be done once a resource has been found, and the designer/developer needs to apply due diligence to the work.

Those from academia may assume that "fair use" standards may apply to an educational context, but the sharing of learning resources in an open context does not meet the requirement of these materials being used in educational institutions for educational purposes (Stim 2018). The safer approaches are to use the more restrictive commercial standards and to not assume exemptions to copyright. It does not take a lot of effort to reach out to copyright holders with boilerplate requests for copyright releases for sufficient cover.

"Safe harbors" do not carry the weight of law but are popular stories of ways to just skirt copyright laws with certain careful practices. One example of a "safe harbor" is to try to find owners of "orphaned works" online before using it without any permission or copyright release.

It would be wrong to assume forgiveness in the space given that copyright laws serve a forcing function by forcing copyright holders to defend their trademarks and brands in court at even small signs of possible infringement or else risk dilution of their brands.

Accessibility In the accessibility space, accessible online contents are par for the course, and these should be built into all learning resources that are broadly shared. One of the main challenges is that accessibility mitigations may be built into particular digital files or platforms, but these may disappear when contents are transcoded or moved.

Media Laws In general, media laws inform on how data may be collected from people and where and the importance of verifying the factuality of information before publishing, particularly as it impacts reputation. The lifeblood of media is facts, and this extends to how imagery and video can be edited (with no factual changes but only jumping colors and cropping for production in still images, and applying highlights or slowing the video to showcase different aspects of video).

Legal and Ethical Research In the research space are a complex mix of laws aimed at ensuring that conducted research is relevant and controlled against potential harms. The complexities of this go well beyond the purview of this chapter.

These can seem very overwhelming because of their complexities and nuances. To avoid being overwhelmed, it helps to translate these into regular practices that may be infused in daily work.

A Checklist of Legal Requirements If legal requirements are requisite (and they are), then breaking the laws would be "showstoppers". In Table 4.1, there is a checklist of requirements that should be met before a work goes live. Checklists can encourage thoroughness in a way that other efforts may miss (Gawande 2009). A few of the factors may be negotiable, but on the whole, these are of sufficient importance to address. No sensitive information should ever be leaked in a learning resource. No intellectual property rights should be contravened. No questionable research should be included in a learning resource. These are just some of the showstoppers. This checklist is conceptualized as a modular one, so it is possible to add to it as well as take away from it as needed.

So what are some practical ways to build "street legal" learning resources? One way is to integrate these awareness's and practices in the regular work at each phase. As a reminder, Fig. 4.2 shows some of the considerations at each stage. (A text version of the applied questions is available in the Appendix.)

Common Legal Shortcomings What are some of the most common legal shortcomings of shared learning resources? See the sidebar box.

Assessing Legality of a Learning Resource

In a perusal of the open-shared learning resources on the Web and Internet, what are some of the most common legal liabilities?

From perusals conducted over a number of years, the most common challenges are two-fold. Foremost, the designer/developers do not clearly source their contents. They make assertions without evidentiary supports, and fact-checking does not often seem to be a priority. Their learning resources lack source citations.

The second most common challenge is that most do not have accessibility accommodations. In a few cases, shared videos may come with auto-voice-to-text closed captioning, but that feature is more a result of the video hosting platform.

It is unclear whether the lack of due diligence is from lack of awareness or lack of interest or both, but many learning objects seem to be snippets derived from textbooks or cobbled open-shared contents from the Social Web.

Within the commercial training space and within academia (such as in massive open online courses), the contents tend to be much better vetted for informational value and intellectual property rights, and these are also often much stronger in terms of accessibility accommodations.

Fig. 4.2 Some legal and ethical considerations in the open-shared learning resources' design-development—launch sequence

Task #1: Protected Data
Go online to find out what different governments consider "protected" or "sensitive" information … by law. Review how information is controlled and restricted in various countries, legally, technologically, and in other ways.

Task #2: Intellectual Property
Media releases come in a range of boilerplates, and they enable individuals to release digital contents that they've created … or digital recordings that they participated in … and others. Capture a dozen media releases available online. Read these. Assess them for effectiveness. Pay attention to how these contractual releases define the rights being signed over and the limitations to the usage of the digital contents.

Task #3: Creative Commons Licensure

Lawrence Lessig's Creative Commons licensure setup enables people to create original contents and then release these in an unretractable way. The licenses come in three "layers" (legal code, human readable form, and machine readable form). At the time of publication, there were six license types, seven if you count the CC0 (public domain) release. The six main licenses have different requirements of the user of the copyrighted contents (https://creativecommons.org/licenses/):

"Attribution" or crediting of the original creator (s) (in the CC BY license);

"Attribution-ShareAlike" (CC BY-SA), so users have to apply the same licensure to whatever they create in a derived way using the shared resource;

"Attribution-NoDerivs" (CC BY-ND), so users can use the work if they credit the original creator (s) but cannot create derived works from this created work;

"Attribution-NonCommercial" (CC BY-NC), so users can use the work if they credit the original creator (s) but cannot use the work in any commercial endeavor;

"Attribution-NonCommercial-ShareAlike" (CC BY-NC-SA), which allows users to "remix, tweak, and build" on the creative work as long as they credit the original creator (s) and share the content with a similar license; (and)

"Attribution-NonCommercial-NoDerivs" (CC BY-NC-ND), which requires users to cite the original creator (s) and refrain from using the created contents in any commercial application and does not allow derived works.

Each ensuing level of the licensure has more restrictions. The most open release is the CC0 or a full release into the public domain … forever.

Review these different options of licensure, and decide which one makes the most sense for the learning resources that you have created or want to create. Why would this particular licensure make the best sense for you?

Or do you prefer a whole other approach? If so, what, and why?

Task #4: Accessibility

Creating accessible online learning requires all sorts of work: closed captioning (which may be done in an automated way), digital file content types, proper coding of HTML data tables, avoiding the uses of color alone to convey information, and other close-in work.

One of the more difficult aspects to creating accessible learning is to apply alternate text (alt-text) to informational imagery. Informational imagery may include visuals like data visualizations, diagrams, drawings, maps, network graphs, photos, and others. The idea is that the alt text has to be informationally equivalent to the visual. By definition, visuals are multidimensional and complex. The space for alt text is limited, and capturing the informational heart of a visual can be challenging.

To get a sense of how difficult this work may be, select a dozen images related to the domain field that you work in. Write 1–2 sentences per visual to convey the crucial information from the visual. (Strive to not give away the learning but help the learner along in his or her learning with your descriptive text. You want learners top work a little to achieve the necessary learning.)

[Note: With advances in machine vision, computers can recognize focal objects in an image. They can recognize public figures. They can recognize the depicted sentiment in the image. Artificial intelligence and machine learning applications are continuing to make strides in this area. That said, the state of the art of automated text descriptions of images—such as through automated tagging—is still very limited.]

Task #5: Privacy Protections

In the current age, some suggest that "privacy" is a no longer possible. With the wide collection of data about people—thousands of datapoints per individual based on their consumer information—and powerful machine learning to find patterns that people may not have even suspected, people's habits and tendencies are being laid bare. Database research has found that people can be re-identified (from anonymized datasets) to a person with only a few datapoints. With a small amount of smart phone locational data, people's locations may be predicted a year from the present moment with about 80% accuracy. Facial recognition applications are common over social networking sites. Much personal information is available on the Deep Web, often for free, and much more intrusively personal information for a nominal sum. In this environment, it becomes much harder to finesse working with human talent and data and digital contents while protecting privacy.

Voice talent and radio personalities use pseudonyms as a matter of course, and many actors use stage names to protect their personal lives. However, the use of their image is already a "tell," and can re-identify them to their actual names. From there, most of the relevant data to their lives is accessible with a few more clicks.

Given the context, how can designer/developers consider the privacy rights of themselves, their team members, their subject matter experts, and their talent? How much effort should they expend in protecting personal data?

If they work with children, whose persons and data require even higher levels of privacy protections, what are some best practices?

Task #6: Media Laws

Media laws—as discussed earlier—cover a range of issues in telecommunications, broadcasting, advertising, information technology, and others. These regulations cover the high brow and the low brow. These address issues of legal ways to report (including rules on privacy rights, newsworthiness, public vs. private figures), protections of individuals against defamation (by libel or slander), when recordings may be made of others (one-party consent, two-party consent, and others), and other issues. First Amendment rights are a critical part of informing media laws, and in the U.S., government has little power in terms of prior restraint or censorship.

Conduct a light review of media laws and how they may affect your building and distribution of an open-shared learning resource.

4.3.1 Legal Requirements for Going Global

Publishing to the world, through the affordances of the Web and Internet, not only results in a potentially large user base but may expose the learning resources to wide-scale perusal and additional requirements. Recently, in the European Union, a new law known as the General Data Protection Regulation (GDPR) went into effect that extends users' privacy rights on websites and that extends user control over their own personal data held by service providers. Users must be notified by the service providers of what exactly is done with their personal information and whether it will be used for profiling.

> The law protects individuals in the 28 member countries of the European Union, even if the data is processed elsewhere. That means GDPR will apply to publishers like WIRED; banks; universities; much of the Fortune 500; the alphabet soup of ad-tech companies that track you across the web, devices, and apps; and Silicon Valley tech giants. (Tiku 2018)

Another idea that arose in Europe and has gained traction is the concept of the "right to be forgotten," also known as "the right to silence on past events in life that are no longer occurring"). Legally, this is a right for Europeans to request that their personal past online information be removed from the Web and Internet.

Beyond legal requirements, there are cultural ones, with sensitivities that may discourage uptake of particular learning resources.

Task #7: Legal and Ethical Research

For those who have conducted research before, they know that there are federal agencies that are responsible for ensuring that all research conducted by U.S. scientists meet stringent guidelines. There are ethical regimes informed by history and theorizing, and the regimes are backed up by federal laws.

All human participants in human subjects research have protections for their well-being. There are rules for their informed consent, and rules against their manipulation (such as by larger incentives for their research participation). For those engaged in animal science research, there are numerous regulations for the protection of animals. There are laws stipulating the handling of dangerous substances. In every circumstance, clear research designs are necessary.

Then, too, there are laws related to the proper and secure handling of research data and limitations on their use and guidance on their maintenance for a particular period of time.

In your subject area, download a few recent published research works, and read for the underlying laws behind the research. Analyze the resulting work to see how the research design, methodology, data reporting, and other aspects were possibly influenced by the regulations and oversight and professional practices. Then, spend some time to explore the actual letters of the law for the professional subject domain.

Task #8: Applicable Laws in other Locales

Different regions evolve in different directions based on their populations, their leadership, their respective histories, and other factors.

Based on the different regions of the world—Africa, East Asia and Pacific, Europe and Central Asia, Latin America and the Caribbean, the Middle East and North Africa, and South Asia (as defined by the World Bank)—identify different approaches to some of the laws regarding intellectual property, accessibility, and media law.

Zooming in, identify a few target countries of interest within these regions, and see how their approaches may be different as well regarding IP, accessibility, and media law.

Where does the U.S. stand in comparison to some of these other countries? Why do you think the U.S. differs in the ways that it does?

Ethical Guidelines for Distributed Open-Shared Learning Objects and Resources Beyond the laws and policies, particular ethics of a domain and the ethics of contributing team members may affect the design and development of open-shared learning resources. These are extra-legal, but they may still be deeply compelling and may affect critical aspects of the designed learning resources.

Applying ethical reasoning to open-shared learning resources requires some assumptions. One is that learning resources released to a global environment will have real-world impacts not only in the present but potentially into the future. Some of these impacts may be anticipated—as direct first order effects, second order effects, and so on, but it is likely that not all potential effects may be anticipated (whether direct or indirect), and not all potentially negative effects may be potentially mitigated. Anticipating harm may require an ability to imagine abuses in the usage of learning resources. Building open-shared learning resources ethically is not costless, and it will require competence, investments, and designer/developer control.

So to generally recap, what are some of the most important moral principles that guide open-shared learning?

1. Consider the well-being of learners. First, do no harm. Consider learners' needs foremost, and take a beneficent approach. Avoid stereotyping learners (to their

detriment), and be as inclusive as possible of learners (through both accessibility and usability). Avoid any manipulation of learners, such as through overt or subliminal messaging. Keep motives pure. Be as transparent as possible. Be responsible for what is released in the public space. Do not collect user data unless there is a research reason to do so, and this is done ethically and soundly and user identities are protected (and there are no identity leaks and no data leaks).

2. Be law-abiding. Adhere to (intellectual property, media, and other relevant) laws, so that others' rights (to privacy, to trespass, to public reputation, to dignity, to creative works, to inventions, to data, to copyright, to credit for original works, and others) are not infringed upon. Acquire permissions appropriately. Cite sources, and give credit where it is due. Avoid misuses of others' resources—whether those of work places or others' data or others' ideas.
3. Get the facts right. Ensure that all information shared is as accurate as possible. Control for misunderstandings and negative learning. Control for false inferences. Control for naïve learning from novices and amateurs. Do not create implied relationships or endorsements where there is none. Avoid hidden motives. Get as close to sources as possible, and do not lead expert sources, and do not speak for others. Let others' voices come through.
4. Treat team members with respect. If there are colleagues and co-contributors to the project, they should be treated with professional respect and care. They should be properly looped on the state of the project, and they should be credited for their contributions. Their influences should be given full play.
5. Ensure availability of the open-shared learning resources over time and space. Once resources are released to the public, they should not be retracted. These should also be protected against slow fires of digital obsolescence where possible. They should also be made available wherever possible in the world. (There are denied areas currently based on political considerations).

For example, particular fields may include particular values that may affect the teaching-and-learning. Many fields involve service learning and ways to improve the world with learner efforts. Some environmental science studies involve pro-environment efforts. In other fields, there are particular habits to improve learner performance. For example, in math, story problems and extensive practice are important. In computer science, creating code and testing it on systems is a critical part of the skillset. In journalism, getting out into the world and reporting news accurately and fairly, and publishing it is part of the learning trajectory. A value of the field involves being the Fourth Estate and holding officials to account. These additional influences may influence the design of learning resources.

Also, the metadata standards for shared learning resources will affect the learning resources. These have to be properly and fully described to enhance the reusability of the learning resources. Various metadata standards are built into authoring tools, which enable an easy way to emplace the proper text in the proper locations. (Different domains have different preferences for which metadata schemas to use.)

In cases where there may be a client or funder, the contractual agreement may have other ethics and values that need abidance (Fig. 4.3).

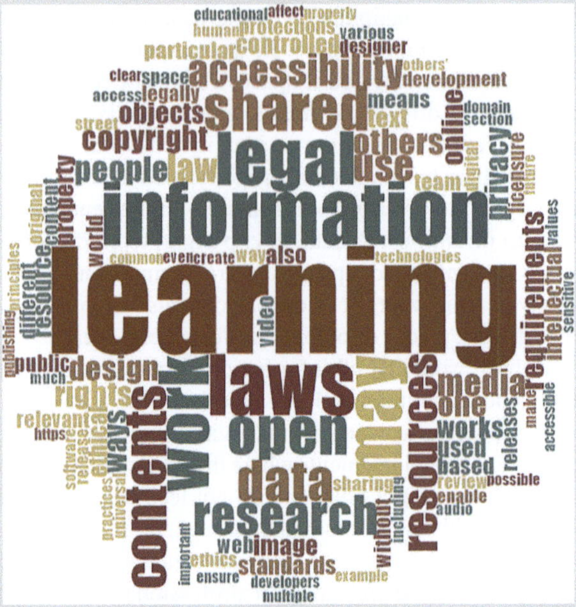

Fig. 4.3 "A Word Cloud of Chapter 04: "'Street Legal' Openly Shared Learning"

What-If: Integrating Partner Work into a Shared Project

You are working with a distributed team to create a learning resource that will be shared broadly and publicly. The communications among the team members have been spotty, but the team members have handed over a zipped folder of contents for you to peruse. You explore the contents, and you find some documentation (including a partial README folder), some raw files, some processed files, and that's it. In the text, the citations are clear and generally professionally done. You know that part of your near-term work will involve chasing details and finding people who may be a little elusive.

You want to make sure that you have the legal rights to use all the provided audio, the imagery, and the video.

What do you do?

Decision point #1: *Stop or advance*. If advance, do you first go with your own due diligence, or do you contact the team members to see if they actually have this data?

You decide to ask your colleagues about the rights releases, and they let you know that what they sent to you was everything they have … and they do not remember what came from where. They just know that they came across the respective resources and thought those would be beneficial to the project. They mostly thought that they accessed open-shared contents under open licensure. Mostly. And good luck.

You start the trawl by accessing a reverse image search to find the origins of the respective images, and you track them down to the earliest original versions, view the licensure releases (and document these by URL, level of licensure release, authors, date of creation, and other relevant information … and saved-to-PDF versions of web pages), and find only a few for which you have to acquire rights. You send out the emails requesting rights and describing your project and the team.

Then you search for videos, and you do that by a text search online and specify the modality. You do the same for the audios. You document what you can in terms of those contents released under open licensure and pursue rights for the others.

Some of the works, though, seem to be orphaned works, without any clear origination. What do you do?

Decision point #2: *Stop or advance*. If advance, how do you establish actual ownership if all responses are coming back "no"? How much effort should be invested in this work?

According to some "safe harbor" approaches, if you show sufficient due diligence in identifying potential copyright holders for "orphaned works" and document these, if a lawsuit arises, you may have some cover. You realize though that "safe harbor" ideas are stories that people tell to enable their risk-taking, and you go with removing those resources without clear copyright holders. You want to substitute works that have clear provenance (origins) and clear release of copyright.

In your work, you explore some content by third-party content providers: stock image distributors, audio distributors, and video distributors. You cost out the work, and you realize that you and the team would be out hundreds of dollars for a learning resource if you were to buy rights. Some of the rights are only for a certain amount of time and date out.

You let the team know what you've found. You ask if they are willing to have you swap out some of the contents. One of the team members suggests using some of the contents with murky sources. Others disagree.

What do you do?

Decision point #3: *Stop or advance*. If advance, what are practical options? What are ways to ensure that the learning resource is fully legally vetted but which still does not cause disgruntlement among the team?

You ask the team member what he/she likes about the particular found resource, and based on those attributes, you find some other legal (and free-to-use) resources that offer some options. The team weighs in, and they agree to the changes.

You realize that some of the images lack alt texting, and the team members themselves do not know the original context of the audio recordings, image captures, and video captures. The authorship is clear and established for the works, but most content creators have not documented the locations of the photos and videos, the topics being depicted in the imagery, the technologies used, and other information that would be helpful for detailed information-rich alt-texting (the providing of alternative text).

You can put in some placeholder information (made by inference and make-believe), which will likely be accepted into the final draft. You can ask the subject matter expert for more information, but he or she will be relying on their more expert guesswork. You can go to the team for more details. You can go back to the links to see if additional information was available that you had somehow missed the first time.

What do you do?

Decision point #4: *Stop or advance*. If advance, what standards will you use for the accuracy of included information?

You decide to track back information on all the prior channels, fix the alt text, and are just about done. Then, you come across a fateful image. The image is a clearly copyrighted one and belongs to a mega corporation. You contact the corporation, and the legal counsel there says that you are not authorized to use any of their imagery. The challenge is that the image was integrated into a slide used as a backdrop in a video. An important point is being discussed during that image's portrayal on the screen.

You can re-edit the video and redact the offending image. Or you can use a transition image that illustrates the point and keep the same timeline and audio in the video.

What do you?

The What-If Debriefing

This what-if scenario provides a sense of the back-and-forth work on a team that does not set standards early on and then has a lot of follow-on make-work because of that oversight. This also shows some best practices in terms of rigor and some of the tradeoffs that arise during the development process. The challenges of finding original copyright holders, reaching out to distributed team members, and other details, are drawn from real life.

Live Examples (On the Web)

This section contains some live resources that relate to some of the issues addressed in this chapter. It is hoped that these will still be live and relevant at publication. If not, these may be used to seed an initial search.

Export Controls and Controlled Information

Overview of U.S. Export Control System (US Department of State): https://www.state.gov/strategictrade/overview/

Intellectual Property

Copyright Law of the United States (U.S. Copyright Office): https://www.copyright.gov/title17/

United States Patent and Trademark Office (USPTO): https://www.uspto.gov/

Trademark Electronic Search System (TESS): http://tmsearch.uspto.gov/bin/gate.exe?f=tess&state=4806:8xrzyu.1.1

Accessibility

IT Accessibility Laws and Policies: https://www.section508.gov/manage/laws-and-policies

National Center on Universal Design for Learning: http://www.udlcenter.org/

Media Law

Media Law Resource Center: http://www.medialaw.org/

Children's Online Privacy Protection Rule ("COPPA") (Federal Trade Commission): https://www.ftc.gov/enforcement/rules/rulemaking-regulatory-reform-proceedings/childrens-online-privacy-protection-rule

Data Protection

Data protection in the United States: overview (Thomson Reuters Westlaw): https://content.next.westlaw.com/Document/I02064fbd1cb611e38578f7ccc38dcbee/View/FullText.html?contextData=(sc.Default)&transitionType=Default&firstPage=true&bhcp=1

European Union General Data Protection Regulation (GDPR) Portal: https://www.eugdpr.org/

Research Ethics

Resources for Research Ethics Education: http://research-ethics.org/

Five Principles for Research Ethics (American Psychological Association): http://www.apa.org/monitor/jan03/principles.aspx

Discussion The risk in creating open-shared learning resources is that it is very easy to upload contents to any number of hosting sites, and these generally do not require any peer review or oversight. Entry into the space is self-opt-in by individual volition alone, so self-proclaimed experts may engage with all due speed. There is very little that stands in the way of an individual or team being inspired to create content and pushing it out to the world.

Instead of speeding to publication, it may be better to focus on long-term wins and learning resources that stand the test of time, professionalism, laws, and ethics … and that not only impress the novices and amateurs but even the experts that happen by.

While retraction is sometimes an option, in many cases, once a work is in the world, it is seen by others and copied. Indexers may capture records of the resource. Take-backs may be expensive.

Where legal requirements affect open-shared learning resources is a dynamic space. With changes in technological enablements, laws have been fairly slow to catch up. The laws may come from any branch of government given the breadth of the space.

How these requirements are addressed have been improved also with various technologies. For example, a popular video-sharing social media platform has a built-in assessment for whether video and audio sequences are copyrighted and will block those elements; the platform also enables blocking of contents to particular regions of the world based on their respective laws. Some learning management systems have built-in accessibility checks, and others are able to accommodate such checks through Learning Tool Interoperability (LTI)-enabled capabilities. Bibliography technologies enable the accurate citation of sources, often in a number of different citation formats. Integrated design styles and color palettes in slideshow software have built-in contrast standards and other accessibility mitigations.

Legal ways to release copyright on original contents has enable broader usages of others' contents for publication, albeit with close attention required for the various conditionals to the releases (unless works are wholly released to the public domain).

Certainly, if learning object (LORs) learning management systems (LMSes) and other platforms had a built-in tests for copyright contravention, that would be a helpful tool. This capability may be something provided by a third-party with access to big data capabilities.

For all the various supports that may be provided through information and technologies, the ultimately responsibility still falls to the designer/developers and the teams. And this work is not only about following the letter of the law, but also the spirit, which means that it is important to understand the underlying values and rationales for the laws.

It makes sense to stand behind the work with one's actual name and to give credit where it is due, based on common practices in the domain for crediting. The lead author should be reachable via email or other means—so as to be the first to hear if there may be unforeseen issues. If there are complaints, they should be responsive, not avoidant, not defensive, and not accusatory. Another consideration is to use disclaimers to lower the amount of legal exposure, even if it is just a little. The designer/developer(s) should maintain accurate records and all files to prove the development sequence of the work, to show originality. One additional way to mitigate legal risk is to release objects through a limited liability non-profit or corporation, so personal resources are not put at risk.

4.4 Future Research Directions

From the open-shared designer/developer perspective, the future research may involve new laws, new technologies, efficient methods for adhering to the respective laws (by integrating these into typical work processes), methods for retrofitting to the respective laws, and other approaches. Many of these may be case-based approaches, with insights on how to actualize the work legally.

4.5 Conclusion

As part of the professional work of creating open-shared learning resources, designer/developers do well to be aware of the relevant laws and practical ways to be in solid compliance. Their work effort would benefit from early due diligence to review the applicable laws and updates to them and then to apply these laws assiduously. To achieve this, individuals must acquire a feel of the street and the rules at play to ensure that their creations are street legal. Not knowing the law is no defense against breaking the law. The due diligence is on the individual and the team to know the space that they're working in. After all, they work in a global space and a litigious environment. To actually contribute open-shared learning contents of value, one has to do so with the real-world standards in place. One should approach this with a "do no harm" approach. And one should engage with a sense of fair play and sound ethics.

4.6 Reviews and Assignments

4.6.1 Main Points Review

- Legal requirements for open-shared learning resources are non-negotiable. They have to be adhered to. If they are not, those should be showstoppers, and the work should stop well short of publication and distribution.
  - Hiding a work behind a password-protected "walled garden" of a learning management system (LMS) or proprietary video-hosting site is no protection. The laws still apply in socio-technical "walled gardens."

- Controlled information is anything sensitive (like technical information, like trade secrets) that is restricted against distribution by export controls laws. Generally nothing sensitive should ever be shared or even suggested.
- Based on the Berne Convention, people automatically own copyright to their creative works, and they do not necessarily need to register their works in order to own those rights.
- Copyright was created to ensure that those who innovate can be motivated to do so and to earn some rewards from their efforts but also to ensure that society benefits ultimately from people's creations.
- "Safe harbors" do not carry the weight of law but are popular stories of ways to just skirt copyright laws with certain careful practices. One example of a "safe harbor" is to try to find owners of "orphaned works" online before using it without any permission or copyright release.
- Trademarks should be correctly identified as "registered" marks or trademarks, using ® or ™.
- Various types of licensure schemes—Creative Commons licensure, GNU, and others—enable those who create contents to set terms for usage of their creations, including rights to remix and revise (use in derivative ways), distribute, use in commercial ways, enable access to underlying code, and others.
- Pirated software should not be used in a project because of the principle of the thing (do not use what you do not own) and because of the degraded performance and informational compromises of such jail-broken packages.
- Web accessibility is required by U.S. federal laws (including Section 508), and these include a range of requirements to ensure that information is communicated in multiple modalities.

  - Images (including figures, photos, maps, data visualizations, and others) need to have alternate text descriptions that are the informational equivalent of the image.
  - Audio and video files require closed captioning and/or transcription.
  - For user interfaces, the interactions should not require mouse actions (since assistive interaction devices require keyboard shortcuts).
  - Color should not be used alone for the conveyance of information.
  - HTML data tables should have coding to enable screen readers to capture the correct column header and row header for each data cell.
  - Simulations and video players require a high level of user controls.
  - Strobe effects should be avoided.
  - The writing should be as clear and simple as possible. The writing should also be as culturally neutral as possible.
  - The file types should be as universal as possible.
  - And others

- If people (their likenesses) are recorded in any form (image, audio, other), they have to give consent. This applies to guest speakers; this applies to students, and so on.

- The Children's Online Privacy Protection Act (COPPA), of 1998, explicitly protects children and youth, in particular about the information that may be captured about them and how it may be used and how it should be handled.
- In alignment with media law, people should not be defamed (have their reputations sullied with false information) or libeled (have something false written about them) with inaccurate information. In general, negative information about others should not be broadcast.
- The common practice of "remix" for mash-ups online can lead to a variety of challenges: contravention of others' copyright, privacy infringements, and other challenges—particularly if the provenance of various digital contents is not known and is not verifiable.
- The laws described in this chapter to make sure that a learning object is "street legal" implies certain values related to human rights, human creativity/innovation, human privacy, human dignity, and other factors. Understanding the underlying values and impetuses may be important. Learning objects should be accessible as a basic requirement (Gkatzidou and Pearson 2008).
- In different parts of the world, there are different laws that affect the publishing and distribution of learning contents. One example is a new privacy law in Europe known as the General Data Protection Regulation.
- Subject domains all generally have their own professional ethical guidelines and professional values. These should be surfaced and adhered to in the design of open-shared learning objects.
- Any included research data should be acquired legally. If the research was conducted by the author, the necessary research oversight should be conducted, for such issues as human subjects research review.

4.6.2 Critical Thinking Questions

Anticipation of future laws

- Based on the given laws, are there ways to anticipate future laws and to mitigate for them in the present designs?
  - For example, is it better to forgo information collection of learners that are identifiable to a person (such as requiring recorded log-ins to access learning contents) than to capture that information but run afoul of potential future privacy laws? Or privacy laws in particular regions?

Upholding standards

- Given the pressures of $0 budgets and limited time and resources, what are ways to be strong and uncompromising in the face of temptations like using others' copyrighted work, using pirated software, ignoring accessibility, playing fast-and-loose with data, and other forms of corner-cutting? What are ways to shore up one's sense of accountability?

   - For you personally, what are the most tempting of these challenges?

- Given the amount of changes occurring simultaneously on all legal fronts, technical fronts, and social media sharing fronts, what are some practical ways to stay up on the relevant changes?
- Are there ways to create work sequences within which are tripwires to indicate that one may have crossed an important line and must revise the work … or end the work?

Checking work

- What are some practical ways to validate/invalidate partner work when working on a team? What are some ways to check for legality/illegality on the various fronts?

Differing national standards

- In a review of the applicable laws around the world, which countries would be the hardest to adapt to, and why? Which countries would be the easiest, and why? Are there some accommodations that you can make that would make your learning resources acceptable anywhere around the world at any time, and if so, what are these? Are these accommodations work making? How expensive are these accommodations?

Ethics of open sharing

- How would you describe the ethics of open sharing? How is this space governed? What are the principles that govern this space?

4.7 Assignments

Directions The Assignments are divided into two sections, Basic and Advanced. The Basic section is for those who may not have much instructional design experience or background in the area of creating instructional contents for open sharing. As such, these are set up to familiarize them with the chapter-related knowledge, skills, and abilities. The Advanced section is for those who already have some knowledge of this general space and who may benefit from more challenging work.

In a formal learning context, these assignments would benefit from expert feedback and further applications of the learning contents. In a nonformal or informal learning context, including self-directed learning, these assignments would benefit from both reflection and practice. These assignments are built to be extensible, to have elements added to benefit the learners. They are designed to be assigned selectively and not in full. The setup of this textbook is as a work sequence, and similarly, the assignments may be set up as tasks to be completed by the learner in a sequential way … that takes them through the fairly complete and sequential *open-shared learning design -> development -> test -> revision -> launch -> post-launch* process.

4.7.1 Basic

Assignment 4.1: Controlled Information Controlled information are those identified as potentially having negative effects on national security and/or trade—that affects the U.S., based on export laws and regulations. Conduct an inventory of the information that you have access to and what the respective rules are in the handling of the data. Are there any "safe" ways to reveal parts of the data, and is there a good learning case that can be made? What are the possible implications in terms of part-worths releases of information or data?

Assignment 4.2: From IP Laws to Practice "Intellectual property" laws were created to encourage people to innovate and benefit from the fruits of their creativity and also to benefit the larger population who would ultimately share in the rewards of innovations (such as when contents are released to the public domain). In an academic environment, there are "fair use" and other exemptions at play. And in the open-source space online, the rules change yet again. Write a summary of your best understandings of intellectual property as applies to "creatives." Describe how IP likely will affect you in your open sharing design and development work.

Extra: If your project were audited for legality, how effectively and efficiently can you access records? What can you do to ensure that you have access to whatever you need to make your case that you've developed the work in a legal way? What are some of the optimal ways to keep records completely and accurately? What sorts of naming protocols would you use, and why? How can you ensure that rights releases were properly attained?

Extra: If you had to plan "law-breaking" for your learning object, what laws would you break and why? How would you effectuate this law-breaking? Will it be by omission or commission? How would you try to mitigate risk in this law-breaking?

Assignment 4.3: From Accessibility Laws to Practice Section 508 defines web-based accessibility guidelines for web publishing and online learning. There are guidelines for how to handle text files, slideshows, audio, video, HTML data tables, and simulations, among others. Some of these issues are handled using universal design approaches and others through accommodative ones. Some common interventions include closed captioning of audio and video, alt texting of imagery, strategic uses of color, labeling text in document hierarchies, and others. How would you set up your work project to accommodate all accessibility requirements?

Extra: If accessibility could not be done by the time the project is due, are there rolling mitigations possible? If so, what? If not, why not?

Assignment 4.4: From Mass Media/Publication Laws to Practice Publication laws touch on a number of rights of individuals, such as their rights to privacy and to not be libeled or defamed, and others. In the creation of an open-shared learning object, the creator acts as an author, an editor, and a publisher—often all-in-one. On websites, the sharing occurs broadly. Because of these realities, it is important to attain media releases when capturing people's likenesses (their image, their voice, their movements, and other representations). Write a short essay about how you would go about considering media law when creating open-shared contents.

Assignment 4.5: Principles Behind "Street Legal" Open-Shared Learning Contents, Courses, and Sequences The export controls laws, intellectual property laws, mass media/publication laws, accessibility laws, research standards, and others that affect open-shared learning content development all have implied values and principles at play. Write a short essay analyzing what these values and principles are. From your experiences, how well do the laws and practices uphold the implied values and principles. An early start is provided here:

- Information is controlled to protect against compromises to national security by those who are in competition to the nation-state and/or who are enemies. Information is controlled against export also to protect trade because many are looking for advantage, and much of the world is zero-sum (a gain by one means a loss by another).
- Intellectual property protections are in place to encourage human innovation by benefitting the original thinkers and inventors for a time but ultimately enabling people's works to be released to the public domain. All along the way, there should be benefits to humanity.
  - Copyrights, patents, and trademarks are to protect the interests of the originators of novel innovations and creative works, so that others do not abscond with their creations and the related benefits.
- Media laws, in part, protect against having reputations harmed by unscrupulous others who spread misinformation about them on any media channels. Privacy protections are in place to enable people to live lives without the sense of others' intrusion or control.
- Research protections are in place to ensure that people and animals are not unnecessarily harmed in the research.

Assignment 4.6: Professional Ethics and Values of the Content Domain to Practice In your particular study or work area, what are some of the main professional ethics and values? How can these be expressed as part of the street legal features of your digital learning object, course, or sequence?

Assignment 4.7: Retrofitting Real-World Learning Objects or Sequences Select digital two learning objects or learning sequences that are publicly available. Assess those learning objects based on the "street legal" standards described in this chapter. Make a note of each "infraction." If you were to retrofit the objects for full "street legal" status, what would you look to do? Why? What are the difficulties in retrofitting a digital learning object or course or sequence fully? Why? How much control is there for a person retrofitting an online learning object or learning sequence? Is there "lossiness" in terms of the quality of contents?

4.7.2 *Advanced*

Assignment 4.8: Ascertaining Relevant Laws in a Different Regional or National Context Select a region of the world (European Union) or a particular country—with a set of defined laws. Review the available laws to understand how those laws may affect instructional designs for open-shared learning objects or learning sequences released in those regions.

Assignment 4.9: Anticipation of Future Laws and Policies If you were to push out the time frame to a year, five years, ten years, what do you anticipate the laws may be for shared learning? Why? Which entities and stakeholders would have interests in the particular laws and policies? Why?

Assignment 4.10: "Street Legal" Open-Shared Learning Contents (or not)? List the top 10 laws and policy rules you can think of that apply to digital learning objects and sequences. Collect a sample of ten learning objects in a particular learning domain. Analyze those objects based on the 10 laws and policy rules. What are some initial conclusion that you can draw about how closely shared learning objects adhere to legal rules. What can you infer about the open-shared space based on what you found? What can you infer about those sharing open-shared learning objects and sequences? Their development?

Assignment 4.11: A Principled Value-Driven Approach The various law and policies applied to online learning objects and sequences are set in place in order to protect people and their interests. These are people who are creators of contents (photographers, writers, developers, designers, and others), publishers, learners, administrators, and others. Summarize the various principles and values behind the extant laws. Based on these principles alone, is it possible to arrive at various ethical and professional practices?

Keyterms and Definitions

Accessibility The conveyance of information on several perceptual channels (sight, hearing, touch, taste, and smell) and via multiple methods of symbolic processing (to enable understanding), usually through communicating through multiple modalities to ensure that those who have differing abilities can still access the information and related learning; the provisioning of information which enables users to maintain as much control over the consumption and learning experience as possible

Closed Captioning Timed text representing verbatim speech for audio and video files

Controlled Information Information (such as technical data, trade secrets, and others) that is sufficiently sensitive to a nation-state so that its export and sharing is restricted

Copyright The legal right to temporary ownership of a creative work that one has created

Defamation Harming a person's public reputation and name through incorrectly shared information through publication (libel) and broadcast (slander)

Intellectual Property A creative work that may be protected under copyright, patent, trademark, or other IP protection

Libel A false statement that is published about a person or entity

Media Rights Release A contract that releases the rights to use the signer's likeness in a recorded medium for particular defined purposes

Right to be Forgotten ("the right to silence on past events in life that are no longer occurring") The ability to request that past online information (text, photos, audio, video, and other modalities) about an individual be removed from the Web and Internet

Universal Design A framework used to "provide multiple means of representation," "multiple means of action and expression," and "multiple means of engagement" in online learning (according to the National Center on Universal Design for Learning)

Appendix: Some Legal and Ethical Considerations in the Open-Shared Learning Resources' Design-Development—Launch Sequence

01 Environmental Scan, Internal Scan, and Local Starts

- Is the information used in the external and internal environmental scans legally accessed (or are they private and protected)?
- Is the handling of this data proper, with required protections?

02 Profiling "Target" and "Potential" Learners

- Are profiles identifiable to a person's personally identifiable information (PII)?
- Do these contravene people's privacy rights?

03 Thinking Learning Design: Theories, Models, Frameworks, and Heuristics

- Are the learning designs based on valid theorizing and research?
- Are the learning designs inclusive (vs. excluding)?

04 "Street Legal" Open-Shared Learning

- Is any of the information used sensitive and restricted against sharing under export controls laws?
- If sensitive information is riding in the metadata of the digital files, have those been cleaned off?

- If research data is used, was the research conducted legally and ethically? Is the data acquired legally? Is it being used within the limits of the legal strictures for their usage?
- Are all the digital contents acquired legally and within the laws of intellectual property?
- Have all talent in the media captures signed media releases? Have they been properly informed and properly compensated?
- Are all the trademarks and registered marks properly labeled? Is it clear which are in the early stages of TM acquisition (as a registered mark) and which are fully registered (as a trademark)?
- Are the contents factually presented?
- Are the contents respectful of persons, without any defamation or libel or mis-representational harms?
- Have all persons' privacy rights been protected?
- Are all the learning contents accessibly rendered for universal access?
- Are sources accurately cited?
- Have all those who contributed been credited?

05 Core Technology Considerations

- Have all technologies (hardware and software) been legally acquired? (No pirated software should be used.)
- If freeware is used, has it been vetted for security?
- Are all the technologies properly credited (if relevant)?

06 Contemporary E-Learning Standards: Evolving Stylebooks, Planning Work

- Does the work align with the e-learning standards that it professes to follow?

07 Early Designs, Prototypes, and Learning Sequences

- Are the early designs, prototypes, and learning sequences original? If they are derived from others' works, are the others credited (and recompensed, if relevant)?

08 Content Development (with Work Documentation)

- Are those who contributed to the work properly credited (and recompensed, if relevant)?

09 Alpha Testing, Beta Testing, and Customized Testing

- Are all those who participate in the beta testing properly informed and recompensed (if relevant)?

10 Open Sharing: Launching, Outreach, Publicity, Usage Monitoring, and Post-Launch Care

- Are the open-shared learning resources accurately presented to the public?
- If learner data is collected, are learners notified? Do the learners have an opt-out? Is the learner data used ethically? Is it stored and handled legally? Is it protected against data leakage?

- If learning resources are updated and retrofitted, are these updates and retrofits legally done? Are these revised based on professional and other relevant ethical standards?

11 Some Possible Futures of Openly Sharing Learning

- Are the learning contents effectively future-proofed to meet the needs of current and future learners?
- Will the creators of the learning resources work hard to ensure that the learning resources do not contravene future laws? Or will they retract published works if they are non-compliant with relevant future laws? (Should such works be expected to be responsive to future laws?)
- Will the content creators ensure future access to the learning resources as much as possible? Will they keep the resources free and open?

References

Al Mahmud A, Braun J, and Martens J-B. Designing to capture and share life experiences for persons with aphasia. In The proceedings of Mobile HCI'10. Sept. 7 – 10, 2010. Lisbon, Portugal. 391 – 392, 2010.

Bissell AN. Permission granted: Open licensing for educational resources. *Open. Learning* 24: 97 – 106, 2009. doi:https://doi.org/10.1080/02680510802627886.

Fitzgerald B. Open Content Licensing (OCL) for open educational resources. In the proceedings of OECD Expert Meeting on Open Educational Resources, Malmö, Sweden. Retrieved May 10, 2018, from http://eprints.qut.edu.au/archive/00003621.1– 24, 2005.

Gawande, A. *The Checklist Manifesto: How to Get Things Right.* New York: Henry Holt & Company. 2009.

Gkatzidou S, and Pearson E. The potential for adaptable accessible learning objects: A case study in accessible vodcasting. *Austalasian Journal of. Educational Technology* 25: 292 – 307, 2009a.

Gkatzidou S, and Pearson E. A transformation, augmentation, substitution service (TASS) to meet the needs and preferences of the individual learner. In the proceedings of the 2009 Ninth IEEE International Conference on Advanced Learning Technologies. 98 – 100, 2009b.

Gkatzidou S, and Pearson E. A vision for truly adaptable and accessible learning objects. In the proceedings of ASCILITE Australasian Society for Computers in Learning in Tertiary Education, Melbourne, Dec. 1 – 3, 2008. Australasian Society for Computers in Learning and Tertiary Education: 340 – 342, 2008.

Poore-Pariseau C. Online learning: Designing for all users. *Journal of Usability Studies* 5*:* 147 – 156, 2010.

Section 508 of the Rehabilitation Act. Level Access. https://www.levelaccess.com/accessibility-regulations/section-508-rehabilitation-act/. 2018.

Stim R. Educational Uses of Non-coursepack Materials. Copyright & Fair Use. Stanford University Libraries. https://fairuse.stanford.edu/overview/academic-and-educational-permissions/non-coursepack/. 2018.

The Three Principles of UDL. National Center on Universal Design for Learning. http://www.udlcenter.org/aboutudl/whatisudl/3principles. 2014.

Tiku N. Europe's new privacy law will change the Web, and more. *Wired Magazine.* https://www.wired.com/story/europes-new-privacy-law-will-change-the-web-and-more/. Mar. 19, 2018.

Additional Reading Section

Burgstahler S.E. *Universal Design in Higher Education: From Principles to Practice.* 2nd Ed. Cambridge: Harvard Education Press. 2015.

Jacob S, and Hartshorne TS. *Ethics and Law for School Psychologists.* 4th Ed. Hoboken, New Jersey: John Wiley & Sons, Inc. 2003.

Kaplin WA, and Lee BA. *The Law of Higher Education: A Comprehensive Guide to Legal Implications of Administrative Decision Making.* 3rd Ed. San Francisco: Jossey-Bass. 1995.

Rest JR, and Narváez D. *Moral Development in the Professions: Psychology and Applied Ethics.* Hillsdale, New Jersey: Lawrence Erlbaum Associates, Publishers. 1994.

Shapiro JP, and Stefkovich JA. *Ethical Leadership and Decision Making in Education: Applying Theoretical Perspectives to Complex Dilemmas.* Mahwah, New Jersey: Lawrence Erlbaum Associates, Publishers. 2001.

Chapter 5
Core Technology Considerations: Equipment, Authoring Tools, Digital Editing Tools, and Hosting Platforms

Abstract Getting from an idea to an actual learning object (or sequence) usually requires some complex technologies, for the research, design, prototyping, development, testing, hosting, and launch. There are the research databases, camcorders, scanners, digital still cameras, the authoring tools, prototyping tools, video editing tools, image editing tools, and much more. This chapter focuses on some common considerations around technologies, such as equipment and tool functionality and interoperability, costs, digital preservation considerations (for files and digital contents), cost mitigations, and feature tradeoffs. Given the dynamic complexities of this topic, this will cover the issue more generally—to enhance generalizability and transfer.

Keywords Authoring tool · Courseware · E-learning toolkit · Learning management system · Online survey platform

> Technology, like art, is a soaring exercise of the human imagination.
> —Daniel Bell, in *The Winding Passage: Essays and Sociological Journeys, 1960–1980* (1980)

> The number one benefit of information technology is that it empowers people to do what they want to do. It lets people be creative. It lets people be productive. It lets people learn things they didn't think they could learn before, and so in a sense, it is all about potential.
> —Steve Ballmer, Microsoft Corp. (1956–)

S. Hai-Jew, *Designing Instruction For Open Sharing*,
https://doi.org/10.1007/978-3-030-02713-1_5

Opening Scenario

Opening Scenario: Know What to Build with and on for the Necessary Capabilities and Functions?

Designing open-shared learning resources requires a wide range of technologies, both hardware (equipment) and software (programs). Together, these are not low-cost tools, even if some freeware may be used in the mix. Various hardware and software tools are used in virtually every phase of the design, development, and deployment process. While tools come with various enablements, they also come with constraints and limitations. Hardware cannot run without software, and vice versa. However, it may help to think about each somewhat separately initially.

The hardware is generally used for two general purposes: (1) recording the world in sound, images, video, and signals, and (2) converting physical resources into digital file formats. In the first group are camcorders, digital still cameras, and others. In the latter are slide scanners, flatbed scanners, vinyl-to-digital turntables, and others.

The software is generally used for two general purposes: (1) post-production of video and editing of captured imagery and audio, and (2) originating "born digital" resources such as diagrams, images, video, slideshows, data visualizations, short and long games, simulations, and other contents.

Oftentimes, the learning curve for the uses of such tools can be quite high. Lifelong users of particular tools may only use some of the more common functionalities and not deal with the more complex ones. The technology can be a high barrier to the open sharing of learning resources.

The technology settings can also affect how high-fidelity the learning objects may have, how usable they are, and what may be done with the objects downstream—such as whether the objects are editable, revisable, and usable. The developers of the learning resources have some control over how much capability and value are handed over to the user. Technologically, how should a particular learning object or learning sequence be shared, and with how much control and capability should be given over to the user?

Some Early Questions to Consider

If you were to list a core set of technology tools for your design and development work, what would they be, and why?

If you were to proceed with a sparse list of tools, what would these tools be? If you could add more tools to your usual set of tools, what would they be, and why?

Do you have social media hosting platforms that you like to use? Online learning object platforms? Learning management systems?

Are you familiar with tools used by virtual teams to collaborate in distributed ways?

Have you heard of the "slow fires" of time that renders both analog and digital contents inaccessible? What are some common digital preservation methods to protect informational contents from becoming inaccessible? What are ways to manage "continuity" even in the cases of service outages and technological aging-out?

Are there freeware that you use that enables work in various stages of the design and development cycle? If so, what are these?

Learning Objectives

Learners will...

Necessary Hardware and Software by Functionality

- List the hardware and software functionalities required for a particular instructional design project (or a typical one if a specific one is not available)
  - Identify the instructional media that may be used to implement the instruction

Candidate Hardware and Software

- Consider the main commercial and free equipment used for digital content creation (scanners, digital still cameras, flatbed scanners, and others)
- Consider collaboration tools for distributed team collaborations
- Consider the main commercial and free tools used for digital authoring, editing, and other project requirements
- Consider the main commercial and free hosting sites (including content-based social sharing platforms)
  - Consider how easy/difficult it may be to port contents off of the respective sites should the sites go down permanently (such as if they go out of business or are no longer a viable business model or ongoing concern)
- Consider the legal (accessibility, for example) and other standards for selecting any of the various technologies

Team Collaboration Technologies

- Identify how technology decisions may best be made in a team context (by global consensus or by subgroup; and other factors)

Technological Requirements: Desirable Features

- List some technological requirements to ensure that learning objects are properly findable, properly informed for findability (by machines and humans), types of standards and metadata standards, that are important for learning object and learning sequences

Digital Preservation Considerations

- Consider some strategies and tactics to ensure that the digital contents of the shared learning object or learning sequence is protected against the "slow fires" of technological changes

Some Practical Cost Mitigations

- Consider some strategies and tactics to ensure that costs related to technologies are mitigated

5.1 Introduction

To actualize various digital and multimedia designs, designers and developers actually use various digital equipment and software tools in various sequences. Common equipment may include the following types: camcorders, digital recorders, digital still cameras, flatbed scanners, text scanners, slide scanners, sound booths, analog-to-digital converters, vinyl to digital turntables, web cams, and others. Common software include the following: diagramming tools, audio recording tools, image editing software, video editing software, simulation software, animation software, screen capture tools, screencasting tools, authoring tools for learning objects, data analytics tools, web page design tools, spreadsheet software, office suite software, and others.

Digital contents for learning are often aggregations or composites of digital information objects (text, imagery, documents, slideshows, videos, podcasts, and others) built into a learning sequence with assignments, practices, and even assessments. Authoring tools have been defined as a range of software products having utilities for composing, editing, assembling, and managing multimedia objects, while the term authoring system refers to a subset of these products allowing multimedia development without having to program (Locatis and Al-Nuaim 1999, p. 63).

"Courseware" refers to "educational, multimedia authoring software" (Kaskalis et al. 2007, p. 135). Modern software for development of learning objects tend to output contents in code that is functional for human users and automated programs, and much of the content is also "mobile-friendly" and suitable for small screens, able to be experienced via Android and iOS operating systems. Also, these authoring tools often handle the learning resource's metadata, packaging requirements, sequencing requirements, performance functionalities, schema standards, and other aspects that enable learning resource reusability and interoperability (between technology systems).

These are just for the basic development tools, and depending on the particulars of the design and the design context, a number of other tools may be relevant as well, such as game development tools, simulation development tools, and others. To create an open-shared learning resource, not all the prior list will be required. In some cases, freeware (no-cost software) may be available to help mitigate some of the costs. That said, a full set of basic resources will run in the many thousands of dollars. Some of the basic functions are summarized in Table 5.1.

Table 5.1 Equipment, authoring tools, digital editing tools, and hosting platforms for designing and developing e-learning

	Capabilities * Enablements * Functions
Equipment	Digitizing or transcoding analog or physical objects Capturing imagery (from the world) Capturing audio (from the world) Capturing video (from the world) Recording in-world phenomenon (in multimedia)
Authoring tools	Drawing diagrams Creating drawings Creating prototypes, externalizing concepts Creating videos Creating simulations Creating animations Creating digital learning objects Creating websites
Digital editing tools	Refining imagery Refining diagrams Refining audio files Refining video
Hosting platforms	Hosting digital files Maintaining metadata Enabling findability of digital files Offering downloadable contents Streaming video

Finally, hosting platforms and applications include content management systems (CMSes), learning management systems (LMSes), massive open online course (MOOC) platforms, web-facing databases, learning object repositories, content-sharing social media sites, digital libraries, wikis, and other applications that store and deliver learning contents. These tools make digital learning contents available for download or streaming. Learning object referatories point to resources hosted elsewhere on others' web servers.

The open-shared learning resource toolkit involves complex abilities and skills, to wield these tools effectively, to keep the technology systems updated and functioning, to troubleshoot challenges, and to ensure that digital contents are handled appropriately at every phase and in every tool.

To show how these tools are accessed for design and development sequences, a real-world creation of a digital poster for a conference is described in Fig. 5.1. In this case, data was extracted from an LMS data portal and analyzed. The designer/developer proposed a basic thesis, and she built a poster around that thesis—to present both as a physical cloth poster with grommets and a digital one hosted off of a slide-sharing website. The sequence shows the technologies accessed for each step in the work. While the general process is linear broadly speaking, it is also somewhat recursive as needed. For example, if an assertion is made on the poster that needs to be checked thoroughly, the designer/developer will have to return to the data portal to access new information and to run the query, for example. The two-headed arrows are included to capture more of a sense of what happens in the real. (The poster titled "Using Large-scale LMS Data Portal Data to Improve Teaching and Learning at K-State"

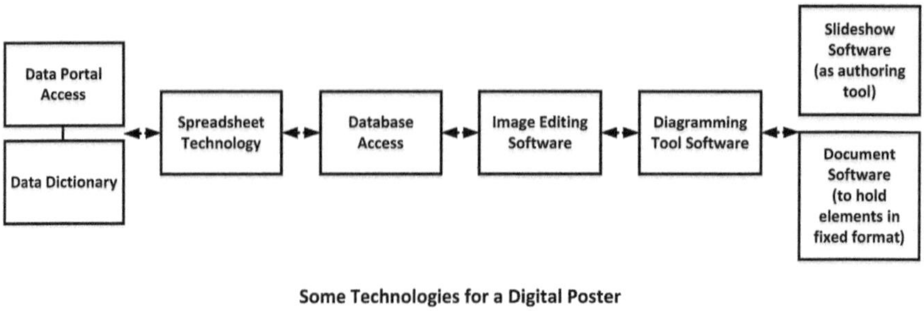

Fig. 5.1 Some technologies for a digital poster

may be accessed off of SlideShare at https://www.slideshare.net/ShalinHaiJew/poster-using-largescale-lms-data-portal-data-to-improve-teaching-and-learning-at-kstate) (Hai-Jew 2017).

Given the critical role of technologies, these need to be defined fairly early in the process (Fig. 5.2).

This chapter addresses some of the basic necessary hardware and software in terms of functionalities. This walks readers through some basic considerations in the selection of technologies. For teams to collaborate, there are additional considerations. Finally, some practical cost mitigations are discussed. No brand-name products are suggested here, but the expressed preferences are for mainline tools by reputable companies as first choices and freeware at the bottom of the list (except for freeware created by large populations of crowds and headed by expert leadership and carefully vetted for updates).

5.2 Review of the Literature

How do designer/developers choose the hardware and software in their toolkits? Do people choose based on some combination of considerations, such as tool capabilities, costs, user interfaces, ease-of-learning, and brand reputation? Do they choose tools by familiarity and name recognition? The lifespans of the respective technologies? Their robustness? Whimsy? The reputation of the hardware or software maker for supporting their users?

Fred Davis' Technology Acceptance Model (1985) and its TAM2 suggest that technologies are accepted when they are easy-to-use and useful and seen to be acceptable in the social context (Legris et al. 2003). One study suggests that the fit of a particular technology to a desired task may be one factor in technology adoption in a "task-technology fit" approach (McGill and Klobas 2009). The co-authors explain:

> Task-technology fit in turn both directly influences performance, and indirectly influences utilization via precursors of utilization such as expected consequences of use, attitude towards use, social norms, habit and facilitating conditions. (McGill and Klobas 2009, p. 498)

Technology performance "is a necessary but not sufficient precursor to task performance" (Parkes 2013, p. 997) because of mediating factors. In authoring tools,

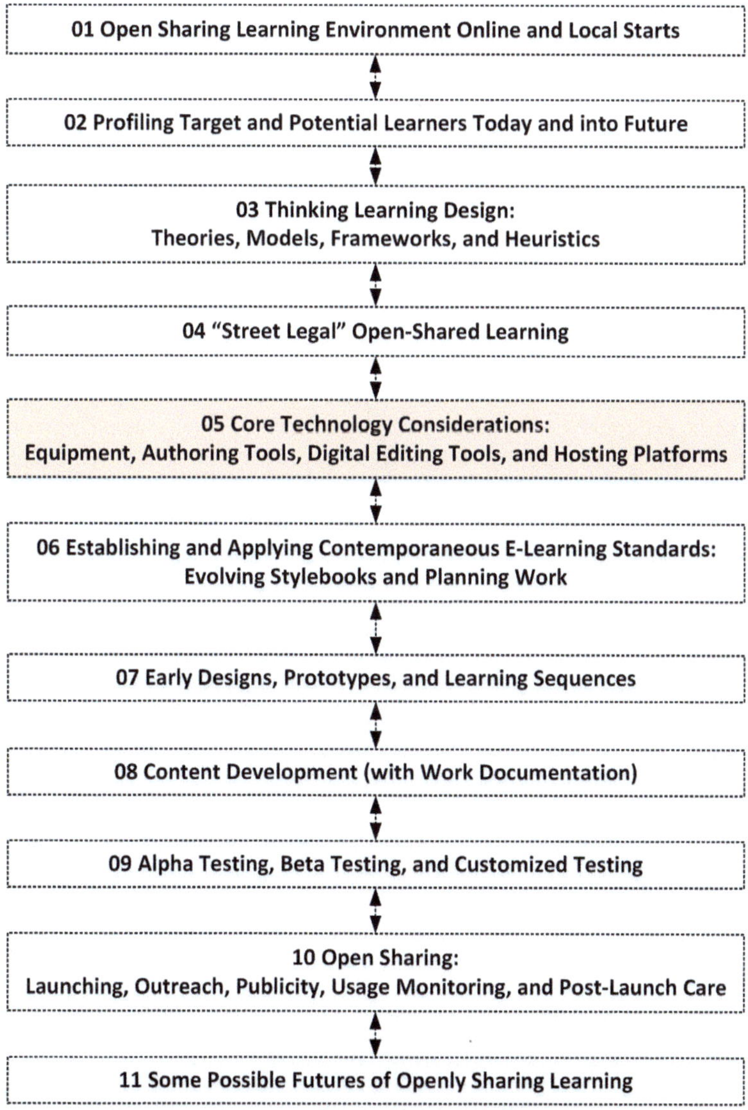

Fig. 5.2 Step 5 in the open-shared learning resource development sequence

perhaps the integration of technology standards enabling interoperability or conceptual models of learning may be the difference (Downes 2001). One research team explains technological features that enhance learning content reuse:

> In order to support a richer set of educational functions and increase their effectiveness, such systems need to interoperate, collaborate and exchange content or re-use functionality. A key to enabling the interoperability is to capitalize on the (1) semantic conceptualization and ontologies, (2) common standardized communication syntax, and (3) large-scale service-based integration of educational content and functionality provision and usage. (Aroyo and Dicheva 2004, p. 60)

The advancements in the field of open-shared learning are based not only in advancements in the hardware and software but also the advancing standards on the Web and Internet.

To be reusable, shared learning resources have to be in universal file formats, so they can be accessed using various technologies. One author suggests the following: "Plain text: Unicode; Images: TIFF (Tagged Image File Format); Audio: MP3 (MPEG-1, Layer 3); Video: MPEG-4" (Note: semicolons added) (Wenk 2010, p. 437). Markup languages are also used for accessible learning resources, such as the use of XML (extensible markup language) along with XSL (eXtensible Stylesheet Language), and these may be created using open-source authoring frameworks (Wenk 2010, p. 437).

Over the years, software makers have worked to simplify the software functions and interfaces, to push technologies close to subject matter experts and content experts. A "noob" or "newbie" in the open-sharing sphere would benefit from the templating, color palettes, design overlays, font face sets, context sensitive help, suggested work sequences, and other supports in software tools; over time, these supports may fall away in the same way cognitive scaffolding does for new learners. As new users become more experienced, they will be able to troubleshoot challenges and use the tools with skill and finesse. They will be able to use the tools in more sophisticated "developer" ways. They will update and patch when needed and will work around the tool's quirks. They may move beyond some of the fixed paths of the software and enable higher degrees of designer/developer freedom. (Some authoring technologies offer canned products that have a revelatory "tell." Many in the instructional design space eschew such technologies because they are so obvious as to the source and are so restrictive in terms of look-and-feel. In other cases, the finalized learning resources cannot be analyzed to understand the technologies that went into their build because the technologies are generalist and are not overbearing in terms of look-and-feel and functionalities.) In general, trusted hardware and software makers keep open channels with their users, and updates will be arrived at in a co-evolved way, based on perceived user needs.

5.3 Core Technology Considerations: Equipment, Authoring Tools, Digital Editing Tools, and Hosting Platforms

The future of e-learning is envisioned as affirming of learners and their interests. It is seen as experiential and interactive and social. The expectations go well beyond the 1990s computer-based learning (CBT) with just a learner by himself or herself in front of a screen. And yet, that concept has not fully disappeared either. Contemporary ideas of online learning through shared open learning addresses the whole person and a wide range of their perceived needs.

Putting a Software (of Interest) Through Its Paces
When considering a new software program, how do you do your due diligence to make sure that the software functions as advertised and will meet your needs in the near- to mid-term? How do you assess the learning curve if you do not have prior experience with the software? How do you ensure that the technology plays well with others in the proverbial sandbox? Do you read the fine print?

Online, there are some fairly trustworthy sites that offer documentation about software. Many software programs are available for trial usage. User experiences are fairly well documented, too, by professed users.

5.3.1 Necessary Hardware and Software by Functionality

A simple way to create a list of necessary technologies is to understand how practical tasks relate to required technologies. What technologies are needed to actualize particular tasks? Recall that in the open-sharing sequence, one may need achieve the following: research, design, prototyping, development, in-world recording and capture, project management, testing, data analytics, and launching, generally speaking. The hardware and software toolkit should enable the work, and the instructional media tools will be cloud-based ones as well as local ones (on one's local machine). (I would be hard-pressed to define a toolkit that is either wholly offline or wholly online.) One piece of equipment or one software may meet multiple needs. Also, a particular required work sequence may require multiple technologies (such as prototyping).

It may help to provide some rough common work sequences and the general technologies required for each. (Fig. 5.3).

Assessments are a common part of an instructional design, whether they are stand-alone or integrated into a learning sequence. They may be formative assessments, to aid the learning, or summative ones, to assess the learner knowledge on the topic. With the advancement of the technology tools in this space, assessments are potentially much more complex and multimodal today than in the near-past (Fig. 5.4).

A video is comprised of a number of different contents—visuals, audio, moving images, and others. The contents may be scripted or not. For this development

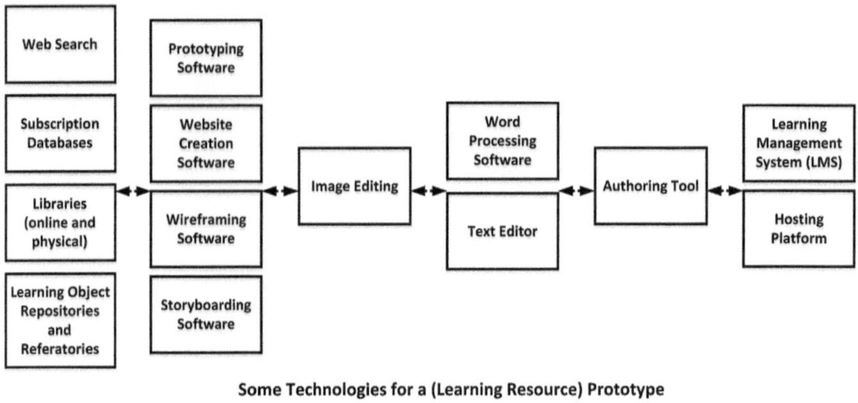

Fig. 5.3 Some technologies for a (learning resource) prototype

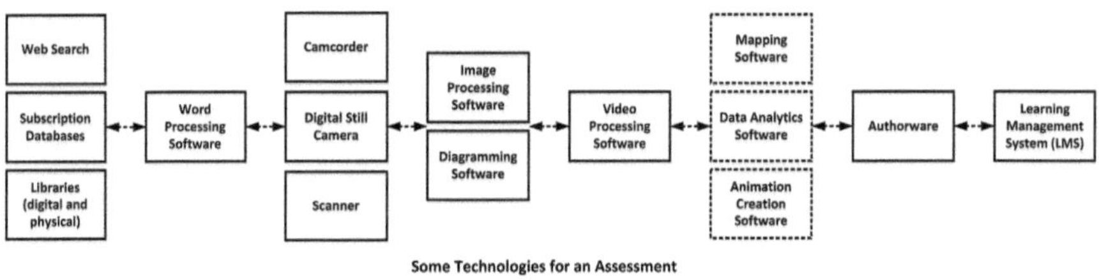

Fig. 5.4 Some technologies for an assessment

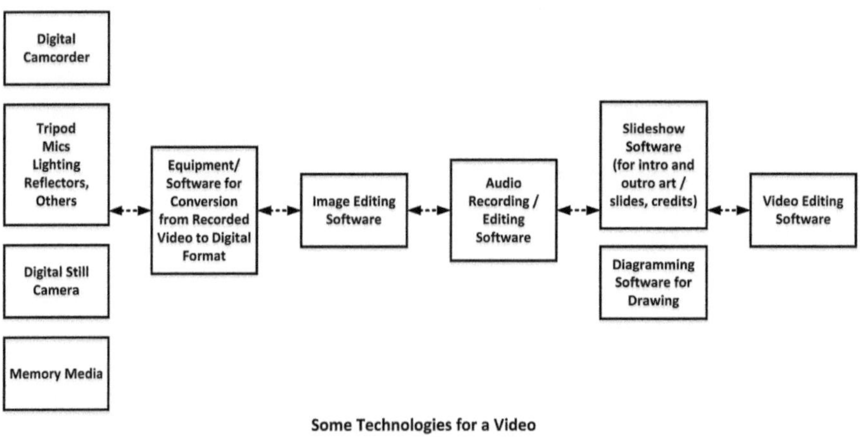

Fig. 5.5 Some technologies for a video

sequence, a number of technologies are required (Fig. 5.5). If there are unique other sequences, more technologies may be needed beyond the basics listed here.

For the creation of a brand logo, various software tools are typically used (Figs. 5.6). Developing an electronic book also requires a wide range of technolo-

Fig. 5.6 Some technologies for a brand logo

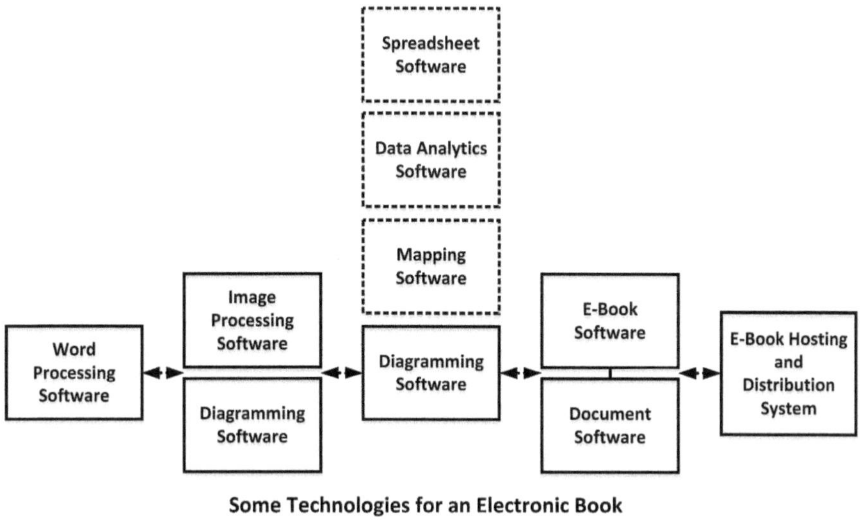

Fig. 5.7 Some technologies for an electronic book

gies, especially given the multimedia richness of the contents, to enable interactivity and engagement (Fig. 5.7).

Conducting a web panel discussion for online learning is a fairly common experience. To record this event is technologically simple (with built-in recording tools for most mainstream web conferencing applications, but It requires attaining signed releases and other coordination. In the live context, accessibility mitigations are advisable—such as having live notetakers during the event. Also, the video needs to be accessible for follow-on users of the resource. Some technologies required in this sequence follow in Fig. 5.8.

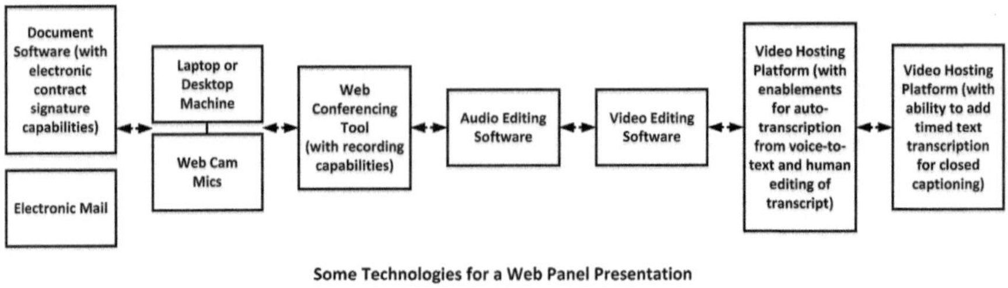

Fig. 5.8 Some technologies for a web panel presentation

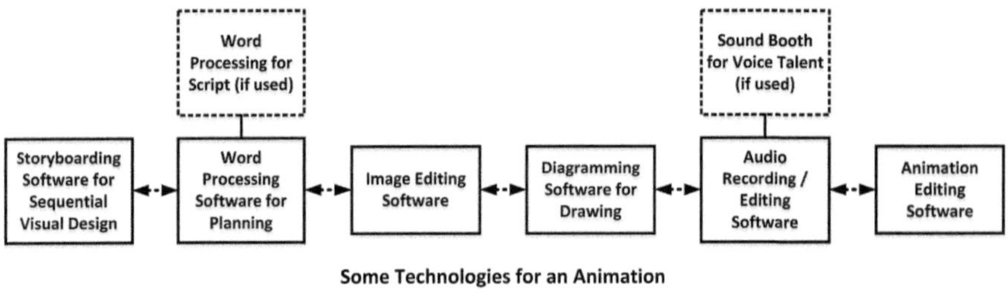

Fig. 5.9 Some technologies for an animation

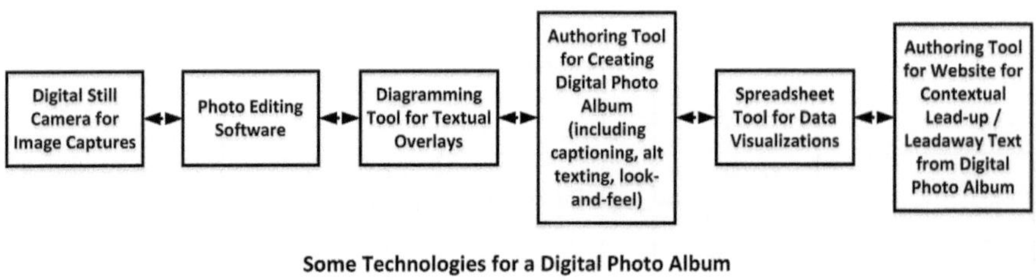

Fig. 5.10 Some technologies for a digital photo album

A basic animation may be actualized with the technologies listed in Fig. 5.9.

Digital photo albums enable users to click through a series of captioned images to understand a phenomenon or story. A technology sequence for such photo albums follows in Fig. 5.10.

Online survey research suites are used for information collection as a mainstay, but they also are harnessed to deliver automated trainings and other work. To these ends, the work begins with research, the creation of contents, testing, and deployment. There are heavy technology requirements along the way and throughout (Fig. 5.11).

For project research, a wide range of tools is needed because of the complexity of the task. This research informs complex decisions and designs. (Fig. 5.12).

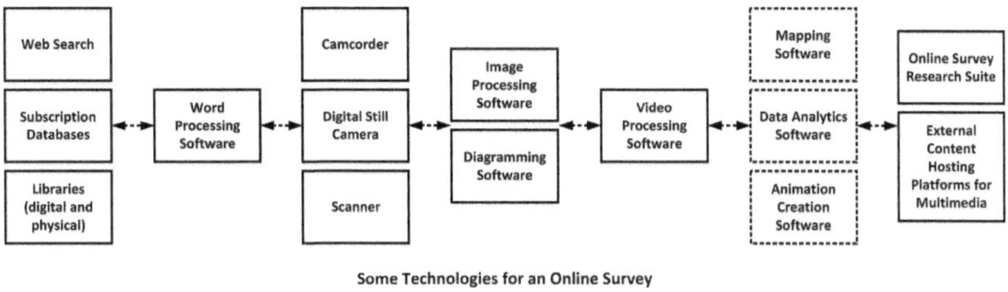

Fig. 5.11 Some technologies for an online survey

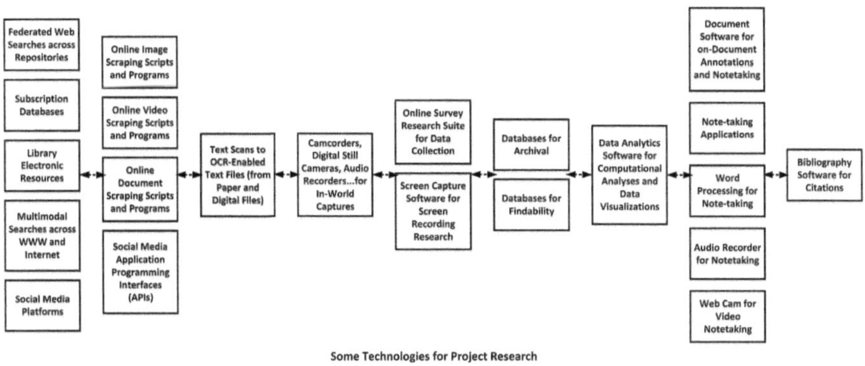

Fig. 5.12 Some technologies for project research

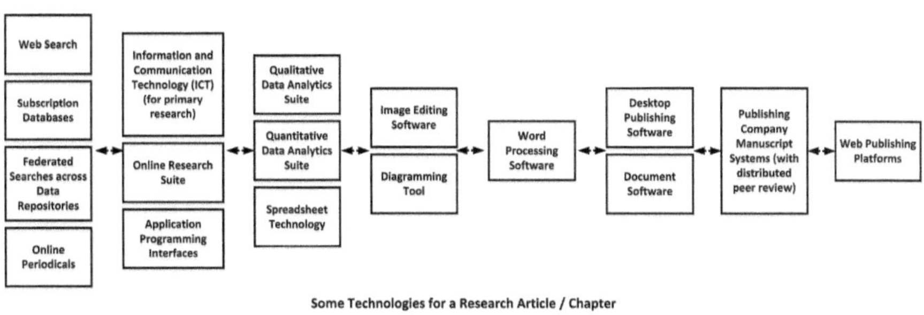

Fig. 5.13 Some technologies for research article/chapter

Creating a research article for open-access sharing [with costs of the share covered by the author and his/her institution of higher education or workplace, but with copyright retained by the author(s)] requires a wide range of technologies (Fig. 5.13). A research article may require hundreds and hundreds of work hours to create from start to finish. In the academic research space, each goes through often-grueling peer review.

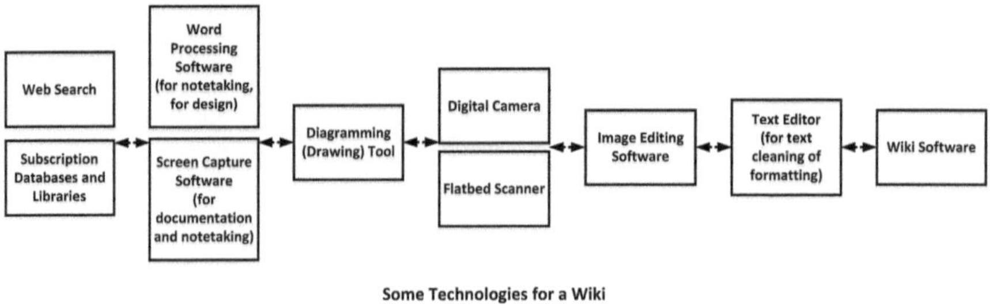

Fig. 5.14 Some technologies for a wiki

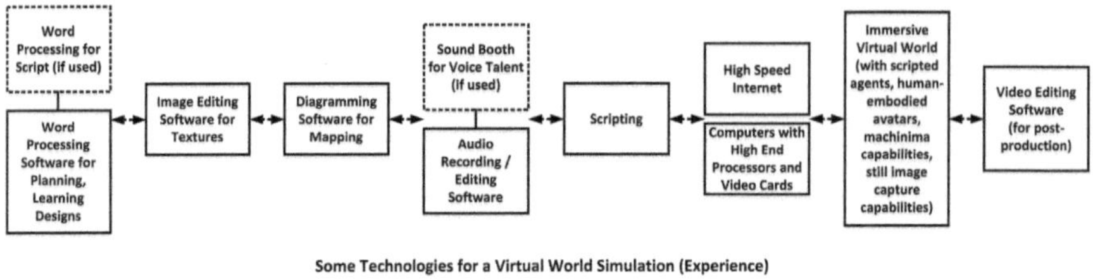

Fig. 5.15 Some technologies for a virtual world simulation (experience)

To create a wiki from scratch, there are some basic required tools, beginning with an initial and continuing need for research, to feed the informational needs of the wiki (Fig. 5.14).

With the movement towards open educational resources, electronic book-writing has become a common practice in higher education. Ostensibly, these save money for students, and they disintermediate the third-party content providers and commercial publishers. Such open-source e-books may be hosted and distributed in learning management systems (LMSes), websites, wikis, learning object repositories, library sites, and others. Some use proprietary electronic book formats. E-books may be highly static (electronic versions of print), or they may be interactive, enabling note-taking, annotations, social information exchange by users, integration with an online learning sequence, user behavior data collection, and others. Depending on the topic, a variety of tools may be needed in addition to the basic technology sequence.

A virtual world simulation involves a fair amount of lead-up work to enable it to go well. A technology sequence based on this scenario is available in Fig. 5.15. This shows the need for some post-production work as well.

Task #1: Listing Technos

The first task is for you to take an inventory of the technology tools that you use normally. For hardware, mention the product, the model, the year of the tool's acquisition, and other relevant information. In terms of the software tools, list the name, the company that created it, the version that you are using, and the operating system that you are using. Then write what sort of licensure you have for the software. Then make a list of the functionalities that you use each of the tools for and why.

How much of your toolkit is commercial? How much is freeware "equivalencies"? Which tools are the competitors in the space?

If you had unlimited resources, what toolkit would you have, and why? What are some practical ways to access at least some of the hardware and software for the idealized toolkit?

Task #2: A Sequence of Required Technologies

Based on the examples of sequencing tasks based on required technologies (Fig. 5.1 and Figs. 5.3 to 5.15), map one of your work sequences and the required technologies. Are any of the technologies used extraneous to the work, and can they be omitted? Why or why not?

5.3.2 Candidate Hardware and Software

This chapter title lists equipment, authoring tools, digital editing tools and hosting platforms. In many ways, those building hosting platforms are striving to disintermediate the other tools, particularly the authoring ones and some equipment. For example, a contemporary learning management system can be the core space where learning contents are captured (through the computer webcam and audio because of the built-in screen recording and web cam applications), the screen capture feature, the light video editing on video hosting platforms, and so on. In a sense, everything can be done online with a mix of cloud-based tools and free applications and the LMS. Of course, if external in-world imagery is required, a digital camera is required. If a diagram is not predrawn, a person only using the cloud-based tools, free applications, and an LMS would be hard-pressed to create one to quality. Also, LMS platforms are being used to deliver e-books built on that platform. There will likely continue to be efforts at disintermediation throughout.

The desirable features of related equipment, software, collaboration sites, hosting sites, and other tools will vary based on individual and team needs. Desirable features would be easy to list here, but they would also date the work. For your local work needs, what tools do you need for digital captures and recordings from the world? For authoring and digital content editing? In terms of team collaboration tools that are respected and usable, which ones are most usable and why? (Table 5.2).

Table 5.2 Technology contenders based on features and other considerations

	Candidate hardware
Video capture	
Image capture	
Audio capture	
Analog to digital capture	
Others	
	Candidate software
Image editing	
Video editing	
Diagramming	
Learning content authoring	
Animation authoring	
Others	
	Team collaboration tools
Web conferencing	
File sharing	
Co-design	

(continued)

Table 5.2 (continued)

Others	
	Hosting platforms
Learning management systems (LMSes)	
Content management systems (CMSes)	
Learning object repositories (and referatories)	
Electronic book distributors	
Content-sharing social media platforms	
Others	

Task #3: One "Courseware" or "Authorware" and its Affordances and Constraints

Identify a courseware or authorware tool that you use regularly. List its affordances (enablements) and constraints. Are its outputs recognizable? Do you prefer fixed paths to the work or more leeway? Why?

Task #4: Hand Coding

Do you enjoy coding by hand? If so, what computing language(s) do you use, and why? How long does it take for you to output the code? How do you test it? What are some strengths and weaknesses to going straight to code?

Task #5: Maintaining Equipment and Software

An important skill involves caring for the physical hardware and equipment as well as the software. What are some of your habits regarding "machine hygiene" and maintenance of equipment? What about your work towards updating (patching) software?

Task #6: Freeware

Freeware (no-cost software) is widely used in some applications and domains. Which ones do you use? How do you vet the freeware that you use? Where do you go to find the best possible applications? Add-ons? Stand-alone tools? How do you validate freeware programs? How do you avoid malware infections on your computers?

Team Collaboration Technologies Other tools may be required to collaborate virtually. For the collaborating cross-functional teams, the resident experts in various aspects of the project should have an outsized responsibility to explain what they need in terms of contents and which technologies should be used for the work. If all the team members will take part in information collection, the standards for the respective contents should be defined clearly in the work documentation (like the project stylebook), so there is no wasted effort or makework. There should be shared resources for the collaboration that all the team members have access to because it is sufficiently rare to have physically co-located teams.

Desirable Features of Authoring Tools A number of authoring tools have built-in technology standards for accessibility (a11y), for learning object metadata, for e-learning reference modeling, for interoperability, and others. These features are usually described in the fine print for the technologies. Those who build hardware and software are well aware of technology standards and strive to build to them to enable their products to achieve particular objectives with the standards.

And professional industries and professional organizations that require such standards in their learning resources will have "go-to" technologies that work with the hosting platforms. These entities may be consulted if one wants to build open-shared learning resources to particular professional communities.

If an individual or team chose the wrong technology, they can treat it as a learning experience to apply more due diligence in the future. Undoing a wrong choice may be costly in time and effort and moneys, but in most cases, teams can recover from such mistakes. The next go-around, though, they may need to consider the strengths and weaknesses of the respective technologies. Also, given the dynamism of the space, some factors may well be outside the hands of the decision makers. For example, software companies do go out of business, and contributors to freeware end supports. As long as the prior work can be somewhat preserved and transcoded, the project is recoverable.

Digital Preservation Considerations In practice, designers/developers protect their digital resources in several ways. First, they maintain a pristine master set of files in their original "least lossy" formats. They maintain the original imagery, video, and other files from the original devices. They also keep a copy of the transcoded files that enable editing of those digital files on desktop computers. When they need to recode a learning resource, they make copies from the pristine master files, so they are using the least lossy version possible (so they are not losing visual and auditory data).

Second, raw proprietary files should also be kept because those also provide a level of editability that would not be available otherwise, even as these require access to the originating software. Rendered finalized and compressed files cannot easily be disaggregated, and revisions would be impossible without the original files. Recreating a learning resource from a compressed file is awkward and rarely successful. Recreating a work from scratch can be time- and labor-intensive.

Third, they version files into standardized and universal file formats: plaintext, HTML, and others. They reversion contents from proprietary file formats to open-source ones that do not require a software tool to access.

Some Practical Cost Mitigations One of the most common cost mitigations is to use organizational ties to access the requisite technologies. The organizations could be workplaces, professional organizations, and others. Ideally, these would enable legal access to the high-end professional tools required for quality work. Acquiring educational licenses may be a job perk for those working in this vertical.

Another approach is to go with trusted open-source technologies. Some cloud-based tools are free. Some database tools are free. There is a freeware version of a popular office suite. Of course, such tools have to be vetted for functionality (many third-party freeware tools do not function as advertised). And it is important to ensure that no malware rides with the respective tools.

Another approach is to harness the available technologies for uses in ways that they may not have been originally designed. A recent new application of PowerPoint is as a storyboard diagram (using the Slide Sorter view).

Interestingly, there are some bargains to be had. Some software makers still enable “eternal” licenses. If a user can muster sufficient usage, these upfront costs may be minimal in the long run.

Designer/developers can pursue a reasonable level of thrift for the equipment and software but not ultimately at the cost of the project. In general, the more originality desired, the higher the costs. After all, if one has to create one’s own images and videos and animations, each object will require technologies and skills and work. The more sophisticated the multimedia, the higher the costs (and the higher the demands on the technologies and requisite skills).

Sometimes, even a lower cost piece of equipment or software can be more expensive in the long term. If the equipment is constantly breaking and needing repair, or if it turns out poor quality files (which require a lot of post-production or rework), the losses can mount. There is also the cost of acquiring new skills. Companies that offer free cloud-based development of contents may make it impossible to download a copy or to host the contents elsewhere through the Terms of Use or End User License Agreements (EULAs). In the fine print, they may acquire rights to the shared contents beyond what is needed for basic hosting and sharing. Further, such terms may change over time, with little warning to users. This is particularly problematic for people who do not read the fine print in depth, and they can be caught up short.

Finally, the relative costs of the technologies may differ if the designer/developer is in an early-, mid-, or late-career context, or a hobbyist context. While some may be tempted to ignore the cost aspect, it seems better to be aware of the costs and to mitigate them legally and sensibly where possible. There are benefits from the work that may be invaluable such as extending skills, exploring personal interests, and sharing knowledge with the world for others’ benefit.

Discussion It is important to have an informed sense of the technology ecosystem and the available technologies in all their categories. It is important to maintain a voice into how technologies advance into the future (especially co-evolved ones like some learning management systems). Customers of software have an importance voice in this space.

5.4 Future Research Directions

The technology space is a highly dynamic one, and there are new practices and standards that arise with regularity. To share learning resources in open ways, those who want to contribute, will have to maintain access to the technologies and the skills to wield them effectively. What would benefit the research would be to have shared methods and processes for various cases, more documentation of the uses of technology tools, and more accurate senses of how relevant software will evolve into the future (based on principles, based on functionalities).

Live Examples (On The Web)

On the Web, there is no shortage of vetting and assessment methods for different classes of technologies.

Go online and explore a particular class of technology that is relevant to your work. Read some of the formal assessments in academic research and journalism. Also, go to the Social Web and read some users' assessments.

Which tool is "best in class"? What standards were used to determine the "best in class"? What metrics were used in the assessment?

Based on your own experiences with the software, what functions and features do you prefer, and why? What are the strengths and weaknesses of the particular software?

Fig. 5.16 A Word Cloud of Chapter 05: "Core Technology Considerations: Equipment, Authoring Tools, Digital Editing Tools, and Hosting Platforms"

What-if: Free but Not Free, Expensive but Not Expensive (Fig. 5.16)
In your open sharing endeavor, you are not starting out wholly without prior resources. You have a basic laptop that is a few years old. It is loaded with basic technologies, such as an office suite of technologies, a multimedia developer suite of tools, and a bunch of freeware. You have some years of instructional design experience. You can save up for more resources and updates on the current software tools, or you can start some work now.

Decision point #1: Stop or advance. If advance, what will you do to make the resulting contents look more contemporary and updated? What are some strategies to make the contents more eye-catching?

You decide to update the tools that you have and focus on the informational contents and the pedagogical design. You create some early designs, some prototypes, and some learning sequences. Then, you realize that you need to be able to create some visuals with alpha channels. Your main image editing software does not enable this. You can go to a commercial tool, or you can go with freeware. You do some research, and you realize that there will be tradeoffs. If you go the commercial route, you'll overstretch your bank account and be under financial stress for the next few months. If you go open source, you can get the images processed for free, but you have to sign up to receive ads for some time. You check out the open source and find that the tool actually has a good reputation. Another option is to use an online site that can process the images, but the entity behind the service will retain a copy of the images. You read their end user license agreement (EULA), and it sounds like the company will retain some rights to whatever has been uploaded to their site.

What do you decide?

Decision point #2: Stop or advance. If advance, what is your best option to process the images? What is an optimal solution that will enable you to re-edit the images as needed?

You decide to buy the commercial software and have software that you trust, even if it means that you'll be frugal for the next half year. You are confident in your project and think that the alpha channels will result in cool visual effects. And with one of the images, you need the background gone, so you can place the visual on a different background.

You are almost done with the learning resource. You receive an email about a local conference where a local expert will be presenting on a topic that relates to your work. You're always looking for ways to improve your skillset, and if you commute and skip hotel fees, you can keep down the costs. You may be able to write off the local conference on your taxes.

Or you can learn about the topic by going online to some video sharing sites, some slide sharing sites, and academic publication sites. There are all sorts of opportunities to hone skills, and with many of the digital media, you can always review and replay.

Decision point #3: Stop or advance. If advance, what will you do about the conference opportunity? Do you pursue open-shared learning resources? How do you ensure that you learn the skills accurately?

You continue…

The What-if Debriefing

This scenario highlights some of the realities of the open-sharing area, with technology tools constantly needing updates at some pretty severe costs (on a freelance budget) and local opportunities to develop professionally (but at a cost). There are risks of letting skills decay, but maintaining the toolset and the skillset will require real efforts and real investments. Falling in love with a certain project may mean some less rational decisions about expenditures, but in the long run, it may all still be worth it… Maybe.

5.5 Conclusion

In this chapter, the role of technologies (hardware, software, and hosting platforms) has been brought to the fore. The equipment, software, and hosting systems are complex, but they are needed to create and serve-up the digital learning resources.

For those building with $0 budgets, now is a very powerful time with a wide range of freeware, free hosting, and a pro-sharing culture online.

5.6 Reviews and Assignments

5.6.1 Main Points Review

- When assessing what hardware and software to use on an open-shared learning object project, it is important to understand both by their functionalities (enablements and constraints) instead of by brand or intended usage. This approach broadens understandings of the tool and can lead to more creative harnessing of the tools. They extend the capabilities of the hardware and software.
- In many cases, the core set of equipment and software will already be set based on what is used in the workplace and/or by the individual at the home office. Decisions may then be made more at the margins in terms of new or additional equipment and the software. For example, a simulation may require additional software, and the toolkit would benefit from the addition of the dedicated simulation capability as needed.
- Conducting an environmental scan of commercially available candidate equipment and software for digital content capture; born digital content creation; digital authoring, editing, and others; digital content hosting; and other functionalities may be important to know what is practically available.

- Whatever equipment and software is chosen has to be used by people, so the learn-ability and usability of the tool has to be considered. Not all team members will have the same facility with various equipment and software, so prior knowledge is relevant.
- Virtual collaboration software is important so that the team may intercommunicate and meet, share resources, collaborate, document their shared work, and achieve other project-based objectives.
- Equipment and software have to enable accessibility as a basic legal standard. Depending on the tool, there are other standards that apply. Workplace standards for technologies should be adhered to generally.
- Distributed teams have to ensure that they can create "interoperable" digital files that are usable by other team members. It is important to identify common technologies that may form the basis of the collaboration as well.
- The Semantic Web has structured information requirements in order to enable the findability of relevant resources. When it is harnessed for learning, people can build Educational Semantic Webs.
  - Various (reference) models and metadata standards may be used to increase the findability of learning objects and sequences and to enable their harnessing for a learning sequence.
- A basic hardware toolkit for designing open-shared learning may include a high-end laptop, digital camcorder, digital still camera, flatbed scanner, audio recorder, and other tools.
- A basic software toolkit for designing open-shared learning may include basic office suite software, multimedia design software, video editing software, image editing software, authoring tools, text editor, and other tools.
- The "slow fires" of technological datedness usually require efforts at digital preservation (as an effort towards "future proofing"). These efforts include maintaining raw digital contents at their most readable and non-proprietary form.
- Some developers prefer to hand-code using high level computer languages. These afford close-in control but require a high level skill set and close attention to details.
- It is helpful to think of cost-cutting measures for open-shared learning projects. Freeware can be one resource to mitigate costs for an open-shared project. However, some freeware has malware riding along, so accessing such resources will require vetting.

5.6.2 *Critical Thinking Questions*

Affordances and Constraints, Tradeoffs, and Costs

- With the selection of any particular equipment and software of a particular class, there will be tradeoffs with its features, capabilities, costs, and other considerations

(both strengths and weaknesses). In each equipment and software category, what are core requirements that cannot be compromised? Which are features that are not directly required?
- Between commercial-proprietary and open-source software programs, which are most preferable for different functionalities: digital recording, digital authoring, digital editing, and others? Why?
- When does it make sense to go with freeware instead of proprietary software, to save on costs?

Distributed Teams and Technology Setups

- In a distributed team context, is it more efficient to have one fully equipped shop for content processing, or distributed locales? Why or why not?
- Does concentration of the software mean a single point-of-failure and excessively concentrated power? Does having all the technologies in all distributed locales mean unnecessary expense?

Avoiding Security Compromises

- Given the wide prevalence of malware, what are some safer ways to deal with free software downloads and with cloud-based software-as-a-service?
- What are the standards that may ensure some level of "trust"?

Outreaches to Potential Learners

- Beyond findability of the learning objects and sequences, what are some ways to target particular audiences with intrinsic interests in the topic? Peripheral interests in the topic? How much effort should be put into attracting larger audiences to using particular learning objects?

Versioning Learning Contents

- Given the challenges of digital preservation, should a project involve multiple versions of particular learning objects and learning sequences? How much effort should go into versioning?
- Should the assumption be that the learning contents will have sufficient value into the future that it should not be allowed to fall into technological disuse? What if the work is in the Great Unread or the Great Unused?

5.7 Assignments

Directions The Assignments are divided into two sections, Basic and Advanced. The Basic section is for those who may not have much instructional design experience or background in the area of creating instructional contents for open sharing. As such, these are set up to familiarize them with the chapter-related knowledge, skills, and abilities. The Advanced section is for those who already have some knowledge of this general space and who may benefit from more challenging work.

In a formal learning context, these assignments would benefit from expert feedback and further applications of the learning contents. In a nonformal or informal learning context, including self-directed learning, these assignments would benefit from both reflection and practice. These assignments are built to be extensible, to have elements added to benefit the learners. They are designed to be assigned selectively and not in full. The setup of this textbook is as a work sequence, and similarly, the assignments may be set up as tasks to be completed by the learner in a sequential way...that takes them through the fairly complete and sequential *open-shared learning design → development → test → revision → launch → post-launch* process.

5.7.1 Basic

Assignment 5.1: Defining Standards for Third-Party-Created Technologies Before defining the hardware and software technologies list, write up a list of the technological requirements based on usability, functionality, outputs, company reputation, and other details. Be as thorough as possible. Consider how the technological affordances and enablements will affect the design possibilities, the work capabilities, and available decisions and choice-making.

Extra: In professional workplaces, there are legal standards that have to be adhered to in the selection of third-party software. These include standards for accessibility, legality, and others. Make a complete lists of such requirements. Write some paragraphs about why these are important and how these standards affect what may/may not be used.

Assignment 5.2: Listing Necessary Hardware (Equipment) and Software Programs Draft a list of all necessary technologies (hardware and software) to build a digital learning object, course, or sequence from end-to-end. Specify the technologies as well as the required software (including versions). Write out a budget for any equipment or software that is not already readily available in the workplace. If possible, identify freeware that may be used in lieu of some commercial-grade software.

Assignment 5.3: Taking Inventory of Technology Resources Define the need for particular deliverables for the current open sharing project. Reverse-engineer what it will require to create these deliverables. Based on the needs of the open sharing project, take inventory of the equipment and software that you have already and those that you will need to acquire. Also, explore freeware that may be used to support the project. Examine the pros and cons of respective freeware programs.

Assignment 5.4: Candidate Hosting Sites Review a number of available candidate hosting sites for the open-shared learning. Create a pros and cons table to evaluate the respective features of each. Read the end user license agreements (EULAs) for each of the potential hosting sites as well. What are the most important features of these hosting sites for your work: technological functionality, reputation, terms of use, interface design, and others?

Assignment 5.5: Working for Digital Preservation Over Time Digital contents are prone to inaccessibility based on "slow fires" and fast-changing technologies. One way to address this issue is through "digital preservation" efforts. What are some basic methods to protect digital contents/information by going with the most simple technological file formats and open-source formats (instead of proprietary file formats)? What are the most basic file format types for text, for imagery, for audio, for video, datasets, and others? What are the most efficient ways to preserve the relevant digital information without make-work?

5.7.2 Advanced

Assignment 5.6: Tapping Outside Design and Development Expertise Write a short essay about when it would make sense to tap outside expertise (with their related technologies) to do part of the instructional design and development work. Explain what standards would be set for the external designs and digital resources. Explain what formats the respective files should come in and why.

Assignment 5.7: Creating and Sharing Code in an Open-Source Way Developers who create software have had a long tradition of sharing their work in an open-source way. They have created licensure for sharing well before the age of Creative Commons licensure. Identify some reputable open-source projects, and examine how these technologies are used. Explore the underlying structures that enable the evolution of such projects. Examine the leadership (Centralized, decentralized? Distributed, non-distributed?) behind such efforts.

Assignment 5.8: Exploring Open Data Some governments and other entities enable the open sharing of data that are byproducts of the work. These data are cleaned (against sensitive data leakage such as personally identifiable information or "PII" and other issues), and metadata are created about each dataset. Read up on the standards for the open sharing of data. What are the rules of engagement? If you were to share a dataset legally, what are the steps that you would have to take, and why? From the recipient point-of-view, what insights can you glean from a dataset shared on data.gov? (Choose one, and find out!)

Assignment 5.9: Learner-Based Customizations and Adaptivity Modern "courseware" enables some level of learner adaptivity—based on learner actions, learner performance, learner profiles, and others—or some combination of the prior. If you were to build branching logic in a simple learning sequence, on what basis would you set up the branching, and how would you ensure that the branching makes sense? How would you make sure that the branching is ethical (that no one is shorted in their learning based on the branching)? How transparent would you be about the branching?

Extra: What about other methods of learner-based customizations have you engaged in? What do you find to be effective?

Assignment 5.10: Scripting and Hand Coding Some code purists prefer to create programs and functionalities by hand, using high-level scripting languages. Over time, these tools have had data visualization and other packages enabled. What are your experiences with scripting and hand coding? What do you tend to use these for, and how? What computer languages do you prefer, and why?

Assignment 5.11: Educational Semantic Web Web 3.0, the Semantic Web, is based on World Wide Web Consortium (W3C) standards to enable common data formats and exchange protocols—to enable machine collection and access to information. Tim Berners-Lee conceptualized the Semantic Web in 1999, with the following quote: "I have a dream for the Web [in which computers] become capable of analyzing all the data on the Web—the content, links, and transactions between people and computers. A "Semantic Web", which makes this possible, has yet to emerge, but when it does, the day-to-day mechanisms of trade, bureaucracy and our daily lives will be handled by machines talking to machines. The "intelligent agents" people have touted for ages will finally materialize" (Berners-Lee and Fischetti 1999, Ch. 12). There have been advancements in the creation of semantic learning webs through learning object metadata standards (Aroyo and Dicheva 2004, pp. 61–62).

What do these standards say? How do they affect the work of creating open-shared learning resources? What are some effective descriptors to describe online learning resources?

Key Terms and Definitions

Authoring Tool A software program that enables the design and creation of born-digital contents (also referred to as "authorware" and "courseware" and other terms in the electronic learning space)

Content Management System A technology that enables the hosting and delivery of various types of digital contents: text, imagery, video, and others

Digital Preservation Enablement of authentic digital contents over time

Freeware Free or no-cost software

Learning Management System (LMS) A technology tool that enables various dimensions of online (and blended and face-to-face) learning including the management of persistent identities, delivery of digital presentations, assignments, assessments, grading, and others

Slow Fire A term (from the library sciences and information sciences) to describe the aging and degrading of paper over time ("paper embrittlement resulting from acid decay"); a term which has also been applied to digital technologies which go defunct resulting in limited access to various contents

Social Media Platform A technology that enables people to create personal profiles in persistent ways, intercommunicate, and interact with others

User-Generated Contents The text, images, audio, video, and multimedia created and shared with others by users of a social media platform

References

Aroyo L, and Dicheva D. The new challenges for e-learning: The Educational Semantic Web. *Educational Technology & Society* 7: 59 – 69, 2004.

Berners-Lee T, and Fischetti M. *Weaving the Web*. Ch. 12. San Francisco: Harper. ISBN 978-0-06-251587-2. 1999.

Downes S. Learning objects: Resources for distance education worldwide. *International Review of Research in Open and Distance Learning* 2: 1 – 35, 2001.

Hai-Jew S. Poster: Using Large-scale LMS Data Portal Data to Improve Teaching and Learning at K-State. 2017. https://www.slideshare.net/ShalinHaiJew/poster-using-largescale-lms-data-portal-data-to-improve-teaching-and-learning-at-kstate.

Kaskalis TH, Tzidamis TD, and Margaritis K. Multimedia authoring tools: The quest for an educational package. *Educational Technology & Society* 10: 135 – 162, 2007.

Legris P., Ingham J., and Collerette P. Why do people use information technology? A critical review of the technology acceptance model. *Information & Management* 40: 191 – 204, 2003.

Locatis C, and Al-Nuaim H. Interactive technology and authoring tools: A historical review and analysis. *Educational Technology Research and Development* 47: 63 – 75, 1999.

McGill TJ, and Klobas JE. A task-technology fit view of learning management system impact. *Computers & Education* 52: 496 – 508, 2009.

Parkes A. The effect of task-individual-technology fit on user attitude and performance: An experimental investigation. *Decision Support Systems* 54: 997 – 1009, 2013.

Wenk B. Open educational resources (OER) inspire teaching and learning. IEEE EDUCON Education Engineering 2010- The future of Global Learning Engineering Education. Madrid, Spain. 435 – 441, 2010.

Additional Reading Section

Clark RC, and Mayer RE. *E-Learning and the Science of Instruction: Proven Guidelines for Consumers and Designers of Multimedia Thinking*. Hoboken, New Jersey: John Wiley & Sons. 2016.

Hai-Jew S. *Constructing Self-Discovery Learning Spaces Online: Scaffolding and Decision Making Technologies*. Hershey, Pennsylvania: Information Science Reference, IGI Global. 2012.

Hai-Jew S. *Digital Imagery and Informational Graphics in E-Learning: Maximizing Visual Technologies*. Hershey, Pennsylvania: Information Science Reference, IGI Global. 2010.

Hai-Jew S. *Open-Source Technologies for Maximizing the Creation, Deployment, and Use of Digital Resources and Information.* Hershey, Pennsylvania: Information Science Reference, IGI Global. 2013.

Hai-Jew, S. *Packaging Digital Information for Enhanced Learning and Analysis: Data Visualization, Spatialization, and Multidimensionality.* Hershey, Pennsylvania: Information Science Reference, IGI Global. 2014.

Hai-Jew S. *Virtual Immersive and 3D Learning Spaces: Emerging Technologies and Trends.* Hershey, Pennsylvania: Information Science Reference, IGI Global. 2011.

Chapter 6
Establishing and Applying Contemporaneous E-Learning Standards: Evolving Stylebooks and Planning Work

Abstract The standards for e-learning are in constant flux, and they come from a range of government entities, educational institutions, professional groups, education researchers, technology companies, learners, and others. These e-learning standards enable more effective learning by ensuring that shared contents are built to quality standards (of factuality, of legality, of design, of functionality, of accessibility, and other features). This chapter explores some individual and team-based ways to control for adherence to e-learning standards during the design and development phases. It describes how to set up an evolving consensus-built project (work) stylebook (statement of work) to co-define the e-learning standards and how to apply these standards in the work. This includes a section on planning the work, and finally, it describes some ways to assess for e-learning quality once the learning resources are drafted.

Keywords E-learning quality standards · Project stylebook (statement of work, proposal of work) · Template · Work plans

> A dream doesn't become reality through magic; it takes sweat, determination and hard work.
> –Colin Powell (1937–)

> Only great minds can afford a simple style.
> –Stendhal (1783–1842)

> Unless commitment is made, there are only promises and hopes, but no plans.
> –Peter F. Drucker (1909–2005)

S. Hai-Jew, *Designing Instruction For Open Sharing*,
https://doi.org/10.1007/978-3-030-02713-1_6

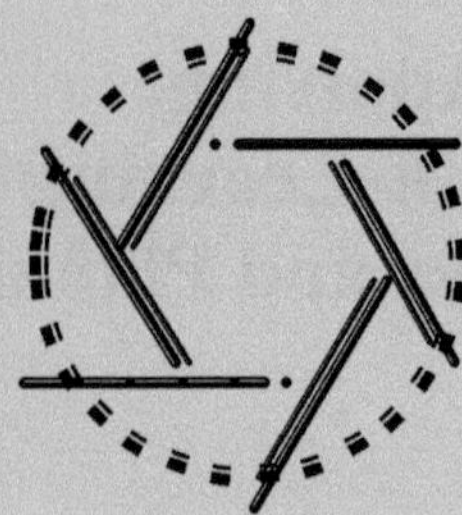

Opening Scenario

Opening Scenario: Got a Workable Plan?

With more complex instructional design and development projects, there are common design aids—project stylebooks (that record the standards that will be used in the project), templates (of the various types of objects used for the learning), and other work supports. These objects help to systematize projects—especially those that tend to be more complex, with geographically distributed team members. This is not to say that what is designed has to be fitted to templates and high constraints. The creativity of the designers and developers should be as little constrained as possible. However, for the sake of legality and basic standards, defining these is important.

How systematically designed should the open-shared learning be, and why?

Some Early Questions to Consider

If you were to sketch a project stylebook for your design of an open-shared learning object, what would you include, and why? What parts of a project should be defined, so that the designs and developments can adhere to particular standards (legal, technological, aesthetic, values, branding, and others)?

If you were to create common templates for an online learning project, what would the templates include? How would you set these up in an effective way to support the project evolution?

If you were to create a timeline, what would be the work sequences, and how much time would each task require?

If you were to draft a real-world budget for the work, what information would that budget include, and why?

Learning Objectives

Learners will…

Contemporaneous E-Learning Quality Standards

- Define sources for contemporary e-learning standards (laws, policies, technology standards; theories, models, and frameworks, and related research; state of the art, quality definitions, project specifics, and others)
- Select the e-learning standards that apply directly to the particular projects

- Consider how the various e-learning standards express in the learning designs and objects, courses, sequences, and resources

Learning Resource Project Stylebook

- Describe the importance of having a consensus-built expert-informed project stylebook, which is evolved through the course of an instructional design project
- Include the selected e-learning standards into the requirements
- List and define the various parts of a project stylebook (with a focus on instructional design and development needs) and explain the applications of a project stylebook
- Draft a project stylebook with all basic required elements, including a real-world budget and schedule
- Include a style section in the stylebook, to include considerations of branding and user acceptance (including visual design, audio design, textual design, logos, and other aspects)
- Describe how identified contraventions of the stylebook requirements will be prioritized and addressed (practically) and which identified issues will not be addressed given limited time and resources

Work Plans

- Produce a practical work plan that aligns with workplace realities in the local context
  - Include work-based tasks, timelines, resources, technologies, budgets, labor, deliverables, professional work-based roles, legal constraints, policy constraints, and so on
- Based on your work plan, conduct a light analysis and see if there are efficiencies that may be practically exploited

6.1 Introduction

This next step begins the work of the actual open-shared learning resource, and it begins with defining some e-learning standards that will be built to. Some of these standards are from the legal realm, others from the technological. Those "givens" are addressed elsewhere in this text. The main focus will be here will be on other standards beyond the requisite ones. Next, based on the custom e-learning standards, those objectives will inform the creation of a project (work) stylebook that will define the work. A projected work plan will be defined to explain how the work will be achieved most efficiently.

This effort is Step 6 of the work sequence (Fig. 6.1). So far, readers have conducted a scan of the open sharing learning environment, profiled target and potential learners, reviewed some of their knowledge about human learning (through exploring some theories, models, and frameworks), and explored the legal requirements in the space. This step now focuses more specifically on the planned learning resource.

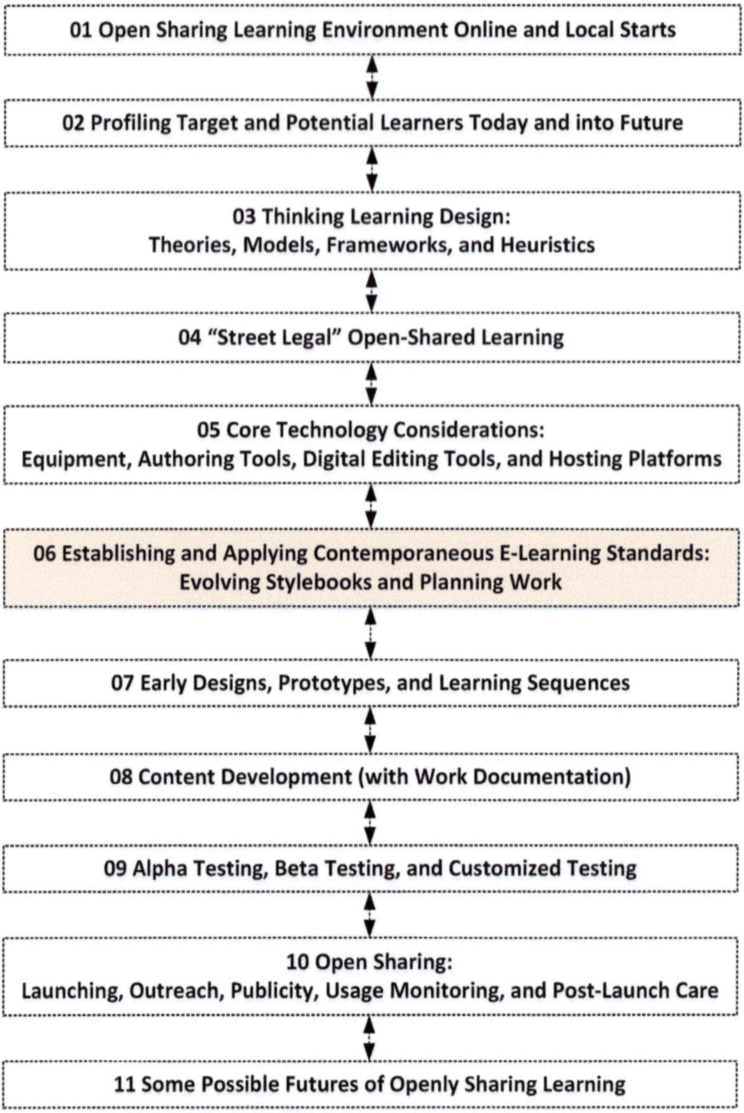

Fig. 6.1 Step 6 in the open-shared learning resource development sequence

6.2 Review of the Literature

This chapter helps move the reader from a general concept with some early reconnaissance work to actual steps that may take them closer to the work of designing and developing an open-shared learning resource. This is a culminating step that draws in part from some of the earlier work in the environmental scan, the learner

Fig. 6.2 Getting from point A to point B in the design and development of open-shared learning resources

profiling, the exploration of secondary research and theorizing, the laws that apply to the space, and some required technologies. All the prior data are generally necessary for informed decision making about whether to advance, pause, or retreat. Those who are up-to-date on the prior information will be able to make faster progress by coming right to this planning phase.

Why is planning important? Planning helps bridge the "say-do" gap. There is a chasm between stated intentionality ("say") and actual actions ("do"), and the planning work in this chapter is one way to help bridge that space from the intangible to the tangible. Abstract intentions require plenty of efforts to instantiate the work in the world (Fig. 6.2).

Project (work) stylebooks are not usually created for the development of one stand-alone learning resource or a one-off share. Rather, these are created for uses in the following circumstances:

- when there is a collection of related learning objects (like for an evolving website or a podcast series)
- when a learning resource project involves a number of distributed collaborative team members
- when a project is a complex multi-year project with many moving parts (and often the need to report out to a grant funder)

A work plan helps an individual or team to actualize the work described in the project stylebook, so the stylebook is a reference resource. In cases where work handoffs are needed, the project stylebooks and work plans may aid in the transition. On a project's completion, these documents may serve as institutional memory. So let's begin with contemporaneous e-learning quality standards.

Contemporaneous E-learning Quality Standards Contemporaneous e-learning quality standards are defined in three categories. One is a "fixed" category of non-negotiables, like legal requirements (which affect controlled information, intellectual property, accessibility, research ethics) instantiated in laws and policies, and technological standards and requirements (which affect how various digital objects function, and how reusable they are).

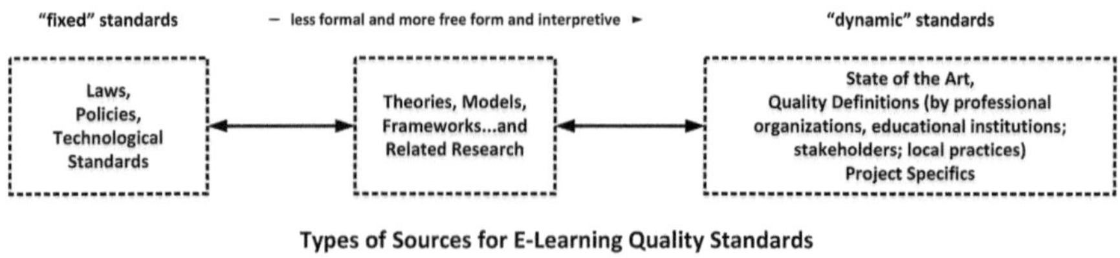

Fig. 6.3 Types of sources for e-learning quality standards

Another category is a category of quality standards from the formal theorizing and research. These include the models, theories, and frameworks in the academic literature, and related research. Based on these findings, there are some semi-fixed understandings of how people learn best. While much of this work is non-prescriptive, many do suggest some advisable ways forward and warn against risky ways forward.

Then, third, there are a more self-defined and "dynamic" category of quality standards, and these are informed by the state-of-the-art practices in the field. This is defined by the formally defined quality standards by professional organizations, educational institutions (K12, higher education, and others), e-learning quality rubrics, quality practices, and more local understandings and practices of e-learning standards (such as among learners and other stakeholders). The design/development team is responsible for collecting the relevant local data for a full understanding of e-learning quality standards that apply to their respective projects. The on-ground realities of the target learners, the learning domain, the learning designs, the harnessed technologies…and other factors…will inform the quality standards dynamically adopted.

In this latter category, there may be standards like the following: a welcoming tone, cultural alignment with potential learner groups, engaging learning experiences, moody atmospherics, research-relevant, common-sensical and applied to a professional context, freeform, high-energy, learning outcomes mapped with the revised Bloom's Taxonomy, attention-getting openings, instructor telepresence, and other ambitions and phrases that signify quality for the particular project. In each step, there is a lessening of formality and a move towards more creative interpretations of quality. There are many right ways to design and create learning resources (Fig. 6.3).

Defining quality standards early helps an individual or team focus the work, and it often saves on retrofitting and make-work. That said, it is wholly possible to discover relevant quality standards during the work. For example, as the individual or team is working on a particular part of the design or development, they may discover new quality standards for the particular type of learning that they are creating. Documenting that and including those new e-learning standards may benefit the project work and the team's professional skills.

There is no accepted across-the-board consensus about what quality e-learning includes separate from particular contexts. The extant standards in the academic literature are for college courses taught online, with particular emphasis on "high-tech high-touch" strategies. There are quality standards suggesting the importance of alignment in design, by ensuring that the learning objectives and learning outcomes align, along with the built assignments and activities. Then, there are standards suggesting the need for learning in a domain to align with the practices of graduates in the field. There are standards related to ensuring that the whole learner is considered in massive open online courses (MOOCs) and other online learning contexts with large numbers of learners. The research is broad and deep, and it is will beyond the purview of this text to even begin to try to summarize some of these.

Of course, the fact that the open-shared learning contents are being built to an open space means that the target learners may be inaccurately defined, with learners coming at the work for informal, nonformal, and formal learning contexts. Given the fungibility of learning objects and resources, the various "use cases" will be potentially broad, such as in F2F contexts, blended, and fully online contexts.

In the learning object space, researchers have looked into how those who might adopt and use others' learning resources evaluate quality. Teachers who took part in a study were aware of a range of quality approaches: "Quality Management (ISO 9000, EFQM)" (46%), "Quality Checklist or Quality Criteria" (41%), "Quality Marks (quality assessment by independent organization)" (38%), "Benchmarking" (27%), "Evaluation (of courses/programs)" (64%), "Accreditation (of University programs)" (46%), "Peer reviewing" (53%), "Rankings (for example giving stars)" (65%), (and) "User recommendations (recommendations from colleagues or friends)" (82%) (Clements and Pawlowski 2011, p. 11) (note: in the order as presented by the original researchers in a horizontal bar chart).

Some researchers have shared about work processes that enable quality. One researcher advises using "a design process modelled after an assembly line" and replacing design documents with "specification sheets" and to use "electronic storyboard templates" in lieu of authoring tools (Roytek 2010, p. 175). In many ways, beyond the "fixed" e-learning standards, the project-specific standards set for particular projects depend a fair amount on interpretation and expression because there is not just one way a particular project feature will instantiate. This means that when assessing for the presence of that quality, the design/development team will have to return to the stylebook and the defined meanings of the respective quality.

For all the various types of definitions of quality for e-learning, defined standards will not necessarily result in similar designs. The concept of a "convergent validity" (the idea that designs will be similar when the same standards are being used) is far-fetched, and there is no actual "equifinality" (a same resultant outcome or end state from different start points). In most learning designs, there are so many design influences and so many designed moving parts that the results are richly divergent and varied. Assessing quality in e-learning designs will require judging the resulting learning resources, to some degree, on their own merits.

Project (Work) Stylebooks In general, project (work) stylebooks are considered internal documentation for projects and the organizations that use them. It is not common practice for these to be published or shared publicly. That is not to say that shared project stylebooks may not be valuable for others' usage, such as for research and analytical purposes. A sparser stylebook template with specific prior project information removed may be helpful for applied project work, without prior project specifics unduly affecting others' works.

The literature may benefit, too, from insights on how to best create and evolve these, and the roles of topical content experts in contributing input and suggestions.

In terms of work mechanisms to help people to be more thorough and quality minded, the humble checklist is used to powerful effects (Gawande 2009), especially given the limits of human cognition, decision making, and memory.

Planning Work Planning and coordination are critical aspects of enabling individuals to work together well as a team. Setting temporal norms early on for self-managing project groups enables more efficient shared work later on (Janicik and Bartel 2003).

Work planning is an inexact science in many fields. In many projects, inaccurate information may mean cost overruns, missed deadlines, wasted resources, political fallout, over-commitments to work, and even ultimately, project non-completion and failure.

The research literature on work planning shows a human tendency towards a "planning fallacy," resulting in underestimations of the resources and time needed to complete work. The "planning fallacy" is a form of "optimism bias," which leads people to take on work because they think it will be easier, less expensive, less effortful, than it actually is. (And some have argued that if self-fulfilling prophecies apply, then maybe an optimistic start may mean actual follow-through and finish… in some cases…but more likely in the minority of cases.) Others have suggested that unwarranted optimism can give people a sense of the doability of a tough project in a shorter amount of time and may make it more likely for them to take it on, so there may be a "utility" or benefit in thinking that a challenging task will take less time than it does (Brunnermeier et al. 2008).

Researchers have long tried to understand why people tend towards optimism bias (having high expectations for achievable work vs. the actual outcome) in work estimations. One study found that people tend to over-estimate task duration for short tasks (less than two minutes in the study) but to under-estimate the necessary time for long tasks "for both remembered and predicted duration," which some researchers attribute to biases in memory (Roy and Christenfeld 2008, p. 202). Others have also found that for atypical tasks, there are time-based nuances, with "unpacking atypical long components" increasing task duration estimates and "unpacking atypical short components" as decreasing task duration estimates; whether an atypical task occurs early or late in a sequence also affect time duration estimates (with early tasks increasing task duration estimates and late components leaving time estimates unaffected (and sequence placement for early or late tasks for typical components did not have an effect on estimates) (Hadjichristidis et al. 2014, p. 45).

In terms of time units, the larger time units are more practically relevant, so think hours and not minutes, days and not hours, weeks and not days, months and not weeks, and years and not months. Variability in task difficulty (for shorter tasks) can lead to over-estimations of the time needed (Rodon and Meyer 2012).

There are social power elements, too, that may cause skews in optimism bias. Those in positions of social power tend to bias individuals towards underestimations of time needed to accomplish particular tasks because of a narrow over focus on the particular goals (Weick and Guinote 2010). Time predictions for completions of tasks "often have little or no influence on completion times" (Buehler et al. 2010, p. 23). Research is ongoing to understand the magnitude and directions of the planning fallacy.

Another contemporary understanding is that people may build their understandings based on an "inside view" of the work and focusing on their own internal "plans and scenarios" and not paying attention to relevant information from the external environment and others' experiences in the space. People may build there understandings based on hopes instead of looking at the experiences of others who have come before them, and they engage in base-rate neglect (they do not look at common probabilities). Expectations for positive outcomes from the future task apparently tend to lead to more optimistic time predictions (Buehler et al. 1997). When people approach projects with too much optimism, they may be blind to "high costs but also to unexpectedly low net benefits" (Flyvbjerg and Sunstein 2015, p. 1). People may be dazzled by their own expectations for positive outcomes ("best case scenarios") and fail to look further. In such cases, they may take on outsized risks without considering the full range possible consequences. Such predictions of future behavior "overweight the strength of their current intentions, and underweight situational or contextual factors that influence the ease with which intentions are translated into action," which would suggest limits to follow-through (Koehler and Poon 2006, p. 517). Or, they may go to the other extreme, with the internal focus amplifying tendencies towards loss aversion (meaning that people will not take what they see as undue risk). Acquiring a proportionate sense of risk requires appropriate research and analysis and risk mitigation.

Humans and Problems of Predictivity One of the predominant theories is that when people make judgments under conditions of uncertainty, they tend towards built-in cognitive biases (Kahneman and Tversky 1996). These biases are expressed in unthinking ways. For example, people tend towards over-confidence in estimations (Kahneman and Tversky 1996). People tend to assume that they have control over phenomenon which they do not have. Further, they tend towards inaccuracy for self-predictions even when these are for factors under the individual's control (Koehler and Poon 2006, p. 517). Researchers suggest that one mitigation is to know when to trigger "thinking slow" (System 2) vs. "thinking fast" (System 1), or when to go analytical vs. unthinking and habitual (Kahneman 2011). The limits to intuitive judgments mean that people need to correct for these (Kahneman and Tversky 1977).

Broadly speaking, Philip E. Tetlock's research suggests that those who have broad knowledge ("foxes") tend to outperform those with fixed ideologies ("hedgehogs") in terms of political predictions (Tetlock 2005). Individuals need to be willing to change their points of view as they receive new information. This reluctance to accept evidence that contradicts "preconceived notions" stems from "confirmation bias" (Kahneman et al. 2011, p. 51), and is one of a litany of cognitive biases built into human decision making. Worse, people with a "negative weighting bias" or negative valence (viewing a thing as aversive, having a negative attitude about something) will avoid challenging their own attitude by engaging in-world experience whereas those with a more "positive weighting bias" will engage to learn more. The researchers explain:

> Those with a more negative weighting bias gave greater weight to negative information that was actually false, avoided testing the associated stimuli, and hence did not discover their true value. Those with a more positive weighting bias gave less weight to the negative information, tested the associated stimuli more fully, and overcame the false negative information. (Rocklage and Fazio 2013, p. 144)

Pre-existing positive and negative associations have real-world effects on "judgment and decision-making, close relationships, the self, and stereotyping" (Rocklage and Fazio 2013, p. 144). The "weighting bias is most impactful in novel situations" (Rocklage and Fazio 2013, p. 145), which suggests that those who have a negative or positive approach to new situations should be aware of their own tendencies and mitigate for those by engaging the world and being open to changing their stances. To use a common colloquialism, people need to "get outside of their own heads." One study looked at whether procrastination tendencies were associated with the planning fallacy. In this study, students who procrastinated in preparing for exams and spent less time preparing than their peers were still fairly accurate in their study time predictions (Pychyl et al. 2000).

Need for Strategic Information-Seeking Not only do they need to seek more information, but the information has to be relevant, and it has to be accurate (so misinformation has to be sifted out and discounted). Researchers write:

> Decision makers have a strong tendency to consider problems as unique. They isolate the current choice from future opportunities and neglect the statistics of the past in evaluating current plans. Overly cautious attitudes to risk result from a failure to appreciate the effects of statistical aggregation in mitigating relative risk. Overly optimistic forecasts result from the adoption of an inside view of the problem, which anchors predictions on plans and scenarios. (Kahneman and Lovallo 1993, p. 17)

The use of "narrow decision frames" isolates the decision making from other considerations. This tendency to "consider decision problems one at a time, often isolating the current problem from other choices that may be pending, as well as from future opportunities to make similar decisions" (Kahneman and Lovallo 1993, p. 19) decontextualizes the decision-making and separates that decision from the real world. (World phenomena do not occur in isolation.) Consciously broadening the focus to a more panoramic view by broadening sources of information may aid the decision making. To these ends, researchers suggest finding similar "classes of cases" that may offer reference points for the current context (Kahneman and Lovallo 1993, p. 25). The use of reference classes to "forecast in practice" (Flyvbjerg 2008) requires that they are actually comparables. Because of the outsized influence of analogies (and cases) on decision-making, researchers have come up with ways to use these analytically to improve their usage by critically and systematically analyzing analogies (cases) and seeing what light they shed on a certain context and considering how much to weight each case (Lovallo et al. 2012).

When people present to others, their self-presentation motives (such as wanting to appear favorably to others) may also influence the planning fallacy. The public attention of others does not apparently increase accountability nor accuracy even if there is awareness that their claims will be necessarily tested (Pezzo et al. 2006, p. 225).

Unpacking Work Another method for trying to correct for the planning fallacy is to have people "unpack" multifaceted tasks so that they may arrive at a more accurate estimate, and this method was found to be helpful for more complex tasks (Kruger and Evans 2004, p. 586). Decomposition of tasks was found to help predictive accuracy in some cases and hurt in others. Spelling out "implementation intentions" was found to reduce the optimistic bias in the planning fallacy and result in higher completion rates (Koole and Spijker 2000).

Going to Groups Another mitigation for engaging human cognitive biases is to go to the "wisdom of crowds" (Surowiecki 2005). In this approach, certain types of issues may be best understood with the inputs of independent individuals in a crowd in a pooled polling approach. In organizations, individual cognitive biases may be mitigated for with more collective decision making (Kahneman et al. 2011, p. 52).

Remembering Past Experiences Another approach to improving prediction accuracy is to bring past experiences top of mind (Peetz and Buehler 2011).

Time Factors In another research project, "individuals predicted earlier completion times for close than distant projects. In contexts that prompted a focus on obstacles, individuals predicted later completion times for close than distant projects" (Peetz et al. 2010, p. 709). In other words, the optimism bias manifested for more salient near-term work than distant future ones. One understanding is that when individuals plan narrowly for particular work, they "neglect other useful information such as previous completion times, potential obstacles, and competing demands for their time (Buehler et al. 2002; Kahneman and Tversky 1979, as cited in Peetz et al. 2010, p. 709). There are risks in focusing too narrowly or concretely on particular defined paths to achieving project aims. Based on temporal construal theory, what is nearer in time is more concrete (and more defined), and what is farther in future time is more abstract (Liberman and Trope 1998; Trope and Liberman 2003, as cited in Peetz et al. 2010, p. 710). Other research has found conflicting results: "Research on predictions in other domains indicates that people become less optimistic and less confident in their predictions about an event as it draws near (Eyal et al. 2004; Gilovich et al. 1993; Savitsky et al. 1998) or is made to seem closer in time (Sanna et al. 2005)" (Peetz et al. 2010, p. 710). There is thinking that focusing on concrete planning but also on obstacles may cancel each other out and result in more accurate time predictions (Peetz et al. 2010, p. 716).

Other research found longer duration times for closer-in work. As people get closer to a task in time (temporally) and in "hypotheticality," duration estimates increased (Kanten 2011, p. 1044). More real tasks were estimated to take longer, and more hypothetical tasks were found to take shorter amounts of time (Kanten 2011). Thinking about tasks only shrunk duration estimates for simple tasks but elongated duration estimates for longer tasks (Siddiqui et al. 2013, p. 184).

If ego-based assessments lead to planning fallacies, would having people think from a third-person point-of-view mitigate such skews? Indeed, participants in four studies predicted longer completion times when exposed to third-person imagery and hew closer to realistic predictions (Buehler et al. 2012, p. 138). Such an approach also focuses away from individual motivations which may affect judgment.

There are corrective benefits of having people connect their future work predictions for length of work with relevant past work experiences (Buehler et al. 1994). More recent research suggests that people's memories of past project durations are biased and not particularly accurate (Roy et al. 2005).

6.3 Contemporary E-learning Standards, Evolving Project Stylebooks, and Planning Work

Formalizing the standards of an instructional design project help an individual or team flesh out their objectives, practical ways to achieve those objectives (to quality), and to advance the work in practical ways.

6.3.1 Part 1: Contemporaneous E-learning Quality Standards

E-learning standards are in constant flux depending on a variety of factors. As noted earlier, there are fixed definitions of such standards based on laws and policies, and technology standards. Then there are standards from theorizing and research. Then, there are standards from the state of the art, stakeholders in the field, and local realities of the project. While standards may be defined early in a stylebook, the sense of quality will evolve as the designer/developers actually engage the work and make decisions on-ground. Where quality standards really matter is on the applied work. Subject matter experts advising on projects will also have insights based on their expertise in the domain.

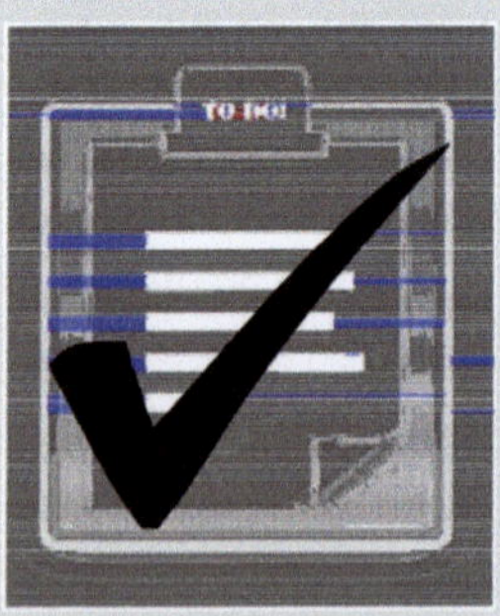

Task #1: E-learning Standards to Use as Generic and Others to Use as Specific

Based on your local context, where would your e-learning projects find the fixed e-learning standards? The semi-fixed learning standards? Dynamic e-learning standards? Do you find overlaps, and if so, where? (Table 6.1)

Table 6.1 Sources for fixed, semi-fixed and dynamic e-learning standards

Sources	Fixed e-learning standards	Semi-fixed e-learning standards	Dynamic e-learning standards
Laws			
Policies			
Technological standards			
Technologies			
State of the art			
Professional organizations			
Educational institutions			
Grant funder			
Learners			
Design/development team			
Others			

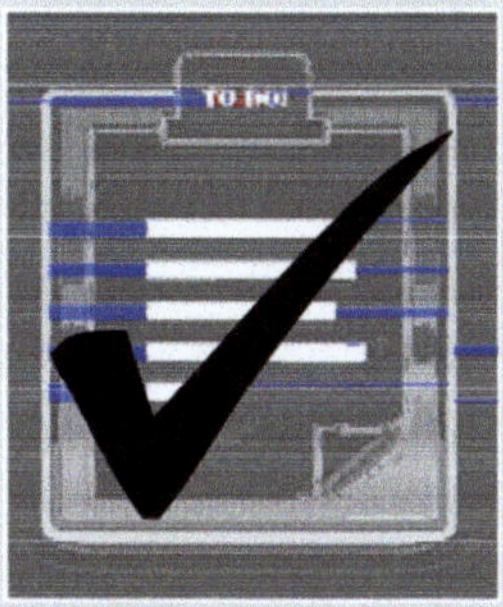

Task #2: Where to Source Updates to E-Learning Standards

The point about going with contemporaneous e-learning standards is that this is a dynamic space with a lot of changes. As new discoveries are made, new technologies are rolled out, new practices are achieved, people's thinking about what is effective changes.

What are some important sources to check for updates to e-learning standards? Why? Which sources are more trustworthy than others? How would you decide which of these standards to adopt and which to leave, for a particular project?

6.3.2 *Part 2: Project (Work) Stylebooks*

"Project (work) stylebooks" (or "statements of work") are usually created for several contexts. One, the first learning resource may be the first of a series of related resources. Here, the project stylebooks help maintain an institutional memory of the standards applied to the project, so the follow-on creations align with the first in terms of standards, look-and-feel, usability, and other features.

Two, the learning design is complex and will require a cross-functional team to actualize. (A cross-functional team is one whose members come at the task with different backgrounds and skills.) Here, a project stylebook helps the team decide on shared standards (and understandings) across different areas of expertise and stay on course in the design and development work. It also helps the team coordinate around a schedule and a budget (if one is available).

Three, the learning resources being created are complex, with longer sequences, mixed sets of learning resources, combinations of short courses, long courses, or series of learning. Here, a project stylebook ensures that the various elements are of-a-piece based on the defined standards. A stylebook also ensures that the work meets technological standards for functionality and optimally that the work stays on schedule.

Project stylebooks are not as common for one-off learning resources. If plans change and follow-on resources are planned, it is possible to "reverse engineer" a project stylebook from the completed resource; however, this would be done inferentially from observations and may not fully represent the intentionality of the designer/developer individual or team.

Project stylebooks may range from the practical to the aspirational, with doable standards for the practical and idealized ones for the aspirational. The point of stylebooks is to enable documentation of standards for the learning resources, and to make the work efficient, and after the first use, somewhat reproducible.

Stylebook Affordances A consensus-built expert-informed project stylebook is critical at the beginning of a project so that all members of the cross-functional team are aware of what the respective requirements are for the different team members. The shared discussions to co-develop the stylebook offers a number of team benefits. They may…

- Help the team members get to know each other
- Enable the team to brainstorm together and bring more creative power to the shared work
- Bring attention to issues of concern
- Help the team members better understand the work of others and how each of their roles inter-mesh
- Encourage future intercommunications and collaborations
- Help the team work more efficiently to defined standards
- Provide each member of the team a work project overview early on, and
- Result in a practically usable project (work) stylebook, among others.

Research suggests that when team members work collaboratively on a specific task over time, their sense of "common ground" increases, with higher amounts of "mutual knowledge, beliefs, and protocols that partners share" (Convertino et al. 2007, p. 225).

Working as part of a team may also help mitigate the cognitive biases of an individual making decisions. Further, there has been work on how to mitigate team-based cognitive biases and instrumentation to address some of these limits. A checklist for different types of team-based cognitive errors include a dozen mitigations. There are the risks of motivational biases (conflicts of interest), the affect heuristic (or "falling in love" with the particular recommendations), groupthink (or a lack of dissenting viewpoints considered), the over-influence of "salient analogies" which come to mind easily but may not be actually comparable, the consideration of "credible alternatives" or not, the review of relevant information ("If you had to make this decision again in a year's time, what information would you want, and can you get more of it now?"), anchoring biases (using unsubstantiated or otherwise-questionable numbers), halo effects (the assumption that a person's success in one area will necessarily transfer to another), "sunk-cost fallacy, endowment effect" or an over attachment "to a history of past decisions," decision making on an optimistic "base case" informed by an optimism bias and planning fallacy and "competitor neglect" (not considering competitor responses to a local action), ignoring the potential for disaster ("disaster neglect"), and loss aversion (a tendency towards over caution) (Kahneman et al. 2011, pp. 54–59). Using a designed checklist to test decision making may benefit enable quality controls to be applied to group decision making and the resulting work.

A stylebook for an instructional design project is not a once-and-done sort of approach. The ecosystem is a highly dynamic one, and the rules of engagement, the technologies, and other factors are in constant flux. New information is coming in constantly to the team, and the team itself is learning constantly—about their work, the learners that they are hoping to serve, the technologies they are using, and so on. A project stylebook has to be sufficiently flexible to accommodate those updates and changes, for when new technological standards come online or new learner groups are added as target learners or new learning objectives are added or a new methodology is being taken up or deadlines change. Sometimes, the changes are small and can be made without much debate. Other times, the changes may be fairly fundamental and high-impact to the project. In general, it makes sense to set standards for when the shared stylebook will be updated and how. Or if the project is a large one, different members of the team will be responsible for different parts of the stylebook, and the team members will notify their counterparts of changes as the work progresses. For some tech teams, the consensus-built stylebook will be maintained in a version-controlled environment.

Figure 6.4 provides a sense of how the project stylebook fits in with the instructional design and development process. As conceptualized, the sources in the middle of the circle inform the development of the stylebook. These include theories, models, and frameworks; e-learning standards; the state of the art (of learning resources); technologies; heuristics (and "best practices"); the subject domain; subject matter experts / content experts; and others. Some of these have been reviewed

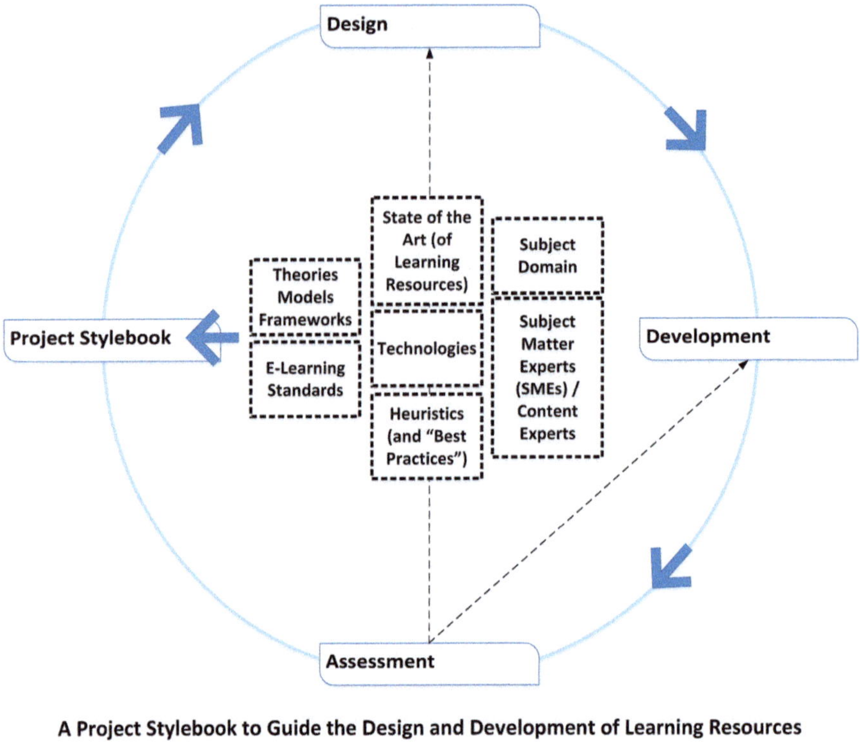

Fig. 6.4 A project stylebook to guide the design and development of learning resources

in prior chapters already. Once the project stylebook has been initially drafted to satisfaction, it may be used to inform the design and the development of the learning resources. The standards described in the project stylebook may be used to design the alpha, beta, and customized tests once the learning resources have been drafted and finalized to a sufficient degree.

Parts to a Project (Work) Stylebook A "project stylebook" is so named because it lists the standards to which technology contents and digital objects may be built. [*Note*: Depending on the work places, these may be referred to as "statements of work" or "proposals of work" (particularly when the project is in a proposal phase while being considered for support or funding; once funded, the "proposal of work" is used to inform the work, and when the project is done, it becomes a "statement of work" and is part of the institutional record of work). If a project is handed off to others when it is partway done, the project stylebook is passed along to the inheriting individual or team. Also, during a grant-funded project, the project stylebook or statement of work or proposal of work may be used as a basis from which to create up-to-date reports. For example, there may be references to the project team members and roles, the project budget, the project timeline, the project deliverables, and such, as baselines against which new information is reported.]

What are the basic parts to a project stylebook? What are their respective functions? What information is required in each?

Some Parts to a Project Stylebook

Project Goals

The main focus and *raison d'être* of a development team is its objectives or goals, its project deliverables. A successful project is one which delivers is promised outcomes on time, under budget, and to quality. These may be listed as measureable objectives and as listed deliverables.

These objectives may come from "authorizing documents," from contracts, competition rules, memorandums of understanding (MOUs) or memorandums of agreement (MOAs), and to other sources. What these documents are may depend on the impetus for the project.

Sometimes, there is a degree of "play" in terms of what project goals are. Sometimes, it is helpful to build some extra potential learning resources into a project goals, so if there is any extra time, those additional resources can be created. There is an importance balance between ambition and what is practically likely to achieve. In that gap is a where a project may complete, with most of what was planned but still some room to do more if the team is so inclined…and resourced…and motivated. Documenting the planned work may restrain the project from project creep (going too far afield by including more work than initially planned).

Project Standards

Project standards may be external ones, which affect the products of the team, and they may also be internal, influencing how the work is done among the team. These standards are determined externally and internally as well.

Learning content development standards. This section defines the legal standards that the contents must meet. These usually include controlled information restrictions, intellectual property, accessibility, media law, research ethics, and others.

Learning object functionality goals. There may be the traditional standards of digital learning objects for technological accessibility (ways to acquire and experience instructional components from a remote location), interoperability (the ability for a resource to function with other tools or platforms), adaptability (the ability to change up features of the learning to local needs and conditions of the users), reusability (the ability to download, access, and or integrate a learning resource into other contexts), durability (the robustness of the resource even when "base technology changes, without redesign or recoding"), affordability (enabling learning for minimal costs, usually of learning resource adoption), assessability (the ability to evaluate the learning resource's "pedagogical effectiveness, price, and usability"), discoverability (the ease of finding the resources online), and interchangeability (the ability to swap one learning object out for another) (Brown et al. 2002). Collectively, these are known colloquially as the "ilities" of digital learning objects and were based in part on software development and systems engineering. How to get to these end stages of functionalities differs depending on the design context, technologies, and other factors.

Work project documentation standards. This section describes the desired levels of documentation for the raw contents and data, such as about the contexts in which digital imagery, audio, and video were captured, the informational relevance of the captures, the dates of the captures, the equipment and technologies used, and other relevant information. How signed media releases and copyright releases are handled should also be noted. There should be standards for cited research. File naming protocols should be defined early on, so that there is not a lot of effort wasted in renaming generically named files, and so work files are easily findable. (A simple e-book chapter, a digital learning object, a slideshow, or a video may involve hundreds of files to actualize.)

Development Teams and Roles

An important part of a stylebook is a listing of the members of the team, their respective roles, and their contact information. Subject matter experts / content experts may also be included in this list. The point is to make sure that everyone is aware of their own roles and those of others, so people will not double up on work or work at cross-purposes.

In some stylebooks, this section will define decision making responsibilities as well. Defining these early help the team follow processes of rule and order when the work gets busier.

Work Sequences

The work sequence section may be represented with work phases and Gantt charts and calendars. This section describes the team's work, the respective tasks of the members, the major decision junctures (when decisions are made individually or in groups or with the whole team) and shared hard and soft deadlines. A "hard" deadline is one that cannot be missed, and a "soft" deadline is one that is suggested but is not a can't miss one.

Resources and Budgets

This section lists the existing resources of the team, including equipment, software; funds; informational contents; and human resources (such as by hours).

Technologies

Project technologies. Oftentimes, even for open-shared learning objects, there are a number of technologies needed to create the learning contents and to deploy them. If data is to be analyzed and processed, those technologies need to be defined, so that work may be shared across distances. Hosting platforms for the learning resources may need to be defined, if those have an implication for how the contents are designed and developed. For distributed teams, there are technologies required to enable the intercommunications and collaborations. If there are intermediary file states that are readable across technologies, then the originating technologies may not be so critical. However, given the proprietary nature of software, sometimes some shared technologies have to be defined, so that teams can collaborate.

In terms of the technologies used, these should also include the versions of technologies…and even the intermediary file types and extensions.

Technological guidelines and file types. One of the more valuable parts to a project stylebook is this section where the technology standards are set for the collection of text, imagery, diagrams, audio, video, simulations, games, assessments, assignments, datasets, and other pieces. For example, in terms of digital imagery captures, what does the team need in terms of resolution, white color balance, image file type, metadata, and other aspects? How much post-processing is desired before it is shared? What sort of processing is needed for the various uses of the imagery? Also, the principle of least-lossiness applies, so there will have to be pristine master copies of all basic media files in their original formats, in case the learning resource has to be rebuilt from ground up (for any number of reasons).

Data Management

What data is captured is also an important part of a project stylebook. Some group projects use special project software to keep a record of the work done and respective team members' contributions. Other team projects use individual or shared work journals. Still others depend on just a documenter who collects data from the various team members and reports out to all. And there are other combinations of approaches as well.

Style

A stylebook wouldn't be one if style were left out. "Style" may refer to the look-and-feel and branding of the respective learning contents. It may include logos and taglines. It may include particular color palettes and other aspects of visual design. Perhaps there are themes in the audio design, the textual design, and the "packaging" of the learning resources. Maybe the learning is delivered through a personality framework or "character," including his / her backstory and voice. Style may refer to throughlines in the learning resources, such as animating and continuing narratives, and characters.

Style may include less obvious features such as the influence of learning theories, models, and frameworks; particular technologies; and other features.

And Niceties

How credits will be handled. The team would benefit from having a policy on how contributors will be credited, based on what is contributed, and where the acknowledgments will be included.

A sparse stylebook may just stop here. However, certainly, stylebooks may include any other sections that would be valuable for the work based on the team's setup and the work ahead of them. For example, there may be other sections including the following:

- Select learning theories, models, and frameworks
- Proposed learning sequences
- Proposed target and potential learning audiences
- Proposed digital learning objects and other content types (and their respective structures and patterns or "templates"), and others

In some senses, the more uses that a stylebook is put to, the richer the documentation needed. The preferences of the designer/developer and the team will play an important role here.

Sometimes, stylebooks can be confidential. For example, a software company may have a portion of a stylebook where they have the copyrighted names of people and faux company names that they can use in their examples and stories to support the software use (without being accused of accidentally defaming someone or causing offense). Perhaps this company had their employees voluntarily submit their names for copyright registration. Such due diligence to not accidentally create a legal issue where there did not need to be one is a sign of professional practice.

The Style in Stylebooks What do project stylebooks look like, and how are these "styled"? Most are written in the third-person objective point-of-view. These generally look like informal reports. Some companies use templates for their stylebooks, so there is some degree of interchangeability between them. Then specific modules and parts may be added to stylebooks to accommodate the other unique aspects of projects. The particulars of projects will also reflect in the data in the different sections of a stylebook.

Meeting Stylebook Standards So what happens when work is submitted without meeting standards. That occurs in any project. In some cases, team members just work around these challenges, which are not uncommon. This is especially so in a context where people are volunteering their efforts, and good will is important. In cases where the work must meet standards, and there is only one source for the contents, it is sent back to whomever sent the work in to begin with for rework and re-assessment.

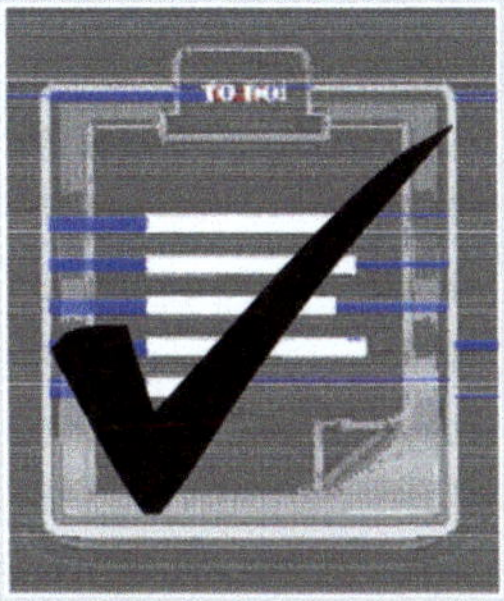

Task #3: Addendum Structures of Learning Project Stylebooks
To radically over-simplify, a learning project stylebook generally contains what the individual or team members need to know to advance thc work.

If the prior contents of a stylebook were all included, what else would be helpful to add for a stylebook to be as supportive of a project as possible? Why? (Use some from-life experiences to complete this task.)

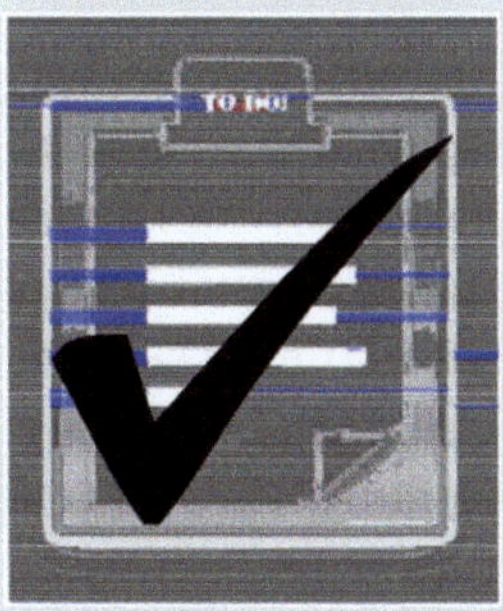

Task #4: Evolution of Project Stylebooks and Decision Junctures
Based on your experiences, if you had a fully informed stylebook at the start of a six-month project, where would you likely have to update information over time? Why? What parts of a real-world project tend to be most dynamic and changing? Why?

Content Forms and Multimodal Templating Based on the standards in the project stylebook, it may be possible to generate some templates for the various types of objects that might be built for the project (such as slideshows, articles, tip sheets, white papers, or other objects). Templates are base "patterns" from which more complex objects are made. What do you see as base requirements for various base forms of learning resources? For example, when you view a video, what do you always expect to see included, and why? (Those are the elements that may appear in a template.) (More on templating follows in Chap. 7.)

6.3.3 Part 3: Planning Work

A work plan helps an individual and / or team to systematically think through what they need to have and to do to achieve their project goals and to create the deliverables to quality standards on deadline. There are different methods to creating work plans.

One basic approach involves beginning with all deliverables from the project and using a backwards design. An example follows in Table 6.2.

Time deadlines may be applied to the work, with general estimates of how long it will take for the setup preparations and the design and development and launch work to be done. If there is a hard deadline, such as if the work is being done for a client or for a competition or a specific rollout, that should be specified. Then, all that deadline is used to figure out what sequential steps have to be done, and the time is allotted given the real-world hard deadline. If there are no external time pressures, then all the deadlines are negotiable soft ones, and work may be done as time allows.

The general steps to this sequence is depicted in a BPMN (Business Process Model and Notation) diagram, with the work split out into three main sections: (1) the collecting and creating of relevant raw digital files, (2) the aggregating of contents and creation of the learning contents, and (3) launching the learning resources and conducting project post mortems (Fig. 6.5). The project objectives, the target and potential learners, supporting backup data, and project deliverables are inferred but not explicitly present in the diagram. The sequence of work is clear, though, with certain contents needed at certain times, in order to enable the work to progress apace. Also, while the arrows show the work moving in what appears to be a linear way, this is not necessarily so. Multiple team members may be working on their respective tasks at any one time, and the work may be recursive, as the project may dictate. For example, research usually does not only happen at the beginning of a project but may arise at any point in the work—based on identified need.

Different visualizations of project work highlight different aspects of the plan. A Gantt chart focuses on the specific amounts of time required for the work, for example, based on a real-world calendar.

Table 6.2 Starting with a target deliverable and backtracking to get there

Deliverable: An interactive slideshow
Required technologies Hardware Software
Required information (and related sources)
Required digital contents (and related sources)
Required work (and related roles and tasks)

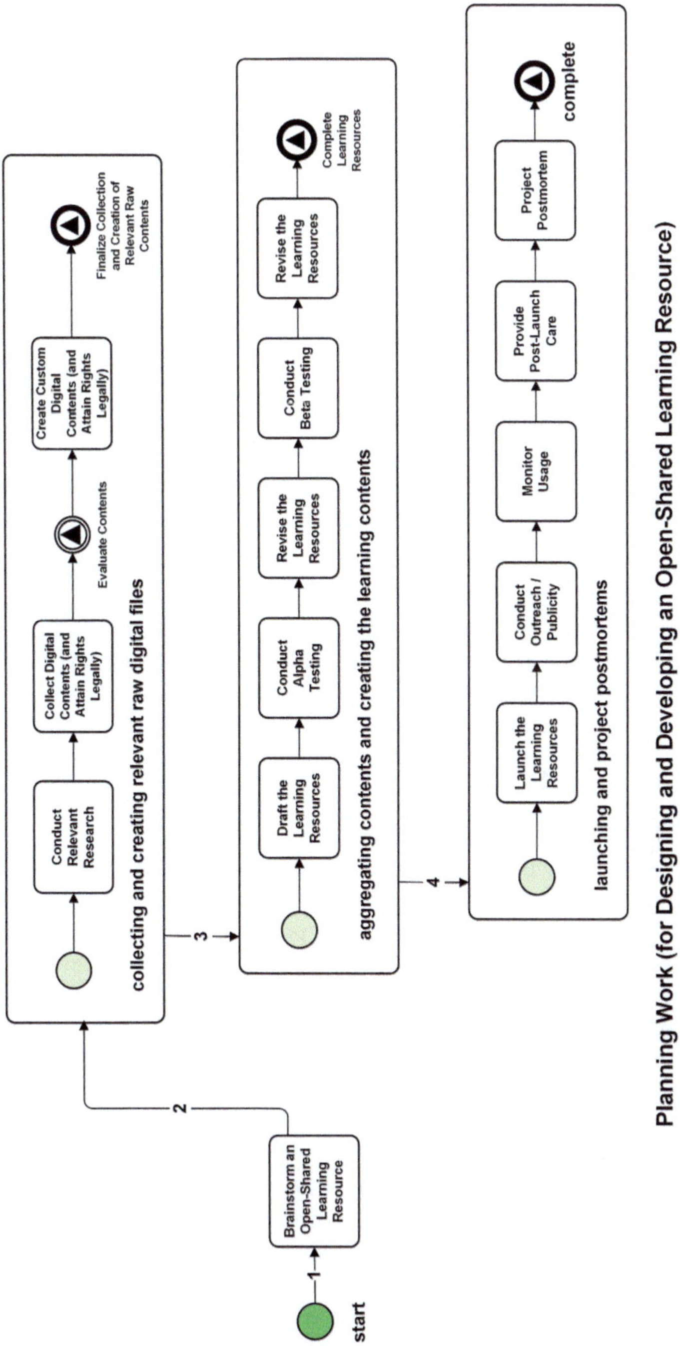

Fig. 6.5 Planning work (for designing and developing an open-shared learning resource)

The work plan is designed to address the work practicalities with necessary sequences addressed, so that whatever needs to be achieved first is done first, and so on, so there are fewer task inefficiencies or cases of make-work. For example, defining the respective professional roles on a team means that there will not likely be multiple people doing the same work. Having a work plan helps an individual or team coordinate the work, and it helps them read in new members of the team as needed. Having a work plan in a tangible form also enables the team members to identify choke points for the work and to create work processes that may be more efficient.

A work plan cannot anticipate all challenges, so building in some extra resources and extra time and even extra talent may be helpful. It helps to acknowledge "uncontrollable risks" and to understand that these risks "are compensated by chances of gain" (Kahneman and Lovallo 1993, p. 17). Anticipating risks may lower some possibilities for negative surprises. It may also help the individual and / or team to anticipate obstacles to the work's completion. And it may encourage planning for contingencies and go-to alternatives if plans change. Sometimes, Plan B's are created on-the-fly as things happen in real time. In others, the design work may be specific enough to be designed into the work.

Practical Budgeting A simple approach is to tally up what resources the individual or team have, what they need to acquire (equipment, software, other technologies, memory devices, information, digital contents, travel costs, services), and what the basic costs are. For an open-shared learning project, the usual assumption is that the budget is $0, so all costs thereafter are out-of-pocket. Every asset entails a practical cost. "Must-haves" will often change to "would-likes" in the framework of a budget. In terms of project planning, there seems to be much less of an underestimation of cost expenditures than for time expenditures on projects (Spiller and Lynch 2010).

Those who like budgeting may want to calculate the actual real costs of an open-shared learning resource. A full calculation may be surprising. Academic research articles that have to be paid for range in prices from about $20–$70 each. Commercial-grade software runs at about $1,000–$3000 each for "forever" licenses. Subject matter experts bill $100–$300 or much higher an hour, depending on their areas of expertise. And so on. Outside the cover of a workplace or an ecosystem that supports open-shared learning contents, this work can get pricey fast. And with multimedia development and coding, the burn rate on expenditures is high.

There does not seem to be any statistics on the success or failure rates of projects related to open-shared learning, whether the projects are small ones to the mega-ones. Regardless, it would be important to set standards for when to "cut bait" if no progress is being made. Sometimes, the discovery may happen early that a project does not have a future; other times, the discovery may not be made until much investment has already been made. In the latter case, "sunk costs" are understood as a part of engaging in the space, and these should be mentally written off (reference: the "nothing ventured, nothing gained" truism).

How Accurate are Stylebooks to the Final Products of a Project?
Learning from project stylebooks and the projects in which these are used would make for engaging research. After all, if planning is a critical part of project success, which are the work stylebooks which enable projects to advance successfully? And which ones are less helpful? What makes for accurate projections in stylebooks? Is it possible to predict success by what project stylebooks look like in their first iterations? How can the creation of stylebooks be improved in the future?

6.3.4 *Work Plans*

Work Plans Aligned to the Workplace Realities Different work contexts have different workplace cultures, values, processes, and individuals. The work plans that may work for one context may not easily transfer to another. One way to see this would be to share work plans between contexts and work places and to see what would transfer well and what wouldn't.

Efficiencies to Be Had? Work efficiencies may be gained when multiple tasks may be addressed simultaneously. For example, if in the digital content collection phase the legal requirements may also be addressed, that will save on work later. Of if the design prototypes may be created in authoring tools, and then the finalized objects created from those prototypes, then multiple tasks have been condensed.

If work is mis-sequenced, that can result in the opposite. For example, if public testers are brought in to analyze drafts and prototypes (that they may have a hard time understanding), that may be an expensive waste of effort. And outside testers will still have to be brought in when the learning contents are finalized and ready for the formal beta testing. Sometimes, it helps to do mental walk-throughs of each of these work sequences to visualize the work and the handoffs and the progress.

If the designer/developers lock in to a version of a learning resource too quickly, without sufficient attention to the underlying information and raw contents, they may end up having to redesign and recode objects. If rights releases were acquired in a sloppy way, or there is poor documentation, that will likely lead to clean-up work and / or legal liabilities. Not vetting outlines and drafts sufficiently may mean re-dos and retrofitting.

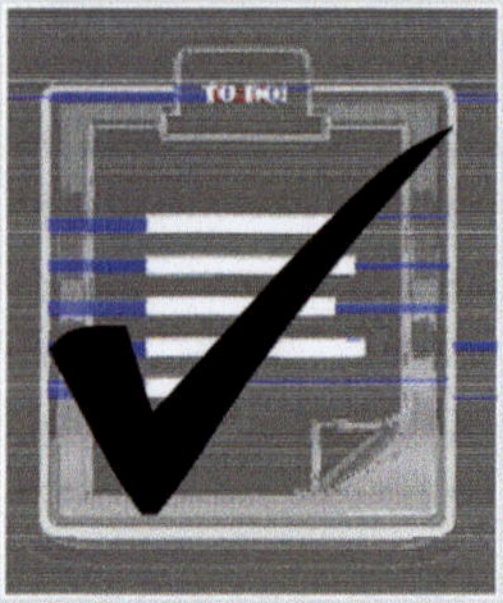

Task #5: Effective Work Plans

A work plan is never 100%. It is a jumping off point only to get work started. Draft a work plan for a design and development task, and follow that plan to the letter. During the work, keep a short "journal" of your work experiences.

How accurate was the work plan? How much did you have to improvise? What were the strengths and weaknesses of your work plan?

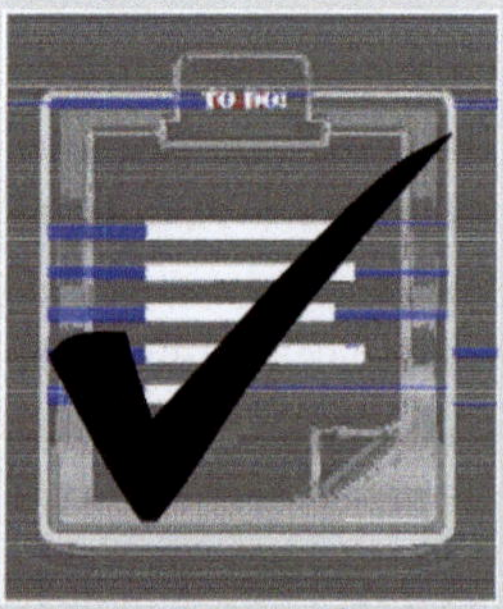

Task #6: Work Sequencing

Documenting work sequences can be a little like recording a favorite recipe. There has to be a listing of the necessary ingredients (content, technologies, and others).

There is a step-by-step sequence of tasks to actualize the work.

There are quality standards that should be achieved with the finished product.

In this spirit, describe a work-based sequence. Review it for missing steps. If you have the inclination, test what you've written to see how this works out.

Discussion This work suggests the importance of defining e-learning quality standards first, to inform the work, and then creating a project stylebook to record the standards, the related technologies, the necessary tasks, deadlines, the work planning, and other relevant information. The difficulty of planning accurately has been well documented in the research literature, along with ways to mitigate some of these.

For some smaller projects, it is possible to go straight to development without pre-planning and then going back to fix errors like instances of contravention of copyright or libel/slander, and so on. If works have been finalized in fixed forms like rendered videos or rendered animations, this work will require going back to raw sources and recoding much of the work. For the few who work in the space full-time and have the lead-up work already done and generally defined and who have quality processes in place, starting with the development and bypassing design may be a proper work sequence for smaller projects. However, in most other cases, going straight to development may be high-risk, low-reward.

6.4 Future Research Directions

Project (work) stylebooks (and statements of work) have been a part of the workspace for decades in private industry and higher education. There is not much written about them in the research literature, however, and examples of these are not widely available for study. Understanding how these are informed from various sources—for quality standards and other objectives—could enhance both knowledge and practice.

Live Examples (on the Web)

Backwards extrapolations of e-learning quality standards from shared learning resources. To benefit from the contemporaneous qualities of the Web, it would help to engage with some of the shared learning resources in order to backwards-extrapolate some of the quality standards that may have informed the work. What are the observable factors that "speak to" particular quality standards?

State of the art. According to the available learning resources, that is the state of the art of the field? What does this say about the adherence to e-learning quality standards?

Updates on formal and semi-formal e-learning quality standards? Also, search for updates on defined e-learning quality standards. Form a list of URLs that are trusted sources for this information. Write a short note about what has updated since the last time you checked (Fig. 6.6).

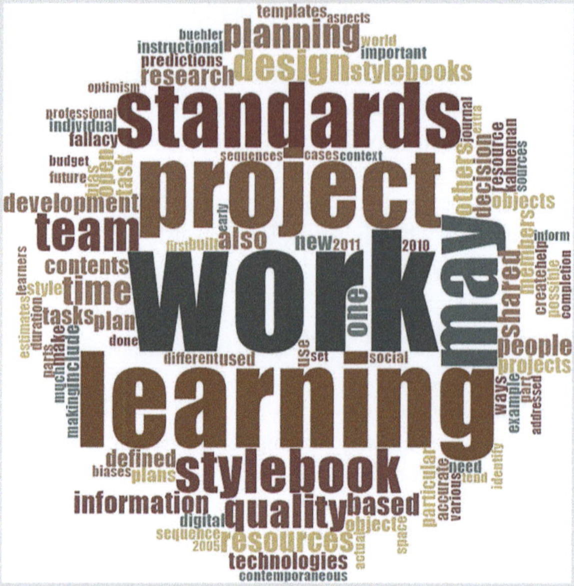

Fig. 6.6 A Word Cloud of Chapter 06: "Establishing and Applying Contemporaneous E-Learning Standards: Evolving Stylebooks and Planning Work" (Version 1)

What-If: Virtual Immersive World Designs and Styling

You have embarked on creating a virtual immersive learning space, replete with artificial intelligence (AI) bots and scripted objects. The platform enables a wide range of design decisions. The "style" design space is large.

You can bring in textures. You can depict the automated humanoid agents in any number of ways. The style should align with the learning and enhance it; it should not detract from it. The various designed elements should also work together and not clash.

There is sound design that may be necessary to evoke parts of the virtual space.

There is interactivity design that also has to be created.

Within the virtual space, there are many regions, and each will have to communicate different learning messages.

Where do you start?

Decision point #1: stop or advance. If advance, how do you create a main theme? How do you decide what the different design elements convey? How will you test your design?

The What-If Debriefing

This is the only what-if scenario that stops at the first decision point. There are so many design and style features in play, and the generality of the scenario, really makes it difficult to move this farther (Fig. 6.7).

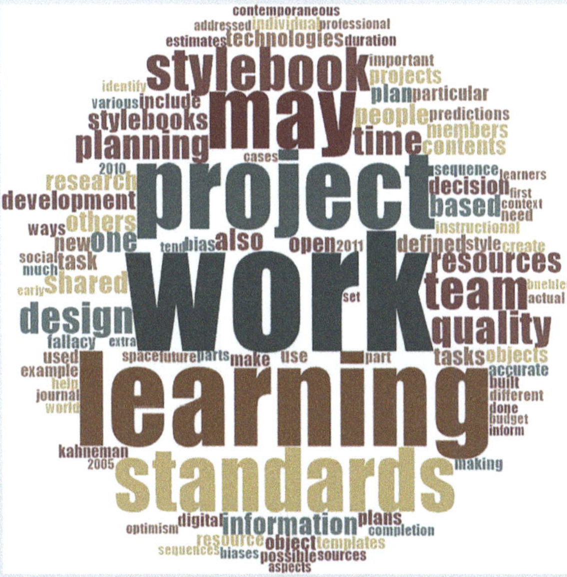

Fig. 6.7 A Word Cloud of Chapter 06: "Establishing and Applying Contemporaneous E-Learning Standards: Evolving Stylebooks and Planning Work" (Version 2)

What-If: Work Efficiencies and Tradeoffs

You have a project stylebook set up and a work plan set up. The work commences. The team is excited to get started, and the idea is that the team will have something to upload in a few weeks (maybe a month). The team is a lean and professional one, and each member has critical work to do.

Just a few days in, one of the team members has a change in her work life, and she has to pull out of the project. The team reconstitutes around her tasks, and everyone is off-and-running again.

Several weeks in, it becomes clear that two of the team members are not pulling their weight. They are missing deadlines, and one of them has gone to silence. When pressed, one wants to continue, and the other does not.

What do you do? Do you decide to stop the project? Do you continue and make further adjustments by resetting the shared goals? Do you bring in other team members with the skills of the one who will be discontinuing the work? What are the possible tradeoffs?

Decision point #1: stop or advance. If advance, you and the team have some decisions to make.

The team decides…

The what-if debriefing

This scenario shows that there are unplanned occurrences. To keep a project on track, there will have to be tradeoffs.

6.5 Conclusion

Refreshing one's knowledge on e-learning quality standards is important to the work, so that these may inform the tasks that follow. A project (work) stylebook and work plans are inert until they are activated with actual efforts and actual work. While work plans are not likely going to be accurate to the letter, that may not be the most critical aspects of the plans. If they are written well and inform follow-on work, then they will be valuable, even if they may be skewed based on planning fallacies and optimism biases.

6.6 Reviews and Assignments

6.6.1 Main Points Review

- Creating an understanding of the e-learning standards that are most relevant at present is important to inform the work
  - Some e-learning standards are "givens," such as those based on applicable laws, applicable policies, technology standards, metadata standards, and others
  - Human learning theories, models, and frameworks may be used to inform on e-learning standards as well
  - More flexible e-learning standards may be understood from the state of the art in the field, formalized quality standards (such as by professional organizations and educational institutions), quality rubrics, quality practices, and project-level realities
- The local context for the open-shared learning resource may also inform the e-learning quality standards
- A consensus-built expert-informed project stylebook needs to be collectively evolved and shared because the stylebook needs to be informed by the varying expertise of the cross-functional team members. Non-expert assumptions about others' spheres of responsibility may often be incorrect or ill-advised.
- The consensus aspect is important because the team members need to collaborate effectively with each other, and that is often done through shared understandings of what each other needs (so as to be more efficient and to save on re-work).
- A project stylebook has to evolve with a project because new information is collected during the course of the work. This new learning would benefit the project. The sooner a team is advised of the change, the more responsive it can be to the change. (Changes to pedagogy- and technology-based projects are common, given the energy and dynamism of the space.)

- A project stylebook has basic components: professional roles, work sequences, timelines, budgets, technological tools, technological standards, legal constraints, policy constraints, and others.
- The "look and feel" of learning contents may be defined in a project stylebook as well. This may include branding principles, visual designs, audio designs, textual designs, logos, and other aspects.
- It is not enough to just have a defined stylebook, but there has to be a clear plan about how to handle contraventions of the stylebook requirements. For example, new workflows may have to be designed around identified work challenges, and so on. Not all shortcomings may be addressed, however, given the fact that all projects are addressed with limited time and limited resources.
- Complementary objects that are used along with stylebooks include "content forms" and "templates." These structures enable building to defined branding and quality by controlling for the fixed aspects of instructional objects, like slideshows, photos, articles, videos, audio files, and others.
- Work plans may be defined separately from a stylebook. These may include considerations external to the design team, such as external partner organizations and grant funding organizations, and others. These may define how outside interactions will be handled.
  - If a stylebook is distributed outside an organization, the work plans may be more closely held, or vice versa. For example, some confidential work documents include those that may have sensitive information—like copyrighted names of individuals and organizations used for the examples in the learning objects.
- One way to lower the cost of an instructional design project is to conduct a work analysis and identify redundancies, unnecessary work sequences, and areas that may be improved. (Lean Six Sigma methods are often applied to identify such challenges.)

6.7 Critical Thinking Questions

Contemporaneous E-Learning Quality Standards

- Contemporaneous e-learning standards (beyond the "givens" from law and technological practice) may be drawn from a number of sources: defined e-learning standards, rubrics, practices, and other information sources. They may also be drawn from the local project. What do you see as universal e-learning quality standards, and why?

Project (Work) Stylebooks

- If a stylebook is consensus-built (all team members contribute) but merit-based (best ideas win), what process should be used to make sure that the best ideas win

out? What evidentiary bases should be used, and why? How should ties be broken? Why?
- When should a stylebook be updated with "new" information? Constant changing may be distracting to team members, but if changes are too slowly adopted, that can hinder the project work. What is a possible happy medium? What are optimal ways to ensure efficient decision making?
- How would you delimit what goes into a "stylebook" vs. a "work plan"? If a stylebook has a public facing side, what more private or confidential information would go into an internal work plan?
- How do you conceptualize a "soft" deadline vs a "hard" one (described in either a stylebook or a work plan, or both)? Are there ways to soften a hard deadline? Ways to harden a soft deadline? And when might such softening and hardening be helpful?
- What factors of a learning object or learning sequence should inform the style? Why?
- How can the respective elements of a learning object or sequence be aligned, including visuals, audio, text, video, character depictions, and others?
- How can the style of a learning object be made non-exclusionary of others' cultures and style preferences? Is it possible to create an unobtrusive style?
- Let's assume that legal and ethical and professional conventions are critical for a learning object or sequence and should be addressed first. What else should be addressed next? Make sure that you have a complete list in descending order (with the most important conventions first).
- Is there a value to creating an idealized and aspirational stylebook with standards that may not be fully achieved (but could be if time and resources allowed)? Or is it better to build a stylebook to real-world standards only and to not go beyond?
- In the spirit of open sharing, should project stylebooks be broadly published for others' usage, critique, research, and study? Should work plans be broadly published? What are the pros and cons of such broad sharing?

Templating

- Templating can be limiting because their use assumes accepted forms and informational structures. What are some ways to extend creativity while using templating? Are there ways to create more flexible templates? Should templating be avoided in some parts of an instructional design project for some of the learning objects? Should templates be used in a hard-and-fast rule sort of way, or should they be used more flexibly? And if more flexibly, how should templates be used without introducing "disorder" or "chaos"?

Work Plans

- In a work plan, what parts do you think are the most changeable and dynamic? (Some common parts include the following: deliverables, schedule, costs, technologies, professional roles, and others.) Why would these particular parts be the most flexible?

- How would you identify potential efficiencies in work sequencing? Would it help to identify dependencies of each work phase and suggest efficient sequencing? Would it help to identify repeated or redundant work? Would it be helpful to identify unnecessary work or "make-work"?
- On what basis should a work plan be created? Given people's tendency to underestimate how much work is required for a project (planning fallacy), what are some ways to make work proposals more accurate to the world and to what is possible? What are some reasons for why people tend to be over-optimistic about what may be achieved (under deadline and within budget)?

6.8 Assignments

Directions The Assignments are divided into two sections, Basic and Advanced. The Basic section is for those who may not have much instructional design experience or background in the area of creating instructional contents for open sharing. As such, these are set up to familiarize them with the chapter-related knowledge, skills, and abilities. The Advanced section is for those who already have some knowledge of this general space and who may benefit from more challenging work.

In a formal learning context, these assignments would benefit from expert feedback and further applications of the learning contents. In a nonformal or informal learning context, including self-directed learning, these assignments would benefit from both reflection and practice. These assignments are built to be extensible, to have elements added to benefit the learners. They are designed to be assigned selectively and not in full. The setup of this textbook is as a work sequence, and similarly, the assignments may be set up as tasks to be completed by the learner in a sequential way…that takes them through the fairly complete and sequential *open-shared learning design → development → test → revision → launch → post-launch* process.

6.8.1 Basic

Assignment 6.1: Defining Contemporaneous E-learning Standards For e-learning, some given standards include legality, accessibility, cultural alignment, learner-centeredness, and other aspects. Some of these aspects are better defined than others, with actual defined standards. Where would you "source" e-learning standards, and how much would you weight each source (value each particular source to total to 100%), and why?

Extra: What of these standards are the most crucial to meet and why?

Extra: In a perusal of open-shared learning resources, which are the standards most commonly met? Why? Which are the standards most commonly unmet? Why?

Assignment 6.2: Drafting a Project Stylebook Based on the empty draft project stylebook, fill in as many of the sections as possible based on the requirements of the project. Try to make this as real-world as possible. Work to close any work gaps, so that the standards are as clear as possible. Evolve this over time as the work for the instructional design project progresses—based on new insights. (If interested, maintain a static copy of your first draft of the stylebook, and contrast that with the evolved one. Identify the differences to see what was missed with the initial conceptualization.)

Assignment 6.3: Templating Based on the projected types of digital contents (slideshows, cases, photo albums, videos, audio files, and others), create templates for each type in the proper format. Be sure to include elements that enable proper language, navigability, consistent style, and other factors. Have clear rationales for why you might create the templates in particular ways.

Extra: If you actualize your instructional design project, compare the actual templates you create and use against those initially conceptualized.

Assignment 6.4: Plan for Maintaining Raw Contents An important part of creating an online learning object involves proper handling of raw digital (and other analog) contents. Raw contents are those materials that contribute to a digital learning object or which later are adapted into a polished digital learning object, such as researched articles, photos, sound files, video files, and so on. It is important for these contents to be easy to find. They have to be properly labeled. There have to be clear records of copyright releases and digital evidence of those releases. The metadata have to be accurate; for example, images have to be labeled with correct "alt text" (alternate text) for accessible learning. The contents have to be in the format that optimizes digital preservation. How would you plan to capture the raw contents aspect?

Assignment 6.5: Testing a Drafted Project (Work) Stylebook Create a simple digital learning object step-by-step, and use a drafted project stylebook in the design. Pay attention to what critical issues are effectively addressed by the stylebook but also those important issues that have not been addressed. Consider some revisions to the project stylebook that may align it with better design and development practices.

Assignment 6.6: Reverse-Engineering a Learning Object Template Capture several open-shared learning objects (slideshows, videos, or other), and identify the important basic features of the particular form. Reverse-engineer a (slideshow, video, or other) template for that form of learning object.

Extra: If you have access to original templates for that learning object or other insider information from the design and development team, test your reverse engineering accuracy in regards to that work. Identify where you were accurate and where you were inaccurate.

Assignment 6.7: Drawing Up a Project Budget Write down the various necessary steps to achieve the design, development, and public launch of an open-shared learning object. Based on the necessary technologies, resources, and work, create a reasonable budget for the work. Calculate the total cost of the project. Be sure to include personnel hours as part of the calculation.

Extra: If the project is actualized, assess how accurate your original budget was against the actual finalized one. Identify why you may have fallen short in some projections and why you were more accurate in others. Think about how you can be more accurate in terms of budgetary assessments in the future.

Assignment 6.8: Drafting a Project Timeline Write down the various necessary steps to achieve the design, development, and public launch of an open-shared learning object. Place the various steps on a reasonable timeline. If you're interested, place this information on a Gantt chart representing both the tasks and the timeline. Review the readings in this chapter about the human tendencies towards "planning fallacies" and "optimism biases."

Extra: If the project is actualized, assess how accurate your original project timeline was against the actual finalized one. Identify why you may have fallen short in some projections and why you were more accurate in others. Think about how you can be more accurate in terms of time assessments in the future.

6.8.2 Advanced

Assignment 6.9: Embedded Style in a Project Stylebook Practically speaking, a project stylebook documents the projected work, the standards that the work will be built to, the deliverables, and so on. A project stylebook can also be a work of the imagination, to capture and communicate idealized *style*, as elegance, as look-and-feel, as branding. Define what aspects of a stylebook may communicate a distinctive and defined style (visual, auditory, textual, font, and others) beyond the basics.

Extra: Explore some of the open-shared learning objects and sequences that you find useful. Analyze a related set of these for the embedded style.

Assignment 6.10: Analyzing a Work Plan for (In)efficiencies and Working to Capture Efficiencies Sometimes, looking at an instructional design project from the work-function view can be helpful in shedding light on where efficiencies may be exploited. For example, during a research phase, multiple research questions may be asked simultaneously. Similarly, when a visual design is being explored, the logo, website banners, learning object players, and other elements may be co-designed at the same time. And when testing is scheduled, local experts may be asked to engage a number of analyses instead of piecemeal work.

The open-shared learning resources may align with the development of current projects, and the contents may be byproducts. Necessary work may be folded into other work sequences. (Sometimes, developing open-shared learning objects is about working at the margins.)

It is important to define work sequences intelligently, so the dependencies in the project do not hold up over steps in the work.

It would be helpful to define security approaches to protect the work, so that accidents and other challenges do not hinder progress.

The essential idea is to create efficiencies where possible, to not make-work (don't do anything unnecessary), and to identify inefficiencies (such as work done twice, maybe by different people) in order to address these.

Assignment 6.11: Evolving an Online Learning Object or Sequence Without a Plan Sometimes, people prefer to just start creating an online learning object or sequence without prior planning. It is possible to just start the draft, and see where it goes. In that spirit, conceptualize a learning object, and start with the development right away. Take the object, and analyze it for internal structure, learning objectives, learning value, and so on. Identify where the work may need more development, and develop it from there.

Key Terms and Definitions

Budget A listing of costs to actualize a learning design balanced against available funds (if any)

Documentation Records, official information

Metadata Data about data

Optimism bias A tendency to view a context in overly positive ways (based on the reality of the context)

Planning fallacy A form of optimism bias in which people tend to underestimate how much time it may take to complete a set task

Project (work) stylebook A project document that describes the requirements for learning resources, including the look-and-feel and functions

Science of instruction A set of research based findings about methods to enhance instruction

Statement of work A project document that describes the work

Storyboard A visual-based planning document that focuses on the sequence of a learning resource

Templating The creation and usage of templates (patterned files) to ensure the quality and uniformity and consistency of learning resources

Work plan A formal document that describes the work that will be achieved during a project and the standards that will be built to

References

Brown J, Larson J, and Meachen E. Tips, techniques and tools for creating sharable learning content objects. In the 18th Annual Conference on Distance Teaching & Learning. Standards by Advanced Distributed Learning. 2002. https://zapdoc.tips/presenters-agenda-your-interests-topics-advanced-distributed.html.

Brunnermeier MK, Papakonstantinou F, and Parker JA. An economic model of the planning fallacy. National Bureau of Economic Research Working Paper No. 14228. Retrieved from http://www.nber.org/papers/w14228. 2008.

Buehler R, Griffin D, and Ross M. Exploring the 'planning fallacy': Why people underestimate their task completion times. *Journal of Personality and Social Psychology* 67: 366 – 381, 1994.

Buehler R, Griffin D, Lam KCH, and Deslauriers J. Perspectives on prediction: Does third-person imagery improve task completion estimates? *Organizational Behavior and Human Decision Processes* 117: 138 – 149, 2012.

Buehler R, Griffin D, and MacDonald H. The role of motivated reasoning in optimistic time predictions. *Personality and Social Psychology Bulletin* (PSPB) 23: 238 – 247, 1997. SAGE Journals.

Buehler R, Peetz J, and Griffin D. Finishing on time: When do predictions influence completion times? *Organizational Behavior and Human Decision Processes* 111: 23 – 32, 2010.

Clements KI, and Pawlowski JM. User-oriented quality for OER: Understanding teachers' views on re-use, quality, and trust. *Journal of Computer Assisted Learning:* 28, 4 – 14, 2011. https://doi.org/10.1111/j.1365-2729.2011.00450.x.

Convertino G, Mentis HM, Ting AYW, Rosson MB, and Carroll JM. How does common ground increase? In GROUP07. Nov. 4 – 7, 2007. Sanibel Island, Florida, USA. 225 – 228, 2007.

Flyvbjerg B. Curbing optimism bias and strategic misrepresentation in planning: Reference class forecasting in practice. *European Planning Studies* 16*:* 3 – 21, 2008.

Flyvbjerg B. and Sunstein C.R. The principle of the Malevolent Hiding Hand, or, the Planning Fallacy writ large. arXiV. Retrieved from https://arxiv.org/ftp/arxiv/papers/1509/1509.01526.pdf. 2015.

Gawande, A. *The Checklist Manifesto: How to Get Things Right.* New York: Henry Holt & Company. 2009.

Hadjichristidis C, Summers B, and Thomas K. Unpacking estimates of task duration: The role of typicality and temporality. *Journal of Experimental Social Psychology* 51: 45 – 50, 2014.

Janicik GA. and Bartel CA. Talking about time: Effects of temporal planning and time awareness norms on group coordination and performance. *Group Dynamics: Theory, Research, and Practice* 7: 122 – 134, 2003.

Kahneman D. *Thinking, Fast and Slow.* New York: Farrar, Straus and Giroux. 2011.

Kahneman D, and Lovallo D. Timid choices and bold forecasts: A cognitive perspective on risk taking. *Management Science* 39: 17 – 31, 1993.

Kahneman D, Lovallo D, and Sibony O. Before you make that big decision… *Harvard Business Review:* 51 – 60. 2011.

Kahneman D, and Tversky A. On the reality of cognitive illusions. Theoretical Notes. *Psychological Review* 103: 582 – 591, 1996.

Kahneman D, and Tversky A. Intuitive prediction: Biases and corrective procedures. Technical Report PTR – 1042 – 77 – 6. 1 – 44, 1977.

Kanten AB. The effect of construal level on predictions of task duration. *Journal of Experimental Social Psychology* 47: 1037 – 1047, 2011.

Koehler DJ and Poon CSK. Self-predictions overweight strength of current intentions. *Journal of Experimental Social Psychology* 42: 517 – 524, 2006.

Koole, and Spijker M. Overcoming the planning fallacy through willpower: Effects of implementation intentions on actual and predicted task-completion times. *Eur. J. Soc. Psychol.* 30: 873 – 888, 2000.

Kruger J, and Evans M. If you don't want to be late, enumerate: Unpacking reduces the planning fallacy. *Journal of Experimental Social Psychology* 40: 586 – 598, 2004.

Lovallo D, Clarke C, and Camerer C. Robust analogizing and the outside view: Two empirical tests of case-based decision making. *Strat. Mgmt. J.* 33: 496 – 512, 2012. https://doi.org/10.1002/SMJ.962.

Peetz J, and Buehler R. When distance pays off: The role of construal level in spending predictions. *Journal of Experimental Social Psychology* 48: 395 – 398, 2011.

Peetz J, Buehler R, and Wilson A. Planning for the near and distant future: How does temporal distance affect task completion predictions? *Journal of Experimental Social Psychology* 46: 709 – 720, 2010.

Pezzo SP, Pezzo MV, and Stone ER. The social implications of planning: How public prediction bias future plans. *Journal of Experimental Social Psychology* 42: 221 – 227, 2006.

Pychyl TA, Morin RW, and Salmon BR. Procrastination and the planning fallacy: An examination of the study habits of university students. Procrastination: Current Issues and New Directions. *Journal of Social Behavior & Personality:* 135 – 150, 2000.

Rocklage MD, and Fazio RH. Individual differences in valence weighting: When, how, and why they matter. *Journal of Experimental Social Psychology* 50: 144 – 157, 2013.

Rodon C, and Meyer T. Searching information on the Web and planning fallacy: A pilot investigation of pessimistic forecasts. *Revue européenne de psychologie appliquée* 62: 103–109, 2012.

Roy MM, and Christenfeld NJS. 2008. Effect of task length on remembered and predicted duration. *Psychonomic Bulletin & Review* 15: 202 – 207, 2008.

Roy MM, Christenfeld NJS, and McKenzie CRM. The broad applicability of memory bias and its coexistence with planning fallacy: Reply to Griffin and Buehler (2005). *Psychological Bulletin* 131: 761 – 762, 2005.

Roytek MA. Enhancing instructional design efficiency: Methodologies employed by instructional designers. *British Journal of Educational Technology* 41: 170 – 180, 2010. https://doi.org/10.1111/j.1467-8535.2008.00902.x.

Siddiqui RA, May F, and Monga A. Reversals of task duration estimates: Thinking how rather than why shrinks duration estimates for simple tasks, but elongates estimates for complex tasks. *Journal of Experimental Social Psychology* 50: 184 – 189, 2013.

Spiller SA, and Lynch JG. Individuals exhibit the planning fallacy for time but not for money. SSRN: https://ssrn.com/abstract=1458380 or https://doi.org/10.2139/ssrn.1458380 2010.

Surowiecki J. *The Wisdom of Crowds.* New York: Random House. 2005.

Tetlock PE. *Expert Political Judgment: How Good is It?* Princeton: Princeton University Press. 2005.

Weick M, and Guinote A. How long will it take? Power biases time predictions. *Journal of Experimental Social Psychology* 46: 595 – 604, 2010.

Additional Reading Section

Ariely D. *Predictably Irrational: The Hidden Forces that Shape our Decisions.* New York: HarperCollins Publishers. 2008.

Gawande A. *The Checklist Manifesto.* New York: Henry Holt and Company LLC. 2009.

Joseph PB, Bravmann SL, Windschitl MA, Mikel ER, and Green NS. *Cultures of Curriculum.* Mahwah, New Jersey: Lawrence Erlbaum Associates, Publishers. 2000.

Kahneman D. *Thinking, Fast and Slow.* New York: Farrar, Straus and Giroux. 2011.

Rothwell WJ, and Cookson PS. *Beyond Instruction: Comprehensive Program Planning for Business and Education.* San Francisco: Jossey-Bass Publishers. 1997.

Shafir E. *Preference, Belief, and Similarity: Selected Writings Amos Tversky.* Cambridge, Massachusetts: The MIT Press. 2004.

Surowiecki J. *The Wisdom of Crowds.* New York: Random House. 2005.

Part III
Design, Development, and Testing

Chapter 7
Early Designs, Prototypes, and Learning Sequences for Exploration and Decision Making

Abstract During the early development phase, designers-developers may process the collected raw data and begin organizing the collected imagery; they may draft various learning objects, with full functionalities, in order to see how the objects look and how well the instantiated item compares with the original plan. They may experiment with item contents, sequencing, functions, style, and other features. This phase may be fleeting for some, but when observed with care, these processes may be informative to the ultimate project and beneficial to the learning. This chapter describes some ways to benefit from early designs and prototypes, to inform individuals of ways forward. After all, designs and plans look appropriate and clean and doable until they are tested in the real, and there are numerous discoveries to be made once the development work actually starts.

Keywords Early designs · Prototyping · Learning object design · Learning sequence design

> The knowledge we get by tinkering, via trial and error, experience, and the workings of time, in other words, *contact with the earth,* is vastly superior to that obtained through reasoning…
>
> –Nassim Nicholas Taleb, in *Skin in the Game: Hidden Asymmetries in Daily Life* (2018)

> Details are not the details. They make the design.
>
> Eventually everything connects—people, ideas, objects. The quality of the connections is the key to quality per se.
>
> –Charles Eames (1907–1978)

> Design is not just what it looks like and feels like. Design is how it works.
>
> –Steve Jobs, 2003, the "Guts of a New Machine" in *The New York Times* (https://www.nytimes.com/2003/11/30/magazine/the-guts-of-a-new-machine.html)

S. Hai-Jew, *Designing Instruction For Open Sharing*,
https://doi.org/10.1007/978-3-030-02713-1_7

Opening Scenario

Opening Scenario: Expressivity for Designs, Prototypes, and Learning Sequences?

As an organic part of the instructional design work, a designer/developer starts to create contents. They start to experiment to various ways to frame and package online learning contents. They experiment with writing and visuals. They set up some sequencing. While some may begin with a full written plan, others may simply start to evolve the learning using drafting, prototyping, and/or authoring tools (software used to create and assemble multimedia objects). For many, early designs and prototypes are created as part of the experimentation, and these may be used to inform the design and development of objects in other parts of the project. In some ways, such early objects may be "notional," or drafts of what would be created if money (and time) were no object. The learning from creating such early "roughs" can be very beneficial to an open-shared learning object or resource.

What are some ways to encourage risk-taking and innovation in the initial designs, to better introduce value to the designs and to enhance the ability to share the learning object when it is complete?

Some Early Questions to Consider

If you were to rough-sketch a learning object, what features would you include, and why?

If you were to fully develop a rough early design or prototype fully, what percentage of the finalized learning object would have been included in your early draft designs? Why?

What features of a learning object or sequence are most critical to understand and define early on? What is most critical to "get right"? Why?

What are some common next steps to advance a design from the early drafting stage?

Learning Objectives

Learners will…

Planning with Early Designs

- Based on imagination alone, create some early designs for the target learning resources

- Identify some conventional structures of digital learning objects, sequences, and learning resources, and use these to create some early designs; also, indicate where certain contents may be placed and in what sequence and modality
- Curate a set of all "street legal" raw files (to be) used in the instructional design project, and use the contents as a starting point for creating early learning designs
- Create some "early designs" of digital learning objects for a specific instructional design project (while adhering to the known laws and other requirements)
  - List some types of early designs

Planning with Learning Object/Resource Prototypes

- Create some "prototypes" of digital learning objects for a specific instructional design project (while adhering to the known laws and other requirements)
  - List some types of prototypes
- Develop various prototypes (first of their kinds for a bespoke or customized learning resource project), and evolve these to a sufficient level of development so that others may visualize what a finalized form may look like
- Using off-the-shelf authoring tools and/or prototyping tools, create some informative prototypes that benefit a design and development project

Learning Sequence Designs

- Design learner experience-based sequences to optimize learning

Applied Learning from Early Designs and Prototypes

- Define how prototypes may be used as exemplars for follow-on designs
- Constructively critique early designs in order to explore relevant aspects and to make project-wide decisions
- Constructively critique draft learning object prototypes and learning sequence designs in order to explore relevant aspects and to make project-wide decisions
- Produce work-based documentation related to this instructional design project that captures the learning from the early designs and prototypes
- Maintain a work journal to pay close attention to the work and what is learned during the design and early development

Overall Project Content Design Informed by Early Designs and Prototypes

- Set up (or revise) an open sharing instructional design project plan (in a project stylebook or work plan) that is practically "doable" within a set time period, with insights and efficiencies from early designs and prototyping

7.1 Introduction

A digital learning object or sequence enables a learner to engage information, interactivity, feedback, and other learning experiences, to ultimately acquire knowledge. Learning designs are complex, and they are informed by learning research, learning theory, technological capabilities, and other factors. Some are informed by the needs and preferences of the target (and potential) learners. Learning designs should enable a range of learning experiences, and they should provide learning value.

An "early design" is defined here as an expressed conceptualization of a learning resource and its structure, general sequence (an outline, a storyboard), target learning contents, technological modality, look-and-feel, and other attributes. Design is how something works, not a veneer, not a surface (Soto 2013). In a learning resource, how it works is how it functions and how it influences the learners. It is "early" in multiple senses. One is that it is done near the beginning of the instructional design work (so "early in a process"). It is also "early" in the sense that no design is finalized until the learning object or sequence is complete. Every design is provisional until the draft work is finalized, any "commits" are provisional and potentially temporary. In designing curricula, it is better not to not go forth with "a mélange of unarticulated methods and purposes" but with articulated objectives and congruous practices (Joseph et al. 2000, p. ix) when creating learning.

There are various design thinking techniques for the design of "learning, teaching and assessment," including the following five: "*metaphors* to assist in conceptualising the educational opportunities we design, *mind mapping* to explore innovative assessment opportunities, *problem posing* to examine innovative assessment challenges, *problem solving* to design innovative assessment solutions, (and) *reflective thinking* to assist in devising ways of integrating sustainable learning with innovative assessment" (Swirski 2010, p. 1)

An early design may be expressed as a series of drawings. It may be a drawing of an interface. It may be a written or aural narrative that describes the learning object. It may be a narrative (with plot, characters, and the classic structure of rising tensions peaking at a climax and resulting in a denouement). Or it may be a story problem. This design may include understandings of target learners in order to build to their needs. In the same way that design-based research is harnessed to advance understandings, research-based designs are often used to advance builds of technologies. One researcher explains:

> Opportunities to learn arise in the course of any design process. These opportunities for learning are the direct result of the specific decisions that must be made in the course of a design" (Edelson 2002, p. 108).

The iterative design process offers "opportunities to learn unique lessons" that have an impact on educational practice (Edelson 2002, p. 105). One thinker differentiates between "high-level design, including prototyping" and "detailed design, including detailed prototyping" (Gery 1991, as cited in Gustafson and Branch 1997, p. 84); whether designs are zoomed-out or zoomed-in affects the types of insights and how they may be practically used. Another sense of prototypes reads: "Prototypes may be shallow or narrow: shallow in the sense that the entire look of a product is replicated minus some functionality, or narrow in the sense that a small segment is completed with all functionality, leaving other whole portions of the final product undeveloped" (Wilson et al. 1993, p. 3). Rapid prototyping is applied in broad ways:

1. to test out a user interface;
2. to test the database structure and flow of information in a training system;

3. to test the effectiveness and appeal of a particular instructional strategy;
4. to develop a model case or practice exercise that can serve as a template for others;
5. to give clients and sponsors a more concrete model of the intended instructional product;
6. to get user feedback and reactions to two competing approaches. (Wilson et al. 1993, p. 3)

Every learning object design is both patterned (and therefore somewhat generalized) and unique (specific to the designer signature, the learning context, and the particular object). In some ways, every instructional design for a particular learning object, sequence, or resource, is at once a unique bespoke design as well as a generic one. No two instructional designs are exactly alike; simultaneously, every design is a variation on a prior one. Too much customization, and a work becomes too costly to create and too unrecognizable for users. Too little customization, and a work is unmemorable and unengaging.

Early designs may be aspirational and ambitious, to set a high bar for the follow-on work, even if those works do not attain the heights of the initial plans. These designs may be conceptualizations and/or instantiated expressions (like prototypes, which are ideas made manifest). These help designer/developers understand what is workable and what is desirable/undesirable. Also, early designs are not considered necessarily holistic but tend to focus on particular objects and object features. Parts of the design may be highly structured and defined, and other parts may be less structured or unstructured altogether. The point is to employ an experimental mindset. The design phase is a powerful one to infuse a work with originality and innovations.

If multiple members of a team will be using the designs, it is important to explain the design and what has informed it because such influences may be invisible and hidden and non-obvious to others. Early designs may be polysemic and ambiguous. Without sufficient built-in descriptions, others may infer why a design contains the ideas and expressions it has, but those may be far-off of accurate.

Another consideration in early designs involves the concept of "ongoing delivery" or "maintenance" of the learning resource (Sims and Jones 2002, p. 4). If the learning resource is a once-and-done piece of content, then continuing attention may not be necessary; however, if it evolves and changes over time, then the design thinking may have to extend beyond the first part of the creation and to longer term considerations.

An early design may take on a number of forms: a drawing or sketch, a visualization, textual outlines, storyboards, audio plans, text-and-image drafts, and others. These should capture the most salient points of the design. On teams, these may be design artifacts around which discussions may occur. How detailed these are will depend on the purpose of the designs, but these vary in terms of the level of "zoom". Sometimes, the designs are the details, so it is important to pay close attention to the close-in design features.

An early plan should be both ambitious and doable, imaginative and grounded, fanciful and real, inspired and practical. These pairs of adjectives, on the surface, may seem to be at counter-purpose, but they are not necessarily so. If a plan is too pie-in-the-sky, it becomes highly daunting to execute on. If it is too practical and uninspired, it may be too boring to actualize. The sweet spot is somewhere in-between ambitious inspiration and doability.

A "prototype," in this context, is the first of an instantiated or expressed form (of learning object), to inform the development work. Another definition reads as "any representation of a design idea, regardless of medium" (Hounde and Hill 1997, p. 3). Prototypes enable designers to "organically and evolutionarily learn, discover, generate, and refine designs" (Lim et al. 2008, p. 7:2), and as such, they enable the designer to explore designs and reflect on their work. Prototypes serve as "filters that traverse a design space and are manifestations of design ideas that concretize and externalize conceptual ideas" (Lim et al. 2008, p. 7:4). Another research team suggests that prototypes are exploratory objects that focus on crucial elements of the design:

> We argue that the purpose of designing a prototype is to find the manifestation that, in its simplest form, will filter the qualities in which the designer is interested without distorting the understanding of the whole. (Lim et al. 2008, p. 7–10)

Prototypes contain foundational defining features of the thing being described. These objects are representational:

> 'Prototypes' are representations of a design made before final artifacts exist. They are created to inform both design process and design decisions. They range from sketches and different kind (sic) of models at various levels—'looks like,' 'behaves like,' 'works like'—to explore and communicate propositions about the design and its context (Buchenau and Suri 2000, p. 424).

Another source defines a prototype as "a *concrete representation* of part or all of an interactive system" (Beaudouin-Lafon and Mackay 2002, p. 1-1). Prototypes do serve different purposes in different design contexts, and they take on different forms. For many, a prototype is able to be run and put through some paces. One team describes this requirement:

> To prototype is to develop an executable version of a product which incorporates key elements of the final version but which is incomplete in many respects, for example, in terms of functionality, robustness, or exception handling. The purpose is to realize the conceptual structure of the product without incurring the expense of the full product development cycle" (Jones et al. 1992, p. 96).

Ultimately, whatever form they take, prototypes are thought to improve "the quality of the final product" (Moonen 1996, as cited in Jones and Richey 2000, p. 65).

In the research literature, there are a wide range of alternate prototype formats used in the design of instruction: "scope/visual prototypes" and "executable prototypes," which each defining various features of the learning resources (Jones and Richey 2000, p. 65). Such prototypes may describe the learning contents, instructional strategies, harnessed media, learning setting, and measurement tools in a "generic template prototype" (Yang 1995, as cited in Jones and Richey 2000, p. 65), or "user and computer interactions" in a "functional" or "technical" prototype (Gray and Black 1994 as cited in Jones and Richey 2000, p. 65), or "labeling conventions, sequencing, clarity of the message, and pacing in a videotape" in a "rough cut prototype" (Appleman et al. 1995, as cited in Jones and Richey 2000, p. 65), among others. There are no consensus-based classifications of prototypes at present in the instructional design space, and the approach seems to be that people will use whatever works for them.

The prototypes may be "throwaway" ones that are just used to answer particular design and development questions. (These are not discarded and remain part of the project documents, but they are not evolved from the original file into a future working prototype and final learning object. All throwaway prototypes serve a use by answering questions and providing insights. They suggest paths to take and not to take.) For many, prototyping work may be seen as ultimately "disposable," with new design insights as the main objective, and the created contents as a byproduct of the process (Petrelli et al. 2014, p. 42). These instantiated designs may be low-fidelity and highly selective in terms of the represented features. These prototypes tend toward minimalism and lightness. Or some prototypes are created only to represent the project direction and inspiration to clients and funders. In these latter cases, the designers and developers often need to clarify what the respective prototypes mean. After all, prototypes are "not self-explanatory" (Hounde and Hill 1997, p. 2).

Prototypes may be characterized by their basic form, from paper prototypes to digital mockups to "virtual prototyping" (creating prototypes in virtual immersive worlds).

Even more explanation may be needed if the prototypes are used with individuals who represent target learner and potential groups. Cooperative prototyping involves users "actively and creatively in design and evaluation of early developed prototypes" (Bødker and Grønbæk 1990, p. 1). Testing new technology features with potential users may shed light on the social acceptability of particular new behaviors for interactions (Rico and Brewster 2010).

Users who participate in cooperative prototyping research were not found to be less responsive to low-fidelity paper vs. computer prototyping (Sefelin et al. 2003). A later study did find user-participants in prototyping to be more satisfied with formal designs than hand-drawn diagrams (Yeung et al. 2007, p. 311). Prototypes inform on the focuses of the learning and the "mix of emphasis…to specific aspects of the experience, such as sensory, physical/spatial, cognitive, social and temporal/dynamic qualities" (Buchenau and Suri 2000, p. 432); to this end, designers/developers need to understand "what the user looks at, feels and hears while using it" (Houde and Hill 1997, as cited in Buchenau and Suri 2000, p. 424).

Or, fairly commonly, these prototypes may be actual early drafts of open-shared learning objects or sequences, which are built on and refined into finalized form. A number of off-the-shelf authoring tools (for the creation of slideshows/slide decks, websites, screencasts and other videos, games, animations, image stories, data stories, image sets, simulations, and other objects) are relatively easy-to-use; many enable built-in scaffolding of content structures and context-sensitive help. There are courseware systems that structure building learning objects that are web friendly; these are often non-agnostic approaches, meaning that the systems have some built-in elements that are informed by particular learning theories. These features of authoring tools enable subject matter experts to build their own contents by closing the gap between a design and a working learning object. Many of these enable WYSIWYG ("what you see is what you get") functionalities, so even tentative and early designs may be built with actual interactivity. These technology tools enable prototypes to morph into finalized learning objects. Identifying a "prototype" involves freeze-framing the learning object or putting the development process in a slow motion view; the item in development necessarily goes through the development phases, and a "prototype" is a cleaned-up version of that object in a certain development phase.

Sizes of Prototyped Objects for Learning? Are there particular sizes of prototypes used in instructional design? A common size is the "learning object," defined as "any entity, digital or non-digital, which can be used, re-used or referenced during technology supported learning" by the IEEE (2004) Learning and Technology Standards Committee. Another definition for learning objects is as "discrete units of learning resources based on agreed standards" and inspired by object-oriented software engineering (Douglas 2001, p. F4E-1). Common objects may be slideshows, games, videos, articles, small applications (applets), programs, simulations, datasets, and so on. There are prototypes for objects smaller than learning objects or sub-objects, such as the design of examples and counter-examples, factuals and counter-factuals, assessments and feedback, assignments and feedback, preparatory modules, and so on. Prototypes may be built for modules and web pages and e-books, which may contain multiple learning objects. Sizes of online learning contents may be understood as relative to each other, but even within the various types, the sizes may be highly variant.

Beyond authoring tools, there are technologies designed for in-depth prototyping and "wireframing" mockups (simulations and designs focused around an object's navigational structure and interactive functionality) of applications and websites. Automated interactive functionalities have also broadened with the advancement of technologies, with interactive data visualizations, interactive digital flashcards, question-answer displays, photo albums, interactive maps, timelines, short games (crossword puzzles, drag-and-drops, ordering activities, jigsaw puzzles, sorting games, and others), and light assessments (with automated feedback).

With the popularization of Cascading Stylesheets (CSS) and other methods for presenting contents on the web, much of the instructional design work surrounds creating the text, video, and other contents, but the overall look-and-feel of an e-book or website or wiki or courseware may be handled within the hosting technology. The visual brand may be a combination of "skins," color palettes, and other contents.

In some contexts, prototyping may be contrasted with other methods of design, with one such contender as a "life cycle approach" based on systems analysis (Alavi 1984, p. 557).

A "learning sequence" (or "learning sequences") refers to the order in which learners experience learning contents. Some learning objects, common stand-alone and linked units of learning, have fixed order time sequence structures: "static" videos, animations, simulations, and slideshows. A common trajectory for learning content is to start with basics and advance to more complex information. Or a sequence may be a problem-solution one. Static contents are more common than dynamic ones.

Then, there are dynamic versions of each of the prior forms as well, that enable users to make choices and take branching paths through "dynamic" videos, animations, simulations, and slideshows as compared to a fixed-order static approach. At the learning module level, there is usually a time structure, such as an initial phase, a middle learning content section, and a concluding phase. There may be transitions or segues designed into the time structure. There may be time loops. For example, a learner may loop back to take a different version of an assessment that he or she wants to review or did not perform well in initially.

Another approach in learning sequencing relates to the learner sequential experience. For example, a learner may first need to be attracted to the open-shared learning object by visual (attraction based on an arresting visual), conceptual (attraction to an idea), curiosity (attraction based on a story) or social means (positive word of mouth). Then, he or she needs to feel welcome. Expectations for the learning may come next. Then the actual learning experiences may ensue. Throughout, the tone will be aligned with the contents. There may be formative and summative assessments offered. And then, there is a transition away from the learning object to other relevant learning resources. Understanding the learner's "walk-through" of the learning resources is important. For learning resources that are fairly complex and demanding, these have to be designed so that learners may come and go at their convenience…and they have to be accommodated for their access behaviors. They should be able to pick up where they left off, for example.

For the more dynamic paths through learning contents, the actual experienced learner sequence may depend on various information: a pre-test, the learner profile, the learner behaviors, the learner performance (such as on assessments), the learner's preferences (including opt-in and opt-out sequences), and other factors. Some adaptive systems deliver customized learning paths based on pre-programmed learner needs, and those are identified from a mix of data sources.

In some cases, learning contents may not have an "learning sequence" per se. For example, an image set may not have a coherent sequence in which the contents may be experienced, but these are commonly released into the public space for learning. The same dynamic may exist for audio sets, curated text sets, knowledge bases, data tables, and multi-modal datasets.

The work phase for creating early designs, prototypes, and learning sequences directly follows, chronologically, the setup of the stylebook and templating (Fig. 7.1). While this high-level sequence may give the sense that early designs and prototypes may occur early in the design/development process, these are relevant at any stage, and the two-headed arrows in the diagram show recursiveness in the processes.

Some Risks…in Early Commitment…in Vacuous Prototypes…in Additional Costs One risk in this work phase is to fixate on an early design idea too early and to miss other more optimized alternatives (Dow et al. 2010). One suggested way to

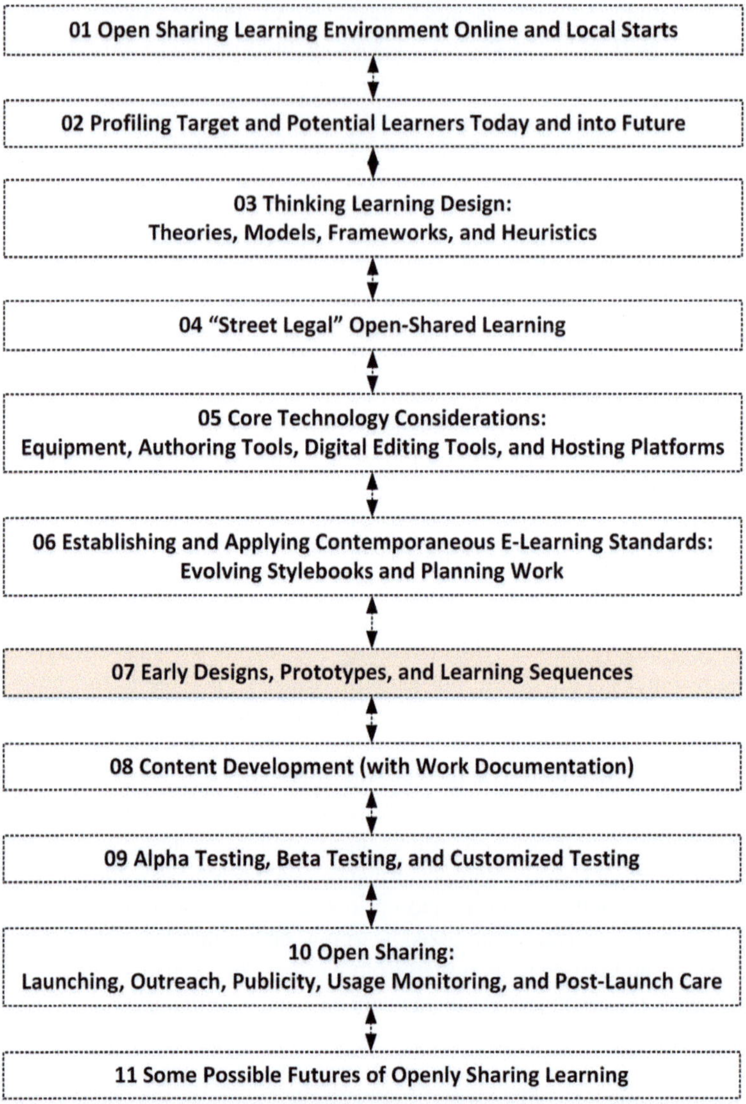

Fig. 7.1 Step 7 in the open-shared learning resource development sequence

avoid early commitment is to engage in so-called parallel prototyping instead of serial linear approaches resulting in more creative possibilities (Dow et al. 2010). This way, multiple ideas are being evolved simultaneously along different channels, and those ideas may compete with each other and highlight different approaches. It is thought that what is considered initially is rarely the best solution for a design challenge, and premature acceptance of an approach simply because the idea came to mind first is a poor way to advance a design (Petrelli et al. 2014, p. 48).

Even before the present age of abundant technologies what offer a dazzling range of prototyping possibilities, researchers have observed the advent of so-called "vacuous prototypes" [described in the following way: "Vacuous prototypes are for the 1990s what 'vaporware' was for the 1970s and early 1980s" (Berghel 1994, p. 49).] The author suggests that prototyping tools were so easy to use that good-looking designs could be created without sufficient thought or effort, and these would lack explanatory or predictive power for the actual work (Berghel 1994, p. 50). Prototyping is prone to "the problems caused by fluid specifications, incongruities, false starts, and administrative distractions" and other challenges (Berghel 1994, p. 54).

To lower the costs of prototyping, rapid prototyping was originated to enable faster results. Early conceptualizations of rapid prototyping explicitly entangled research and design, given the prescriptive role of prototypes: "Rapid prototyping continues with the parallel processes of design and research, or construction and utilization. It is assumed that full understanding of needs, content, and objectives is a result of the design process and not an input into it" (Tripp and Bichelmeyer 1990, p. 39). Earlier forms of prototypes were critiqued for not pleasing users with the end products, for not lowering project time, for not enabling proper decision making, and not reducing project costs (Tripp and Bichelmeyer 1990, p. 36). In ensuing years, there has been more focus on how to apply prototypes in effective ways to solve more real-world design and development challenges. This rapid prototyping method "hinges on an iterative, overlapping approach to design, instead of a linear approach" in the instructional systems design (ISD) space (Daugherty et al. 2007, p. 2). Rapid prototyping has long had applications in other areas, too. "For ideation to be successful an idea must be explorable (sic) in hours if not minutes" (Agustin et al. 2007, p. 36). Fast "explorative prototypes" may be done on-the-fly with the potential users of the objects in order to elicit their initial responses. In an instructional design context, rapid prototyping may inform the design phase with feedback on "technical issues, creative treatment, and effectiveness of instruction" (Boulet 2009, p. 5).

In the spirit of the #failfast ethos, fast or rapid prototyping is thought to help designers achieve insight faster—by "formulating a concept, selecting the technology, designing the form, critically evaluat(ing) the outcome and reflect(ing) on the findings" (Petrelli et al. 2014, p. 47). In this scenario, designers and developers get some actionable information sooner rather than later. Designers and developers may make provisional small commits to aspects of early designs and prototypes but evolve their creations with new information and technologies and inspirations.

On the one hand, the "incompleteness" of a prototype is a strength because it enables the examination of an idea "without building a copy of the final design. Prototypes are helpful as much in what they do not include as in what they do" (Lim et al. 2008, p. 7:7). Some designers and developers can read possibilities in the sparsity and abstractness of the prototypes. In other ways, prototypes may be more high fidelity, concretely detailed, evocative, and explicated, but these are more costly to create and may lock the designer/developers into a particular course of design action (because of sunk costs and expended efforts). Bringing a prototype to production-level quality requires a high level of expenditures. Different designers and developers may have different preferences between barebones prototypes vs. more fleshed-out ones.

Another potential application of the prototype is as an initial "proof of concept" to show that something can actually be created as conceptualized or that it is infeasible. A prototype is a compromise from the ideals of an ambitious design, but it at least shows do-ability. If a designer tends towards pie-in-the-sky thinking, prototypes should bring that focus back to earth, to working and workable models.

Another application of prototypes is as a hedge haphazard work, something unthinking, inarticulate, or non-purposive. The prototypes enable a designer/developer (individual or team) to draw out and externalize their ideas. It brings out assumptions to the surface to enable interactions with those ideas. Also, prototypes are a hedge against a failure to meet standards. Appropriate prototypes may serve as "guardrails" for effective projects. These can be especially useful as the learning resources are serialized or extended, so newly developed works align with the first set.

"Early designs," "prototypes," and "learning sequences" stand to provide a historical record about how designs were arrived at, what thoughts went into each, the inspirations, the design concepts, and other details. These documents and objects may provide a provenance of the learning resources; they may serve as proof of contributions of respective team members and of the work's originality.

While it may seem like the creation of prototypes is an extra step and make-work, it may be understood as merely an early state in the design of a learning object. If the prototype is to be shared with clients/funders, the design team, or used with external groups for early testing, these have to achieve some level of coherence before they are used. Certainly, low-tech paper prototyping has long been used to elicit responses to the designs before the development work (Snyder 2001). Otherwise, early and intermediate prototypes can be as rough cut and awkward as the designers/developers need, on the way to a refined resource. (Those who have not had a lot of experiences building learning objects may want to keep some copies in some early and intermediate stages to better understand how these develop. This information can be used to improve their work processes. Effective prototypes will cohere and clarify over time.)

How "early designs" and "prototypes" and "learning sequences" are defined and expressed will depend on the particulars of the local context and particularly the needs of the design and development team and the design questions that the team wants answered. As may be seen in this introduction, there is much room to maneuver, and there are many correct ways to create designs as long as they inform an effectively designed learning resource. Others may suggest that theoretical alignment to select educational theories, academic research, and instructional design approaches may be critical requirements as well. How the early designs, prototypes, and learning sequence designs inform the actual work and the resulting learning contents may vary greatly because the designs themselves and how they are used are highly variant.

7.2 Review of the Literature

Instructional design "is engaged in to create means for human learning; doing so involves performing a set of basic processes; and the product, whether simple instruction or an elaborate environment, is a coherent set of conditions for learning" (Rowland and DiVasto 2013, p. 9). Arriving at the proper "conditions for learning" through design, though, is a contested and complex space. A basic truism seems to be that there are as many instructional development models as there are "practitioners of instructional development" (Gustafson and Branch 1997, p. 73). There has long been a sense that there is not "a well-developed design field in education" (Resnick 1999, as cited in Reeves 2000, p. 1).

From a high-level view, there are paradigms in education and training designs. They have been identified as instrumental [by providing "planning and tracking mechanism"(s)], communicative (eliciting feedback from stakeholders and co-creating "shared design specifications"), pragmatic (introducing efficiencies in work processes), and artistic (enabling the creation of "unique and creative products") (Visscher-Voerman and Gustafson 2004, p. 87). Each of the paradigms have weaknesses as well, with resulting designs that may be too fixed to accommodate new insights, those which are not "theoretically sound," those that may result in conflicting visions for the learning resource, and over-focusing on the designer's vision at a cost to other stakeholders (Visscher-Voerman and Gustafson 2004, p. 87).

The lack of a learning design consensus may be logically explained. There are multiple reasons for this, including the fact of many moving parts: types of learning, applications of learning, identities of learners, complex learner needs, technologies used to build the learning, and others. While the decisions may theoretically be mapped (because the numbers are large but finite), the degrees of freedom are many, and the combinatorial complexity may be high. Then, too, there are many competing and conflicting educational theories, learning models, learning frameworks, along with mixed research findings, and competing ideas for how to optimally design instructional objects. Those who design instruction are engaged in…

> …a chess game, in which players engage in an intellectual activity for which there is no one set of appropriate moves. . . . The order, and manner, [in which design skills are used] depends upon the character of the problem, and the aim in mind. There is no one best way, and no one way of proceeding. Neither is there one optimal solution. Everything depends upon the situation, and the skills available. (Davies 1978, pp. 22–23, as cited in McDonald 2011, p. 53)

The state of the field itself is seen as undeveloped or underdeveloped. Instructional design was a "formal educational discipline in the 1940s" and much of its focus has been on adult learners (Desrosier 2011, p. 135). For years, datedness linear "assembly-line instructional design models" were common (Gayeski 1998, p. 36). The field borrowed from other disciplines, such as Agile development methodologies from software design and the concept that the created software/learning resource "meets the customer needs, no more, no less" (Rawsthorne 2005, p. 4).

There are no given widely accepted standard approaches except some general principles. The accepted ideas, in practice, seem to be that instructional design…

- should build on the best known empiric-based research-based information about how people learn (in their particular developmental phases);
- should be based off of the defined learning objectives and learning outcomes;
- should align the instructional design with the learning contents and contexts;
- should be learner-centered and have their best well-being at heart;
- should be informed by professional ethics and applicable values;
- and others.

If instructional designers have a predominant epistemology, theory of how knowledge may be captured and built, it is very closely informed by academic research practices. The realist objectivist assumption of research applies in instructional technology practices as well (Reeves 1993, as cited by Reeves et al. 2005, p. 102). Ideally, how learners engage with various learning sequences would be studied, and that feedback could be used to improve the particular learning designs and learner experiences and possibly generalize to similar contexts.

The term for conducting research to inform designs is "design research." Here research is not academic in the popular sense of the word meaning not particularly practical but informs a design. One author team writes: "Design research requires that faculty members explore significant educational problems, rather than conduct research for its own sake" (Reeves et al. 2005, p. 109). There are practical design applications, like defining "a pedagogical outcome and create(ing) learning environments that address it" (Reeves et al. 2005, p. 109). Design research objectives include work to…:

- "Emphasize content and pedagogy rather than technology.
- Give special attention to supporting human interactions and nurturing learning communities.
- Modify the learning environments until the pedagogical outcome is reached.
- Reflect on the process to reveal design principles that can inform other instructors and researchers, and future development projects" (Reeves et al. 2005, p. 110)

Another applicable term is "developmental research" from instructional design and development practice. The co-authors explain:

> The crux of developmental research is to systematically examine our products, tools, processes, and models in order to provide reliable, usable information to both practitioners and theorists. It is research, however, that is intricately connected to real world practice. It creates a loop with practice informing research and research, in turn, informing practice (Richey and Klein 2005, p. 35).

Public Learning Objects Meeting Standards? A bare minimum conceptualization of necessary standards may be that the learning resources fulfill basic requirements for being a "learning object" (defined in Wikipedia as "a collection of content items, practice items, and assessment items that are combined based on a single learning objective") ("Learning object 2017). One study found that in a survey of learning objects (LOs) on four learning object repositories that most of those assessed did not meet basic definitional standards:

> A survey of objects contained in existing repositories, however, reveals that relatively few can strictly be defined as LOs at all, being of a basic CO (content object) type and not useable on a stand-alone basis to bring about intentional learning. These objects need to be aggregated with other materials in order to achieve specific objectives. Their quality also varies greatly, and in some cases calls into question the professionalism associated with the learning materials of which they are a part. The current review indicates that the effective development of LOs requires the clear definition of an instructional process addressing the unique characteristics of LO technologies, within the structured process stressed by ID principles. If such principles are not heeded, learning repositories will gain a reputation for amateurish content, rather than credibility as worthwhile educational resources. (Harvey 2007)

The standards for this research were basic—that learning objects should have two main elements: learning contents and related metadata (data about those learning contents), and that they should be sufficiently stand-alone to enable re-use (Harvey 2007). If learning resources are not executable on multiple platforms, and they do not interplay well with other learning objects, their reusability and *raison d'etre* is in question.

Within e-learning, there are a range of standards defined through a variety of forms. The group defines them as follows:

- *Official standard*: a set of definitions, requirements, formats, and design guidelines for elearning systems or their components that a recognized standards organization has documented and approved (see the "Standardization Bodies" sidebar for a detailed list of organizations).
- *De facto standard*: the same as an official standard, but widely accepted only by the community and industry—that is, lacking formal approval from a recognized standardization body.
- *Specification*: a document on the same issues as an official standard, but less evolved; usually developed and promoted by organizations or consortia of partners from academia, industry, and educational institutions. It captures a rough consensus in the e-learning community and is used as a de facto standard in system and content development.
- *Reference model*: an adapted and reduced version of a combination of standards and specifications focusing on architectural aspects of an e-learning system, definitions of parts of the system, and their interactions (Devedžić et al. 2007, p. 17)

From these requirement types come standards for learning object packaging, metadata labeling, and others, to enable the usability of the objects and their proper performance.

How Professionals Arrive at Designs Only half of respondents in a study regularly used theories to make instructional strategy decisions, and many were "eclectic in their underlying philosophical assumptions" (Christensen and Osguthorpe 2004, p. 45). These researchers explored how instructional designers decide on which instructional strategies to use and how theories inform that work. In one study, the researchers found that the most informative "Theory/Theorist/Model" mentioned by the research participants were the following, in descending order:

> Gagné; Gagné, Briggs, & Wager;
> M.D. Merrill: Component Display Theory; Pebble in a Pond Theory, etc.;
> Dick & Carey;
> Keller's ARCS Motivational Model;
> Instructional Models (Generic & ADDIE);
> Problem-based Learning, Project & case-based instruction;
> Cognitive Theories;
> Institution-Specific ISD Process;
> Rapid Prototyping;
> Harless's ABCD-Outcomes-based model;
> Rothwell & Kazanzas: Systems Design;
> Behaviorism;
> HTP;
> Mager & Pipe;
> Smith & Ragan: Instructional Design;
> Cognitive Apprenticeship;
> Layers of Necessity;
> Clark & Mayer: e-Learning;
> Constructive ideals (Christensen and Osguthorpe 2004, p. 56).

Useful learning theories, represented in general categories, were listed in the following descending order of relevance: "Constructivism, Social Constructivism; Cognitive Theories; Instructional Theories; Motivational Theories; Behaviorism, S-R Theories; (and) Andragogy Theories" (Christensen and Osguthorpe 2004, p. 57). In terms of actual influences, these researchers found a heavy reliance on "interaction with others both as a means of making instructional-strategy decisions and of learning about new theories, trends, and strategies" (Christensen and Osguthorpe 2004, p. 45).

Besides direct reportage by the professional designers, some of the artifacts that they create may inform on their work. For example, externalizations of "expert mental imagery can play an important role in the design reasoning of high-performance teams" (Petre 2010, p. 171).

Researchers have coined a term for the necessary flexibility of those who design instruction and draw inspiration from a range of sources. "Critical flexibility" refers to the following:

> a fundamental openness to one's own conceptual design sense and alternatives; it seeks to achieve this ideal not only through its commitment to the use of whatever conceptual resources seem useful in practice, but also in its acknowledgement of conceptual design sense as a way of being involved in one's work that should be explicated to whatever degree possible for critical examination. At times, perhaps often, critical flexibility will require that potentially useful conceptual tools be reconstructed or modified to cohere with existing background values and assumptions; conversely, one's conceptual design sense will, at times, need to be reconsidered and revised to better accommodate potentially useful conceptual tools and meet the needs of practice. Critical flexibility thus embraces the idea of

> conceptual guidance, but requires that this guidance be fluid, evolving, and adjustable or transformable as designers gain experience and continually adapt to the contextual demands of their work. Practitioners, then, are not ideologues or technicians who rigidly apply standard principles, but agents of design seeking continuous improvement through critical reflection and the coherent appropriation of whatever may facilitate practice. In this way, critical flexibility offers a means of moving between, and indeed, beyond, the problems of eclecticism and orthodoxy. (Yanchar and Gabbitas 2011, pp. 395–396).

In a sense, diverse theories may be brought to bear on learning designs even if they are contradictory: "Difficult judgments about diverse theories are then avoided as design work is enriched by all perspectives" (Yanchar and Gabbitas 2011, p. 384).

Learner-Centeredness and Agency An important aspect of open-shared learning resources is to decide how much agency and decision making to enable for learners. Some learning tracks are fixed-path ones with limited learner interactions (Beaudouin-Lafon and Mackay 2002, p. 1–5). Others are much more interactive, with branching paths. Some open-shared learning enables a wide range of learner agency and choice making. One researcher has described "pedagogical levels of 'freedom' or 'openness'" as high when learners can determine their own "objectives of learning and methods" and low if the learning systems are "closed, one-way, transmissive, and reproductive" (Ehlers 2011, p. 4).

A culturally "inclusive curriculum" involves teaching not from a monoculture but from cross-cultural ones. In one constructivist learning design, inclusive tactics enable learners to "adopt different learning approaches and have different levels of prior knowledge"; focus on "authentic" assessments, and harness "cultural differences and perspectives" as "assets, not liabilities" (McLoughlin 2001, p. 22). The focus is on learner experiences and outcomes in safe learning environments (McLoughlin 2001, p. 18). Core tools involve collaborative ones that enable learners to engage in learning communities surrounding "teaching and support processes, learning activities, learning outcomes, (and) assessment" (McLoughlin 2011, p. 13).

Recent research has focused on the need to introduce social factors in the designs. Initial considerations for learners as individuals came about because of their decision making power. Learners are a critical factor because of their decision making role as a potential adopter. Ernest Burkman's User-Oriented Instructional Development (UOID) model suggested the importance of social factors in "instructional products" and pointed to the importance of "user-friendly products" (Surry and Farquhar 1996, pp. 4–5). Individual decision making has been found to be influenced by their social networks. Connectivist massive open online courses (MOOCs) are built around principles of connectivity "connectivism (autonomy, diversity, openness and interactivity)" (Rodriguez 2013, p. 1), focusing on human social aspects of engagement and learning.

Technology-Informed Designs Various technologies—authoring tools, learning management systems, courseware systems, content management systems, and others—also affect the learning design. While some technologies aim to be "agnostic" or "neutral," researchers have suggested that such agnosticism may be somewhat illusory since technology functions may be suggestive of what is important. For example, a slideshow authoring tool may offer a range of features to define the tool—by enabling headers, contrastive colors for accessibility, slide numbering for easy referencing, and other elements. Another example may be the templated module with certain types of contents enabled in a learning management system.

The user interface design may be informed by many of the technologies as well based on built-in templating, items menus, color palettes, available functionalities, and others. Technologies enable handing over varying controls and decisions to users, which may enhance the design of the user (learner) experience. Also, designing a user interface with clarity—for easy orientation and easy navigation—is thought to increase usability (by lessening the mental load to use the learning resource). Interestingly, "interface-aesthetics did not affect perceived usability" (Tuch et al. 2012, p. 1604), but poor user interface designs resulted in lower usability and resulting user frustration. [For those outside of the field, a lot of inputs go into user interface designs: "Designing the instructional interface is a challenging endeavor requiring knowledge and skills in instructional and visual design, psychology, human-factors, ergonomic research, computer science and editorial design" (Lohr 2000, p. 161).] For learner interfaces, beyond basic orientation and navigation, some researchers propose simplification, with focuses on common core tasks of "instructional presentation" and "learner practice" (Sugrue and Clark In Press, as cited in Lohr 2000, p. 168).

At more close-in levels, say, at the level of "learning object," it seems that there is compelling research on optimized design for designing particular types of learning, such as problem-based learning (Malopinsky et al. 2000), case-based learning, simulation-based learning and simulation pedagogy, game-based learning (serious games), and for harnessing multimedia for learning (Clark and Mayer 2016). In each of the areas, there is empirical research around effectiveness for learning.

Meeting Ethical Standards Values may be expressed in particular designs in a number of ways—by the selectivity of what is important and the leaving off of what is not important, by the depicted values (which are desirable, and which are not), by how people are depicted, by how learners are addressed, and a number of other factors. One team explains some of the values:

> Prototypes are intricately intertwined with the evolution of design ideas throughout the design process. We constantly evaluate and reflect on the values of what we design—if those designs are socially responsible, economically viable, experientially pleasing, culturally sound, operationally usable, technologically compatible, and functionally error-free. These are some of the important values that designers try to satisfy. (Lim et al. 2008, p. 7:8)

The practice of education itself is seen as a "virtue" that promotes pro-individual and pro-social learning (Kabisch and Williams 2012, p. 343).

Efficiencies and Cost Savings Some ways to introduce efficiencies in the instructional design involve modeling the design process after "an assembly line" and replacing design documents "with specification sheets" and using "storyboard templates" in lieu of authoring tools (having a pre-formed structure) and other approaches (Roytek 2010, p. 175). The technology skill set is a critical competency for instructional designers (Roytek 2010, p. 178). Instructional design requires project management skills (van Rooij 2010), and these include intelligent budgeting. In a $0 budget context for enabling open-shared learning, having the necessary skill set and ability to use complex technologies provides a crucial head start.

Historically, prototyping has been a core practice in various types of design for decades: industrial, computing, and other fields (Petrelli et al. 2014, p. 41). In the design of interactive computer artifacts, prototypes have been harnessed to represent "different states of an evolving design" (Hounde and Hill 1997, p. 1). Prototypes may be created from analog objects, like paper (Hounde and Hill 1997, p. 6), and also digital ones, by computer. With the advent of HTML objects for interactive prototypes (Vaidyanathan et al. 1999), prototypes can be experienced as part of the analysis. Some design sequences may move between paper and digital, with an initial draft on paper, then a move to digitization of some ideas, some initial testing, then further designs. Within digital itself, there are a range of modalities to use, visual, auditory, multimodal, and others.

In human-computer interaction studies, video prototyping has long been a common technique to test human-computer interfaces. These approaches require expensive "recording and editing equipment, actors, sets, props and special effects" for believable scenarios (Bardzell et al. 2006, p. 433), leading many to go to *machinima* (machine + cinema, referring to videos taken in immersive virtual world environments) for prototyping. This authoring team defines *machinima* as "both a filmmaking technique and a film genre"…"in which some or all elements are staged, recorded and produced within the virtual environments found in many video games" (Bardzell et al. 2006, p. 433).

Prototypes have been categorized by the technologies used to create them, the levels of detail offered, the closeness of the prototype to its finalized form, and other features. These characteristics may be misleading. Two co-authoring researchers observe:

> Finished-looking (or -behaving) prototypes are often thought to indicate that the design they represent is near completion. Although this may sometimes be the case, a finished-looking prototype might be made early in the design process (e.g., a 3D concept model for use in market research), and a rough one might be made later on (e.g., to emphasize overall structure rather than visual details in a user test). Two related terms are used in this context: "resolution" and "fidelity". We interpret resolution to mean "amount of detail", and fidelity to mean "closeness to the eventual design". It is important to recognize that the degree of visual and behavioral refinement of a prototype does not necessarily correspond to the solidity of the design, or to a particular stage in the process. (Hounde and Hill 1997, p. 3)

They suggest that the optimal way to represent prototypes is by "what it prototypes" (what it designs) and not by more incidental or peripheral descriptions (Hounde and Hill 1997, p. 1).

One approach focuses on four dimensions of prototypes in order to describe them.

- *Representation* describes the form of the prototype, e.g., sets of paper sketches or computer simulations;
- *Precision* describes the level of detail at which the prototype is to be evaluated; e.g., informal and rough or highly polished;
- *Interactivity* describes the extent to which the user can actually interact with the prototype; e.g., watch-only or fully interactive; and
- *Evolution* describes the expected life-cycle of the prototype, e.g. throwaway or iterative. (Beaudouin-Lafon and Mackay 2002, p. 1–2)

While prototypes may be informed by imagination, experience, individual style, and whimsy, essentially, they exist to solve design questions and offer alternate paths for the design. Those who design instruction ultimately focus on the practical:

> The phrase *creative spirit of design* is meant to evoke three characteristics instructional designers may exemplify, that can help them resist the pull towards unproductive procedure or formula. These characteristics are *imagination*, being *creation-oriented*, and *interdisciplinary action*. (McDonald 2011, p. 53)

Because prototypes are externalized expressions of concepts, they are able to be shared with others to see if the original idea is valid and well received (Pniewska et al. 2013). In many cases, end users may be brought in to see how receptive they are to the design prototype (Pniewska et al. 2013, p. 3).

Data Collection Monitoring for learner engagement on massive open online courses (MOOCs) including user behaviors, linguistics data from expressions, structural data (from "forum-interaction" and temporal data ("user activity over time"). (Ramesh et al. 2014, p. 157)

7.3 Early Designs, Prototypes, and Learning Sequences for Exploration and Decision Making

The review of the literature shows the instructional design space as fairly silent on some aspects of early designs, prototypes, and learning sequences. Exploring design ideas early on in a design and development process enables those ideas to infuse the follow-on work and ensure some coherence. (Legal standards and other requirements are usually handled in the project stylebook, and these do not usually vary between learning resource projects.)

Part 1: Early Designs Early designs refer to a range of preliminary thinking about how learning resources will function, what they will look like, what they will provide to learners, and so on. The designs may be begun in a top-down way (from objectives, from goals, from theories, and so on), or a bottom-up way (from detailed learning contents, from "scratch"). They may be composed in a free-build way, without reference to theories, models, or frameworks…or research…or heuristics.

7.3.1 *Planning with Early Designs*

Early learning designs may be informed by the human imagination, by extant learning object structures in the world, by available raw files, and other approaches. In terms of the human imagination, that is open, and if designer/developers use a range of prompts, they may come up with a wide range of ideas. In terms of conventional structures, these are built into authoring tools, courseware tools, website building tools, and other technologies. Starting with contents enables a design/development team to conduct an audit of what resources they have to build with, and oftentimes, some natural ways to present that information may arise, and then the learning can be built around that. For example, the availability of an image set may enable image-based learning based on slideshows, digital photo albums, photo essays, and other contents. Or if there are audio interviews available, maybe learning built around audio podcasts may work. And so on. Or if the team has access to real-world cases, they may be able to use these fact-based cases around scenario-based learning, supported by engaging multimedia.

In practice, what early designs look like and what they achieve, will depend a lot on the preferences of the designer/developer. A barebones practical approach may answer some basic questions:

- Who are the target learners? What do we assume that their level of knowledge is? Their level of enthusiasm for this learning?
- What is the appropriate level of challenge to build to for learners?
- What general contents will be covered?
- How can the learning resource be sufficiently stand-alone?
- What are some common ways to present the contents coherently?
- What technologies would be optimal, and why?
- What sorts of practices are helpful for learners?
- What sorts of interactivity would promote learner learning?
- What sorts of formative assessments would promote learner learning?
- What sorts of summative assessments would be informative about the learners' overall learning?
- How should learners be addressed? How would they like to be treated? What are some specific learning and other needs they might have?
- Should the subject matter experts or others on the team be personality-forward or not? Should there be a character or persona who stands in for the content experts and content creators? Why or why not? If yes, how should the character be defined?
- Are there particular cultural aspects to include? If so, how so?
- What should a general branding design look like? What should the general look-and-feel be?
- What are the optimal learner experiential paths and content outcomes?
- What downloadables should be included?

The above questions are answered for the particular learning design context. Because these are for a certain group of learners and with dated learning contents, the early designs are thought to be dated as well. The idea is to invest sufficient time and effort to create the designs but not to refine beyond what is necessary. Simplicity trumps ornamentation. Any energy after the initial designs should next go to creating prototypes or instantiated versions of the designs.

The making of early instructional designs requires both creative and critical (analytical) faculties. During the creation phase, the critical faculties need to be suppressed (so as not to squelch the brainstorming); during the critical faculties, the creativity may have to be somewhat restrained to focus on practical considerations.

The essential design question is generally: What are the most effective ways to package and present the target learning contents to a particular target (or potential) learning audience (while using the available informational resources, while staying legal to intellectual property requirements, while ensuring accessibility…with the affordable technologies…and within the constraints of the design and development environment)? (Tables 7.1 and 7.2).

Table 7.1 A blank table about what is addressed in "early designs" vs. "prototypes" (based on designer/developer preferences)

Variables	Early designs (plans)	Prototypes (expressed or instantiated designs, exemplars, first drafts)

Table 7.2 A filled-in table about what is addressed in "early designs" vs. "prototypes" (based on author preferences)

(Variables)	Early designs (plans)	Prototypes (expressed or instantiated designs, exemplars, first drafts)
Pedagogical concerns	Target learners Learning needs Learner-centered design Learning objectives Learning outcomes Learning designs Assignments Assessments Learning sequences (learner experiential sequences)	(Instantiations)

(continued)

Table 7.2 (continued)

(Variables)	Early designs (plans)	Prototypes (expressed or instantiated designs, exemplars, first drafts)
Instructor social presence	Personality framework	(Instantiations)
Information sources	Standards for information Acquisition strategies Respected sources Self-developed primary information Information processing	(Instantiations)
Communications	Substance Tone Modality	(Instantiations)
Technologies	Hosting platforms Modalities/multimedia	Authoring tools (for web page building, for slideshow building, for animations, and others) Prototyping tools
Look and feel	Atmospherics design	Expressed look-and-feel
Object-based design	Conventions of the Respective forms	E-books Q&As Slideshows Animations Articles Diagrams

Another way to think of early designs is as visual expressions: flowcharts, concept maps, diagrams, mind maps, and others. These maps may be unexecuted early conceptualizations that are purely conceptual. One type of conceptualization may be merely a product of a brainstorm. Perhaps a learning sequence is expressed as a game board with different types of learner experiences. Or it is a safari map with learning along the way. A rough mind map of what an instructional designer club could provide participants and the larger organization is expressed in a rough concept map (Fig. 7.2).

Another kind of map visualization may show an evolved informational structure (Fig. 7.3). This latter example shows an auto-mapped article-article network evolved around the target node "Instruction_design" article (Mediawiki page) on Wikipedia. This is a one-degree network that shows direct outlinks from the target article, and the relational closeness of the informational linkage sheds light on the target topic. Such networks show structurally linked informational relationships. (A full ego neighborhood would require not only outlinks but inlinks or the articles that point to the "Instructional_design" article, too.)

Learners may not notice the organizational structures and designed elements of their learning resources unless they take a critical thinking approach.

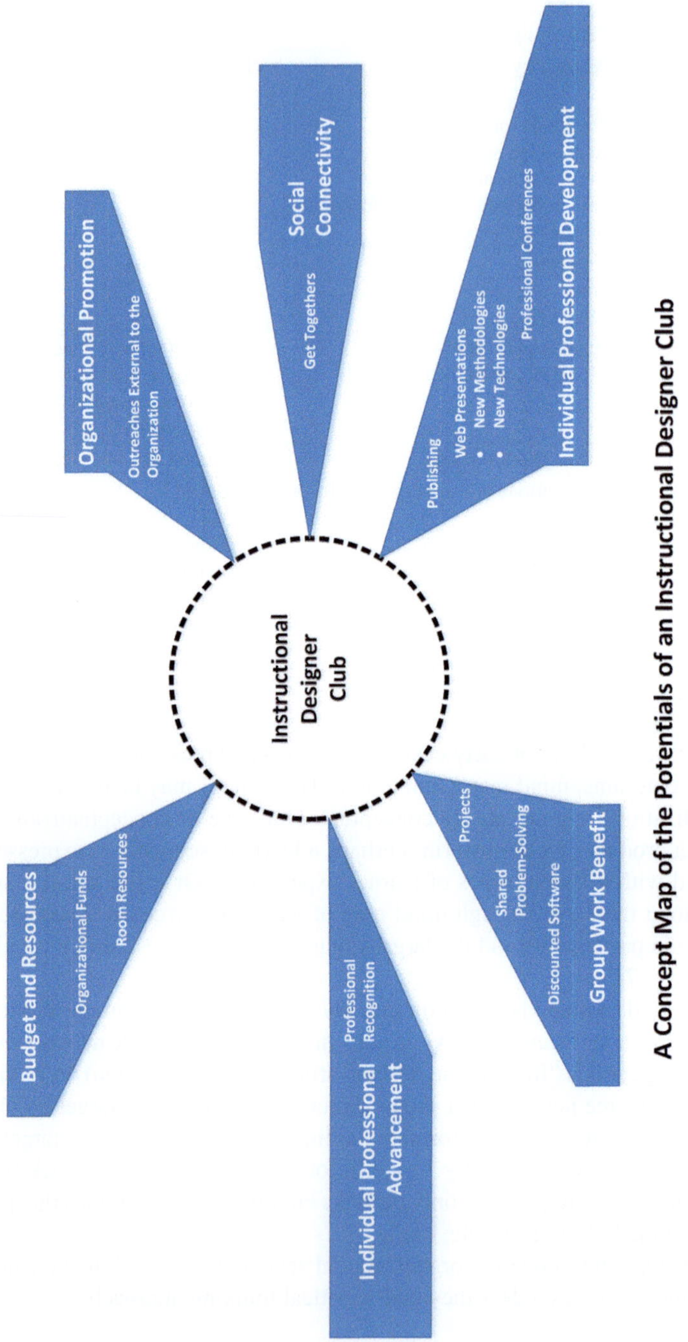

Fig. 7.2 A concept map of the potentials of an instructional designer club

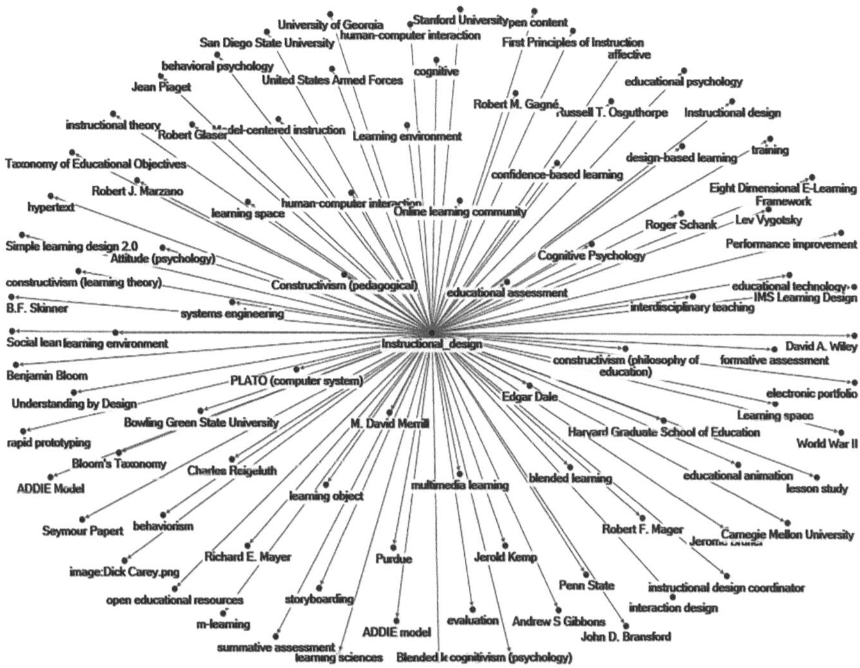

Fig. 7.3 An article-article network for "instructional_design" on Wikipedia as an evolved learning resource (one-degree)

Task #1: Early Designs
If one rationale for early designs is to offer alternatives and options, then it may make sense to create multiple designs for one learning object and then to compare them in order to see which design features (or designs) come to the fore as the most preferable (based on practical and other standards).

Based on these ideas, identify learning contents around which to create a learning object. Conceptualize six different ways to design the learning, and create some simple but informative early designs around the concepts. Do include a range of different digital and form modalities within this set of instructional designs. Digital modalities include different digital file types; and form modalities refer to different structured learning objects like slideshows, photo albums, short games, and others.

Finally, you may describe what you want from early designs. What sorts of information do you find useful, and what sorts do you find not useful?

Task #2: Designing to Stand-Alone

For shared learning resources to be "reusable," they have to play well with other learning resources. They have to hold their own in a learning sequence with other learning components, whether those sequences are human-created or computer-created. The question is how to make a learning object or sequence "stand-alone."

To be stand-alone, a learning resource needs to be a complete unit of learning for the particular topic, with sufficient content coverage. It should be sufficiently self-explicating. Vocabulary terms and concepts should be disambiguated. Learners using the resource should be able to acquire sufficient help for basic learning through the object itself. Technologically, it should have as few dependencies as possible; it may be of a piece or multiple but solidly and robustly connected pieces. As a unit, it should enable the achievement of the defined learning objectives around which it was built. Its metadata should be sufficiently descriptive for understanding its contents.

What are some other features of "stand-aloneness" for digital learning resources? How can this stand-aloneness be achieved in design and then in development?

Part 2: Prototypes A prototype is the first of its kind, and serves potentially as a model of something; follow-on objects may be developed from that initial prototype (which becomes canonized as a reference object).

7.3.2 Planning with Learning Object/Resource Prototypes

Prototypes may be informed by early designs, or they may be created on-the-fly. In a sense, the prototype may be a middle-step or bridge between the concept of the object and the finalized learning resource. Prototypes are usually instantiated designs of particular learning objects, such as slideshows, games, interactive videos, simulations, and others. The prototypes may be built using the authoring tools for those objects, some other sort of prototyping tool, and/or symbolically and representationally, through design artifacts (flowcharts, storyboards, mock-ups, wireframes, all of which have their own design cues). Prototypes may be built to particular courseware or learning management systems or immersive virtual worlds, in which case, the larger ecosystem is somewhat pre-defined. The level of details (resolution) and the closeness to the complete and refined learning object form (fidelity) will vary depending on the uses of the respective prototypes.

Some design features are already built into some of the authoring tools used for development. Prototypes should not be forced into particular structures and functions based on the authoring tools used, and creative work-arounds enable more creative learning objects. Also, prototypes do not have to be treated as their own discrete step, but as the learning objects are being developed, it may help to pause to see what the design looks like and even to explore how effective it may be. In this sense, evolving objects in development are becoming both higher-resolution (level of details) and higher-fidelity (closeness to the finalized designed form) as the work progresses. Each step makes the learning resource more real (unless design decisions nullify some core aspects of the designs).

The common questions answered in instructional prototypes may include the following: How doable is this project? How expressible are the design concepts into actual instantiated learning resources? What do the actual objects will look and feel like? How do they function? How appealing would these be to learners? Where will the challenges be in the creation and deployment of these learning resources, and what are some ways to mitigate some of the anticipated costs and work? How may these challenges be mitigated for, practically? In the local context, are there sufficient resources, will, talent, interest, and commitment to follow through on the original plan? In other words, the considerations are almost wholly practical.

Prototypes have an anticipatory or predictivity role: "Prototypes are a tangible attempt to view a design's future impact so that we can predict and evaluate certain effects before we unleash it on the world" (Lim et al. 2008, p. 7–8).

An important angle to consider is how learning objects are used in public space. One factor is how screenshotting enables the disaggregation of slideshows and videos and websites into still images separate from the other parts. Images may be taken out of slideshows, videos, and simulations and virtual world spaces. Audio tracks may be extracted from podcasts (syndicated audio productions), vodcasts (video podcasts), videos, and video games. This ability to disaggregate learning resources into constituent parts suggests the importance of designing learning thoughtfully so that the pieces and parts may still retain some coherence. The easy ability to reintegrate digital contents into mash-ups also affects this space. This ability to recompose means that those who are malicious may reuse contents in derogatory or harmful ways. The design should enable some value to each part of the learning resource even if it is disaggregated, and its design form should make its original whole available for discovery.

Task #3: Image Prototyping

There are a range of different ways to create prototypes. One approach is to borrow from what is in the world at least for some ideas to start. In the spirit of an environmental scan, review a number of online learning objects, and take screenshots of the features that you think would be helpful in your design. Annotate the screenshots with red rectangles and labels to express what you like and why. Riff off of the ideas from the world, and brainstorm some inspired design concepts of your own.

Create a sequence of these screenshots to introduce your prototyping ideas to a group of colleagues. Share some of your own original ideas as well.

Part 3: Learning Sequences A learning sequence, the order of the learning, may be conceptualized in a number of ways. The order of presentation can have outsized effects on how understandable the learning may be because learners have to make sense of the contents. Those going through learning sequences as a novice (a new learner to a learning sequence in a domain that he or she aspires to achieve expertise in), an amateur (a new learner to a learning sequence in a domain that he or she does not aspire to achieve expertise in), and an expert (a new learner to a learning sequence in a domain that he or she has expertise in) will differ.

Also, in the actual experience of learning, there will be a number of overlapping and interacting sequences in both the actual design (in a slideshow, there may be chronological sequences of information as well as un-time-structured data tables and designed step sequences of learning)…and in the experience of the learning (learners have a say in how they consume learning). If a learning resource is harnessed for formal learning, it may be incorporated into a larger learning sequence that may be wholly invisible to the original designers of the original learning resources.

7.3.3 Learning Sequence Designs

Some types of open-shared learning are not sequenced, such as shared image, quantitative, text, and multimodal datasets.

Some shared resources are built for exploratory learning. In such cases, learners may choose any of a number of start points, and they can take any path as long as every piece of learning is satisfactorily covered.

In other contexts, information may be revealed strategically. This often occurs in scenario-based learning and case-based assessments. Here, the content creators will reveal information of a case in a controlled manner, so those solving the real-world issue have limited information in a time sequence. The slow reveal informs the learning.

Other learning contents may involve fixed-path sequences, such as non-interactive videos and static slideshows. Here, learners have a pre-set sequence that they follow and not a lot of dynamic versions or branching options.

side bar

Getting to Know Yourself as a Designer/Developer

When you approach a learning design challenge, what information sources do you seek out to understand how to approach the work? What criteria do you use to make your design decisions? What subject domains are you most comfortable engaging in terms of design and development? What are some of your go-to design solutions and technologies for conveying information to learners?

The readers of this text come at this book with a wide range of different backgrounds: life experiences, formal and informal education, and professional experiences. Some may have never created learning resources of any kind before. Others may have many years of professional experiences in instructional design. There are likely many who are somewhere in between those extremes.

In an open shared learning context, the self is a core place from which to understand motivations, worldviews, teaching and learning, creativity, and the role of sharing. There is a benefit, too, in understand oneself as a designer/developer because that can inform us on how to get past "creator's block," how to work with our respective strengths and weaknesses, and what knowledge, skills, and abilities (KSAs) to work on to enhance our capabilities.

Who am I as a learner? Most of us have preferred learning styles and contexts. Some types of learning appeal to us more than others. We tend to enjoy certain modalities of learning than others. And whether consciously or unconsciously, our fallback design positions may be to what we find appealing and what is familiar to us.

What motivates and inspires me? Because the cost of creating open-shared learning resources is so high, and the need for long-term effortful work so necessary, it helps to know what values and issues are motivating. After all, the rewards for such work start at 0. If this work is not personally meaningful, it will be hard to get such endeavors off-the-ground and actual achievements to be made. What sorts of social justice issues are meaningful, and why? In creative work, there are times when progress is slow. Getting through such lulls is important, and it helps to know which ways to self-manage stress, work frustrations, and creator's block (a version of writer's block).

To get at the above information, it may help to write some narratives exploring the questions.

Inspirations, if they cannot be acted on, are inert. To actually execute on the work, an individual needs to have certain skills and follow-through, especially in contexts of self-imposed soft deadlines.

What knowledge, skills, and abilities do I apply to my design and development work? What KSAs do I need to acquire and/or improve? A personal "KSA" audit helps a designer/developer to know where to focus attention and effort. Professional development is required in every field, and it is especially critical in one with fast-changing technologies and skills requirements.

The "know thyself" here has to translate into updated KSAs. This ability to function outside one's comfort zone, in an environment of risk, is important.

Being aware of one's familiar go-to's should encourage expanding beyond that space. Knowing of one's habits should inform one on which habits to reinforce, and which ones to break.

If you have a body of work in the open sharing space (or even just in the work space, it may help to examine your work portfolio and *curriculum vitae* (CV) for patterns. What projects do you tend to take on? What target learner groups are most common in your work? What are the domain fields of focus? What inspires you about the particular topics? What technologies do you tend to use, and what learning objects do you tend to create? Where does the value lie in terms of what you've created? How open are you to others' feedback and critique?

To add value to this approach, play a form of "Never Have I Ever…" and work to change up the list of "nevers" by acquiring new professional work skills and experiences.

How much of me do I put out there, and what am I sharing about myself? In the age of the Social Web, many are very comfortable in public space, and many have the necessary sophistication to know what to share and what not to. In terms of shared learning contents on the Web and Internet, some of this may be shared wholly without byline or only with a handle, without obvious connection to personally identifiable information (PII). For others, they use their real names and real photos and enable identification of shared learning resources back to themselves.

How much of yourself do you share to the broad public, and why? What does your personality frame look like? How much do you backstop your presence online with follow-on behaviors when others reach out to you? Where are your redlines beyond which you do not share, and why?

What is my design and development signature? In the same way artists are thought to have a distinctive hand in their work, the creatives who create learning resources may also have some unique authorship "tells." The unique aspects come from a range of factors: the designer's worldview, personality, expressiveness, design and development methods, sense of taste, and other features. (Users of learning resources may infer from what they see and experience who the person is behind the particular work.)

What of you goes into the design and development of learning resources? What makes a design and developed object by you different than someone else's?

Using Analog (Physical) or Non-Digital Means to Create an Early Learning Design and/or Prototype

Clay has been used to depict characters in Claymation sequences. Folded paper has been used to design a wide range of objects in industrial design.

For contemporary instructional designers, their designs and prototypes are usually designed using various combinations of equipment, technologies, and software. Very rarely do designers create "early designs" and "prototypes" for learning resources using non-digital resources. Sometimes, the medium used for design may inspire insights that may not be possible otherwise.

Some materials enable individuals to engage various perceptual senses: their auditory sense, their visual sense, their tactual sense, their olfactory sense…or some mix or combination of these senses.

Think of various common materials in the world used for creative modeling, and think about how they may be harnessed for creative learning designs. [There is not always a clean differentiation between analog and digital since there are so many designed overlaps and integrations. Think of the Internet of Things (IoT.)]

Then, too, there are a variety of dynamic sequences based on various data inputs or scripted designs. One way to think about learning sequences is in a componentized way, with some initial drawing of learners into a learning experience, delivering various sequences of learning, and wrapping up the learning with a conclusion or finale Fig. 7.4. This illustration takes an á la carte approach. This figure does not suggest any time length for the learning or any pacing, and those may be added to a custom visualization with the selected "menu" items.

7.3.4 Applied Learning from Early Designs and Prototypes

An important part of informatizing prototypes is to use a prototype (a first of its kind) to inform follow-on designs. Here, a prototype slideshow is used to inform follow-on slideshows for that particular learning resource, and so on, for the various

Starts

- Welcome
- Topic intro
- Learning objectives
- Organization, sequence
- Learning outcomes
- Attention getters
- Attraction, allure
- Amusement, humor
- Assessment (pre and post)

Middle Sequences

- Developmental sequence (simple to complex; complex to simple; other)
- Problem-solution
- Data -> analysis
- Project-based learning
- Mystery (controlled reveal / slow discovery; data set and exploration-based interpretation; story structure; others)
- Chronology (time-based organization)
- Design-based learning
- Narrative structure (buildup of tension to climax and denouement)
- Scenario-based learning
- Simulations
- Case analysis
- Collaborative work

Conclusions

- Review
- References to follow-on resources
- Contact information
- Open challenges
- Anticipated future
- Lessons
- Brand message
- Solution(s), debriefing
- Assessment (pre and post)

(and various combinations within classifications)

An Á La Carte Menu of Learning Sequence Options (by Function)

Fig. 7.4 An Á La Carte menu of learning sequence options (by function)

types of digital contents. This templatizing is not to be done in a mindless way, but in a thinking way.

One of the more common approaches is to take a created prototype and extract a template from it. Templatizing a prototype is an act of simplification, including stripping out any custom contents, and using what remains.

As such, prototypes may inform on template structures, sequences, interactions, functions, looks-and-feels (visual branding), labeling, font faces and sizes, image handling, layout, language, citation methods, legal requirements, and other elements. The extracted templates may already contain scripting and coding for interactions and functions. They may have emplaced required elements, either as required elements or as placeholders for custom contents. There may be latent design features included in the template (Fig. 7.5).

For different design and development teams, they may have different experiences with early designs, prototypes, and (draft) learning sequences. Some may go with some fast discussions and go right to development. They may expend more energy in the revision phase to correct for errors from a lack of a coherent design approach. (In general, if major errors have been made, and they are discovered in the assessment process, the retrofitting may be quite labor-intensive and costly. One required change may beget others. If videos have to be re-shot or to go into post-production, all of these efforts will entail further costs.)

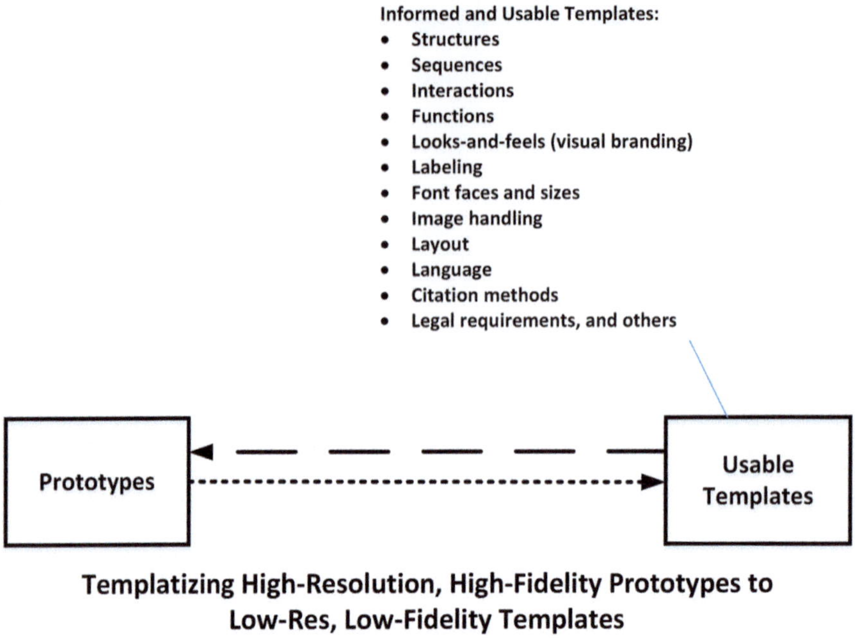

Fig. 7.5 Templatizing high-resolution, high-fidelity prototypes to low-res, low-fidelity templates

Or the instructional or learning design may be left to the principals working on respective different parts of the project. Others may go through more of a design phase when alternatives are created, decisions are thought-through, and some designs are prioritized over others.

One way to develop a critical assessing mindset in relation to early designs is to look at some created by others. The reason for this may be in part that people can be more critical of others' works than one's own. It may also be that others build designs that make sense to them in the way that one makes designs that make sense to oneself, and the frictions between those may provide insights.

Another way to develop an assessing approach to design artifacts is to do a pre- and post-. Here, an early design/prototype/learning sequence is created, and after an instructional design project's completion, the early design is assessed for how informative it was…and what it left off…in relation to the final created contents. What did the designs fail to understand or anticipate? What miscues did they contain? The thinking here is that whatever makes a final cut is considered valuable, and whatever is left on the proverbial cutting-room floor was deemed unimportant (Fig. 7.6). Misdirections in designs may be expensive if they are not identified sufficiently early.

Another way to informatize the design work is to maintain a contemporaneous work-based journal to capture insights about the work as it happens. Also, it helps to make a point to analyze these design artifacts in a project postmortem (after action analysis).

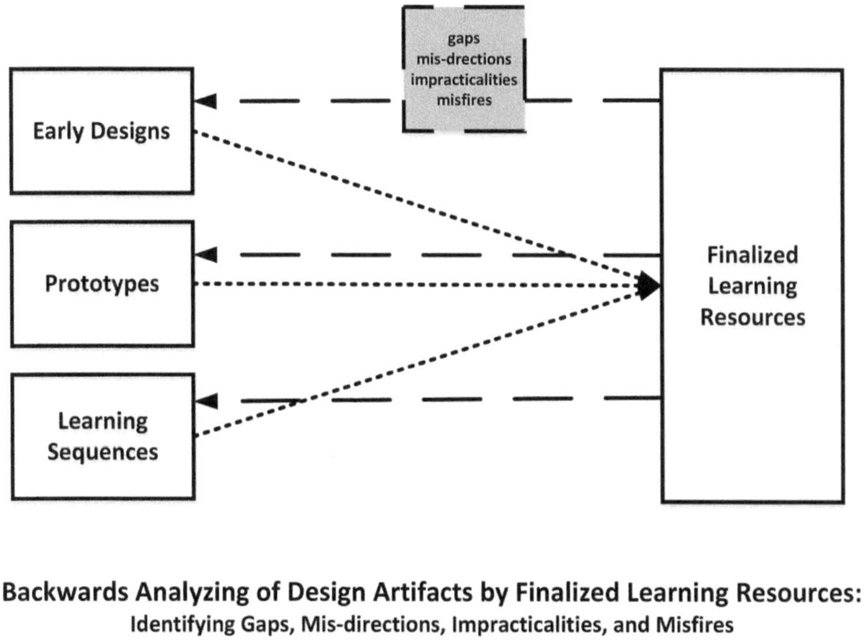

Fig. 7.6 Backwards analyzing of design artifacts by finalized learning resources: identifying gaps, mis-directions, impracticalities, and misfires

7.3.5 Overall Project Content Design Informed by Early Designs and Prototypes

Now that the learning designs have been created—whether as an early design, prototype, or learning sequence, or mix of the priors—it is important to see how practicable and applied these are. You need to "operationalize" the design.

Select one of your designs, and extract required tasks from these to get from the plan to the finalized object. Include as many related and necessary tasks as possible, and avoid any task gaps. (It is not uncommon to forget to include tasks and to find that tasks and costs have to be added to an actual real-world project. Do not assume that any digital resources will be available without the necessary work to create them. It is not uncommon to assume that work will somehow be easier and of lower cost than the work turns out to be. Do not assume that reviews of learning object resources will find nothing that needs to be revised. Sunny optimism is great for some things, not this.)

If this is part of a team project, define the timelines for the tasks to ensure that all the lead-up pieces to a particular learning object are completed in time for the assembly and collation of the composite contents. In other words, if there are various team members engaged in photography, research, writing, interviewing, and videography, all the resultant pieces needed to create a learning resource should be sufficiently aligned time-wise, so that these are ready when the instructional designer/developer needs them to integrate. The hard deadlines are the ones that the team members should aim for, and these should be defined clearly to organize the work. In teamwork, everyone is working on somewhat parallel tracks. For open-shared learning that may not involve *actual* hard deadlines, team members may be somewhat more loosely coupled even as they work in tandem. Various timeline visuals may be made to aid in the work (such as Gantt charts).

Cost these out to find out how much the equipment, software, expert time, contents, and other resources will require. Figure out how much time the respective required tasks will take. Try to use real-world data as much as possible. Write this up in a basic memo. If the opportunity presents, put your plan into action, and keep a record of the challenges that come to light in the work. See how closely your extracted sense of costs and timelines were.

Task #4: Learning Sequences

To focus on what learning sequences may be like experientially, select a few learning objects that are of interest to you. Before you start the learning experience, open up a digital file and use it to take notes to describe your learning sequence. From your observed learning sequence, how do you think the learning object was designed in order to enable that experience? Was the object sufficiently designed and developed for your learning experience?

Now, do the same thing with a few other learning objects. What have you learned from this experience?

Can you conceptualize alternate sequences that would be more effective? If so, do describe these, and analyze why different ordering might result in more effective learning for you (for that particular learning object-based experience).

Task #5: Transferability of Early Designs, Prototypes, and Learning Sequences

One expects the learning designs for local contexts to be quite particular to the context, the designer/developer individual or team, local cultures, local resources, and local learners. For early designs, prototypes, and learning sequences to be transferable for others to inherit and use, they must be in a more generalizable form, oftentimes.

What are some common ground features of early designs, prototypes, and learning sequences that may enhance their inheritability by other designers and developers?

What are outlier features and unique elements that may make designs more original and "signature" and styled? Why?

Do you think these design objects are practically reusable? Why or why not?

Further, do you think these learning design artifacts may have academic and applied research value? If so, what, and why?

Live Examples (on the Web)

This "Live Examples (on the Web)" section serves as a way to update knowledge in this realm given the static nature of a printed book. This section enables users to update their knowledge based on what is in the world, to inform their work. At present, the contemporaneous Web does not offer much in the way of early designs, prototypes, or learning sequence designs, for public consumption. What it does offer is a wide range of shared learning objects, which may be seen as the culmination of designer/developer conceptualizations, intentions, skills, decision making, and actions. These finalized objects may be analyzed by backwards analysis for the extraction of inferred learning designs.

In this backwards analysis sequence, an individual looks at the finalized learning resource…disaggregates it into pieces and parts…and infers the design that may have informed the building of that work. This approach requires abductive reasoning, or the use of observations from the real world and the assertability of insights from those observations (without further validation/invalidation efforts).

The observed learning sequences may inform on how the learner experience was designed. This is not to say that experiences are easily explicated or observed. In a work about experience prototyping, the authors observe: "Experience is a very dynamic, complex and subjective phenomenon. It depends upon the perception of multiple sensory qualities of a design, interpreted through filters related to contextual factors" (Buchenau and Suri 2000, p. 424).

The written language, the forms of address to the learners, the designed learning experiences (the learning objectives, the learning outcomes, the learning contents, the assignments and assessments, and others), the learner discretion and decision making, and other elements may show the attitude towards the target and potential learners. The amount of transparency in the design may indicate respect for the learning audiences. These details may inform on the perceived level of knowledge and intellect of the learners. These may inform on the perceived relationship between the creator of the learning contents and the potential users.

The learning contents and their presentation, the abidance by laws, the factuality of the contents, the following of design conventions for particular modes of information, may show something about the professional hand behind the learning resource.

The selection of the presented information and access to privy and relevant information may show something of the expertise of the content source. Costly signaling (vs. cheap talk) may indicate something of the seriousness of the original source.

The expression of personality of the content sources may be for any number of reasons: pro-learning, self-promotion, manipulation, or other purposes.

The amount of investment into the learning contents may show something of the designer/developer (Beneficence? Access? Interests?).

This approach is not to suggest that designer/developers and users of the open-shared learning resources in the world can be purists and have out-of-this-world demands. What this suggests though is that the world is a competitive space, and being in the top few pages of a Web search out of millions of contenders requires that learning resources be designed in thoughtful ways, so they may be actual destination learning sites. Users are reading into the shared contents and drawing some conclusions—some accurate, some not. However, knowing how the various aspects of a learning resource may be read and understood is important to creating competitive works (Fig. 7.7).

Fig. 7.7 A Word Cloud of Chapter 07: "Early Designs, Prototypes, and Learning Sequences for Exploration and Decision Making"

What-If: Creating a Related Learning Design and Module Prototype for Open Sharing

One day, seemingly out of the blue, you are struck by an inspiration to create a module on a topic in which you specialize. You are focusing on adult learners, from hobbyists to experts, because this niche topic is fairly unique, and it has applications to individuals in different domains. You start to collect research. You start creating some digital contents. You start considering different digital modalities to harness to create the contents. You want to give this idea and effort some time to gel, but in the meantime, you decide to doodle some early design concepts. This will require some in-depth efforts, but it will give you a sense of direction for the development. You open up a blank word processing document, and you start the brainstorming and write-up. You capture screenshots. You doodle on a drawing app and drop those images into your Word file. You use screen recording software to capture a video about how some interactive parts of the learning could work. You also conduct some light research to inform your design thinking.

Decision point #1: stop or advance. If advance, what topic will you address, to what degree, and where will you acquire your sourcing information? Who are your target learners (as subgroups), what are their respective needs, and how will you accommodate their needs? What learning contents are widely available in the world for them, and how will your contribute fill a gap and serve a need (with niche information)? How will you make the learning experience original? What sort of learning sequences will make sense to your target learners? What sorts of interactive learning experiences would they respond to?

You write out some of your insights. Some of these are intuitions. Some of these are based on academic and other research. You ask a few colleagues for ideas. You explore some of the online contents that are available for your identified target learner groups.

You take as a given that whatever you create should follow all applicable laws. The contents should be factual and cited. At minimum, learning materials "in any medium" should be "clear, unbiased, and accurate" (Leacock and Nesbit 2007, p. 45). You take as a given that all contents will have to be accessible. All of these assumptions are normative and par for the course.

You started from the outside-in in your thinking…by defining the larger context for the learning resources and then focusing in on particular possible learning resources. You finally decide on a topic-based module and want a draft prototype. A "module" is a digital container with learning contents within, whether the contents are sequenced or not. You decide that sequencing makes sense for your purposes.

Given the basic container, you have some conventions of learning modules that you can use or not. You create several alternative designs.

Decision point #2: stop or advance. If advance, when do you know you have arrived at a workable design? What standards should you use to select a design to operationalize and develop?

You begin by setting some standards for selecting an effective design. The designs should show a clear understanding of the target and potential learners. They should show a clear understanding of the topical domain. They should show how to achieve the desired learning objectives. They should be practically executable with the available resources. They should define a clear learner path through the learning. They should be accommodative of a wide range of learners. They should not require any part of the design to be inaccessible, illegal, or inappropriate. They should not enable negative learning or misconstruals of the core information. They should not contain stereotypes. As you look through the proposed designs, you find that you can remove a few based on potential costs because of some ambitious simulations included in one and some protected photos and videos in another.

You have to select between the remaining designs. Here, you have less foundational standards. The learning should be appealing and attractive to learners. The learning object should be differentiated from other contents in the space. The learning design should have an actionable sense of expressed style. The learning design should fit within the designer's sensibilities and resources. Finally, you choose one as the best. You revise this one based on some cool features that you borrowed from some of the rejected designs.

Then, based on your prior experiences, you estimate the related tasks, costs, and investments needed to actualize a design. You can go "standard," or you can pull out all the stops and go "extravagant." Either path will require expenditures and effortful work, but the "extravagant" path will be expensive and set you back.

Decision point #3: stop or advance. If advance, should you build only what your resources enable you to without too much stretching, or should you pull out all the stops, go extravagant, and throw some expensive resources at this? If you invested more, you could really create an eye-popping resource that can make splash in public space.

You remember your given earnings of $0 and decide that a basic effort will suffice. You'll not have overspent, and those in public who have interest in a resource will one extra resource that they would not have had before.

You work on the learning resource, and along the way, you have to make compromises. Some resources that you thought would be easy to find in the open-source realm turn out to be elusive. You track down research that you'd read that would apply to the work, and you find that a lot of what you accessed before online is still available. You take a flexible approach in your evolving learning module, and the prior design informs some of it. Other parts are unaddressed by the design. And the directions you take in your work may be seen as conflicting with some initial design thinking, but the impetus is to go with what works and where the available resources are.

You also decide to change the didactic features in the initial design because these are turnoffs in the open social space. You're aware that people's preferences may change, but this might be one of those truisms with staying power.

You update the low-fidelity modular design itself as you go because you are learning about the realities of the build—the enablements and the constraints. You try to keep the revised modular prototype design as general as possible. You know that it makes little sense to prematurely freeze a design until the very last moment, of public launch.

You review and proof the learning resource, based on understood standards in the field. You upload it to a hosting site and test its functionalities. Before you go public, you decide to run the learning module by a few colleagues. You want them to be as free as possible to share their ideas, no holds barred. You collect their responses, and you update the resource based on their comments. One of them suggests that you also test this with members of the learning public. What do you do?

Decision point #4: stop or advance. If advance, what are your basic options? If you go formal, you need to identify target learners, incentivize them to engage in the testing, conduct the research, analyze the data, and apply the new insights on the learning module. If you go informal, you need to go through the same motions but maybe with less rigor. Or you can let this suggestion for a beta test pass.

You decide to do a light and informal beta test by recruiting a convenience sample of target and potential learners. They review the draft module and provide feedback. You update the learning resources.

After one final walk-through, during which you still find a typo, you decide that this is ready for prime time. You need to find a social media platform or hosting site on which to upload the open-shared learning module.

There are several practical contenders. Some are relatively "free."

- An LMS-specific commons that you can access through work channels, but this limits the use of the module to the users of the LMS, created by a commercial company
- Several social media accounts which host contents, but which are not specifically set up for the sharing of open-source learning contents
- A slide sharing site that enables the upload of slide contents but which disallows revisions and re-uploads

Others involve a nominal but continuing cost.

- Several generic web hosting services that can be used as a centralized location from which various elements of the module may be linked or inline-framed (iframed)
- Several cloud hosting services

Your goal is to ensure that the contents are hosted stably and in a discoverable and accessible way. Your goal is also to minimize costs. You goal is also to enable the targeted and potential learning communities to know about your efforts.

Decision point #5: stop or advance. If advance, will you go frugal or will you incur some continuing expense?

You decide to go frugal. You choose a free hosted solution that is findable. You can now reach out to targeted and potential learner communities with news of the release of your learning module...so you…

The What-If Debriefing

This scenario highlights some aspects of the instructional design-for-open-sharing experience. Here, several initial designs are created, one is promoted and executed on, and the resulting module is its own designed object. This work shows some best practices—such as adhering to given standards, eliciting feedback from others, and not unthinkingly committing to early design ideas. There is the lesson that the world does not conform to the design imagination per se, but also that within limits, the world may enable the full expression of the imagination. The recurrence of the $0 budget helps keep designs and developments grounded in the real, and the trajectory of the decision making here strives to protect some designer/developers from letting their imaginations get away from them and costing them big in the self-funding realm.

Discussion This chapter presented some design approaches that may be used in designing and developing open-shared learning contents. Its order suggests starting with design concepts, then learning object designs, and finally learning sequences (which may take into account the interaction effects between the various objects). There are other perfectly fine ways to change up this sequence. For example, one can conceptualize and draft early prototypes of learning objects, sequence these in different learning sequences, and then come out with a reverse-engineered conceptual design. Some of the variations are depicted in Fig. 7.8. Work preferences and preferred mental modeling approaches matter.

Sometimes, a designer/developer has a spark of an idea—about a technology, an instructional design plan, a storyline—and he/she is off full-bore into development! In such cases, designs may be better to capture from the created objects, sequences, and resources, by extracting the design from the works. Top-down coding is based on conceptual design that informs the prototypes and learning sequences, and bottom-up (emergent) coding is based on created prototypes and created learning sequences that inform the conceptual designs. The order of operations often affect the follow-on design work.

Early designs, prototypes, and learning sequences may be harnessed to enable more purposefully created learning resources for open sharing. Given the different objectives and focuses of learning resources, these design efforts may not necessarily result in convergence on particular tactics and methods, but they may enable a more coherent and reasoned approach than a straight-to-development one. How much time is spent creating early designs, prototypes, and learning sequences may vary, but even something fairly light can be informative. After the initial designs and/or prototypes are created, they may be assessed for learning effectiveness—through consultations within the development team, with other professionals, and with learners. Another design factor is the need to differentiate the learning resource from others available in the space, in order to compete...while being sufficiently complementary to be added to others' learning sequences. The designs—whether created from concepts or others' in-world designs (as inspiration) or created contents—serve to inform the current instructional design project but also follow-on projects and serialized works.

Finally, the systematized design phase is not about make-work; it has to add value to the project planning, the design, and the development. Anything that is too complex or convoluted may be less useful. Anything that does not help a team advance its work is not so useful. What a design and development individual or team would want from an early design or prototype or learning sequence may vary, but it is important to list some helpful features: inspirational, informative, pedagogically sound, creative, original, efficient, engaging, learner-centered, practical, and others. There are many potential questions to ask of an early design, a prototype, or a learning sequence design; however, what is required will differ based on the individual or team...their context...their available resources...their target learners, and other factors. In a comparison between how expert instructional designers work in practice as compared to novice designers, based on a think aloud protocol, a researcher

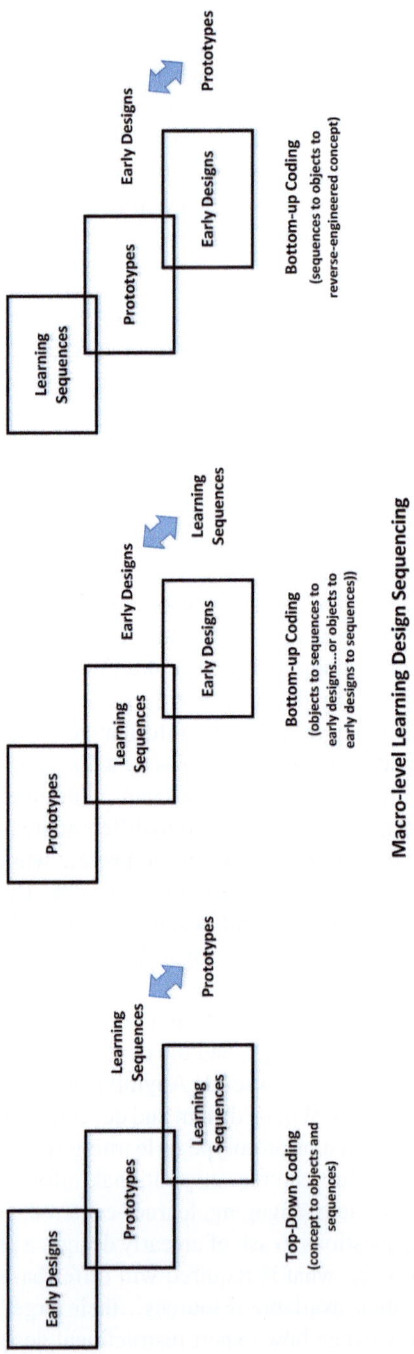

Fig. 7.8 Macro-level learning design sequencing

found that experts rely on experience for future designs, with some pattern matching (Rowland 1992, p. 65). Instructional design patterns found to be effective for learning may be re-used in other contexts (Douglas 2006). These research works suggest that there may be some benefit in sharing such patterns.

Beyond the design and development functions of these designs, there are issues of external validity. If some designs are better than others for development, this may not necessarily mean that the designs are better for external validity (the learner experience, the learning objectives, the learning outcomes, or the learning value).

There are no optimal designs that will meet the needs of all learners. Also, learners who want to engage with open-shared learning resources need to engage with a variety of learning designs, even those which are not necessarily to their exact preferences. Even if a user interface design is unfamiliar, learners need to make the efforts to adjust to these and to learn how to navigate them, even if the organization does not fit their own mental models. In every learning context, there will be some degree of the unfamiliar vs. the familiar. This is a necessary caveat.

Some suggest that there are preferred sequences in terms of design and development work. One instructional designer suggests the following of more formalized trainings:

> Design your assessments first to align directly with your objectives. Revise the objectives as needed so that they are measurable. Then design activities to support the learner in successfully meeting the objectives. Evaluate all materials and resources. *Do they support the activities, the assessments?* If not, consider eliminating them or identifying them as optional. Using this process can promote alignment so that learners can focus on meeting objectives successfully. (Holder 2013, p. 2)

Certainly, open-shared learning resources do not often include summative assessments.

Going to Heuristics Also, beyond informal and formal designs, those who create learning objects, courses, resources, and sequences have practical heuristics that they apply to their work to enable structure, values, learner-centeredness, engagement, and quality. Exploring these heuristic practices may be helpful in addition to exploring early designs, prototypes, and learning sequences. A downside to merely considering heuristics is that these are often unique to the designer and only address parts of the instructional design process.

The following consists of one instructional designer's heuristics:

Thorough Research

- Conduct thorough research about the topic until saturation. Keep the data as relevant as possible. Strive for as up-to-date information as possible.
  - Vet all data for accuracy.
  - Capture full source citations in the citation method used on the project.

Actual Expertise and Standing to Address

- Only tackle subject matter about which one has some level of basic expertise. Make sure one has standing to address the particular issue in public.

Collecting Available Digital Contents on the Web and Internet

- Collect raw digital contents that may be legally attained (such as from the public domain and through generous Creative Commons licensure).
  - Keep a README file that helps maintain provenance of all collected digital contents to enable legal usage.

Accurate and Thorough Documentation

- Keep a document file of all signed media releases, contracts, Creative Commons licensure releases, and other official documentation.

Local Self-Created Contents

- Create relevant raw data that may be used in slideshows, videos, web pages, e-books, and other learning objects.

Pristine Datasets and Collections

- Maintain a pristine dataset of all raw digital resources, in the highest fidelity and most pristine state possible. Likewise, keep a pristine collection of all raw data collected for the project (prior to data cleaning).

Informational Value

- Provide new information where possible.
- Explain a little more than less given the rarity of learners reaching out to content creators and the need for the learning resource to be stand-alone and generally self-explanatory.
- Be selective about what information to include, but backstop the whole learning resource with a lot of research (even if most of it is not directly cited).

Organization and Structure

- Organize the learning contents in an understandable sequence. Chunk similar data.
- Structure the data in a logical way.
  - Time data may be placed on a timeline or a chronological sequence or a narration.
  - A biography may be sequenced in a narrative structure.
  - An ordered list may be set up in ascending or descending order by relevance.
  - Or, if there are overarching organizational methods, those may be applied.
- Present the data in familiar constructs and logical and ordered formats to learners, so learner extraneous cognitive load is kept to a minimum (per cognitive load theory).

Accessibility

- Ensure that the learning contents are as accessible as possible.

  - Provide proper informational alt texting for imagery.
  - Ensure that audio and video are transcripted and/or close-captioned.

Revise, Revise, Revise

- Use attuned and nuanced language. Use language that you are comfortable with. It is okay to be informal.
- Iterate through the design contents for sensemaking and logic. Read for implications. Read for subtext messaging.
  - Read as a novice. Read as an expert. Control for negative learning or possible misunderstandings. Make adjustments as necessary.
- Always spell check.
- Always grammar check.
- Enable easy reference to contents by numbering slides and pages and using informational naming.

Transparency

- Strive for transparency. If there are conflicts of interest, surface these and mitigate them. However, these are best avoided.

Cost Controls

- Keep costs low. Do not invest moneys in shared learning objects when possible.

Crediting

- Give credit where it is due.

Author Hand

- Strive for originality as much as possible, but avoid self-indulgence.
- The content creators should keep a low profile but be findable and reachable by the users of the contents.
- Keep motives simple.
- Keep opinions out of the work. Use an objectivist hand.

Creator Neutrality

- The learning contents should be non-distractive.
- The learning contents should be non-offensive.

Implications

- First, do no harm. Consider all possible implications when releasing contents to the public.

Straight to Live

- Make sure all assertions are defensible (legally, logically, and otherwise). Resist any over-reach.

- Even if you are "ghost-writing" a work, make sure you can still stand by it, and assume your identity is wholly public.
- Go right-to-live after the vetting. Pre-review tends to be time-consuming and expensive.

Light Usage Monitoring

- The published contents should be lightly monitored to better understand learner usage, public interests, and other insights.
- If learning analytics are capture-able, that data should also be collected and analyzed (in part to improve future shared learning resources).

Recordkeeping

- Keep records and documentation over extended time.
- Keep raw files over extended time to enable future revising (without lossy files or files with degraded or lost data, such as due to file compression, edits, and/or transcoding).

Even though these rules of thumb were acquired over decades of professional work, a basic read-through of these suggests gaps.

Moustakis (1990) described a more formalized method of heuristic research, which requires focused exploration. He writes:

> Heuristic research is an extremely demanding process, not only in terms of continual questioning and checking to ensure full explication of one's own experience and that of others, but also in the challenges of thinking and creating, and in the requirements of authentic self-dialogue, self-honesty, and unwavering diligence to an understanding of both obvious and subtle elements of meaning and essence inherent in human issues, problems, questions, and concerns. (p. 37)

Non-learning Objectives The learning resources themselves likely have objectives beyond the learning objectives and learning outcomes. There may be considerations for attracting learners, winning their trust, providing for their needs, and maintaining their interest over time. Perhaps there may be efforts towards burnishing the credentials and reputations of the designers/developers and the sponsoring organization. Perhaps there are interests in advancing a particular field or supporting a particular learning community online and in the real. In participatory (cooperative) designs, would-be learners may contribute to designs—so the objectives may also be evolving and dynamic given a mix of interests.

Learning objects may be conceptualized to meet simultaneous needs in the public/private and commercial spaces simultaneously; they may be created in "short time frames but also to meet institutional quality standards while fulfilling marketplace needs for innovative new educational content" (Desrosier 2011, p. 135). These elements may be written into the designs—whether they are in the early designs, the prototypes, and the learning sequences.

7.4 Future Research Directions

Those who may want to pursue future research in this space may focus on a wide range of potential topics. Some are questions about how to best create early designs, prototypes, and learning sequence designs. Others are about learning from such artifacts.

- early designs and prototypes and learning sequences designed for specialized instructional design projects for open sharing (maybe as cases);
- ways to increase the generalizability and transferability of such designs to enhance other projects;
- fast prototyping methods from real-world open-shared learning projects;
- analyses of early designs;
- analyses of prototypes;
- analyses of learning sequences;
- applied technologies for the creation of prototypes;
- methods for vetting early designs and prototypes and learning sequences for applied work;
- ways to assess the internal validity of such designs;
- ways to assess the external validity of such designs;
- ways to improve project stylebooks with insights from early designs and prototypes (particularly for stylebooks related to complex series learning resources),
- applied heuristics to designing learning,
- and others.

This list is just a start, and many other topics may be added to this.

7.5 Conclusion

It can be hard to know what will strike a chord with learners. And yet, there is a benefit in being aware of what is going into a design and to know what the "rules" are even if one breaks them now and again judiciously for effect.

What are the guiding objectives of the respective learning contents, and what strategies and tactics are harnessed to attain those objectives? What information should be shared and what held back (and why)? What are optimal ways to frame information? And in what sequence? How should people be portrayed? What sort of language should be used—for visuals and for text? What are the values that inform the learning design? How should assignments and assessments be created? How can the learning resources be future proofed? This chapter covered the harnessing of early designs, prototyping, and learning sequences to inform the design and development of learning resources created for open sharing. It introduced a range of methods for creating these, and it emphasized the importance of learning from these individual and team creations to systematize the design of instruction and to think through design challenges. These design artifacts may also inform on learning designs, the parts that work and those that do not.

Certainly, there are other ways to "start" open-shared learning resources as well. One common approach is with a basic audit of available materials and building from those contents. This is straight to development. Bypassing design is generally the *status quo* in this space for many. If designer/developers can articulate the design, retroactively, all the better, but that is not always the case. For many who are highly practiced, they can go straight to build without too many problems, particularly if they follow that up with proofing, testing, and revisions. In a sense, most of developer work is up-close and detailed work. Designs are important, but they only go so far. The harder work is solving problems to the designed objects one by one.

Finally, there is room for designers to "add to the canon by exploring the cutting and sometimes precipitously bloody edge of the pedagogical envelope" (Harding and Ingraham 2007, p. 150).

7.6 Reviews and Assignments

7.6.1 Main Points Review

- Early designs are conceptualizations or instantiated/expressed conceptualizations of various learning resources. They are used for various purposes: to inform the instructional design and development work, to communicate with clients, to run early user testing with target learners, and others.
  - Early designs may be built conceptually or evolved from raw informational materials.
  - In general, it is a good idea to keep in-house designs legal and to avoid using any contents for which one does not have copyright because if copyrighted contents accidentally slip into a design, there may be unnecessary liabilities. Using professional standards in every phase of a project also encourages professional practices in every other part of the work.
- Prototypes are the first of a kind of various learning objects that are instantiated designs. These may be used to answer design questions. These may also be evolved into refined finalized learning resources.
  - Prototypes may be used by the design team to co-evolve designs. In some cases, prototypes may be used to elicit feedback from groups that represent "target" learners as well as "potential" learners.
- Learning prototypes (of objects and sequences) may be evolved to describe critical design features of each. They may serve as exemplars for follow-on designs.
- Early designs and prototypes vary in terms of level of detail (resolution) and level of fidelity (closeness to the finalized format).

- Technologically, authoring tools and specialized prototyping and wireframing tools enable rich expressions of early learning object designs and prototypes.
- Early designs and prototypes may be used with target learners for early developmental-stage beta-testing with individuals representing target learner groups.
- Effective uses of early designs and prototypes may inform designers and developers of a range of important details:
  - Creative brainstormed potential elements and sequences
  - Variations for possible designs
  - Effective/ineffective presentation sequences
  - Various interface designs
  - Various navigational designs
  - Effective/ineffective language use
  - How various elements of a learning design work together
  - Branding strategies
  - Proper look and feel
- Early designs and prototypes may inform on project management aspects, including about how long the actual work may take to develop, on preferred technologies, on effective work sequences, on required resources, and other features

7.6.2 Critical Thinking Questions

The imagination and designs

- Some people begin early designs with their imagination. What parts of your imagination might be helpful to evoke particular early designs…that are "wildly creative"? That are "fun"? That are "complex"? What are conditions that are especially conducive to your creativity?
  - What are ways to elicit such imaginative early designs for you? For your colleagues? For your team?
  - How can highly imaginative early designs be used even if some of these may not be directly used to build out a learning object?

Content and data to inform designs

- Some people create early designs by first collecting a large amount of available information and seeing what may be built from those contents. Others begin with an empty shell or outline or storyboard, and then they seek those contents to actualize the design. Which approach do you find more appealing, and why? Which approach is more effective for your work? Why? Or do you find combinations of content and structure helpful in creating early designs?

Solving problems and answering questions with designs, prototypes, and sequences

- What sorts of questions do "early designs" answer for you in your instructional design work?
- Prototypes, as first of their kind (in form), are instantiated designs. What sorts of prototypes are most informative to you and why? What sorts of questions do "prototypes" answer for you in your instructional design and development work?

Right to development

- If you prefer to go right to development by using an authoring tool to start building contents, how can you use such early expressions as "early designs" and as "prototypes"? At what stage in the development do you find optimal for pulling "early designs" and "prototypes"? (For example, when I create slideshows, I conduct thorough research first on the topic and think through internally what I want to achieve with the slideshow. Then, I generally create a basic understandable sequential structure and start populating contents into the slideshow. At some early point maybe an hour or two into the work, I have an early design, with the object built towards particular defined learning objectives and related learning outcomes. Then, an hour or two after that, I find I have an instantiated prototype with most of the contents emplaced. Thereafter, I review the work multiple times to make sure that all the contents are accurate, the http links are live, the language is correct, and the look-and-feel aligns with the contents. A fair amount of prior research work has to be done before I start working on the draft, but once I start, it is fairly easy to sequence the information because I already "see" a coherent logical structure about what learners need to know and in what sequence.)
- What are some go-to sequences of learning that you have found useful in the past? How can you build on these ideas for effective learning?

Transferring early designs, prototypes, and learning sequences

- Which learning design ideas transfer or generalize better to other unrelated projects? Why? How can you recognize the relevance of particular design ideas and practices?
- What are some things you can do to protect your ideas against being forgotten or lost to time? (Some ideas may not be useful for the project at hand, but they may have value and traction on others.)
- Do you find "early designs" and "prototypes" and "learning sequences" better if they are sparsely defined or more fully explicated?
- Do you prefer the creation of "early designs" and "prototypes" and "learning sequences" as a separate and discrete phase, or do you prefer to have these as part of the development work (maybe as "rapid prototyping")?

Practical considerations for designs

- How can you tell how doable a particular "early design" is? A "prototype"? A "sequence"? How can you tell something is "doable"? How can you estimate time investments? How can you extract technological needs from early designs and prototypes?

7.7 Assignments

Directions The Assignments are divided into two sections, Basic and Advanced. The Basic section is for those who may not have much instructional design experience or background in the area of creating instructional contents for open sharing. As such, these are set up to familiarize them with the chapter-related knowledge, skills, and abilities. The Advanced section is for those who already have some knowledge of this general space and who may benefit from more challenging work.

In a formal learning context, these assignments would benefit from expert feedback and further applications of the learning contents. In a nonformal or informal learning context, including self-directed learning, these assignments would benefit from both reflection and practice. These assignments are built to be extensible, to have elements added to benefit the learners. They are designed to be assigned selectively and not in full. The setup of this textbook is as a work sequence, and similarly, the assignments may be set up as tasks to be completed by the learner in a sequential way…that takes them through the fairly complete and sequential *open-shared learning design* → *development* → *test* → *revision* → *launch* → *post-launch* process.

7.7.1 Basic

Assignment 7.1: Identifying Inspirations Start work on a digital learning object or digital learning sequence. While you are drafting the work, consider ways that you find inspiration. What inspires learning designs for you? What sorts of objects? What perceptual channels are most effective (Visual? Auditory? Tactual? Olfactory? Taste? What combinations?) What seems to slow the inspiration? Are there methods to jump-start stalled creative projects?

Assignment 7.2: Learning from an Early Design of Yours (As Exemplar) The effort of creating an early design enables designers and developers to attain a real-world sense of the design challenges; this preliminary work informs the decision making on how to proceed with a committed design. An early design is an example of a learning object (like a slideshow or video or simulation, for example) populated with contents. To these ends, create a draft learning object based on an area of specialty. Then, analyze the draft design for insights. For example, what is your "author hand" in terms of early designs? What are reasonable paths to take for the future design and development work, and what are unreasonable paths? Why?

Assignment 7.3: Learning from a Prototype A "prototype" is a first or early model of a particular thing. From this initial design, other real objects may be created from it. A prototype usually consists of the structure of the design but generally without informational or media contents (unless the contents inform others of how to treat various elements, such as the imagery or the video or the particular text types; in other words, the contents may be placeholders or stand-ins). To these ends, build a prototype of a particular form of learning object. Explore this prototype for design and development insights. What parts of the prototype are actionable and useful, and which parts are not, and why? Write up a short essay to describe this.

Extra: For the prototype design phase, use several different mediums: stylus and tablet, pen and paper, wireframing software, diagramming software, website development software, mind mapping software, code, or other mediums. Explore the influences of the different mediums on the prototypes. Which mediums do you find most amenable for your thinking and exploration? Which mediums do you find most difficult for your thinking and exploration? Why? Which mediums are the most freely? Which mediums are the most restrictive and constraining?

Assignment 7.4: Learning from a Design Plan Draft a design plan for a particular learning object type. Include the sequencing of the research, content creation (and/or collection), the writing/content creation, the scripting, the testing, and so on. Then, walk the plan through in the real world, and then revisit the plan to see what worked and what didn't work. How does a conceptualized plan differ from actual execution of the plan? Why? What are some ways to ensure that future work plans are more accurate to the world?

Assignment 7.5: Reverse Engineering an Early Design/a Prototype/or a Work Plan Identify an open-shared learning object, course, or learning sequence. Experience this object as a learner. Based on the artifact and your learning experience, reverse engineer any one of the following: (1) an early design, (2) a prototype, or (3) a work plan that *could* have been used to create that online learning object(s) and experience.

Extra: If you have a method to test your work in reverse engineering, test your assumptions. How accurate were you? Where were you accurate? Where were you inaccurate?

Assignment 7.6: Evaluating a Learning Object, Course, or Learning Sequence for Reverse-Engineered Design Identify an open-shared learning object, course, or learning sequence. Based on what you can see of the design, what sort of teaching and learning was being aspired to, and who are the members of the learning audience for that object. Why? How well was the open-shared online learning designed? Why?

7.7.2 Advanced

Assignment 7.7: Theoretically Redesigning an Extant Learning Object, Course, or Learning Sequence Identify an open-shared learning object, course, or learning sequence. Experience this as a learner. Write up a reasonable re-design plan to enhance this learning object for pedagogical purposes based on knowledge of human learning research.

Assignment 7.8: Analyzing an Early Online Learning Object or Learning Sequence Design Capture a design or prototype used to design a learning object or learning sequence. How was the prototype conceptually informative of the finalized learning object or learning sequence? What parts of the prototype were used, and what parts were not used? Why do you think those particular design and development decisions were made? What sorts of prototypes seem to be the most informative for learning object design and development? Learning sequence design and development? Do you have some initial ideas on how to improve prototypes to be more effective for learning design and development? What parts of the final design were left out of the prototype?

Extra: Slow down the process of development by first building a prototype for a learning object…saving a pristine version for later analysis…and then evolving the prototype over time. What steps are usually taken to advance a prototype design? Is information added? Are new features added? Do the presentation and style change? Does the tone change?

Assignment 7.9: Drafting Possible Learning Sequences Define a particular learning design context, with learning topics, learning objectives, and target learners. For this context, draft between five to 10 different possible sequences. Consider the strengths and weaknesses of each of the sequences. Analyze why some are more preferable than others. Are there some generic sequences that seem to make more sense (for learning) than others? How so, and why?

Extra: Find an open-shared learning sequence. Map this sequence out in an outline or a timeline or some other visual form. When looking at the learning sequence this way, is it possible to identify gaps in the learning?

Assignment 7.10: Considering Alternatives In every instructional design context, there are a number of possible alternatives for early designs or prototypes and the ensuing paths to actualize the work. Define a basic start point, and document a half-dozen possible paths from that point. Analyze the pros and cons, benefits and risks, costs and gains, of the respective paths. Which alternatives come to the fore as the most doable and positive to pursue, and why?

Key Terms and Definitions

#failfast A silicon valley value to test new ideas quickly and identify quickly whether they will or will not work in order to advance to more constructive approaches

Curation Management of a set or collection of object types

Draft A preliminary version

Early designs Any of an initial series of instantiated or expressed concepts for a particular (instructional) plan

Evolutionary prototype An early design that evolves as understandings (of user needs, of technological contexts, and other information) change

Exemplars An excellent or typical example

Learning object A reusable component-based resource used for learning in different contexts

Paper prototyping Using paper and pencil/pens for early designs comprised of drawings and text usually

Prototype The first of a type or form, a model, an archetype

Throwaway prototype An initial design created for learning and not for implementation, available for discarding

Wireframe A digital prototype (of a website, application, or software program) that enables some observable behaviors/functionality and structures that mimic a real object

WYSIWYG "What You See is What You Get" as a kind of technological design interface for authoring

References

Agustin M, Chuang G, Delgado A, Ortega A, Seaver J, and Buchanan JW. Game sketching. In the proceedings of the 2nd International Conference on Digital Interactive Media in Entertainment and Arts (DIMEA '07). Perth, Australia. Sept. 19 – 21, 2007. 36 – 43, 2007. https://doi.org/10.1145/1306813.1306829.

Alavi M. An assessment of the prototyping approach to information systems development. *Computing Practices* 27: 556 - 563, 1984.

Bardzell J, Bardzell S, Briggs C, Makice K, Ryan W, and Weldon M. Machinima prototyping: An approach to evaluation. In NordiCHI 2006. Oslo, Norway. Oct. 14 – 18, 2006. 433 – 436, 2006.

Beaudouin-Lafon M, and Mackay W. Prototyping tools and techniques. In *The Human-Computer Interaction Handbook*. Ch. 52. 1006 - 1031, 2002. Hillsdale, New Jersey: Lawrence Erlbaum Associates Inc. https://dl.acm.org/citation.cfm?id=772136/.

Berghel H. New wave prototyping: Use and abuse of vacuous prototypes. *Interactions:* 49 – 54, 1994.

Bødker S, and Grønbæk K. Cooperative prototyping – Users and designers in mutual activity. *International Journal of Man-Machine Studies.* 1 – 23, 1990.

Boulet G. Rapid prototyping: An efficient way to collaboratively design and develop e-learning content. Navy e-learning center of excellence. 1 – 6, 2009. http://faculty.mercer.edu/codone_s/tco620/2013/Rapid_prototyping.pdf.

Buchenau M, and Suri J.F. Experience prototyping. DIS '00. Brooklyn, New York. 424 – 433, 2000. https://hci.stanford.edu/dschool/resources/prototyping/SuriExperiencePrototyping.pdf.

Christensen TK, and Osguthorpe RT. How do instructional-design practitioners make instructional-strategy decisions? *Performance Improvement Quarterly* 17: 45 – 65, 2004.

Clark RC, and Mayer RE. *E-Learning and the Science of Instruction: Proven Guidelines for Consumers and Designers of Multimedia Learning*. 4th Ed. Wiley. 1 – 528, 2016.

Daugherty J, Teng Y-T, and Cornachione E. Rapid prototyping instructional design: Revisiting the ISD model. https://files.eric.ed.gov/fulltext/ED504673.pdf. 1 – 8, 2007.

Desrosier J. Rapid Prototyping Reconsidered. *The Journal of Continuing Higher Education* 59: 135-145, 2011. https://doi.org/10.1080/07377363.2011.614881.

Devedžić V, Jovanović J, and Gašević D. The pragmatics of current e-learning standards. IEEE Internet Computing. 16 – 24, 2007.

Douglas I. Instructional design based on reusable learning objects: Applying lessons of object-oriented software engineering to learning systems design. In the proceedings of the 31st ASEE/IEEE Frontiers in Education Conference. Oct. 10 – 13, 2001. Reno, Nevada. F4E-1 – F4E-5, 2001.

Douglas I. Issues in software engineering of relevance to instructional design. *TechTrends* 50 28 – 35, 2006. https://eric.ed.gov/?id=EJ774616.

Dow SP, Glassco A, Kass J, Schwarz M, Schwartz DL, and Klemmer SR. Parallel prototyping leads to better design results, more divergence, and increased self-efficacy. *ACM Trans. Comput.-Hum. Interact* 17: 4, 1 – 24, 2010. https://doi.org/10.1145/1879831.1879836

Edelson DC. Design research: What we learn when we engage in design. *The Journal of the Learning Sciences* 11: 105 – 121, 2002.

Ehlers U-D. Extending the territory: From open educational resources to open educational practices. *Journal of Open, Flexible and Distance Learning:* 15, 2011.

Gayeski DM. Out-of-the-box instructional design. *Training & Development* 52: 36+, 1998.

Gustafson KL, and Branch RM. Revisioning models of instructional development. *Educational Technology Research & Development* (ETR&D) 45: 73- 89, 1997.

Harding D, and Ingraham B. The art of design. Ch. 11. In H. Beetham and R. Sharpe's *Rethinking Pedagogy for a Digital Age: Designing and Delivering E-Learning.* Routledge. 142 – 152, 2007.

Harvey B. 49. Learning Objects and Instructional Design. Technical evaluation reports. *The International Review of Research in Open and Distributed Learning* 6: 2007.

Holder D. Instructional design strategy for achieving alignment: Which comes first, activities or assessments? E-Learning Industry.com. https://elearningindustry.com/instructional-design-strategy-for-achieving-alignment. 2013.

Hounde S, and Hill C. What do prototypes prototype? In M. Helander, T. Landauer, P Prabhu (eds.): Elsevier Science. Amsterdam. 1 – 16, 1997. *Handbook of Human-Computer Interaction* (2nd ed.)

Jones MK, Li Z, and Merrill MD. Rapid prototyping in automated instructional design. *Educational Technology Research and Development (ETR&D)* 40: 95 – 100, 1992.

Jones TS, and Richey, RC. Rapid prototyping methodology in action: A developmental study. *Educational Technology Research and Development (ETR&D)* 48: 63 – 80, 2000.

Joseph PB, Bravmann SL, Windschitl MA, Mikel ER, and Green NS. *Cultures of Curriculum.* Mahwah, New Jersey: Lawrence Erlbaum Associates, Publishers. 2000.

Kabisch E, and Williams A. Vice interfaces. In the proceedings of TEI 2012. Kingston, Ontario, Canada. Feb. 19 – 22, 2012. 343 – 346., 2012

Leacock TL, and Nesbit JC. A framework for evaluating the quality of multimedia learning resources. *Educational Technology & Society* 10: 44 – 59, 2007.

"Learning object". Wikipedia. https://en.wikipedia.org/wiki/Learning_object. Dec. 19, 2017.

Lim Y-K, Stolterman E, and Tenenberg J. The anatomy of prototypes: Prototypes as filters, prototypes as manifestations of design ideas. *ACM Transactions on Computer-Human Interaction* 15: 7:1-7:27, 2008. https://doi.org/10.1145/1375761.1375762

Lohr LL. Designing the instructional interface. *Computers in Human Behavior* 16: 161 – 182, 2000.

Malopinsky L, Kirkley J, Stein R, and Duffy T. An instructional design model for online problem based learning (PBL) environments: The Learning to Teach with Technology Studio. In *Annual Proceedings of Selected Research and Development Papers Presented at the National Convention of the Association for Educational Communications and Technology:* 1-2. Denver, CO. Oct. 25 – 28, 2000.

McDonald JK. The creative spirit of design. *TechTrends* 55: 53 – 57, 2011.

McLoughlin C. Inclusivity and alignment: Principles of pedagogy, task and assessment design for effective cross-cultural online learning. *Distance Education* 22: 7 – 29, 2001. https://doi.org/10.1080/0158791010220102.

Moustakis C. *Heuristic Research: Design, Methodology, and Applications.* Newbury Park, California: SAGE Publications. 1990.

Petre M. Mental imagery and software visualization in high-performance software development teams. *Jrn of Visual Languages and Computing* 21: 171 – 183, 2010.

Petrelli D, Dulake N, Marshall M, Willox M, Caparrelli F, and Goldberg R. Prototyping tangibles: Exploring form and interaction. In 8th International Conference on Tangible, Embedded and Embodied Interaction (TEI'14). Feb. 16 – 19, 2014. Munch, Germany. 41 – 48, 2014.

Pniewska J, Adrian WT, and Czerwoniec A. Prototyping – Is it a more creative way for shaping ideas. In MIDI '13. June 24 – 25, 2013. Warsaw, Poland. 1 – 8, 2013.

Ramesh A, Goldwasser D, Huang B, Daumé III H, and Getoor L. Uncovering hidden engagement patterns for predicting learner performance in MOOCs. Atlanta, Georgia. Mar. 4 – 5, 2014. In L@S 2014. 157 – 158, 2014.

Rawsthorne P. Agile methods of software engineering should continue to have an influence over instructional design methodologies. Cape Breton University & Memorial University of Newfoundland. Research paper. 1 – 14, 2005.

Reeves TC. Enhancing the worth of instructional technology research through 'design experiments' and other development research strategies. In International Perspectives on Instructional Technology Research for the 21st Century. SIG/Instructional Technology at the Annual Meeting of the American Educational Research Association. New Orleans, Louisiana. 1 – 15, 2000.

Reeves TC, Herrington J, and Oliver R. Design research: A socially responsible approach to instructional technology research in higher education. *Journal of Computing in Higher Education* 16: 96 – 115, 2005.

Richey RC and Klein JD. Developmental research methods: Creating knowledge from instructional design and development practice. *Journal of Computing in Higher Education* 16: 23 – 38, 2005.

Rico J, and Brewster S. Gesture and voice prototyping for early evaluations of social acceptability in multimodal interfaces. In the proceedings of ICMI-MLMI'10. Nov. 8 – 10, 2010. Beijing, China. 1 – 8, 2010.

Rodriguez CO. MOOCs and the AI-Stanford like courses: Two successful and distinct course formats for Massive Open Online Courses. *European Journal of Open, Distance and E-Learning.* 1 – 13, 2013.

Rowland G. What do instructional designers actually do? An initial investigation of expert practice. Performance Improvement Quarterly 5: 65 – 86, 1992. https://doi.org/10.1111/j.1937-8327.1992.tb00546.x.

Rowland G, and DiVasto T. Instructional design and powerful learning. *Performance Improvement Quarterly* 26: 9 – 42, 2013.

Roytek MA. Enhancing instructional design efficiency: Methodologies employed by instructional designers. *British Journal of Educational Technology* 41: 170 – 180, 2010. https://doi.org/10.1111/j.1467-8535.2008.00902.x.

Sefelin R, Tscheligi M, and Giller V. Paper prototyping – What is it good for? A comparison of paper- and computer-based low-fidelity prototyping. In CHI 2003 New Horizons. Apr. 5 – 10, 2003. Ft. Lauderdale, Florida. 778 – 779, 2003.

Sims R, and Jones D. Continuous improvement through shared understanding: Reconceptulaizing instructional design for online learning. In *Winds of change in the sea of learning: Proceedings of the 19th Annual Conference of the Australasian Society for Computers in Learning in Tertiary Education.* Auckland, New Zealand. Dec. 8 – 11, 2002. UNITEC Institute of Technology. ASCILITE. http://www.ascilite.org/conferences/auckland02/proceedings/papers/162.pdf. 1 – 10, 2002.

Snyder C. Paper prototyping. IBM DeveloperWorks. https://www.csee.umbc.edu/courses/undergraduate/345/spring12/mitchell/readings/paperPrototyping_Snyder.pdf. 2001.

Soto VJ. Which instructional design models are educators using to design virtual world instruction? *MERLOT Journal of Online Learning and Teaching* 9: 1 – 11, 2013.

Surry DW, and Farquhar JD. Incorporating social factors into instructional design theory. In M. Bailey, & M. Jones, (Eds.) *Work, Education, and Technology:* 6.1-6.8, 1996. DeKalb, IL: LEPS Press.

Swirski T. Unleashing the imagination in learning, teaching and assessment: Design perspectives, innovative practices and meaning making. ATN Assessment Conference. Australia. Retrieved from https://www.uts.edu.au/sites/default/files/Swirski.pdf. 2010.

Tripp SD, and Bichelmeyer B. Rapid prototyping: An alternative instructional design strategy. *Educational Technology Research and Development* 38: 31 – 44, 1990.

Tuch AN, Roth SP, Hornbæk K, Opwis K, and Bargas-Avila JA. Is beautiful really usable? Toward understanding the relation between usability, aesthetics, and affect in HCI. *Computers in Human Behavior* 28: 1596 – 1607, 2012.

Vaidyanathan J, Robbins JE, and Redmiles DF. Using HTML to create early prototypes. In CHI 99. May 15 – 20, 1999. 232 – 233, 1999.

Van Rooij SW. Project management in instructional design: ADDIE is not enough. *British Journal of Educational Technology* 41: 852 – 864, 2010.

Visscher-Voerman I, and Gustafson KL. Paradigms in the theory and practice of education and training design. *Educational Technology Research & Design (ETR&D)* 52: 69 – 89, 2004.

Wilson B, Jonassen D, and Cole P. Cognitive approaches to instructional design. In G.M. Piskurich (Ed.), *The ASTD Handbook of Instructional Technology.* New York: McGraw Hill. 21.1 - 21.22, 1993.

Yanchar SC, and Gabbitas BW. Between eclecticism and orthodoxy in instructional design. *Education Tech Research Dev* 59: 383 – 398, 2011.

Yeung L, Plimmer B, Lobb B, and Elliffe D. Levels of formality in diagram presentation. In the proceedings of OzCHI 2007 Proceedings. Nov. 28 – 30, 2007. Adelaide, Australia. 311 – 317, 2007.

Additional Reading Section

Budhai SS, and Skipwith KB. *Best Practices in Engaging Online Learners through Active and Experiential Learning Strategies.* New York: Routledge. 2017.

Clark RC, and Mayer RE. *E-Learning and the Science of Instruction: Proven Guidelines for Consumers and Designers of Multimedia Learning.* 4th Ed. Hoboken: John Wiley & Sons, Inc. 2016.

Dirksen J. *Design for How People Learn.* 2nd Ed. London: New Riders, Peachpit Press, Pearson Education. 2016.

Moustakis C. *Heuristic Research: Design, Methodology, and Applications.* Newbury Park, California: SAGE Publications. 1990.

Chapter 8
Content Development (with Work Documentation)

Abstract Taking a concept, making a plan to actualize that concept, and building to that plan involve a lot of skill, resources, technologies, and hands-on work. This chapter focuses on what the actual work entails, through the typical development phases: collecting digital contents, creating digital contents, drafting a learning object by integrating raw contents and information, writing, illustrating, creating assignments, creating assessments, adding a style overlay, sequencing the learning, refining the work, and so on. There may be work building context-sensitive help, so those using the learning resources may access the cognitive scaffolding at various points in their learning. There may be downloadables created to enable learners to refresh on the subject matter long after their learning experiences. Finally, work documentation is commonly included in the development work, to enable learning from the development…and to report to grant funders…to enable project handoffs to others…and to leave a historical record for later reference. If there is a point where designer/developers hesitate, it is at this crucial implementation step because the work is hard, and the costs are high. This is where concepts actualize or fail to realize.

Keywords Content development · Work documentation · Designer/developer signature

> Individual commitment to a group effort—that is what makes a team work, a company work, a society work, a civilization work.
>
> –Vince Lombardi (1913–1970)

> Opportunity is missed by most people because it is dressed in overalls and looks like work.
>
> –Thomas A. Edison (1847–1931) in a book by John L. Mason titled *An Enemy Called Average* (1990, p. 55)

S. Hai-Jew, *Designing Instruction For Open Sharing*,
https://doi.org/10.1007/978-3-030-02713-1_8

Opening Scenario

Opening Scenario: Executing on the Work?

The thinking and planning are now harnessed for building the digital learning object(s) and/or sequence. This development work often involves research, writing, image integration, video/motion graphics capture, audio capture, accessibility mitigations, and other elements. During the work, a designer/developer is constantly assessing, to see how the learning object is evolving and testing to see whether the elements are coalescing into a whole object. The work is not a linear development one. For example, if a gap in information is found, then an instructional designer/developer may have to return to conduct more research. If the design does not look like it is working out, then he or she may have to go back to the design phase and start there…at least for part of the work. This is a critical phase, where the actual learning objects coalesce.

If the early designs seem like ephemera, this phase deals with actual digital contents: photos, diagrams, audio files, video files, and other elements. The originality and informativeness of the raw "information objects" and contents contribute to the value of the shared learning object or learning sequence.

Where lighter value learning objects share interpretations of publicly available contents or remakes of existing information (which involves freeriding others' contents), truly effective learning objects share original contents and pro-learning ways to access those contents. The actual development deals with the base value of a shared learning object or sequence. This Is the moment of truth, when plans progress and function, or they fall apart. If a designer/developer cannot execute, all the prior work is just a grand thought experiment.

This phase deals with what the designers and developers are actually sharing as learning objects and sequences.

Some Early Questions to Consider

Based on your experiences, what are some typical steps required in the development of a learning object? Why are the steps in this particular order or sequence? Are there ways to re-sequence the work in order to save on time invested because of mistakes?

How much recursiveness do you go through to create a suitable learning object ready for prime time?

What are some reasons why you have to return to the design to rework the learning object?

What standards are you using when you have to rework part of a learning object? What criteria do you use before you can sign off on the public release of a digital learning object? Why?

What are some elements of a learning design that are desirable but not absolutely required? Why?

What sorts of work documentation do you engage in during the development of the learning resources?

What sorts of work documentation do you do for grant funder purposes?

Are there some automated ways to create work documentation integrated with the work procedure?

Learning Objectives

Learners will…

Project Development Work

- Consider how a conceptualized learning object or learning sequence or design can lead to practical development ideas that have traction (and preserve these ideas for possible action)
- Draft design and work notes related to the development of a particular learning object and/or sequence (such as in a timeline, outline, script, decision-tree, or storyboard)
- Create raw materials for a digital learning object from scratch (e.g. take photos, create diagrams and drawings, research and write content, and so on)
  - If there are trusted raw contents with clear provenance released through Creative Commons licensure or other appropriate licensure, collect these with the highest level of fidelity (and least lossiness) and maintain a record of creators (for attribution), licensure, publication date, and relevant factual information
- Select an object or two from the instructional design plan set up earlier, and build the planned learning resource (while using all known legal standards)
- Design a style-based approach for an online learning object, course, or sequence, and analyze what is being communicated through that style (style should generally be in service of the learning and the learner)
- Upload the planned online e-learning contents onto a hosting site, and sequence the objects appropriately for learning (and build segues between the respective objects)
  - Ensure that there is a rational, consistent, and principled approach to the learning sequence
- Create some downloadable files for learners to enhance the value of a particular learning object, course, or sequence

Project Documentation Work

- Define what work-based information is relevant for record-keeping (for work improvement, for enhanced future designs, for reporting to administrators and to grant funders, to enhance academic research, and other purposes, etc.)
  - Capture information typical to grant reportage, such as work progress, changes to work plans, costs, partnerships, major decisions, and relevant collected data, among others
- Maintain a design and development work journal to record the work, encountered challenges, decision junctures and decisions, and work-based insights
  - Be sure to highlight ways to improve future work based on these from-life insights
- Consider whether project documentation is most effective in real-time (during the work) or post-work (afterwards); by effective, the documentation would have to be accurate, detailed, and comprehensive
- Identify technological features and technology systems that enable the capture of event log data that may enhance project documentation work

Designer/Developer Signatures

- Describe the elements of a designer/developer signature based on a single work or a body of work
- Select which elements of a designer/developer signature are most relevant and why
- Identify which elements of a designer/developer signature are most malleable and able to change and why

8.1 Introduction

You are developing a slideshow…*as part of a learning sequence. You collect the relevant research by going through a number of subscription databases and Google Scholar. You read through the resources and vet them for relevance, and you take notes as you go. You decide some information is more important than others. As you read further, you also explore follow-on sources, like videos and other contents. You start formulating a sense of how the slideshow may be sequenced and how the contents should be chunked for working memory limitations, pacing, and learner comprehension. You have a better informed sense about how the learning objectives may be rewritten in a way that aligns with the contents. The revisions in the learning objectives will also affect the learning outcomes, and you revise those as well. You find gaps in information and conduct a custom interview to collect custom information.*

You open up a slideshow software program (from a local client on your computer or a cloud-based tool). You create a working title, and you start drafting the slide-

show. You realize that some of the data may be more intuitively presented as a table, so you build the tables. You draw diagrams to express other information that are more informative as visuals. You take screenshots of websites and software programs as needed. Some of the data tables work better as data visualizations, so you convert those. You create some maps to go into the sequences. For some of the visuals, you need to overlay some labels on them for clarity.

Based on the learning objectives and the learning contents, you discover that some important learning points need to be made. Because the slideshow is a bit of a longer one and because it will be hosted on a platform that enables an interactive slideshow, you emplace some multiple-choice questions at important junctures in the slideshow, to ensure that the learners are paying attention and to ensure that important points are clarified and emphasized, and muddy points are addressed.

Several video snippets available on the Social Web are relevant to the learning and may benefit learners, so you use embed text to include those after ensuring that both have been closed-captioned already on this site. Both sources seem to be trustworthy ones, and the outros from the videos seem benign.

After most of the contents have been put into place, you go through the slideshow multiple times to ensure that the contents are clear, that the sequence makes sense, that functional features work, and so on. If you have branching sequences, you test every path. You also check to see how this slideshow might fit with the lead-up learning coming before it and that coming after it. You make some adjustments for fit. The segues to the pre- and post-learning contents should hold, you decide. And there is sufficient play to enable the slideshow to stand on its own even if the sequence changes.

Then, you go through and ensure the slideshow is fully accessible. This involves making sure that all images have alt-texting with the informational equivalent of the visual included. You ensure that colors included are high-contrast ones. You make sure that colors alone are not used to convey information. You check that all links to articles are to articles in formats that are machine readable (no image-based .pdfs, for example). You strive to make sure that all information is conveyed in more than one perception channel: visual, auditory, and touch.

You create some reference slides to give credit where it is due and to stay legal and professional. You emplace the slide numbers for clear referencing by users. At some point you apply the look-and-feel of the slideshow either based on the built-in designs or some custom version. You run it through a spell and grammar-check, as a typical matter of course. (If you are working with a team, you have to run the slideshow by them and have them "alpha-test" it for you.)

You render the slideshow in the format that you want and re-test. You upload the slideshow to the hosting platform, add the proper metadata, test it again for function on multiple devices, and you're good to go.

You are developing a video…*that is part of a fictional game. The game has been brainstormed among a small group, and they have a script in mind. Two of the principals on the team agree to be in a video for the project, and they have signed releases. The location where the videotaping will take place is, fortunately, an indoor location—a basic soundstage.*

You have a light script with basic scenes described. The lines are not too complicated. The individuals though have to use their imaginations because they are acting against a green screen, for chroma key compositing capabilities. The two characters are going to be shown in different locations with different backgrounds, and those will be edited in later. The studio where the videography and photography is happening has controls for lighting and for sound. One of the "actors" brings in some pieces of her wardrobe, and both individuals (who are not actors) dress themselves from the pile. The videographer captures the video against a green screen background for chroma key compositing. Several hours later, the videotaping is done. The videography involved multiple camcorders, and the photography involved several digital still cameras. The work has involved professional skills to ensure that the scenes were properly lit and the sound accurately captured.

There is plenty of post-production work. The video editor has to capture stills from the videos. He has to use different video backgrounds for the scenes to fit the fictional narratives. He designs the sound, and he brings in some sound effects from open-source sources. He builds a visual look-and-feel around the videos to align with the game. He and his team manage to bring in one (very funny) visual joke. He runs the snippets by the team and gets approval for the finalized videos.

Those are integrated into a Web-based game. The elements are checked to ensure that they work together. When adjustments have to be made, they are made to the script and not the video because the cost of reshooting and post-production would be prohibitive besides the fact that the talent has moved on to other projects, and neither one would be available by the time this all launches. This work has been realized by a cross-functional team because a range of skills are required.

These two examples show some of the thought and the effortful work that goes into actualizing learning designs. There is setup work, pre-production, captures, and post-production. There are legal issues in consideration at virtually every phase. Even with the help of technologies, many designed functionalities require highly trained effort. For any multimedia object, a number of raw files are needed, and for video and simulations, each media minute requires many visuals and effects. The image-audio-video captures need to be accurate from the beginning, without much margin for error. (There is no effective correcting for unfocused video or image-captures, for example. No amount of heroic work can mitigate poor quality in original digital captures.) The rendered files have to have the proper and precise settings and codecs. The various digital files have to interoperate in precise ways for smooth operations. These requirements are so for a range of digital learning resources: image sets, podcasts (subscribable syndicated audio broadcasts), vodcasts (subscribable syndicated video broadcasts), datasets, simulations, games, and others.

If there is any point in the sequence that may be the point where open-shared projects falter, it seems to be at the point of implementation or the actual work. There can be high intentions, insightful planning work, and some preparation, but unless the work can be actualized to a usable state, all the prior work would generally be for nothing.

What are some of these common skills that are required, and when are they required? One way to conceptualize this is as skill-based intensifications during this

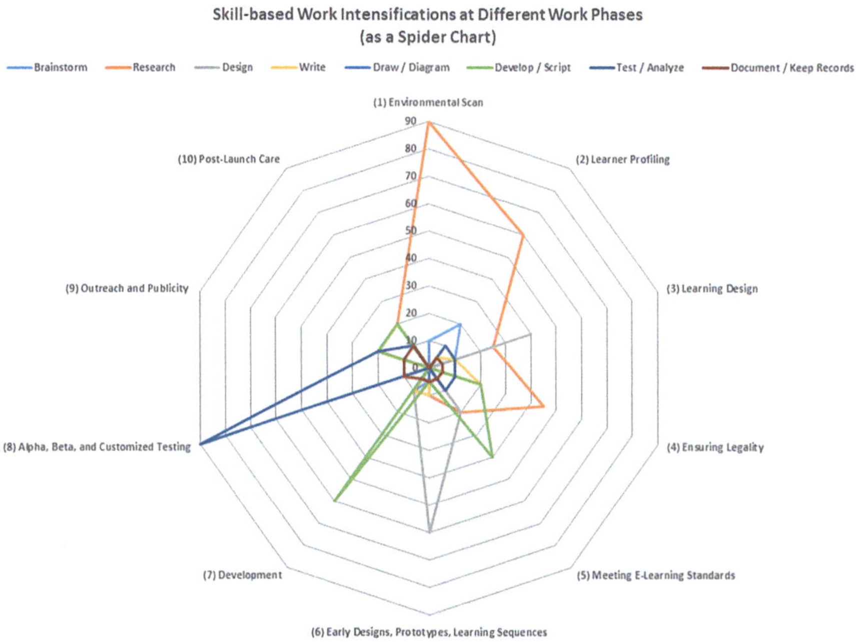

Fig. 8.1 Skill-based work intensifications at different work phases (as a spider chart)

sequence to design and create open-shared learning contents (Fig. 8.1). During the environmental scan, research comes to the fore, and it continues to be important during the learner profiling stage and ensuring the legality of the learning resource. Then, over time, as the project gets underway further, research is still done, but it is less critical. As research fades, design comes to the fore, and then development, and then testing and analysis. To keep an open-shared project on course, it helps to say productive and to understand these various ebbs and flows of focuses and efforts. It also helps to be sufficiently self-aware to get past mental blocks in healthy ways—with relaxing music, walks around the block, reading, or talking with family and friends. Sometimes, something simple like printing out a draft and working that may help a developer get past a mental block. Also, where designs and work plans come in helpful is that they can suggest ways forward when a person or team feels like they have hit an inspiration roadblock. For example, if one part of the work is not advancing, an individual can move on to a different necessary task. It also helps to think of the project to create open-shared learning materials almost as a paid project, as just other work, instead of a volunteer gig. It also helps to note that any progress is still progress, going from raw data to processed data, from unshaped content to shaped, one small bit and byte at a time.

These dynamics may be clearer in Fig. 8.2, which portrays the same information as a horizontal stacked bar chart.

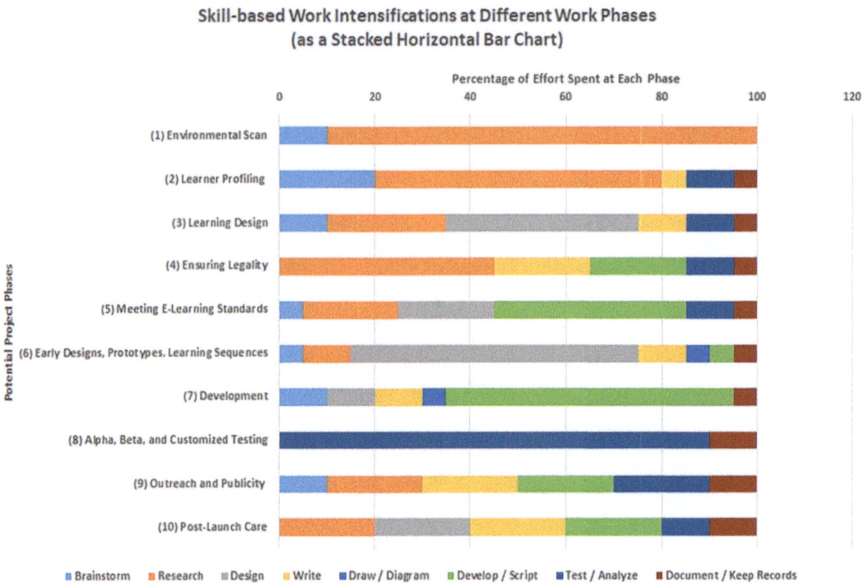

Fig. 8.2 Skill-based work intensifications at different work phases (as a stacked horizontal bar chart)

Finally, the conceptual (and actual) "say-do" gap is wide, and many with good intentions but without the resources or skills or the willpower to make the designs real will fail to achieve any usable work. In this book, content development is the eighth step (Fig. 8.3).

A caveat: A "learning object" is a term of art in instructional design and has particular implications. That is not necessarily how it is used here. In this work, the focus is on the most simple sense of "object" as a tangible "thing." While the theorized work behind a formal "learning object" is solid and helpful, there are too many overlapping and conflicting models in play, so using the generic definition seems more appropriate.

8.2 Review of the Literature

In many ways, in the academic literature, direct writing about instructional development for e-learning seems to be addressed indirectly. There are abstract approaches, including normative models, theories, and frameworks. (Some of these are addressed in Chap. 3). There are shared development experiences described in applied cases. There is research on some testing of the learning resources for their efficacy/inefficacy for learning.

In terms of published research that gets closer to development, there are sources that address some of the technologies used. To actualize various digital and multimedia designs, designers and developers actually use various digital equipment and software tools in various sequences. Common equipment may include the following

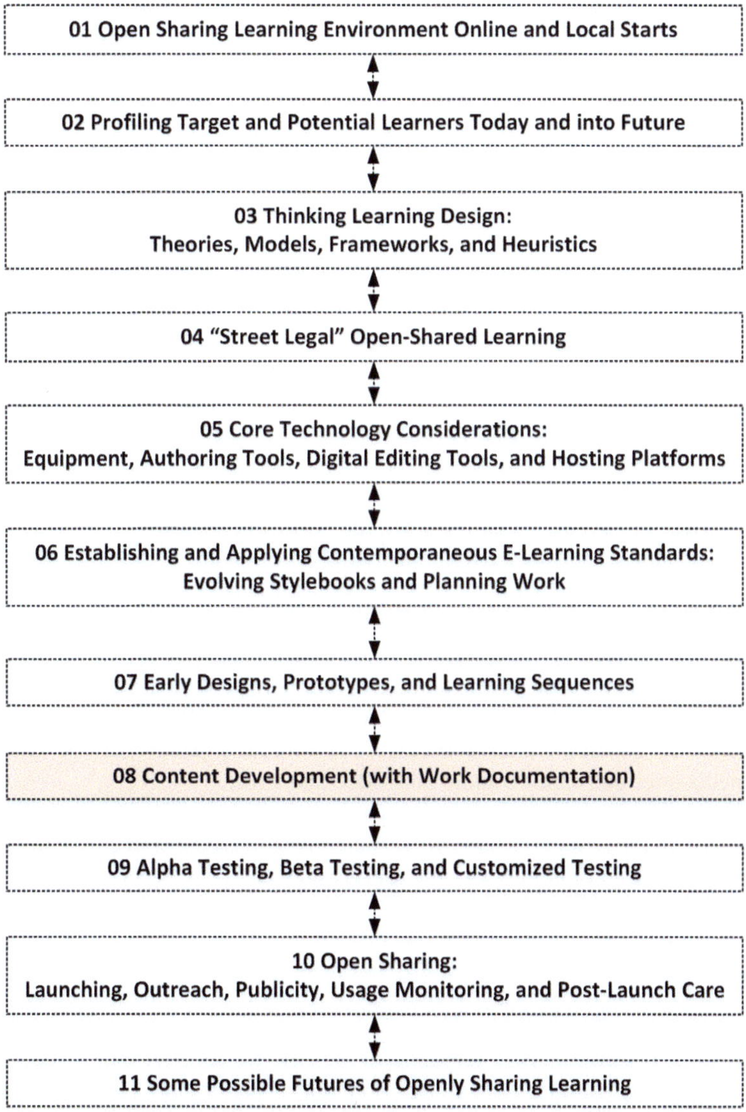

Fig. 8.3 Step 8 in the open-shared learning resource development sequence

types: camcorders, digital recorders, digital still cameras, flatbed scanners, text scanners, slide scanners, sound booths, analog-to-digital converters, vinyl to digital turntables, web cams, and others. Common software include the following: diagramming tools, audio recording tools, image editing software, video editing software, simulation software, animation software, screen capture tools, screencasting tools, authoring tools for learning objects, data analytics tools, web page design tools, spreadsheet software, office suite software, and others. These are just for the base development tools, and depending on the particulars of the design and the design context, a number of other tools may be relevant as well, such as game development tools, simulation development tools, and others. (Some of these were addressed in Chap. 5.)

To over-simplify, development involves collecting and creating digital information and contents in order to actualize the learning designs. (A more sophisticated explanation of the actual steps to development and the actual tasks follows in the main body of this chapter.) Contents may be collected from the open Social Web, with so much contents in the public domain (Creative Commons 0 or "CC0" licensure releases), as well as delimited Creative Commons licensure releases. They may be requested from copyright holders, but each of these will require direct outreaches and the exchanges of contracts and co-signings. They may be captured by transcoding analog contents into some sort of proxy digital format. For instance, vinyl records and eight-track tapes may be turned into digital audio files. Or paper files may be scanned into optical character recognized (OCR-ed) digital files. Older "legacy" digital files may be opened in a later version of the software used to create it, and if the new software was designed with finesse, it can go back some versions and open old files and update them to current file types and standards.

Another approach to capturing contents involves using digital recording technologies. In smart classrooms, passive capture approaches may be used to capture video (motion graphics) and audio from the room. So while videography can be labor intensive and complex, there is also automated videography, which may lessen some of the human workload. Or drone flyovers may be done to capture audio and video. Or digital still cameras may be used to capture still images. Digital audio recorders may capture sounds and voices. The initial captures may be integrated multimedia ones and capture audio and video and stills.

After the initial capture, there is also post-production required to ensure that the raw files are in the proper formats, are sufficiently well edited, and communicate the information desired (without changing the actual basic facts of the contents). Some systems go right to live, with the captured videos uploaded to servers and made available on the Web as soon as the rendering is complete. In other cases, multimedia authoring tools, game design tools, and web design tools are used to integrate the pieces into a coherent learning resource.

The advent of "multimedia technology allows richer, more varied, and more dynamic means for presenting information, along with the potential for displaying more kinds of information than was possible before" (Schank et al. 1995, p. 633). These have enriched the types of learner experiences enabled through packaged online learning. Interactive multimedia scenarios may enable teaching and learning well beyond linear storylines. Advanced compression algorithms have enabled the preservation of visual and audio information even as images and videos could be made sufficiently lightweight for web delivery and streaming.

Over the years, multimedia authoring research has focused on making "authoring complex multimedia titles as easy as using a word processor or drawing program" (Rowe and Jain 2005, p. 1). Such efficiencies bring the technologies closer to the actual subject matter experts or content experts. They enable the creation of coded objects with user-friendly "middleware" tools that enable coding without programming backgrounds.

Common tool types used to aggregate digital information and objects are known as authoring tools. One pair of researchers describes an "authoring tool" as follows:

> …a range of software products having utilities for composing, editing, assembling, and managing multimedia objects, while the term authoring system refers to a subset of these products allowing multimedia development without having to program. (Locatis and Al-Nuaim 1999, p. 63)

Multimedia authoring may be built in automatic, semi-automatic, and fully manual ways (Falkovych and Nack 2006, p. 227). Software used for creating learning contents are sometimes known as "courseware," defined as "educational, multimedia authoring software" (Kaskalis et al. 2007, p. 135). The tool selected depends on what the development team thinks is important for functionalities (Kaskalis et al. 2007), and "many factors affecting the selection and use of authoring software are exogenous to the technology itself" (Locatis and Al-Nuaim 1999, p. 63).

A review of some of the available authoring software shows a very dynamic space, with many of the former products not around a little more than a decade later.

From the development side, for example, the interfaces are much easier to use. In tools that enable the development of "hypermedia" and "active multimedia," tools enable developer visualizations of temporal relations on a timeline, including simultaneity. In tools that enable branching logic, visual storyboards are often built into the tool. Another software enables the harnessing of a pre-designed player with spaces for downloadables, built-in context-sensitive help, designed looks-and-feels, and user control features.

One authoring team defines the terms:

> *Hypermedia* implies store-and-forward techniques where user actions, typically mouse-selections on hotspots, cause the system to retrieve a new "page" of data which could be an image, text, video etc. There are usually no temporal relationships between media. *Passive multimedia* implies a fully synchronized document that "plays itself back" in time, synchronizing all media objects together. *Active multimedia* implies that there are hypermedia-type choices presented to users during the playback of a multimedia document which allow the user's interaction to "drive" the playback. (Hirzalla et al. 1995, p. 25)

Some tools enable the creation of digital storytelling, a narrative conveyed via digital media. This is challenging and nontrivial work, to write a script, record it, edit digital photos and videos around the script, to create a coherent story. There are dedicated software programs for particular aims, including multimedia authoring for game design, slideshow creation tools, and other tools. The lines between the various multimedia development tool types are blurring though, with slideshow software enabling rendering as videos, and presentation web tools on the cloud enabling downloads as slideshows, and so on.

There are new information-rich approaches to authoring. One approach known as "immersive authoring" enables a WYXIWYG ("what you experience is what you get") design approach. There are new tools harnessing augmentations to reality through head-worn displays and handheld devices.

Beyond dedicated tools, there are general ones used for digital content captures and editing (for post-production of imagery, audio, and video). There are general data analytics tools that enable outputs in datasets and data visualizations, both of which are often used for learning. In general, within software content categories, there are only a few real choices of technologies in a space. Given the learning curve of many of these tools, most designer/developers will only master one or a few of the software tools in each category.

One of the basic heuristics is to build to the users, in part, based on the technologies that they are using: their devices, their operating systems, their browsers, their applications, and so on. Learning management systems (LMSes), e-learning systems, social media platforms, online research suites, all capture data about what devices and systems and browsers and apps users are using to access the resource. This provides important information to developers to know what to build to.

In selecting a system to handle the hosting of the learning contents and to manage the learning, faculty should not just be inheriting the technology in a passive way but engaging in reconfigurations and other adaptations for the "interfaces, interactions, and contents"(Wang et al. 2013, p. 147). How well people will accept a technology may be understood using the task-level Technological Acceptance Model, or based on how well the user's task needs are met by the technology (Schoonenboom 2014). User intentionality frames the points of view and preferences of users in relation to an LMS (Schoonenboom 2014).

The adaptations to learners where they are does not end with their technologies of course. Learner expectations for the learning and their accessing the relevant parts of the learning resources are important predictors of learner success (Paechter et al. 2010). The level of learner self-regulation in the learning and their ability to engage collaboratively around the learning are also important learner success factors (Paechter et al. 2010), so these enablements of learner agency should be developed.

There are a number of sequences that are suggested in development but usually in broad terms (like analysis coming before design in the ADDIE Model or the "Analysis, Design, Development, Implementation, and Evaluation" model). One instructional designer describes his preferred design-development sequence:

> Design your assessments first to align directly with your objectives. Revise the objectives as needed so that they are measurable. Then design activities to support the learner in successfully meeting the objectives. Evaluate all materials and resources. *Do they support the activities, the assessments?* If not, consider eliminating them or identifying them as optional. Using this process can promote alignment so that learners can focus on meeting objectives successfully. (Holder 2013, p. 2)

This approach is still based around the given learning objectives, which is a core tenet in instructional design, but it describes the real-world aspect of how change in one area affects changes in others, and whatever was laid down as a solid part of the design may change as new information is available.

8.3 Content Development and Sequencing

An early design, a prototype, and a learning sequence may be created as sparse outlines and drafts of a learning design. Based on either a design or on some inspiration, designer/developers may begin the work. What does this work look like, generally speaking?

8.3.1 Part 1: Project Development Work

What is the "development" sequence comprised of? One way to think about this is as the seven-step sequence in Fig. 8.4. There is both lead-up work and lead-away work to the development sequence. The lead-up work offers some guidance on the development. The lead-away work shows follow-on endeavors to promote the learning resources to learning audiences, to serve the actual learners of the learning resources, and also to plan for post-launch revisions as needed.

Lead-up Work: Research, Instructional Design, and Early Designs and Prototypes

1. Content collection and acquisition, analog content transcoding, raw content creation
2. Content revision, content editing, post production; accessibility mitigations
3. Writing, illustrating
4. Structuring and organizing contents into learning objects and sequences; writing code, scripting
5. Initial refinement, application of look-and-feel
6. Testing and assessment
7. Revising, finalization

Lead-away Work: Deployment and Launch; Post-launch Refinement; Usage Monitoring; Project Postmortem/After Action Review; Project Archival

Infused in the development sequence are e-learning standards, legal considerations (for privacy laws, accessibility considerations, intellectual property considerations, and others) and work documentation.

Reading a design and understanding how to develop from that design is not necessarily obvious. After all, one is conceptual and sparse, and the resulting development should be tangible and finely detailed. The challenges in development are several-fold.

First, a plan is fairly vague, and it asserts what should be achieved in the development, but it does not spell out how oftentimes or what informational contents to use or what technologies to use. By definition, plans are sparse, and that sparsity leaves room for interpretation. Some designs may be wispy inspirations, and how to fulfill those may result in very different outcomes for deliverables. The design conceptualizations are necessarily incomplete by design and by accident. As an illustration, the design may identify target learners, but it may not offer comprehensive research to better understand their needs. There may be parts missing, such as the many "use cases" for the particular learning contents in an open-shared ecosystem. The designer/developers will not have any control over when or how any of the contents are used.

The plan may be built with wrong understandings of practically available data and practically available resources. A plan cannot anticipate what materials are available for harvesting or for capture. Harvested open-source contents may be open-source and free-to-use in many cases, but their provenance is not often available, and their informational value, then, becomes less clear. In the cases of digital captures (photography, videography, audio recording, etc.), those are fairly costly endeavors because of the expensive equipment needed, the human costs in time and

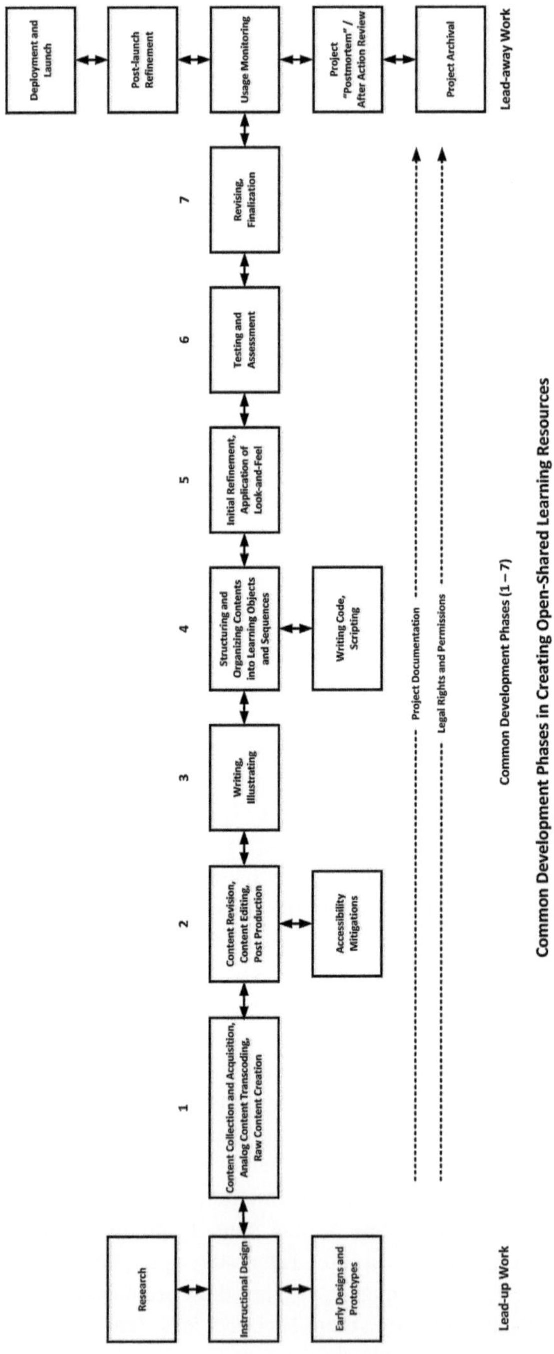

Fig. 8.4 Common development phases in creating open-shared learning resources

effort and skill, and so on. It would be rare to have all items needed at the start of development, and every endeavor and task will involve real costs and effort. Many such gaps may not become clear until the work actually starts. In an even more challenging scenario, a design may be overly ambitious, without clear understanding of just how much work is necessary to actualize a design to quality.

So right at the start, equipment and technology decisions have to be made because this work requires a fairly comprehensive toolkit. The technologies may come in a mix of suites and combinations, but a strong set of technologies would include thousands of dollars of commercial equipment and memory devices and batteries and cords and software, all of which need to be maintained and updated. Technologies are often selected for their functionalities and their robustness and their brand (reputation). It is also important to anticipate how technologies may evolve into the future. Each new advance may mean costly changes.

Hardware and software technologies can be complex and finicky. For digital files to be readable between tools, the file formats have to be exactly correct. There are many dependencies required for technologies to run smoothly on a computer. Various updates and installations can result in unintended malfunctions. In learning contents, there are a lot of moving parts and a lot of potential for issues to arise. Also, people who use technology tools regularly build a sense of each tool and how they interact, and they become much more savvy about creating and using workarounds based on the enablements of the respective tools. (They are able to think beyond the designed and intended functions of the tool and apply the technologies in different ways. They also see the patterns between the tools in terms of interfaces and functionalities.) For many who want to build to public space, and share openly, they may have to use whatever they own at the moment of their inspiration because acquisitions are expensive.

The skills in a toolkit generally should already be in place for the most part before the development phase of a learning resource. The learning curves are fairly high for using the respective tools and for instructional design (requiring graduate degrees oftentimes). Learning while developing is going to happen because of the complexities of the work challenge and the technologies…but having major gaps in the skillset would be negative for the context.

The seven development steps are listed as follows. What do each of these steps entail in terms of the experienced work, and what are some of the most effective practices based on experiential knowledge and abductive reasoning?

1. Content Collection and Acquisition, Analog Content Transcoding, Raw Content Creation
2. Content Revision, Content Editing, Post Production; Accessibility Mitigations
3. Writing, Illustrating
4. Structuring and Organizing Contents into Learning Objects and Sequences; Writing Code, Scripting
5. Initial Refinement, Application of Look-and-Feel
6. Testing and Assessment
7. Revising, Finalization

More details follow about the finer points about each of the seven "development" steps. The first step involves collecting and creating digital contents.

1. Content Collection and Acquisition, Analog Content Transcoding, Raw Content Creation

An early step involves collecting and creating digital contents and taking stock of what one has and what else is needed.

Content Collection On the surface, collecting digital contents may seem like something fairly simple. After all, there are literally tens of billions of images online at present, and many of these have been released to the public domain by aging out of copyright protections and by copyright releases (such as the CC0 licensure). The challenges, though, are multi-fold in this scenario.

First, while there may be many images, the free and open-source ones may not fit the bill by style, by contents, or by information. Images are high-dimensional objects with a wide range of embedded information. Is the image photorealistic or not? Is it taken in the location of interest? Does it communicate the desired information without distracting or extraneous other information? Does the diagram show the model in the way one means it to be? Does the socially shared video communicate the information accurately throughout?

If one does seem to fit, one has to track the image down to the actual owner, read the release guidelines, and follow the guidelines to the letter. Many released images require giving credit to the original photographer or diagram creator…and many the rules of academic citation require a full citation (such as the American Psychological Association source citation format both in-text and in the References list). Users of open-source contents have to keep accurate files in order to use these with minimal liability. Editing rights may be released or held, and there are limits to the commercial usages of many of the released imagery.

Using such images also introduces problems of provenance or where the image actually came from and what it actually depicts. (A reverse image search may be done online, but that is still time spent on work that could be better spent doing something else! And a search is not definitive per se but more suggestive and inferential. It is hard to know how well such a search would hold up in a court of law.)

Many released images do not come with metadata, and when it does, sometimes the metadata are uninformative or misleading. In some cases, metadata and tags are auto-applied by the image-sharing social media platform and not the original photographer.

The original photographer may have edited the original image, cropped it, compressed it, and introduced artifacts (errors in this context). Or some malicious actors may have put hidden images in the shared imagery as part of malicious pranking.

In some rare cases, with sensitive (in a government sense) imagery, there may be exif ("exchangeable image file" format) data riding on the image that should be scrubbed for sensitivity (and/or protection against reputational harms).

Then, too, some simulations require users to download proprietary software on their respective machines. These downloads may be prohibited on public library computers or university computers. And for personal ones, the download may take up excessive space and result in outreaches from the commercial companies behind the simulation players.

Content Elicitation What about crowd-sourcing? There are platforms that enable tasking based on micro-payments and/or free content creation. The same challenges of quality crop up and not knowing the principals doing the work. The liability falls to the author, not the crowd…and not the paid agent (unless he/she can be tracked down to a known person). In some cases, these may be valid options, but the coordination requires effort.

Content Transcoding Another approach is to legally acquire analog contents and digitize those contents legally and include those in the designed learning resources. This is done but usually for background research, to enable digital notetaking and annotation…to enhance the design and some aspects of development. Taking paper text to digital text requires ensuring the optical character recognition (OCR) is enabled, so that search and find capabilities are enabled.

Third-Party Research and Write-Ups Third-party peer-reviewed research often adds plenty of value to a learning resource, but users have to apply the gold standard for information sourcing, selection, and citation. They should do their best to avoid plagiarism.

Raw Content Creation If the raw content creation work is not too expensive, going with self-created contents may be optimal, as long as the individual knows the rules of the game and is willing to abide by them. He or she or they can acquire the images at the highest resolution and quality, maintain a pristine master in storage, crop and edit ethically, and use the images without worries. If people are in the imagery or video, he or she can acquire the media releases. He or she can avoid shooting on private property. He or she can vet images and video and audio for background imagery and sounds and video that cannot be used legally. And so on. If recordkeeping is kept well, the provenance is trackable. Similarly, self-created diagrams and drawings may be more informative and designed to the local usage.

Raw Data Creation In circumstances where the designer is a researcher or works closely with one, they can acquire original data that can add value to the shared learning resource. Of course, these efforts all require proper training, proper permissions (if human research is being done), and so on. (In terms of shared learning resources, it is not so common for people to share original research except now and again, and usually from those in academia and some corporations. Individuals without these ties often do not have the resources or training to acquire valid data or to present the data with sufficient qualifiers and nuances.)

2. Content Revision, Content Editing, Post Production; Accessibility Mitigations

After the raw contents have been collected and/or created, and the documenting README files have been created (about where the contents were collected from and other critical data for citations and backtracking to a source), and the pristine master sets of the raw contents have been created (to preserve the least-lossy image formats in case of future development needs), then the designer/developer has to start revising and editing the raw contents.

Images have to be cropped, alt-texting, and reversioned for the respective uses. Raw audio has to be cleaned and edited. Raw video has to be cleaned, cropped, edited, and spliced; sound design has to be introduced. Closed captioning has to be captured through semi-automated means. Diagrams, maps, and other visuals have to be revised for accuracy. If there are branding standards, those should be adhered to.

3. Writing, Illustrating

Writing is a critical device to organize the learning contents and to convey the meaning to a learning audience—even though multimedia means are also critical to engaging learners and conveying multi-dimensional information. The writing work involves drafting an outline and then filling it with informational contents.

For accessibility purposes, the writing should be as clear as possible and should optimally stand up to auto-translations into a number of languages (180+ enabled on the WWW currently). Provocative or distancing or emotional trigger language should not be used. Everything here should be spelling- and grammar-checked.

Illustrations and visuals need to be integrated clearly into the learning. The various parts of an image require proper and accurate labeling. Every diagram or labeled image should also be spell checked.

Data visualizations should follow understood conventions for the data handling and the representations. Likewise, geographical maps should follow conventional standards.

4. Structuring and Organizing Contents into Learning Objects and Sequences; Writing Code, Scripting

One of the more challenging aspects in the development phase involves organizing the contents into coherent learning objects and sequences. If an original design "breaks," this is generally where it happens. Real learning resources are built on the available information and the available resources in the world (or the resources that can be made from the world in reasonable time with reasonable resources).

In a way, development work is like working a multi-dimensional jigsaw puzzle to chunk learning into manageable sizes (given all people's relatively limited attentional and cognitive resources) and in ways and forms that learners would appreciate and understand. These learning resources are presented through clear user interfaces and in sequences that enable learning. Excessive complexity should be hidden through encapsulation (enclosing the complexity in the technology or the sequence or the activity). Another reason why this phase brings a design into the real is because of the complex interplay between technologies and digital file types. For each type of resource, there are varying parameters for quality and resolution, balanced against unwieldy file sizes (which affect how digital files portray online).

For this step, it helps to be aware of different organizational structures for information: narratives, chronologies (forwards and backwards), problem-solution,

Q&A, most to least, least to most, contrasting, and so on. Using alphanumeric ways to indicate structures can also be highly effective. Organizational structures are relevant whether or not learners themselves are consciously aware of the applied organization.

It also helps to see information in a hierarchy of relative importance and differing roles in relation to other information. It helps to see information by styles (headings, body, and other types). Is the information a high level organizing title? Is the information a supporting detail? I

And it helps to see information as a form and a type. Is this information better presented as a table, a matrix, a list, a data visualization, a map, a song, a video, a game, or something else altogether? What form conveys the information in the way that is most accurate and understandable and with the least distortion?

What are some common heuristics for learning sequences?

- Depending on the domain field and the learners, the designer/developer has to attract learners and bypass their natural apathy. They have to "woo" learners with an engaging question, a mystery, a compelling story, a personality, a visual, a game, a riddle, or a compelling fact. They may have to harness charm and humor and encouragement to maintain some engagement during tough learning periods.
- People sometimes respond to others' personalities, enthusiasms, knowledge, and humanity. That connection between people can be highly attractive, particularly if the subject matter expert (SME) has a lot of charisma and charm. The personality frame can be deeply compelling.
- While interactivity can be valuable, it can also be annoying too people who want to experience a learning resource without interruptions and without being asked to respond to questions or prompts. There are always tradeoffs.
- In the creation of learning objects, there seems to be a balance between the vision of the content creator and learner needs (a mix of self-serve and other-serve). The right mix has to be decided by the designer/developer, but both points of view are important. For the open-sharer, it is important not to have mixed motives, so the share does not get muddied with the commercial interests or potential other conflicts of interest.
  - If a designer/developer and/or content sharer wants to be personality-forward, there are pros and cons to this. What will be important is knowing what each path entails and the risks-benefits of each. Some degree of flare may be positively attention-getting, but beyond a certain point, it can be self-indulgent and distracting, irritating, and even offensive.
  - Whether or not to go with a byline is not really about personality. It is more about having a named person who is responsible for the shared contents and who is reachable for answering questions, should those arise.
- Learning contents should be built in a fairly non-disaggregate-able way, so that the learning may occur of-a-piece. This is not to say that people won't disaggregate contents themselves (they'll take screenshots, they'll take screengrabs of videos, they'll download and edit videos into snippets), but it's better to design in a coherent and cogent and unified way.

- Any harnessing of specific teaching and learning methods (problem-based learning, project-based learning, tabletop simulation learning, serious games learning…) should be informed by the latest research, which is specific, focused, empiric-based, and often valuable. The research may be comprised of works which specify theorizing, applied designs (usually in specific cases), efficacy testing on learners, meta-analyses, and others.
- Multimedia-based design resources based on human cognition is also valuable.
- Assignment design should be backstopped with the latest research on methods and human learning research.
- Assessment design also has widely available and informed research-based resources.
- Examples should be designed with care and thoughtfulness. The selected exemplars should be applicable. Counter-examples should serve particular purposes. There are strong academic papers about how to design examples effectively for a variety of outcomes and learning contexts.
- Feedback provided to learners need sufficient explanatory power, and they should be right-sized for the learning context.
- Both examples and feedback are some controls for misinterpretations and the management of some ambiguity in learning.
- There will not be perfection in this area or any, and knowing what is "good enough" and "satisficing" is important.
- Every design should be built to be competitive in the space; otherwise, it will be a wasted effort.
- Use proper metadata for the learning resources to enable their sequencing. Use proper technological standards to enable sequencing and proper reporting of learner performance to the e-learning hosting system.
- Build to learner expectations because learners are informed by prior experiences and conventions.

Aggregating Learning Objects and Elements Once the respective learning objects and other contents have been created and vetted to satisfaction, they are sequenced in learning paths (some fixed, some dynamic, some adaptive)…or lessons…or modules…or short courses…or long courses…or collections of learning contents (without sequential order). Once the elements are placed in relation to each other, they each reflect off each other, and their interoperations come to the fore. The granularity of focus also changes to a higher level of abstraction.

Interestingly, at this phase, oftentimes, there is still need to rework some parts: the naming protocols; the segues and transitions; the sequencing order; the learning objectives and outcomes, and so on. Some "load balancing" may need to be done, with objects moved outside the learning sequence is the content is excessive for a particular sequence. Some parts may be seen to be missing and so need to be designed and developed. There may be reordering. Some of the learning contents may have to be revised. What becomes clear in a holistic ordering of learning resources is that repeated sections suddenly come to notice. A lead-away text in one object suddenly becomes inaccurate because the follow-on object does not align with the prior description. The point of view (POV) may shift between parts of the learning sequence. Or central verbiage shifts between learning resources. A narrative may be found to be inconsistent logically. Consistency may seem like a very basic requirement, but it requires a lot of effort and attention to details. Some of these challenges may be headed off with a clear design and high work standards, but there will still be errors that slip through. These need to be addressed before anything goes live.

An online learning object or resource is usually thought of as something that is experienced online once-through, maybe a few times if the learner is particularly interested, and the learner may not return to the resource unless they want to refresh on a part of it. (Some open-shared learning resources are packaged in live MOOCs, and these are only offered a few times a year—often in alignment with university quarters or semesters. If a learner drops out partway, they will need to wait until the next live iteration. Or even if they finish one iteration but want to re-reference original materials, they will have to wait. One way to get around some of this is to encourage learners to consume the learning in part by accurate notetaking and digital recording/screen-shotting, to extend the learning experience.) Some ways to extend the learning, from a design point of view, is to create downloadable files that refresh the learning, enhance learner memory, lower skills decay, and serve as a reference. Examples of downloadables may be checklists, procedure charts, decision flows, maps, and other information-rich resources. Downloadables are designed to be downloaded and printed in many cases…or made to be available on mobile devices for easier access and usage. While hosted learning resources may be updated with ease, downloadable files (for print) once downloaded are beyond the reach of the designer/developers. This would suggest that these resources should go through very very close analysis before release.

Teaching Manuals and Learner Notes? One formality from education involves the creation of analogs to teaching manuals and learner notes. Teacher manuals accompany textbooks to let teachers know how to effectively deploy the learning contents. These are especially helpful for long learning sequences, short courses, and long courses. For learners, learning notes may be baked into the preliminary information and the directions. Too much more may feel belabored. Or a designer may choose to make such notes available in an encapsulated way (such as making the information available via an unobtrusive link or pop-up window)

5. Initial Refinement, Application of Look-and-Feel

An initial refinement may involve running the contents through a spell- and grammar-check. It may include the application of a design overlay for a look-and-feel and sense of polish.

6. Testing and Assessment

The testing phase is conceptualized as including alpha testing (in-house testing to defined standards for the respective learning resources), beta testing (testing with members of the general public who represent the "target" and "potential" learners), and customized testing (testing based on the unique aspects of a particular learning resource and the exclusive requirements of the design). (More about these three testing methods follow in Chap. 9.)

The main observation here is that tests have to be defined early on in order to benefit a project, so that the standards may be "baked in" to the work. This is not to say that standards cannot be applied later in a project or at the end, but by then, the costs of retrofitting a project can be extremely expensive; in some cases, it can be impossible to correct errors introduced in the design and development processes.

Also, testing with live learners can be informative. For example, in a learning sequence, there may be benefits in conducting role plays and human-driven simulations in virtual immersive worlds. Scripted objects may be deployed in the space with particular learning contents, and guest speakers may join in in character from anywhere around the world (as long as they have a fast processor and solid video card and speedy connectivity to the Web and Internet). Such sessions can be recorded through *machinima* (machine + cinema) and still image captures. However, the learning curve about how to create digital avatars in online spaces and how to enable them to navigate, speak, interact, and share information may be prohibitive.

7. Revising, Finalization

This last development stage is about revising the learning resources based on the collected insights from the alpha, beta, and customized testing and applying a final layer of polish. At this point, if the learning resources require versioning for mobile or different learner groups or other contexts, those changes should be put into play now.

The "seven steps" of development can be a kind of shorthand. These are not linear steps and may be recursive, with developers moving backwards and forwards in this space, to achieve the ultimate resources. Some designer/developers prefer to design and develop episodically and may "play it by ear" based on what resources are available.

The design of instruction is too big of a field to be doctrinaire about what works and what doesn't in every case. Part of expertise requires the ability to "play by ear." Rules are only artificial guideposts, and many may be broken for effect, as long as the designer is doing so on purpose for designed effects.

About Style The question of "style" is a challenging one because the style should serve the learning. It should make the learning resources appealing, indicate the brand of the resources, and not be distractive. In many cases, the built-in styles and color palettes of authoring tools are used in lieu of a professional graphic artist-designed proposal. Oftentimes, "style" is applied as an afterthought, just so learners don't feel its absence.

That said, style rarely (never?) trumps substance. After the initial pop of color and "wow!" learners will still expect some substance.

With advancements in Cascading Stylesheets (CSS) and other methods, it is possible to create the contents and use CSS to apply the design packaging and presentation. The style may be designed, and then web developers may create the desired look-and-feel and apply it to the web-facing object (depending on how the object was built and what the object is).

Task #1: Design ↔ Development
During the design, there is a reciprocal relationship between the original design and the development, and each informs the other. A design does not fully specify how to develop the learning resources, and the development work may inform a design (the applied work shows what works better than the initial conceptualization, oftentimes).

In the development phase of an online learning object and/or sequence, a designer/developer often makes a lot of discoveries. What are some of these discoveries for you? How do you arrive at these discoveries? What are some ways to enhance your learning and learning awareness during the development phase?

How do you use each (design and development) to benefit the other during the development phase? Describe this phenomenon in a development journal to enhance your work, in both future designs and future developments. How informative should a design be, and what parts of work should be defined in the design and what parts in the development, and why?

Using your own design is one thing because you generally know what you meant when you created the design, or you can sort of guess afterwards. In cases where you inherit someone else's vision and sense of design, how can you develop contents that meets their conceptualization? What are ways that you can iterate the development with check-ins with the designer? What are ways that you can iterate the development without check-ins with the original designer?

A final note: A common "rookie" mistake is to hold too tightly and literally to an original design and to not actually interpret the design.

Task #2: Riffing off a Design and Other Inspirations
A design is almost never the only inspiration for development work, in part because a design is so purposefully sparse.

For this task, focus on a conceptualized learning object/sequence design. Ruminate over it for about a week, and during this time, record all inspirations and ideas that arise. Identify the ideas that have development traction. Preserve all the ideas, and do not prematurely discard any. Sometimes, an idea that does not seem relevant may turn out to be the solution for a difficult challenge.

In your development work, how much inspiration do you take from the design, and how much do you take from other inspirations during the development process? How much do you stay "true" to a particular design (and why)?

About Time For open-shared learning, unless there are external drivers like competitions or publisher deadlines, the designer/developer generally sets the pace and the quality standards that have to be achieved (the main defining factor for when something is done). In the seven steps, which ones tend to take the most time, and which the least? Well, the answer really depends on the project. But a general estimate might be the following in Fig. 8.5. Generally, the work is frontloaded to the initial steps, and the work lightens in the last few. This assumes that the decisions made in the early steps were generally in the ballpark and would not require major work in retrofitting and correcting.

1. Content collection and acquisition, analog content transcoding, raw content creation
2. Content revision, content editing, post production; accessibility mitigations
3. Writing, illustrating
4. Structuring and organizing contents into learning objects and sequences; writing code, scripting
5. Initial refinement, application of look-and-feel
6. Testing and assessment
7. Revising, finalization

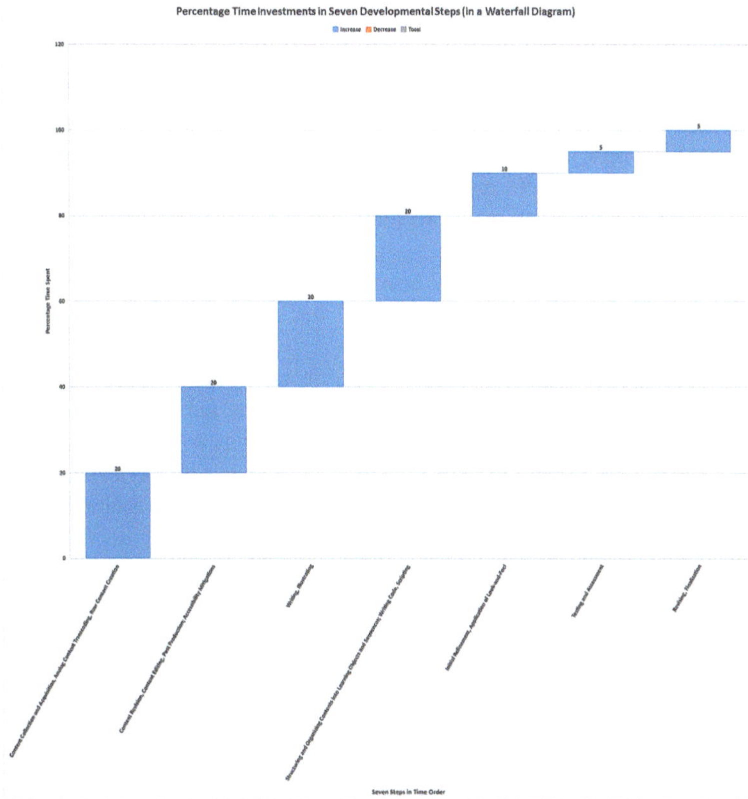

Fig. 8.5 Percentage time investments in seven developmental steps (in a waterfall diagram)

To get more specific, there are general time estimates that can be made for particular learning objects in a particular domain space. The time investment will depend on the quality that is being built to and with what tools and the skill sets of the individual and team. Of course, teams involve multiple human hours in simultaneous time, so the time estimates can go up very quickly in those contexts.

For most designer/developers, they have multiple projects going on at any one time. Then, they also have projects next on-deck that they may be collecting contents for as time allows while they are directly focusing on other projects. The subconscious mind is constantly working on design and development challenges, and side projects benefit from accruals of ideas over time even when the direct work focus is elsewhere. In general, once a project is started, it is important to keep it in the active workspace until it is completed to satisfaction and released to the public. It seems like a bad idea to start something and not finish it and leave it lying around on a messy digital workbench. If time drags on too long without progress, there does arrive a point in time (and in investment) when the will breaks, and plans change. It helps to run an internal clock for when something should be complete.

8.3.2 Part 2: Project Documentation Work

Work-based information is usually recorded to accomplish a mix of objectives: improve future work, inform project planning (and budgeting), enhance future instructional designs, report information to administrators and/or grant funders, enhance academic research, and other purposes. Proper data management may make it easier to track necessary information down, for individuals and for teams (especially).

Documentation of work should be accurate and informative, but this effort should also be unobtrusive. Documentation should not detract from the main work of development.

During the developmental work processes, decisions are constantly being made; experiments are constantly being run; designer intents are being considered, and learner experiences are being considered. There is no way to remember every single nuance, and yet, it is important to be able to track back to critical decision junctures to advance to work, to satisfy administrators and funders, and to maintain a sense of institutional memory.

For some types of project documentation, it may be easier to capture the information during the work. This ensures that small details are captured, and it is helpful to have this captured contemporaneously to the work especially on long developmental projects. Some of this work documentation may be built off of the event logging of various technology systems. For contemporaneous recording, a work journal may help capture the most important insights. For some, having a structured work journal may be more effective than a wholly freeform one. For example, the journal may include guidance on the work challenges, problem solutions, decision junctures and decisions, and technology discoveries. It would help to have a freeform space available as well. These digital work journals may include sketches and drawings, audio recordings, text notes, short videos, and other ways to capture the inspirations in multimodal ways.

In other cases, documenting the project work may be most effective and least intrusive post-development work.

Post-Project Record-Keeping If the record-keeping is done at the end of the project, then maintaining raw and finished files fairly comprehensively may be important, for later review. It will be important to use proper naming protocols for the respective files, proper folders and folder structures, and plans to enable continuing access to proprietary files after the end of a project. (Poor digital content management can be challenging when trying to conduct a project post-mortem.) The point about the proprietary files showcases the importance of "digital preservation" (ensuring that digital files are accessible into the future and not fall to "slow fires" or inaccessibility due to loss of access to particular proprietary software). If one only has digital files in the raw format with the unusual file extensions (think .camproj, .avi, .nvpx, .vsdx, and others) and not one in a universal file format, then it is wholly possible that some files and the related data will be lost to history and the individual/team.

Some of the design artifacts may be somewhat informative of decision making, especially if there is record-keeping of iterations (such as through version control). Storyboards may be suggestive of decisions. Individual or group calendars may be informative of work progress and scheduling and time usage. However, turning these into objective and verifiable information may require time and effort. There may be more efficient ways to collect relevant documentation. However, saving the documentation to the end of the project may mean some lossiness of information.

Organizations that provide moneys for open-shared projects, particularly larger-scale ones, will require clear and objective definitions of the work, standards of the work, an approved design plan, a budget, defined team roles, hard deadlines, defined deliverables, and other details. They may require sample work. They will require regular check-ins. Often, grant funders will want to know about changes in the design and development. As a standard, grant reportage may be an effective guide against which to collect and report information.

Live Examples (on the Web)

Go online and identify a half-dozen grant funders in the open-shared learning space…from anywhere in the world. Read the standards for the grant applications. Focus also on the reportage requirements. What sorts of project data are the funding organizations or agencies or entities requiring? Why? What form do they want the information in? What controls do these organizations maintain over the contents (if any)?

For some, project documentation seems most effective during the work. Designer/developers may keep a running work journal that they update daily, or they may post information in their work calendars, and other approaches. Others find that they document best after a project is done, and they will make notes from their memory and from project artifacts.

Some technologies enable the capture of "log data" (records of people's behaviors and actions on the systems). This data may be offer validated work documentation with a precision that may not be available from other sources. The point of documenting work is to provide research- or work-based insights, so not all data will be valuable.

Task #3: Project-based Documentation

Documentation is an important part of an instructional design project for a number of reasons: to enhance the work, to report to grant funders, to keep team members apprised, to ensure legality with the various media releases and intellectual property releases, to maintain "institutional memory" around the work, and others.

How would you go about documenting an instructional design project? What types of information would be relevant for you to keep? What are ways to use work byproducts for part of that documentation?

Task #4: Notetaking

While notetaking may seem like a simple sort of skill, effective notetaking (accurate, relevant, comprehensive) is often a lot harder than many people realize. Go through a development work sequence, and maintain notes about the effort. Use any of the recording enablements that technology affords today—with digital notetaking, diagraming, photography, audio recording, video recording, screen capturing, screencasting, and others. What combinations of these approaches are most accurate and most effective for you? What information seems relevant in the notetaking in the near-term? the mid-term? the long-term?

8.3.3 *Part 3: Designer/Developer Signatures*

One of the assertions in this text is that sharing learning resources can be seen as an extension of self-expression and even artfulness. An extension of this idea is that a designer/developer's style may be part of his/her personality frame and may be (un) attractive to learners.

This begs the question of what a designer/developer signature may look like, based on an analysis of a single work or a body of individualized work. Which elements of a work are most revelatory of a signature and why? Of these indicators, which are most malleable and able to be changed?

Based on some decades in the field, I identified eight common areas that may be revelatory of a learning design hand: information, pedagogical design, engagement, technology, legal adherence, tone, personality forwardness, and polish (Table 8.1). These are not conceptualized as comprehensive but only as a start to answering this question. Beyond these may be affectations and tells, and other more nuanced overlays of voice and expression.

Table 8.1 Some aspects of designer/developer signatures

1. Information	
Data richness	How much data and information are provided in the learning resource
Novelty	How rare and unusual the provided information is
Value	How informationally valuable the information is (for research, for commerce, for understanding, etc.)
Originality	How uniquely the information is presented
2. Pedagogical design	
User centered	How much learner needs are considered in the design and development
Sophisticated	How elegant and effective the learning design and development are
Didactic	How obviously designed for teaching the learning resource is
Depth	How complex or profound the learning is
Ambition	How high of a bar is set for the learning
3. Engagement	
Interactivity	How many interactive opportunities are there in the designed learning resource
Social learning	How much users of the learning resource are expected to interact with others
4. Technology	
Sophistication	How expertly the technologies are wielded to create and implement the learning resource
5. Legal adherence	
Accessibility	How accessible and accessibility-compliant the learning resource is
Intellectual property	How intellectual property-compliant the learning resource is

(continued)

Table 8.1 (continued)

6. Tone	
Formal, conventional	How conventional and official the learning resource is
Seriousness	How solemn the learning resource is
7. Personality forwardness	
Values based	How much principles and standards are at the forefront of the learning
Subjectivity	How much personal feelings are present in the learning resource
Friendliness	How much warm communications are present in the learning resource
Voice	How much an original voice comes through in the learning resource
Opinion sharing	How much opinions are shared in the learning resource
Humor	How much humor is shared in the learning resource
8. Polish	
Refinement	How well presented (revision, editing, look-and-feel) a learning resource is

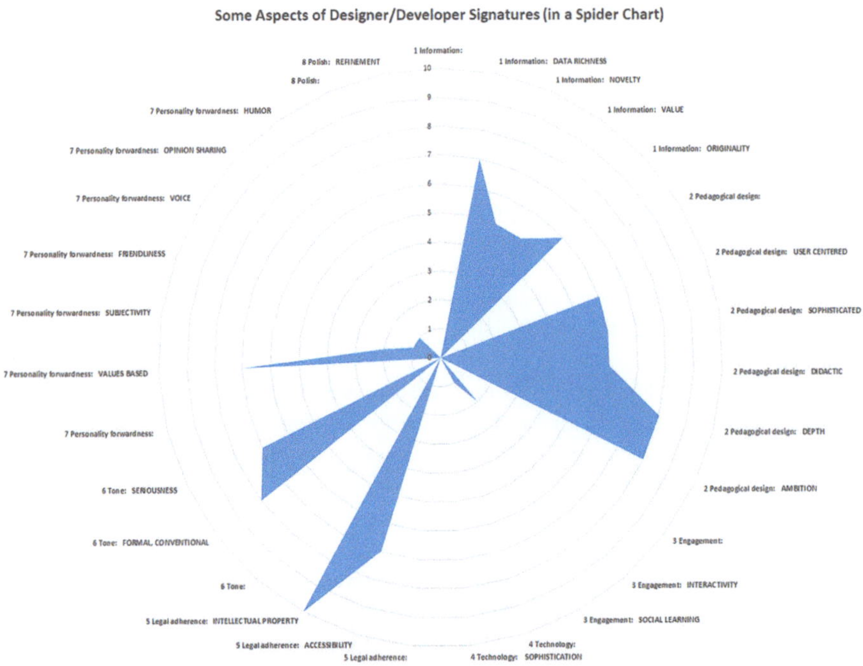

Fig. 8.6 Some aspects of designer/developer signatures (in a spider chart)

The same eight areas and related sub-elements may be seen in Fig. 8.6. In this spider chart, the various aspects are measured for one instructional designer and her unique hand. The filled shapes may give the sense that based on these respective dimensions that each instructional designer may have a unique expressed persona and related signature and style. Perhaps certain styles may result in better design and development outcomes for certain kinds of teaching and learning. This conceptualization suggests that a designer/developer signature stems from his/her relationships to information, pedagogical design values, social sensibilities, technological skills, attention to legal constraints, expressed emotional states, personality, and attention to details. An instructional design signature is revealed by how an individual solves design challenges and problems and expresses into the space.

Individual signatures can be highly forward and present, such as bravura performances, or they can be receding and quiet, such as behind-the-scenes work.

Task #5: Your Design/Development Signature

Some instructional designs require close adherence to rules and defined templates and other structures. Other designs are more freeform and enable more experimentation. Regardless of the guidelines, there is often still something of the author hand or developer "signature" from the individual. This is in part because there is not actual equifinality in terms of instantiation of designs; rather, any number of potential learning resources may be built from a learning design. Designers/developers are often fairly self-aware of their own signatures and how they instantiate into a field as a designer/developer. A person's reputation may be based in part on his/her signature and public persona.

Please review some of your work, and then define your own signature. What are your go-to's and habits? Where are your areas of comfort and confidence (and then the converses of these)? How do you work through difficulties here?

In descending order, list the most salient aspects of your signature. Explain why these are most salient.

Of these, what are most important to you, and why? Create another list of the features from most important to least important.

Are there aspects of your signature that you dislike and want to change? Why?

How would you practically go about strengthening the parts of your signature that you appreciate and improving on the parts of your signature that you do not?

Task #6: Design/Development Signatures from Group Work
In some ways, as with authors, it may be easier to extract senses of unique signatures and styles from individual works. Those works can be interpreted through biographical frames, worldview frames, personality cues, psychological frames, core values, and other aspects of identity. For works that are group designed and group authored, the signatures may be more elusive. How would you go about understanding a group-developed learning resource and the group authoring hand/signature? How would you begin to understand how group minds might work and result in creative endeavors and outputs?

Inspiration, Starting, a Long Grind, Some Crunch Times, and Beyond
It seems that there are regular phases in an open-shared learning project that prove challenging, albeit in different ways. Understanding these challenges and how to get through them can be helpful for the work.

At the beginning, there is the challenge of getting inspired. What topic will be addressed and how?

Once an idea has been arrived at, there is the challenge of starting the design and development work, which tend to be closely intertwined.

Then, the work commences, and for the longest time, it feels like little progress is being made. Frustrations may arise, and the work may seem somewhat futile. For some, they may want to just scotch the plan and give in to their negative impulses. It seems that the developed contents are not yet taking on the shapes of the design or any other structure for that matter. At this stage, it is not clear at all that the object will make or that it will coalesce. Then, suddenly, it feels like a corner is turned and the resistance seems to break, and it feels like the project will "make". It is not that the work lessens, but the respective digital elements start fitting and falling into place. There is a clear way forward. And sometime after that, the work seems easier, the slog is no longer uphill but includes some downhills. (In the same way, if a project has versions of learning contents, the work is much easier once an accepted and working prototype is created from which all the other versions are created.)

There are different difficult phases with other open-shared project types. With deadline-heavy projects, such as deadline driven ones, there are high-pressure crunch times and intensifications of work. Something like this may be a contest or a publication related to open-shared learning.

With some group projects, waiting on others can be the challenge. The dependencies in such projects mean an enforced patience.

Meeting the Challenge

What are some ways to meet these challenges? For practical purposes, it helps to know oneself sufficiently to know where to find inspiration early on. It helps to know how to manipulate oneself to get started on projects ("It's on your calendar, so do it" or "If you start the project, you will be rewarded with an hour of time reading" or whatever is a healthy reward for you). It helps to be able to deal with the hard work of the actual slog…and the best way to appreciate this is to both keep the ultimate goal in mind (and the target and potential learners) and to sort of masochistically enjoy the work. It helps to believe in the original design and one's skills as well, to achieve the "proof of concept" (evidence of the feasibility of the design). In these middle phases of a project, a designer/developer has to be comfortable with ambiguity and complexity because learning resources can go through phases when the contents are shapeless and chaotic.

The point is to keep the work moving. In times of frustration, it helps to walk around from the work for a while, self-soothe, and do other distractive activities. If the work is stuck, work towards a redirect and work past impasses. (There are always ways around instructional design challenges.)

During crunch times, have the discipline and the space in your schedule to be able to intensify.

In the cases of team development, be patient, be supportive, and work around others' schedules where possible; where not possible, on deadline, always have backup plans and substitute other work for peer work. Be fair, be transparent, and give other people their due.

It helps to know that the ultimate decision maker is you and your team on open-shared projects, unless, of course, you're working with a client. In that case, there may be external sources of pressures and additional standards beyond the basic ones. No matter! You've got this!

8.3.4 *Discussion*

Taking a design through development to a finalized learning resource for open sharing requires a fairly high level of skill and experience. In this chapter, the steps are the following, informed by lead-up work, and supported by lead-away work.

Lead-up work: research, instructional design, and early designs and prototypes

1. Content collection and acquisition, analog content transcoding, raw content creation
2. Content revision, content editing, post production; accessibility mitigations
3. Writing, illustrating
4. Structuring and organizing contents into learning objects and sequences; writing code, scripting
5. Initial refinement, application of look-and-feel
6. Testing and assessment
7. Revising, finalization

Lead-away Work: Deployment and Launch; Post-launch Refinement; Usage Monitoring; Project Postmortem/After Action Review; Project Archival

This work requires close-in knowledge of the technologies, which are evolving at a fast clip. (The finer points of technologies will not be engaged in this book because readers will end up "in the weeds" very quickly.) This work also requires awareness of pedagogical design, learning research, learning theory, and domain knowledge. Project documentation is important for the work, and for project postmortems. These resources may be evaluated for research value.

8.4 Future Research Directions

There does not seem to be any published research on how an instructional design or prototype or learning sequence is interpreted to inform the creation of a developed learning object or resource. After all, a design is polysemic, and its many layers of meanings can be interpreted in different ways with different technologies and different sensibilities. Also, there may be ways to analyze the sufficiency of the developed resources as compared to the designs—not only at the level of the specific project but in a more general sense. (For example, how comprehensive are the shared contents? The clarity of the messaging? The alignment with the applicable laws? The technological functionality? The correctness of the verifiable data? The strength of the logic? The orientation and navigability?)

The field would benefit from how to enhance the effectiveness and efficiency of development methods. Expert designers and developers and designer/developers may be interviewed to better understand their work processes.

This chapter focuses on self-aware development of open-shared learning objects and sequences and documentation of that work. This chapter informatizes the development artifacts, the objects used to structure and create the remote online learning. What may seem just like a folder of raw files can have informational value and may offer practical insights. Some of the files may contain templates that may be re-used. In cases where the learning contents are wholly original, such as with boutique projects, there may still be learning from such outliers based on their uniquenesses.

Follow-on work to this chapter may include formalization of just what aspects of the development cycle benefit from documentation for various uses: work improvement, future designs, reportage to grant funders, academic research, and others.

This chapter seems to assume the use of a general design and/or prototype and/or learning sequence. A common scenario is for a designer/developer to go straight-to-build, based on the momentum of an idea or a tasking. Some unfolding events may encourage the immediacy of a straight-to-build. These are valid approaches, too, depending on the learning context that is being built to. So while the formal approach is "scaffolding and then building," there are many instances of "building and then scaffolding" (extracting a design from the built object, in a form of reverse engineering). More work in this area would be potentially beneficial, for both knowledge and practice (Fig. 8.7).

Fig. 8.7 A Word Cloud of Chapter 08: "Content Development (with Work Documentation)"

What-If: Development and Decision Making

You have created (or inherited) a plan for learning resources. Some parts of it are explicitly clear, and others are somewhat vague but still informative, at least in terms of a general direction. You begin by collecting relevant research and reviewing the already collected research. The amounts of information, at least in some areas of the content, are overwhelming; in others, you find gaps. To create an effective organization, you begin to chunk the data into learnable sequences. (The designs suggest slideshows for some of the contents and videos for others. You start thinking strategically about what contents would be best expressed in which format.)

You collect digital contents within the legal guidelines of intellectual property restrictions. You capture required photos, diagrams, audio, video, and other contents. You start to structure the contents using outlines and storyboards once you have sufficient contents.

Along the way, you also create assignments and assessments. The contents inform the assignments and assessments, and vice versa. After all, you cannot ask people to be responsible for learning that you do not address, and you do not want to build out too much in the way of learning that learners do not have to show responsibility for. Each filters the other. At every stage in the design, there are decisions about what contents to select as relevant and what contents to de-emphasize. The standards are to build as-if you are to go public as soon as possible, to ensure that the contents are legally usable and precise, to ensure that no placeholder contents are offensive if exposed (no sarcastic humor), and to ensure readiness if deadlines shift.

Progress is being made, but you realize that parts of the plan will be infeasible. When the plan was written, it was informed in part by assumed access to particular information. That information turns out to be sensitive and held by only a few entities in the world. What do you do?

Decision point #1: stop or advance. If advance, would you pursue access to that information from those who may have it? Would you gloss over the lack of information? Would you acknowledge the gap in information but indicate how much or how little is known publicly? Would you read into the publicly available information and make some unsupported assertions?

You initially reach out to the potential sources to ask for access to the contents. Most of them ignore you, but a few contact you, and two provide some contents to you with legal releases to use the contents. You agree to handle the information as the sources suggest and give information where requested (and obscure names where needed). You also acknowledge where the gaps are. You add a small piece to anticipate information that may come, but you are very clear about the limits of your assertions.

You are careful about giving away advantage where you do not need to. You are also aware of how people can read into shared information and misread it, so you control for negative learning.

During the design work, to "break up the gray," you consider illustrating some of the concepts. Creating original diagrams and imagery requires time, but you do so because those efforts inform the learning. However, there are other contexts where you cannot think of what illustration to use, and you think something like an open-source image or some stock imagery might be in order. What do you do?

Decision point #2: stop or advance. If advance, what criteria will you use for the selection of a relevant illustration? How do you try to ensure that the image has informational value (while also breaking up the gray)? How can you ensure that there is a consistent look-and-feel or visual style to the images used in the learning resources?

You review some stock imagery. If you do use stock imagery, there is a cost, and often, the rights released are for a narrow band of usage. Also, these images do not come with clear provenance, and their glossy look-and-feel may contrast badly with the other imagery in the learning resources that lack the marketing sheen.

You consider using some open-source imagery, which are at least free. However, you are not always sure about provenance. You are not sure that those posting the images for usage are the actual owners, at least not without some due diligence (like reverse image searches to check for earlier appearances of the same images on the Web and Internet, like reaching out to the apparent owners, and others). There are costs regardless of what path is chosen—whether in costs, risks, lacks of information, or development costs.

You make a variety of decisions along the way and develop the project.

You build to standards of accessibility along the way. You want to make sure to follow the legal requirements for accessibility, and you want to include as many potential users as possible.

As you work, you realize that you have a knowledge gap.

Decision point #3: stop or advance. If advance, do you conduct more research to make up for your knowledge gap? If so, this will require effort and access to the research. Or you can gloss over this gap and just aim for a smaller part of the domain topic. You can reframe the focus. Or you can bring in a content expert to fill in the gap.

You make your decisions and proceed.

You have an initial draft completed. You have proofed the contents. The links all work. The learning sequences make sense. The language seems appropriate for your target learners. The various learning resources are consistent in terms of approach, language, look-and-feel, and other aspects. It all looks good to you. What do you do next?

Decision point #4: stop or advance. If advance, do you run this through alpha, beta, and/or customized testing? Do you have in-house others evaluate the work (alpha testing)? Do you bring in representatives of target learners to assess the work (beta testers)? Do you engage in customized testing?

If you bring in others to assess, you will have to give them credit on the work. You will also have to conduct some revisions based on their critiques and reviews. Some of the ones you ask will turn you down because they are busy people.

If you bring in those from the public to engage in beta testing, you will have to motivate them to respond. You may have to pay for some compensation. You do not have social capital to draw on in these cases.

You can go straight to launch, but you may be missing some ways to enhance the work.

You make your decisions and continue. You do check the drafted works against the original plans. You do check for legality. You check for spelling and grammar. You make sure that you are well rested and fresh before each iteration because you want to be as careful and attentive as possible. If the cases where you can run automated assessments, you do.

You are close to launching…so you conduct some research on the potential hosted platforms for the learning contents. You find that several of them are no longer available. Some have turned from free platforms to pay ones. The space has been highly dynamic. You're generally back to square one. What do you do?

Decision point #5: stop or advance. If advance, what are the standards that you would use with a hosting platform?

You decide to begin with a list of ideal features and functions. A hosting platform should be free into perpetuity if possible because of your $0 budget. It should have a sufficient track record, so the access to the site is continuous and uninterrupted. The organization should have a strong reputation, so there are no negative associations in relating contents with the hosting platform. The tool should enable hosting of various types of digital contents, so as not to limit the design and development decisions of those who use it. It should have intelligent integrations with other tools. The tool should have sufficient archival capabilities and search functions (so digital contents are not left to molder). And these are just for starters.

You create a spreadsheet/grid. You collect a list of all the potential hosting organizations and technologies. You evaluate pros and cons of each. You consider your best options. You update the information as new information becomes available. You are confident that you will have a few options when you are ready to launch.

You continue with your work. You continue to refine and polish the work. You iterate through the resources until you are hard-pressed to find anything else to change.

All along the way, you have been maintaining pristine raw files, pristine datasets, legal releases, and other documentation.

You go to launch.

Right after launch, several people contact you with different queries. Some want more information about particular aspects of the learning. One is confused about the user interface (and you think that context-sensitive help might address this, but it would require your rebuilding some of the learning objects with an additional layer of cognitive scaffolding). Others have questions about technologies you used to build the resources. Some want follow-on resources created as a next step in the learning. (No one is throwing money at you, but they are making requests and offering some kudos.)

You have to decide whether you want to offer post-launch care or remain silent (which is the default).

Decision point #6: stop or advance. If advance, what standards will you use for post-launch care of users of your learning resources? What standards will you use for revising the resources? When will you conduct the revisions, and based on what thresholds and to what standards?

You decide…

The What-If Debriefing

This scenario offers several insights. Effective instructional design work does not only require the skills to create learning but to make the right decisions at the respective junctures. The designer/developer will be making design and development decisions at each phase of the work, and there are tradeoffs at every phase. The instructional design plan is usually limited, and from the first steps in the development, the plan becomes much more ideational and aspirational. There is rarely anything in the world that is built-to-order already, even in a world with lots of shared digital resources. In a world of $0 budget and project advancement by good will, the plan is only a start. What matters is how the plan is expressed and manifested.

In this framework, proofing seems normal, but alpha, beta, and customized testing may seem much more costly and add-on. This scenario shows the importance of having priorities and standards throughout because those are the things that will drive quality in the learning design and development (along with a deep sense of professional skill). Good habits—like staying legal, like going with project documentation throughout the work, like learning from one's experiences, and such—also are important to keep the project on course and in good stead. In the work, there is almost always a sense where more investment into an open-shared project does not make practical sense.

Projects can stall at any point, and a developer can "defect" instead of "cooperate" at any stage. ("Defection" here means an end to the endeavor, and "cooperation" means continuing with the development work. The ideas of defection and cooperation come from a classic game theory concept of the iterated Prisoner's Dilemma.) He or she can lose will or focus at any stage. He or she may be stumped by particular challenges. So this is about having an actionable plan (especially one that enables work efficiency gains) and the skills to back it up and the will to make this all real. In an open-shared context, there is no actual rush to finish. Those who may wish to may slow down the process and enjoy the work (unless procrastination is a problem).

Less directly, those who would build open-shared learning contents should not be put off or intimidated by the competition. They also should not be squeamish about creating their own resources and being their own supply chain (as long as they are sure about the underlying information). Having clear provenance of contents in the supply chain is a net positive as well. And when they face headwinds, they should go heavy on the self-encouragement and not engage in self-blame with the inevitable dead-ends and occasional flubs.

This what-if scenario was written in an open-ended way with any number of decisions being potentially correct for the project but with basic fixed requirements for legality, accessibility, and so on. This aligns with reality in which a number of potential solutions would work to meet the design needs of the learning resource. Often it does take working a design to see where the challenges are and how to solve the respective design issues. Sticking with a challenging effort requires grit and working a problem *ad nauseam.*

This approach suggests some of the "best practices" in development.

8.5 Conclusion

Moving from a design to an instantiated developed object is no mean feat. As noted, the interpretation of the designs is important, and how that interpretation is then translated into something tangible is even more critical. After all, there are a number of assessments, decisions, technologies, and processes, that connect a design to its (defensible) expressed form. The $0 budget will result in constraints and will cause preferences towards the lower-cost options.

If planning an open-shared learning resource is "cheap talk," then actualizing the learning resources through development and sharing the work are "costly signaling." This is where an individual (or team) evidences the commitment and the skills to make something real. This is where real costs are incurred and real moneys spent. This phase requires effort and focus. As shown, the work itself is complex and demanding, and ultimately, very satisfying.

8.6 Reviews and Assignments

8.6.1 Main Points Review

- In some cases, building a learning object may be done with just the authoring tool and the subject matter expert's thinking and maybe some light notes. Sometimes, when the inspiration to create a work strikes, it is optimal to just start getting some contents down in recorded form. In other cases, when the learning is more complex, it may help to use any of a number of tools to help plan and structure the work before any effort is made towards creating the particular learning object or sequence.

  - In the cases of fast on-the-fly development, it may help to "version" the object, to maintain a sense of history about how the object evolved over time.

- Designing a learning object or sequence with draft documents can ensure that the evolving work is thought through and sequentially sound. These draft documents need to be thoroughly vetted and revised before production commences because production is costly.
- Designing learning sequences also benefits from a systematized and principled approach, to ensure that the sequence makes sense for learners developmentally, topically, and otherwise. Each of the components of the sequences should also be stand-alone as well because some learners will access the learning objects piecemeal.
- Downloadable files are augmentations to online learning and help extend the work. These may include notes, tip sheets, described processes/steps, and other approaches.
- A designed learning object is often created from design documents that help structure the work.

  - For example, a video may be backstopped by a script, a case study with case notes, a complex learning sequence by a decision tree, an audio lecture by an outline, an interview by a questions list, a timeline visualization by a timeline, and so on. Having access to the rough notes behind a learning object can be informative of the design and the intentionality behind the design.

- During the development of the learning objects and sequences, it helps to maintain a meta-awareness of the work in order to learn from this work phase.
- Project documentation is a critical part of the design of open-shared learning objects and sequences. Most commonly, this is to advance the design and development work, and it is for grant funding reportage. Less commonly, such documentation may be used for academic research.
- For some types of project documentation, it may be easier to capture the information during the work. This ensures that small details are captured, and it is helpful to have this captured especially on long developmental projects. Some of this work documentation may be built off of the event logging of various technology systems. In other cases, documenting the project work may be most effective and least intrusive post-development work. Often, this will require reviewing available files and other information sources. However, saving the documentation to the end of the project may mean some lossiness of information.
- Designer/developer signatures may be fairly unique to the person, his/her worldview (and sensibility), his/her way of approaching the learning domain, and his/her problem solving in the design and development space. His or her skill level with technologies may also inform the design and development. His or her aesthetics may be informative as well.

8.6.2 *Critical Thinking Questions*

Creativity and Practicality

- What are ways to balance unconstrained creativity and innovation and originality with the constraints of a particular creative form (like learning objects and learning sequences)?
  - What are ways to be inspired by creations and activities outside the topical learning domain?
- What are some effective ways to capture ephemeral ideas and thoughts in fixed ways that evoke the original concepts?

Ideas with Traction

- How do you know which ideas will have traction on a project? What criteria do you use to determine this? How do you avoid prematurely scotching ideas that may have traction?

Modalities for Design and Development

- What are the most comfortable modalities that you use to capture your ideas in fixed form: text, doodles and sketches, photos, screenshots, audio recordings, short videos, multimodal captures, or others? Why do you find particular modalities more useful than others? Which other modalities are you open to trying to capture concepts dynamically and at any time-of-inspiration?

Transitions from Designs to Development

- In terms of development, what sorts of design documents do you prefer, and why? What are some ways to enhance those design documents with additional information? Additional expressiveness? Other design features?
- What are some up sides to using raw digital materials created from scratch? What are some down sides to using raw digital materials created from scratch?
- What sorts of analog objects have you digitized for the creation of learning objects? What are some up sides to using raw analog objects for digitization? Down sides?
- What sorts of open-shared raw digital contents do you use for the creation of learning objects? How do you determine what is usable: provenance of the contents, reputation of the content creator, quality of the contents, proper metadata, licensure, and others? Which features are most important, and which are least important, and why?
  - Have you ever conducted a reverse image search to understand how an image has been used on the WWW and Internet? Would muddy ownership of an image be a deal breaker in terms of the use of the image?
  - Do you know of other ways to check provenance of other digital contents?
  - What are deal breakers for you in terms of the possible uses of other-created raw contents for the creation of a learning object or a learning sequence?

In terms of how you create learning objects, how easy or difficult is it to swap out a third-party created image or audio or video or other contents?

- In the development phase of an online learning object and/or sequence, a designer/developer often makes a lot of discoveries. What are some of these discoveries for you? How do you arrive at these discoveries? What are some ways to enhance your learning during the development phase?

Understanding the Hard Work

- What are some of the main challenges you encounter during the development phase of a learning object/learning sequence?
- When you apply a visual/textual/other style to your designed learning objects and sequences, how do you decide what style to go with? Do you use the pre-packaged color palettes and style templates of the respective software tools? What informs your style? Do you consider learner needs when applying style(s)? How consistent are your styles?
  - What is the role of branding in your applied styles?
- When you create a sequence of learning, what information informs your choices? Why?
- What sorts of downloadable files have you created, and why? What learner needs are met with downloadable files? How do you tend to structure downloadables? What file formats do you tend to use? Do you monitor downloads to better understand usage through usage statistics?

Documenting Work

- What are the most common forms of work documentation do you create? To what purposes? (How readable and interpretable are your notes? Why? What are some ways to improve the readability of your notes?)
- What are the most effective methods for collecting work documentation, and why?
- If you have worked on grant-funded projects and created documentation for grant applications, grant reports, and other elements, what have those experiences been like? What are some challenges in creating documentation about work for grant funders? What are some challenges that stem from having regular fact-based check-ins?
- Have you ever used work documentation for academic research? Academic publishing? How does this context and this audience affect the requirements for work documentation? What are the standards for including work documentation?

Designer/Developer Signatures

- For many designer/developers, their "signature" is an unplanned byproduct of how they think in the world, how they approach the topical domain, their facility with technologies, and their aesthetics. It is not something that they consciously build. If you were to consciously evolve your own signature through your design and development work, what would that signature be? What adjectives would you want to have applied to your signature? How distinctive would your signature be, and why? Do you think signatures are changeable, or are they organically evolved from the individual?

- How do signatures of team members change in a group design and a group development context? How are different sensibilities integrated, and why? What are effective processes to enable a variety of inputs for group projects?

8.7 Assignments

Directions The Assignments are divided into two sections, Basic and Advanced. The Basic section is for those who may not have much instructional design experience or background in the area of creating instructional contents for open sharing. As such, these are set up to familiarize them with the chapter-related knowledge, skills, and abilities. The Advanced section is for those who already have some knowledge of this general space and who may benefit from more challenging work.

In a formal learning context, these assignments would benefit from expert feedback and further applications of the learning contents. In a nonformal or informal learning context, including self-directed learning, these assignments would benefit from both reflection and practice. These assignments are built to be extensible, to have elements added to benefit the learners. They are designed to be assigned selectively and not in full. The setup of this textbook is as a work sequence, and similarly, the assignments may be set up as tasks to be completed by the learner in a sequential way…that takes them through the fairly complete and sequential *open-shared learning design* → *development* → *test* → *revision* → *launch* → *post-launch* process.

8.7.1 Basic

Assignment 8.1: Content Development: Available Open-Source Contents To avoid "reinventing the wheel," it makes sense to conduct an environmental scan to see what extant raw materials and other contents may be available for developing share-alike online learning. To this end, conduct an environmental scan to identify sources of openly-shared and public domain contents that may be useful for a particular target instructional design project.

Assignment 8.2: Content Development: Scoping Out the Competition If there is an attention economy in which content creators are competing with each other for the attention of a general public, it may be helpful to have a sense of who the competition is and what sorts of contents they are sharing. To this end, conduct a review of the competing contents for the open-shared learning object or content that you are creating.

Assignment 8.3: Downloadables One way to enhance the experience of online learning is to offer contents that learners may download for later reference, for memory refreshing, for protecting learning and newly acquired skills against decay, and others. What are some possible useful downloadables that you might create to ensure that those who use your learning resource benefit from it. Why? What are some contents that would be important to know and remember but which may not be easily captured in downloadables?

Assignment 8.4: Lead-Up Module For more complex learning sequences and courses, learners who approach the learning are expected to have prior knowledge, skills, and abilities. Oftentimes, to enable a more fair start to a learning sequence, lead-up or priming modules are created. These may help learners refresh their memories and understand some of what may be in store in the forthcoming learning. Consider what learners are expected to know before they encounter your particular learning object or course or online learning sequence. If you were to create some lead-up contents, what would they include? How would you design a lead-up module to help learners acclimate to the forthcoming topic and learning?

Assignment 8.5: Content Sequencing Select a topic about which you have expertise. Consider some aspect of learning that you could create an open-shared learning object about. Conceptualize a portion of learning, and break that learning out into some manageable units of learning. (Remember that you're an expert teaching new learners.) Conceptualize a sequence that you could create. Look closely at the sequence and consider why the materials may be addressed this way. Consider alternate sequencing as well. Consider how you would pace the learning in the sequence.

Assignment 8.6: Technology Tools and Content Development The available technologies for digital content developments—authoring tools, editing tools diagramming tools, screen capture software, video-recording software, and others—can affect the types of contents that may be created. Identify one tool that you use, and describe its affordances and limitations in depth. Consider how your skill in using that tool affects what you can create.

8.7.2 Advanced

Assignment 8.7: Metadata Practice Identify an image set released for public use by the U.S. government (or any other government with quality contents). Identify the types of metadata used to label the imagery and how these contribute to understandings of the shared resources. Define the conventions of the metadata labeling and the respective data fields. If you were to add resources to that data collection, what fact-based data would you need, and where would you obtain the data? Or, use a collection of videos, or articles, or other objects, and indicate what sorts of metadata would be helpful for those resources.

Extra: Work on developing metadata for the learning objects you have created. Identify where the best sources of data will be for the respective data fields. Identify the optimal ways to present the metadata for clarity and for usability by others.

Assignment 8.8: Attracting Target Learner Attention and Meeting their Needs Part of the development work for learning objects requires some planning for target learners and some thinking about how to get learning objects to that target audience in terms of platforms and other means. Please write a short paper about how these considerations may affect the development of the particular learning objects/learning sequences. What are some ways to consider target learner needs, especially as these evolve and more is known about the respective learners?

Assignment 8.9: Assessments Assessments for open-shared learning objects tend to be fairly simple, are only sometimes recorded, and sometimes result in feedback to learners. These are also usually formative assessments even if summative assessments may occasionally be included. Select a learning object, and create a simple formative assessment to go along with that learning object. Assess the assessment for its efficacy for teaching and learning. Revise and refine it to improve the work.

Assignment 8.10: Examples Examples are important aspects of learning because they fill in gaps of understanding of ideas and abstractions by illustration. Examples serve as instances of concepts, and they help clarify these concepts and to add dimensionality to them. The creation of examples may draw from hypotheticals and models and concepts, as well as real-world example sets. How the examples are set up and described is important to the learning. Identify a concept that will benefit from illustration, and "source" half a dozen examples from models as well as from real-life. Examine each example, and decide how to frame them for learners. Decide what facts to include and which ones not to. Identify which of these examples may be most effective for the particular learning and what sequence they may be presented in for the highest levels of learning efficacy. Also, consider counterfactuals and what these may show about the particular topic.

Assignment 8.11: Multiple Approaches to Learning Objective(s) For any learning objective or set of related learning objectives, there are a number of ways to create the learning. Create multiple instantiations of a learning objective or a set of learning objectives, and then evaluate which one works best for a particular context and why. (This is a time- and effort-costly approach as an assignment, and it is not often done in a professional context. However, it is useful in helping readers see how various approaches focus on different aspects of a topic and how various learning objects are more effective for some audiences than others.)

Assignment 8.12: Style Variations for Learning Objects and Learning Sequences The efficacy of a learning object or learning sequence may be affected, in part, by the variations in presentation and style. The "look and feel" of a work may be appealing and attractive, or it may be the converse. Choose a half-dozen learning objects that are in the world, and describe the style of the objects. Use clear examples, and articulate the design features with as much clarity as possible. Do these mostly use pre-made style overlays and color palettes, or are there unique and customized details?

Assignment 8.13: Designer/Developer Signatures Identify a particular author of open-shared learning resources, such as those on a MOOC, hosted on a website, shared on a social media platform, or in a digital learning object repository. Capture multiple examples of this person's work, and write a description of his/her signature. What makes him/her unique in his/her approach to the topic? How personality-forward is he or she? How distinctive is this signature? Is there an identifying "tell"? How predictive is this "tell"?

Assignment 8.14: Your Own Designer/Developer "Signature" Collect a body of your own work in the learning space. (If you have a sufficient body of work, you can limit this to the learning resources in the open-shared learning space.) Analyze this for a "signature," or a distinctive authorship. Write your observations down. Ask a professional in the space to evaluate your works for a signature. Compare the two versions of senses of a signature, and identify how these are different (Fig. 8.8).

1. Collect created learning objects and resources created by oneself (or open-shared ones only if those are available)
2. Analyze the learning resources for signature. Write up the analysis
3. Have another professional also evaluate the works for signature. Request that they write up the analysis
4. Contrast the two evaluations. What are the differences? Why?
5. Create a Venn diagram to see what the shared insights may be

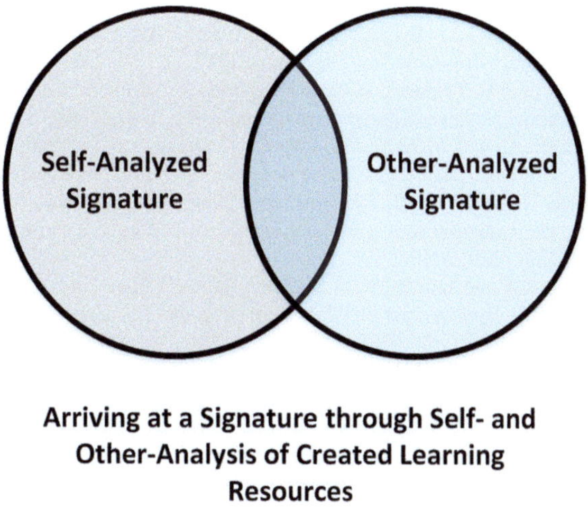

Fig. 8.8 Arriving at a signature through self- and other-analysis of created learning resources

Key Terms and Definitions

Authoring tool The software used to create digital contents

Data collection The collating of relevant information and data

Data visualizations The expression of concepts and data in image format

Deliverable The finalized digital contents to be launched or distributed to the general public

Digital contents Any of a number of digital format files (expressed as images, text, audio, video, and others; multimedia slideshows, games, simulations, and learning objects; others

Digital learning object (DLO) A digital file or aggregation of files and functionalities to enable the acquisition of knowledge, skills, and abilities

Downloadable A digital file that may be downloaded (and often printed)

Online learning sequence The designed (and/or actual) experiential learning sequence for learners

Proof of concept Evidence that shows that a design is feasible, usually applied to new inventions that are shown to work by research in a lab or in the field

Short course A formal or informal online learning sequence of limited duration (usually an hour or two)

Tranclusion Including parts of one document to another through hypertext pointing (such as by automated or manual means)

References

Falkovych K, and Nack F. Context aware guidance for multimedia authoring: Harmonizing domain and discourse knowledge. *Multimedia Systems* 11: 226 – 235, 2006.

Hirzalla N, Falchuk B, and Karmouch A. A temporal model for interactive multimedia scenarios. *IEEE Multimedia* 2: 24 – 31, 1995.

Holder D. Instructional design strategy for achieving alignment: Which comes first, activities or assessments? E-Learning Industry.com. https://elearningindustry.com/instructional-design-strategy-for-achieving-alignment. 2013.

Kaskalis TH, Tzidamis TD, and Margaritis K. Multimedia authoring tools: The quest for an educational package. *Educational Technology & Society* 10: 135 – 162, 2007.

Locatis C, and Al-Nuaim H. Interactive technology and authoring tools: A historical review and analysis. *Educational Technology Research and Development* 47: 63 – 75, 1999.

Paechter M, Maier B, and Macher D. Students' expectations of, and experiences in e-learning: Their relation to learning achievements and course satisfaction. *Computers & Education* 54: 222 – 229, 2010.

Rowe LA and Jain R. ACM SIGMM Retreat Report on future directions in multimedia research. *ACM Transactions on Multimedia Computing, Communications and Applications* 1: 3 – 13, 2005.

Schank RC, Korcuska M, and Jona M. Multimedia applications for education and training: Revolution or red herring? *ACM Computing Surveys* 27: 633 – 635, 1995.

Schoonenboom J. Using an adapted, task-level technology acceptance model to explain why instructors in higher education intend to use some learning management system tools more than others. *Computers & Education* 71: 247 – 256, 2014.

Wang J, Doll WJ, Deng X, Park, K, and Yang MG. The impact of faculty perceived reconfigurability of learning management systems on effective teaching practices. *Computers & Education* 61: 146 – 157, 2013.

Additional Reading Section

Angelo TA, and Cross KP. *Classroom Assessment Techniques: A Handbook for College Teachers.* 2nd Editioin. San Francisco: Jossey-Bass Publishers. 1993.

Clark RC, and Mayer R.E. *E-Learning and the Science of Instruction.* Hoboken: Wiley. 2016.

Chapter 9
Alpha Testing, Beta Testing, and Customized Testing

Abstract Once some digital learning contents have been created and provisionally "finalized," these are ready to be put through more formal review and revision. This chapter deals with development-based assessments, commonly termed "Alpha Testing, Beta Testing, and Customized Testing." These include internal and external assessments. The typical work of the in-house alpha (α) test involves various elements, including legal requirements, ethical requirements, pedagogical design, accessibility, usability, informational accuracy, technological functionalities, device playability, language(s) clarity, metadata accuracy and completeness, research and usage monitoring, branding, and others. The work of the beta (β) test, which involves the bringing in of outside representative target users, involves testing for user interactivity, user experiential learning, user feedback for learning, social aspects in support of learning, and others. This chapter also addresses other types of customized tests that may be written for particular unique features of specific learning resources, based on their designs, versioning, and adaptations, and other aspects. After the testing, revisions are made to the learning resources albeit not usually a full redesign or retrofitting (based on expense). If anything, unless fundamental errors were made, the revisions and edits will be piecemeal and at the margins. Finally, there is a section on how to assess the practical efficacy of the respective alpha, beta, and customized tests.

Keywords Alpha testing · Beta testing · Customized testing · Pilot testing (pretesting) · Meta-assessment

> The life-and-death rule was check it out before calling it in.
> –Seymour M. Hersh, *Reporter: A Memoir* (2018, p. 8)

> Testing leads to failure, and failure leads to understanding.
> –Matthew Gionta, 2005, in David H. Freedman's "Entrepreneur of the Year" featuring Burt Rutan in *Inc.* (https://www.inc.com/magazine/20050101/eoty-rutan.html)

S. Hai-Jew, *Designing Instruction For Open Sharing*,
https://doi.org/10.1007/978-3-030-02713-1_9

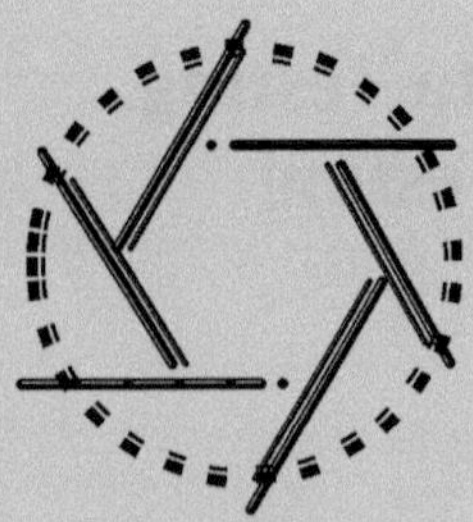

Opening Scenario

Opening Scenario: Testing for Function and Quality and Learner Fit?
You have drafted the online learning object with all the elements you think are required. Now, it is important to check it for quality, to ensure that it will meet requirements before it is released on the Web for broad use. The so-called "alpha (α) testing" involves first-stage in-team testing of the learning resources for adherence to relevant laws, professional ethics, content accuracy, pedagogical design, technological functionalities, and other critical aspects. Generally, the "beta (β) testing" involves bringing in testers from outside of the organizers who stand in for the potential learners of the general public to elicit their experiences with the learning object, to ensure that the work may be accepted by the learners. These processes are about first getting the basics right and then adding further touches to make the object more usable. Because learning objects have a lot of moving parts, it is often important to have structured and systematized ways to assess learning objects to ensure that nothing is missed.

Before a learning object or sequence is shared, it goes through several checks as part of the development, termed alpha and beta testing.

Some Early Questions to Consider
What tests would you use to ensure that all the information included in the learning object are as accurate as possible, in the present moment?

What tests would you use to ensure that the functionality of the learning object is effective?

What sorts of checklists or rubrics would you use to ensure that your learning objects meet legal standards? (For intellectual property? For publication? For accessibility? For other requirements?) For technological functionality? For learning value? For informational accuracy? For a whole range of standards? (alpha testing)

What sorts of tests would you use to understand how well learners accept your online e-learning object? The designed user interface? The usability of the learning resources? And how much learning they can actually achieve? How would you measure the achieved learning? (beta testing)

What sorts of customized tests would you create for particular learning objects and learning sequences? For what reasons?

Learning Objectives
Learners will…

Why Testing of Learning Objects/Sequences?

- Consider some practical reasons to conduct testing of online learning objects and sequences
- Research for and list some automated tests for online learning objects and sequences
- Research for and list some manual tests for online learning objects and sequences
- Consider some methods to control for costs and increase time and other efficiencies with testing learning objects
- Think about when alpha-, beta-, and customized tests should be created (prior to the design and development? after the design and development?) and whether or not they should be used to guide the design and development work

Alpha (α) Testing

- Define the elements of an in-house "alpha test," which should include the following: legal requirements, ethical requirements, learning data and contents, pedagogical design, usability design, technological functions, functioning on various devices, language, metadata, research and usage monitoring, branding, and others
- Set objective and observable standards for the decision making for accepting or rejecting draft designs and prototypes (as well as finished objects)
- Apply the standards to the built digital objects to evaluate them, and return a detailed evaluation
- Revise and edit the learning designs, and offer clear rationales for the decision making
- Apply a level of polish to the learning objects, courses, and sequences

Beta (β) Testing

- Define the elements of a public-inclusive "beta test," to understand how a learning resource is received by learners and to understand how to increase their learning efficacy and learning experiences
  - based on user-computer interactivity, user experiential learning, user received feedback for learning, harnessing of sociality in support of learning, and learning value
  - based on identifying target learner groups (and how to access representative individuals and groups for the beta testing)
- Apply the learning from users to revise the digital learning objects and digital learning sequences

Other Customized Testing

- Define additional required customized testing for the particular digital learning objects/sequences/resources, which may be based on a personality frame, unique features, versioning and adaptations, and other aspects

- Design these tests and subtests
- Apply these tests to some or all of the designed and developed digital learning objects and digital learning sequences

Assessing the Assessments

- Create some quality criteria for the respective alpha, beta, and other customized tests
- Assess the test instruments for their insightfulness and contribution to the project

9.1 Introduction

The building of learning resources for open sharing involves a fair amount of complexity. Learning objectives and target learning audiences are used to inform the design and development work. There are a large number of sources of information, both primary and secondary. There are underlying design files, such as storyboards and scripts and slideshow drafts. In many cases, learning object prototypes are created, and these are often evolved into finalized versions of learning resources (built with various components like imagery, audio, video, and other contents). There are many "moving parts." For instructional designers and developers, they may have some defined work processes to ensure quality at each phase. There may be vetting at every phase to ensure that the choices made are the optimal ones, given the known information and the available resources.

As a matter of course, draft learning contents also require some level of testing before anything is published to the public. A simple test may be based on editorial rigor, grammar, and spelling, and basic technological functions. More formal assessments may involve alpha testing for a range of features: legal requirements, ethical requirements, learning data and contents, pedagogical design, technological functions, functioning on various devices, language, metadata, research and usage monitoring, branding, and others. Alpha (α) tests are conducted in order to refine learning objects to a polished state. Next comes beta (β) testing, which involves bringing in people from outside to serve as beta testers to better understand learner needs, their learning experiences, their sense of the user interfaces, and other aspects. After the feedback from beta testing is collected, revisions and updates are made. If further testing is needed due to unique aspects of the learning object, then that is done through customized testing, and further refinements are made, and then the learning resources are released to the public. The general approach is to iterate phase-through-phase until no mistakes are found, within the time and human resources limits of the project. The human mind has limits to how much may be focused on at a time, and having a particular objective for each pass-through enhances the work. (For some digital learning objects, automated tested may be conducted using automated programs. Some programs are built into particular platforms. They are used to assess accessibility, for example. That said, the automated tests are not commonly used, and most are applied to very limited attributes currently.)

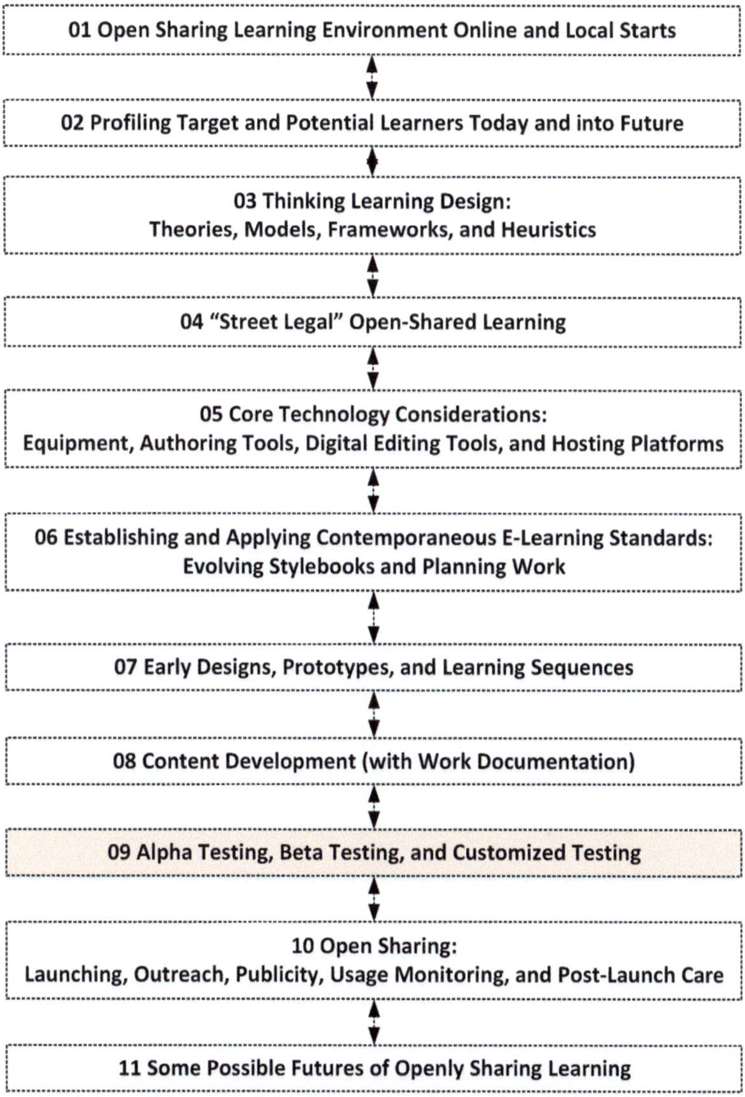

Fig. 9.1 Step 9 in the open-shared learning resource development sequence

This testing phase is scheduled after the initial contents are developed (Fig. 9.1).

Finally, the alpha, beta, and customized tests can be themselves evaluated for efficacy, comprehensiveness, and usefulness. Essentially, are they assessing the right things? Are they enabling quality in the learning resources? Are they practically useful? Do they effectively identify leads to further unscripted and un-preplanned testing?

9.2 Review of the Literature

In the academic research literature, there is not research about formalized tests for open-shared online learning resources in a general sense. In particular cases of particular learning designs, there may be testing described as part of the development process, but none of these have been captured and generalized to a range of contexts. There is no inherency in terms of what goes into an alpha, beta, or customized test. The basic guidelines are that an alpha test is done in-house and usually assesses standards guiding the design, and the beta testing is done with individuals from outside the organization and focuses on issues related to user adoption. Customized testing is even more generic and is a catch-all approach.

Some early references to alpha testing in the academic literature describes preliminary testing to get a software product to a state that it can be tested outside (Noack 2000). Often, these first runs are done by the development team or within the organization. Beta testing, which follows, involves the engagement of individuals who represent the target users or constituents. The members of focus groups are carefully recruited to address issues of interest, and these groups need to be inclusive of the respective constituencies (Krueger and Casey 2009, p. 63). These focus groups are "interviewed" through a variety of activities and elicitations. In some cases, beta testing may "be intertwined with the later stages of alpha testing" (Johnson and Schleyer 2003, p. 1216). Other forms of evaluation, such as in the interactive multimedia design and production processes, involve a "continuous evaluation and revision approach" (Liu et al. 1998, p. 260), in lieu of discrete processes. The major phases in content creation may be described as the following: "funding, planning, designing, production, testing, (and) marketing" (Liu et al. 1998, p. 260), often practiced in a recursive semi-linear sequence.

9.3 Alpha Testing, Beta Testing, and Customized Testing

The first learning object is a slideshow, and it purports to offer privy insights on a technological issue of the day. The authorship is set up as a group of hard-nosed investors, and they introduce their positionality to the topic early on. In the background is a stock image of the stars as a stand-in for the idea of promise and the future. Overlaid over this background are screenshots of text (not screen readable) and data snippets, interpreted in short phrases. Initially, it is unclear where the data come from. Some of the images have some visual skew and seem stretched, with inaccurate aspect ratios. Logos and icons have been cut and pasted in as well. The font types and sizes are variant. In terms of data visualizations, there are bar charts and treemap diagrams. In the treemap diagram, the text labels on the shape vary in size but not in correct relationship with the sizes of the frequency-sized rectangles (which breaks data visualization conventions). Later on, there are finer details about the data. While the canvas size of the slides are the same, there are differing amounts of data. At full screen, the numbers and text are readable without pixelation. An early impression of the superficiality of summary data and the sense of sell resolves to a more serious back-end and the clearer credibility of the information source, which has conducted the primary research as a part of their business and does have unique insights to share. The slides themselves are unnumbered, so referencing specific contents may be difficult. While the source checks out, the presentation has given more of a sense of amateurism and fast design.

Another learning resource is a video by a company that produces nature films for television. The macro-videography (the videotaping of small objects to enable their viewing at large sizes) shows various insects in life-and-death encounters in the wild, demonstrations of wildlife "red in tooth and claw." The information is portrayed in narrative format with two entomologists describing various physical aspects of the insects. The insects are imbued with personalities. There are 3D visualizations of each of the insects, glowing against a black background, and these visuals show these animals' physical structures built for defense and offense. There are slow motion sequences that demonstrate how insect-on-insect attacks may occur. Each encounter is set up as a dramatized encounter between animals in a real-life cage fight. The sound design is vivid, with the insects growling and snarling, and when one insect eats another, there are some fairly graphic chewing sounds overlaid on the video. Music is employed to emphasize certain points. Occasionally, there are digital re-enactments of insect locomotion or other features of insect form and function. From a viewer sense, the videography would suggest painstaking work in the field. When insects are referred to, they are referred to by their colloquial names and not their full formal ones. The narration is breathless and dramatic, and these encounters involve nothing less than combat, with survival on the line. The framing of the insect encounters read like fictionalized dramatizations.

Another learning resource is a podcast focused on the work of spies in various contexts: government, military, corporate, sports, and others. This is an extension of educational services for a physical museum based in the capital of the U.S. These audio podcasts, which sometimes are released with video versions, include presentations, talks, interviews, panel discussions, and other approaches. While a majority of the topics are fact-based, a few are of popular culture (movies, fictional books, and others). A common theme that runs through these presentations are that these are insiders sharing their insights, and the hosts are informed and do their homework before the encounters with the guests. The personalities of the respective participating individuals often come through, and there is a sense of unvarnished personhood behind the encounters. There are references to a part of the audience as young people who may be interested in pursuing a place in the intelligence community. In terms of political issues of the day, each participant acknowledges his/her stance, and controversial positions are not shied away from. A core value of fact-based reasoning seems to run through the audio podcasts. The podcasts are to educate and inform the public, to raise the profile of the museum, to drive traffic to the physical museum, and to encourage job applicants to consider working in the IC.

Another source is an open-source e-book, which is now in Version 2. There is a published version at a nominal cost to cover the paper and ink and then a free downloadable .pdf version. This book is about a version control system in popular use among a wide number of developers around the world. The book is co-authored by two super users, who have nuanced understandings of the technological func-

tions. Theirs is a welcoming and inclusive tone, with writing in the first-person point-of-view. They pace the book slowly, and they use simple two-dimensional imagery to communicate ideas. They set the record straight about the history of the technology. They take open-source as a critical informing value, which is a core aspect of the featured software and of the open-source book. The co-authors acknowledge readers who have provided the authors with errata reports by thanking them and listing their names to give them credit. It seems that small updates have been made along the way. The book has over 500 pp.

The next open-shared learning resource is an "island" in a virtual immersive world. This space is advertised as an artificial intelligence (AI) space, and indeed, there are humanoid conversation 'bots that approach the human-embodied digital avatars in this world. They are chat bots that will engage in text-based conversations with the visiting humans. Some look like characters from "Star Wars." The physical spaces enable human-embodied digital avatars to interact with each other. The automated characters move around particular regions only though, and, none of them track with the live humans that interact with them. There are no automated agents for sale here. The virtual space feels more like an experimental one, with a coder behind the respective avatars trying out his or her coding skills.

Another learning object is a long-form slideshow. Early on, the author is clear that he is telling a story about a coder who is using some contemporary codes and methods. A pattern emerges early on varying between screenshots of computer code and depictions of a line drawing of an individual who has bubble thoughts and emotional expressions. This character is a stick figure that is generally non-descript but reads male. This individual represents both the author and the potential audience. It is unclear where the images came from, and a reverse image search shows that there are 2165 of the same images already on the Internet (based on a trawl of 29.6 billion images). The user is not the owner of the images, and the sharing of these images may contravene copyright. The story told is about the character's challenge in facing a code issue and experiencing frustration and lost time…and discovering a solution that addresses the issue in a helpful way. The backgrounds vary from a white to a black background, and the font colors change depending. The font set is consistent, and the sizes are consistent. For a slide deck with over 150 slides, there is no table of contents for the slides, and there are no slide pagination numbers, but the slideshow player does include a slide numbering at the bottom. The humor helps bring in readers with the sense that the author empathizes with them about code issues. A third of the way into the slide deck, the author suggests that most coders mal-attribute the problem, and he suggests a different way to approach the issue. The story turns out to be a problem-solution wrapped inside the narrative. Once the solution is realized, the slides suddenly have cleaner layout. There is a black-and-white photo of the presenter, book covers of books he has written, and an increasing sense of his credibility based on track record. There is a URL to access his slides. This looks like self-promotion and book-selling in the guise of problem-solving for the general public. (Note: There was no #ad for "advertisement" or #spon for "sponsored message" in sight.) Open-shared learning resources may be understood as promotion of the author's interests balanced against consideration of the public interest, and there is a lot of tendency towards self-interests.

The above real-world "analyses" are described anecdotally and informally. However, they collectively make an important point: When a digital learning resource is finalized to the public, it is a kind of moment-of-truth. The learning resources embody a culmination of intentionality and planning, design and development skills, and technological resources. From a casual evaluation angle, it is easy to make inferences about the following (based on initial impressions) (Tier 3):

- The apparent original intentions in the design (and whether the goal is achieved or over-reach occurred)
- The target (and potential) learning audience

Essentially, the above two bullet points involve a light assessment: What informational contents are being shared, in what mediums, why, and who is the original communicator addressing and to what apparent ends?

A more formal and esoteric assessment (Tier 2) may bring out the following:

- The (un)original information source(s)
- The apparent filtering and selectivity in the inclusion of particular information (and the information left out or not included)
- The likely (inferred) learning design (if any)
- The development inputs
- The likely technologies used
- The general learning value (the explanatory power, the clarity, the designed learning), and other aspects

The above points elaborate on the initial assessment and result in more solid evidentiary supports. Targeted expert assessments (Tier 1) may draw out even more complex insights, including the following:

- The adherence to applicable laws (intellectual property, media, privacy, and others)
- The legal user accessibility of the learning resources
- More sophisticated insights about the likely general and applied research behind the learning resources, and
- An identifiable signature or style of the designer/developer.

At each additional level of analysis, the analyst has to bring more sophisticated knowledge to the task.

Tier 3 is about initial impressions, and these inferences are not directly tested. Tier 2 is more objectively evidence-based and explores the sourcing and learning design and development. Tier 1 is also evidence-based and includes analysis of legality and legal accessibility, research, and author hand/style (Fig. 9.2). Also, for Tiers 2 and 1, there may be application of analytical technologies. For example, various testing technologies may be applied to assess learner achievements from the uses of the learning objects. Or, for Tier 1 analysis, images used in learning resources may be run through reverse image searches to track ownership and online usage and image ownership. Stock images are fairly easily identified to the commercial source. Open-source images are fairly easily identified as such. Original imagery without a record of online usage may be much less easy to identify to an actual source, but this

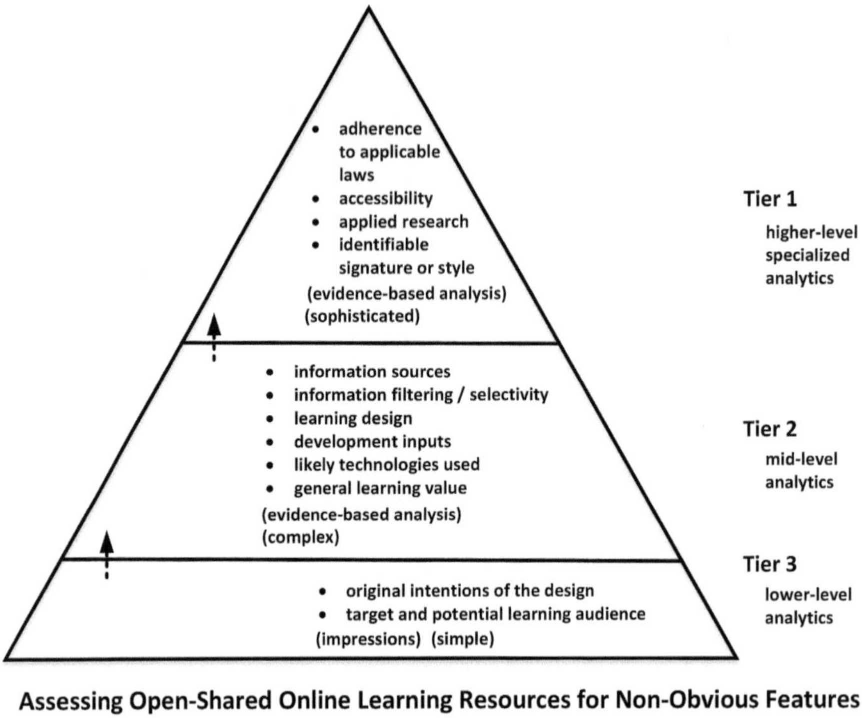

Fig. 9.2 Assessing open-shared open learning resources for non-obvious features

would depend on how forthcoming and responsive people are who host the source websites or who post contents to the particular sites.

There are clearly heightened levels of sophistication moving from Tier 3 to Tier 1. For most learners who use online learning resources, they may not pursue this depth of analysis, not even as Tier 3. However, for those who build learning objects, or those who aspire to contribute some original learning resources to this space, it helps to be able to critique others' works…in order to improve critiquing skills on one's own work. An application of the three-tiers of analysis to learning resources by different designers and developers will not necessarily result in convergence to agreement. The thin surfaces of learning resources may result only in lightly provisional assertions, and without further investigations, the insights themselves may not be provable. However, such analyses may offer leads for further exploration. Few if any works will be "perfect" and check every box. However, understanding where there are shortcomings in shared online learning may be informative of the field and those contributing works to it.

As an instructional designer for the past dozen years and with decades of work in higher education prior, I have rarely found learning objects, sequences, courses, and resources that fit the high standards of the prior list. Intended learners themselves may be murky or poorly defined. In terms of Tier 2, the original information sources may be from third-party shared contents (in mash-ups), and the learning designs may not be explicitly clear. A "perfect" exemplar is a rarity, particularly in terms of adherence to applicable laws and accessibility builds. Part of the challenge comes from the available technologies, which contribute to the state of the art.

Task #1: Searching for the Learning Object Unicorn
Explore a dozen self-selected available learning resources online, and identify the one that you see as having the highest quality among them. Analyze that object or sequence for the prior listed factors, and write up your findings. Does the work meet a basic minimum threshold of having learning value and being "street legal"? Why or why not? Why is an object that meets all basic requirements a "unicorn" (at least from this author's perspective)?

Don't Be that Person Who... So to use an Internet meme, knowing the strengths and weaknesses of some of the open-shared learning resources, it is important not to be that person who puts out learning resources that are poor quality, self-serving, self-promoting, unclear, non-functioning, and/or ineffectual. For personal well-being, definitely do not be the person who releases learning objects to the public space that do not meet legal standards.

A trawl through some publicly available opens-shared learning objects regularly show misstatements of fact, non-functional technological functionalities, unoriginal contents, unaligned imagery selections, poor writing, inaccessible aspects (lack of captions, lack of alt text, and others), broken links, misspellings, and other challenges. The state of many shared learning objects may be a product of the free-wheeling mash-up culture and the rush to publish from social media culture (think-tweet, feel-share, think-act). Many who create such objects and sequences may go through only rudimentary learning design or skip that step altogether. For those who train in the formal creation of learning objects, they may at least hesitate before releasing the work and conduct some lightweight proofing, but they, too, sometimes fall into the trap of offering something both premature and incomplete. There is room for improvement in terms of the learning resources that are shared openly. One way to work towards quality is to formalize a thorough testing and revision/editing cycle, in which the testing informs the revision/editing work.

With so many "moving parts" to learning resources, and the very human limits of individuals and teams, and complex harnessed technologies, going through alpha, beta, and/or customized testing before publication is advised. One simple way to think about these assessments is as a pre-launch set and a post-launch set. Pre-launch assessments (alpha, beta, and some customized tests) inform what needs to be revised before the learning resource goes live; post-launch assessments (some customized tests) may inform on the overall quality of the learning resource (with a resulting validation or invalidation), and on research and future designs. Research should inform work processes for increased learning resource quality, so the *modus operandi* of designers and developers may be changed based on empirical information. The first set of assessments are formative ones, and the latter set are summative ones (Fig. 9.3). These are not pro forma assessments but should lead to revisions and updates and some thought-through actions, after the initial feedback and comments are vetted. This does not mean that there should be high reactance as a response to one comment, but there should be some constructive responses. Once these become regular practice, they become much easier to conduct to inform follow-on revisions. Note that some of the two-headed arrows indicate recursiveness in this process, based on the project needs.

In general, an alpha (α) test refers to an in-house assessment that may address a range of basic issues: legal requirements, learning data and contents, pedagogical design, technological functions, functioning on various devices, language, metadata, research and usage monitoring, branding, and others. For testing draft trainings, after the alpha test-informed changes are made, the learning contents are assessed with real-world learners:

> The final procedure of formative evaluation that brings closure to the training development process is the pilot test. Pilot testing is the process of assessing instructional materials with end users in the actual learning environment, prior to the implementation of the instruction, and provides empirical support regarding the efficacy of the proposed instruction. Thus, subsequent decisions can be made from an informed position. (White and Branch 2001, p. 75)

This phase is described analogically to a "test drive," and these may be done in various social contexts: one-to-one, one-to-many, small groups, and others (White and Branch 2001, p. 76). Beta testing may also be done at a distance. A beta (β) test refers to testing contents with external users, and these may include aspects such as user interactivity, user experiential learning, user feedback for learning, social in support of learning, and others. The alpha and the beta are just the "a" and "b" equivalents from the Greek ("α" and "β"). The general features described in this paragraph are generally understood meanings of these respective tests, but teams may define these differently based on their testing needs.

Finally, beyond the classic alpha and beta testing, there can be various types of customized testing based on various features. One may be an original personality frame (the teacher as a personality), by style aspects, and by expressivity, if the

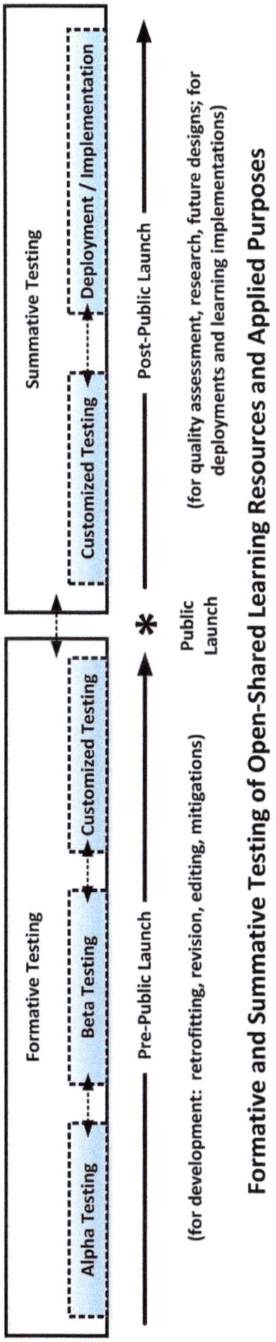

Fig. 9.3 Formative and summative testing of open-shared learning resources

teaching is achieved through a person (whether a real person or a fictionalized character). There may be unique features of a learning sequence. There may be various types of versioning and adaptations of the learning resources. These customized tests go beyond the alpha and beta tests by focusing on issues beyond legality and functionality and correctness (alpha testing) and beyond user experiences (beta tests). These customized tests may be done internally in the organization or external to the organization or in some combination. These customized tests may be predesigned a priori, or they may be exploratory (without pre-defined features for testing). More details will follow on each of these approaches. (These are not to be confused with A/B testing, which involves trial testing presentation variants in web analytics to see which ones people respond better to.)

Also, the "deployment" and "learning implementation" of the learning resource may be studied as part of the learning effectiveness of the resource as applied—in face-to-face (F2F), blended, and online learning contexts, with particular learning groups.

"Audience fidelity" is thought to increase as development teams move from the developer group (in alpha testing) to the public individuals (who work with the beta testers).

There is a preferred order of operations. An alpha test is conducted first to ensure that the learning resources are ready for outside yes, and a beta test follows to include external reviewers. If a design and development team are comfortable with attaining public feedback earlier, then the order may be changed up. However, the typical practice (and logic) is that α comes before β. An alpha test is conducted in-house, so that any aspect of it that is not ready for primetime is addressed. A more finished or refined object or sequence then may be assessed with external test groups using beta tests. If beta tests are run before the learning resources alpha test-informed clean-up, then they may need to be run again after the clean-up, which is repeated make-work. Also, if beta tests are run before some level of refinement is achieved, the respondents may misfocus on the alpha test contents and spend their energies on legalities, technological functionalities, language, and other aspects.

So, tests can run in any order, but logically, efficiencies would suggest an alpha test first and then a beta test sequence. Within those broad categories, there may be other preferences. For example, teams may have different preferred alpha testing sequences. For example, some may follow some sort of order of importance, with a focus on the most important to the least important, with the deal breakers addressed first. Legal considerations may trump branding, for example.

The first time quality controls are applied to open-shared learning contents is *not* at the point of the alpha test. The design and development work all contain quality control aspects (Fig. 9.3). As to what informs the quality, these come from a range of sources:

- Pedagogical designs
- Technological systems
- The legal ecosystem
- Language rules
- Domain systems
- Usability guidelines, and others.

In cases of funded learning resources, the funding agency will often have additional requirements spelled out in the authorizing documents. To over-simplify, and at the cost of sounding doctrinaire, there are guidelines that define quality, and anything less is off-true. To create quality, at minimum, a developer/designer or team needs to be aware of the quality standards, have the skills and will to create to quality, and have the resources and time to practically achieve these.

Practically speaking, the designer/developer or team members need to have a plan for what to do with the findings of the respective tests. Depending on the findings of the alpha test, the beta test, and the customized test(s), what will be revised and how? Design and development include stepwise processes, and it can be difficult to return to an early stage prior to development and prior to design. There are real limits to the revisions possible from the testing. For example, if content is found to be copyrighted and unusable, the follow-on choices may be to remove the contents and to use other contents in lieu of the offending ones. If a particular technology was adopted, the strengths and weaknesses of that technology are a given (with limited tradeoffs and limited accommodations). If one pedagogical theory or framework is challenged in the beta testing process, going back through the learning object and reframing aspects of the learning may have to be done (assuming that the originating team agrees with the different assessment…there is room for differences). What learners apparently need is a contested space. If there has been effort invested into designing learning characters and avatars, changing out respective features may be expensive. If a narrative designed for learning is seen to be ineffective or offensive, changing that core structure may involve a range of follow-on changes throughout the learning contents. Sweeping changes cannot generally be made with impunity. Added learning objectives will likely have implications throughout a learning resource, including learning outcomes, pedagogical methods, learning contents, assessments, look-and-feel, and so on. The lock-in occurs because of the sunk costs in the design and development, the learning curve in going to different technologies, and the effort to unwinding built work. Some aspects of a learning object may not be possible to update or to recreate. Designs should not be committed to in an early sense because of this very fixedness once the development process starts. In part, this is because the designer/developers assume certain design questions have been settled. If a learning object is part of a learning sequence and is integrated with other learning objects, the challenges of updates may reverberate throughout a sequence.

9.3.1 Part 1: Alpha (α) Testing

An important formative assessment is the alpha test. Alpha testing is considered a required step in the creation of learning contents because the designer/developers have to be sure that what was created reaches a basic threshold of quality. The issues addressed in an alpha test should generally be those defined early on in the project such as those defined in the project stylebook (and by authorizing documents such as from the grant funders). They may include legal requirements, ethical requirements, learning contents, pedagogical design, usability design, technological functionality, device functionality, language, metadata, research and usage monitoring, and branding, among others. There are some must-achieves, such as the legal requirements, learning contents, technological functionalities, and language values. If any of the prior fall short, they may be "showstoppers" (serious problems) that end the project. Knowing when to scuttle a work is important. There are other issues that may be less defined and less definable (such as pedagogical designs, which are open to interpretation and which may be informed by a wide range of research and theories/frameworks). In some cases, the issue may be less critical depending on individual or team objectives. For example, "branding" may be less of an issue for some individuals and teams. (Each designer/developer has a signature and a public reputation, which is part of an individual "brand," too. That reputation should be of some importance to create, express, and ultimately protect. A designer/developer needs to be a known quantity to the public in order to build trust and followership.)

Once the alpha testing is completed, varying levels of work may follow. A major retrofitting may involve work that affects broad pieces and parts of the project. Lesser and more common works may involve recoding, revisions, and basic editing. It is important to note that proofing and updates should be done by trained professionals to particular defined standards; otherwise, amateur proofers may introduce their own errors in the process. In the testing stage, it helps for members to approach the work in an emotional "cold state," so they can focus on details and facts.

Another alpha testing approach may involve evaluations by panels of experts, who can speak to a range of issues. Ideally, experts would be brought in sufficiently early before a work has gone into fixed form. For example, if errors are baked into a simulation or a video, corrections may be difficult or costly to address. (That said, animation artworks may be difficult to change, but the coding itself for the actions may not. Also, corrective notes may be added to a video.) Content experts may identify areas where learners may misunderstand contents, where naïve learners may stumble in the learning, where there are gaps in the learning sequence; they may see better ways to present and package learning contents. They may know of other human- and inanimate resources for uses in the learning, and they may have the professional connections to make the right introductions. They may have solid and actionable ideas about how to expand the learning resources. They may be able to identify nuances in the assignment and assessment language. They may imbue the learning resources with a sense of their own passions for the field. These subject matter experts from outside of the project may provide different points of view and insights. For their contribution, these professionals may be credited for their evaluations. If they contribute more, they should be credited for that as well. (This is not to say that in academia or elsewhere that experts just make themselves available. Usually, whoever is creating the learning resources will need some major connections and social capital to make this happen.)

It is never a good idea to go straight to release unless the hosting site enables constant updating while enabling the maintenance of the original URL…and the design/development team have the wherewithal and resources to conduct an alpha test shortly after the upload, with corrections soon to follow. This is a rolling release, with iterations of the resource (v. 1, 1.1, etc.); however, the first version should be as solid as possible, and follow-on changes should not be fundamentally different (generally speaking). A logical argument for an infused quality-testing approach during the entire design and development process is that some interventions may only be done during these work phases, and a post-development alpha and beta test will not surface particular mistakes such as those of factual errors necessarily or those of an improperly captured media release, and so on.

Task #2: Alpha Testing Design

Based on the needs of your particular instructional design and development project, create a basic alpha test that you think will meet your needs.

Use that alpha test on the learning resource you have created.

For extra work, add an "inclusivity design" add-on to ensure that all learners in a potential learner population are included in the learning through depictions of individuals in the learning contents. Add analysis of all the media and the top-level as well as the subliminal messaging.

9.3.2 Part 2: Beta (β) Testing

Once the learning resources have been revised and polished after the alpha testing, they may be ready for primetime (public release). For simpler learning resources, these are mostly released to the public, for learners to respond as they will.

For better-funded and more complex projects, a beta test may follow. In general, a beta test involves testing with public individuals from outside the development team (and its organization), in order to better understand potential user receptivity to the resources. This testing is different because it harnesses the different perspectives from people in different positions relationally to the learning objects. The learners have fresh eyes. Those who design and develop learning contents have been working with content experts for a period of time, and they have some familiarity with the topic. Learners from outside the design/development team may have differing levels of expertise and points-of-view. In the same way that experts may forget what a naïve point of view (POV) looks like in relation to a learning topic or skill, designers and developers may not understand a naïve learner sensibility. Reaching out to potential users may enable a refreshing of that perspective, which may better inform the learner design. Practically speaking, beta tests let designers/developers know what hurdles users may perceive in their use of the learning resources.

Those who have not experienced a peer review process of their work would do well to consider a few insights. One is that the invited beta testers are doing the designer/developers a favor by providing unanticipated insights. If the respondents come at the process with candor and no ulterior motives, their responses should be treated with plenty of respect and seriousness. It is often a fair assumption that critiques that are submitted during beta testing will likely be observed by users of the learning resources if they are not addressed in the development phase.

More specifically, beta tests may involve explorations of user-computer interactivity, user experiential learning, user received feedback for learning, the harnessing of sociality for learning, and the (perceived) learning value. In other words, do the users have an easy time engaging with the learning resource through the user interface? Are they able to navigate easily through the learning resources? Do the learning sequences make sense to them? Are they satisfied with the amount of and contents of the feedback from their own work (if relevant)? Do they find value in the social interactions related to the use of the learning resources? Is the actual learning clear and useful to them? In these field tests, there tend to be multiple assessment methods, and qualitative and quantitative and mixed methods approaches to capturing data. At core, such assessments are evidence-based.

Beta testing is critical for many projects because they enable an early sense of how the larger public may respond to a learning object, and these—if defined well—may suggest necessary revisions before anything is irretrievably released. Beta testing may be conducted in face-to-face (F2F), blended (combination of F2F and online), or wholly online means. Those conducting such tests may use a variety of approaches, such as focus groups, interviews, eye-tracking, system monitoring, and other techniques and tools. The conductors of beta tests may be individuals who represent particular target groups, or they may be the general public. Crowd-sourcing formalized tests of learning resources may be done through sites that enable micropayments for assessors or through other elicitations and means. In the same way that open-source software "generally means higher security and higher reliability" and more "robustness, clear flexibility and higher quality" than their closed counterparts (Dinevski 2008, p. 117), going open-source and broadly public in the social marketplace may enhance assessments of learning objects and sequences built for open sharing. Most evaluators are asked to sign non-disclosure agreements (NDAs) in order to take part. Some may want answers to particular design questions (top-down research question-based studies), and others may want general target user responses (discovery learning study).

In the same way that quality controls may be instantiated in the work processes (in support of the goals of alpha testing), pilot testing with the targeted potential end users may be done with drafts and prototypes during the design and development phases of the work (in support of the goals of beta testing). The participants in such beta tests have to be able to understand the draft designs and prototypes, however; for many people, such objects may not make sense or may not seem authentic. Their imaginations may not enable them to read into the draft objects in a clear way. Still, such preliminary engagements may help inform user-centered designs.

Task #3: Beta Testing Design

There are formalized methods for conducting beta testing, but these are usually specific to a particular software or object. For this tasking, you will be asked to go through some of the basic steps.

First, who are the target learners for your open shared learning resource? Why? What are some practical ways to access these target individuals to participate in a beta test? What incentives can you use to encourage their participation?

Second, what should the informed consent involve (and what other human subjects research should you address before conducting this research)? If you use a non-disclosure agreement (NDA), what should it say, and why?

Third, what do you want to know and learn from the potential users of this learning resource? What are the best ways to get at this information—through direct means and asks or indirect means and asks (or a combination)? How can you ask confirming and disconfirming questions in order to acquire relevant revision information? Prior to running the tests, what would you see if a learning resource works? What would you see if a learning resource does not work?

Fourth, if you were to select parts of the learning designs to assess, what would they be? How would you set up the research so as to enable learner-based insights but without the learner fatigue?

Fifth, from your research, what of the learner feedback do you find to be relevant, and why?

Sixth, how do you plan to revise the learning resources? What are ways to not over-react to user responses and re-designing learning objects that may exclude others?

Finally, can you take your beta tests and apply them to different assessment contexts, with other learning resources? What parts of your beta tests are transferable and generalizable? Why? Which parts are specific to your learning resources and non-transferable, and why?

How can others parse through these resources and harness them for their own local usage?

9.3.3 Part 3: Customized Testing

Finally, beyond what is covered in the alpha and beta tests, there may be some idiosyncratic standards from other sources, such as the funders, project partners, and others. Or, the learning resources may be versioned and adapted for different use cases: for different learner groups, or by language, by culture, specialized designs, technological adaptations, and others. These versions may require different customized testing specific to the learning source and the context.

If particular aspects of objects are being focused on, it may help to suppress other channels. For example, if the visuals of a video are being assessed, it may help to turn off the sound. And when the sound is being assessed, it may help to isolate that as one channel.

For example, in a cultural learning context, are there offensive messages (of disrespect? of discouragement of learning?) Are males and females depicted in appropriate ways (and with equal encouragement for learning)?

If downloadables are available, are they useful for learning, for usage in different learner contexts?

If learning objects are being used into the future, are there ways to future proof them?

If the learning needs to acquire a large-scale audience, is it up to the task (with the idea that non-attention is a death knell for an open-source or open-access project)? If the designers/developers have unique professional standards, are those standards met in the designed works?

If data is collected about the learners and their performances, it is important to have a data plan in place to notify learners of the information collection, to collect the data, to securely manage the data, and to properly use the data for improving the learning resource and/or to advance academic and applied research.

Some designer/developers may forgo both alpha and beta testing and go with their own customized test regimen. They may have a section that covers some of the territory of alpha testing and beta testing, and then they may add the specifics features that are of special interest to them. For my own personal customized assessment, I would add some of the following values: memorability, originality, factuality, simplicity, practicality, style, and others.

In the same way that there may be phases to alpha testing and beta testing, customized testing may occur as either a one-off or as a phased approach.

Task #4: Customized Testing Design
Based on the given definition of a customized test for open shared learning resources, please design your own custom test.

Set up this text in the most easily applied way as possible. For example, if you like checklists or rubrics or automated assessments, set your customized test up in a form.

Apply your customized test to the learning object/sequence/resources for which it was designed.

Take an extra step and revise your customized test based on what you saw in this analysis. (What did you learn when you applied the test to an actual learning object or sequence or resource?)

For open sharing, a designer/developer should be satisfied with contents that are the best that they can create in a given time period with the available resources. No single learning resource will meet every need for every potential learner. In many ways, there are not hard and fast rules for quality (outside of being legal and of being clear and factual). The contents of an alpha, beta, and customized test are summarized in Table 9.1. Some of the elements may be addressed in a particular test, and other elements may be left off. Parts of the sequences may be human-led, and others may be automated. There may be discretized phasing of some sequences in some cases or amorphous phasing in others.

The main points of alpha, beta, and customized testing of learning resources is to ensure that the works are of sufficient quality for others' usage and for public release.

Once an instructional work is out in out in public, it will be experienced and assessed in different ways, both formal and informal. For example, an "Instructional Quality Profile" may be used to evaluate curriculum (and suggest design improvements) (Merrill et al. 1979).

Testing for Deployments and Learning Implementations How learning resources are deployed may also affect how constructive the learning experiences are for the learners. So far, the alpha, beta, and customized testing approaches are focused on formative testing insights to update the learning contents, and then sum-

Table 9.1 Components of alpha, beta, and customized testing for open-shared learning resources

Alpha (α) testing	Beta (β) testing	Customized testing
Legal requirements Intellectual property Accessibility Data security	*User-computer interactivity* User interface design (from usability testing) User-computer interactivity	*Personality frame* By personality By style By expressivity
Ethical requirements Transparency Disclosure of interests Beneficence	*User experiential learning* User experiential learning sequences User decision making and choice-making User agency	*Unique features* By special features (of the learning resources)
Learning contents and data All likely questions that may be reasonably asked about the topic Accuracy Clarity of representations Proper focus Control for inferences and possible misperceptions Source citations	*User received feedback for learning* Assignments Assessments	*Versioning and adaptations* By target learner groups By language and culture By related specialized designs for different learning contexts By technological adaptations for different learning platforms and contexts By other versioning and adaptations
Pedagogical design Learning design (problem based learning, project based learning, case based learning, simulations, and others) Learning experiences for learners Learner feedback Sequencing	*Harnessing of sociality in support of learning* Intercommunications Collaborations Designed interactivity/ mediated sociality Informal enabled interactivity	*Deployments and learning implementations* By F2F usages By blended usages By fully online usages
Usability design Acceptance by learners User interface design(s)	*Learning value* User perceived learning value	
Technological functions Focus Fidelity Interactivity Integrations Scoring (if relevant) Data reporting Branching sequences and logic User controls Modalities		
Functions on devices Mobile devices Laptops		
Language Clarity and coherence Grammar Syntax Spelling Punctuation		
Metadata Accuracy Format		
Research and usage monitoring Data collection Data logging Data security		
Branding Branding messaging Branding consistency Branding look-and-feel		

mative testing once the learning resources are released to the public to understand how effective the resources are. Within the post-public launch phase, the resources may be deployed and harnessed in different ways, and that deployment and harnessing may affect the learning efficacy. The mitigations of these tests may be revisions to the deployments and learning implementations (such as in live and F2F and blended usages).

9.3.4 A Menu of Tests

Depending on the needs of the designer/developers, they may find that certain menus of tests work the best for their processes and their final published learning objects. There may be other assessments outside of the alpha (α), beta (β), and customized testing as well, and the customers/clients may themselves conduct their own testing based on their own requirements. Once the tests are run and the updates are applied at each phase, there can be one last brief check before it all goes live. Test plans are designed to the needs of the team and the project, to ensure that the optimal learning resource is created.

And again, once the learning resources have been released, they may be used in a variety of contexts and methods, in F2F, blended, and fully online applications. The harnessing methods may affect the learning efficacy of the learning resources and may be studied to extend the effectiveness of the learning resources.

side bar

An Informal Back-of-the-Napkin Lightweight Testing Approach

This sidebar introduces a simple way to create an informal testing approach to assessing learning resources. This is Option 4, beyond the alpha, beta, and customized testing…but it is also inclusive of some elements.

Basic "givens". One is to define the givens that have to be correct for any learning resource. These include issues of legality and ethics…factuality of contents… learning value…and technological functionality, among others. A core standard has to be quality of the writing and grammar and syntax, for a basic proofing. Optimally, another critical standard is acceptance by the target users. These standards have to be achieved for a work to "make."

In the next section are desired standards based on the unique learning resource and related conventions.

Learning object-based assessments. Next, define the actual learning object or sequence or resource. Identify unique aspects of this resource, and link those to standards. For example, if the learning involves problem-based learning, does the object align with the research in the field for problem-based learning? Or if the object is a simulation, is it clear to learners what is being simulated and the limits of that simulation? Is there appropriate debriefing? The intuition behind this second aspect involves the respective conventions of different learning objects and the empirical-data and research-based insights that inform the building of particular objects.

9.3.5 Why Testing of Learning Objects/Sequences?

It would be dangerous and inaccurate to suggest a doctrinaire approach to testing learning objects because of the broad variety of learning contents in the open shared space, the variety of wholly appropriate approaches to design and development, and the contention over appropriate and inappropriate approaches. For many of the following sections, the answers may be, "It depends."

Essentially, testing online learning objects and sequences helps identify shortcomings and gaps in the designed and developed learning resources, so that these may be addressed. Having a discrete testing phase enables a focused approach to assessing various dimensions of the resources to check for legality, ethical considerations, informational quality and accuracy, pedagogical value, technological functionality, branding, and other features. In the same way that grammar and spell checks are necessities for all text documents, some level of testing is generally required for learning resources.

At the code level, automated tests may be created for features that may be addressed with code and other remediation. Some of these include accessibility tests, for example. There are some publicly available tests, such as those built for learning management systems. Others are individual coded ones distributed in the open-shared space. And team members may sometimes roll their own scripts to test for particular aspects of the learning.

Currently, there are no broadly accepted generalized manual assessments for online learning objects and sequences. However, there are general standards in the field for legality (based on intellectual property laws, media laws, and federal accessibility requirements), factuality, pedagogical values, and others. From the various standards, tests may be derived.

The later in a design and development process a revision or retrofit is, the most costly it often is because prior work has to be undone or removed. In general, it is better to start with a list of quality standards and build to those from the beginning, so the work is less effortful, and time and other efficiencies may be maintained. Building quality in from the beginning means that the formalized or informalized testing phase is much easier, too, as well as the follow-on revisions from that testing.

Practically speaking, not all design specifications for a digital learning resource are known at the start. Those that are should be recorded and built to.

Other add-on tests may be created during the development of the contents (such as with the discovery of new technological standards that are relevant). Given the dynamism of the space, with the changing pedagogical and human learning research, evolving technologies, and new discoveries, it is wholly possible to have assessments arise even after a project has been drafted. The point is to be as adaptive and responsive as possible to the changing demands. Designer/developers also have the right to change their minds about focuses and what is important, particularly as they learn during the work process.

9.3.6 Alpha (α) Testing

The specific alpha tests applied to particular learning objects will be tailored to the designed learning resource, because of the specific features of the objects and sequences. One of the best ways to understand what alpha tests to use will be to do assessment walkthroughs of the respective contents and paying attention to what is being evaluated. It helps to have outside individuals assess the resources as well in order to attain fresh insights to inform the creation of a general alpha test for local use.

Not all suggested changes can necessarily be made given resource, effort, energy, and time-constrained environments. Without a clear plan for how to handle the feedback and data from the formalized assessments, it would be easy to lose the potential benefits of the respective tests. For this part, what are the bare minimum quality standards that have to be achieved on a number of dimensions for a learning object to be published with the designer/developer byline and the organizational brand? What orders should the revisions be done in to ensure that the works reach quality? And what are the standards that—if not met through revision—would render the learning resource unusable?

When building alpha, beta, and customized tests, some features may be understood as a simple binary: present or not present, to standard or not to standard, and so on. In terms of other attributes, the measures may be more of a continuous variable, maybe something between a 0 and a 1 (with some set threshold for quality within that range). Some of the assessments may have built-in suggestions for improvements.

Also, many will have spaces for open text-based commenting, so that particular open observations may be made. These are especially helpful to have early on in a review process, so that nuanced commentaries may be captured, and changes may be made. If the comments are especially astute, they may be integrated into the test instrument as another variable to apply to learning resources.

An assessment should optimally return information that is usable for improving the learning resource. To that end, it helps to test an assessment by applying it to actual objects and seeing what it returns and how usable that feedback can be.

Not all feedback is equal, though, so deciding what is most important to address and then listing the fixes in descending order would be important. Using a reasoned structure to identify the most critical fixes is important, too. Usually, criticality is important, as are related costs.

Formalized testing of learning resources should contribute to their improvement, so the prioritizing of the changes and the actualizing of the work serves to close the loop. Achieving the fixes is important as well as documenting how each prioritized issue was addressed.

Raw contents that inform a learning object design may include a wide range of content types. There may be extant contents like published articles, image sets, and other resources (both digital and analog). There may be contents created by the team: primary interviews, fresh photographs, audio files, videos, and others. There may be design files, plans, storyboards, and paper prototypes. These all contribute to the created learning objects and sequences. A raw draft learning object or sequence is identifiable by its scaffolding, side notes, placeholder areas, incompleteness, and unedited look and feel. Depending on the stage of the development, the draft objects may range from being very rough-cut to somewhat polished.

Refinement comes from how thought-through the learning resource is…and the efficacy of the sequences, the clarity of the writing, the solidity of the logic, the appropriateness of the imagery, the engagement and informativeness of the videos…and the absence of mistakes. In terms of look-and-feel, consistency and informed design are key elements.

In terms of the design and development phases, the refinement stage generally is not a goal until the fundamentals are sound (the pedagogical designs, the originality of the raw contents, and so on). Every quality and aspect of a learning design will have a cost because it involves human effort and skill (expensive) and technologies.

9.3.7 *Beta (β) Testing*

Running a beta test involves a basic sequence that may express something like this.

1. Design a beta test plan and beta test instrument. (If there is time, assess the instrument and refine it further before it is used. Ensure that the proper questions are asked, that the proper research methods and technologies are harnessed, and that the resulting data may be informative and actionable to the design/development individual or team.)
2. Identify target learners for whom the learning is designed. Identify their proxies in the public space, and design a way to reach out to them to acquire their participation in beta testing.

3. Conduct the beta test.
4. Clean the information, so it may be harnessed for decision making and revisions of the learning resources. Have a clear rationale for the follow-on revisions.
5. Apply the beta test insights to actually retrofitting or revising the learning resources.
6. Test again, or move forward to the public release.

Earlier, it was noted that beta tests should result in "actionable" information. The best way to acquire this experience is to review the feedback, filter it for relevance, and apply the relevant feedback to an actual revision or redesign.

9.3.8 Other Customized Testing

As noted above, customized tests may be complementary to alpha and beta tests. In other contexts, they may subsume the alpha and beta tests and be applied alone.

The customized tests may be inspired from any number of sources for standards setting (including funding agencies), unique personal standards of the designers/developers, and so on. The unique features of the respective learning objects or sequences or sets of related objects may inform the structure and function of customized tests. Spinoffs of learning resources—such as versions and adaptations and such—may also benefit from some custom testing to address some unique features.

9.3.9 Assessing the Assessments

A meta-assessment approach involves analyzing the various test instruments for their efficacy. After all, if the assessments are incomplete or poorly designed, those failings will affect the data collected and the follow-on redesign and re-development work. Validating or invalidating parts or wholes of these tests may help improve the quality of these tests…and their role in instructional design and development. Such tests work as an aid to getting to the desired end state.

There are no widely accepted ways to assess alpha tests, beta tests, and customized tests for open shared learning resources. There are some possible approaches from the testing of research instruments that may inform this space. For example, construct validity measures from survey instruments may be informative to assess some survey-based testing methods. Test-retest reliability methods may be applied as well, to see how consistent findings are in a test-retest context. Another assessment angle may be how comprehensive the assessment is (if that is a goal), or how targeted to particular issues of interest (if that is a goal). The desirable features of an assessment are based on the needs of the team, so observations from applied uses of such assessments in action research may also be informative.

What complicates test assessment is that there are varying ways to get to certain understandings. In some cases, direct questions may be helpful, but there are risks of respondent bias and mis-reporting. How information is elicited can affect what is captured. On e-learning systems and within learning objects, performance data may be captured that sheds light on other aspects of the learning resource. How individuals are selected for alpha, beta, and customized testing may affect outcomes. A more practical and applied approach may involve what aspects of an assessment are most usefully informative for revising the particular learning resources. These may be specific to a particular learning object and a learning case or situation. Colloquially, a simple back-of-the-napkin approach is to ask: If a test is a tool, what do I want the tool to achieve, and how well does this tool meet my needs?

Each project may have "showstoppers," an old-school term that refers to serious problems that are project-ending. These are non-negotiable issues that prohibit a learning resource from being shared in public if that issue cannot be satisfactorily addressed.

If a work is not "street legal" and will not pass muster, that may mean that it never leaves the development phase for production.

Official signoffs are necessary. If a work does not meet client requirements, for funded projects, it will not be released. If a subject matter expert who has worked on the project does not sign off on it, it will not go public.

If a work becomes controversial, that may be sufficient to stop the work.

If a work is not culturally palatable, that may be yet another showstopper.

Defining the must-achieve thresholds and standards is important for the project's direction.

Having a particular standard to build to can inform where analytical attention should go and how to analyze the learning object. For example, the standard of having accessible hierarchical text in learning contents may mean the following:

- Slideshows should be built into templates with hierarchical text labeling.
- Articles and other documents should be tagged with style tags (like headers and body text, among others) to indicate the document's textual hierarchies.
- Web pages should include tags to indicate the document structure.
- Built into some recorded speech and writing, there may be indicators of structure.

Using this idea that standards may be used one-by-one for evaluative purposes, identify a standard, and apply it to the learning resource that you are building (or some learning resources you have from the public space).

Based on feedback from the tests, some ideas may come to the fore for how to improve the designs. A walkthrough of such decision making may provide ideas not only for improving the particular learning object but also for creating improved designs in the future.

The testing applied to the learning resources should offer some direction and ideas about what parts of a project need further attention. What aspects of learning objects create a sense of finish or polish, and why? And which parts are the most low-cost ones to engage for an effective outcome?

Live Examples (on the Web)

In terms of live examples, there are a wide range of examples of open-shared learning resources shared on the Web and Internet. These include formalized learning sites like those hosting massive open online courses (MOOCs), learning object repositories and referatories, learning management systems (LMSes), courseware systems, and social media platforms.

People may seek these resources out and apply alpha, beta, and customized tests to them.

Where Do Common Mistakes Come from in the Creation of Learning Resources? So why would there need to be an alpha, beta, and customized testing phases? The basic thinking is that each serves a critical role in each phase of development and then the post-launch analysis. The different focuses enable different analyses of different aspects of the learning resources at different times and enables revisions of particular aspects as needed and with the proper granular depth needed. Human focus and attention require structural supports to enable higher level work.

In terms of larger-scale errors, involving poor pedagogical designs, inappropriate learning sequences, inappropriate technologies, and/or misuses of third-party content resources, these often stem from poor information, inappropriate decision making, insufficient content area expertise (or instructional design expertise), a failure to anticipate project needs, and other challenges. Individuals and teams may not have considered particular necessary objectives or outcomes sufficiently early. These challenges may also come from project scope: if projects are ambitious and sprawling, it helps to have work documents and templates to shape the work. If project drift affects a project, then original plans may be stretched, sometimes to beyond breaking points. Project drift is especially a potential issue for longer-term projects and those with changing leadership. Distributed project teams may also experience some drift based on the leadership. Good designers and developers can be over-matched by the challenges of the project. In some cases, the resources applied to a project may be insufficient, and that can result in quality gaps. Very tight deadlines may result in over-focus on some aspects and under-focus on others. The more ambiguity that exists in the design and building of learning contents, the more likely for there to be required mop-ups. Less-serious errors may include small coding challenges, omitted digital elements, incorrect images, typos, and misspellings.

These imperfections are par for the course. For example, a designer/developer may plan a particular learning sequence. As he/she/they are populating the outline with contents, they may realize that the learning object is much longer and more complex than they intended. They may decide to split the object or present some of the information in a different way. There are many right ways to design learning that is effective. Or maybe a learning sequence finally coalesces, and the designer/developer has to make sure it is all of a piece once the respective elements are designed. Or a particular part of a design may somehow trigger a target audience of users with unintended messaging, so that has to be removed.

Practically speaking, there are real-world limits to what may be corrected in this phase. The reason for this is often how much build-up occurs to reach a fairly finalized state of a project. If a mistake is introduced early, it may be hard to scrub it out of an integrated object like a video or a simulation or a game. Certainly, there are possible mitigations, but these post-production endeavors are effortful and often somewhat annoying. A worse error would be to leave identified errors unfixed. Shifting from one technology to another results in a range of intended and unintended consequences and surprises. One change may engender others. This is why it is better to take the design and development work slowly, so the work is thought –through to save on later and most costly revision efforts. If critical errors are found that cannot be addressed, such as anything involving legal liability or factual accuracy, the team may be faced with a "go" or "no-go" decision, and publication may be withheld. In this extreme case, the prior investments are just sunk costs. In the rare cases that the team may need to, they may have to start from scratch and redesign from a blank file and a blinking cursor.

side bar

Rookie Mistakes in Open-Shared Learning

So if mistakes are generally par for the course, are there special errors that tend to be common among rookies? Indeed, there are.

(1) *Building from the other and the external or the self?* Rookies will not put sufficient thought into what they build. They do not engage in suffi-

cient self-reflection to think about what they have to contribute in a unique way. Many build from whatever they can find in the environment. They do not think about how they want to self-portray in the near-term and the long term. They do not consider their learners and their needs and build to those needs.

Neophytes will emulate those that they admire, and they focus much less on creating their own sense of voice. They are short-changing themselves by merely emulating others and not working to discover their own voices and to make unique contributions. Stepping out in public requires confidence, and the best confidence is an earned one based on created expertise over time.

(2) *Global competition.* Beginners tend to underestimate how competitive the space is. They are dazzled by the potentials of big numbers, and they assume that if they create anything that they can drive traffic to their resource and make some greenbacks. The shtick for populist attention getting is not the formula for creating effective learning. Riding attention streams and fads like air currents does not make for a long-term strategy against the pulls of gravity. They do not use sufficient strategies and efforts to create a quality resource that can be differentiated from other resources and can compete in the space.

Creating relevant resources is hard work. If a person will contribute in the long term, they have to plan for and play to the long game. (Note: "Global competition" may be a bit of a stretch, but the competition comes from patches of expertise in various parts of the world for that topic.)

(3) *Actual expertise.* Often, rookies do not differentiate between actual expertise and I'm-an-expert-because-I-like-the-topic. It is not enough to just have access to some open-source contents, some freeware, and an idea…to offer learning resources that actually have value. Information has to be vetted for accuracy (with a healthy skepticism), and sources have to be cited. Something that is cobbled together on-the-fly looks like it. Mash-ups are low-hanging fruit, and they can as easily be created by anyone else. They forget that there will likely be actual experts trawling the space.

(4) *Investment. Bring it.* With a budget of $0, novices expect that they can put in little effort and have something passable. After all, they are merely trying to attract attention, aren't they? Relying on inspiration is a losing proposition; rather, building the necessary skill set through discipline is critical. A $0 budget usually means more effort and more investments are needed, not less. From the outside, it is easy to underestimate the work required.

Related to this, some will assumes that others owe them because of their quest to share, and they will send requests and make demands of others whom they do not know at all and have no relationship to. That presumption does not advance their cause.

(5) *Giving away something that is rare and valuable.* In most cases, once information has been used for an open-shared learning resource, it does not have much usage in copyrighted publications and other works. It is one-

time-use. A momentary inspiration to share work precludes its formal use elsewhere. The allure of attention can lead to misjudgments about what should be shared. (Human time and effort are precious, too, and these should not be spent without forethought.)

(6) *Assuming others' learning is experienced as intended.* Newcomers to the space may assume that those who encounter their learning resource will use it as intended and experience it as intended. They will not test the resource with others before releasing it to the public. (They will not "beta test" it.)

(7) *Proofing for errors.* Rookies forget to proof their work. They do not check their images for aspect ratios and stretching and resolutions. They don't verify information. They fail to connect with external experts where needed, for consultations. They will cut corners, and they will share works that are error-ridden. They will not go back and fix errors even when these have been noticed by others and mentioned to them.

(8) *Not me. Yes me.* Rookies will use handles and assume that their works cannot be re-identified back to them. They are creating a legacy without realizing it, and the reputations that they are creating may not suit them in the long term. They forget that the Internet has a version that is "forever."

A handle is very thin cover, and it is only one step out from actual re-identification (through various and simple means). Also, public disavowal of a work does nothing to mitigate legal liabilities for that work.

(9) *Legal risks.* Rookies do not consider the legal jeopardy they put themselves in when they use pirated software, plagiarized texts, copyrighted imagery (belonging to others), copyrighted video, careless representation of facts, inaccurate handling of others' reputations, self-plagiarism, and so on. A freewheeling online social media ecosystem may give the sense that anything goes and that people can just "wing it," but not so much (In academia, any four words used in the original order without quotation marks and source citations is plagiarism. Sloppy handling of information is no defense.).

(10) *Monitoring on one dimension.* If new designer/developers in the space measure any response to their learning resource, it is usually a rough measure: counts. Going with one metric is highly limited, and little can actually read into that one measure. Comments on sharing sites may be another measure. Emails from users may be another. Building more informative feedback loops may be helpful, in the learning object design and in elicitations.

These all can be simplified to a basic concept. Those who have developed professional skills in one or more parts of their professional lives may have much to share with the general public in the open-shared learning resource space, but they have to apply their professional standards in the creation and sharing of these properties. It is not enough to come at the work like rookies. Open-sharing on $0 budget does not mean cost-free or risk-free or quality-free.

Structuring Tests for Optimal Applicability Separate from the contents of the alpha, beta, and customized testing, it is important to think about how to structure the tests (whether these are on paper or digital). Checklists are a basic form for the most simple assessment, essentially a binary, such as "yes/no," "present/not present," "sufficient/insufficient," with space for related commenting (involving observations and suggestions for follow-on work, if necessary).

A checklist assessment may look something like the following in Table 9.2 This depiction suggests a checklist for the usability of social imagery into a project. The attributes in the row headers are numbered for easier referencing. The Non-applicable column is an opt-out

Another form of testing may be rubrics. A rubric contains evaluative criteria in combination with levels of quality. In terms of layout, in general, the column head-

Table 9.2 A Sample checklist approach for assessing legal and practical usability of socially shared imagery

	Yes, sufficient	No, insufficient	Commenting (optional)	Non-applicable (N/A)
1. Established provenance (origin)				
2. Established reputation of the source for professionalism (legally signed media releases for the initial image capture)				
3. Informationally relevant				
4. Editable				
5. Released through creative commons or other licensure				
6. Release with time requirements (released usage for certain amount of time only, then renewal required)				
7. Release with attribution or crediting requirements				
8. Release with custom requirements				
9. Resolution				
10. Wide usage on the Web and Internet (reverse image search test; image search test)				
11. Sensitive content or data leakage [in foreground or background, in Exif (exchangeable image file format) or other metadata]				

(continued)

Table 9.2 (continued)

	Yes, sufficient	No, insufficient	Commenting (optional)	Non-applicable (N/A)
12. Presence of personally identifiable information (PII)				
13. Presence of trademark or registered mark data and/or visual branding				
14. Alignment of messaging with the goals of the instructional design project				
15. Others				

Table 9.3 A sample rubric approach for assessing cognitive scaffolding and help of an online learning resource

	Excellent	Satisfactory	Incomplete	Commenting (optional)	Non-applicable (N/A)
1. Lead-up module (optional)					
2. Glossary of terms					
3. Clear directions					
4. Context-sensitive help (with relevant information available)					
5. Examples for learning					
6. Opportunities for learner practice					
7. Learning feedback					
8. Intelligent tutoring agent					
9. Wisdom of crowds access					
10. Lead-away module (optional)					
11. Other					

ers contain the attributes, and the row headers contain the quantitative measures. However, the reverse may be used depending on the amount of attributes and readability. This latter layout is used in the draft example (Table 9.3). The measures may be discrete summary ones as in the example, or they may be continuous (such as slider values), and others. The Commenting column enables textual insights to be shared. The cells may be used for commenting in lieu of a separate column, with only one of the cells fillable with text per row. Or, there can be numerical values indicating range, such as: Excellent (10–9), Satisfactory (8–7), Incomplete (6–0), so relative intensities of excellence, satisfaction, and incompleteness may be indicated numerically. This all depends on how granularly detail-oriented the assessments need to be for the development team. The Non-applicable column is an opt-out, so as not to unnecessarily force a response.

An add-on column can be one that records the "fix" for the particular identified issues. These items should be included to the respective assessments if they will be addressed or fixed. If these are included just to pay attention to a particular feature (for the informational value), then they may stay on the respective assessments; however, in general, these should be as practical as possible.

There may be other forms of assessments as well, such as mixed modal forms, such as checklists and rubrics combined, for example. Or aspects of assessments may be expressed as scripted tests, when those work for the particular assessed features. The idea is to continuously evolve and improve these assessments to strengthen their applicability. The two prior examples of testing mostly come from the alpha testing space.

In terms of beta testing with target learners, such assessments may be conducted F2F, in a blended fashion, or fully online. Table 9.4 shows the use of a design

Table 9.4 A sample questionnaire for assessing learner experiences with a learning resource

What did you expect with this learning experience? Were your expectations met with this learning experience? How so? How not?
How familiar were you with the particular technologies used to deliver the learning?
When you first started using the learning resource, how clear was it how to use the learning resource?
How comfortable were you in navigating through the learning resource? What challenges did you have with orientating yourself (if any)?
During the learning, did you feel in control or not? Why or why not?
Did you find the directions clear? If not, what would be more helpful?
How would you describe your background with this particular topic? What prior learning experiences have you had regarding this topic?
What do you think about the sequence of learning? What was useful? What was not useful?
In terms of the feedback about your performance that you received during the learning, how helpful was it? Did you want more or less feedback? What did you think of the explanatory power of the feedback?
Did this learning experience provide you with useful information? Is the learning helpful for your studies? Your work?
Did you identify any gaps in the provided information? What else would you have wanted to learn about, and why?
What did you think of the pacing of the learning? Was it comfortable for you? If not, how may this be improved?
When you needed more information and engaged in help-seeking, were you able to acquire the help you needed within the learning resource? Outside the learning resource?
What were some of your predominant emotions during this learning experience? Did you experience anxiety? Pressure? Frustration?
Do you feel that the learning resources focused sufficiently on important information or on less important information?
What are some ways to improve this learning resource?

research questionnaire to assess learner experiences with a learning resource. These questions may be elicited in focus groups, in interviews, in in-person or online survey format, and other means. This list of questions may be understood as general issues of interest in a learning experience-based beta test. Their phrasing here is more of a pragmatic research-based kind and not likely the verbiage that would be used in actual interactions with learners.

An automated beta test may examine, in part, how users engaged respective items in the learning object, such as how much time they spent on each item and how well they performed. Or automated eye tracking may be suggestive of what parts of a computer-user interface is engaged with and in what sequence. These outputs are usually both quantitative data and data visualizations from that data.

A full alpha or beta or customized test may be comprised of a series of small checklists and rubrics and others pieces and parts to ensure sufficient coverage of the necessary issues.

Discussion Such alpha, beta, and customized tests for learning resources are not box-checking; they should link to actual follow-on work to revise and update the learning contents. Beta tests do not have to be one-offs. Retests may be done with new groups. The cycle of testing and revision and deployment and re-testing, revisioning, and re-deployment, can be set up like a continuing spiral. The real-world limiting factors are time and costs. Ultimately, what passes muster of these stress tests will be released to the broader public.

Beyond the particular learning resource, the team should consider work processes to address potential errors and blind spots in future design and development process that enabled the mistakes, so that such issues may be headed off on future projects. The drafted alpha, beta, and customized tests can be used as pretests at the beginning, so people can build to that known quality. One critical aspect is to define a regulatory and quality regime for a learning resource. There are healthy practices that may enhance instructional design and development projects. For example, designs should be invested in fully and vetted in depth before going to development; if not addressed, these will be make-work. All data should be checked before they are included as facts. All support contents—images, audio, video, and others—should be the property of the design/development team, and all should be legally acquired (with proper media release and contract-based signoffs). Many of the known challenges can be handled during the work processes.

Also, having an alpha test, a beta test, and/or a customized test does not mean that there cannot be checks and verifications along the way. Whatever challenges are handled in development do not have to be addressed at the conclusion of the project. In some cases, it may not be possible to conduct an alpha test until near launch. For example, an organization or individual may not want to pay for a commercial service to host the learning objects early on until the objects are near-completion. However, this late start on the hosting site may mean less time for functionality testing of how the various objects play together and individually in the particular environment. There should be a focus on quality through individual/team awareness, work processes, and checks and double-checks. There are many practical ways to create quality.

9.4 Future Research Directions

The typical advice for a design and development team is to under-promise and over-deliver, so that the respective funders or clients are satisfied. At the same time, teams benefit from having high aspirations, so they may contribute something of true value. Having tests to ensure quality may benefit the resulting learning resources. As noted, "alpha" and "beta" and even "customized" tests are somewhat placeholder terms, and designer/developers may develop (or co-develop) such assessments for particular projects. The practitioners operationalize those terms by writing and applying those tests on learning resources—often on-the-fly. What are their experiences with creating such assessments for learning objects? What learning and other theories, models, and frameworks are relevant to these assessments? Are there optimal applications of the alpha, beta, and customized tests? Are there optimal thresholds for such tests?

This area offers plenty of opportunities exploratory research. There are no formalized alpha, beta, or customized tests currently in the literature for online learning resources. This is not to say that professionals do not use them, but these are usually created by the design and development teams for internal usage. Some of these may be "privy" and not broadly shared. Sharing these publicly and evolving them may benefit the larger community of practitioners, and further, academic researchers.

Also, there are automated code tests for the efficacy of code, and these may be further evolved to work on the code of online learning objects—for a particular set of programs and for particular features.

At present, there is also nothing in the academic research literature about assessing the alpha, beta, and customized tests applied to online learning resources. More on effective methods and criteria for determining effective assessments would enhance the field as well. Another important question is how transferable alpha tests can be (Fig. 9.4).

Fig. 9.4 A Word Cloud of Chapter 09: "Alpha Testing, Beta Testing, and Customized Testing"

What-If: Going in Cold Without Any Testing

You've decided to create several interrelated open shared learning objects which while not sequential are somewhat interrelated topically. You have done a quick analysis and realize that you are tight on time, and if you are going to achieve your ambitions, you will have to cut some corners. You've decided to leave off formalized testing. No alpha testing, no beta testing, and not even light customized testing. The idea is that you'll do a grammar check and maybe a spell check, and you'll call it good.

Your contents are drafted. You have a host site that you plan to upload the contents to. You have built learning objects before, and you feel like you have an internal sense of what works. You feel comfortable in public spaces. You will play this by ear.

Decision point #1: stop or advance. If advance, will you go for a hard launch (wide publicity) or a soft launch (directed or targeted publicity)? How much signaling will you do to encourage commenting by the learners, so you can use the live launched contents as a way to elicit feedback from learners?

You decide to upload the contents and share some links to these contents in directed emails. You also share some microblogging messages to advertise these. You share these among your social network. Based on an initial look at the uptake, it does not look like the learning objects are going to set the world on fire, but there is some interest. A few of the resources have garnered some initial accesses, but it is hard to tell if any of them will "go viral," to use the terminology of the day.

You decide to allow rankings (0–5 stars), and you decide to allow commenting (both anonymized and with identified sign-ins). In the text description of the learning objects, you add a small invite for commenting and your contact email. In general, the world is a quiet one as regards responses to your learning contents, and you decide to take some light risks. (You figure that people will have opinions anyway, but it's better to hear what they are in public than to not hear them. Your inclusion of your email also enables a private channel in case people do not want to post to a public venue.)

Then one day, several months later, you revisit the postings, and you realize that one of the objects has attracted several thousand views. Another object still has only less than ten. And you have found some star ratings…and you have some actual comments. Some of the comments are garbled and do not seem to reflect on the actual contents. Some seem to be from scripted agents or chatbots. Then, you find that some of the public comments are surprising and substantive. No one has emailed you thus far, but you could find the identifiers for those who commented and reach out to them to discuss their comments in more depth. What do you do?

Decision point #2: stop or advance. If advance, what sorts of information do you want to know from this public user? How will you portray yourself to a learner without causing offense or potential intimidation? How do you signal that you want some information but not a continuing social relationship online?

You find the contact information to the individuals who have reached out to you, and you decide to use their emails as less public channels. Some ask for further resources, and you oblige where you can. You engage multiple of the respondents, and you start to hear some common themes. One common theme is that they want some lead-up learning resources to refresh their knowledge on a particular topic. Another is that they want more explication about a particular data table. What do you do?

Decision point #3: stop or advance. If advance, should you build learning objects by request by the general public? What if you find other resources that are available in public? Do you refer the learners on to other resources? Do you revise your learning object with more explication on the data table to anticipate others' potential needs?

You decide to point several respondents to an external open shared resource that fits the bill for their learning needs. Then, you also decide to elaborate on the data table because you agree that you should have added more information initially.

As more time passes, you realize that an unknown individual has usurped some of your contents without attribute, counter to your licensure request. You can decide to reach out to them and request credit, or you can just leave it. The social context only enables people to do mash-ups, and it is a lax environment, but you also feel like you should get credit for what you created and not benefit others who either claim credit or earn moneys from your work. What do you do?

Decision point #4: stop or advance. If advance, what sort of tone should you strike—to get their proper attention and legal behavior? How far do you plan to push this if the individual does not respond? Should you watermark your work or put access controls on it, so you don't feel used? Or do you just accept that there will be some abuses, and overall, the system is working?

You decide to give the individual a chance to respond and notify the individual in polite terms about this discrepancy. A few weeks pass without a response, so you decide to let it go.

You go on to other projects. Then, one day, you come across an image that you thought was an open-source one. As you explore further, you realize that the image is actually a copyrighted one. You find the original via a reverse image search tool. You can write to the copyright holder and ask for permission, or you can swap out the image for a different open-source one or an original one that you took, or you can pretend that you didn't see this. Or you can retract the whole learning object. What do you do?

The What-If Debriefing

This scenario gives somewhat of a real-world sense of what it may be like to go live with a set of learning resources, after conducting only a light proofing and review and no formal testing. Contents that are put out in the world will attract learners at varying rates, and often with the wide disparities of the numbers above, even on the same hosting platform. In general, learner commenting is actually fairly rare. There may be occasional emails from users, usually with agendas (they want to advertise on a platform, or they want a job opportunity, or they want free access to a commercial technology, or they have a problem that they cannot troubleshoot, and so on).

9.5 Conclusion

There are many right ways to create open-shared learning objects in the world, and not all of them will require in-depth alpha, beta, and customized testing. Depending on the experiences of the design and development team (or individual), it may be that the required checks may only require some vigilant design and development work, some light user testing, and grammar and spell checks. It is possible to wholly bypass the formal testing. However, the more requirements that are placed on an open shared project, the higher the risk that nothing may be ultimately created and shared.

The *status quo* current involves a rapid build cycle and a release to the world, and its treatment in public is its own testing, often without any follow-on revisions. This approach is a high stakes one because errors may then go unaddressed and so propagate. To shore up such common approaches, some relevant testing may be designed in the work sequence to close the loop and ensure a level of accuracy, legality, learning value, and other forms of quality.

Finally, designer/developers benefit from applying the highest standards to their work, which are the commercial standards, so that in-depth revisions are not required after launch. The external world does not offer obvious guardrails for the design and development of learning resources for quality, so those who would develop to this space would do well to learn to standards and create work supports that enable them to achieve excellence.

9.6 Reviews and Assignments

9.6.1 Main Points Review

- Learning objects and sequences, before they are released to the public, would do well to be assessed for various quality standards through various tests. After the assessments, the learning resources should be revised to address those standards.
- An "alpha (α) test" is typically set up for in-house (in-team) testing of digital contents, and it is usually based on the *a priori* standards set by the team at the beginning of a project.
- A "beta (β) test" is typically set up for testing of digital contents with an invited target audience (such as of target learners to test a learning object). Oftentimes, beta tests address how well received a particular audience will be to a particular object or technology or piece of media content.
- The in-house test team is considered somewhat less accurate to "audience fidelity" than the targeted learners from the public in the beta test phase.
- The testing sequence usually moves from in-house to the public because of the need to offer fairly polished and refined contents to test audiences. This also makes the external evaluations more applicable based on the relative completeness of the learning resources.
- Customized tests may be written to test for particular aspects of open-shared learning objects not addressed in an alpha test and a beta test. The customizations may be based on the more unique features of the specific learning resources.
- For the respective assessments to work, the various dimensions have to be generally objectively observable and often measureable.
- The assessment instruments for the respective open-shared learning objects and sequences may themselves be assessed for practicality and effectiveness. For example, they may be assessed for

  - how thoroughly they address the particular evaluative dimensions…
  - the comprehensiveness of the assessed constructs (validity)…

- the consistency of the assessments (reliability)…
- and other features.

9.6.2 *Critical Thinking Questions*

Alpha (α) testing

- Alpha testing is conducted based on "objective" and "observable" factors. Why is it necessary to have "objective" and "observable" features that may be recorded?
- Similarly to the expenditure of time on design, small-scale and preliminary pilot testing is often done to save on development costs. Why is pilot testing so effective at informing what needs to be developed, and what does not need to be developed?

Beta (β) testing

- How should people be recruited to serve on a beta test? Which individuals are most representative of a population of potential learners for open-shared learning? Why? What sorts of small incentives are considered appropriate? What are possible "conflicts of interest" to pay attention to?

Remote testing

- What are effective ways to conduct remote alpha and beta and customized testing?

Customized testing

- Customized tests are usually specific to the unique aspects of the particular learning resources being created. What aspects of a learning resource may be unique to it?
- A summative assessment may be done around the deployment of a learning resource. What are some effective ways of conducting such a summative assessment?

Proofing

- In a normal course of building learning resources, there is usually a revision or proofing stage to ensure that the resource meets standards of accuracy and clarity. There are checks for legality and other requirements. Explicitly defining a formal testing phase emphasizes the importance of meeting standards.

Thresholds for quality

- After the tests are complete, additional work is often required to ensure that learning resources achieve quality and identified shortcomings are addressed. What are ways to set basic thresholds for quality for open-shared learning resources? What features should be prioritized, and why?

- While alpha, beta, and customized testing may enhance the open-shared learning resources, there may be research benefits to analyzing the captured information. What are some approaches to harnessing the test information for academic research?
- Practically, assessments of learning resources enable the designer/developers to achieve quality. Which tests are most effective for these purposes, and why? Beyond their support for quality online learning resource designs, what other research contributions are there from such assessments? Why?

9.7 Assignments

Directions The Assignments are divided into two sections, Basic and Advanced. The Basic section is for those who may not have much instructional design experience or background in the area of creating instructional contents for open sharing. As such, these are set up to familiarize them with the chapter-related knowledge, skills, and abilities. The Advanced section is for those who already have some knowledge of this general space and who may benefit from more challenging work.

In a formal learning context, these assignments would benefit from expert feedback and further applications of the learning contents. In a nonformal or informal learning context, including self-directed learning, these assignments would benefit from both reflection and practice. These assignments are built to be extensible, to have elements added to benefit the learners. They are designed to be assigned selectively and not in full. The setup of this textbook is as a work sequence, and similarly, the assignments may be set up as tasks to be completed by the learner in a sequential way…that takes them through the fairly complete and sequential *open-shared learning design* → *development* → *test* → *revision* → *launch* → *post-launch* process.

9.7.1 Basic

Assignment 9.1: Running an Alpha (α) Test and a Faux Beta (β) Test on a Public Learning Object Choose a learning object in the target domain of interest. Using a draft alpha test [testing for legality (IP, accessibility, media law, and others), technological functionality, and other features], write up a short critique of the learning object. How well did the object meet the alpha test guidelines? How much was knowable? How much was unknowable? What does this assignment reveal about the open-shared learning objects available in the public? What sorts of advice is most helpful for the instructional designers to create learning objects and sequences to quality?

Extra: If you have the interest, download the target learning object, and see how editable and revisable it is. How hard is it to get it to quality?

Assignment 9.2: Alpha (α) Testing Create an alpha test to address legalities, technological functionality, writing clarity, and others. Use this test against 1-3 learning objects, and use the learning from those objects to refine the alpha test further. Then, as follow-on work, consider how you might apply what was learned in the alpha test to update a learning object. How would the alpha test feedback be prioritized? Why?

Extra: Create an alpha test that is sufficiently general to apply across a range of online learning objects.
Extra: Create an alpha test that is sufficiently general/specific to apply to particular types of learning objects.
Extra: Create an alpha test that is sufficiently general/specific to apply to a particular learning domain, in terms of informational value.

Assignment 9.3: Beta (β) Testing Create a beta test for a target "public" population sample to experience a learning object/course/sequence. What back-end data would you include in the data collection, and how would you use this data to understand learner actions and experiences? What sorts of questions would you ask potential learners directly, and why? How would you analyze to understand the learning efficacy of the designed learning? As a follow-on work, consider how you might apply what was learned in the beta test to update a learning object. How would the beta test feedback be prioritized? Why?

Extra: Create a beta test that is sufficiently general to apply across a range of online learning objects. Remember that the focus of the beta test is on users.
Extra: Create a beta test that is sufficiently general/specific to apply to particular types of learning objects.
Extra: Create a beta test that is sufficiently general/specific to apply to a particular learning domain, in terms of informational value.

Assignment 9.4: Creating Customized Tests Some features of an open-shared learning object or learning sequence may fall outside the typical purview of an alpha test or a beta test. For example, there may be relevant questions such as the following: How useful is the learning object or sequence when it is auto-translated and used in a different culture? How effective is the learning object or sequence when the Internet connectivity is low? How mobile-friendly is the learning object when using particular devices, particular apps (if relevant), and so on, in particular contexts?

Extra: How transferable are customized tests for others' learning objects and sequences? Or are customized tests one-offs just applicable to the local context?
Extra: The different tests applied to a learning object or sequence highlight different aspects of the learning content. Use one learning object and two different assessments, and explore how the different assessments affect the way the learning object/sequence is experienced and seen.

Assignment 9.5: Polish of the Learning Objects Given the wide range of media that may be consumed today, many learners expect a certain level of polish and sheen to their online learning as well. What are some elements that learners look to for "polish"? How can those designing online learning contents build digital objects and online learning experiences with a sufficient level of polish or sheen? What are some work-arounds to achieve this level of sheen? Why?

9.7.2 Advanced

Assignment 9.6: Learner Adoption of Open-Shared Learning Objects, Courses, and Sequences If those who create learning objects are in competition with others for the attention of those who might adopt learning objects, what are some ways for you to be competitive for learner attention? How would you encourage learners to adopt your open-shared learning objects, courses, and sequences? What standards would you build to? What reputation do you want to create (and how)?

Assignment 9.7: Versioning for Different Learner Groups Based on your conceptualization of your main target learner group, you have designed a particular learning object. Consider what you might do to version the learning object for the second largest potential learner group. What factors would you consider in versioning the online learning? Why? How many changes would you have to make in order to enable the online learning to be effectively used by multiple groups?

Assignment 9.8: Assessing the Assessment for the Learning Object/Learning Sequence When assessments are used in research contexts, they are often measured for various efficacy features, such as construct validity and test-retest reliability (consistency of test results, over time). Besides the internal validity of the test, are there ways to assess external validity, such as by measuring how well the assessment corrects a learning object or sequence? What are some valid ways to assess the validity of the alpha test or beta test or the customized assessment, and why? What are some invalid ways to assess the validity of the respective test, and why?

Extra: Some assessments may be scripted or automated ones. Explore several automated assessments (such as for accessibility). Identify the strengths and weaknesses of each one.

Assignment 9.9: Prioritizing What to Fix or Revise Based on the findings from the alpha testing, the beta testing, and the custom testing, what do you see as the top ten most critical things to fix? Why? Likewise, what are the top ten least critical things to fix, and why? Are there ways to change the work processes to catch these quality issues earlier and not only after once a draft has been achieved? How so? (Strive to be as practical as possible.)

Assignment 9.10: Planning Follow-On Learning Objects If you were to build follow-on learning objects to the initial one that you've created and shared, what would it be? What would it look like? Who would it be designed for? How would you apply the learning from the alpha testing, the beta testing, and the customized testing to ensure that this follow-on object achieves similar or improved quality to the first open-shared object/sequence?

Assignment 9.11: Testing Open-Shared Learning Resources for Learning Efficiencies And Effectiveness Assessing the effectiveness of open-shared learning resources may be much easier for massive open online courses (MOOCs) than for stand-alone learning objects and resources. In the first case, the data is captured as a matter of course on the learning system, often with large numbers of learners, and with the ability to apply various algorithms and statistical analytics approaches to the data. For the stand-alone learning objects, the learners are scattershot as a population; the data collected is sparse; the learning context is not particularly clear, and both analysis and assertability can be elusive. Even with those limits, though, it would be helpful to capture some initial insights about the quality of the learning objects based on learner responses (and not just a general evaluation to see how closely the learning object aligns with a particular design approach).

Key Terms and Definitions

Alpha (α) testing In-house testing of learning objects for whether they meet predefined standards (for such issues as legality, accessibility, technological functionality, and others)

Audience fidelity The faithfulness or alignment of a test group with the actual users who will be using the learning resources, how representative a particular group is in representing the target audience

Automated testing The uses of applied scripts to assess particular features of learning objects and sequences

Beta (β) testing Testing of learning objects with select public audiences to test for learning efficacy and public acceptance as well as other features

Customized testing Adaptive and unique testing specific to particular learning objects or projects

Digital preservation Work of re-versioning digital files into formats that may be more accessible or usable over time (even in light of the "slow fires" of technological change)

Interactivity The interactions between a user (or users) and technology systems

Metadata Data about data

Porting Moving contents from one technology platform to another

Showstopper A problematic factor in a work (or learning resource, in this case) that prevents it from being used because of the seriousness of this issue or challenge
Universal file format An openly accessible file type that proprietary file formats may be converted to or from
User interface A designed screen through which users may interact with technology systems

References

Dinevski D. Open educational resources and lifelong learning. In the proceedings of the ITI 2008 30th International Conf on Information Technology Interfaces. June 23 – 26, 2008. Cavtat, Croatia. 117 – 122, 2008.
Johnson LA, and Schleyer TKL. Developing high-quality educational software. Educational Methodologies. *Journal of Dental Education* 67: 1209 – 1220, 2003.
Krueger RA, and Casey MA. *Focus Groups: A Practical Guide for Applied Research.* 4th Ed. Los Angeles: SAGE. 2009.
Liu M, Jones C, and Hemstreet S. Interactive multimedia design and production processes. *Journal of Research on Computing in Education* 30: 254 – 280, 1998. https://doi.org/10.1080/08886504.1998.10782226.
Merrill MD, Reigeluth CM, and Faust GW. The Instructional Quality Profile: A curriculum evaluation and design tool. In H.F. O'Neil's *Procedures for Instructional Systems Development.* Ch. 6. Academic Press, Inc. 165 – 204. 1979.
Noack D. So you wanna be a beta tester? *Link-up* 17: 8, 2000. Nursing & Allied Health Database.
White BS, and Branch RM. Systematic pilot testing as a step in the instructional design process of corporate training and development. *Performance Improvement Quarterly* 14:, 75 – 94, 2001.

Additional Reading Section

Abbott A. *Methods of Discovery: Heuristics for the Social Sciences.* New York: W.W. Norton & Company. 2004.
Creswell JW. *Research Design: Qualitative, Quantitative, and Mixed Methods Approaches.* 2nd Ed. Thousand Oaks, California: SAGE Publications. 2003.
Gall MD, Gall JP, and Borg WR. *Educational Research: An Introduction.* 7th Ed. Boston: Pearson Education Inc. 2003, 1996, 1989, 1983, 1979, 1971, 1963.
Glaser BG, and Strauss AL. *The Discovery of Grounded Theory: Strategies for Qualitative Research.* New York: Aldine de Gruyter. 1967, 1995, 1999.
Hai-Jew S. *Techniques for Coding Imagery and Multimedia: Emerging Research and Opportunities.* Advances in Knowledge Acquisition, Transfer, and Management Book Series. Hershey, Pennsylvania: IGI Global. 2018.
Krueger RA, and Casey MA. *Focus Groups: A Practical Guide for Applied Research.* 4th Ed. Los Angeles: SAGE Publications. 2009.
Miles MB, Huberman AM, and Saldaña J. *Qualitative Data Analysis: A Methods Sourcebook.* 3rd Ed. Los Angeles: SAGE Publications. 2014, 1994.
Moustakis C. *Heuristic Research: Design, Methodology, and Applications.* Newbury Park, California: SAGE Publications. 1990.
Norman GR, and Streiner DL. *PDQ Statistics.* 2nd Ed. Hamilton, Ontario: BC Decker Inc. 1999.

Ruel E, Wagner WE III, and Gillespie BJ. *The Practice of Survey Research: Theory and Applications*. Los Angeles: SAGE Publications Ltd. 2016.

Saldaña J. *The Coding Manual for Qualitative Researchers*. 2nd Ed. Los Angeles: SAGE Publications Ltd. 2013.

Taylor SJ, and Bogdan R. *Introduction to Qualitative Research Methods: A Guidebook and Resource*. 3rd Ed. New York: John Wiley & Sons, Inc. 1998.

Part IV
Launching to an Open-Shared Future

Chapter 10
Open Sharing: Launching, Outreach, Publicity, Usage Monitoring, and Post-Launch Care

Abstract Once an open-shared learning object or learning sequence has been designed to standards and polished and refined, it is published to the world, to achieve its fortunes (or not). This chapter surfaces some of the issues that will arise. A "soft" launch involves sharing the resources to smaller target groups, and a "hard" launch involves sharing to the broad general public. Both approaches may be employed to bring attention to the released object or sequence. Or neither approach may be used: some learning objects are open-shared without any fanfare. This chapter describes how to create mainstream media and social media "buzz" through publicity plans and how to attract publicity and measure the effectiveness of the media outreach. Learner usage monitoring of the learning resources is described to enable awareness of the usage. Finally, there is important discussion of post-launch care—to consider how much continuing support to provide to users, and to consider whether or not to revise the released work and/or build follow-on learning.

Keywords Post-launch care · Cognitive scaffolding · Learning object retrofitting · Outreach · Media plan · Post-launch learner supports

> Without publicity there can be no public spirit, and without public spirit every nation must decay.
>
> —Benjamin Disraeli (1804–1881)

> I don't know why people are so keen to put the details of their private life in public; they forget that invisibility is a superpower.
>
> —Banksy (1973–), graffiti artist

S. Hai-Jew, *Designing Instruction For Open Sharing*,
https://doi.org/10.1007/978-3-030-02713-1_10

Opening Scenario

Opening Scenario: Crossing the Rubicon into Public Space?

Your digital learning object/sequence/resource has been designed, developed, assessed, revised, and approved for release. It is now ready to be shared with the larger world, whether through a broad public launch (hard launch), or direct invitations for usage to defined subgroups (soft launch) or through some combination of outreach. Such objects may be released on a single platform (single-sourcing) or released on multiple platforms. It/they may be published broadly and ignored, or further supported. It may be updated after certain time periods. Going live is a major moment in the lifespan of a digital learning object for several reasons: (1) the object has been made available to a broad public audience, and (2) the object is in a somewhat fixed form (or in a fully permanent form) [revisable or non-revisable]. The public space is a proving ground, where an object will make or not make. Those that make are relevant and come to public attention and have an outsized positive effect for a period of time. The vast majority are in the long tail of the works that are part of the Great Unread or the Great Unused.

How successful a learning object is depends on a variety of factors, but the core meta-factor is value for the users. Value here comes from the learning benefit and the learning experience. Ideally, the information provided would be accurate and timely; the digital contents would be novel; the framing would be beneficial to the learning; the accommodations would be targeted to the learners; the creators would be professional and credible; the production values would be high.

For some designers of instruction, they are familiar with what to expect with such releases. In the open-shared space, many will engage with the learning objects in fairly predictable ways. They will generally use the learning objects for a just-in-time perceived need, and they use it often quietly, without social comment (whether positive or negative). In some cases, some users will reach out to the object creators, through social media or emails or telephone, or other means, to send along information, make suggestions, request more information, acquire help for troubleshooting a learning problem, or send some other messages. Some messages are one-directional only, such as a user telling the designer/developer what his/her experience was, and others are interactive and bi-directional or multi-directional, with expectations of interchanges between the discussants. The creators of open-shared learning objects need to consider how much post-launch care they will provide.

Going live is the ostensible point of no return, or crossing the Rubicon. With sufficient splash, the shared object will be accessed, and often copied, and occasionally, it will find a broad audience. Going live is the share, both intended and unintended.

Some Early Questions to Consider

Given that there tends to be low adoption rates of others' created learning objects, what will be your launch strategies and launch channels? Why?

Who would you reach out to? Why?

How would you appeal to learners who may use open-shared learning resources?

How would you measure the success of your outreach?

How would you measure continuing usage of the learning resources after initial adoption?

How much interaction will you maintain with those who use your open-shared learning object, and why?

Do you think a learning resource should be once-and-done, or should it be revisable and update-able? (Historically, if publication is an analogical practice, once-and-done is more common. This way, when people cite a source, it is a static one, not one that changes.)

If you were to create an updating plan for your shared learning resources, how would you structure it? How often would you update the learning object (if at all)? When would you update it? Why would you update it? Would you create add-on information to the original learning object (along with revisions) or create a new follow-on learning resource? Or both?

Learning Objectives

Learners will …

Defining Target Learner Audiences (as Groups)

- Based on your target learner profiles (Chap. 2), describe who the respective target audiences are (and who they are not)
- Identify how these audiences may be reached through formal mass media and informal social media, and other means
- Identify target leaders and influencers of respective groups who may be important contacts and touchpoints for various online communities

Objectives for Outreaches and Publicity

- Define the practical objectives for the outreaches and media plans
- Create accurate ways to measure the efficacy of the respective outreaches to achieving the various objectives (and to what thresholds)

Media Plans for Publicity

- Create a media plan to reach out using efforts like press releases, interview offers, media-friendly events, and other efforts, and ensure that these elements are aligned and coherent (with talking points, principled messaging, speaker preparation, and others)
- Design a clear message about the resource, the makers of the resource, the intended users, and appeals for attention
- Execute the media plan
- Define what "success"/"failure" looks like in terms of the media plan
- Measure the effects of the publicity plan
- Fine-tune the publicity plan for Version 2.0
- Tailor the media plan messages (and strategies) to different technologies and audiences

Project Launching (Hard and Soft) and Outreach

- Define a "teaser" to raise interest about a learning resource with a future roll-out date
- Define (and design) a "hard launch" to publicize the rollout of an open-shared digital learning object or digital learning sequence
  - Define the large-scale audience which is being reached out to
  - Define what "success"/"failure" of this marketing campaign and event and other efforts looks like (in objectively observable ways)
- Define (and design) a "soft launch" to publicize the rollout of an open-shared digital learning object or digital learning sequence
  - Define the targeted smaller-scale audience which is being reached out to
  - Define what "success"/"failure" in this soft launch looks like in objectively observable and measureable ways
- Consider several ways to create an "event" for mainstream media and social media "buzz" around the launch of the learning contents
  - Define attentional "hooks" for public attention
- Anticipate possible challenges with going deeply public, and work to address possible challenges

Mapping Learning Object (or Sequence) Usage/Monitoring

- Capture baseline data about usage of similar open-shared digital learning objects and sequences
- Design some practical methods for capturing accurate real-world data about how the learning object (or sequence) is being used in the wild (and/or in controlled environments if this is deployed that way)
- Consider what usage patterns over time may mean for the particular open-shared learning object or sequence

- Review ways to improve usage monitoring and surveillance to be more informative
- Consider what usage patterns may suggest for future instructional designs of similar objects and learning resources

Post-Launch Care of Learners and the Shared Learning Resources

- Take on the role of the learner, and anticipate what their learning needs may be with the learning object, course, or learning sequence, and create a plan for addressing anticipated learner needs
  - Describe some methods for creating authentic empathy with various types of learner groups
  - Define some ways to test that empathy (Do your senses of learner needs align with those among actual real-world learners?)
- Explain what parts of learner needs are integrated in the main body of the learning object, and which parts are add-ons as cognitive supports
- Make a list of when the shared learning contents may need updating, the indicators for the readiness for updating, and how the updating may be achieved; write this up as an informal updating plan for the learning contents and/or sequence

10.1 Introduction

In every design and development project, there is a certain point at which the content creators sense that the handoff is close. The mental countdown begins: just a few more passes to refine the resources, and it's done!

Once the learning resources are ready for prime time (after having been properly vetted), the next step is reaching out to "targeted" and "potential" learners via both private and public channels. The targeted learners are the main ones for whom the original learning contents were created and intended, and potential learners are those who find the learning resources and hopefully benefit from the resource. In the design and development sequence, this sharing step is the final one (Fig. 10.1).

This chapter addresses some steps to defining the target learner audiences and ascertaining who the potential ones may be, how to set objectives for outreaches and publicity, what some media plans may look like (harnessing both social media and traditional media), and how to conduct a "hard" and a "soft" launch and measure the respective effectiveness of each outreach. Further, this addresses some methods of monitoring usage of the learning resource to enable revisions (if applicable) and to improve future designs. At the end, this explores the idea of post-launch care of both learners and of the learning object—and discusses ways to strategize and plan for these efforts.

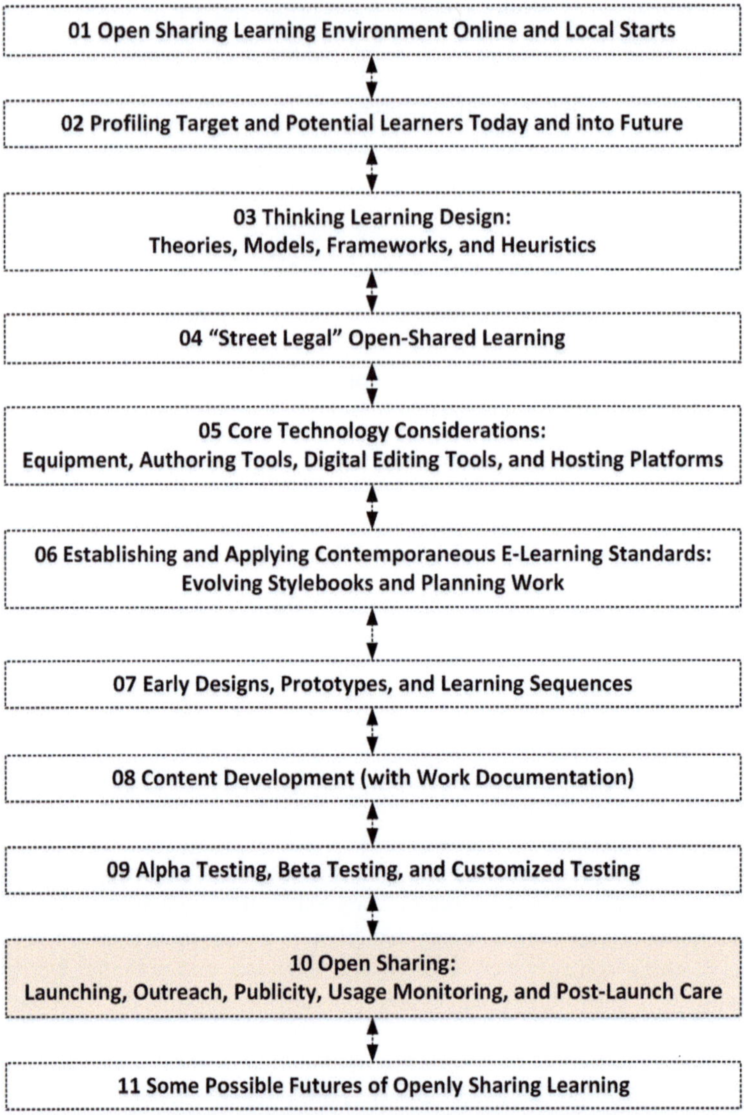

Fig. 10.1 Step 10 in the open-shared learning resource development sequence

10.2 Review of the Literature

In the open-shared learning environment, the learners are a critical part of the equation. They are the *raison d'etre* for the creation of the open-shared learning resources, and in a $0 budget environment and no channels for income, the main metric for the success of an object is how many users use it and to what constructive purposes. Some released learning contents have no takers (Kanwar et al. 2010, p. 69), and in terms of learning object adoption, only about 20% find adopters (Ochoa 2008, 2011). Going in with inflated hopes and neglecting this base-rate would be a mistake.

The early work in profiling "target" and "potential" learners for the learning resources may be reviewed and built upon to understand how to reach out to them. The learning resource adaption model identifies five phases for teachers who use open resources: the search phase, the evaluation phase, the adaptation phase (to modify "the educational resource to the use and context"), the use phase, and then the share phase when "the newly adjusted resource" is reshared to the community (Pawlowski and Zimmermann 2007, as cited in Clements and Pawlowski 2011, p. 5).

Another study focused on how adopters found relevant learning resources for re-use: by "*browsing on topics and subjects*" (89%), "*recommendations from colleagues*" (82%), *recommendations from personal friends*" (71%), resource rankings (56%), positive organizational reputations (58%) (Clements and Pawlowski 2011, p. 9). The researchers identified barriers to adoption, such as incompatibility with the local curriculum (74%), copyright (52%), subject variations "between countries" (48%), and others (Clements and Pawlowski 2011, p. 9). For open educational resources (OER), a wide range of quality approaches may be used as indicators of learning resource quality, including technology standards, quality checklists, benchmarking, peer review, user evaluations, accreditation of sponsoring organizations, rankings, and user recommendations (Clements and Pawlowski 2011, p. 11).

Common reuse revisions and edits include the following, in descending order: visual and technical changes (51%), general editing (24%), collaboration-related changes (11%), metadata changes (8%), modularisation (sic) 1%), language translations (1%), and "miscellaneous reuse behaviors" (as a catch-all) (6%) (Petrides et al. 2008, p. 110). This suggests that open-shared learning resources may not necessarily be seen as in final form and that adopters have to invest some serious work to make the fit happen. In this space, "consistent author users" tended to create more shared contents over longitudinal time (5 years in this study) as compared to "intermittent use" author users and "eventual non-use" author users (Petrides et al. 2008, p. 106).

A common option for releasing open-shared learning objects is merely to upload the contents and make them available to the general public and let potential users find their way to the objects through Web search and some built-in search tools on the hosting repository or learning management system site or social media platform. This approach is a passive one. More active measures are possible and even advisable: a "hard" launch involves a media campaign to reach a wide public audience, and a "soft" launch involves one to reach targeted audiences. Some informal outreach may be to share about the shared resources via professional electronic mailing lists, trade publications, microblogging sites (like Twitter), social networking sites (like Facebook), and other types of narrowcasting. With Web 2.0 and so much of learner works being enacted in public space (Gray et al. 2010) and the advent of E-Learning 2.0 (online learning with Social Web features), the social media angle may be understood as par for the course. Then, too, there may be broadcast efforts through press releases, media events, interviews, and other efforts through more formal mass media channels (with complementary social media efforts). A media campaign may involve an initial launch and no other activities, or there may be multiple follow-on activities to keep public focus on the topic and to keep the resource top-of-mind and to bring in more potential users.

The post-launch care phase is conceptualized as a two-fold one: How are actual learners (both the intended targets and the potential ones) supported in their use of the learning resource? How is the learning resource maintained over time?

The first part involves how the designer/developers (as individuals and as team members) interact with learners who have questions or who comment publicly (or privately). The second part involves how learning resources may be updated and kept relevant (if at all). Some use a "once and done" approach and will not revise contents once it has been uploaded. Some will revise if the object itself is easily revisable and if there is a rolling publishing cycle (like for some e-books).

The commitment to open-shared learning may continue with the particular released object or resources because of the need for maintenance:

> The amount of work to develop educational resources (e.g. documents, graphics, images, videos, laboratory exercises, compatible learning units) is high. Moreover, all these resources have to be maintained and to be developed further as technologies or curricula change (Wenk 2010, p. 435).

There may be frameworks for when to update a learning resource. One design conceptualization conceives of instructional designs as comprising various layers, which age out on different timetables (Gibbons 2003, p. 23).

Another approach is a four-fold one, based on four areas of focus, depicted as the following central questions:

1. Have legal guidelines and relevant policies that might affect the course revision changed?
2. What progress or change in the domain field might inform the course revision?
3. What updates in teaching and learning methodologies might be relevant?
4. What updates in relevant technologies could improve the course? (Hai-Jew 2010, p. 2).

In this four-fold approach, there is a suggested sequence by importance of the topic, with an initial focus first on (1) Legal Guidelines and Relevant Policies, (2) Progress /Change in the Domain Field (and in related cross-disciplinary or multi-disciplinary fields), (3) Course Curricular Strategies/Teaching and Learning Methodologies, and (4) Relevant Updated Technologies (Hai-Jew 2010).

10.3 Open Sharing: Launching, Outreach, Publicity, Usage Monitoring, and Post-Launch Care

Sharing a learning resource in public, for some, may feel like a point of no return. After all, once materials are released, others may find it and post comments and judge it. Most digital materials online may be downloaded or copied. If one's name is out in the world, people may go to the Deep Web and explore one's private life. In the real, releasing learning contents may be more of a let-down, with very muted responses. If one retracts a learning object, that action may well be met with silence. In general, some learning objects may attain a few views, and others may rank in the hundreds and thousands. In terms of contacts by potential users, most will not reach out, but a few may call one's work telephone or send an email with a query or an offer (of free contents). That is not to say that WYSIATI (what you see is all there is), but some of what you see is about the extent of usage. Professionally speaking, shared learning resources are not usually citable in a *curriculum vitae* (CV) but do benefit one's professional work skills. Before releasing a work to the public though, it is important to make sure that everything is done to legal requirements and to quality. If going public feels awkward, then use an initial learning object release as a test case, evaluate the experience, and decide how to proceed from there. One truism is that the public is an important audience for various human endeavors, including learning.

At the time of release, the designer/developers may have to decide whether or not to offer their byline or to use a pseudonymous "handle" (which may/may not be trackable back to them through personally identifiable information or "PII). Certainly a number of works shared in the social learning space are ghost-written. How "forward" a content creator is depends in part on personal preferences. That said, just avoiding having a name on a work does not lessen any legal liabilities for that content.

Going a step further, one may consider executing a media plan to draw wide public attention to the learning resource and to raise its impact factor. This effort may enable unanticipated learners to find their way to the resource. Outreaches can help break the ice between potential users of a resource and that resource; these serve as a bridge to usage in the same way that trailers can lead to full-legnth movies and reviews to full-length books. Going public benefits work by bringing a wider set of eyes on the resources and enabling broader usage. However, here, too, there may be some ambivalence. Going public also bring unwanted attention, whether it is obsessive parasocial follower relationships and harassment, trolling, or other unintended effects.

What is in public may be interpreted many ways by a wide range of people. If there is a wide range of people who can access a resource, there will be both benevolent and malevolent actors and people with mixed motives. The original creators of contents cannot control for how their shared contents may be used, may be disaggregated, may be framed, and may be spun. For many, they may see taking on a public role as a high-risk choice, and they may dismiss this path out-of-hand. However, it would be hard to be totally stealthy and still have a high impact in the people space. Some of the potential pros and cons of going public based on observations and abductive reasoning are listed in Table 10.1.

The contents of the table are shared because sometimes people go into this with a fantastical sense of what publicity will achieve for them. They assume that they will be "discovered," that their dreams will come true, that they'll create a monetary stream or some other fairytale benefit, and that they will change the world. (In the few cases of a person's "discovery," the exceptions prove the rule.) This myth of "going public = fame and glory" can be highly alluring and deceptive. One way to ground this in reality is to see the past as prologue and ask, "What have others who have come before me experienced?" and to understand the "survival bias" in the high profile individuals they see and the many silent ones who never make.

10.3.1 Defining Target Learner Audiences (as Groups)

In Chap. 2, "targeted" and "potential" learners were profiled in a number of ways. Based on the best informed of these profiles, consider how these particular audiences may be reached through formal mainstream media and informal social media. Explore social media platforms and identify high influence individuals ("influencers") who may disseminate information to others effectively.

Table 10.1 Understanding the public as a "forgiving" and/or "unforgiving" environment

	Pros: public as a "forgiving environment"	Cons: public as an "unforgiving environment"
Attention...	Is piecemeal and limited Can feel personally affirming Is non-intrusive in most cases	Can be unrelenting and feel intense Can involve second-guessing and negative interpretations from a distance Can be hyper-critical Can feel personally disconfirming Can be brutal if a person's name is connected with a hot-button political or controversial issue Can be intrusive with explorations in the Deep Web
Emotional tone...	Can be supportive Can include superficial "cheap talk" kudos	Can be impersonal Can be demanding Can be presumptive Can be manipulative Can be motivated by jealousies and *schadenfreude*
Privacy...	May be possible with careful curation of one's social and online presences (and with the cooperation of one's family, friends, and colleagues) May seem possible with selective consumption of online contents	Can be elusive in the face of intrusions Can be lost with the spread of personal information (available on the Deep Web and elsewhere, at negligibly low costs and for free in many cases)
Accuracy...	Can be maintained with trusted entities and agents who have truth as a lived standard Can be created with triangulated sourcing	Can be elusive when people online assign themselves roles as sleuths, and worse, as trolls
Risk...	Can be partially mitigated and managed	Can be hard to anticipate given the size of the world and the ranges of human motives
Public criticism...	Can be constructive Can be insightful Can improve work Can be informative	Can be personal Can be brutal Can be dismissive Can be misfocused Can be a massive pile-on
Forgetting...	Is not an uncommon feature of the online space, where issues appear and disappear with alacrity	Is not possible for issues that are considered of long-term interest and high controversy Is challenging when the internet "never forgets"

Task #1: Editable Learning Resource or Not?
One of the key dimensions of re-usability of shared learning resources has been their revisability and editability. These issues are explicitly addressed as one of the variable in the Creative Commons licensure approach. Teachers who use shared learning objects often want to be able to change up the learning resource to fit their particular contexts. Some designer/developers enable usage of their learning objects but not any revision or editing. They are concerned by how others might represent their work, and they are concerned of potential changes to the quality of the learning resources.

Consider the pros and cons of enabling the revision and editing of your own created open-shared learning resources, and consider how much power you plan to give over to potential users. What sort of licensure release do you see as optimal for your comfort? Elaborate.

10.3.2 Objectives for Outreaches and Publicity

Some practical objectives for media outreaches and media plans for open-shared learning resources may be the following:

- Raise awareness of available open-shared learning resources
- Encourage usage of available open-shared learning resources (to drive traffic)
- Burnish the image of various egos (individuals) and entities (organizations)
- Attract collaborators and co-researchers for open-shared learning projects
- Build a learning community around the usage of particular learning resources in a learning domain
- Promote particular ideas and practices in a particular domain, and others.

To assess the effectiveness of an outreach and/or a media campaign, figure out ways to capture data and metrics about usage. For example, how would one know that awareness was raised about available open-shared learning resources? By usage numbers? By back-end system analytics counts?

Task #2: Formal Media Channels or Less Formal Social Media Channels? Or Both? Or Academic Publishing?

The common path of going through formal media channels generally involves creating a media press release and distributing that to newspaper publishers, television stations, radio stations, magazine publishers, and hoping that there may be a few who may choose to do a story about the issue. The competition for column inches and air time is fierce, and there are many entities sharing information in that space. Open-shared learning resources are not common fodder for mass media. The 24-h news cycle runs on adrenalin and some hype, and unless there is a tie to an issue of the moment, learning resources will not likely make the cut (for relevance). [What makes a story "newsworthy"? It has to be relevant, attention-getting, timely, important for society, interesting, and dramatic, among other things.]

In terms of sharing on social media, this effort usually involves creating messaging and digital contents, and sharing these on social networking sites, microblogging sites, blogs, audio podcasts, video podcasts (vodcasts), websites, electronic mailing lists, and others. It is easy enough to get a message out, but there is still a challenge of driving attention to that message. If the information is newsworthy, though, it is possible for the story to go from social media into mainstream media.

There can be a mix of formal and less formal methods of outreach.

A fourth path may be to publish in academic publications and going the path of academic publicity.

For each approach, there may be a need for versioning similar messages but in different digital mode formats. These efforts are not cost-free. Also, it will be important to measure impacts of the respective outreaches.

Consider these various options, and draft a basic media plan for your particular goals and context.

10.3.3 Media Plans for Publicity

A basic media plan defines the following:

- The respective objectives of the media plan
- The target media organizations (both from mass media and from social media)

- The basic message to be conveyed
- The methods to convey that message
- Any interview offers from principals to advance the story
- Any media events to promote the learning contents, and so on

Typically, there would be budgets related to media plans, too. The individuals carrying out a media plan would do well to have shared talking points, so that the message is perceived as a coherent and focused one. Mixed messages would muddle the message and make it more difficult for recipients of the message to understand what is being shared and to whom. For open-shared learning resources, some basic questions may include the following:

- What is this learning resource? What is its purpose? What makes this noteworthy/newsworthy? What makes this timely?
- Who is this learning resource for?
- Why was it created?
- When was it created?
- Who created it? Who funded it?
- How was it created?
- Where was it created?
- Where can people go to learn more about this resource?

The idea is to get the message right the first time and to backstop the outreaches by having available staff on hand to share accurate information. It is important to get the right kind of attention, not just any attention. With outreaches to target groups vs. mass media, the messaging should be more specifically tailored to the specific audiences.

A media plan is comprised of both internal documents (used by the organization for planning) and external documents (released to the media organizations and general public). A press release usually contains the following elements:

- A headline
- A story written in upside-down triangle order (~to news stories) and in the third-person objective point-of-view
- A dateline (the place and date of the writing)
- A byline (authorship)
- The date of release of the press release
- The press officer (person to contact for more information)
- Telephone and email and other contact methods to reach the press officer
- Organization branding

Images, audio, video, and other digital media and multimedia may be released along with the press release. If there may be follow-on learning resources, it may help to turn the approved press releases as templates for future releases. It also helps to learn from the experiences with the press.

After the plan is created, the individual and/or team should execute on the plan … and use objectively observable measures to decide whether or not the media outreach was successful or not. How many were reached? How clear was the messaging (both intended and unintended)?

And finally, it makes sense to learn from this initial foray into the press space and fine-tune publicity plans for v. 2.0, 3.0, and so on.

Task #3: Strategic Messaging

An effective message has to first positively capture the attention of the individuals and groups who are the target; otherwise, people may merely skip over the contents. The message cannot come across as negative or biased. It should be factual, without over-claiming and without misrepresentation. After all, part of the work of strategic messaging is to control for expectations. All basic questions that may be asked by the recipients have to be answered: who, what, when, where, why, and how? If the recipient audiences require specific tailored information, that should be provided in an anticipatory way.

For television stations, there should be video that may be legally broadcast to support the story. For radio stations, there should be audio that may be legally broadcast to support the coverage. The written press releases should have usable quotes and the names of individuals who may be contacted as further sources. And there should be easy ways to contact individuals who are responsible for handling the press from the originating organization.

It helps to have some experiences in the field to understand how much information to include in a press release (how much is enough, and how much is TMI). To this end, it helps to review some of the many press releases available in electronic format online. Please go online, find a dozen recent press releases related to the topic of your open-shared learning resource. Download these, and read them over. Make a note of some features of these press releases and what makes them effective/ineffective.

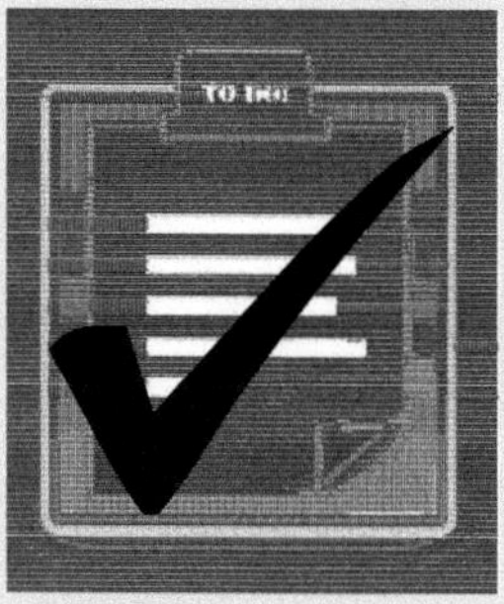

Task #4: Public Relations Planning
Public relations management focuses on how an ego (individual) or entity (group, organization, company) maintains positive relationships with the public and communicates its positive aspects to the broad public: its savvy, its beneficence, its generosity, and other features.

How can you create a public relations plan for your brand and/or your organization? How can you create a positive reputation for your brand? Your organization? Your open-shared learning endeavors?

10.3.4 Project Launching (Hard and Soft) and Outreach

One less-common approach in terms of publicity is to "tease" the release of an open-shared learning resource by offering some early information about the future release data. "Teasers" raise awareness, build curiosity, direct attention, and built up public anticipation for a near-future rollout. To be effective a teaser cannot leave the message recipients indifferent. Through humor, question posing, story-telling, name-dropping, emotional appeals, and other attention-getting measures, teasers create a sense of anticipation. Timing does matter, so such releases benefit from aligning with a larger movement or event; however, these are expensive to create, and serendipitous time alignments rely too heavily on chance.

A "hard launch" is a media campaign that strives to communicate with a large public audience; a "soft launch" is one that strives to communicate with targeted groups. Hard launches are achieved through both formal mass media and social media, and soft ones are usually achieved in more targeted fashion through emails, electronic mailing lists, narrowcast microblogging, and others.

Consider some ways to create an "event" that may merit media coverage and social media buzz. Having a guest speaker from afar may be one lower-cost way to create an event, or having this done via a web conferencing tool may be even lower-cost.

Finally, it may make sense to anticipate some possible challenges with going public and to plan to mitigate those challenges.

Task #5: Self Promotion and Popularity Waves

In some cases, an early work may capture the public's imagination, and that word of mouth (WOM) may drive learner traffic and encourage usage of the particular learning resources. Those who would folk-tag learning resources into amateur folksonomies will also affect and drive traffic. High-influence individuals (aka "mayors of the hashtag") may also drive attention. Such fame may make the reputations of the creator and/or creating team. Extreme fame is rare, and it is "bursty" and only lasts for a time before dropping off steeply or fading slowly, leaving behind some residual effects. People, in general, go through a notice-pay attention-forget cycle.

One way to ride a popularity wave is to promote the learning resources even more to ensure that the resource becomes a recognizable "thing" on social media. If a social phenomenon becomes too hot, it may overtake the individual or team, and they may find that they have to build careers around the initial work. (An example may be dominant models that are created by researchers, who then spend decades elaborating on that main work.) Fame can lock in individuals and teams to particular points-of-view and personas. Fame may also attract critics and detractors.

Would you prefer to be high profile or low profile? A high profile approach means that you will be personality-forward and sharing of some personal aspects of your life in order to connect with the learner audiences and general public. It means that you may share photos and video and audio of yourself to convey personal charisma, expertise, likeability, and appeal. A low profile may be a more impersonal approach even as the contents are shared openly. For your domain topic, which is preferable? For your personality, which is preferable?

Given the various tradeoffs, where would you like your work to land on the fame spectrum? Why? If you had a public-facing persona, what aspects of your personality would you like to be represented? Why? (Fig. 10.2).

What are some ways you would mediate the upsides and downsides of each position on the spectrum?

Extra: Research into online virality shows that a message has to be captured and shared beyond an initial social network, and it has to cut across

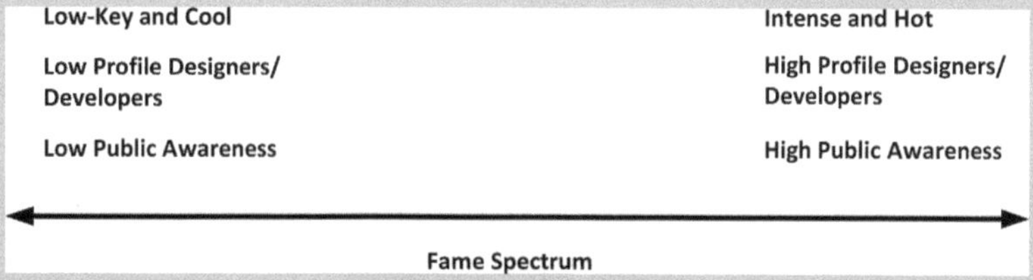

Fig. 10.2 Fame spectrum

multiple social networks in short order, to achieve the "escape velocity" and gravitational pull of the local. Such messages, on social media, require some attention-getting shock value. For learning resources, what are ways to try to achieve viral social sharing and awareness? Why? What are methods you would use to attract attention, and what are your limits or redlines beyond which you would not go for capturing attention?

Oftentimes, virality may be achieved with the championing of the resource by a high influence individual. Are you aware of such individuals who may be contacted to advocate for a particular resource? Do you have a message that would encourage him/her/them to support your work?

Also, would you create follow-on learning resources to extend the focus on the select topic? How would you ensure that a work is "newsworthy" (if further courting of the press will occur then)? Are there ways to show a public interest in the topic?

10.3.5 Mapping Learning Object (or Sequence) Usage/ Monitoring

Sometimes, to understand how well a particular learning resource is doing, it helps to set a baseline for usage of similar open-shared learning resources. It is possible to set baselines for usage by evaluating similar learning resources and paying attention to usage counts and other usage data.

When a learning resource is shared—in the wild or in closed or controlled-member spaces—there are different ways to capture usage statistics. Conducting reconnaissance on these methods early may be helpful for when objects are deployed, so that the designer/developer can capture that information. Such data may not only be from a particular slice-in-time but may be collected over time, to see how usage fluctuates. The public commenting on learning resources, emails sent to the content creators, and other channels may enable further usage insights.

Finally, it makes sense to apply the usage pattern data to improve the instructional designs of similar learning resources. For example, if particular learning sequences are especially appealing to learners, maybe that information may be helpful for future designs. Likewise, if there are particular complaints about a learning object, that information may be useful, too.

Task #6: Making a Plan for Usage Monitoring and Learner (User) Responses

Usage monitoring points to the capturing of metrics and qualitative data about user experiences with particular open-shared learning resources. Generic measures may include counts of views over time as a rough measure. More specific measures may include user behavior with the particular learning resources. There may be pre- and post-test measures of learner performance. Various hosting platforms for learning contents may enable other insights to user accesses and experiences. Learner commenting, star rankings, and other channels may be informative as well. Some learners will also reach out directly to the content creators via email, phone, and social media.

No matter what is collected, learner identities should not generally be captured, and people's data have to be handled with care.

For this task, do some exploration about the types of data collectable for usage monitoring in your particular context, and write up a brief usage monitoring plan.

10.3.6 Post-Launch Care of Learners and the Shared Learning Resources

For user-centered design, it is important for the designer/developer to serve as an "empath" with learners, so that the learning contents are designed to learner needs. This ability is also important after learning contents have been finalized and released to the world. "Post-launch care" is understood as comprising two main elements here: (1) the support of past, current, and future users of an open-shared learning resource and/or (2) the maintenance and updating of learning resources into the future with necessary revisions and retrofitting. In traditional "once and done" approaches, designer/developers may merely create contents and share it and be done. The post-launch care may not be necessarily followed. Over time, though, the space has changed to where either or both of the care elements may be important.

For the support of learners, usually, learners have to reach out to the content creators for support. Some instructors will purposefully reach out to learners and even travel to meet learners around the world in their massive open online courses (MOOCs), but that level of dedication is more an exception.

While shared learning resources may have been initially future-proofed, there are real limits to what may be done to ensure the relevance of learning resources over time. In terms of the maintenance of the learning resources, the maintenance may be required due to the sunsetting of particular technologies rendering the learning object non-functional. The hosting platform may have gone out of business. Or there may be new information in the domain field that would enhance the learning resource. Regardless of the reasons, in many cases, the designer/developers may no longer have access to the original team that created the original contents. The original technologies themselves may not be available. Depending on how project documentation was done, some of the original project files may be unavailable.

Maintaining learning resources may become more challenging as time passes. And treating a shared learning resource as a work-in-progress may require more commitment than the designer/developers already have to invest. If a work is no longer relevant or usable without excessive investment, a simple solution may be to sunset it and take it off of the server.

If there is still interest in supporting a learning resource, it may be good to build an add-on to meet some understood learner needs post-launch.

Also, if there is continuing commitment to the learning resource over time, it may help to have a plan for when to update the contents, list the objective indicators for readiness for updating, and how that updating may be achieved.

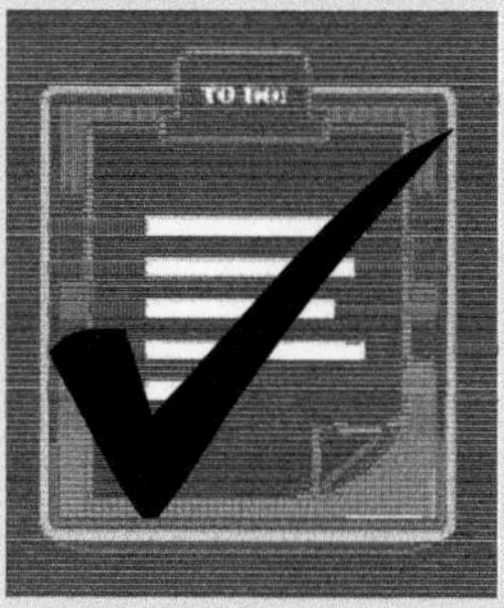

Task #7: Post-Launch Care

In this work, the post-launch care is comprised of two elements. The first is the support for users of the learning resources (learners, administrators, and others), and the second relates to the amount of maintenance of the respective learning objects going forward (updates, protection against digital extinction, and other factors).

Please define how much you are willing to be "on call" to users of the learning resources. If you are asked to solve a technical coding issues similar to your designed object, do you respond?

Do you believe in a once-and-done approach to the learning resource? If not, what are the thresholds you would use to know when to revise a learning resource? Why? What are your limits in terms of how much work you will put into revisions into the future?

Live Examples (On the Web)

It is possible to piece together others' outreach plans to the public by reviewing email messages from massive open online course (MOOC) course providers … professional organizations related to open-shared learning resources, and other messages. Collect as many of these messages as you can find over a 5-day period, and analyze them for strategic messaging.

Creating, Executing, and Assessing an Informal "Soft Launch" Outreach Plan

You have identified a target learner group that you've worked with in the past. You know some of the members from a non-profit professional organization that you've been involved with for some years, and some of the members are familiar with you, too. You decide to create a message for the electronic mailing list, which is human-moderated.

Your goal is to raise awareness of the availability of the learning resource, and you hope to convert some of the email recipients into users of the resource. You have read that a 1% conversion rate is about what you can expect. You think that even if you do not achieve more than the 1%, you at least will have written this information into the records.

You begin with an apology if there is any cross-posting. This is pro forma but also necessary given how quickly information moves and how generous people can be about forwarding messages.

You describe the resource and how it may benefit users, and you include some information about your history with the organization. You let readers know where to access the resource. You provide a little history about the creation of the resource for human interest. You include contact information. After double-checking the writing and the links, you send it to the list.

You will measure the success of this message by how many new users you see on the site … and by how many emails you get back.

10.3.7 Discussion

This work shows the importance of understanding what going live and public may mean for shared learning resources and some of the cautions that are understood whenever engaging with others online. It is helpful to have a plan going forward to attract public attention and to handle that attention in a logical and professional way. The point-of-launch is also critical in another sense because this is a good time for post-project reflection for the designer/developer and/or team. This reflection is important to improve future work, and it may also inform whether anyone continues on to future open-shared learning projects. Some useful questions to ask include the following: What was learned? What new technologies were used, and what new methods were engaged, and what new skills were acquired? What was enjoyable about the work? What was done well, and what could have been done better? What actual contributions were made to the larger environment with the open-shared learning resources? What were the actual inputs and outputs (I/O) to the project, and the cost-benefit calculations? How aligned was this work with the respective contributors' professional (and personal) goals? If this were to have been done differently, what would the approaches have been?

10.4 Future Research Directions

At present, there does not seem to be research on how to effectively launch publicity for open-shared learning objects and sequences. These topics may include the identification of target learner groups, the creation of media plans, "hard" and "soft" launches, monitoring of publicity efforts for effectiveness, ways to improve media outreaches, the post-launch care of users of the learning resources, updates to the shared learning resources post-launch, and related topics. There is likely plenty of extant experiences in this area. Open-shared learning resources have been around for decades. Research in these areas stand to benefit on-ground decision making, publicity designs, and other practical applications.

Also, in the same way that there are automated, blended, and manual ways to assess instructional designs in formalized online learning courses, there will be ways to assess stand-alone open shared learning resources. Beginning with the data available off of the hosting platforms and the learning resources themselves is a start (Fig. 10.3).

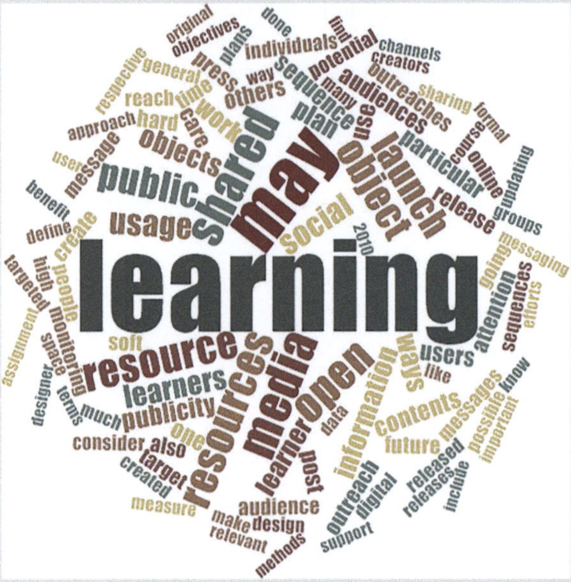

Fig. 10.3 A Word Cloud of Chapter 10: "Open Sharing: Launching, Outreach, Publicity, Usage Monitoring, and Post-Launch Care"

What-if: Connecting with Learners of Open-Shared Learning Resources

So you have released an open-shared learning resource to the public, and you've followed that up with some messages to professional email lists and messaging on social media. You encouraged a professional organization to create and release a press release to its membership. You move on to other projects, but you plan to monitor usage with a simple counting tool on the platform and messaging to your email and social media accounts (given that you did include contact information in the presentation).

Based on numbers of views alone, you see an early burst of visits based on the publicity, and a month or two after the release, you find that usage has settled to a dozen or so accesses a month. You decide not to sweat this because the resource may be discovered sometime in the future by others, and the numbers will accrue over time. Also, you know that the "sunk costs" are gone and irrecoverable, so the numbers alone are not going to be the difference one way or another.

The hosting platform enables access to more information about learners if you pay for a more expensive subscription cost. If you do, you could learn more about the usage. You may be able to find some insights that may enhance the learning object. You may even create something publishable in the research literature. However, this may be news to potential users that you can collect this type of information about their online learning behaviors. What do you do?

Decision point #1: Stop or advance. If advance, and you decide to collect more information, how will you let learners know of this data collection (so you don't break trust)? If not, you can still use other informational channels to capture learner usage data.

You decide to notify learners of the enhanced data collection. Several of them reach out after this communication, and they have some suggestions on how to improve the learning resource to meet their needs. Some of the ideas would enhance the learning resource over all. Some of the ideas are very niche and specific to the individuals.

Decision point #2: Stop or advance. If advance, what are some standards you would use to revise the resources? How would you let some know that their ideas will be accepted and others that their ideas will not?

You decide to thank all the learners for their comments and honestly let them know that you will consider their suggestions. You decide to update the resource based on some of the suggestions … and on some of the other data.

Over time, some of the learners start asking some personal questions. Or they indicate that they are assuming intimacy where none exists. You can confront them and let them know that such approaches are unwanted. Or you can let the interactions go to silence ….

Decision point #3: Stop or advance. If advance, how do you control for the interchange going off the rails? ….

The What-If Debriefing

The general public on the WWW and Internet are individuals from around the world, and they come at resources with a wide range of backgrounds and expectations. Engaging with the public requires hearing people out and responding respectfully, even when some of the requests are inappropriate (requests for copyrighted manuscripts, requests for software licenses, and so on). Sometimes, in reading between the lines, it is clear that the communicator has incorrect assumptions about the content creators, and their propositions are invariably self-serving.

In some cases, silence is the proper response.

10.5 Conclusion

If you want to carve a niche in this open-shared learning space, in all likelihood, you will have that niche, and it will likely go unchallenged in part because of how much work it takes to contribute. A key insight about reusability is that people will not want to reinvent the wheel!

Considering launching an open-shared learning resource to the public can be daunting. A learning resource never seems quite perfectly ready, but waiting on that perfection may well stand in the way of a good basic resource. No one should be aiming for perfection because if he or she did, nothing would ever get done. Crossing the Rubicon by publishing a work may seem less momentous than a mental buildup might suggest. If nothing else, this chapter should have provided some assurances that individuals and teams may share learning resources to public space with confidence in the solidity of their open-shared learning resources, and they can control the outreach to better target their learner audiences while ensuring that the broad general public is welcome, too. Also, this work raises some questions about what happens after going public—and how much responsibility the content creators may have for the learners who use their contents and for revising and updating the released contents into the future.

To wrap, though, those who reach this "finish line" for the particular small race really should celebrate. In my years, I have had many projects start, progress, and wrap—without any in-team or private fanfare. This strikes me as misguided. For the amount of work that it takes to achieve some of these projects, the celebrations should be held, even if it is only a no-host meal out at a local restaurant or coffee shop!

10.6 Reviews and Assignments

10.6.1 Main Points Review

- Media plans are built around objectives for that media. A core need is to raise awareness of the open-shared learning resource in order to heighten its usage.
- Outreaches to both targeted and potential users of the respective open-shared learning objects and sequences may be done through traditional mass media, social media, direct person-to-person outreaches, and other means.
- Different target learner audiences may be reached in different ways.
- High social influencers may be important points-of-contact to reach out to a number of virtual communities.
- Teasers may be created to raise interest about the future launch of a forthcoming learning object. These are not generally released unless the learning resources are near completion.
- Larger-scale media plans (for hard launches) will require a combination of efforts: writing and distributing press releases, offering individuals for interviews, conducting media-friendly events, and others.
- Media plans should be followed up with objective ways to measure the efficacy of the outreaches to know if the audience was reached … with the accurate message … and behavioral responses were followed-through on. There should be ways to assess relative "success" and "failure". There should be assessments about how to run future publicity plans. Also, there should be insights about how to tailor future media plan messages and strategies to different technologies and audiences.

- A "hard launch" is usually about publicizing the rollout of an open-shared digital learning object or learning sequence (or series). Hard launches are used to reach out to large-scale audiences.
- A "soft launch" is usually about publicizing the rollout of an open-shared digital learning object or learning sequence (or series) to a defined target audience.
- Media-friendly events are about creating a sense of excitement or buzz. They are "friendly" to media because of the invitation of media, offers of specialized tours, press passes, and other aspects. These events may include anything newsworthy and attention-getting.
  - Event-based outreaches are soft launches, to geographically local individuals.
  - For the sake of security, it would be helpful to target outreaches and also ensure basic security to any events.
- Sometimes, going deeply public can be risky by attracting detractors and others who do not have direct interest in the open-shared learning resources.
- Once a learning object is made public, it is helpful to understand how it is being used through monitoring or surveillance. Such information may inform future instructional designs of similar learning objects and learning sequences (resources).
- How users of the learning objects and sequences are cared for in terms of their learning may be part of the post-launch care.
- Have a plan about when a released learning object or sequence may be updated and why. This would be for more substantive updates.

10.6.2 Critical Thinking Questions

Defining Target Learner Audiences (as Groups)

- What are the target learner audiences for the particular designed learning object and/or learning sequence? (And who are not? And why not?) Who are some possible "surprise" target audience members who may not have been conceptualized initially?
  - What are some creative ways to reach out to the respective communities? What social media platforms attract certain members of the target audience vs. others?
  - What are ways to tailor messages to the specific communities? What messages may be more resonant with some communities vs. others?
- What are ways to identify powerful "influences" (people, memes, messages, images, and others) on certain social media platforms? Certain virtual communities? (For example, "high degree" and "high network centrality" are some ego measures that may show influence in a social network, using social network analysis.)

Project Launching and Outreach

- How will your outreaches and messaging differ between formal mainstream media and social media? Will your tone be different and why?

Objectives for Outreaches and Publicity

- What are the practical objectives for your outreaches and media plans related to the learning resource? Are there interests in promotion of the individual developer/designers, the design team, the organization, and other egos and entities? The learning resource as a stray one-off or as a sequence? Particular methods, technologies, and ideas? Learning communities? Is there interest in merely driving use of the learning resource? Or is there interest in achieving more?
- What are accurate ways to measure how well the respective objectives are met (and to what threshold standards)?

Media Plans for Publicity

- In terms of publicity for learning resources, is the goal virality (a huge burst of high-level publicity and then follow-on positive word-of-mouth messaging, with reputational gains, and gradual diminishment of attention) or a slow burn of regular attention and usage over time? Which would be preferable and why? If both together is possible, would that be desirable? Finally, what are some ways to attract attention (authentically and non-manipulatively) months and years after a learning resource has originally been launched?
- Given that a media plan may entail disparate elements like press releases, speakers, interview subjects, events, and other efforts, what would some of your main talking points be? Some of your main principles? How would you make sure that there is a coherent message?
- What parts of a learning object or sequence would be most salient to the general public and to potential learners? Why? How can you design messaging to highlight these points?
- What are measureable ways to know that you are successful with a media outreach? How would you measure that level of success? What are ways to tell if you have been unsuccessful with a media plan, and how would you measure that level of lack of success? How would you capture ideas for ways to improve the publicity? How would you fine-tune a "rolling" publicity campaign to be more effective as you go?

Project Launching (Hard and Soft) and Outreach

- What sorts of teasers for short-term lead-ups to a project resource release may be most effective for particular audiences? Would these work better to a closed audience or a broad general public, and why? What are social media channels most amenable to such teasers, and why? How can such messages be mysterious and yet informative?
- Most "hard launch" publicity outreaches are to a broad-scale audience. How would you define desirable recipients of the message, and what features would

they have, and what would their behavioral response be? What about unwanted responses, and why would these be undesirable? How can you tailor the outreach to encourage wanted behaviors vs. unwanted ones?
- Most "soft launch" publicity outreaches are to target limited-scale audiences. How would you define desirable recipients of the message, and what features would they have, and what would their behavioral response be? What about unwanted responses, and why would these be undesirable? How can you tailor the outreach to encourage wanted behaviors vs. unwanted ones?

Mapping Learning Object (or Sequence) Usage/Monitoring

- What are some effective quantitative ways to measure public learner usage of a particular open-shared learning resource? What are some effective qualitative ways to measure public learner usage of a particular open-shared learning resource? How assertable and accurate are the results from each of the measures? What are ways to learn how to improve future learning objects and sequences from learner usage patterns?
- If learner behaviors are captured using learning object technologies (like xAPI) and e-learning platform technologies, how should learners be notified of the tracking? How can such information be used effectively without compromising learner privacy?

Post-launch Care of Learners and the Shared Learning Resources

- Should open-shared learning objects just be created once, released to the public, and left alone without any further investment by the designer/developer(s) in terms of the support of the learning community or any revisions to the learning object? Or does the release of an open-shared learning resource presage a longer-term commitment? (If the commitment lasts longer, would that be too expensive for potential designers/developers?).
- When learning objects and sequences go public, there is not only the voice from the center (the creators) but also voices from the periphery (the users of the learning object, reviewers, and others). Do the original creators have a role to harmonize the conversations? Mediate? Respond? Why or why not? How much should the original designers/developers engage (or not)? (Fig. 10.4).
- When should a public learning resource be updated and why and how?
- When should a follow-on learning object or sequence be built to a prior extant learning object or sequence? How can an established "user base" be built upon if there is some followership and established loyalty?

10.7 Assignments

Directions The Assignments are divided into two sections, Basic and Advanced. The Basic section is for those who may not have much instructional design experience or background in the area of creating instructional contents for open sharing.

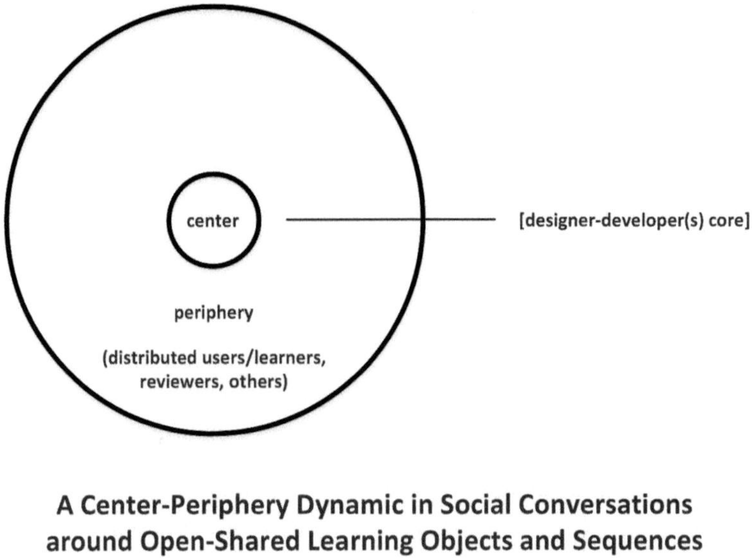

Fig. 10.4 A center-periphery dynamic in social conversations around open-shared learning objects and sequences

As such, these are set up to familiarize them with the chapter-related knowledge, skills, and abilities. The Advanced section is for those who already have some knowledge of this general space and who may benefit from more challenging work.

In a formal learning context, these assignments would benefit from expert feedback and further applications of the learning contents. In a nonformal or informal learning context, including self-directed learning, these assignments would benefit from both reflection and practice. These assignments are built to be extensible, to have elements added to benefit the learners. They are designed to be assigned selectively and not in full. The setup of this textbook is as a work sequence, and similarly, the assignments may be set up as tasks to be completed by the learner in a sequential way … that takes them through the fairly complete and sequential *open-shared learning design → development → test → revision → launch → post-launch* process.

10.7.1 Basic

Assignment 10.1: Teasers A teaser is like a movie trailer, which is released prior to a feature film's rollout. This pre-release is designed to create excitement, interest, and anticipation; it is designed to enable audiences to identify themselves. Explicitly, audiences may pre-register to be notified through online sign-ups, for example.

Implicitly, audiences may have heightened awareness of the forthcoming resource. What are some effective ways to tease a forthcoming learning resource on electronic mailing lists, social networking site poststreams, microblogging messages, blog messages, news press releases, and others?

Assignment 10.2: Hard Launch A "hard launch" usually refers to the general release of a new learning object to the general public. This usually requires some manufactured fanfare, such as an event, public releases, advertisements, social media outreaches, and other efforts. Ensure that these messages are fairly aligned and coherent. List ten methods for conducting a hard launch to reach relevant learner audiences for your conceptualized open-shared online learning. What alliances can you benefit from? How would you drive traffic to your learning object? How would you introduce your learning object to a "cold" audience without background to your learning object? Is it more important to have a lot of users, or is it the quality of user which is more important?

Extra: After the initial hard launch, what are some ways to reach out further and acquire a sense of "second wind" for the learning resources? Who are non-traditional potential user-audiences that may be contacted?

Assignment 10.3: Soft Launch A "soft launch" refers to the release of the learning object to a restricted audience, such as a dedicated group of people or virtual community. A soft launch usually does not require large-scale outreach or huge electronic word of mouth (e-WOM); it usually does not require advertising dollars. List ten methods for conducting a soft launch to reach relevant learner audiences for your conceptualized open-shared online learning. How would you introduce your learning object to a "cold" audience without background to your learning object? What are some attentional hooks that might create buzz about the learning object?

Extra: After the initial soft launch, what are some ways to reach out further and acquire a sense of "second wind" for the learning resources? Who are non-traditional audiences that may be contacted?

Assignment 10.4: Reaching Out Through Connected and Influential Individuals ("Social Influencers") There are individuals who have high "degree" and "high centrality" in social networks. Within their respective social communities, these are individuals who have high influence within that community. How would you identify these individuals and reach out to them to win their support to share your open-shared learning object? Further, how would you identify stakeholder communities to the particular domain and by extension your learning object?

Assignment 10.5: Post-launch Care of the Shared Objects/Sequences And of Learners Consider what learners might need to use the open-shared learning contents. (This assumes that multiple strategies, including cognitive scaffolding, were already used in the design of the original learning.) Where do learners need support, information, feedback, and advice? Where do learners need social support? How forward-leaning should the respective creators of learning objects and sequences be? How public should they be? How much should they encourage interactions with the respective users?

Extra: One aspect of post-launch care involves what happens to the learning object and/or sequence after its rollout and broad publication. Should such objects or sequences be updated? If they are updated, what parts should be updated, and why? Further, how should users be notified of the updating (versioning)? Or should these be once-and-done? And should focuses then be on follow-on learning objects and sequences? Which approach seems more broadly applicable and why?

Assignment 10.6: Learning Object/Course/Sequence Retrofitting Plan Create a reasonable plan for when the particularly open-shared learning object, course, or sequence should be retrofitted. Further, what should be looked at to be retrofitted, and what sorts of retrofitting actions should be taken? What standards should be applied to the retrofitted object, and why? What should the intervals be for checking on the state of the learning object? What sorts of automated feedback should be collected around the usage of the learning object? What are efficient ways to monitor the learning object and its usage?

Extra: When online learning objects become defunct, should they be revised for newer technologies? Why or why not? Who should have responsibilities for this?

10.7.2 Advanced

Assignment 10.7: Risks with Reaching a Wide Audience? A Small Audience? Anticipate some possible risks with releasing your learning object to a broad and public audience. Consider as many dimensions as possible. Consider what ways there may be to mitigate some of these risks. Also, what are some risks with reaching a small audience? Consider a breadth of possibilities in each of the cases.

Assignment 10.8: Terms of Learning Object /Sequence Retraction If you were running a repository for open-shared learning objects or sequences, what rules would you set to encourage as many interested and informed people to participate as possible? Also, if you were managing such a site, what would be the bases for your pulling or retracting a shared object (assuming there is an open submission system)? Would it be on the basis of controversy (the challenging of social norms)? Awkward inferences? Law-breaking? What would be your ethical grounds for retracting a work? Your legal grounds? Ethical grounds? Values? How would you set up policies to protect your decision making in this context?

Extra: Conversely, as a designer and developer, what are some bases on which you would pull an open-shared learning object or sequence? What information would you leave behind to explain the retraction?

Assignment 10.9: Open-Shared Digital Learning Objects and Sequences as Historical and Retro Information? Digital learning objects and sequences will "date out" at different rates and for different reasons (content, design, technological, learner populations, and so on). What are some ways that such learning objects may offer research value? Historical insight?

Extra: Step forward 5 or 10 years, and consider how such objects may shed light on the current present and be informative to people in the future. Or informative to our future selves. What sorts of objects and sequences would be most informative from a historical perspective?

Assignment 10.10: Post-release Monitoring of the Learning Objects and Sequences How much monitoring would you place on the particular open-shared learning objects and sequences? What sorts of feedback would you want to know, and why? Would you collect learner information, and if so, what kind? Would you collect personally identifiable information (PII)? Why or why not? What sorts of information would be ultimately helpful for future designs, and why?

Assignment 10.11: Others' Harnessing of the Open-Shared Resources? Based on the open-shared learning object or sequence you created and shared broadly, what are some usages of that resource by others that would concern you? Why? What sorts of licensure would you apply to protect the rights you want to protect and release those which are less worrisome? Are you open to others using what you've created for commercial purposes? Are you open to others revising and editing your work? Are you open to others taking credit for your work? Are you comfortable with others leaving your byline off of your work? And so on. More importantly, write out any sort of follow-on enforcement plan if others do mis-use the open-shared work. Will you use cease-and-desist letters? Take further action?

Key Terms and Definitions

Broadcast To send a message to a wide audience through technology
Curation The collection, selection, management, and presenting of relevant contents in a set
Hard Launch A full release of a new learning resource to the general public
Narrowcast To send a message to a relatively small audience
Post-Launch Care (1) the support of past, current, and future users of an open-shared learning resource and/or (2) the maintenance and updating of learning resources into the future with necessary revisions and retrofitting

Potential Learners The individuals and groups who may benefit from a particular learning resource but who were not the original intended focuses of the design and development

Press Release A structured and official statement on a particular topic by an organization, individual, or company released to the public (and which may often be used verbatim, and which includes contact information about the press officer who may be contacted for more information)

Public Relations The external communications of an ego or entity to promote a positive public reputation

Publicity The distribution of information to the general public or to targeted groups

Publicity Campaign A concerted endeavor to reach the public or targeted groups with particular messages (to induce the public to awareness, behavior, or other volitional actions)

Social Media Socio-technical spaces that enable people to create persistent personality profiles, interact, intercommunicate, share digital resources, and achieve shared goals

Soft Launch A partial release of a new learning resource to targeted or restricted audiences as either the full publicity endeavor or as a prelude to a hard launch

Targeted (Focal) Learners The individuals and groups for whom a learning resource is intended (and was designed and developed for)

Usage Monitoring The act of checking on the amount of usage a learning resource receives along with other usage information

References

Clements KI, and Pawlowski JM. User-oriented quality for OER: Understanding teachers' views on re-use, quality, and trust. *Journal of Computer Assisted Learning* 28: 4 – 14, 2011. DOI: 10.1111/j.1365-2729.2011.00450.x.

Gibbons AS. What and how do designers design? A theory of design structure. *Tech Trends* 47: 22 – 27, 2003. https://link.springer.com/content/pdf/10.1007/BF02763201.pdf.

Gray K, Thompson C, Sheard J, Clerehan R, and Hamilton M. Students as Web 2.0 authors: Implications for assessment design and conduct. *Australasian Journal of Educational Technology* 26: 105 – 122, 2010.

Hai-Jew S. An instructional design approach to updating an online course curriculum. *Educause Review.* https://er.educause.edu/articles/2010/12/an-instructional-design-approach-to-updating-an-online-course-curriculum. 2010.

Kanwar A, Kodhandaraman B, and Umar A. Toward sustainable open education resources: A perspective from the Global South. *The Amer. Jrn. of Distance Education* 24: 65 – 80, 2010. DOI: 10.1080/08923641003696588.

Ochoa X. Learnometrics: Metrics for Learning Objects. Slideshow. Retrieved May 18, 2018, from https://www.slideshare.net/xaoch/learnometrics-metrics-for-learning-objects-presentation. 2008.

Ochoa X. Learnometrics: Metrics for Learning (Objects). In the proceedings of LAK 2011. Retrieved from https://www.slideshare.net/xaoch/learnometrics-keynote-lak2011. 2011.

Petrides L, Nguyen L, Jimes C, and Karaglani A. Open educational resources: Inquiring into author use and re-use. *Int. J. Technology Enhanced Learning* 1: 98 – 117, 2008.

Wenk B. Open educational resources (OER) inspire teaching and learning. IEEE EDUCON Education Engineering 2010- The future of Global Learning Engineering Education. Madrid, Spain. 435 – 441, 2010.

Additional Reading Section

Hiam A. 2009. *Marketing Kit for Dummies*. Hoboken: Wiley Publishing, Inc.

Chapter 11
Some Possible Futures of Openly Sharing Learning

Abstract If it is true that the present age shows a retreat from globalism in a G-Zero world, then it may be that the appeal of creating online learning contents and learning sequences for free for the betterment of others may be a non-starter. If the ecosystem is about everyone for themselves, why start in a dominated position and sure-lose strategy? This chapter asks a critical question about what the future of open sharing may look like, and why. What would be the optimal (aspirational?) scenario (s) for humanity? What are some possible futures at the macro-, meso-, and micro- scales, and why? What are ways to reconfigure incentives and disincentives for the optimal outcomes? And most importantly, how does the reader see himself or herself (or themselves) in this space into the near-future, mid-term future, and long-term future, and how do they plan to get themselves into their desirable future?

Keywords Open-shared learning · Projected futures · Sustainability · Learning object economy

> The sea is selective, slow at recognition of effort and aptitude but fast in the sinking of the unfit.
>
> —Felix Riesenberg's "Riesenberg Saying" (1879–1939)

> You must never confuse faith that you will prevail in the end—which you can never afford to lose—with the discipline to confront the most brutal facts of your current reality, whatever they might be.
>
> —Jim Stockdale (1923–2005), as cited in Jim Collins' *Good to Great: Why Some Companies Make the Leap ... and Others Don't* (2001)

> Leaders must encourage their organizations to dance to forms of music yet to be heard.
>
> —Warren Bennis, Professor of Business (1925–2014)

> "The public is the only critic whose opinion is worth anything at all."
>
> —Mark Twain, Author (1835–1910)

S. Hai-Jew, *Designing Instruction For Open Sharing*,
https://doi.org/10.1007/978-3-030-02713-1_11

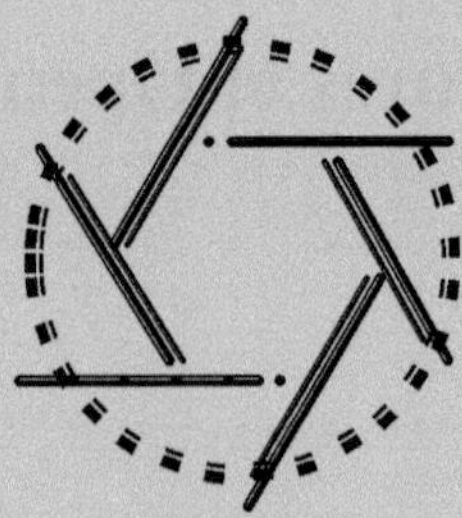
Opening Scenario

Opening Scenario: Thinking Ahead? Redux?

You have now gone through a process of conceptualizing, designing, developing, releasing, and publicly launching an open-shared learning object. This has been your "side gig" for a period of time. Early on, you had considered what you would gain from this work process and from sharing the learning resource broadly.

Now that the project is complete, you realize that the work may have been somewhat disruptive but also fulfilling. The shared object may not have fully instantiated in the way you might have expected at the beginning, but it "ticks the boxes" in many ways. You have learned a few new skills or reinforced some of the existing ones. You have contributed to curating your reputation online.

After taking a breather, you realize you have some other ideas for projects that would be rewarding to you. However, you are aware that there are opportunity costs (other endeavors that you cannot engage in) with taking on such side projects. You are aware of some rewards and some risks.

Do you want to continue creating for open sharing? How do you handle such transactions where you take on a majority of the cost and the risks, and strangers benefit?

Some Early Questions to Consider

What do you think about the future of open sharing … and how viable it may or may not be? How do you envision your potential place in the open sharing learning space? What do you see yourself contributing?

Would you take on a new open-shared project based on the work experience alone, regardless of how the initial object or resource is received or not?

Would you have to receive encouraging messages from users? How would you respond to discouraging messages or critiques?

Do you have a threshold number of learners within a certain timeframe that you would need to have as an audience before you feel justified in your investment of time, effort, expertise, and reputation? Why would you set a user threshold at this particular level?

What sorts of infrastructure do you see in place for promoting the future of open-shared learning objects? What sorts of infrastructure should be put into place to support open-shared learning? How much of the necessary infrastructure is already in place?

What do you see about incentives and inducements to open sharing?

Learning Objectives
Learners will …

Ideal Desirable Futures for Open-Shared Learning

- Define some desirable futures for open-shared learning and explain why a particular conceptualized future is "desirable"
  - List some ways to change up the incentives and remove disincentives for contributing to open-shared learning at macro-, meso-, and micro-/local (organizational) scales to achieve some of these desirable futures
  - List some ways to head off undesirable futures with open-shared learning such as poor quality, derivative works, illegal works, non-factual works, and so on
  - List some ways to change up personal incentives for contributing to open-shared learning on a personal level
- Consider some ways that open-shared learning may be sustainable into the future

Your Possible Futures in Relation to Open-Shared Learning Resources

- Define your various roles in relation to open-shared learning resources (for example, as a user, as a designer, as a developer, as a review, and others)
  - Separate out the positive and negative experiences in each of the relevant roles
- Consider how you want to see yourself in the future in each of the respective roles and based on how you anticipate the future of open-shared learning to unfold
- List ways to improve your ability to learn from open-shared learning resources
- List ways to improve your ability to contribute learning resources to open-shared learning holdings

Some Possible Futures for Open-Shared Learning Resources

- List some pros and cons of open-shared learning resources for entities (commercial companies, including third-party content creators; for institutions of higher education; for K12 institutions; for nonprofit organizations; for government or the public sector; for learning communities) and for egos (learners, for teachers, administrators, and others) and for others based on stakeholder roles in relation to the issue)
  - Consider some ways to magnify the pros
  - Consider some mitigations for the cons
  - Consider some first order effects and some second order effects
- Consider some possible futures of open-shared learning at a macro Web and Internet scale, and use some objectively observable indicators and evidence to support this possible future

  - List some of the elements that support an infrastructure for open-shared learning at Web level (incentives, social recognition, social norms, socio-technical structures, authoring technologies, resource catalogs, intellectual property release licensure, and other factors)
- Ponder some possible futures of open-shared learning at a meso-domain-level scale, and use some objectively observable indicators and evidence to support this possible future
  - List some of the elements that support an infrastructure for open-shared learning at meso- or domain-level scale (incentives, social recognition, social norms, socio-technical structures, authoring technologies, resource catalogs, intellectual property release licensure, and other factors)
- Think about some possible futures of open-shared learning at a micro or local organizational (and /or individual) scale, and use some objectively observable indicators and evidence to support this possible future
  - List some of the elements that support an infrastructure for open-shared learning at micro- or organization-level and individual-level scale (incentives, social recognition, social norms, socio-technical structures, authoring technologies, resource catalogs, intellectual property release licensure, and other factors)

11.1 Introduction

So what is the future of open-shared learning resources, their creation and sharing, their usage, and their forms? A common tendency is to predict the future of a phenomenon, and that applies to the open sharing of learning resources as well. The initial "gold rush" strategy of getting into the space seems to have passed, and many who are engaging now focus more on strategy, user-centered design, and learning efficacy and value. To borrow from Gartner's Technology Hype Cycle visualization, when a new enablement rises in the public mind, there is a Peak of Inflated Expectations initially, which drops to a Trough of Disillusionment. Then, expectations eventually rise along a Slope of Enlightenment, and there is a Plateau of Productivity. This dynamic seems to apply generally to open-shared learning resources.

In this space, a designer/developer may think that a free learning resource will necessarily garner wide attention and enthusiastic uptake; it might go viral. In the real, the uptake may be slow, and a learning resource may garner users slowly over time, or it may remain in obscurity. Understanding the competition in the space can be challenging as well as the inertia of wide swaths of the population as regards learning. Playing the long game and aiming to find a learning audience ultimately may be the dominant or winning strategy. The initial outsized expectations do initially settle into some level of equilibrium and consistent output. Individual

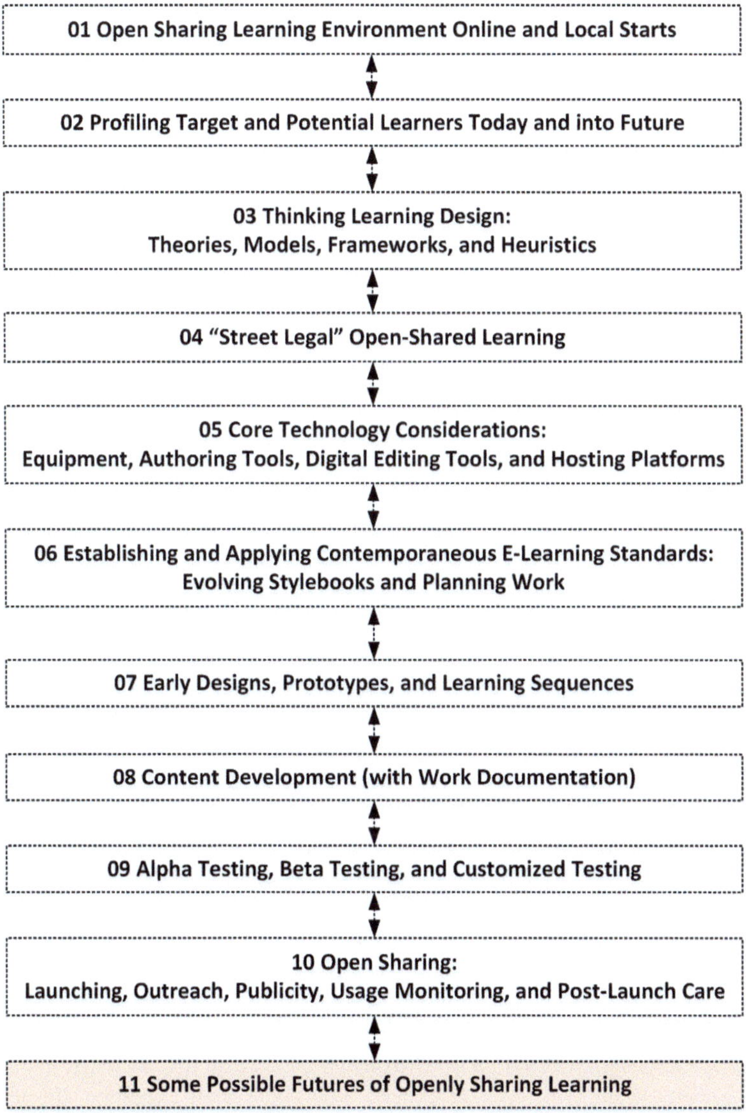

Fig. 11.1 Step 11 in the open-shared learning resource development sequence

designers/developers may experience the same initial sense of heightened possibilities, then disappointment at the limits, and then arrive at some maintainable level of productivity. The environment itself has enablements and constraints.

This last chapter focuses on some possible futures of open-shared learning (Fig. 11.1).

This work explores some desirable futures of open-shared learning and efforts to advance this effort, at the macro-, meso-, and micro- (individual) levels.

11.2 Review of the Literature

In the research literature, the "open" in open-shared learning resources may refer to different concepts: cost (low-cost, affordable, or free), convenience (easy-to-find), effectiveness (for learning), sustainability (sufficient resources to create and maintain), accredited (marked with the imprimatur of quality), distribution (broad, without barriers), reusability (adoption by others), modifiability (often with some or full editing rights), and other dimensions (Downes 2007, pp. 31–32), including "an open source attitude" (Súilleabháin and Coakley 2007). Certainly, not all shared learning resources check all the boxes based on the compilation of features from different models and conceptualizations. As yet, there is not a consensus on what open-shared learning objects are, except that they are broadly available for usage without cost but with rights retained by their creators.

The question about the possible futures of this practice of creating and sharing learning resources openly (online and otherwise) is not a light one. At a systems level, the challenge is to avoid the so-called "tragedy of the commons," which refers to situations where a common resource is available to all and where the temptation is to exploit this resource to such an extent that everybody (including one self) is worse off over time because the resource can no longer support continued use. Examples of commons tragedies are readily observable in the modern world faced with ecological disasters: rain forests, the air, fish populations. (Brosnan 2005, p. 107).

If individuals make the selfish choice to use the public goods but never contribute, then this requires contributors to play a "dominated strategy," or an ultimately losing one (also known as playing a sucker while others free-ride the creators and the system). The goal is to create a virtuous cycle dynamic that may be self-sustaining at a certain level of stability (or equilibrium). If the right mix may be created, various stakeholder groups may benefit from having open-shared learning resources: the designer/developers who design and create the contents, the subject matter experts (SMEs) or content experts who share their expertise, the learners who extend their knowledge and skills and abilities, the work places that benefit from higher skilled employees, the universities with lower costs for their learners, the foundations that fund such endeavors and benefit from the tax writeoffs of their contributions, and so on. In a virtuous cycle, everyone pays in, but everyone benefits (albeit not equally), so there is sufficient motivation for participation. There are self-reinforcing cycles that trend towards the constructive and the positive. Using a systems view, one author described what is needed for open educational resources (OERs) to work as a movement, requiring "volunteers and incentives, community and partnerships, co-production and sharing, distributed management and control" as well as “funding, technical, and content” (Downes 2007). The social aspect of people enables aspects of this interchange:

> Learning takes place in communities, facilitated by artifacts, which in turn sustain the communities that generate them (Stahl 2002, p. 1).

There are social organization endeavors that may be used to get past social dilemmas like the tragedy of the commons. People are much more willing to cooperate when they are in close communication with each other (Kollock 1998, p. 194, as cited in Brosnan 2005, pp. 108–111), when they share a group identity, when they maintain ongoing relationships, when people have reputational histories of past behaviors, and there are mechanisms for “supporting resource exchange,” such as in a “learning object economy” (Brosnan 2005, pp. 108–110). “Socializing tasks” may be harnessed to encourage individuals to create open-shared learning resources, in part to please others and maintain social goodwill and comity. Much research informs the work of building and maintaining environments “conducive to sharing and reuse” (Philip and Cameron 2008, p. 1). The sharing exists at a meta-level beyond the learning resources, with the sharing of “learning designs” as a way to advance higher education (Oliver 2007) and e-learning courses (Koper and Olivier 2004).

The online sharing space provides “digital abundance” (Batson, et al. 2008), and with the “constant increasing of resources on the Web (both static documents and functional components and software) it becomes almost impossible for the learners, authors and instructors to get an overview of all the available information relevant to their current needs, tasks, roles and goals” (Aroyo and Dicheva 2004, p. 60). There are efforts to harness the “educational semantic web” for more “effective information storage and retrieval” and to use “nonhuman autonomous agents to augment the learning and information retrieval and processing power of human beings” (Anderson and Whitelock 2004, as cited in Aroyo and Dicheva 2004, p. 60).

Technologically, the social aspects of the Social Web are also critical to shared e-learning:

> In fact, in the world of e-learning, it is more widely recognised that how learning content is used and distributed by learners might be more important than how it is designed. In the last few years, there has been an increasing focus on social software applications and services as a result of the rapid development of Web 2.0 concepts. (Chatti et al. 2007, p. 404)

The authors note that “Learning and knowledge are social, personal, flexible, dynamic, distributed, ubiquitous, complex and chaotic in nature,” which requires new thinking of learning management and knowledge management (Chatti et al. 2007, p. 411). In this conceptualization, based on connectivism, knowledge is socially co-created and builds on current knowledge (Chatti et al. 2007, pp. 411–412).

Technologies may be leveraged “to promote better sharing and discussing of learning and teaching ideas and designs” to further enable the sharing of learning resources and their adoption (Conole 2010, p. 141). Researchers have created aids to help would-be adopters be aware of and make decisions regarding shared learning resources. One is the Learning Object Review Instrument (LORI), which was designed "to balance assessment validity with efficiency of the evaluation process" (Leacock and Nesbit 2007, p. 44).

Individuals who participate in "do it yourself" (DIY) culture also share learning contents in a non-commercial way on the Social Web. These "expert amateurs" create, modify or repair objects themselves, without professional input (Kuznetsov and Paulos 2010, p. 1). The "amateur" only refers to the fact that their efforts are non-commercial and do not necessarily reflect skill level (Kuznetsov and Paulos 2010, p. 1). Many often share their skills as part of common practice, and their enthusiasms tide them through the work.

11.3 Some Possible Futures of Open Sharing Learning

In the research literature, there are some glimmers that open sharing may be sustainable not only in the near-term but the mid- and the long-terms. Based on the $0 budget idea, it is a hard case to argue for investing the time in producing public goods because of the time sink. However, if there is a sufficient level of "unpaid global cooperation" (Brosnan 2005, p. 107), it is possible for the dilution of individual responsibility to enable the work because each person takes on only a small part of the responsibility, and the economies of scale may be the difference. In reality, though, the Pareto principle (aka "the law of the vital few") tends to apply with only a small percentage of the population (20%) responsible for 80% of the effects. In actual practice, the numbers of actual contributors to the open-shared space may be closer to the lower single digits (if workplace participations are any indication).

11.3.1 Ideal Desirable Futures for Open-Shared Learning

There are a range of ways to interpret what a desirable future of open-shared learning would optimally look like and then how to change up the incentives to achieve that future. Taking a generalist point-of-view, complete Table 11.1. Consider how the respective levels of interests may result in differing interests. The phenomenon of open-shared learning offers different equities for people at different levels of organizational size.

Figure 11.2 offers a partially filled fishbone diagram of causes that may advance open-shared learning and barriers to this endeavor.

Table 11.1 Brainstorming desirable futures for open-shared learning resources at the macro, meso and micro scales

	Desirable futures
Macro-scale (web- and internet-scale)	
Meso-scale (domain)	
Micro-scale (local, organizational)	

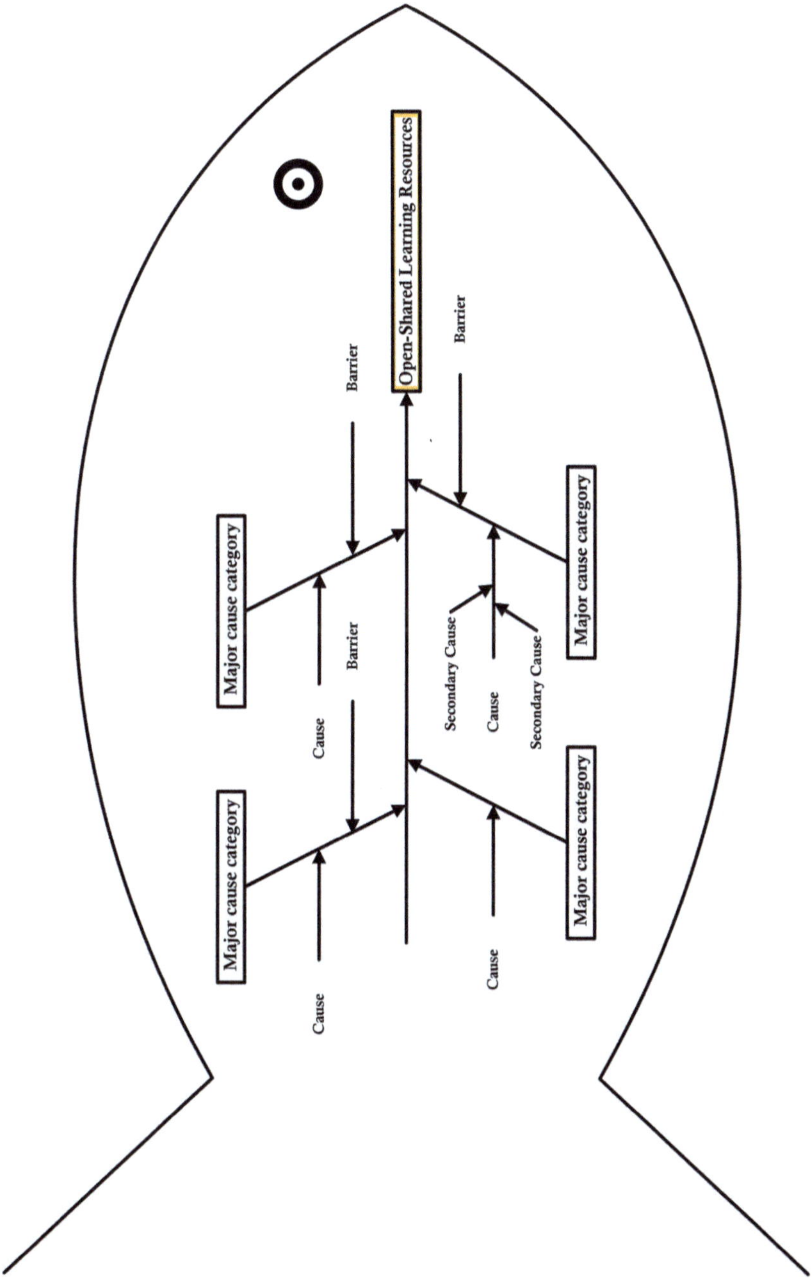

Fig. 11.2 A partially filled fishbone diagram to define factors that advance (and hinder) open-shared learning resources

Table 11.2 Identifying supporting and hindering factors in the future of open-shared learning at varying scales

	Supports open-shared learning	Blocks or hinders open-shared learning
Macro-scale (web- and internet-scale)		
Meso-scale (domain)		
Micro-scale (local, organizational)		

Another way to brainstorm where this cultural practice may be going is to engage Table 11.2.

Anticipating Potential Disruptive Effects It may help to spend some time musing on potential disruptive effects to open-shared learning. A creatively destructive technology, per Schumpeter, may be automated creation of learning contents using artificial intelligence, and the deployment of automated agents may make expert collation unnecessary.

There are funding endeavors by third-party commercial companies that may discourage open sharing of created contents because these may be held under contract into practical perpetuity (within the limits of copyright law).

If new laws are put into place affecting what may be included for publishing and if these raise liabilities (which can be highly expensive), these may discourage engagement.

Extensive free ridership may also discourage participation of content creators to the space.

Task #1: Promoting Future Open Shared Learning by Considering Stakeholder Needs

A simplified approach to understanding the open-shared learning context is to conceive of various user groups surround this issue. A partial list may include the following:

- Learners (novices, amateurs, and experts) … in various contexts
- Administrators in institutions of higher education … government offices … K12 … private organizations … and others
- Makers of technologies (authoring tools, online learning systems, and social media systems)
- Third-party content providers (publishers, courseware makers, and others)
- Designers/developers
- Subject matter experts (SME)/content experts
- Funders of open-shared learning resources

Beyond these basic roles, individuals may of course play several roles. A designer/developer may also be a learner and also a subject matter expert, and so on.

Based on the brainstorm (feel free to add additional groups and subgroups), define what you see as each group's main incentives. Why are they engaging in this space, and what are their main interests?

What changes in practices, policies, technologies, and funding … might promote each of their respective needs? Why?

How can each stakeholder group be affirmed? Supported?

Task #2: Building Future Learners/Users of Open-Shared Learning Contents

If sustainability is about building content creators, there is also an argument for the need to build future learners or users of open-shared learning contents. These are the individuals and groups that are the "target" and "potential" learners whom content creators design and build to and for. As noted earlier, these may be novices, amateurs (including hobbyists), and experts. They may be engaging in formal learning (accredited learning), nonformal learning (non-credit learning), and informal learning (learning as a byproduct of other activities). They may be lifelong learners.

Think of practical ways to build such future learners, so that there is a consuming audience to "demand" such resources. User demand is the main rationale for sustaining open educational resource initiatives (Harley 2008). Learners also need to be understood because of their centrality in the social aspects of learning (Chatti et al. 2007, p. 412). Users of open-shared learning resources are expected to bring knowledge and skill to locate relevant learning contents (in a sea of online contents), adapt these to their needs, and deploy for their own and others' learning. Having a savvy learner audience means that those who build for them can be held to account, to a degree. Having learners using open-shared learning resources lessens the chances of learning resources ending up in the Great Unread and the Great Unused. It helps to have a mutual collective mindset around open-shared learning resources, so people can play and interact well in this space.

11.3.2 Your Possible Futures in Relation to Open-Shared Learning Resources

The typical assumed path of a person who would contribute open-shared learning resources is that he or she likely initially started out as a consumer of shared contents—to meet information needs, for entertainment, for work, and so on. Then, he or she transitioned at some point to share some expertise in the social space, whether that expertise came from work or hobby or some other source. This pivot point at which a net consumer comes a "prosumer" (producer and consumer) is a critical one for the sustainability of open-shared learning. Understanding one's various interests is important.

Regardless of whether this practice catches fire and becomes part of a larger continuing movement, individuals and teams and organizations can decide to create contents for open sharing. They can engage the supply-side and worry about potential demand later. The greater public may benefit from local innovations and the positionality of content experts from a number of fields. Sometimes, in life, events come down to an individual (or group) who has access and knowledge who is willing to share. And thinking out a degree or two about the potential and even likely impacts of one's contributions may be important before releasing learning resources into the public space. All said, creating open-shared learning contents may be part of living one's best life, by caring for others and giving in a real way. There is power in speaking into this space and making a unique contribution or a portfolio of contributions.

In this book, the process for designing and developing the learning resources is thought to take over ten steps, and with experience, these may seem like over-think. In Fig. 11.3, the absolutely necessary steps are identified as only five: conceptualizing the design, ensuring the legality of the contents and work, developing the learning resources, conducting some light proofing and testing, and then launching. An environmental scan, learner profiling, core technology analysis, reviewing contemporary e-learning standards, creating early designs, and such, are extras.

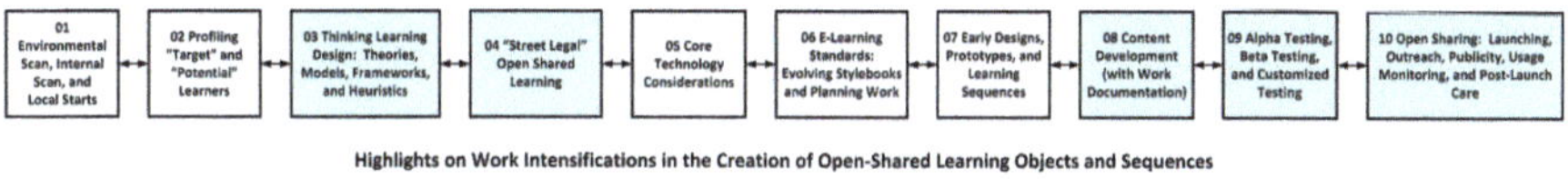

Fig. 11.3 Highlights on work intensifications in the creation of open-shared learning objects and sequences

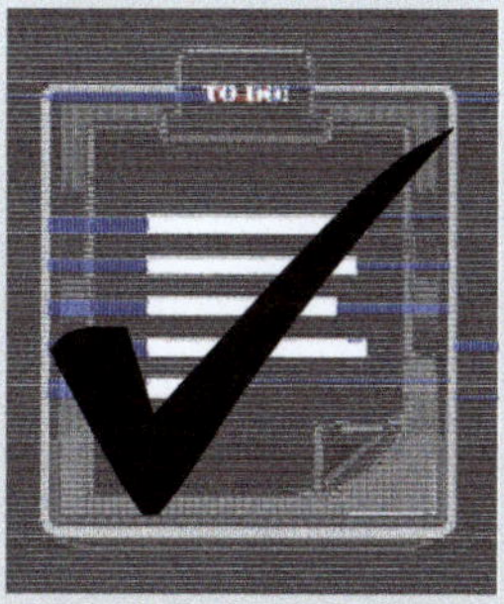

Task #3: My Future Self and Open-Shared Learning

One part of personal planning for the open sharing future may be to conduct a light self-assessment. Based on your prior experience in creating an open-shared learning resource, what did you find pleasurable? What did you find unpleasant?

Based on your "positionality" in relation to various topics, what unique equities do you bring to this task?

If you were to pursue low-hanging fruit in this space, what would that involve?

11.3.3 *Some Possible Futures for Open-Shared Learning Resources*

To understand the interests of various stakeholder groups, it may help to consider how the release of learning contents in an open-shared way may affect various people groups (entities) and individuals (egos) (Table 11.3).

Table 11.3 How to project pros and cons of possible changes in the open sharing learning spaces on various stakeholders

	Pros	Cons
Entities		
Commercial companies (including third-party content creators)		
Institutions of higher education		
K12 institutions		
Nonprofit organizations		
Government/public sector		
Learning communities		
Egos		
Learners		
Teachers		
Administrators		
Others		

Some what-ifs to use with Table 11.3 follow. These should be treated as individual scenarios. If desired, though, combinations of these factors may be brought into play for a more complex and possibly real-world experience. Where possible, please use facts to back-up the effects that you think will occur.

- What are ways to magnify the advantages and minimize the disadvantages?
- What are effective ways to think through first order and second order effects?

Scenario 1: Open-shared learning popularizes and is the main provider of academic e-texts.

Scenario 2: The technologies used in a shared learning resource outclasses what is available in the world.

Scenario 3: Social media platforms decline to host the contents for open-shared learning objects.

Scenario 4: The respective commercial platforms hosting the free learning contents start charging fees for the usage of the learning resources.

At the Macro Scale Changes at the Web and Internet scale may also affect this environment. For example, the rollout of an educational semantic web may have far-reaching implications for the findability of learning resources and their usage. What are some other possible changes at this level? What if social recognition for contributing is more widely recognized? What if shared online social norms encourage self-expression and sharing? What if authoring technologies are cloud-hosted and free? What if federated resource catalogs for learning contents were more informative and usable? What if there are automated ways to check intellectual property rights of objects to enable broader harnessing and usage? And so on. Certainly, there are other rules that may come into play that may discourage the creation of open-sharing and have chilling effects.

At the Meso Scale The meso scale is defined here as the domain level, various changes in the open sharing space may have effects. For example, if learning contents become available, they may disintermediate third-party content providers. If there are advances in data visualizations and simulations, that may change how teaching is done in the field. If there are effective online practices, how students learn may change. If an evocative film is created about the field, that may drive learners to pursue particular courses of learning actions. The possible futures of open shared learning resources are directly affected by people's awarenesses, behaviors, and actions.

At the Micro Scale The micro scale is defined here as at the scale of the individual and his/her local organizations (work places and other contexts). Changes in the open sharing space may include individual and local interests, incentives, projects, technologies, and other factors. After all, the individual persons and teams have to decide whether they want to be serial contributors in this space; they decide whether to put in a 40-h workweek of a 60-h one, whether to contribute time, talent, and treasure, and whether to donate evenings and weekends to these efforts. Often, ideas for projects come from individual's areas of interest, their workplaces, their colleagues, and their social networks. The individual has much more influence in the space from the local level, but to engage the open sharing space, they have to be aware of the meso- and macro-levels.

Scale here matters because different and relevant issues come to the fore at different levels of granularity. It is not enough to work only at one scalar level or another but requires the combination.

Task #4: Keeping the Lights On
Sustainability refers how well something may be maintained over time. For open-shared learning to continue, members have to play various constructive roles in the space and in relationship to each other … to maintain an ecological balance.

Task #5: Effective Designs and the Future

Go online, and spend an hour or two reviewing open-shared learning objects and resources. Identify a dozen or so that strike you as "futuristic" (something that will last over time, something indicative of where the future of open-shared learning is headed).

Record the URLs. (If specific directions are needed to access the contents, record these as well.)

Then, analyze the identified learning objects, and write up why you think these learning resources are indicative of the future. How are they similar from each other? How are they different from each other?

Task #6: Near-Term, Mid-Term, Long-Term Futures

So much of what is shared in the open realm is because of individuals and small teams and the respective local work contexts. In that spirit, based on your prior experiences and knowledge, anticipate what a near-term, mid-term, and long-term future may look like for

you as an individual;
your design and development team as a group;
your workplace as a supporter of open-shared learning contents.

For the purposes of this tasking, near-term is a month to a year; mid-term is about 2 years, and long-term is about 5 years. If these time frames do not make sense of your conceptualizations, feel free to redefine them for this exercise. How do you see yourself, a development team, and your workplace playing the short game and the long game? Why?

Conceptualizing Open-Shared Learning Resources as Multi-Generational Use Ones … with Ripple Effects

The Lindy effect is a concept that the future life expectancy of some non-perishable things (an idea, a practice, a technology, or others) is proportional to their current age, so that every additional period of survival implies a longer remaining life expectancy. This concept may apply to the practice of open sharing of learning resources … and to the shared contents themselves.

[The Lindy effect (1964) is attributed to Albert Goldman, who wrote about this in an article titled "Lindy's Law" in *The New Republic*. This concept has evolved over time, with contributions by Benoit Mandelbrot (1982) and Nassim Nicholas Taleb (2007, 2012)].

This concept brings up the idea of an expanded life of a learning resource that is shared digitally. If there is the possibility of digital ∞ eternity, a work may have potential value into extended time.

What are some paths to a learning resource's rediscovery after an initial release and usage? How can newcomers to the Web and Internet be served with all the learning contents? How can new generations of users from around the world have their needs met?

Beyond the usable lifespan of a work, it may help to consider "first order" and "second order" effects. First order effects are direct consequences of the release of a shared learning resource. These may include direct learning applications and learner actions/decision making and so on. Second order effects are those effects stemming from the first order ones.

side bar

Working Through Open Sharing Burnout

In longer-term projects, initial enthusiasms may wear off, and designer/developers need to stay on track, refresh and renew themselves, and ensure strategic completion of their projects.

Of greater concern is an analogical longer-term (and even lifetime) burnout … that may lead to full stoppage of contributions in the open-sharing space. One of the work risks in creating learning resources for open sharing is work-based burnout or fatigue. The work of designing and developing learning is complex and challenging, and the rewards may be fairly limited (and sometimes non-existent). Overwork, poor work-life balance, and other challenges may lead to fatigue and a lack of interest in continuing to contribute. If the burnout continues, it can mean the loss of many potential productive years of contributions.

The question then is how to refresh in this work in times of tiredness.

1. Think of why you got into this work in the first place. Who were you trying to support, and how? What issues were you engaging in, and why? How did open-shared design and development work help you engage with the world constructively? (Sometimes, it helps to review the contributions through an online search for the hosted contents.)
2. Work on self-awareness about how you like to refresh yourself from hard work. Do you enjoy taking a meditative walk? A bicycle ride? Enjoy a political thriller? Give yourself that time and that space to relax and recover from tough work. Set deadlines further out, and remove the sense of pressure from the work.
3. Experience some of the shared learning objects that others have created. Appreciate how others solve shared instructional design challenges or frame topics or code a learning object/resource. See how others contribute, and understand your place as one contributor among many. See how others are paying it forward and helping others. Other people's works and being can be deeply inspiring.
4. Conceptualize the sharing of learning resources as a form of authorship, self-expression, and personal style. Use the learning object as a palette on which the individual self-expresses. Use the work as a form of self-

affirmation. Explore your own portfolio of contributions in that light (with the work as an extension of the self).

5. Reconnect with the users of the learning resources. Engage with them to better understand their experiences. In the present day, there are generations of learners using open-shared learning resources as part of their K12 and higher education studies.
6. Keep work pressures under control (if you do not thrive under pressure). You can make some choices that can ease some of the work pressures:

   In terms of the open-shared content creation, it helps to have a sense of control over one's own project choices. When strangers and others ask for free work, give yourself permission to decline them politely. Be selective about what you take on.

   With every project, make a list of what you gain from the work and the publicity, the sharing with learners, and the domain.

   If there are professional partnerships you can enter into the actualize the work, so the responsibility does not just rest on you, that may also alleviate some of the pressures.

   If you enjoy competition, set up a friendly competition with colleagues to build respective learning resources, and go for broke!
7. Have fun! Choose projects that provide thrills, chills, and surprises. Build up an appreciation for the "hard fun" that leads to "flow".

Finally, the future "you" will be a different one than the present "you." It may be that the open-sharing space may meet some needs today but different ones tomorrow, and it may be that your interests in this space eventually age-out. If and when it does, then go with it. This exercise does not assume that continuance is necessarily the only right answer.

Live Examples (On the Web)

To enhance this chapter with live examples from the Web, readers will have to go on a pursuit for sources that may provide indications as to the future of open-shared learning resources. This assignment is fairly open-ended. After all, what would they look for? Design methodologies that seem compelling and may gain traction in the future? Technologies with momentum and name recognition? Learning communities on multiple social media platforms? Leaders who may have a sense of where the future is on this issue? Shared learning resources with cachet and respect? Potent models of learning resources? Engaging software programs? Are these early indicators of the future or lagging ones?

How can one tell that the data point contains more signal than noise as to indicating the potential future of open-shared learning? Based on these signals, what does the future portend?

Further, what are some ideas about the future of open sharing albeit not informed by what exists today? What is nascent?

Discussion In work environments, it can be very easy to make the argument that learning contents are for defined and limited usage, and skillsets and capabilities belong to the organization. Even in academic environments, with works funded by tax dollars, some principal investigators (PIs) will break apart learning object into discrete pieces and encapsulate them into learning objects and emplace all sorts of hindrances for access and download. There is fear that others will take credit, will misuse the learning resources, will harness the original contents for their own gain, or will cause problems. Releasing something to the public feels to some like a loss of control. There are serious mistakes to being too overly protective and unsharing, especially when the works for funded by the public for the public. If the information stands to benefit others and is not sensitive, and if there are permissions to release such contents, all those efforts at obfuscation and hiding, blocking and tackling, and putting up roadblocks seem excessive.

A possible future for the designer/developer depends on how well he or she maintains the skillset (the techniques and methods, the technological fluency), the knowledge (the standards, the state of the art), the sense of the learner audience, the social sharing space, and the peer colleagues who can serve as project collaborators. Each person has strengths and weaknesses in their designs and developed resources. If left unpracticed, the knowledge, skills and abilities will begin to decay, so keeping these fresh will be important.

The chapter focuses on the potential futures of open-shared learning, which may take a number of forms. Some of them are more positive than others, with more potential benefits across the board for the various stakeholders. There is so much potential for benefits to humanity in general by encouraging learning shares, so people can achieve their potential, even outside the competitive strictures of money-based work and formalized roles.

This chapter is not about making future predictions per se but more about enabling a systems view around open-sharing, so people may decide how to participate in these endeavors in a supportive and sustainable way. The possible futures are not fated and not pre-determined, but what emerges will be the individual and collective results from individual and group decisions and actions made daily. It is unfolding even now moment to moment. Readers stand to gain from contributing and being a small part. After all, there is not going to be anyone else in the world who can approach a topic with their worldview, skills, and positionality to the topic.

side bar

Micro-Scale Characteristics that Align with this Work

Profiling individual personality types for particular professional roles and jobs has been done through the years, with mixed effects. What personality traits might line up with effective instructional design work, as conceptualized, for open-shared learning resources? What work experience preferences should such individuals have?

With the benefit of hindsight, seeing the work in total for the first time, some basic ideas follow.

Those who would appreciate this work are those who have a close attention to details. They would have comfort with a wide range of complex technologies and the ability to continually update skills in wielding these singly and together. They would be well versed in exploring information and data and what is shared online and brings a healthy skepticism to information. They would do well to be highly selective and "picky" in terms of the work and have the patience and focus to follow through on achieving the work to quality. They have to have an otherworldly patience to work on projects that start with a blank slate and goes through phases where the work is nebulous and ill-formed and messy in the nascent stages, before ideas start to take form, and the work starts to take shape. Throughout all this, they need to maintain a high level of grit and resilience. In most cases, there is no external encouragement to do this work, and the budget is $0 in the best scenario and usually $-1000 by the time everything is added up in terms of resources, time, and other investments. They would have to go with where the research takes them but also have the nerve to go beyond. They have to develop their own sense of seeing in order to create works that have not existed before but not in a way that is unheeding of history.

This sidebar box is not about, "Does this profile look like you?" Rather, this is more about, "Is this what you want to sign up for?" "Does this sound like the 'hard fun' you want?" "Do you want to speak your truths /skills /talents/knowledge into this space with the given rules and realities?"

[This sidebar box is not about wanting to socially reproduce others who tend to be this way. Rather, my years in this space of staring into the abyss has also meant that the abyss has stared back at me, and some aspects of me have come more to the fore than others. The open sharing space is no abyss, but the disciplines of instructional design for release to the public writes the standards into a person. If he or she continues in the space, he or she has to adapt; if he or she cannot, then it's on to other things. Also, if one has part of the skillset and not the whole, that would be a solid reason to partner with trusted others to collaborate around the work.]

Ready, set, go!

Fig. 11.4 A Word Cloud of Chapter 11: "Some Possible Futures of Openly Sharing Learning"

What-if: Pursuing Follow-On Work? (Fig. 11.4)

You have created your first shared learning resource. You followed standards, and you created quality. Now, you have a small niche contribution of your own on the WWW and Internet. You have an idea for a follow-on object, but you do not want to commit to extra work just yet. Your memory of how much work went into the first object is still too fresh. However, you realize that the freshness of the prior project can be a net positive because you have the standards that you're building to top-of-mind, and you have templates that you can use from the initial project.

Decision point #1: Stop or advance. If advance, what will you carry forward, and what will you leave behind in terms of the earlier design files, the design values, the templates, and other aspects? Do you plan to create a learning object that is a direct follow-on from the initial work, or will you use an empty slate approach and appeal to new learner groups? Or both?

You decide to pursue follow-on work. You have some digital contents that are left over from the initial project that you can use. You start with a back-of-the-napkin design and draft the learning object. Over time, it is developed into a finalized form. You put it through its paces through some alpha, beta, and customized testing. It is ready to launch.

Decision point #2: Stop or advance. If advance, do you host it in close proximity to the first learning resources? Do you use the same publicity channels as before for the first one? Do you look for other potential learners and reach out to them as well through other channels?

You go for broke and launch broadly. And you start looking for other aspects of your work that are share-able.

The What-If Debriefing

This what-if scenario is about moving on from one created learning resource and maybe ensuring that that is not a one-off or just an early proof-of-concept (a sort of trial-run object). This captures the sense that things get easier over time and with practice. This suggests that the first work or an earlier work may inform future ones. For all the sense of achievement with one work, there is so much more potential beyond.

11.4 Future Research Directions

Prior research on open-shared learning has focused on defining terms in the space (like, "What is a learning object?"), sustainability, different technologies, learning object repositories and referatories, evaluative measures, usage and adoption, learning efficacy, and other issues. Some of these studies have been case-based ones focused on localized contexts. Updates on many of these issues may be in order, given how dated some of the research has been. Since then, of course, there has been focuses on larger-scale projects like massive open online course (MOOC) platforms and global-scale endeavors for open learning.

What are some extant research questions that may be addressed in this space? Some ideas follow:

- What are effective learning designs for automated learning in the open-shared learning space?

- What are effective methods to infuse quality in critical aspects of open-shared learning resources?
- What are strategies to encourage the sustainability of open-shared learning?
- What are effective ways to adapt learning resources to the needs of respective learners in automated ways?
- What are effective ways to evaluate open-shared learning resources, given the variations in the space?
- How are various countries and regions engaging with open-shared learning? What are legal and policy approaches that various governments have taken, and which ones are most effective?
- What have been the roles of learning communities around the practices of open-shared learning?
- What are some technological means to collate learning resources through algorithms and programs, to benefit individual learners and groups of learners?
- How can digital badging (or other types of public crediting) be brought to the fore to motivate human learners?
- What can machines learn from human-created and machine-created open-shared learning resources?

To the question of open sharing, what are the motivations of serial contributors to the space? What external factors encourage their continuance in contributions?

The core research question posed here involves ways to incentivize participation in the open-shared learning space to ensure sustainability. For example, what are policies to put into place to protect open-shared learning? Technologies? Technological standards? Reviewer assessments of works? Are there socio-technical systems that may be set up to enable bringing together learners and designer/developers in social marketplaces where people may barter and transact based on their respective interests? Are there local innovations that may benefit the global, and vice versa?

The most important concept in this chapter is the idea of human agency, that people can influence the future in positive ways and need to plan for and act in those directions.

11.5 Conclusion

So what is the most likely future of open sharing learning resources? What will this mean for the world's "knowledge-based economies"? The current meta-narrative is a positive one, with a sense that some of the world's excess capacity in information sharing is being drawn to the space, to the benefit of many. This is an accurate narrative. A lesser narrative, which is equally true, is that there are many who can contribute to this space who do not.

A conservative estimate is that there is some level of inelastic demand at present, but given smaller and smaller budgets for education, the demand for such contents will likely continue to rise. There is a current stable level of learning "supply," but these resources are overlapping, and there are whole areas about which there is little contents or only highly generalist contents.

As more people are read into the space, there may be some more contributions, although it is hard to imagine that these will rise to the level of actual demand. Free work is not an appealing proposition for most. (Think about how hard it can be to ask a favor of a stranger, or even a colleague, for that matter.) And yet, people are social. This space rewards through social means, with people able to take on a variety of roles in this space (as both creators and as users, among others). Open-shared learning resources are crowd-sourced, are folk-tagged, shared, commented on, and are collaboratively filtered for people's usage.

As many have observed, the future does not unfold in a linear or predictable way. There are always wildcard factors and butterfly effects and black swan events. How the future of open-shared learning resources is unclear.

Historically, the methods for funding open resources have been by the following models: "endowment, membership, donations, conversion (to a paying customer), contributor-pay model, sponsorship, institutional, governmental, partnerships and exchanges" (Downes 2007, pp. 34–36). In the near-term, there have been efforts by various public and private sector entities to promote the advancement of open-shared content development and usage. Their support may continue, or not, but many organizations are working to create sustainable models for the usage of open-shared learning resources after the initial seeding funds dry up. Interestingly, the cost model for open-shared learning resources is somewhat analogical to that of academic publishing, with high inputs and demanding skillsets to create and often relatively low returns.

This space is a dynamic one. Culturally, this movement has gone through a number of names and evolutions. In all likelihood, the practice of creating learning resources for open sharing will morph into other movements and be repackaged with new leaders and new ideas and new practices. Perhaps this space will become some version of the gig economy, with people engaged in low-wage side projects on commission. Perhaps this will become a boutique space with learners commissioning specific products designed to their own needs. Or there may be more direct elicitations of such creations from organizations, individuals, and other providers. Perhaps advancements in technology will enable more automated setups for collating objects for new assemblages for learning.

The future of open-shared learning will be an emergent one, based on decisions made by individuals and groups and systems. Designer/developers are jacks-and-jills of all trades and masters of none, in some senses, with so many complexities to their work. The future will be co-created by all who express into this space, which has room for all voices, and which can benefit a world of learners all with different sensibilities (and with unique abilities to learn in different ways). While this book has mostly been about method, at its heart, this book is about caring deeply about what one does and sharing that with others, for everyone's betterment. This chapter concludes with a call to pave the way for diverse others to participate constructively to secure a productive open sharing future.

11.6 Reviews and Assignments

11.6.1 Main Points Review

- What is perceived as an idealized future may well depend on the role or roles one has in relation to open-shared learning. For a phenomenon to work over time, multiple stakeholder groups have to benefit from the *status quo*.
- Anticipating the future can be difficult because people's affairs do not advance in an easily predictable way, and there are outsized effects of small occurrences per chaos theory. Linear assumptions about the future are often wrong. Computational simulations can only address very limited numbers of variables, and these often have severe limits out in time. Given all these caveats, projecting the future of open-shared learning should be handled with humbleness and plenty of caveats.
- A number of phenomenon may change up the incentives and behaviors in this open-shared learning object space, such as funding or bartered resources for open-shared learning objects. Other disruptions may come from technologies that lower the cost of the work.
- Thinking about open-shared learning objects as only a net positive might be too simplistic. There may be negatives as well, such as the distribution of poor quality learning objects that may spread inaccurate ideas. There may be disruptions to commercial markets related to human learning and trainings, for example. Some mitigations may be made for recognizable downsides.
- To understand where the future may be going, in terms of open-shared learning resources, there may be some available indicators. For example, people may analyze the quality of the shared learning resources, the amount of refreshing of the learning contents, the enthusiasm of various funders and funding organizations to this endeavor, the popularity of adopting these resources, the enthusiasm of users of the learning resources, and others.
- The macro level of open-shared learning may be understood as global and web-scale, the meso-level as domain-level, and the micro level as the local (individual or organization) level.
- The future for open-shared learning is unknown and quite hazy, given the lack of clear funding streams.
- Those who conceptualize of human knowledge as public goods for the benefit of the world's citizens may conceptualize of a desirable future in open-shared learning as robust and energized, with all participants as beneficiaries—including designers, developers, object users, instructors, and others.
- For open-shared learning to be sustainable, all who engage in it must have some perceived gains. One major challenge is to incentivize the design and creation of open-shared learning objects and sequences, and another is to incentivize the usage of such resources.

11.6.2 Critical Thinking Questions

About Desirable Potential Futures

- What is an ideal future in terms of open-shared learning objects? In terms of a Kantian ethical sense, in terms of the greater good, what are some universals about open-shared learning resources that should be protected? What would the greater good look like in terms of people's access to learning? To self-actualization? What roles could open-shared learning resources contribute to this?
- What would an ideal future look like on a macro web-scale, a meso-domain-scale, and a micro local scale? Why?

Winners and Losers: Idealized for Whom?

- When considering idealized desirable futures for open-shared learning, it is wholly possible that the perceptions of the possible futures will vary based on an individual's role in relation to the open-shared learning. While this space may not be zero sum, there may be a sense of winners and losers.
  - What are idealized futures for designers/developers? Users? School administrators? Hosting sites [such as social media, such as learning object repositories and referatories, such as learning management system (LMS) makers]? Third-party commercial content providers?
  - How can these interests change in the near-term? The mid-term future? The long-term future?
- Governments, universities, corporations, and non-profit entities (foundations, organizations, and others)…and individuals have all provided seed funds to enable the creation of open-shared learning resources. How may these entities be encouraged to continue their support of such endeavors? What do they get out of the deal?

About Open-Sharing Stakeholders

- For *learners* who use open-shared learning resources, what are some things they should consider when using shared learning resources? What should they know about the quality of the resources? How would they differentiate the high-quality learning resources from the low-quality ones? What sorts of learning self-regulation should they consider in terms of their self-directed learning? How can they sustain their learning over time and engage their own motivation to advance, even in the face of frustrations and occasional befuddlement? What sorts of learning self-regulation should they consider in terms of learning? What are some risks that learners may be taking on?
- Likewise, for *instructors* who use open-shared learning resources, what are some issues they should consider? What should they know about the quality of the resources? What sorts of scaffolding should they put around various online learning resources to improve the uses of the resources? How can adopted learn-

ing objects be aligned with formal learning objectives? Informal learning objectives?

- What should *administrators* consider when using open-shared learning resources? What quality issues should they be aware of? How can they mitigate some of these challenges?
- What should *educational technologists* know about open-shared learning resources? How can they accommodate different types of learning resources? How can they insure proper integrations across different platforms?

About Designers/Developers

- What are some "utils" that designers/developers may gain by creating open-shared learning objects and resources?

About Undesirable Potential Futures

- There are some down sides to open-shared learning resources. For example, some people who design and share these may not be experts in that area, and they may pass along inaccurate information. Or open-shared objects may compete for market share with commercial companies, or they may lower the labor value for those who create learning objects commercially. What are some explicit "cons" of open-shared learning objects for various stakeholders?
- What would a less-than-ideal or negatively disruptive future look like on a macro web-scale, a meso-domain-scale, and a micro local scale? Why?

About Infrastructures

- What elements are "infrastructures" for open-shared learning resources? Policies (such as leave time to create such contents)? Technologies (Hosting platforms? Authoring tools? Social media?)? Social norms? Others?
- Lack of quality can be a deal-breaker in this space. What are some ways to ensure that quality is achieved with the shared learning resources?

About Personal Considerations and Resilience

- To consider whether you may participate in the open-shared learning space in the future, consider your varying roles in this area as a contributor and as a user (of the contents). What are drivers for your actions, and why? Based on your current calculus, what needs of yours must be met for your to continue as a contributor? As a user?
  - What are potential deal-breakers that would end your participation in the open-shared learning space?
- What are some ways to help an individual stay fresh, so that they do not burn out on open-source development?
- What are some ways to help a team stay fresh, so that they do not burn out on open-source content development?

11.7 Assignments

Directions The Assignments are divided into two sections, Basic and Advanced. The Basic section is for those who may not have much instructional design experience or background in the area of creating instructional contents for open sharing. As such, these are set up to familiarize them with the chapter-related knowledge, skills, and abilities. The Advanced section is for those who already have some knowledge of this general space and who may benefit from more challenging work.

In a formal learning context, these assignments would benefit from expert feedback and further applications of the learning contents. In a nonformal or informal learning context, including self-directed learning, these assignments would benefit from both reflection and practice. These assignments are built to be extensible, to have elements added to benefit the learners. They are designed to be assigned selectively and not in full. The setup of this textbook is as a work sequence, and similarly, the assignments may be set up as tasks to be completed by the learner in a sequential way… that takes them through the fairly complete and sequential *open-shared learning design → development → test → revision → launch → post-launch* process.

11.7.1 Basic

Assignment 11.1: Defining Desirable Futures Regarding Open-Shared Learning Resources Consider the optimal desirable futures for each of the members in the following stakeholder groups surrounding open-shared learning resources:

- funders (foundations, organizations, corporations, higher education, and others)
- learners (individuals and groups, in the global North or the global South, engaged in formal, nonformal, or informal learning, from certain demographic slices of the world's population)
- designers of instruction
- developers of instruction
- technology-makers, and others

Define each of their most desirable futures. After you're done, analyze their desired futures, and show where their interests overlap. Does this exercise suggest what an optimal desirable future is for humanity *en masse* or not? Why or why not? What should the guiding forces be?

Assignment 11.2: Some Possible Futures at Either the Macro, Meso, or Local Level Write a short essay about "possible futures" for open-shared learning—at either the macro (Web), meso-(domain level), or local (organizational) level. Use evidence to support your interpretations of the future.

Extra: Consider possible near-term futures, mid-term futures, and long-term futures, for open-shared learning objects and sequences. (Define what the near-, mid-, and long-term futures mean in terms of actual time spans first.)

Assignment 11.3: Personal Future in Open-Shared Learning Development Write a short personal essay about the "possible futures" of open-shared learning development for you as an individual. Explain what factors would lead you to continue to create and share open-shared learning online. Also, explain what factors would be barriers to your continuing to create and share. How would you actualize your full self with future learning objects, and why? What new learning do you plan to acquire? What sort of reputation do you hope to build?

Extra: If you wish, express this sense of a personal future as an open-shared learning designer/developer as a fishbone diagram. Remember that the bones are expressed as positive and negative towards certain outcomes. What would encourage you to continue in this direction? What would discourage you to continue in this direction?

Extra: What are the necessary skills for creating learning objects, courses, or sequences for open sharing? What are some practical ways to maintain these skills and to prevent skills decay? How can you maintain motivation for designing and developing open-shared learning resources? The public space is one that is rife with judgment and often criticism. What are ways to engage in this space and still keep a balanced sense of what is important?

Extra: What mindset is required to engage in open sharing? What are ways to keep this mindset fresh and constructive? What parts of this work do you enjoy? What parts do you dislike? Why?

Assignment 11.4: Which Open-Shared Learning Futures for the Human Good? For the human good, what "possible futures" would be optimal for open-shared online learning. Why? Consider this issue from a macro level.

Assignment 11.5: Defining a "Personality Frame" for Open-Shared Learning One appeal of others' created digital learning objects, courses, and sequences depends on the "personality frame" of the instructor. What parts of a personality frame do you find appealing in terms of online instructors and/or content experts? Why? What parts of a personality frame do you find off-putting? Why? In terms of an "author hand," what do you look for in experts? What makes such an "author hand" unique? What makes such an "author hand" generic?

11.7.2 Advanced

Assignment 11.6: Assessing the Impact of the Created Open-Shared Learning Track the release of the open-shared learning contents, and define several objective and observable measures (metrics) that may serve as indicators of the learning object/course/sequence's success or failure. Define observations that may indicate other aspects of how the object is received (Learner communications? Others). What is a "win" in the public space, and what is a "fail," and why?

Assignment 11.7: Affecting the Possible Futures of Open-Shared Learning What do you see as the optimal possible futures of open-shared learning? Based on your skills and vision, what role can you play in affecting the various possible futures to the good? In advancing your sense of what an optimal possible future may be? What do you need to improve on—in terms of learning, skills, public spaces, data analytics, and others?

Extra: What is the most likely future of open-shared resources for learning? Why?

Assignment 11.8: Open Sharing Learning Resources in a World Without Work A current meta-conversation is occurring currently about a possible human future in which robots and artificial intelligence (AI) may take over people's jobs and render a human future without necessary work for survival. Do you think the creation of open-shared learning may be done by machine and machine intelligence? What sorts of learning needs would people have if they did not have to learn for work? How would a world without learning motivated by survival work? What sorts of open-shared learning would be created? (Would it look more like entertainment?)

Assignment 11.9: The Semantic Web and Open-Shared Learning Objects As humanity moves forward to Web 3.0 or the Semantic Web, and computer programs are used to identify and deliver learning resources, what tendencies do you think will occur in terms of how such objects are located and delivered? What features will help open-shared digital learning objects and learning sequences stand out as desirable and attractive resources? How will a digital learning object or learning sequence be seen to have value?

Assignment 11.10: Risks of the "Great Unused" ("Great Unread") If open-shared learning objects are analogical to the so-called Great Unread, the reams of human production in writing which are not consumed by humans but which may be perused by computing machines only, should such learning resources be created and shared? Is it enough to benefit those who may have designed and developed the learning objects with new awarenesses and skills? What are some ways to encourage development of useful learning objects but avoid the often-costly development of non-useful ones?

Key Terms and Definitions

Lindy's Law (Lindy Effect) A concept that the length of time that something non-perishable has existed will suggest how much longer it will continue (longer survival rates of an object may indicate continuing longer term survival or life expectancy)

Open Sharing The combination of open-access, open-source, and social-sharing of originally-created objects (in this case, learning objects and learning sequences)

Open Source Availability of original source code

Point of View (POV) A subjective perspective, a unique worldview

Possible Futures Potential alternate (and somewhat mutually exclusive) prospects in the near-term, mid-term, and future term

References

Aroyo L, and Dicheva D. The new challenges for e-learning: The Educational Semantic Web. *Educational Technology & Society* 7: 59–69, 2004.

Batson T, Paharia N, Kumar MSV. A harvest too large? A framework for educational abundance. Ch. 6. In T. Iiyoshi and M.S. V. Kumar's *Opening Up Education: The Collective Advancement of Education through Open Technology, Open Content, and Open Knowledge.* Cambridge, Massachusetts: The Carnegie Foundation for the Advancement of Teaching and The MIT Press. 89–103, 2008.

Brosnan K. Developing and sustaining a national learning-object sharing network: A social capital theory perspective. ASCILITE 2005. 105–114, 2005.

Chatti MA, Jarke M, and Frosch-Wilke D. The future of e-learning: A shift to knowledge networking and social software. *Int. J. Knowledge and Learning* 3: 404–420, 2007.

Conole G. 2010. Facilitating new forms of discourse for learning and teaching: Harnessing the power of Web 2.0 practices. *Open Learning* 25: 141–151, 2010.

Downes S. Models for sustainable open educational resources. *Interdisciplinary Journal of Knowledge and Learning Objects:* 1–16, 2007.

Harley D. Why understanding the use and users of open education matters. Chapter 13. In T. Iiyoshi and M.S. V. Kumar's *Opening Up Education: The Collective Advancement of Education through Open Technology, Open Content, and Open Knowledge.* Cambridge, Massachusetts: The Carnegie Foundation for the Advancement of Teaching and The MIT Press. 197–211, 2008.

Koper R, and Olivier B. Representing the learning design of units of learning. *Educational Technology & Society* 7: 97–111, 2004.

Kuznetsov S, and Paulos E. Rise of the expert amateur: DIY projects, communities, and cultures. In NordiCHI 2010. Oct. 16–20, 2010. Reykjavik, Iceland. 1–10, 2010.

Leacock TL, and Nesbit JC. A framework for evaluating the quality of multimedia learning resources. *Educational Technology & Society* 10: 44–59, 2007.

Oliver R. Reusing and sharing learning designs in higher education. In the proceedings of HERDSA Annual Conference. Adelaide. 1–11, 2007.

Philip R, and Cameron L. Sharing and reusing learning designs: Contextualising (sic) enablers and barriers. In Proceedings of Ed-Media World Conference on Educational Media, Hypermedia and Telecommunications, Vienna, Austria, 30 June - 4 July 2008.

Stahl G. Introduction: Foundations for a CSCL community. In Stahl's *Computer support for collaborative learning: Foundations for a CSCL community*. In the proceedings of CSCL 2002. Boulder, Colorado. Jan. 7–11, 2002. 2002.

Súilleabháin GO, and Coakley D. SLOOP: The attempt to progress the learning economy through an open source attitude. In *Sharing Learning Objects in an Open Perspective*. 57–69, 2007.

Additional Reading Section

Lessig L. *Free Culture: How Big Media Uses Technology and the Law to Lock Down Culture and Control Creativity*. New York: Penguin Group. 2004.

Epilogue

There are numerous evocations around open learning on the Web, and in open shared spaces (Fig. A.1). Optimally, *Designing Instruction for Open Sharing* has added some new angles and perspectives even though this work is by no means exhaustive.

I want to wrap this work with an anecdote. Some years ago when I was taking some post-graduate level courses, one of my professors would highlight a theory that was originated by a major thinker in the field. She would note that that individual had won a Nobel Prize for the idea, and she would marvel that they had won a prize for such simple ideas. She presented these insights as an encouragement—that anyone could conceptualize potent insights and ultimately win a Nobel Prize.

Fig. A.1 A word cloud from the Open_learning article in Wikipedia

S. Hai-Jew, *Designing Instruction For Open Sharing*,
https://doi.org/10.1007/978-3-030-02713-1

Some years later, she has continued to publish but not really contribute an earth-shaking idea and so far nothing that would fundamentally change her field. Some of her students have earned their doctorates, and others have not. She has since moved to multiple other institutions of higher education. Why this matters to me is that it is a cautionary tale about how deceptively simple others' achievements may be and really how hard it is (realistically and statistically) to make a large difference in the world—through research and thought. Having ambitions is critical to achievement, but it is not sufficient alone. Much of the context required for high achievement is beyond the direct control of an individual. Actual disruptive achievements are rarities. Writing this book, even though it's based on decades of work in this area, was a challenge, and it is a work that will garner some limited attention and maybe affect a few in their work and volunteerism. This all is harder than it looks. Ambition should be tempered with facts and *realia*. They should be tempered by a real world sense of actual costs and difficulty. And then, after the work is done, there is value to forgetting how hard it all was, so the next challenge may be taken on. And a person should not care too much about outcomes beyond his / her / their control.

Reader Achievements The making of a relevant open shared learning object is much more humble than originating a paradigm-shifting concept that attains elite recognition and acceptance. However, it does require original work, creativity, effort, and some seriously costly investments (per the research, the technologies, and the work).

If readers have used the book as envisioned, they will now have already achieved the following:

- read the main informational contents (in 4 parts and 11 chapters) and explored the data and visuals;
- explored the open-shared learning environment through an environmental scan (to get a feel of "the street");
- explored their local up-close work environment through an internal scan;
- considered their readiness to create open-shared learning objects legally and to quality (and to personal standards);
- profiled "target" and "potential" learners today and into the future;
- conceptualized ways to reach the respective learners via the Web and other electronic means;
- considered various theories, models, frameworks, and heuristics that may affect a learning design;
- identified some research that may affect their learning objects and resources;
- reviewed the laws for making "street legal" open-shared learning resources;
- planned ways to adhere to the relevant laws in the local context and further abroad;
- reviewed the various types of equipment, authoring tools, digital editing tools, and content hosting platforms for the design, development, and sharing of online learning objects;
- created relevant and applicable evolving project stylebooks, templates, and work plans;

- drafted early designs, prototypes of online learning objects, and learning sequences for exploration and decision making;
- developed online learning resources, such as individual objects and as learning sequences;
- created relevant related work documentation to accurately represent the work;
- created and implemented alpha tests, beta tests, and customized tests, to the learning objects;
- launched the open shared learning objects and sequences (with both "hard" and "soft" launches);
- conducted effective outreach to potentially interested parties for the learning objects;
- monitored usage of the learning content;
- set a plan for post-launch care of the users of the learning objects and sequences and of the open-shared online learning resources themselves;
- set aside some resources for post-launch care of the users of the learning resources;
- followed through on the post-launch care plan;
- considered some possible futures of open-shared learning, and most importantly,
- considered their possible future as an open-shared contributor, consumer, and participant…and other activities.

Ideally, this sequence was attempted and achieved by many, including those with varying levels of experiences in instructional design and open sharing. I hope this book introduced some new ideas and work processes.

Beyond the obvious, to contribute learning resources to this open-space requires some less obvious build-up. There has to be relevant expertise, access to recent data and research, connections to professionals in the field, and an interest in learners. There has to be some willingness to do the hard work, even though the world offers up all sorts of temptations to other work and fun. The decay rate of knowledge and skills in cutting-edge spaces can be especially fast. There has to be an inner drive and self-motivation to engage. There has to be technological skills to actualize the work. There has to be a lack of unnecessary fear (beyond what is prudent) in engaging the public. There has to be a sense of sharing and a willingness to invest the real into an endeavor that may or may not bear fruit in easily observable ways. Potential contributors need to restrain any internal motivations to showboat or brag, if they are so inclined, and they need to restrain the self-motivation, all of which are turn-offs to potential users of the shared learning contents.

While each reader has been using *Designing Instruction for Open Sharing*, I assume that the reading experience was unique to each reader because their custom experiences inform their understandings. Further, their projects likely flavored their reading because different parts of the book become more or less salient based on their applications. Every effort was made to make the book as consistent and clear as possible, within very real-world limits. Optimally, this book introduced some new and less-evident but nevertheless relevant practices.

This book took a slow motion approach to engaging the various explicit work steps. Some of these listed tasks may be more salient than others, some skipped, and some steps taken not mentioned in this textbook. There are very legitimate branches and alternate paths. For example, readers may be parts of development teams and only have a part of the work sequence in their purview. Various authoring systems, particularly hosted ones, may mitigate some parts of this sequence, such as systems that may check for legal requirements with system built-ins. Hopefully, along the way, there have been positive surprises, enhanced work skills, and ultimately solid contributions into the lives of learners and the broad public. I also hope that there is an object or set of objects about which the designer/developer can be proud.

This instructional design work for open sharing can be painstaking at times, but in a professional environment, the length of time needed to actualize this is actually much less than one might assume. With practice, this can be done in condensed time, and a polished object or resource may be available to the world in short order.

I hope readers adopt the parts that are useful to them and ignore the rest. I hope that they use a variety of other texts that may be informative to their endeavors. This topic is broad and complex, and the evocations of open learning, open social sharing, open access, and other instantiations of "open" on the Web are myriad. One article-article outlink network around "Open_learning" on Wikipedia shows how diverse the associations may be even in a one-degree network (Fig. A.2).

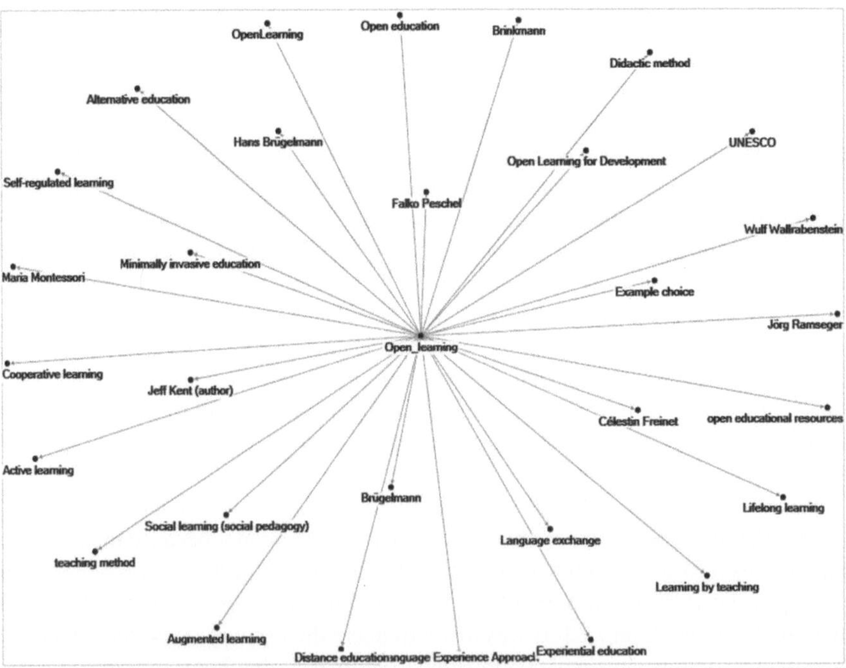

Fig. A.2 "Open_learning" article-article network on Wikipedia (1 deg.)

I hope that they continually expand their skills and that they read and experiment broadly and deeply. I hope that they engage the world with due caution but not fear, ambition but not over-reach. I want them to avoid the naïve illusion of costlessness in providing free open-shared learning contents. "Cheap talk" is low-cost and even free, but "costly signaling" is expensive. When acquaintances and strangers ask for free work, with all their charm and "woo" turned on, these are not low-cost asks. If there will be actual contribution, there has to be actual work and actual value created. Also, there is power in seeing instructional design work and sharing as creative and artful endeavors, an aspect of expressivity.

Writing this Textbook In the Preface, I described my original inspiration for this work and how my professional experiences have informed this. I summarized some of my *bona fides* for the work, from decades in higher education and instructional design. It does help to be able to knock around a space for a while and to learn through directed learning and osmosis. In social network theory, the "bias" of egos (personalities) is calculated into some models. Here, I want to own up to some of my leanings related to instructional design and open sharing. In open sharing, I follow the general precepts and macro strategies:

1. *Learn from the world.* This instructional design for open sharing work is practical, and it has to be informed by the world: its practices, its values, its potential learners, and its technologies.
2. *Go with individual passions and inspirations.* Projects have to turn the designer/developer on…or inspire him/her. Without that spark, the work no longer motivates, and it feels like a waste of attention and concentration and head space; the work becomes too difficult to actualize. (This work is not costless, and there are numerous "opportunity costs" to engage. If the time is better spent on other pursuits, people should pursue those. If they do not, they may become embittered at spending their time, talent, and treasure on unpaid work.)
3. *Work from strengths and expertise.* Designer/developers work from a space of expertise and familiarity. While taking risks and trying new things are important, reaching too far out beyond expertise is an unnecessary risk.
4. *Work efficiently.* The work should be achieved as efficiently as possible. Keep the resource burn rate on a slow burn. Build smart. Self-indulgences get expensive. Poor designs and poorly-conceptualized plans get spendy.
5. *Learn constantly.* Designer/developers need to learn constantly because the field requires it, with ever-changing technologies and new research on human learning and other related fields. Professional development through formal and informal channels is important.
6. *Keep it simple.* With the powerful technologies it hand, it is easy to go complex without thinking. In general, it is better to go with the least possible complexity (irreducible levels of complexity) regarding the technologies so as not to introduce errors.
7. *Meet standards.* Anything released to the public has to meet threshold standards…of legality, accessibility, accuracy, and others. Having a sense of stan-

dards is an important protection against turning out lackluster or substandard work.

8. *Avoid finalizing work too early.* One of the easiest ways to "make work" is to freeze a resource or project too soon. It is good practice to be constantly researching and reviewing what is occurring in the world in case something comes up that is relevant to your project. Then update the work, so it is as fresh as possible, until the work is launched to the public…and is therefore somewhat frozen in fixed form. (If a topic is highly dynamic and changing, then I would go for post-launch maintenance and keep updating as long as that is possible on the hosting platform.)
9. *Proof and test.* "Perfection" is not a natural state. It does not just result from normal work. In every context, run the learning resources through multiple iterations of proofing and testing, to ensure that the work is to standard and to quality. If a complete retrofitting is needed, even if it will be effortful and challenging, it may well be worth doing—so that once a work is released to the public—it is in the best possible shape.
10. *Control your "public you".* Going public is a necessity, but this can be loud or quiet, depending on the context. Those who share learning contents do not have to share any more of themselves than they want to. They can write their own rules and not feel buffeted by the context.
11. *Do not get used.* In public space, people are always trying to trade nothing for something or low-cost efforts for high-cost efforts. There are all sorts of *faux* promises and professions of "friendship". People will insinuate themselves in your publicly announced projects by saying that they are publicizing it through their social networks, and in trade, they want the hundreds of hours of work it takes to research and write a chapter for one of their projects. Strangers will reach out to "task" you with their own work. They will try to offer something for "free"—which is never free and not particularly useful—like co-authorship on projects about which you have no role.
12. *Forget fairytales.* Do not be a fantasist about going public and what you will get from it. People are people, and having many eyes on a thing does not change the basics of the world and the fact that people act on self-interest most of the time. People should advocate for and protect their own interests. Any who would design and develop open-shared learning contents should advocate their own interests, too, and not go at any work with illusions. This is not to say that an occasional surprise cannot happen and that there are not occasional instances of altruism, but these are rare.
13. *Strive for personal bests.* The competition is you. Each time you finalize a work, it should be better than prior work. You need to learn from each project and improve the next one, even if it is only in small ways. Strive for your own personal bests (what you can best achieve given the environmental affordances and constraints). Choosiness is a strength, not a weakness.
14. *Celebrate, but don't rest on your laurels.* Creating an open-shared work from scratch and building it to quality, to the point of launch, is no small feat, and it should be personally recognized. However, after the bit of celebration, a person

should move on to the next thing. Imagine a clock running inexorably, and even a short hesitation can be costly in lost opportunities in the long term.

15. *The competition is the world.* If you cannot offer something of actual and observed value, then your time may be better spent doing something else. And that's okay!

Writing this work was a kind of debriefing. It turns out that a lot of what I knew on the surface was easily captured in the first weeks, and thereafter, for the year in development, it was a tough slog, with frequent writer's block and mere incremental advancements. I learned how important it is to have trusted fallback processes that enable the work to continue even around moments of project stalls. (If you can't write, read. If you need a solution, bring out some scrap paper and Sharpie pens… and doodle…and write…and then shred the notes when done. If you can't make a solid assertion, don't, or use plenty of qualifiers. If you have no specific ideas in particular, revisit every chapter file and update them each, even if it is something small like a grammar-check and a spell-check. Whenever there is an update, be sure to go through every chapter and make every change right away…or make a note to do so as soon as possible.)) It helped that my daily work in instructional design informed the writing. It helped that during the regular workweek that I had an ongoing meta-cognitive observation going and could make observations in the manuscript, which I evolved in a folder on my laptop.

Then, there were the unexpected challenges. Midway through this project, on May 22, 2018, after a dozen years of false fire alarms caused by dust and the occasional over-micro-waved food, Hale Library suffered a devastating attic fire stemming from roofing work. For the next seven hours after the initial fire alarm, fire fighters poured water into the building, and internal fire suppressant systems also triggered. Fire fighters doused the building for potential hotspots. Between the fire, the smoke damage, and the water, the building was uninhabitable for the next indeterminate period—the school president hoped it would be months, but the building professionals suggested upwards of 2 years or longer. This resulted in major disruption and further financial exigencies and work pressures. Personally, my own cubicle escaped larger scale damage, and my thousands of dollars of personally-purchased books were dry in their shelves and undamaged (and ultimately wheeled out in hard-side luggage). Also, thankfully, I had the work updated to the day before and backup copies to draw on. (Any newbie designer knows to have backups against any number of contingencies and potential disasters. What was non-obvious though was that it is not only the "slow fires" of technological aging-out to be wary of but of fast and stealthy fires with actual smoke.)

Then, there were the expected challenges. Of course, I fell into some of the "don't do's" in the writing, such as not sufficiently pounding and questioning the Table of Contents sufficiently to head off multiple revisions to chapter titles, resulting in necessary updates to a dozen visuals multiple times as well as other changes. I added new elements to chapters as the book manuscript evolved, and that added work and some make-work.

Otherwise, though, if this book were a learning object, I have generally tried my best to follow the optimal approaches. In general, I sequenced the work sensibly. I met deadlines. I knew when to push through fatigue and when to just take a break and focus on other things. I knew how to keep myself inspired and diligent but not overworked. I was clear-eyed about costs and used reasonable calculations for the work. I was cautious about what information to include and made sure I had clear provenance for everything. I knew that the work was hard but necessary—and certainly nothing to fear. I knew to carve out a space in my life for this work but not to give up too much of the real for it.

Not My First Rodeo I have always known that one can only do the best one can do in a given circumstance, and while 100% might be dandy, practicality says that 70% may have to be the most practicable aim. I cannot help but wonder if more time and resources were available, what additional topics would and should have been addressed? Would the order of the Table of Contents (TOC) have changed? What would I have done differently?

In this alternate universe, this book would have more sidebars; it would include more voices from the world of open-shared learning designs. A wider range of technologies would be described. I would focus more on history to augment the practical. If my work experiences were different, I might engage more with blended and face-to-face learning, supported with open shared learning resources. I would have brought in more about large-scale learning repositories. I would address massive open online course (MOOC) experiences more directly. Once something is committed to writing, alternate outcomes are not as readily considered. It makes sense to expand the thinking space, though, before, during, and after a project.

There is something to be said about slowing the book writing process and extending the time period over which the work is developed. This enables authors to steep in the process, so the ideas can fully bloom, and so practical questions may be asked and re-asked. Ultimately, with time and incremental advances, the offered work is more thought-through, solid, and practically applied.

About Openly Sharing Learning Resources At the completion of *Designing Instruction for Open Learning*, I am tempted to apply some of the same standards of digital learning objects and online learning sequences to this work. I want to think about the journey it has taken to arrive at this point, from the beginning when this was a mere book idea to the present, with a completed work.

The design and development of open-shared learning resources requires painstaking planning, analysis, research, design, writing, object creation, delivery, and assessment, often in semi-recursive order. This book was similar in terms of the painstaking focus, but the main challenge was slowing down the instructional design process and taking a meta-perspective view in order to document the actual sequences and thinking. This book is sufficiently general in order to transfer to others' work contexts and situations. As with learning objects and sequences, I consider how "future-proofed" this work is, given the dynamism of the space and the changing professional roles, technologies, methods, and subject matter areas. Of course, this question is a bit of a conceit. It is hard enough to be relevant for the now, much less the future.

For those who disagree with open sharing, I would just say that it is a very limited and somewhat boring life to just focus on the self. There are constraints in living a life in which one only acts when one is paid. Contributing to public space can be highly alluring, and speaking into the future can be powerful. This is not to say that there is not room for potential misuse, with others freeriding on one's hard work. There, too, is the risk of the designer/developer cutting corners because this is not paid work (please do not participate if some basic level of quality cannot be managed). Giving to another (the public, strangers) at some level has to be an act of altruism and care and even love. To maintain the ability to give over time and sustainably, it helps to make giving a habit, and it helps to protect the creative ego, so the work feels costless even when the mind knows that the costs are high, often irretrievably so.

In some ways, this work is autobiographical. In my career, I have found that it is helpful to set aside some time for professional development and for giving back. These efforts make for a fuller life. I really hope that readers find this open-shared learning development work enjoyable and beneficial. I hope that they not only take part in this open-shared learning space as contributors but also as consumers (to use a faddish term, as "prosumers" or producer-consumers).

In our work, we engage with so much relevant information in the world, and if given the chance, this overflow can be harnessed to positive aims. And in workplaces which are project-based, there are times of over-capacity, which may be harnessed for building open-shared learning objects.

There are times and places for withholding and protectionism, privacy and hiding, silence and stealth, but there are occasions, too, for global-scale sharing and generosity, publicity, and even tell-alls In this work, I have learned the importance of commitments and recommitments. I have seen the importance of protecting harnessed creativity. We have to take responsibility to stay inspired and innovative, to maintain good will and caring towards others, to stay fresh and disciplined in our skills and work, to explore broadly, and to share when it makes sense to do so. One of the powerful aspects of open-shared learning is that it can be a one-off, or it can be more. The decision is up to the individual and/or the team.

Creating open-shared learning objects and sequences is one way for those with particular knowledge and a tendency to share and maybe even to teach…to reach out to others with something that they created. This approach offers a lot of freedom for professional development and self-expression. Such work, while challenging, can be deeply satisfying. The challenge involves finding a way in, identifying a topic around which to contribute, cultivating a personal sense of inspiration, and firing up the motivation to create learning contents. Ultimately, these contributions may be seen in the rearview mirror, and one's real and lived passions will be made apparent.

On to the next one…

Index

S. Hai-Jew, *Designing Instruction For Open Sharing*,
https://doi.org/10.1007/978-3-030-02713-1

M

MIX
Papier aus verantwortungsvollen Quellen
Paper from responsible sources
FSC® C105338

If you have any concerns about our products,
you can contact us on
ProductSafety@springernature.com

In case Publisher is established outside the EU,
the EU authorized representative is:
Springer Nature Customer Service Center GmbH
Europaplatz 3, 69115 Heidelberg, Germany

Printed by Libri Plureos GmbH
in Hamburg, Germany